Real GDP Growth

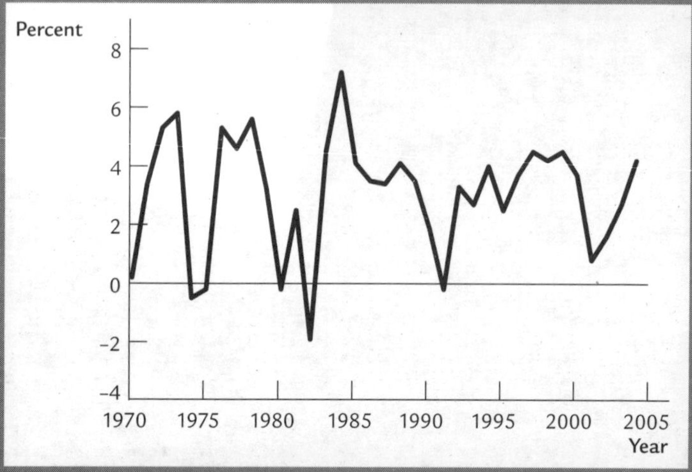

Source: U.S. Department of Commerce

Unemployment Rate

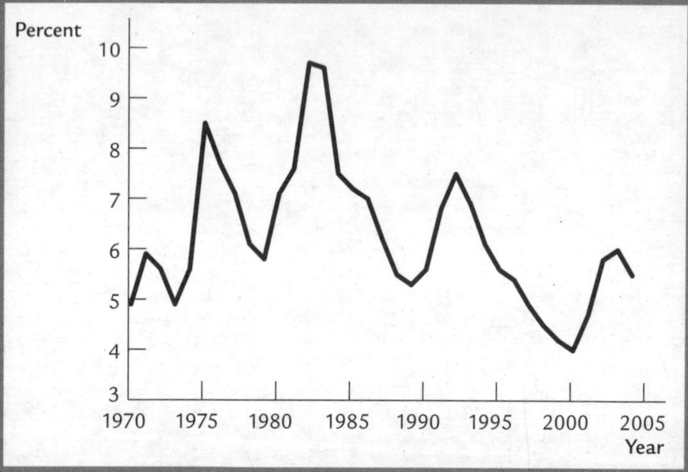

Source: U.S. Department of Labor

Inflation Rate
(GDP Deflator)

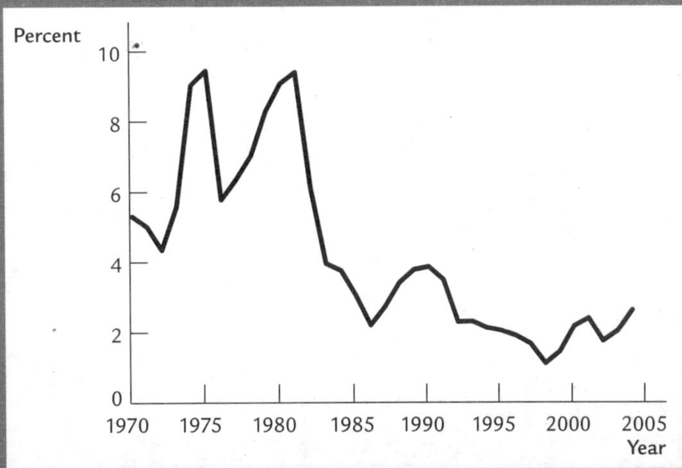

Source: U.S. Department of Commerce

Nominal Interest Rate
(Three-Month Treasury Bills)

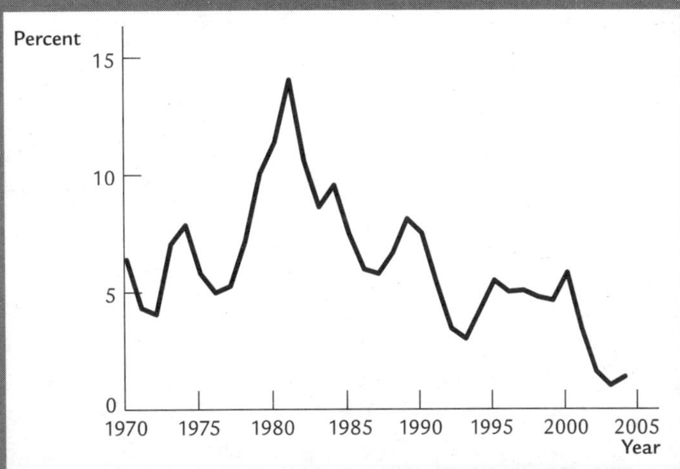

Source: U.S. Federal Reserve

MACROECONOMICS

MACROECONOMICS

SIXTH EDITION

N. GREGORY MANKIW

HARVARD UNIVERSITY

WORTH PUBLISHERS

Publishers: Catherine Woods and Craig Bleyer
Senior Acquisitions Editor: Charlie Van Wagner
Development Editor: Jane Tufts
Associate Managing Editor: Tracey Kuehn
Project Editors: Kerry O'Shaughnessy and Ye Jin Lee (Scribe)
Associate Editor: Marie McHale
Marketing Manager: Scott Guile
Production Manager: Barbara Anne Seixas
Art Director; Babs Reingold
Cover and Interior Design: Vicki Tomaselli
Author Photo: Hilary Rochelle
Composition, Illustrations, and Layout: TSI Graphics
Printing and Binding R. R. Donnelley & Sons Company

ISBN 978-0-230-22492-6

Library of Congress Control Number: 2006902233

Reprinted 2008 (Twice), 2010, 2011

Printed in India by Replika Press Pvt. Ltd.

Worth Publishers
41 Madison Avenue
New York, NY 10010
www.worthpublishers.com

about the author

N. Gregory Mankiw is Professor of Economics at Harvard University. He began his study of economics at Princeton University, where he received an A.B. in 1980. After earning a Ph.D. in economics from MIT, he began teaching at Harvard in 1985 and was promoted to full professor in 1987. Today, he regularly teaches both undergraduate and graduate courses in macroeconomics. He is also author of the popular introductory textbook, *Principles of Economics* (Thomson South-Western).

Professor Mankiw is a regular participant in academic and policy debates. His research ranges across macroeconomics and includes work on price adjustment, consumer behavior, financial markets, monetary and fiscal policy, and economic growth. In addition to his duties at Harvard, he has been a research associate of the National Bureau of Economic Research, a member of the Brookings Panel on Economic Activity, and an adviser to the Federal Reserve Bank of Boston and the Congressional Budget Office. From 2003 to 2005 he was chairman of the President's Council of Economic Advisers.

Professor Mankiw lives in Wellesley, Massachusetts, with his wife Deborah; children Catherine, Nicholas, and Peter; and their border terrier Tobin.

To Deborah

Those branches of politics, or of the laws of social life, on which there exists a collection of facts sufficiently sifted and methodized to form the beginning of a science should be taught *ex professo*. Among the chief of these is Political Economy, the sources and conditions of wealth and material prosperity for aggregate bodies of human beings. …

The same persons who cry down Logic will generally warn you against Political Economy. It is unfeeling, they will tell you. It recognises unpleasant facts. For my part, the most unfeeling thing I know of is the law of gravitation: it breaks the neck of the best and most amiable person without scruple, if he forgets for a single moment to give heed to it. The winds and waves too are very unfeeling. Would you advise those who go to sea to deny the winds and waves—or to make use of them, and find the means of guarding against their dangers? My advice to you is to study the great writers on Political Economy, and hold firmly by whatever in them you find true; and depend upon it that if you are not selfish or hard-hearted already, Political Economy will not make you so.

—*John Stuart Mill*

1867

brief contents

Preface xxv

part I
Introduction

Chapter 1 The Science of Macroeconomics 2

Chapter 2 The Data of Macroeconomics 16

part II
Classical Theory: The Economy in the Long Run

Chapter 3 National Income: Where It Comes From and Where It Goes 44

Chapter 4 Money and Inflation 76

Chapter 5 The Open Economy 115

Chapter 6 Unemployment 159

part III
Growth Theory: The Economy in the Very Long Run

Chapter 7 Economic Growth I: Capital Accumulation and Population Growth 186

Chapter 8 Economic Growth II: Technology, Empirics, and Policy 216

part IV
Business Cycle Theory: The Economy in the Short Run

Chapter 9 Introduction to Economic Fluctuations 252

Chapter 10 Aggregate Demand I: Building the *IS-LM* Model 278

Chapter 11 Aggregate Demand II: Applying the *IS-LM* Model 303

Chapter 12 The Open Economy Revisited: The Mundell-Fleming Model and the Exchange-Rate Regime 334

Chapter 13 Aggregate Supply and the Short-run Tradeoff Between Inflation and Unemployment 373

part V
Macroeconomic Policy Debates

Chapter 14 Stabilization Policy 406

Chapter 15 Government Debt 431

part VI
More on the Microeconomics Behind Macroeconomics

Chapter 16 Consumption 456

Chapter 17 Investment 487

Chapter 18 Money Supply and Money Demand 510

Chapter 19 Advances in Business Cycle Theory 528

Epilogue: What We Know, What We Don't 547

Glossary 555

Index 565

contents

Preface xxv

part I Introduction

Chapter 1 The Science of Macroeconomics 2

1-1 What Macroeconomists Study 2

▶ CASE STUDY *The Historical Performance of the U.S. Economy* 3

1-2 How Economists Think 6

Theory as Model Building 6

▶ **FYI** *Using Functions to Express Relationships Among Variables* 10

A Multitude of Models 11

Prices: Flexible Versus Sticky 11

Microeconomic Thinking and Macroeconomic Models 12

▶ **FYI** *Nobel Macroeconomists* 13

1-3 How This Book Proceeds 14

Chapter 2 The Data of Macroeconomics 16

2-1 Measuring the Value of Economic Activity: Gross Domestic Product 17

Income, Expenditure, and the Circular Flow 17

▶ **FYI** *Stocks and Flows* 19

Rules for Computing GDP 19

Adding Apples and Oranges 20

Used Goods 20

The Treatment of Inventories 20

Intermediate Goods and Value Added 21

Housing Services and Other Imputations 21

Real GDP versus Nominal GDP 22

The GDP Deflator 23

Chain-Weighted Measures of Real GDP 24

▶ **FYI** *Two Arithmetic Tricks for Working With Percentage Changes* 25

The Components of Expenditure 25

▶ **FYI** *What Is Investment?* 26

▶ CASE STUDY *GDP and Its Components* 27

Other Measures of Income 28

Seasonal Adjustment 30

2-2 Measuring the Cost of Living: The Consumer Price Index 30

The Price of a Basket of Goods 31

The CPI versus the GDP Deflator 31

▶ CASE STUDY *Does the CPI Overstate Inflation?* 33

2-3 Measuring Joblessness: The Unemployment Rate 34

The Household Survey 35

▶ CASE STUDY *Trends in Labor-Force Participation* 36

The Establishment Survey 38

2-4 Conclusion: From Economic Statistics to Economic Models 39

part II Classical Theory: The Economy in the Long Run

Chapter 3 National Income: Where It Comes From and Where It Goes 44

3-1 What Determines the Total Production of Goods and Services? 46

The Factors of Production 46

The Production Function 47

The Supply of Goods and Services 47

3-2 How Is National Income Distributed to the Factors of Production? 48

Factor Prices 48

The Decisions Facing the Competitive Firm 49

The Firm's Demand for Factors 50

- The Marginal Product of Labor 50
- From the Marginal Product of Labor to Labor Demand 51
- The Marginal Product of Capital and Capital Demand 53

The Division of National Income 53

▶ CASE STUDY *The Black Death and Factor Prices* 54

The Cobb-Douglas Production Function 55

▶ CASE STUDY *Labor Productivity as the Key Determinant of Real Wages* 58

3-3 What Determines the Demand for Goods and Services? 59

Consumption 59

Investment 61

Government Purchases 62

▶ **FYI** *The Many Different Interest Rates* 63

3-4 What Brings the Supply and Demand for Goods and Services Into Equilibrium? 63

Equilibrium in the Market for Goods and Services: The Supply and Demand for the Economy's Output 64

Equilibrium in the Financial Markets: The Supply and Demand for Loanable Funds 65

Changes in Saving: The Effects of Fiscal Policy 67
An Increase in Government Purchases 67
▶ CASE STUDY *Wars and Interest Rates in the United Kingdom, 1730–1920* 68
A Decrease in Taxes 69
Changes in Investment Demand 69
3-5 Conclusion 71

Chapter 4 Money and Inflation 76

4-1 What Is Money? 77
The Functions of Money 77
The Types of Money 78
▶ CASE STUDY *Money in a POW Camp* 79
How Fiat Money Evolves 79
▶ CASE STUDY *Money and Social Conventions on the Island of Yap* 80
How the Quantity of Money Is Controlled 81
How the Quantity of Money Is Measured 81
▶ **FYI** *How Do Credit Cards and Debit Cards Fit into the Monetary System?* 83
4-2 The Quantity Theory of Money 83
Transactions and the Quantity Equation 83
From Transactions to Income 84
The Money Demand Function and the Quantity Equation 85
The Assumption of Constant Velocity 86
Money, Prices, and Inflation 86
▶ CASE STUDY *Inflation and Money Growth* 87
4-3 Seigniorage: The Revenue From Printing Money 89
▶ CASE STUDY *Paying for the American Revolution* 90
4-4 Inflation and Interest Rates 91
Two Interest Rates: Real and Nominal 91
The Fisher Effect 91
▶ CASE STUDY *Inflation and Nominal Interest Rates* 92
Two Real Interest Rates: *Ex Ante* and *Ex Post* 94
▶ CASE STUDY *Nominal Interest Rates in the Nineteenth Century* 94
4-5 The Nominal Interest Rate and the Demand for Money 95
The Cost of Holding Money 95
Future Money and Current Prices 96
4-6 The Social Costs of Inflation 97
The Layman's View and the Classical Response 97
▶ CASE STUDY *What Economists and the Public Say About Inflation* 98
The Costs of Expected Inflation 99
The Costs of Unexpected Inflation 100
▶ CASE STUDY *The Free Silver Movement, the Election of 1896, and the Wizard of Oz* 101
One Benefit of Inflation 102

4-7 **Hyperinflation** 103
The Costs of Hyperinflation 103
▶ CASE STUDY *Life During the Bolivian Hyperinflation* 104
The Causes of Hyperinflation 105
▶ CASE STUDY *Hyperinflation in Interwar Germany* 106
4-8 **Conclusion: The Classical Dichotomy** 108
Appendix: The Cagan Model: How Current and Future Money Affect the Price Level 112

Chapter 5 The Open Economy 115

5-1 **The International Flows of Capital and Goods** 116
The Role of Net Exports 116
International Capital Flows and the Trade Balance 118
International Flows of Goods and Capital: An Example 120
▶ FYI *The Irrelevance of Bilateral Trade Balances* 120
5-2 **Saving and Investment in a Small Open Economy** 121
Capital Mobility and the World Interest Rate 121
Why Assume a Small Open Economy? 122
The Model 123
How Policies Influence the Trade Balance 124
Fiscal Policy at Home 124
Fiscal Policy Abroad 125
Shifts in Investment Demand 126
Evaluating Economic Policy 127
▶ CASE STUDY *The U.S. Trade Deficit* 127
▶ CASE STUDY *Why Doesn't Capital Flow to Poor Countries?* 130
5-3 **Exchange Rates** 131
Nominal and Real Exchange Rates 131
The Nominal Exchange Rate 131
▶ FYI *How Newspapers Report the Exchange Rate* 132
The Real Exchange Rate 133
The Real Exchange Rate and the Trade Balance 134
The Determinants of the Real Exchange Rate 135
How Policies Influence the Real Exchange Rate 136
Fiscal Policy at Home 136
Fiscal Policy Abroad 136
Shifts in Investment Demand 137
The Effects of Trade Policies 138
The Determinants of the Nominal Exchange Rate 139
▶ CASE STUDY *Inflation and Nominal Exchange Rates* 140
The Special Case of Purchasing-Power Parity 141
▶ CASE STUDY *The Big Mac Around the World* 143
5-4 **Conclusion: The United States as a Large Open Economy** 145
Appendix: The Large Open Economy 149

Net Capital Outflow 149
The Model 151
The Market for Loanable Funds 151
The Market for Foreign Exchange 152
Policies in the Large Open Economy 153
Fiscal Policy at Home 153
Shifts in Investment Demand 155
Trade Policies 155
Shifts in Net Capital Outflow 156
Conclusion 157

Chapter 6 Unemployment 159

6-1 Job Loss, Job Finding, and the Natural Rate of Unemployment 160

6-2 Job Search and Frictional Unemployment 162
Public Policy and Frictional Unemployment 163
▶ CASE STUDY *Unemployment Insurance and the Rate of Job Finding* 164

6-3 Real-Wage Rigidity and Structural Unemployment 165
Minimum-Wage Laws 166
▶ CASE STUDY *The Characteristics of Minimum-Wage Workers* 167
Unions and Collective Bargaining 168
Efficiency Wages 170
▶ CASE STUDY *Henry Ford's $5 Workday* 171

6-4 Labor Market Experience: The United States 172
The Duration of Unemployment 172
Variation in the Unemployment Rate Across Demographic Groups 173
Trends in Unemployment 174
Demographics 174
Sectoral Shifts 174
Productivity 174
Transitions Into and Out of the Labor Force 175

6-5 Labor Market Experience: Europe 176
The Rise in European Unemployment 176
Unemployment Variation within Europe 178
▶ CASE STUDY *The Secrets to Happiness* 179
The Rise of European Leisure 180

6-6 Conclusion 182

part III Growth Theory: The Economy in the Very Long Run

Chapter 7 Economic Growth I: Capital Accumulation and Population Growth 186

7-1 The Accumulation of Capital 187
The Supply and Demand for Goods 187
The Supply of Goods and the Production Function 188
The Demand for Goods and the Consumption Function 188
Growth in the Capital Stock and the Steady State 190
Approaching the Steady State: A Numerical Example 192
▶ CASE STUDY *The Miracle of Japanese and German Growth* 194
How Saving Affects Growth 195
▶ CASE STUDY *Saving and Investment Around the World* 196

7-2 The Golden Rule Level of Capital 198
Comparing Steady States 198
Finding the Golden Rule Steady State: A Numerical Example 202
The Transition to the Golden Rule Steady State 203
Starting With Too Much Capital 204
Starting With Too Little Capital 205

7-3 Population Growth 206
The Steady State With Population Growth 206
The Effects of Population Growth 208
▶ CASE STUDY *Population Growth Around the World* 209
Alternative Perspectives on Population Growth 210
The Malthusian Model 211
The Kremerian Model 211

7-4 Conclusion 212

Chapter 8 Economic Growth II: Technology, Empirics, and Policy 216

8-1 Technological Progress in the Solow Model 217
The Efficiency of Labor 217
The Steady State With Technological Progress 218
The Effects of Technological Progress 219

8-2 From Growth Theory to Growth Empirics 220
Balanced Growth 220
Convergence 221
Factor Accumulation Versus Production Efficiency 222
▶ CASE STUDY *Is Free Trade Good for Economic Growth?* 223

8-3 Policies to Promote Growth 224
Evaluating the Rate of Saving 225

Changing the Rate of Saving 226
Allocating the Economy's Investment 227
Establishing the Right Institutions 229
▶ CASE STUDY *The Colonial Origins of Modern Institutions* 229
Encouraging Technological Progress 230
▶ CASE STUDY *The Worldwide Slowdown in Economic Growth: 1972–1995* 231
Measurement Problems 232
Oil Prices 232
Worker Quality 232
The Depletion of Ideas 233
▶ CASE STUDY *Information Technology and the New Economy: 1995–????* 233

8-4 Beyond the Solow Model: Endogenous Growth Theory 235
The Basic Model 235
A Two-Sector Model 236
The Microeconomics of Research and Development 237
▶ CASE STUDY *Economic Growth as a Process of Creative Destruction* 239

8-5 Conclusion 240
Appendix: Accounting for the Sources of Economic Growth 244
Increases in the Factors of Production 244
Increases in Capital 245
Increases in Labor 245
Increases in Capital and Labor 245
Technological Progress 246
The Sources of Growth in the United States 248
▶ CASE STUDY *Growth in the East Asian Tigers* 248

part IV Business Cycle Theory: The Economy in the Short Run

Chapter 9 Introduction to Economic Fluctuations 252

9-1 The Facts about the Business Cycle 253
GDP and Its Components 253
Unemployment and Okun's Law 255
Leading Economic Indicators 258

9-2 Time Horizons in Macroeconomics 259
How the Short Run and Long Run Differ 260
▶ CASE STUDY *The Puzzle of Sticky Magazine Prices* 260
The Model of Aggregate Supply and Aggregate Demand 261

9-3 Aggregate Demand 262
The Quantity Equation as Aggregate Demand 263
Why the Aggregate Demand Curve Slopes Downward 264
Shifts in the Aggregate Demand Curve 264

9-4 **Aggregate Supply 265**
The Long Run: The Vertical Aggregate Supply Curve 265
The Short Run: The Horizontal Aggregate Supply Curve 267
From the Short Run to the Long Run 268
▶ CASE STUDY *Gold, Greenbacks, and the Contraction of the 1870s* 270

9-5 **Stabilization Policy 270**
Shocks to Aggregate Demand 271
Shocks to Aggregate Supply 272
▶ CASE STUDY *How OPEC Helped Cause Stagflation in the 1970s and Euphoria in the 1980s* 274

9-6 **Conclusion 276**

Chapter 10 Aggregate Demand I: Building the *IS-LM* Model 278

10-1 **The Goods Market and the *IS* Curve 280**
The Keynesian Cross 280
Planned Expenditure 280
The Economy in Equilibrium 282
Fiscal Policy and the Multiplier: Government Purchases 283
Fiscal Policy and the Multiplier: Taxes 285
▶ CASE STUDY *Cutting Taxes to Stimulate the Economy: The Kennedy and Bush Tax Cuts* 287
The Interest Rate, Investment, and the *IS* Curve 288
How Fiscal Policy Shifts the *IS* Curve 289
A Loanable-Funds Interpretation of the *IS* Curve 290

10-2 **The Money Market and the *LM* Curve 292**
The Theory of Liquidity Preference 292
▶ CASE STUDY *Does a Monetary Tightening Raise or Lower Interest Rates?* 295
Income, Money Demand, and the *LM* Curve 295
How Monetary Policy Shifts the *LM* Curve 297
A Quantity-Equation Interpretation of the *LM* Curve 298

10-3 **Conclusion: The Short-Run Equilibrium 299**

Chapter 11 Aggregate Demand II: Applying the *IS-LM* Model 303

11-1 **Explaining Fluctuations With the *IS-LM* Model 304**
How Fiscal Policy Shifts the IS Curve and Changes the Short-Run Equilibrium 304
Changes in Government Purchases 304
Changes in Taxes 305
How Monetary Policy Shifts the *LM* Curve and Changes the Short-Run Equilibrium 306
The Interaction Between Monetary and Fiscal Policy 307
▶ CASE STUDY *Policy Analysis With Macroeconometric Models* 309
Shocks in the *IS-LM* Model 310

▶ CASE STUDY *The U.S. Recession of 2001* 311

What Is the Fed's Policy Instrument—The Money Supply or the Interest Rate? 312

11-2 *IS-LM* as a Theory of Aggregate Demand 313

From the *IS-LM* Model to the Aggregate Demand Curve 313

The *IS-LM* Model in the Short Run and Long Run 315

11-3 The Great Depression 317

The Spending Hypothesis: Shocks to the *IS* Curve 318

The Money Hypothesis: A Shock to the *LM* Curve 320

The Money Hypothesis Again: The Effects of Falling Prices 321

The Stabilizing Effects of Deflation 321

The Destabilizing Effects of Deflation 321

Could the Depression Happen Again? 323

▶ CASE STUDY *The Japanese Slump of the 1990s* 324

▶ **FYI** *The Liquidity Trap* 325

11-4 Conclusion 326

Appendix: The Simple Algebra of the *IS-LM* Model and the Aggregate Demand Curve 329

The *IS* Curve 329

The *LM* Curve 330

The Aggregate Demand Curve 331

▶ CASE STUDY *The Effectiveness of Monetary and Fiscal Policy* 332

Chapter 12 The Open Economy Revisited: The Mundell-Fleming Model and the Exchange-Rate Regime 334

12-1 The Mundell-Fleming Model 335

The Key Assumption: Small Open Economy With Perfect Capital Mobility 336

The Goods Market and the *IS** Curve 336

The Money Market and the *LM** Curve 338

Putting the Pieces Together 338

12-2 The Small Open Economy Under Floating Exchange Rates 340

Fiscal Policy 340

Monetary Policy 342

Trade Policy 343

12-3 The Small Open Economy Under Fixed Exchange Rates 344

How a Fixed-Exchange-Rate System Works 345

▶ CASE STUDY *The International Gold Standard* 346

Fiscal Policy 347

Monetary Policy 348

▶ CASE STUDY *Devaluation and the Recovery From the Great Depression* 349

Trade Policy 349

Policy in the Mundell-Fleming Model: A Summary 350

12-4 Interest-Rate Differentials 351
Country Risk and Exchange-Rate Expectations 351
Differentials in the Mundell-Fleming Model 352
▶ CASE STUDY *International Financial Crisis: Mexico 1994–1995* 353
▶ CASE STUDY *International Financial Crisis: Asia 1997–1998* 355
12-5 Should Exchange Rates Be Floating or Fixed? 356
Pros and Cons of Different Exchange-Rate Systems 356
▶ CASE STUDY *Monetary Union in the United States and Europe* 357
Speculative Attacks, Currency Boards, and Dollarization 358
The Impossible Trinity 359
▶ CASE STUDY *The Chinese Currency Controversy* 360
12-6 From the Short Run to the Long Run: The Mundell-Fleming Model With a Changing Price Level 361
12-7 A Concluding Reminder 364
Appendix: A Short-Run Model of the Large Open Economy 368
Fiscal Policy 369
Monetary Policy 371
A Rule of Thumb 372

Chapter 13 Aggregate Supply and the Short-run Tradeoff Between Inflation and Unemployment 373

13-1 Three Models of Aggregate Supply 374
The Sticky-Price Model 375
The Sticky-Wage Model 377
▶ CASE STUDY *The Cyclical Behavior of the Real Wage* 379
The Imperfect-Information Model 380
▶ CASE STUDY *International Differences in the Aggregate Supply Curve* 382
Summary and Implications 383
13-2 Inflation, Unemployment, and the Phillips Curve 385
Deriving the Phillips Curve From the Aggregate Supply Curve 385
▶ FYI *The History of the Modern Phillips Curve* 387
Adaptive Expectations and Inflation Inertia 387
Two Causes of Rising and Falling Inflation 388
▶ CASE STUDY *Inflation and Unemployment in the United States* 389
The Short-Run Tradeoff Between Inflation and Unemployment 390
▶ FYI *How Precise Are Estimates of the Natural Rate of Unemployment?* 392
Disinflation and the Sacrifice Ratio 392
Rational Expectations and the Possibility of Painless Disinflation 393
▶ CASE STUDY *The Sacrifice Ratio in Practice* 395
Hysteresis and the Challenge to the Natural-Rate Hypothesis 396

13-3 Conclusion 397

Appendix: A Big, Comprehensive Model 401

Special Case 1: The Classical Closed Economy 401

Special Case 2: The Classical Small Open Economy 402

Special Case 3: The Basic Model of Aggregate Demand and Aggregate Supply 402

Special Case 4: The *IS-LM* Model 402

Special Case 5: The Mundell-Fleming Model With a Floating Exchange Rate 402

Special Case 6: The Mundell-Fleming Model With a Fixed Exchange Rate 402

part V Macroeconomic Policy Debates

Chapter 14 Stabilization Policy 406

14-1 Should Policy Be Active or Passive? 407

Lags in the Implementation and Effects of Policies 407

The Difficult Job of Economic Forecasting 409

▶ CASE STUDY *Mistakes in Forecasting* 409

Ignorance, Expectations, and the Lucas Critique 411

The Historical Record 412

▶ CASE STUDY *Is the Stabilization of the Economy a Figment of the Data?* 413

▶ CASE STUDY *The Remarkable Stability of the Modern Economy* 413

14-2 Should Policy Be Conducted by Rule or by Discretion? 415

Distrust of Policymakers and the Political Process 416

The Time Inconsistency of Discretionary Policy 416

▶ CASE STUDY *Alexander Hamilton Versus Time Inconsistency* 418

Rules for Monetary Policy 419

▶ CASE STUDY *Inflation Targeting: Rule or Constrained Discretion?* 420

▶ CASE STUDY *John Taylor's Rule for Monetary Policy* 421

▶ CASE STUDY *Central-Bank Independence* 423

14-3 Conclusion: Making Policy in an Uncertain World 425

Appendix: Time Inconsistency and the Tradeoff Between Inflation and Unemployment 428

Chapter 15 Government Debt 431

15-1 The Size of the Government Debt 432

▶ CASE STUDY *The Troubling Outlook for Fiscal Policy* 434

15-2 Problems in Measurement 435

Measurement Problem 1: Inflation 435

Measurement Problem 2: Capital Assets 436
Measurement Problem 3: Uncounted Liabilities 437
Measurement Problem 4: The Business Cycle 438
Summing Up 438

15-3 The Traditional View of Government Debt 439
► **FYI** *Taxes and Incentives* 440

15-4 The Ricardian View of Government Debt 441
The Basic Logic of Ricardian Equivalence 442
Consumers and Future Taxes 443
Myopia 443
Borrowing Constraints 443
► **CASE STUDY** *George Bush's Withholding Experiment* 444
Future Generations 444
► **CASE STUDY** *Why Do Parents Leave Bequests?* 446
Making a Choice 446
► **FYI** *Ricardo on Ricardian Equivalence* 447

15-5 Other Perspectives on Government Debt 448
Balanced Budgets Versus Optimal Fiscal Policy 448
Stabilization 448
Tax Smoothing 448
Intergenerational Redistribution 448
Fiscal Effects on Monetary Policy 449
Debt and the Political Process 449
International Dimensions 450
► **CASE STUDY** *The Benefits of Indexed Bonds* 451

15-6 Conclusion 452

part VI More on the Microeconomics Behind Macroeconomics

Chapter 16 Consumption 456

16-1 John Maynard Keynes and the Consumption Function 457
Keynes's Conjectures 457
The Early Empirical Successes 458
Secular Stagnation, Simon Kuznets, and the Consumption Puzzle 459

16-2 Irving Fisher and Intertemporal Choice 461
The Intertemporal Budget Constraint 461
► **FYI** *Present Value, or Why a $1,000,000 Prize Is Worth Only $623,000* 463
Consumer Preferences 464
Optimization 465

How Changes in Income Affect Consumption 466
How Changes in the Real Interest Rate Affect Consumption 467
Constraints on Borrowing 468
▶ CASE STUDY *The High Japanese Saving Rate* 470

16-3 Franco Modigliani and the Life-Cycle Hypothesis 471
The Hypothesis 472
Implications 472
▶ CASE STUDY *The Consumption and Saving of the Elderly* 475

16-4 Milton Friedman and the Permanent-Income Hypothesis 476
The Hypothesis 476
Implications 477
▶ CASE STUDY *The 1964 Tax Cut and the 1968 Tax Surcharge* 478

16-5 Robert Hall and the Random-Walk Hypothesis 478
The Hypothesis 479
Implications 479
▶ CASE STUDY *Do Predictable Changes in Income Lead to Predictable Changes in Consumption?* 480

16-6 David Laibson and the Pull of Instant Gratification 481
▶ CASE STUDY *How to Get People to Save More* 482

16-7 Conclusion 483

Chapter 17 Investment 487

17-1 Business Fixed Investment 488
The Rental Price of Capital 489
The Cost of Capital 490
The Determinants of Investment 492
Taxes and Investment 494
The Stock Market and Tobin's *q* 495
▶ CASE STUDY *The Stock Market as an Economic Indicator* 496
Alternative Views of the Stock Market: The Efficient Markets Hypothesis Versus Keynes's Beauty Contest 497
Financing Constraints 499
▶ CASE STUDY *Banking Crises and Credit Crunches* 500

17-2 Residential Investment 501
The Stock Equilibrium and the Flow Supply 501
Changes in Housing Demand 502
▶ **FYI** *What Price House Can You Afford?* 503
The Tax Treatment of Housing 504

17-3 Inventory Investment 504
Reasons for Holding Inventories 504
The Accelerator Model of Inventories 505
Inventories and the Real Interest Rate 507

17-4 Conclusion 507

Chapter 18 Money Supply and Money Demand 510

18-1 Money Supply 510

100-Percent-Reserve Banking 511

Fractional-Reserve Banking 512

A Model of the Money Supply 514

The Three Instruments of Monetary Policy 515

▶ CASE STUDY *Bank Failures and the Money Supply in the 1930s* 516

18-2 Money Demand 518

Portfolio Theories of Money Demand 518

▶ CASE STUDY *Currency and the Underground Economy* 519

Transactions Theories of Money Demand 520

The Baumol-Tobin Model of Cash Management 520

▶ CASE STUDY *Empirical Studies of Money Demand* 523

Financial Innovation, Near Money, and the Demise of the Monetary Aggregates 524

18-3 Conclusion 525

Chapter 19 Advances in Business Cycle Theory 528

19-1 The Theory of Real Business Cycles 529

The Economics of Robinson Crusoe 529

The Interpretation of the Labor Market 531

▶ CASE STUDY *Looking for Intertemporal Substitution* 532

The Importance of Technology Shocks 533

▶ CASE STUDY *The Solow Residual and the Business Cycle* 534

The Neutrality of Money 535

▶ CASE STUDY *Testing for Monetary Neutrality* 536

The Flexibility of Wages and Prices 537

19-2 New Keynesian Economics 537

Small Menu Costs and Aggregate-Demand Externalities 538

▶ CASE STUDY *How Large Are Menu Costs?* 539

Recessions as Coordination Failure 539

The Staggering of Wages and Prices 541

▶ CASE STUDY *If You Want to Know Why Firms Have Sticky Prices, Ask Them* 542

19-3 Conclusion 544

Epilogue What We Know, What We Don't 547

The Four Most Important Lessons of Macroeconomics 547

Lesson 1: In the long run, a country's capacity to produce goods and services determines the standard of living of its citizens. 548

Lesson 2: In the short run, aggregate demand influences the amount of goods and services that a country produces. 548

Lesson 3: In the long run, the rate of money growth determines the rate of inflation, but it does not affect the rate of unemployment. 549

Lesson 4: In the short run, policymakers who control monetary and fiscal policy face a tradeoff between inflation and unemployment. 549

The Four Most Important Unresolved Questions of Macroeconomics 550

Question 1: How should policymakers try to promote growth in the economy's natural level of output? 550

Question 2: Should policymakers try to stabilize the economy? 551

Question 3: How costly is inflation, and how costly is reducing inflation? 552

Question 4: How big a problem are government budget deficits? 553

Conclusion 554

Glossary 555

Index 565

preface

An economist must be "mathematician, historian, statesman, philosopher, in some degree. . . . as aloof and incorruptible as an artist, yet sometimes as near the earth as a politician." So remarked John Maynard Keynes, the great British economist who, as much as anyone, could be called the father of macroeconomics. No single statement summarizes better what it means to be an economist.

As Keynes's assessment suggests, students who aim to learn economics need to draw on many disparate talents. The job of helping students find and develop these talents falls to instructors and textbook authors. When writing this textbook for intermediate-level courses in macroeconomics, my goal was to make macroeconomics understandable, relevant, and (believe it or not) fun. Those of us who have chosen to be professional macroeconomists have done so because we are fascinated by the field. More important, we believe that the study of macroeconomics can illuminate much about the world and that the lessons learned, if properly applied, can make the world a better place. I hope this book conveys not only our profession's accumulated wisdom but also its enthusiasm and sense of purpose.

This Book's Approach

Although macroeconomists share a common body of knowledge, they do not all have the same perspective on how that knowledge is best taught. Let me begin this new edition by recapping four of my objectives, which together define this book's approach to the field.

First, I try to offer a balance between short-run and long-run issues in macroeconomics. All economists agree that public policies and other events influence the economy over different time horizons. We live in our own short run, but we also live in the long run that our parents bequeathed us. As a result, courses in macroeconomics need to cover both short-run topics, such as the business cycle and stabilization policy, and long-run topics, such as economic growth, the natural rate of unemployment, persistent inflation, and the effects of government debt. Neither time horizon trumps the other.

Second, I integrate the insights of Keynesian and classical theories. Although Keynes's *General Theory* provides the foundation for much of our current understanding of economic fluctuations, it is important to remember that classical economics provides the right answers to many fundamental questions. In this book I incorporate many of the contributions of the classical economists before Keynes and the new classical economists of the past three decades. Substantial coverage is given, for example, to the loanable-funds theory of the interest rate, the quantity theory of money, and the problem of time inconsistency. At the same time, I recognize that many of the ideas of Keynes and the new Keynesians are necessary for understanding economic fluctuations. Substantial coverage is given also to the *IS–LM* model of aggregate demand, the short-run tradeoff between inflation and unemployment, and modern theories of wage and price rigidity.

Third, I present macroeconomics using a variety of simple models. Instead of pretending that there is one model that is complete enough to explain all facets of the economy, I encourage students to learn how to use and compare a set of prominent models. This approach has the pedagogical value that each model can be kept relatively simple and presented within one or two chapters. More important, this approach asks students to think like economists, who always keep various models in mind when analyzing economic events or public policies. (The cover of this edition illustrates the approach: the painting, like a collection of models, shows different perspectives on the same phenomenon.)

Fourth, I emphasize that macroeconomics is an empirical discipline, motivated and guided by a wide array of experience. This book contains numerous case studies that use macroeconomic theory to shed light on real-world data or events. To highlight the broad applicability of the basic theory, I have drawn the case studies both from current issues facing the world's economies and from dramatic historical episodes. The case studies analyze the policies of Alexander Hamilton, Henry Ford, Alan Greenspan, and George Bush (both of them!). They teach the reader how to apply economic principles to issues from fourteenth-century Europe, the island of Yap, the land of Oz, and today's newspaper.

What's New in the Sixth Edition?

The positive response to the previous edition of this text suggested that radical change was neither necessary nor desired by instructors—and, indeed, this sixth edition retains the same broad structure as the fifth. I have, however, improved the book in numerous ways. Most obviously, the book has been updated, but I have also refined the pedagogy and coverage. Although the basics of macroeconomic theory are much the same as they were four years ago, enough has changed in the details and practice of macroeconomics to warrant putting out a new edition.

Here is a list of the major changes in the order that they appear:

- Chapter 1 has a new FYI box on Nobel-Prize-winning macroeconomists.
- Chapter 2 has a new section that discusses the establishment survey of labor-market conditions and contrasts it with the household survey. It also has a new Case Study about long-term trends in labor-force participation.
- Chapter 3 has incorporated the Cobb-Douglas production function into the main text, rather than leaving it for an appendix. It also includes a new Case Study about the link between labor productivity and real wages.
- Chapter 4 has a new FYI box on the role of credit and debit cards in the monetary system.
- Chapter 5 has a new FYI box that explains the irrelevance of bilateral trade balances, a new section motivating the assumption of a small open economy, and a new Case Study on why capital doesn't flow to poor countries.
- Chapter 6 has a new Case Study on the characteristics of minimum-wage workers. It also has a much expanded discussion of European labor markets, focusing on the variation of unemployment rates across countries and the decline in hours worked over time.

- Chapter 7 has a new section discussing alternative perspectives on the role of population growth in the process of economic growth.
- Chapter 8 has a new Case Study analyzing the impact of trade on growth, as well as a new section on the role of institutions in fostering economic prosperity; this new section includes a new Case Study on the colonial origins of modern institutions. In addition, the chapter has a new Case Study about Joseph Schumpeter's concept of "creative destruction," including both historical and recent applications.
- Chapter 9 begins with a more extensive discussion of business-cycle facts to introduce the subject of short-run economic fluctuations.
- Chapter 12 has a new section on the "impossible trinity"—the inconsistency of allowing free flows of capital, conducting independent monetary policy, and fixing the exchange rate—including a new Case Study on the debate about the Chinese currency.
- Chapter 15 has a thoroughly revised Case Study on the outlook for fiscal policy and a new FYI box on how taxes affect incentives.
- Chapter 16 contains a new Case Study about what behavioral economics has to say about policies to increase saving.
- Chapter 17 has a new section on alternative views of the stock market, discussing both the efficient markets hypothesis and Keynes's analogy of the beauty contest.
- Chapter 19 has a new Case Study summarizing research on the magnitude of menu costs in supermarket chains.

All the changes that I made, and the many others that I considered, were evaluated keeping in mind the benefits of brevity. From my own experience as a student, I know that long books are less likely to be read. My goal in this book is to offer the clearest, most up-to-date, most accessible course in macroeconomics in the fewest words possible.

The Arrangement of Topics

My strategy for teaching macroeconomics is first to examine the long run when prices are flexible and then to examine the short run when prices are sticky. This approach has several advantages. First, because the classical dichotomy permits the separation of real and monetary issues, the long-run material is easier for students to understand. Second, when students begin studying short-run fluctuations, they understand fully the long-run equilibrium around which the economy is fluctuating. Third, beginning with market-clearing models makes clearer the link between macroeconomics and microeconomics. Fourth, students learn first the material that is less controversial among macroeconomists. For all these reasons, the strategy of beginning with long-run classical models simplifies the teaching of macroeconomics.

Let's now move from strategy to tactics. What follows is a whirlwind tour of the book.

Part One, Introduction

The introductory material in Part One is brief so that students can get to the core topics quickly. Chapter 1 discusses the broad questions that macroeconomists address and the economist's approach of building models to explain the world. Chapter 2 introduces the key data of macroeconomics, emphasizing gross domestic product, the consumer price index, and the unemployment rate.

Part Two, Classical Theory: The Economy in the Long Run

Part Two examines the long run over which prices are flexible. Chapter 3 presents the basic classical model of national income. In this model, the factors of production and the production technology determine the level of income, and the marginal products of the factors determine its distribution to households. In addition, the model shows how fiscal policy influences the allocation of the economy's resources among consumption, investment, and government purchases, and it highlights how the real interest rate equilibrates the supply and demand for goods and services.

Money and the price level are introduced in Chapter 4. Because prices are assumed to be fully flexible, the chapter presents the prominent ideas of classical monetary theory: the quantity theory of money, the inflation tax, the Fisher effect, the social costs of inflation, and the causes and costs of hyperinflation.

The study of open-economy macroeconomics begins in Chapter 5. Maintaining the assumption of full employment, this chapter presents models to explain the trade balance and the exchange rate. Various policy issues are addressed: the relationship between the budget deficit and the trade deficit, the macroeconomic impact of protectionist trade policies, and the effect of monetary policy on the value of a currency in the market for foreign exchange.

Chapter 6 relaxes the assumption of full employment by discussing the dynamics of the labor market and the natural rate of unemployment. It examines various causes of unemployment, including job search, minimum-wage laws, union power, and efficiency wages. It also presents some important facts about patterns of unemployment.

Part Three, Growth Theory: The Economy in the Very Long Run

Part Three makes the classical analysis of the economy dynamic by developing the tools of modern growth theory. Chapter 7 introduces the Solow growth model as a description of how the economy evolves over time. This chapter emphasizes the roles of capital accumulation and population growth. Chapter 8 then adds technological progress to the Solow model. It uses the model to discuss growth experiences around the world as well as public policies that influence the level and growth of the standard of living. Finally, Chapter 8 introduces students to the modern theories of endogenous growth.

Part Four, Business Cycle Theory: The Economy in the Short Run

Part Three examines the short run when prices are sticky. It begins in Chapter 9 by examining some of the key facts that describe short-run fluctuations in economic activity. The chapter then introduces the model of aggregate supply and aggregate demand as well as the role of stabilization policy. Subsequent chapters refine the ideas introduced in this chapter.

Chapters 10 and 11 look more closely at aggregate demand. Chapter 10 presents the Keynesian cross and the theory of liquidity preference and uses these models as building blocks for developing the *IS-LM* model. Chapter 11 uses the *IS-LM* model to explain economic fluctuations and the aggregate demand curve. It concludes with an extended case study of the Great Depression.

The study of short-run fluctuations continues in Chapter 12, which focuses on aggregate demand in an open economy. This chapter presents the Mundell-Fleming model and shows how monetary and fiscal policies affect the economy under floating and fixed exchange-rate systems. It also discusses the debate over whether exchange rates should be floating or fixed.

Chapter 13 looks more closely at aggregate supply. It examines various approaches to explaining the short-run aggregate supply curve and discusses the short-run tradeoff between inflation and unemployment.

Part Five, Macroeconomic Policy Debates

Once the student has command of standard long-run and short-run models of the economy, the book uses these models as the foundation for discussing some of the key debates over economic policy. Chapter 14 considers the debate over how policymakers should respond to short-run economic fluctuations. It emphasizes two broad questions. Should monetary and fiscal policy be active or passive? Should policy be conducted by rule or by discretion? The chapter presents arguments on both sides of these questions.

Chapter 15 focuses on the various debates over government debt. It gives some sense about the magnitude of government indebtedness, discusses why measuring budget deficits is not always straightforward, recaps the traditional view of the effects of government debt, presents Ricardian equivalence as an alternative view, and discusses various other perspectives on government debt. As in the previous chapter, students are not handed conclusions but are given the tools to evaluate the alternative viewpoints on their own.

Part Six, More on the Microeconomics Behind Macroeconomics

After developing theories to explain the economy in the long run and in the short run and then applying those theories to macroeconomic policy debates, the book turns to several topics that refine our understanding of the economy. The last four chapters analyze more fully the microeconomics behind macroeconomics. These chapters can be presented at the end of a course, or they can be covered earlier, depending on an instructor's preferences.

Chapter 16 presents the various theories of consumer behavior, including the Keynesian consumption function, Fisher's model of intertemporal choice, Modigliani's life-cycle hypothesis, Friedman's permanent-income hypothesis, Hall's random-walk hypothesis, and Laibson's model of instant gratification. Chapter 17 examines the theory behind the investment function. Chapter 18 provides additional material on the money market, including the role of the banking system in determining the money supply and the Baumol-Tobin model of money demand. Chapter 19 discusses advances in the theory of economic fluctuations, including the theory of real business cycles and new Keynesian theories of sticky prices; these recent theories apply microeconomic analysis in an attempt to better understand short-run economic fluctuations.

Epilogue

The book ends with a brief epilogue that reviews the broad lessons about which most macroeconomists agree and discusses some of the most important open questions. Regardless of which chapters an instructor chooses to cover, this capstone chapter can be used to remind students how the many models and themes of macroeconomics relate to one another. Here and throughout the book, I emphasize that despite the disagreements among macroeconomists, there is much that we know about how the economy works.

Alternative Routes Through the Text

Although I have organized the material in the way that I prefer to teach intermediate-level macroeconomics, I understand that other instructors have different preferences. I tried to keep this in mind as I wrote the book, so that it would offer a degree of flexibility. Here are a few ways that instructors might consider rearranging the material:

- Some instructors are eager to cover short-run economic fluctuations. For such a course, I recommend covering Chapters 1 through 4 so students are grounded in the basics of classical theory and then jumping to Chapters 9, 10, 11, and 13 to cover the model of aggregate demand and aggregate supply.
- Some instructors are eager to cover long-run economic growth. These instructors can cover Chapters 7 and 8 immediately after Chapter 3.
- An instructor who wants to defer (or even skip) open-economy macroeconomics can put off Chapters 5 and 12 without loss of continuity.
- An instructor who wants to emphasize the microeconomic foundations of macroeconomics can teach chapters 16, 17, and 18 early in the course, such as immediately after chapter 6 (or even earlier).

Experience with previous editions suggests this text complements well a variety of approaches to the field.

Learning Tools

I am pleased that students have found the previous editions of this book user-friendly. I have tried to make this sixth edition even more so.

Case Studies

Economics comes to life when it is applied to understanding actual events. Therefore, the numerous Case Studies (many new or revised in this edition) are an important learning tool, integrated closely with the theoretical material presented in each chapter. The frequency with which these Case Studies occur ensures that a student does not have to grapple with an overdose of theory before seeing the theory applied. Students report that the Case Studies are their favorite part of the book.

FYI Boxes

These boxes present ancillary material "for your information." I use these boxes to clarify difficult concepts, to provide additional information about the tools of economics, and to show how economics relates to our daily lives. Several are new or revised in this edition.

Graphs

Understanding graphical analysis is a key part of learning macroeconomics, and I have worked hard to make the figures easy to follow. I often use comment boxes within figures that describe briefly and draw attention to the important points that the figures illustrate. They should help students both learn and review the material.

Mathematical Notes

I use occasional mathematical footnotes to keep more difficult material out of the body of the text. These notes make an argument more rigorous or present a proof of a mathematical result. They can easily be skipped by those students who have not been introduced to the necessary mathematical tools.

Chapter Summaries

Every chapter ends with a brief, nontechnical summary of its major lessons. Students can use the summaries to place the material in perspective and to review for exams.

Key Concepts

Learning the language of a field is a major part of any course. Within the chapter, each key concept is in **boldface** when it is introduced. At the end of the chapter, the key concepts are listed for review.

Questions for Review

After studying a chapter, students can immediately test their understanding of its basic lessons by answering the Questions for Review.

Problems and Applications

Every chapter includes Problems and Applications designed for homework assignments. Some of these are numerical applications of the theory in the chapter. Others encourage the student to go beyond the material in the chapter by addressing new issues that are closely related to the chapter topics.

Chapter Appendixes

Several chapters include appendixes that offer additional material, sometimes at a higher level of mathematical sophistication. These are designed so that professors can cover certain topics in greater depth if they wish. The appendixes can be skipped altogether without loss of continuity.

Glossary

To help students become familiar with the language of macroeconomics, a glossary of more than 250 terms is provided at the back of the book.

Supplements for Students

Worth Publishers and I have been delighted at the positive feedback we have received on the supplements that accompany the book. Students can use the following tools to test their understanding of core concepts and practice further in preparation for tests and quizzes.

Student Guide and Workbook

Roger Kaufman (Smith College) has revised his superb study guide for students. This guide offers various ways for students to learn the material in the text and assess their understanding.

- *Fill-In Questions* give students the opportunity to review and check their knowledge of the key terms and concepts in the chapter.
- *Multiple-Choice Questions* allow students to test themselves on the chapter material.
- *Exercises* guide students step by step through the various models using graphs and numerical examples.
- *Problems* ask students to apply the models on their own.
- *Questions to Think About* require critical thinking as well as economic analysis.
- *Data Questions* ask students to obtain and learn about readily available economic data.

Companion Web Site (www.worthpublishers.com/mankiw)

Murat Iyigun (University of Colorado) has updated the innovative software package for students (originally created by David Weil, Brown University). The companion Web site provides a range of activities to aid and motivate the student throughout the course.

- *Self-Tests.* Students can test their knowledge of the material in the book by taking multiple-choice tests on any chapter or combination of chapters. After the student responds, the program explains the answer and directs the student to specific sections in the book for additional study. Students may also test their knowledge of key terms using the Flashcards.

- *Data Plotter.* Students can explore macroeconomic data with time-series graphs and scatterplots.
- *Macro Models.* These modules provide simulations of the models presented in the book. Students can change the exogenous variables and see the outcomes in terms of shifting curves and recalculated numerical values of the endogenous variables. Each module contains exercises that instructors can assign as homework.
- *2009: A Game for Macroeconomists.* The game allows students to become President of the United States in the year 2009 and to make macroeconomic policy decisions based on news events, economic statistics, and approval ratings. It gives students a sense of the complex interconnections that influence the economy. It is also fun to play.

Student Tutorials

Mannig Simidian has developed *Mankiw's Macroeconomics Modules: A Powerpoint Tutorial,* an animated set of tutorial slides for students. For each chapter, key points are highlighted, and students are offered another way to learn the material. Dynamic macroeconomic models come alive with shifting curves, colorful equations, graphics, and humor. The tutorial is available on the Web site and on the *Instructor's Resource* CD-ROM.

Supplements for Instructors

Additional supplements are available from Worth Publishers to help instructors enhance their courses.

Instructor's Resources

Robert G. Murphy (Boston College) has revised the impressive resource manual for instructors. For each chapter of this book, the manual contains notes to the instructor, a detailed lecture outline, additional case studies, and coverage of advanced topics. Instructors can use the manual to prepare their lectures, and they can reproduce whatever pages they choose as handouts for students.

Solutions Manual

John Fernald (Federal Reserve Board) has updated the solutions manual for all of the Questions for Review and Problems and Applications. The manual also contains the answers to selected questions from the *Student Guide and Workbook.*

Test Bank

Nancy Jianakoplos (Colorado State University) has updated and revised the *Test Bank* so that it now includes over 1,500 multiple-choice questions, numerical problems, and short-answer graphical questions to accompany each chapter of the text. The *Test Bank* is available both as a printed book and on a CD-ROM. The CD includes our flexible test-generating software which instructors can use to easily write and edit questions as well as create and print tests.

PowerPoint Slides™

Ron Cronovich (University of Nevada at Las Vegas) has prepared PowerPoint presentations of the material in each chapter. They feature graphs with effective animation, careful explanations of the core material, additional case studies and data, helpful notes to the instructor, and innovative pedagogical features. Designed to be customized or used "as is," they include easy instructions for professors who have little experience with PowerPoint. They are available on the Web site and on the *Instructor's Resource* CD-ROM.

Transparency Masters

Instructors can download from the Website four-color master copies of all the figures and tables in the text in order to print overhead transparencies for use in lecture presentations.

Instructor's Resource CD-ROM

This CD-ROM contains all the instructor's tools available on the companion Web site as well as the student tutorials.

Image Gallery

On the companion Web site, instructors have access to every figure and table in the new edition in "high-resolution" JPEG files and PowerPoint format. These textbook images may be used to build classroom presentations or enhance online courses.

Translations

The English-language version of this book has been used in dozens of countries. To make the book more accessible for students around the world, editions are (or will soon be) available in 15 other languages: Armenian, Chinese, French, German, Greek, Hungarian, Indonesian, Italian, Japanese, Korean, Portuguese, Romanian, Russian, Spanish, and Ukrainian. In addition, a Canadian adaptation co-authored with William Scarth (McMaster University) is available, and a European adaptation co-authored with Mark Taylor (University of Warwick) will soon be available. Instructors who would like information about these versions of the book should contact Worth Publishers.

Acknowledgments

Since I started writing the first edition of this book in 1988, I have benefited from the input of many reviewers and colleagues in the economics profession. Now that the book is in its sixth edition, these individuals are too numerous to list in their entirety. However, I continue to be grateful for their willingness to have given up their scarce time to help me improve the economics and pedagogy of this text. Their advice has made this book a better teaching tool for hundreds of thousands of students around the world.

I would like to mention those instructors whose recent input shaped this new edition:

Temisan Agbeyegbe
(Hunter College)

David Aschauer
(Bates College)

Christopher Baum
(Boston College)

Joydeep Bhattacharya
(Iowa State University)

Ducan Black
(University of California, Irvine)

Frank Bonello
(University of Notre Dame)

William Branch
(College of William and Mary)

Mary Burfisher
(United States Naval Academy)

David Butler
(University of Western Australia)

Ricardo Cavalcanti
(Pennsylvania State University)

Wei Chen
(University of California, Santa Cruz)

William Collins
(Vanderbilt University)

Paul Cowgill
(Duke University)

Troy Davig
(College of William and Mary)

A. Edward Day
(University of Texas, Dallas)

Saubnik Deb
(Rutgers University)

David DeJong
(University of Pittsburgh)

David Dilts
(Purdue University)

John Driscoll
(Brown University)

Amitava Dutt
(University of Notre Dame)

Michael Everett
(Quinnipiac University)

Dave Findlay
(Colby College)

Eric Fisher
(Ohio State University)

Sean Flynn
(Vassar College)

Bodhi Ganguli
(Rutgers University)

James Gapinski
(Florida State University)

Harvey Gram
(Queens College)

Cary Heath
(University of Louisiana)

Chris House
(University of Michigan)

Yi Jin
(University of Kansas)

Georgios Karras
(University of Illinois, Chicago)

John Keating
(University of Kansas)

Miles Kimball
(University of Michigan)

Kenneth Koelln
(University of North Texas)

Oleg Korenok
(Rutgers University)

Michael Krause
(Tilburg University)

R. Vijay Krishna
(Pennsylvania State University)

Dirk Krueger
(Stanford University)

Agim Kukeli
(Colorado State University)

Jaehee Lee
(Pennsylvania State University)

Steve McCafferty
(Ohio State University)

Michael McPherson
(University of North Texas)

Diego Mendez-Carbajo
(Illinois Wesleyan University)

Bruce Mizrach
(Rutgers University)

Douglas Morgan
(University of California, Santa Barbara)

Robert Murphy
(Boston College)

Ilan Noy
(University of Hawaii)

Kevin Reffett
(Arizona State University)

Charles Revier
(Colorado State University)

Felix Rioja
(Georgia State University)

Michael Samson
(Williams College)

Majid Sani
(Rutgers University)

Alden Shiers
(California Institute of Technology)

Anthony Sindone
(University of Notre Dame)

Abdulhamid Sukar
(Cameron University)

Mark Thoma
(University of Oregon)

Ed Tower
(Duke University)

Anne Villamil
(University of Illinois)

In addition, I am grateful to Noam Yuchtman, a graduate student at Harvard, who helped me update the data, refine my prose, and proofread the entire book.

The people at Worth Publishers have continued to be congenial and dedicated. I would like to thank Charlie Van Wagner, Acquisitions Editor; Barbara Reingold, Art Director; Kerry O'Shaughnessy, Project Editor; Marie McHale, Associate Editor; Vicki Tomaselli, Design Manager; Barbara Seixas, Production Manager; Ye Jin Lee, Electronic Book Editor (Scribe); Gail Naron Chalew, Copy-editor (Scribe); Eve Conte, Supplements Editor; and Stacey Alexander, Supplements Manager.

Many other people made valuable contributions as well. Most important, Jane Tufts, freelance developmental editor, worked her magic on this book once again, confirming that she's the best in the business. Alexandra Nickerson did a great job preparing the index. Deborah Mankiw, my wife and in-house editor, continued to be the first reader of new material, providing the right mix of criticism and encouragement.

Finally, I would like to thank my three children, Catherine, Nicholas, and Peter. They helped immensely with this revision—both by providing a pleasant distraction and by reminding me that textbooks are written for the next generation.

N. Gregory Mankiw

Cambridge, Massachusetts
January 2006

PART I

Introduction

CHAPTER 1

The Science of Macroeconomics

The whole of science is nothing more than the refinement of everyday thinking.

— Albert Einstein

1-1 What Macroeconomists Study

Why have some countries experienced rapid growth in incomes over the past century while others stay mired in poverty? Why do some countries have high rates of inflation while others maintain stable prices? Why do all countries experience recessions and depressions—recurrent periods of falling incomes and rising unemployment—and how can government policy reduce the frequency and severity of these episodes? **Macroeconomics**, the study of the economy as a whole, attempts to answer these and many related questions.

To appreciate the importance of macroeconomics, you need only read the newspaper or listen to the news. Every day you can see headlines such as INCOME GROWTH REBOUNDS, FED MOVES TO COMBAT INFLATION, or STOCKS FALL AMID RECESSION FEARS. Although these macroeconomic events may seem abstract, they touch all of our lives. Business executives forecasting the demand for their products must guess how fast consumers' incomes will grow. Senior citizens living on fixed incomes wonder how fast prices will rise. Recent college graduates looking for jobs hope that the economy will boom and that firms will be hiring.

Because the state of the economy affects everyone, macroeconomic issues play a central role in national political debates. Voters are aware of how the economy is doing, and they know that government policy can affect the economy in powerful ways. As a result, the popularity of the incumbent president often rises when the economy is doing well and falls when it is doing poorly.

Macroeconomic issues are also at the center of world politics, and if you read the international news, you will quickly start thinking about a variety of macroeconomic questions. Was it a good move for much of Europe to adopt a common currency? Should China maintain a fixed exchange rate against the U.S. dollar? Why is the United States running large trade deficits? How can poor nations raise their standard of living? When world leaders meet, these topics are often high on their agenda.

Although the job of making economic policy belongs to world leaders, the job of explaining how the economy as a whole works falls to macroeconomists. Toward this end, macroeconomists collect data on incomes, prices, unemployment, and many other variables from different time periods and different countries. They then attempt to formulate general theories that help to explain these data. Like astronomers studying the evolution of stars or biologists studying the evolution of species, macroeconomists cannot conduct controlled experiments in a laboratory. Instead, they must make use of the data that history gives them. Macroeconomists observe that economies differ from one another and that they change over time. These observations provide both the motivation for developing macroeconomic theories and the data for testing them.

To be sure, macroeconomics is a young and imperfect science. The macroeconomist's ability to predict the future course of economic events is no better than the meteorologist's ability to predict next month's weather. But, as you will see, macroeconomists do know quite a lot about how economies work. This knowledge is useful both for explaining economic events and for formulating economic policy.

Every era has its own economic problems. In the 1970s, Presidents Richard Nixon, Gerald Ford, and Jimmy Carter all wrestled in vain with a rising rate of inflation. In the 1980s, inflation subsided, but Presidents Ronald Reagan and George Bush presided over large federal budget deficits. In the 1990s, with President Bill Clinton in the Oval Office, the economy and stock market enjoyed a remarkable boom; the budget deficit shrank and even turned into a budget surplus. But as Clinton was leaving office, the stock market was in retreat, and the economy was heading into recession. When President George W. Bush moved into the White House in 2001, he reduced taxes, which helped end the recession but also contributed to a reemergence of budget deficits. The basic principles of macroeconomics do not change from decade to decade, but the macroeconomist must apply these principles with flexibility and creativity to meet changing circumstances.

CASE STUDY

The Historical Performance of the U.S. Economy

Economists use many types of data to measure the performance of an economy. Three macroeconomic variables are especially important: real gross domestic product (GDP), the inflation rate, and the unemployment rate. **Real GDP** measures the total income of everyone in the economy (adjusted for the level of prices). The **inflation rate** measures how fast prices are rising. The **unemployment rate** measures the fraction of the labor force that is out of work. Macroeconomists study how these variables are determined, why they change over time, and how they interact with one another.

FIGURE 1-1

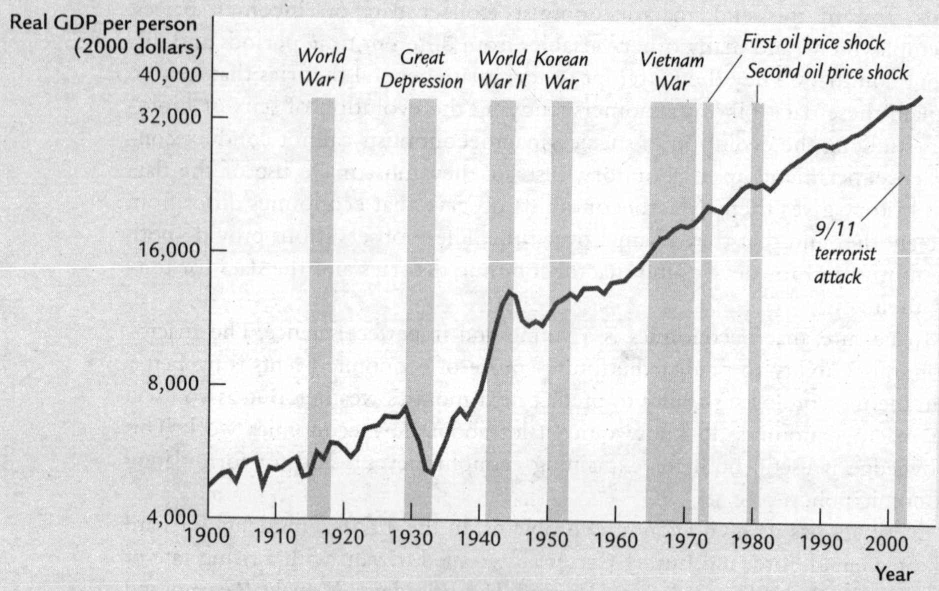

Real GDP per Person in the U.S. Economy Real GDP measures the total income of everyone in the economy, and real GDP per person measures the income of the average person in the economy. This figure shows that real GDP per person tends to grow over time and that this normal growth is sometimes interrupted by periods of declining income, called recessions or depressions.

Note: Real GDP is plotted here on a logarithmic scale. On such a scale, equal distances on the vertical axis represent equal *percentage* changes. Thus, the distance between \$4,000 and \$8,000 (a 100 percent change) is the same as the distance between \$8,000 and \$16,000 (a 100 percent change).
Source: U.S. Department of Commerce and Economic History Services.

Figure 1-1 shows real GDP per person in the United States. Two aspects of this figure are noteworthy. First, real GDP grows over time. Real GDP per person today is about eight times higher than it was in 1900. This growth in average income allows us to enjoy a much higher standard of living than our great-grandparents did. Second, although real GDP rises in most years, this growth is not steady. There are repeated periods during which real GDP falls, the most dramatic instance being the early 1930s. Such periods are called **recessions** if they are mild and **depressions** if they are more severe. Not surprisingly, periods of declining income are associated with substantial economic hardship.

Figure 1-2 shows the U.S. inflation rate. You can see that inflation varies substantially over time. In the first half of the twentieth century, the inflation rate averaged only slightly above zero. Periods of falling prices, called **deflation**, were

FIGURE 1-2

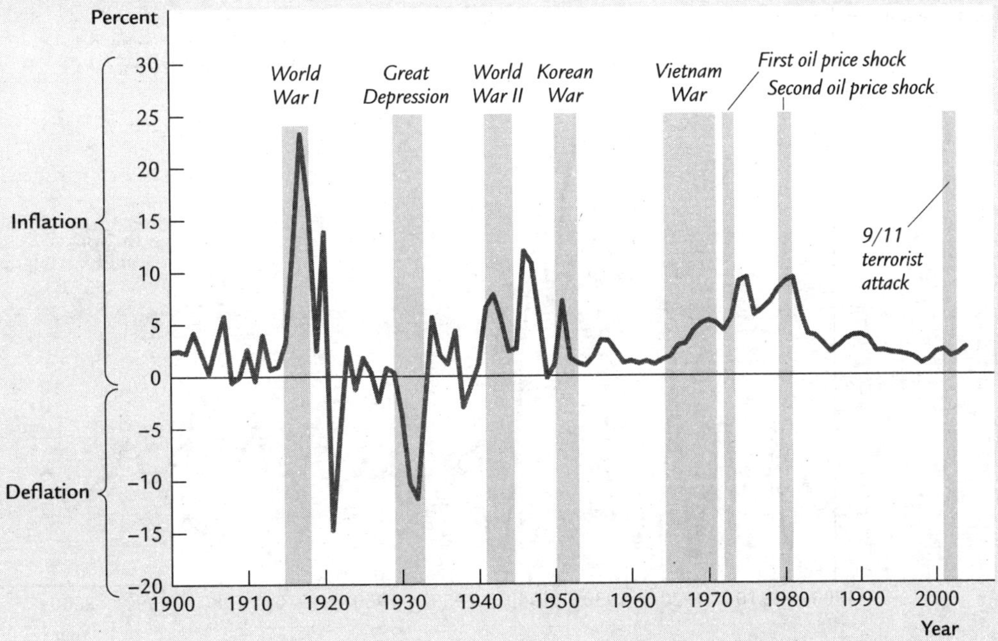

The Inflation Rate in the U.S. Economy The inflation rate measures the percentage change in the average level of prices from the year before. When the inflation rate is above zero, prices are rising. When it is below zero, prices are falling. If the inflation rate declines but remains positive, prices are rising but at a slower rate.

Note: The inflation rate is measured here using the GDP deflator.
Source: U.S. Department of Commerce and Economic History Services.

almost as common as periods of rising prices. In the past half century, inflation has been the norm. Inflation became most severe during the late 1970s, when prices rose at a rate of almost 10 percent per year. In recent years, the inflation rate has been about 2 or 3 percent per year, indicating that prices have been fairly stable.

Figure 1-3 shows the U.S. unemployment rate. Notice that there is always some unemployment in the economy. In addition, although there is no long-term trend, the amount of unemployment varies from year to year. Recessions and depressions are associated with unusually high unemployment. The highest rates of unemployment were reached during the Great Depression of the 1930s.

These three figures offer a glimpse at the history of the U.S. economy. In the chapters that follow, we first discuss how these variables are measured and then develop theories to explain how they behave.

FIGURE 1-3

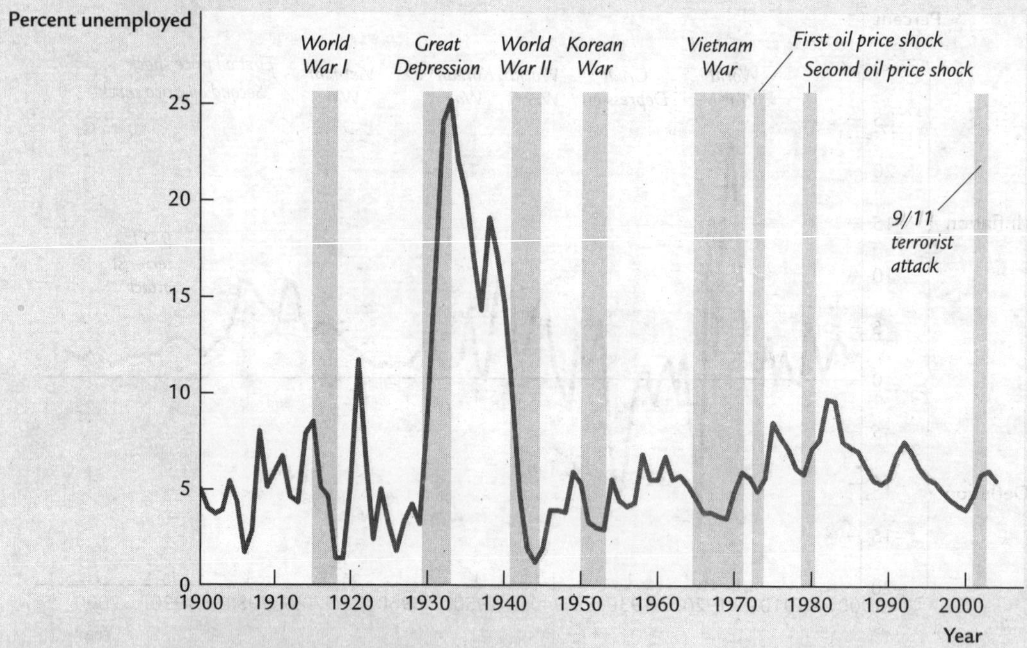

The Unemployment Rate in the U.S. Economy The unemployment rate measures the percentage of people in the labor force who do not have jobs. This figure shows that the economy always has some unemployment and that the amount fluctuates from year to year.

Source: U.S. Department of Labor and U.S. Bureau of the Census (*Historical Statistics of the United States: Colonial Times to 1970*).

1-2 How Economists Think

Although economists often study politically charged issues, they try to address these issues with a scientist's objectivity. Like any science, economics has its own set of tools—terminology, data, and a way of thinking—that can seem foreign and arcane to the layman. The best way to become familiar with these tools is to practice using them, and this book affords you ample opportunity to do so. To make these tools less forbidding, however, let's discuss a few of them here.

Theory as Model Building

Young children learn much about the world around them by playing with toy versions of real objects. For instance, they often put together models of cars, trains, or planes. These models are far from realistic, but the model-builder learns a lot from them nonetheless. The model illustrates the essence of the real object it is designed to resemble. (In addition, for many children, building models is fun.)

Economists also use **models** to understand the world, but an economist's model is more likely to be made of symbols and equations than plastic and glue. Economists build their "toy economies" to help explain economic variables, such as GDP, inflation, and unemployment. Economic models illustrate, often in mathematical terms, the relationships among the variables. They are useful because they help us to dispense with irrelevant details and to focus on important connections. (In addition, for many economists, building models is fun.)

Models have two kinds of variables: endogenous variables and exogenous variables. **Endogenous variables** are those variables that a model tries to explain. **Exogenous variables** are those variables that a model takes as given. The purpose of a model is to show how the exogenous variables affect the endogenous variables. In other words, as Figure 1-4 illustrates, exogenous variables come from outside the model and serve as the model's input, whereas endogenous variables are determined within the model and are the model's output.

FIGURE 1-4

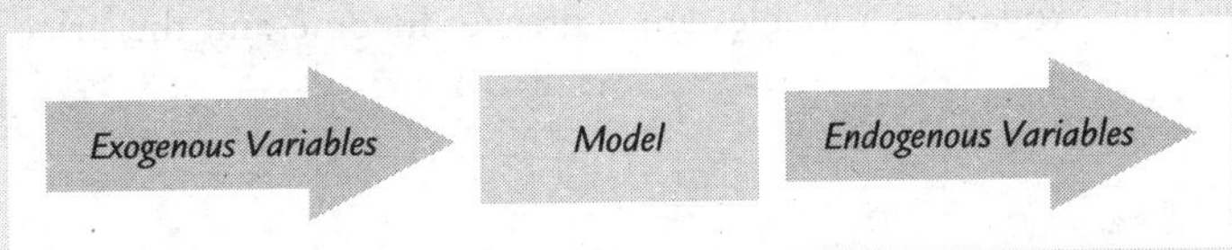

How Models Work Models are simplified theories that show the key relationships among economic variables. The exogenous variables are those that come from outside the model. The endogenous variables are those that the model explains. The model shows how changes in the exogenous variables affect the endogenous variables.

To make these ideas more concrete, let's review the most celebrated of all economic models—the model of supply and demand. Imagine that an economist were interested in figuring out what factors influence the price of pizza and the quantity of pizza sold. He or she would develop a model that described the behavior of pizza buyers, the behavior of pizza sellers, and their interaction in the market for pizza. For example, the economist supposes that the quantity of pizza demanded by consumers Q^d depends on the price of pizza P and on aggregate income Y. This relationship is expressed in the equation

$$Q^d = D(P, Y),$$

where $D(\ )$ represents the demand function. Similarly, the economist supposes that the quantity of pizza supplied by pizzerias Q^s depends on the price of pizza

P and on the price of materials P_m, such as cheese, tomatoes, flour, and anchovies. This relationship is expressed as

$$Q^s = S(P, P_m),$$

where $S(\ )$ represents the supply function. Finally, the economist assumes that the price of pizza adjusts to bring the quantity supplied and quantity demanded into balance:

$$Q^s = Q^d.$$

These three equations compose a model of the market for pizza.

The economist illustrates the model with a supply-and-demand diagram, as in Figure 1-5. The demand curve shows the relationship between the quantity of pizza demanded and the price of pizza, while holding aggregate income constant. The demand curve slopes downward because a higher price of pizza encourages consumers to switch to other foods and buy less pizza. The supply curve shows the relationship between the quantity of pizza supplied and the price of pizza, while holding the price of materials constant. The supply curve slopes upward because a higher price of pizza makes selling pizza more profitable, which encourages pizzerias to produce more of it. The equilibrium for the market is the price and quantity at which the supply and demand curves intersect. At the equilibrium price, consumers choose to buy the amount of pizza that pizzerias choose to produce.

This model of the pizza market has two exogenous variables and two endogenous variables. The exogenous variables are aggregate income and the price of

FIGURE 1-5

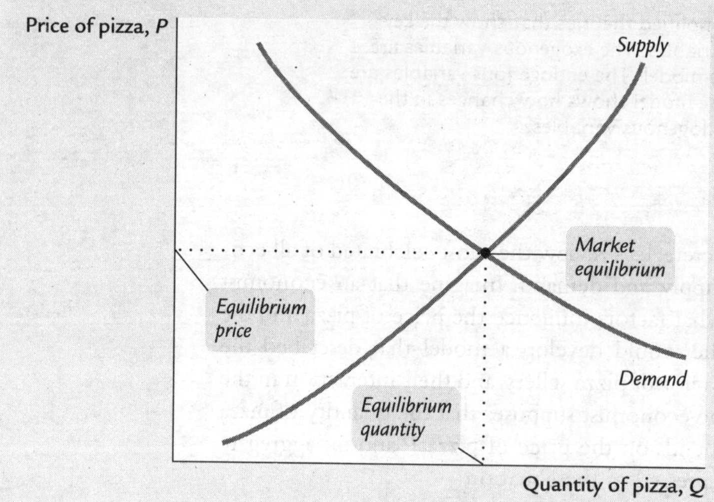

The Model of Supply and Demand The most famous economic model is that of supply and demand for a good or service—in this case, pizza. The demand curve is a downward-sloping curve relating the price of pizza to the quantity of pizza that consumers demand. The supply curve is an upward-sloping curve relating the price of pizza to the quantity of pizza that pizzerias supply. The price of pizza adjusts until the quantity supplied equals the quantity demanded. The point where the two curves cross is the market equilibrium, which shows the equilibrium price of pizza and the equilibrium quantity of pizza.

materials. The model does not attempt to explain them but takes them as given (perhaps to be explained by another model). The endogenous variables are the price of pizza and the quantity of pizza exchanged. These are the variables that the model attempts to explain.

The model can be used to show how a change in one of the exogenous variables affects both endogenous variables. For example, if aggregate income increases, then the demand for pizza increases, as in panel (a) of Figure 1-6. The model shows that both the equilibrium price and the equilibrium quantity of pizza rise. Similarly, if the price of materials increases, then the supply of pizza decreases, as in panel (b) of Figure 1-6. The model shows that in this case the

FIGURE 1-6

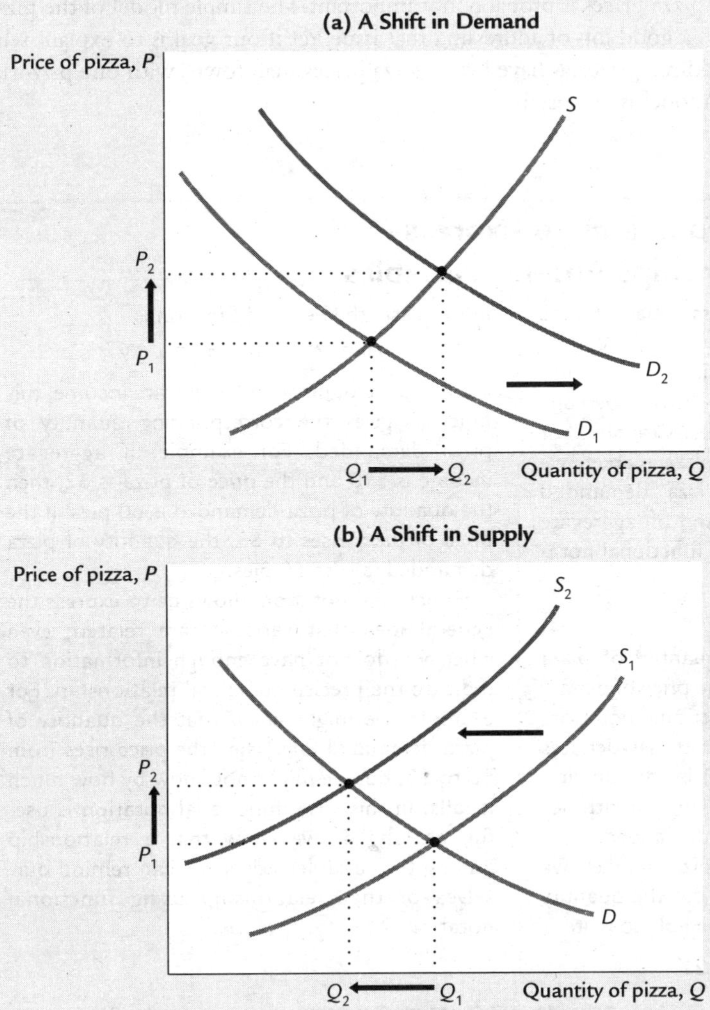

Changes in Equilibrium In panel (a), a rise in aggregate income causes the demand for pizza to increase: at any given price, consumers now want to buy more pizza. This is represented by a rightward shift in the demand curve from D_1 to D_2. The market moves to the new intersection of supply and demand. The equilibrium price rises from P_1 to P_2, and the equilibrium quantity of pizza rises from Q_1 to Q_2. In panel (b), a rise in the price of materials decreases the supply of pizza: at any given price, pizzerias find that the sale of pizza is less profitable and therefore choose to produce less pizza. This is represented by a leftward shift in the supply curve from S_1 to S_2. The market moves to the new intersection of supply and demand. The equilibrium price rises from P_1 to P_2, and the equilibrium quantity falls from Q_1 to Q_2.

equilibrium price of pizza rises and the equilibrium quantity of pizza falls. Thus, the model shows how changes in aggregate income or in the price of materials affect price and quantity in the market for pizza.

Like all models, this model of the pizza market makes simplifying assumptions. The model does not take into account, for example, that every pizzeria is in a different location. For each customer, one pizzeria is more convenient than the others, and thus pizzerias have some ability to set their own prices. Although the model assumes that there is a single price for pizza, in fact there could be a different price at every pizzeria.

How should we react to the model's lack of realism? Should we discard the simple model of pizza supply and pizza demand? Should we attempt to build a more complex model that allows for diverse pizza prices? The answers to these questions depend on our purpose. If our goal is to explain how the price of cheese affects the average price of pizza and the amount of pizza sold, then the diversity of pizza prices is probably not important. The simple model of the pizza market does a good job of addressing that issue. Yet if our goal is to explain why towns with three pizzerias have lower pizza prices than towns with one pizzeria, the simple model is less useful.

FYI Using Functions to Express Relationships Among Variables

All economic models express relationships among economic variables. Often, these relationships are expressed as functions. A *function* is a mathematical concept that shows how one variable depends on a set of other variables. For example, in the model of the pizza market, we said that the quantity of pizza demanded depends on the price of pizza and on aggregate income. To express this, we use functional notation to write

$$Q^d = D(P, Y).$$

This equation says that the quantity of pizza demanded Q^d is a function of the price of pizza P and aggregate income Y. In functional notation, the variable preceding the parentheses denotes the function. In this case, $D(\ )$ is the function expressing how the variables in parentheses determine the quantity of pizza demanded.

If we knew more about the pizza market, we could give a numerical formula for the quantity of pizza demanded. We might be able to write

$$Q^d = 60 - 10P + 2Y.$$

In this case, the demand function is

$$D(P, Y) = 60 - 10P + 2Y.$$

For any price of pizza and aggregate income, this function gives the corresponding quantity of pizza demanded. For example, if aggregate income is \$10 and the price of pizza is \$2, then the quantity of pizza demanded is 60 pies; if the price of pizza rises to \$3, the quantity of pizza demanded falls to 50 pies.

Functional notation allows us to express the general idea that variables are related, even when we do not have enough information to indicate the precise numerical relationship. For example, we might know that the quantity of pizza demanded falls when the price rises from \$2 to \$3, but we might not know by how much it falls. In this case, functional notation is useful: as long as we know that a relationship among the variables exists, we can remind ourselves of that relationship using functional notation.

The art in economics is in judging when a simplifying assumption (such as assuming a single price of pizza) clarifies our thinking and when it misleads us. Simplification is a necessary part of building a useful model: any model constructed to be completely realistic would be too complicated for anyone to understand. Yet models lead to incorrect conclusions if they assume away features of the economy that are crucial to the issue at hand. Economic modeling therefore requires care and common sense.

A Multitude of Models

Macroeconomists study many facets of the economy. For example, they examine the role of saving in economic growth, the impact of minimum wage laws on unemployment, the effect of inflation on interest rates, and the influence of trade policy on the trade balance and exchange rate.

Although economists use models to address all these issues, no single model can answer all questions. Just as carpenters use different tools for different tasks, economists use different models to explain different economic phenomena. Students of macroeconomics, therefore, must keep in mind that there is no single "correct" model that is useful for all purposes. Instead, there are many models, each of which is useful for shedding light on a different facet of the economy. The field of macroeconomics is like a Swiss army knife—a set of complementary but distinct tools that can be applied in different ways in different circumstances.

This book presents many different models that address different questions and make different assumptions. Remember that a model is only as good as its assumptions and that an assumption that is useful for some purposes may be misleading for others. When using a model to address a question, the economist must keep in mind the underlying assumptions and judge if they are reasonable for studying the matter at hand.

Prices: Flexible Versus Sticky

Throughout this book, one group of assumptions will prove especially important—those concerning the speed at which wages and prices adjust to changing economic conditions. Economists normally presume that the price of a good or a service moves quickly to bring quantity supplied and quantity demanded into balance. In other words, they assume that markets are normally in equilibrium, so the price of any good or service is found where the supply and demand curves intersect. This assumption is called **market clearing** and is central to the model of the pizza market discussed earlier. For answering most questions, economists use market-clearing models.

Yet the assumption of *continuous* market clearing is not entirely realistic. For markets to clear continuously, prices must adjust instantly to changes in supply and demand. In fact, many wages and prices adjust slowly. Labor contracts often set wages for up to three years. Many firms leave their product prices the same for long periods of time—for example, magazine publishers typically change their newsstand prices only every three or four years. Although market-clearing models assume that all wages and prices are **flexible,** in the real world some wages and prices are **sticky.**

The apparent stickiness of prices does not make market-clearing models useless. After all, prices are not stuck forever; eventually, they do adjust to changes in supply and demand. Market-clearing models might not describe the economy at every instant, but they do describe the equilibrium toward which the economy gravitates. Therefore, most macroeconomists believe that price flexibility is a good assumption for studying long-run issues, such as the growth in real GDP that we observe from decade to decade.

For studying short-run issues, such as year-to-year fluctuations in real GDP and unemployment, the assumption of price flexibility is less plausible. Over short periods, many prices in the economy are fixed at predetermined levels. Therefore, most macroeconomists believe that price stickiness is a better assumption for studying the short-run behavior of the economy.

Microeconomic Thinking and Macroeconomic Models

Microeconomics is the study of how households and firms make decisions and how these decisionmakers interact in the marketplace. A central principle of microeconomics is that households and firms *optimize*—they do the best they can for themselves given their objectives and the constraints they face. In microeconomic models, households choose their purchases to maximize their level of satisfaction, which economists call *utility*, and firms make production decisions to maximize their profits.

Because economy-wide events arise from the interaction of many households and many firms, macroeconomics and microeconomics are inextricably linked. When we study the economy as a whole, we must consider the decisions of individual economic actors. For example, to understand what determines total consumer spending, we must think about a family deciding how much to spend today and how much to save for the future. To understand what determines total investment spending, we must think about a firm deciding whether to build a new factory. Because aggregate variables are the sum of the variables describing many individual decisions, macroeconomic theory rests on a microeconomic foundation.

Although microeconomic decisions underlie all economic models, in many models the optimizing behavior of households and firms is implicit rather than explicit. The model of the pizza market we discussed earlier is an example. Households' decisions about how much pizza to buy underlie the demand for pizza, and pizzerias' decisions about how much pizza to produce underlie the supply of pizza. Presumably, households make their decisions to maximize utility, and pizzerias make their decisions to maximize profit. Yet the model did not focus on how these microeconomic decisions are made; it left these decisions in the background. Similarly, although microeconomic decisions underlie macroeconomic phenomena, macroeconomic models do not necessarily focus on the optimizing behavior of households and firms, but instead sometimes leave that behavior in the background.

FYI Nobel Macroeconomists

The winner of the Nobel Prize in economics is announced every October. Many winners have been macroeconomists whose work we study in this book. Here are a few of them, together with some of their own words about how they chose their field of study:

Milton Friedman (Nobel 1976): "I graduated from college in 1932, when the United States was at the bottom of the deepest depression in its history before or since. The dominant problem of the time was economics. How to get out of the depression? How to reduce unemployment? What explained the paradox of great need on the one hand and unused resources on the other? Under the circumstances, becoming an economist seemed more relevant to the burning issues of the day than becoming an applied mathematician or an actuary."

James Tobin (Nobel 1981): "I was attracted to the field for two reasons. One was that economic theory is a fascinating intellectual challenge, on the order of mathematics or chess. I liked analytics and logical argument . . . . The other reason was the obvious relevance of economics to understanding and perhaps overcoming the Great Depression."

Franco Modigliani (Nobel 1985): "For awhile it was thought that I should study medicine because my father was a physician. . . . I went to the registration window to sign up for medicine, but then I closed my eyes and thought of blood! I got pale just thinking about blood and decided under those conditions I had better keep away from medicine. . . . Casting about for something to do, I happened to get into some economics activities. I knew some German and was asked to translate from German into Italian some articles for one of the trade associations. Thus I began to be exposed to the economic problems that were in the German literature."

Robert Solow (Nobel 1987): "I came back [to college after being in the army] and, almost without thinking about it, signed up to finish my undergraduate degree as an economics major. The time was such that I had to make a decision in a hurry. No doubt I acted as if I were maximizing an infinite discounted sum of one-period utilities, but you couldn't prove it by me. To me it felt as if I were saying to myself: 'What the hell.'"

Robert Lucas (Nobel 1995): "In public school science was an unending and not very well organized list of things other people had discovered long ago. In college, I learned something about the process of scientific discovery, but what I learned did not attract me as a career possibility. . . . What I liked thinking about were politics and social issues."

George Akerlof (Nobel 2001): "When I went to Yale, I was convinced that I wanted to be either an economist or an historian. Really, for me it was a distinction without a difference. If I was going to be an historian, then I would be an economic historian. And if I was to be an economist I would consider history as the basis for my economics."

Edward Prescott (Nobel 2004): "Through discussion with [my father], I learned a lot about the way businesses operated. This was one reason why I liked my microeconomics course so much in my first year at Swarthmore College. The price theory that I learned in that course rationalized what I had learned from him about the way businesses operate. The other reason was the textbook used in that course, Paul A. Samuelson's *Principles of Economics*. I loved the way Samuelson laid out the theory in his textbook, so simply and clearly."

If you want to learn more about the Nobel Prize and its winners, go to www.nobelprize.org.[1]

[1] The first five quotations are from William Breit and Barry T. Hirsch, eds., *Lives of the Laureates*, 4th ed., Cambridge, MA: MIT Press, 2004. The last two are from the Nobel Web site.

1-3 How This Book Proceeds

This book has six parts. This chapter and the next make up Part One, the Introduction. Chapter 2 discusses how economists measure economic variables, such as aggregate income, the inflation rate, and the unemployment rate.

Part Two, "Classical Theory: The Economy in the Long Run," presents the classical model of how the economy works. The key assumption of the classical model is that prices are flexible. That is, with rare exceptions, the classical model assumes that markets clear. Because the assumption of price flexibility describes the economy only in the long run, classical theory is best suited for analyzing a time horizon of at least several years.

Part Three, "Growth Theory: The Economy in the Very Long Run," builds on the classical model. It maintains the assumption of market clearing but adds a new emphasis on growth in the capital stock, the labor force, and technological knowledge. Growth theory is designed to explain how the economy evolves over a period of several decades.

Part Four, "Business Cycle Theory: The Economy in the Short Run," examines the behavior of the economy when prices are sticky. The non-market-clearing model developed here is designed to analyze short-run issues, such as the reasons for economic fluctuations and the influence of government policy on those fluctuations. It is best suited to analyzing the changes in the economy we observe from month to month or from year to year.

Part Five, "Macroeconomic Policy Debates," builds on the previous analysis to consider what role the government should take in the economy. It considers how, if at all, the government should respond to short-run fluctuations in real GDP and unemployment. It also examines the various views of how government debt affects the economy.

Part Six, "More on the Microeconomics Behind Macroeconomics," presents some of the microeconomic models that are useful for analyzing macroeconomic issues. For example, it examines the household's decisions regarding how much to consume and how much money to hold and the firm's decision regarding how much to invest. These individual decisions together form the larger macroeconomic picture. The goal of studying these microeconomic decisions in detail is to refine our understanding of the aggregate economy.

Summary

1. Macroeconomics is the study of the economy as a whole—including growth in incomes, changes in prices, and the rate of unemployment. Macroeconomists attempt both to explain economic events and to devise policies to improve economic performance.
2. To understand the economy, economists use models—theories that simplify reality in order to reveal how exogenous variables influence endogenous vari-

ables. The art in the science of economics is in judging whether a model captures the important economic relationships for the matter at hand. Because no single model can answer all questions, macroeconomists use different models to look at different issues.

3. A key feature of a macroeconomic model is whether it assumes that prices are flexible or sticky. According to most macroeconomists, models with flexible prices describe the economy in the long run, whereas models with sticky prices offer a better description of the economy in the short run.

4. Microeconomics is the study of how firms and individuals make decisions and how these decisionmakers interact. Because macroeconomic events arise from many microeconomic interactions, all macroeconomic models must be consistent with microeconomic foundations, even if those foundations are only implicit.

KEY CONCEPTS

Macroeconomics
Real GDP
Inflation and deflation
Unemployment
Recession
Depression
Models
Endogenous variables
Exogenous variables
Market clearing
Flexible and sticky prices
Microeconomics

QUESTIONS FOR REVIEW

1. Explain the difference between macroeconomics and microeconomics. How are these two fields related?
2. Why do economists build models?
3. What is a market-clearing model? When is it appropriate to assume that markets clear?

PROBLEMS AND APPLICATIONS

1. What macroeconomic issues have been in the news lately?
2. What do you think are the defining characteristics of a science? Does the study of the economy have these characteristics? Do you think macroeconomics should be called a science? Why or why not?
3. Use the model of supply and demand to explain how a fall in the price of frozen yogurt would affect the price of ice cream and the quantity of ice cream sold. In your explanation, identify the exogenous and endogenous variables.
4. How often does the price you pay for a haircut change? What does your answer imply about the usefulness of market-clearing models for analyzing the market for haircuts?

CHAPTER

2

The Data of Macroeconomics

It is a capital mistake to theorize before one has data. Insensibly one begins to twist facts to suit theories, instead of theories to fit facts.

— Sherlock Holmes

Scientists, economists, and detectives have much in common: they all want to figure out what's going on in the world around them. To do this, they rely on theory and observation. They build theories in an attempt to make sense of what they see happening. They then turn to more systematic observation to evaluate the theories' validity. Only when theory and evidence come into line do they feel they understand the situation. This chapter discusses the types of observation that economists use to develop and test their theories.

Casual observation is one source of information about what's happening in the economy. When you go shopping, you see how fast prices are rising. When you look for a job, you learn whether firms are hiring. Because we are all participants in the economy, we get some sense of economic conditions as we go about our lives.

A century ago, economists monitoring the economy had little more to go on than these casual observations. Such fragmentary information made economic policymaking all the more difficult. One person's anecdote would suggest the economy was moving in one direction, while a different person's anecdote would suggest it was moving in another. Economists needed some way to combine many individual experiences into a coherent whole. There was an obvious solution: as the old quip goes, the plural of "anecdote" is "data."

Today, economic data offer a systematic and objective source of information, and almost every day the newspaper has a story about some newly released statistic. Most of these statistics are produced by the government. Various government agencies survey households and firms to learn about their economic activity—how much they are earning, what they are buying, what prices they are charging, whether they have a job or are looking for work, and so on. From these surveys, various statistics are computed that summarize the state of the economy. Economists use these statistics to study the economy; policymakers use them to monitor developments and formulate policies.

This chapter focuses on the three statistics that economists and policymakers use most often. **Gross domestic product**, or **GDP**, tells us the nation's total income and the total expenditure on its output of goods and services. The **consumer price index**, or **CPI**, measures the level of prices. The

unemployment rate tells us the fraction of workers who are unemployed. In the following pages, we see how these statistics are computed and what they tell us about the economy.

2-1 Measuring the Value of Economic Activity: Gross Domestic Product

Gross domestic product is often considered the best measure of how well the economy is performing. This statistic is computed every three months by the Bureau of Economic Analysis (a part of the U.S. Department of Commerce) from a large number of primary data sources. The purpose of GDP is to summarize in a single number the dollar value of economic activity in a given period of time.

There are two ways to view this statistic. One way to view GDP is as *the total income of everyone in the economy*. Another way to view GDP is as *the total expenditure on the economy's output of goods and services*. From either viewpoint, it is clear why GDP is a gauge of economic performance. GDP measures something people care about—their incomes. Similarly, an economy with a large output of goods and services can better satisfy the demands of households, firms, and the government.

How can GDP measure both the economy's income and its expenditure on output? The reason is that these two quantities are really the same: for the economy as a whole, income must equal expenditure. That fact, in turn, follows from an even more fundamental one: because every transaction has a buyer and a seller, every dollar of expenditure by a buyer must become a dollar of income to a seller. When Joe paints Jane's house for $1,000, that $1,000 is income to Joe and expenditure by Jane. The transaction contributes $1,000 to GDP, regardless of whether we are adding up all income or adding up all expenditure.

To understand the meaning of GDP more fully, we turn to **national income accounting**, the accounting system used to measure GDP and many related statistics.

Income, Expenditure, and the Circular Flow

Imagine an economy that produces a single good, bread, from a single input, labor. Figure 2-1 illustrates all the economic transactions that occur between households and firms in this economy.

The inner loop in Figure 2-1 represents the flows of bread and labor. The households sell their labor to the firms. The firms use the labor of their workers to produce bread, which the firms in turn sell to the households. Hence, labor flows from households to firms, and bread flows from firms to households.

The outer loop in Figure 2-1 represents the corresponding flow of dollars. The households buy bread from the firms. The firms use some of the revenue

FIGURE 2-1

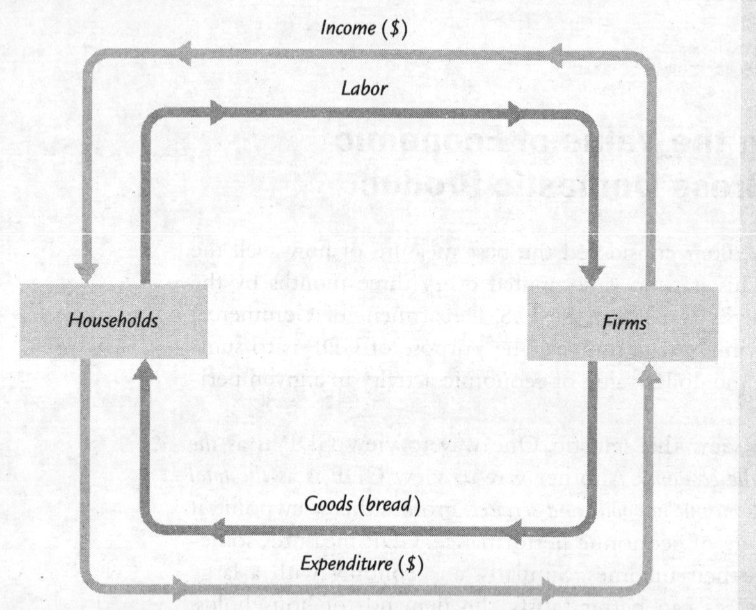

The Circular Flow This figure illustrates the flows between firms and households in an economy that produces one good, bread, from one input, labor. The inner loop represents the flows of labor and bread: households sell their labor to firms, and the firms sell the bread they produce to households. The outer loop represents the corresponding flows of dollars: households pay the firms for the bread, and the firms pay wages and profit to the households. In this economy, GDP is both the total expenditure on bread and the total income from the production of bread.

from these sales to pay the wages of their workers, and the remainder is the profit belonging to the owners of the firms (who themselves are part of the household sector). Hence, expenditure on bread flows from households to firms, and income in the form of wages and profit flows from firms to households.

GDP measures the flow of dollars in this economy. We can compute it in two ways. GDP is the total income from the production of bread, which equals the sum of wages and profit—the top half of the circular flow of dollars. GDP is also the total expenditure on purchases of bread—the bottom half of the circular flow of dollars. To compute GDP, we can look at either the flow of dollars from firms to households or the flow of dollars from households to firms.

These two ways of computing GDP must be equal because the expenditure of buyers on products is, by the rules of accounting, income to the sellers of those products. Every transaction that affects expenditure must affect income, and every transaction that affects income must affect expenditure. For example, suppose that a firm produces and sells one more loaf of bread to a household. Clearly this transaction raises total expenditure on bread, but it also has an equal effect on total income. If the firm produces the extra loaf without hiring any more labor (such as by making the production process more efficient), then profit increases. If the firm produces the extra loaf by hiring more labor, then wages increase. In both cases, expenditure and income increase equally.

FYI Stocks and Flows

Many economic variables measure a quantity of something—a quantity of money, a quantity of goods, and so on. Economists distinguish between two types of quantity variables: stocks and flows. A **stock** is a quantity measured at a given point in time, whereas a **flow** is a quantity measured per unit of time.

A bathtub, shown in Figure 2-2, is the classic example used to illustrate stocks and flows. The amount of water in the tub is a stock: it is the quantity of water in the tub at a given point in time. The amount of water coming out of the faucet is a flow: it is the quantity of water being added to the tub per unit of time. Note that we measure stocks and flows in different units. We say that the bathtub contains 50 *gallons* of water, but that water is coming out of the faucet at 5 *gallons per minute*.

GDP is probably the most important flow variable in economics: it tells us how many dollars are flowing around the economy's circular flow per unit of time. When you hear someone say that the U.S. GDP is $10 trillion, you should understand that this means that it is $10 trillion *per year*. (Equivalently, we could say that U.S. GDP is $317,000 per second.)

Stocks and flows are often related. In the bathtub example, these relationships are clear. The stock of water in the tub represents the accumulation of the flow out of the faucet, and the flow of water represents the change in the stock. When building theories to explain economic variables, it is often useful to determine whether the variables are stocks or flows and whether any relationships link them.

Here are some examples of related stocks and flows that we study in future chapters:

- A person's wealth is a stock; his income and expenditure are flows.
- The number of unemployed people is a stock; the number of people losing their jobs is a flow.
- The amount of capital in the economy is a stock; the amount of investment is a flow.
- The government debt is a stock; the government budget deficit is a flow.

FIGURE 2-2

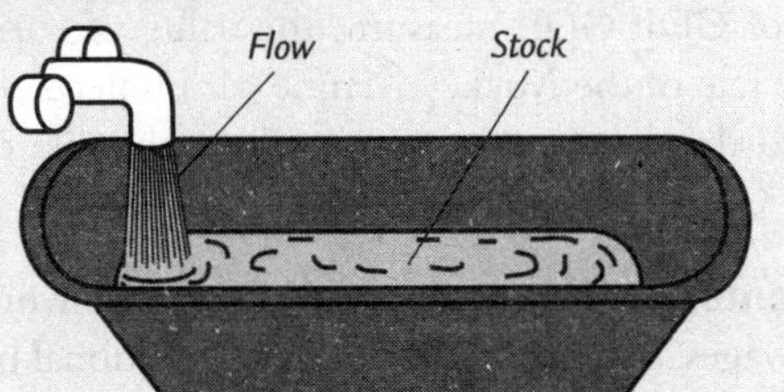

Stocks and Flows The amount of water in a bathtub is a stock: it is a quantity measured at a given moment in time. The amount of water coming out of the faucet is a flow: it is a quantity measured per unit of time.

Rules for Computing GDP

In an economy that produces only bread, we can compute GDP by adding up the total expenditure on bread. Real economies, however, include the production and sale of a vast number of goods and services. To compute GDP for such a complex economy, it will be helpful to have a more precise definition: *Gross domestic product (GDP) is the market value of all final goods and services produced within an economy in a given period of time.* To see how this definition is applied, let's discuss some of the rules that economists follow in constructing this statistic.

Adding Apples and Oranges The U.S. economy produces many different goods and services—hamburgers, haircuts, cars, computers, and so on. GDP combines the value of these goods and services into a single measure. The diversity of products in the economy complicates the calculation of GDP because different products have different values.

Suppose, for example, that the economy produces four apples and three oranges. How do we compute GDP? We could simply add apples and oranges and conclude that GDP equals seven pieces of fruit. But this makes sense only if we thought apples and oranges had equal value, which is generally not true. (This would be even clearer if the economy had produced four watermelons and three grapes.)

To compute the total value of different goods and services, the national income accounts use market prices because these prices reflect how much people are willing to pay for a good or service. Thus, if apples cost $0.50 each and oranges cost $1.00 each, GDP would be

$$\begin{aligned} \text{GDP} &= (\text{Price of Apples} \times \text{Quantity of Apples}) \\ &\quad + (\text{Price of Oranges} \times \text{Quantity of Oranges}) \\ &= (\$0.50 \times 4) + (\$1.00 \times 3) \\ &= \$5.00. \end{aligned}$$

GDP equals $5.00—the value of all the apples, $2.00, plus the value of all the oranges, $3.00.

Used Goods When the Topps Company makes a package of baseball cards and sells it for 50 cents, that 50 cents is added to the nation's GDP. But what about when a collector sells a rare Mickey Mantle card to another collector for $500? That $500 is not part of GDP. GDP measures the value of currently produced goods and services. The sale of the Mickey Mantle card reflects the transfer of an asset, not an addition to the economy's income. Thus, the sale of used goods is not included as part of GDP.

The Treatment of Inventories Imagine that a bakery hires workers to produce more bread, pays their wages, and then fails to sell the additional bread. How does this transaction affect GDP?

The answer depends on what happens to the unsold bread. Let's first suppose that the bread spoils. In this case, the firm has paid more in wages but has not received any additional revenue, so the firm's profit is reduced by the amount that wages have increased. Total expenditure in the economy hasn't changed because no one buys the bread. Total income hasn't changed either—although more is distributed as wages and less as profit. Because the transaction affects neither expenditure nor income, it does not alter GDP.

Now suppose, instead, that the bread is put into inventory to be sold later. In this case, the transaction is treated differently. The owners of the firm are assumed to have "purchased" the bread for the firm's inventory, and the firm's profit is not reduced by the additional wages it has paid. Because the higher wages raise total income, and greater spending on inventory raises total expenditure, the economy's GDP rises.

What happens later when the firm sells the bread out of inventory? This case is much like the sale of a used good. There is spending by bread consumers, but there is inventory disinvestment by the firm. This negative spending by the firm offsets the positive spending by consumers, so the sale out of inventory does not affect GDP.

The general rule is that when a firm increases its inventory of goods, this investment in inventory is counted as an expenditure by the firm owners. Thus, production for inventory increases GDP just as much as production for final sale. A sale out of inventory, however, is a combination of positive spending (the purchase) and negative spending (inventory disinvestment), so it does not influence GDP. This treatment of inventories ensures that GDP reflects the economy's current production of goods and services.

Intermediate Goods and Value Added Many goods are produced in stages: raw materials are processed into intermediate goods by one firm and then sold to another firm for final processing. How should we treat such products when computing GDP? For example, suppose a cattle rancher sells one-quarter pound of meat to McDonald's for $0.50, and then McDonald's sells you a hamburger for $1.50. Should GDP include both the meat and the hamburger (a total of $2.00), or just the hamburger ($1.50)?

The answer is that GDP includes only the value of final goods. Thus, the hamburger is included in GDP but the meat is not: GDP increases by $1.50, not by $2.00. The reason is that the value of intermediate goods is already included as part of the market price of the final goods in which they are used. To add the intermediate goods to the final goods would be double counting—that is, the meat would be counted twice. Hence, GDP is the total value of final goods and services produced.

One way to compute the value of all final goods and services is to sum the value added at each stage of production. The **value added** of a firm equals the value of the firm's output less the value of the intermediate goods that the firm purchases. In the case of the hamburger, the value added of the rancher is $0.50 (assuming that the rancher bought no intermediate goods), and the value added of McDonald's is $1.50 – $0.50, or $1.00. Total value added is $0.50 + $1.00, which equals $1.50. For the economy as a whole, the sum of all value added must equal the value of all final goods and services. Hence, GDP is also the total value added of all firms in the economy.

Housing Services and Other Imputations Although most goods and services are valued at their market prices when computing GDP, some are not sold in the marketplace and therefore do not have market prices. If GDP is to include the value of these goods and services, we must use an estimate of their value. Such an estimate is called an **imputed value.**

Imputations are especially important for determining the value of housing. A person who rents a house is buying housing services and providing income for the landlord; the rent is part of GDP, both as expenditure by the renter and as income for the landlord. Many people, however, live in their own homes. Although they do not pay rent to a landlord, they are enjoying housing services similar to those that renters purchase. To take account of the housing services enjoyed by homeowners, GDP includes the "rent" that these homeowners "pay" to themselves. Of course, homeowners do not in fact pay themselves this rent. The Department of Commerce estimates what the market rent for a house would be if it were rented and includes that imputed rent as part of GDP. This imputed rent is included both in the homeowner's expenditure and in the homeowner's income.

Imputations also arise in valuing government services. For example, police officers, fire fighters, and senators provide services to the public. Giving a value to these services is difficult because they are not sold in a marketplace and therefore do not have a market price. The national income accounts include these services in GDP by valuing them at their cost. That is, the wages of these public servants are used as a measure of the value of their output.

In many cases, an imputation is called for in principle but, to keep things simple, is not made in practice. Because GDP includes the imputed rent on owner-occupied houses, one might expect it also to include the imputed rent on cars, lawn mowers, jewelry, and other durable goods owned by households. Yet the value of these rental services is left out of GDP. In addition, some of the output of the economy is produced and consumed at home and never enters the marketplace. For example, meals cooked at home are similar to meals cooked at a restaurant, yet the value added in meals at home is left out of GDP.

Finally, no imputation is made for the value of goods and services sold in the *underground economy*. The underground economy is the part of the economy that people hide from the government either because they wish to evade taxation or because the activity is illegal. Domestic workers paid "off the books" is one example. The illegal drug trade is another.

Because the imputations necessary for computing GDP are only approximate, and because the value of many goods and services is left out altogether, GDP is an imperfect measure of economic activity. These imperfections are most problematic when comparing standards of living across countries. The size of the underground economy, for instance, varies widely from country to country. Yet as long as the magnitude of these imperfections remains fairly constant over time, GDP is useful for comparing economic activity from year to year.

Real GDP Versus Nominal GDP

Economists use the rules just described to compute GDP, which values the economy's total output of goods and services. But is GDP a good measure of economic well-being? Consider once again the economy that produces only apples and oranges. In this economy GDP is the sum of the value of all the apples produced and the value of all the oranges produced. That is,

$$\begin{aligned} \text{GDP} = {} & (\text{Price of Apples} \times \text{Quantity of Apples}) \\ & + (\text{Price of Oranges} \times \text{Quantity of Oranges}). \end{aligned}$$

Notice that GDP can increase either because prices rise or because quantities rise.

It is easy to see that GDP computed this way is not a good gauge of economic well-being. That is, this measure does not accurately reflect how well the economy can satisfy the demands of households, firms, and the government. If all prices doubled without any change in quantities, GDP would double. Yet it would be misleading to say that the economy's ability to satisfy demands has doubled, because the quantity of every good produced remains the same. Economists call the value of goods and services measured at current prices **nominal GDP**.

A better measure of economic well-being would tally the economy's output of goods and services and would not be influenced by changes in prices. For this purpose, economists use **real GDP**, which is the value of goods and services measured using a constant set of prices. That is, real GDP shows what would have happened to expenditure on output if quantities had changed but prices had not.

To see how real GDP is computed, imagine we wanted to compare output in 2006 with output in subsequent years for our apple-and-orange economy. We could begin by choosing a set of prices, called *base-year prices,* such as the prices that prevailed in 2006. Goods and services are then added up using these base-year prices to value the different goods in each year. Real GDP for 2006 would be

$$\begin{aligned}\text{Real GDP} = {} & (\text{2006 Price of Apples} \times \text{2006 Quantity of Apples}) \\ & + (\text{2006 Price of Oranges} \times \text{2006 Quantity of Oranges}).\end{aligned}$$

Similarly, real GDP in 2007 would be

$$\begin{aligned}\text{Real GDP} = {} & (\text{2006 Price of Apples} \times \text{2007 Quantity of Apples}) \\ & + (\text{2006 Price of Oranges} \times \text{2007 Quantity of Oranges}).\end{aligned}$$

And real GDP in 2008 would be

$$\begin{aligned}\text{Real GDP} = {} & (\text{2006 Price of Apples} \times \text{2008 Quantity of Apples}) \\ & + (\text{2006 Price of Oranges} \times \text{2008 Quantity of Oranges}).\end{aligned}$$

Notice that 2006 prices are used to compute real GDP for all three years. Because the prices are held constant, real GDP varies from year to year only if the quantities produced vary. Because a society's ability to provide economic satisfaction for its members ultimately depends on the quantities of goods and services produced, real GDP provides a better measure of economic well-being than nominal GDP.

The GDP Deflator

From nominal GDP and real GDP we can compute a third statistic: the GDP deflator. The **GDP deflator**, also called the *implicit price deflator for GDP,* is the ratio of nominal GDP to real GDP:

$$\text{GDP Deflator} = \frac{\text{Nominal GDP}}{\text{Real GDP}}.$$

The GDP deflator reflects what's happening to the overall level of prices in the economy.

To better understand this, consider again an economy with only one good, bread. If P is the price of bread and Q is the quantity sold, then nominal GDP is the total number of dollars spent on bread in that year, $P \times Q$. Real GDP is the number of loaves of bread produced in that year times the price of bread in some base year, $P_{base} \times Q$. The GDP deflator is the price of bread in that year relative to the price of bread in the base year, P/P_{base}.

The definition of the GDP deflator allows us to separate nominal GDP into two parts: one part measures quantities (real GDP) and the other measures prices (the GDP deflator). That is,

$$\text{Nominal GDP} = \text{Real GDP} \times \text{GDP Deflator.}$$

Nominal GDP measures the current dollar value of the output of the economy. Real GDP measures output valued at constant prices. The GDP deflator measures the price of output relative to its price in the base year. We can also write this equation as

$$\text{Real GDP} = \frac{\text{Nominal GDP}}{\text{GDP Deflator}}.$$

In this form, you can see how the deflator earns its name: it is used to deflate (that is, take inflation out of) nominal GDP to yield real GDP.

Chain-Weighted Measures of Real GDP

We have been discussing real GDP as if the prices used to compute this measure never change from their base-year values. If this were truly the case, over time the prices would become more and more dated. For instance, the price of computers has fallen substantially in recent years, while the price of a year at college has risen. When valuing the production of computers and education, it would be misleading to use the prices that prevailed ten or twenty years ago.

To solve this problem, the Bureau of Economic Analysis used to update periodically the prices used to compute real GDP. About every five years, a new base year was chosen. The prices were then held fixed and used to measure year-to-year changes in the production of goods and services until the base year was updated once again.

In 1995, the Bureau announced a new policy for dealing with changes in the base year. In particular, it now emphasizes *chain-weighted* measures of real GDP. With these new measures, the base year changes continuously over time. In essence, average prices in 2006 and 2007 are used to measure real growth from 2006 to 2007; average prices in 2007 and 2008 are used to measure real growth from 2007 to 2008; and so on. These various year-to-year growth rates are then put together to form a "chain" that can be used to compare the output of goods and services between any two dates.

This new chain-weighted measure of real GDP is better than the more traditional measure because it ensures that the prices used to compute real GDP are never far out of date. For most purposes, however, the differences are not important. It turns out that the two measures of real GDP are highly correlated with each other. As a practical matter, both measures of real GDP reflect the same thing: economy-wide changes in the production of goods and services.

FYI Two Arithmetic Tricks for Working With Percentage Changes

For manipulating many relationships in economics, there is an arithmetic trick that is useful to know: *the percentage change of a product of two variables is approximately the sum of the percentage changes in each of the variables.*

To see how this trick works, consider an example. Let P denote the GDP deflator and Y denote real GDP. Nominal GDP is $P \times Y$. The trick states that

$$\text{Percentage Change in } (P \times Y) \approx (\text{Percentage Change in } P) + (\text{Percentage Change in } Y).$$

For instance, suppose that in one year, real GDP is 100 and the GDP deflator is 2; the next year, real GDP is 103 and the GDP deflator is 2.1. We can calculate that real GDP rose by 3 percent and that the GDP deflator rose by 5 percent. Nominal GDP rose from 200 the first year to 216.3 the second year, an increase of 8.15 percent. Notice that the growth in nominal GDP (8.15 percent) is approximately the sum of the growth in the GDP deflator (5 percent) and the growth in real GDP (3 percent).[1]

A second arithmetic trick follows as a corollary to the first: *The percentage change of a ratio is approximately the percentage change in the numerator minus the percentage change in the denominator.* Again, consider an example. Let Y denote GDP and L denote the population, so that Y/L is GDP per person. The second trick states

$$\text{Percentage Change in } (Y/L) \approx (\text{Percentage Change in } Y) - (\text{Percentage Change in } L).$$

For instance, suppose that in the first year, Y is 100,000 and L is 100, so Y/L is 1,000; in the second year, Y is 110,000 and L is 103, so Y/L is 1,068. Notice that the growth in GDP per person (6.8 percent) is approximately the growth in income (10 percent) minus the growth in population (3 percent).

The Components of Expenditure

Economists and policymakers care not only about the economy's total output of goods and services but also about the allocation of this output among alternative uses. The national income accounts divide GDP into four broad categories of spending:

- Consumption (C)
- Investment (I)
- Government purchases (G)
- Net exports (NX).

Thus, letting Y stand for GDP,

$$Y = C + I + G + NX.$$

---

[1] *Mathematical note:* The proof that this trick works begins with the chain rule from calculus:

$$d(PY) = Y\,dP + P\,dY.$$

Now divide both sides of this equation by PY to obtain:

$$d(PY)/(PY) = dP/P + dY/Y.$$

Notice that all three terms in this equation are percentage changes.

GDP is the sum of consumption, investment, government purchases, and net exports. Each dollar of GDP falls into one of these categories. This equation is an *identity*—an equation that must hold because of the way the variables are defined. It is called the **national income accounts identity**.

Consumption consists of the goods and services bought by households. It is divided into three subcategories: nondurable goods, durable goods, and services. Nondurable goods are goods that last only a short time, such as food and clothing. Durable goods are goods that last a long time, such as cars and TVs. Services include the work done for consumers by individuals and firms, such as haircuts and doctor visits.

Investment consists of goods bought for future use. Investment is also divided into three subcategories: business fixed investment, residential fixed investment, and inventory investment. Business fixed investment is the purchase of new plant and equipment by firms. Residential investment is the purchase of new housing by households and landlords. Inventory investment is the increase in firms' inventories of goods (if inventories are falling, inventory investment is negative).

Government purchases are the goods and services bought by federal, state, and local governments. This category includes such items as military equipment, highways, and the services that government workers provide. It does not include transfer payments to individuals, such as Social Security and welfare. Because

FYI What Is Investment?

Newcomers to macroeconomics are sometimes confused by how macroeconomists use familiar words in new and specific ways. One example is the term "investment." The confusion arises because what looks like investment for an individual may not be investment for the economy as a whole. The general rule is that the economy's investment does not include purchases that merely reallocate existing assets among different individuals. Investment, as macroeconomists use the term, creates new capital.

Let's consider some examples. Suppose we observe these two events:

- Smith buys for himself a 100-year-old Victorian house.
- Jones builds for herself a brand-new contemporary house.

What is total investment here? Two houses, one house, or zero?

A macroeconomist seeing these two transactions counts only the Jones house as investment. Smith's transaction has not created new housing for the economy; it has merely reallocated existing housing. Smith's purchase is investment for Smith, but it is disinvestment for the person selling the house. By contrast, Jones has added new housing to the economy; her new house is counted as investment.

Similarly, consider these two events:

- Gates buys \$5 million in IBM stock from Buffett on the New York Stock Exchange.
- General Motors sells \$10 million in stock to the public and uses the proceeds to build a new car factory.

Here, investment is \$10 million. In the first transaction, Gates is investing in IBM stock, and Buffett is disinvesting; there is no investment for the economy. By contrast, General Motors is using some of the economy's output of goods and services to add to its stock of capital; hence, its new factory is counted as investment.

transfer payments reallocate existing income and are not made in exchange for goods and services, they are not part of GDP.

The last category, **net exports**, takes into account trade with other countries. Net exports are the value of goods and services exported to other countries minus the value of goods and services that foreigners provide us. Net exports are positive when the value of our exports is greater than the value of our imports and negative when the value of our imports is greater than the value of our exports. Net exports represent the net expenditure from abroad on our goods and services, which provides income for domestic producers.

CASE STUDY

GDP and Its Components

In 2005 the GDP of the United States totaled about $12.5 trillion. This number is so large that it is almost impossible to comprehend. We can make it easier to understand by dividing it by the 2005 U.S. population of 296 million. In this way, we obtain GDP per person—the amount of expenditure for the average American—which equaled $42,123 in 2005.

How did this GDP get used? Table 2-1 shows that about two-thirds of it, or $29,507 per person, was spent on consumption. Investment was $7,095 per person.

TABLE 2-1

GDP and the Components of Expenditure: 2005

	Total (billions of dollars)	Per Person (dollars)
Gross Domestic Product	**$12,485.7**	**$42,123**
Consumption	**8,746.2**	**29,507**
Nondurable goods	2,564.6	8,652
Durable goods	1,026.5	3,463
Services	5,155.1	17,392
Investment	**2,103.1**	**7,095**
Nonresidential fixed investment	1,330.6	4,489
Residential fixed investment	755.8	2,550
Inventory investment	16.6	56
Government Purchases	**2,363.4**	**7,973**
Federal	877.8	2,961
Defense	587.2	1,981
Nondefense	290.6	980
State and local	1,485.6	5,012
Net Exports	**−726.9**	**−2,452**
Exports	1,301.6	4,391
Imports	2,028.6	6,844

Source: www.bea.gov

Government purchases were \$7,973 per person, \$1,981 of which was spent by the federal government on national defense.

The average American bought \$6,844 of goods imported from abroad and produced \$4,391 of goods that were exported to other countries. Because the average American imported more than he exported, net exports were negative. Furthermore, because the average American earned less from selling to foreigners than he spent on foreign goods, he must have financed the difference by taking out loans from foreigners (or, equivalently, by selling them some of his assets). Thus, the average American borrowed \$2,452 from abroad in 2005.

Other Measures of Income

The national income accounts include other measures of income that differ slightly in definition from GDP. It is important to be aware of the various measures, because economists and the press often refer to them.

To see how the alternative measures of income relate to one another, we start with GDP and add or subtract various quantities. To obtain *gross national product (GNP)*, we add receipts of factor income (wages, profit, and rent) from the rest of the world and subtract payments of factor income to the rest of the world:

$$\text{GNP} = \text{GDP} + \text{Factor Payments from Abroad} - \text{Factor Payments to Abroad}.$$

Whereas GDP measures the total income produced *domestically,* GNP measures the total income earned by *nationals* (residents of a nation). For instance, if a Japanese resident owns an apartment building in New York, the rental income he earns is part of U.S. GDP because it is earned in the United States. But because this rental income is a factor payment to abroad, it is not part of U.S. GNP. In the United States, factor payments from abroad and factor payments to abroad are similar in size—each representing about 3 percent of GDP—so GDP and GNP are quite close.

To obtain *net national product (NNP),* we subtract the depreciation of capital—the amount of the economy's stock of plants, equipment, and residential structures that wears out during the year:

$$\text{NNP} = \text{GNP} - \text{Depreciation}.$$

In the national income accounts, depreciation is called the *consumption of fixed capital.* It equals about 10 percent of GNP. Because the depreciation of capital is a cost of producing the output of the economy, subtracting depreciation shows the net result of economic activity.

The next adjustment in the national income accounts is for indirect business taxes, such as sales taxes. These taxes, which make up about 10 percent of NNP, place a wedge between the price that consumers pay for a good and the price that firms receive. Because firms never receive this tax wedge, it is not part of their income. Once we subtract indirect business taxes from NNP, we obtain a measure called *national income*:

National Income = NNP − Indirect Business Taxes.

National income measures how much everyone in the economy has earned.

The national income accounts divide national income into five components, depending on the way the income is earned. The five categories, and the percentage of national income paid in each category, are

- *Compensation of employees* (71.3%). The wages and fringe benefits earned by workers.
- *Proprietors' income* (9.5%). The income of noncorporate businesses, such as small farms, mom-and-pop stores, and law partnerships.
- *Rental income* (1.4%). The income that landlords receive, including the imputed rent that homeowners "pay" to themselves, less expenses, such as depreciation.
- *Corporate profits* (12.4%). The income of corporations after payments to their workers and creditors.
- *Net interest* (5.4%). The interest domestic businesses pay minus the interest they receive, plus interest earned from foreigners.

A series of adjustments takes us from national income to *personal income,* the amount of income that households and noncorporate businesses receive. Three of these adjustments are most important. First, we reduce national income by the amount that corporations earn but do not pay out, either because the corporations are retaining earnings or because they are paying taxes to the government. This adjustment is made by subtracting corporate profits (which equals the sum of corporate taxes, dividends, and retained earnings) and adding back dividends. Second, we increase national income by the net amount the government pays out in transfer payments. This adjustment equals government transfers to individuals minus social insurance contributions paid to the government. Third, we adjust national income to include the interest that households earn rather than the interest that businesses pay. This adjustment is made by adding personal interest income and subtracting net interest. (The difference between personal interest and net interest arises in part because interest on the government debt is part of the interest that households earn but is not part of the interest that businesses pay out.) Thus, personal income is

Personal Income = National Income
− Corporate Profits
− Social Insurance Contributions
− Net Interest
+ Dividends
+ Government Transfers to Individuals
+ Personal Interest Income.

Next, if we subtract personal tax payments and certain nontax payments to the government (such as parking tickets), we obtain *disposable personal income*:

Disposable Personal Income
= Personal Income − Personal Tax and Nontax Payments.

We are interested in disposable personal income because it is the amount households and noncorporate businesses have available to spend after satisfying their tax obligations to the government.

Seasonal Adjustment

Because real GDP and the other measures of income reflect how well the economy is performing, economists are interested in studying the quarter-to-quarter fluctuations in these variables. Yet when we start to do so, one fact leaps out: all these measures of income exhibit a regular seasonal pattern. The output of the economy rises during the year, reaching a peak in the fourth quarter (October, November, and December), and then falling in the first quarter (January, February, and March) of the next year. These regular seasonal changes are substantial. From the fourth quarter to the first quarter, real GDP falls on average about 8 percent.[2]

It is not surprising that real GDP follows a seasonal cycle. Some of these changes are attributable to changes in our ability to produce: for example, building homes is more difficult during the cold weather of winter than during other seasons. In addition, people have seasonal tastes: they have preferred times for such activities as vacations and Christmas shopping.

When economists study fluctuations in real GDP and other economic variables, they often want to eliminate the portion of fluctuations due to predictable seasonal changes. You will find that most of the economic statistics reported in the newspaper are *seasonally adjusted*. This means that the data have been adjusted to remove the regular seasonal fluctuations. (The precise statistical procedures used are too elaborate to bother with here, but in essence they involve subtracting those changes in income that are predictable just from the change in season.) Therefore, when you observe a rise or fall in real GDP or any other data series, you must look beyond the seasonal cycle for the explanation.

2-2 Measuring the Cost of Living: The Consumer Price Index

A dollar today doesn't buy as much as it did twenty years ago. The cost of almost everything has gone up. This increase in the overall level of prices is called *inflation*, and it is one of the primary concerns of economists and pol-

[2] Robert B. Barsky and Jeffrey A. Miron, "The Seasonal Cycle and the Business Cycle," *Journal of Political Economy* 97 (June 1989): 503-534.

icymakers. In later chapters we examine in detail the causes and effects of inflation. Here we discuss how economists measure changes in the cost of living.

The Price of a Basket of Goods

The most commonly used measure of the level of prices is the **consumer price index (CPI)**. The Bureau of Labor Statistics, which is part of the U.S. Department of Labor, has the job of computing the CPI. It begins by collecting the prices of thousands of goods and services. Just as GDP turns the quantities of many goods and services into a single number measuring the value of production, the CPI turns the prices of many goods and services into a single index measuring the overall level of prices.

How should economists aggregate the many prices in the economy into a single index that reliably measures the price level? They could simply compute an average of all prices. Yet this approach would treat all goods and services equally. Because people buy more chicken than caviar, the price of chicken should have a greater weight in the CPI than the price of caviar. The Bureau of Labor Statistics weights different items by computing the price of a basket of goods and services purchased by a typical consumer. The CPI is the price of this basket of goods and services relative to the price of the same basket in some base year.

For example, suppose that the typical consumer buys 5 apples and 2 oranges every month. Then the basket of goods consists of 5 apples and 2 oranges, and the CPI is

$$\text{CPI} = \frac{(5 \times \text{Current Price of Apples}) + (2 \times \text{Current Price of Oranges})}{(5 \times \text{2006 Price of Apples}) + (2 \times \text{2006 Price of Oranges})}.$$

In this CPI, 2006 is the base year. The index tells us how much it costs now to buy 5 apples and 2 oranges relative to how much it cost to buy the same basket of fruit in 2006.

The consumer price index is the most closely watched index of prices, but it is not the only such index. Another is the producer price index, which measures the price of a typical basket of goods bought by firms rather than consumers. In addition to these overall price indices, the Bureau of Labor Statistics computes price indices for specific types of goods, such as food, housing, and energy.

The CPI Versus the GDP Deflator

Earlier in this chapter we saw another measure of prices—the implicit price deflator for GDP, which is the ratio of nominal GDP to real GDP. The GDP deflator and the CPI give somewhat different information about what's happening to the overall level of prices in the economy. There are three key differences between the two measures.

The first difference is that the GDP deflator measures the prices of all goods and services produced, whereas the CPI measures the prices of only the goods and services bought by consumers. Thus, an increase in the price of goods bought only by firms or the government will show up in the GDP deflator but not in the CPI.

The second difference is that the GDP deflator includes only those goods produced domestically. Imported goods are not part of GDP and do not show up in the GDP deflator. Hence, an increase in the price of a Toyota made in Japan and sold in this country affects the CPI, because the Toyota is bought by consumers, but it does not affect the GDP deflator.

The third and most subtle difference results from the way the two measures aggregate the many prices in the economy. The CPI assigns fixed weights to the prices of different goods, whereas the GDP deflator assigns changing weights. In other words, the CPI is computed using a fixed basket of goods, whereas the GDP deflator allows the basket of goods to change over time as the composition of GDP changes. The following example shows how these approaches differ. Suppose that major frosts destroy the nation's orange crop. The quantity of oranges produced falls to zero, and the price of the few oranges that remain on grocers' shelves is driven sky-high. Because oranges are no longer part of GDP, the increase in the price of oranges does not show up in the GDP deflator. But because the CPI is computed with a fixed basket of goods that includes oranges, the increase in the price of oranges causes a substantial rise in the CPI.

Economists call a price index with a fixed basket of goods a *Laspeyres index* and a price index with a changing basket a *Paasche index*. Economic theorists have studied the properties of these different types of price indices to determine which is a better measure of the cost of living. The answer, it turns out, is that neither is clearly superior. When prices of different goods are changing by different amounts, a Laspeyres (fixed basket) index tends to overstate the increase in the cost of living because it does not take into account that consumers have the opportunity to substitute less expensive goods for more expensive ones. By contrast, a Paasche (changing basket) index tends to understate the increase in the cost of living. Although it accounts for the substitution of alternative goods, it does not reflect the reduction in consumers' welfare that may result from such substitutions.

The example of the destroyed orange crop shows the problems with Laspeyres and Paasche price indices. Because the CPI is a Laspeyres index, it overstates the impact of the increase in orange prices on consumers: by using a fixed basket of goods, it ignores consumers' ability to substitute apples for oranges. By contrast, because the GDP deflator is a Paasche index, it understates the impact on consumers: the GDP deflator shows no rise in prices, yet surely the higher price of oranges makes consumers worse off.[3]

---

[3] Because a Laspeyres index overstates inflation and a Paasche index understates inflation, one might strike a compromise by taking an average of the two measured rates of inflation. This is the approach taken by another type of index, called a *Fisher index*.

FIGURE 2-3

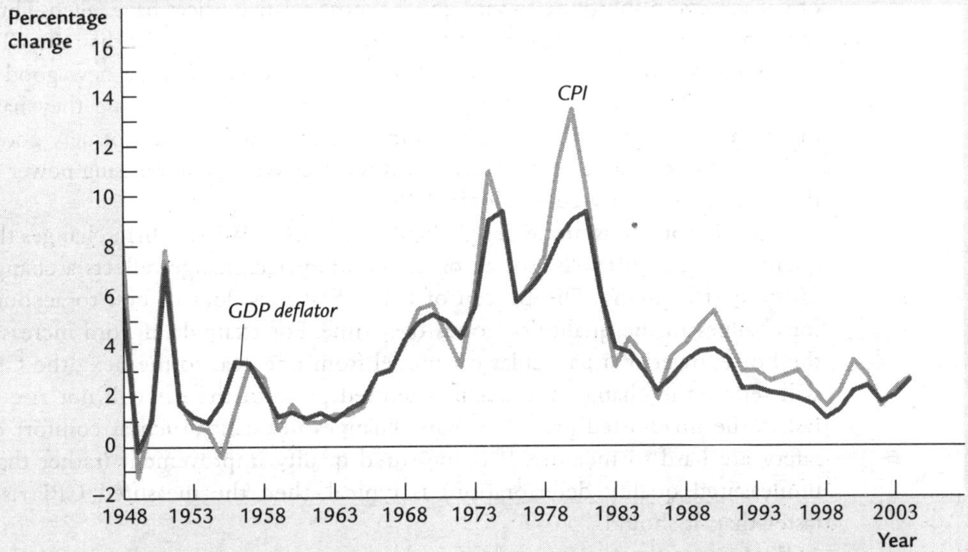

The GDP Deflator and the CPI This figure shows the percentage change in the GDP deflator and in the CPI for every year since 1948. Although these two measures of prices diverge at times, they usually tell the same story about how quickly prices are rising. Both the CPI and the GDP deflator show that prices rose slowly in most of the 1950s and 1960s, that they rose much more quickly in the 1970s, and that they rose slowly again in the 1980s and 1990s.

Source: U.S. Department of Commerce, U.S. Department of Labor.

Luckily, the difference between the GDP deflator and the CPI is usually not large in practice. Figure 2-3 shows the percentage change in the GDP deflator and the percentage change in the CPI for each year since 1948. Both measures usually tell the same story about how quickly prices are rising.

CASE STUDY

Does the CPI Overstate Inflation?

The consumer price index is a closely watched measure of inflation. Policymakers in the Federal Reserve monitor the CPI when choosing monetary policy. In addition, many laws and private contracts have cost-of-living allowances, called *COLAs*, which use the CPI to adjust for changes in the price level. For instance, Social Security benefits are adjusted automatically every year so that inflation will not erode the living standard of the elderly.

Because so much depends on the CPI, it is important to ensure that this measure of the price level is accurate. Many economists believe that, for a number of reasons, the CPI tends to overstate inflation.

One problem is the substitution bias we have already discussed. Because the CPI measures the price of a fixed basket of goods, it does not reflect the ability of consumers to substitute toward goods whose relative prices have fallen. Thus, when relative prices change, the true cost of living rises less rapidly than the CPI.

A second problem is the introduction of new goods. When a new good is introduced into the marketplace, consumers are better off, because they have more products from which to choose. In effect, the introduction of new goods increases the real value of the dollar. Yet this increase in the purchasing power of the dollar is not reflected in a lower CPI.

A third problem is unmeasured changes in quality. When a firm changes the quality of a good it sells, not all of the good's price change reflects a change in the cost of living. The Bureau of Labor Statistics does its best to account for changes in the quality of goods over time. For example, if Ford increases the horsepower of a particular car model from one year to the next, the CPI will reflect the change: the quality-adjusted price of the car will not rise as fast as the unadjusted price. Yet many changes in quality, such as comfort or safety, are hard to measure. If unmeasured quality improvement (rather than unmeasured quality deterioration) is typical, then the measured CPI rises faster than it should.

Because of these measurement problems, some economists have suggested revising laws to reduce the degree of indexation. For example, Social Security benefits could be indexed to CPI inflation minus 1 percent. Such a change would provide a rough way of offsetting these measurement problems. At the same time, it would automatically slow the growth in government spending.

In 1995, the Senate Finance Committee appointed a panel of five noted economists—Michael Boskin, Ellen Dulberger, Robert Gordon, Zvi Griliches, and Dale Jorgenson—to study the magnitude of the measurement error in the CPI. The panel concluded that the CPI was biased upward by 0.8 to 1.6 percentage points per year, with their "best estimate" being 1.1 percentage points. This report led to some changes in the way the CPI is calculated, so the bias is now thought to be under 1 percentage point. The CPI still overstates inflation, but not by as much as it once did.[4]

2-3 Measuring Joblessness: The Unemployment Rate

One aspect of economic performance is how well an economy uses its resources. Because an economy's workers are its chief resource, keeping workers employed is a paramount concern of economic policymakers. The unemployment rate is the statistic that measures the percentage of those people wanting to work who

[4] For further discussion of these issues, see Matthew Shapiro and David Wilcox, "Mismeasurement in the Consumer Price Index: An Evaluation," *NBER Macroeconomics Annual,* 1996, and the symposium on "Measuring the CPI" in the Winter 1998 issue of *The Journal of Economic Perspectives.*

do not have jobs. Every month the U.S. Bureau of Labor Statistics computes the unemployment rate and many other statistics that economists and policymakers use to monitor developments in the labor market.

The Household Survey

The unemployment rate comes from a survey of about 60,000 households called the Current Population Survey. Based on the responses to survey questions, each adult (16 years and older) in each household is placed into one of three categories:

- *Employed:* This category includes those who at the time of the survey worked as paid employees, worked in their own business, or worked as unpaid workers in a family member's business. It also includes those who were not working but who had jobs from which they were temporarily absent because of, for example, vacation, illness, or bad weather.
- *Unemployed:* This category includes those who were not employed, were available for work, and had tried to find employment during the previous four weeks. It also includes those waiting to be recalled to a job from which they had been laid off.
- *Not in the labor force:* This category includes those who fit neither of the first two categories, such as a full-time student, homemaker, or retiree.

"Well, so long Eddie, the recession's over."

Notice that a person who wants a job but has given up looking—a *discouraged worker*—is counted as not being in the labor force.

The **labor force** is defined as the sum of the employed and unemployed, and the **unemployment rate** is defined as the percentage of the labor force that is unemployed. That is,

$$\text{Labor Force} = \text{Number of Employed} + \text{Number of Unemployed},$$

and

$$\text{Unemployment Rate} = \frac{\text{Number of Unemployed}}{\text{Labor Force}} \times 100.$$

A related statistic is the **labor-force participation rate**, the percentage of the adult population that is in the labor force:

$$\text{Labor-Force Participation Rate} = \frac{\text{Labor Force}}{\text{Adult Population}} \times 100.$$

The Bureau of Labor Statistics computes these statistics for the overall population and for groups within the population: men and women, whites and blacks, teenagers and prime-age workers.

FIGURE 2-4

Population: 223.4 million
(16 years and older)

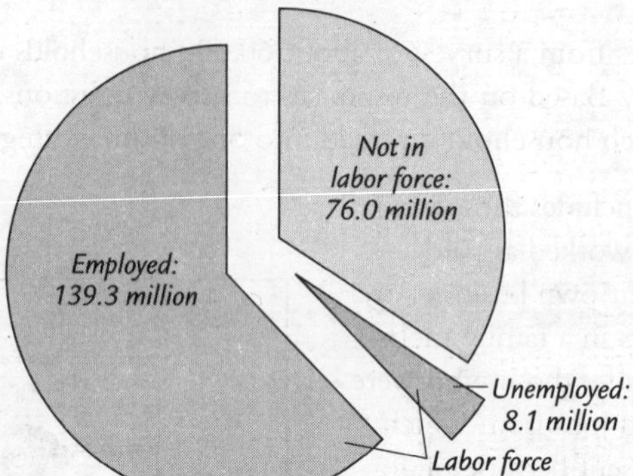

The Three Groups of the Population When the Bureau of Labor Statistics surveys the population, it places all adults into one of three categories: employed, unemployed, or not in the labor force. This figure shows the number of people in each category in 2004.

Source: U.S. Department of Labor.

Figure 2-4 shows the breakdown of the population into the three categories for 2004. The statistics broke down as follows:

$$\text{Labor Force} = 139.3 + 8.1 = 147.4 \text{ million.}$$

$$\text{Unemployment Rate} = (8.1/147.4) \times 100 = 5.5\%.$$

$$\text{Labor-Force Participation Rate} = (147.4/223.4) \times 100 = 66.0\%.$$

Hence, about two-thirds of the adult population was in the labor force, and about 5.5 percent of those in the labor force did not have a job.

CASE STUDY

Trends in Labor-Force Participation

The data on the labor market collected by the Bureau of Labor Statistics reflect not only economic developments, such as the booms and busts of the business cycle, but also a variety of social changes. Longer-term social changes in the roles of men and women in society, for example, are evident in the data on labor-force participation.

Figure 2-5 shows the labor-force participation rates of men and women in the United States since 1950. Just after World War II, men and women had very different economic roles. Only 33 percent of women were working or looking for work, in contrast to 87 percent of men. Since then, the difference between the participation rates of men and women has gradually diminished, as growing numbers of women have entered the labor force and some men have left it. Data for 2004 show that 60 percent of women were in the labor force, in contrast to 73 percent of men. As measured by labor-force participation, men and women are now playing a more equal role in the economy.

FIGURE 2-5

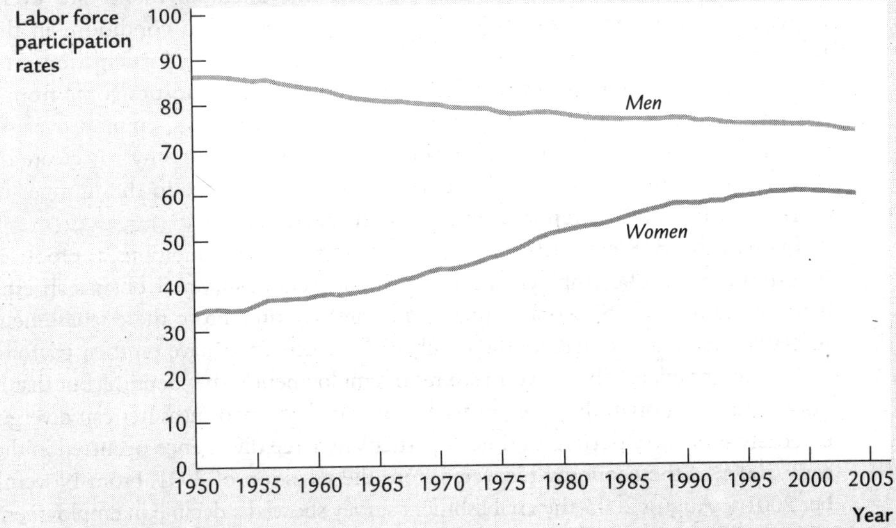

Labor-Force Participation Over the past several decades, the labor-force participation rate for women has risen, while the rate for men has declined.

Source: U.S. Department of Labor

There are many reasons for this change. In part, it is due to new technologies, such as the washing machine, clothes dryer, refrigerator, freezer, and dishwasher, which have reduced the amount of time required to complete routine household tasks. In part, it is due to improved birth control, which has reduced the number of children born to the typical family. And in part, this change in women's role is due to changing political and social attitudes. Together these developments have had a profound impact, as demonstrated by these data.

Although the increase in women's labor-force participation is easily explained, the fall in men's participation may seem puzzling. There are several developments at work. First, young men now stay in school longer than their fathers and grandfathers did. Second, older men now retire earlier and live longer. Third, with more women employed, more fathers now stay at home to raise their children. Full-time students, retirees, and stay-at-home fathers are all counted as out of the labor force.

Looking ahead, many economists believe that labor-force participation for both men and women may gradually decline over the next several decades. The reason is demographic. People today are living longer and having fewer children today than did their counterparts in previous generations. As a result, the elderly are representing an increasing share of the population. Because the elderly are more often retired and less often members of the labor force, the rising elderly share of the population will tend to reduce the economy's labor-force participation rate.

The Establishment Survey

When the Bureau of Labor Statistic reports the unemployment rate every month, it also reports a variety of other statistics describing conditions in the labor market. Some of these statistics, such as the labor-force participation rate, are derived from the Current Population Survey. Yet other statistics come from a separate survey of about 160,000 business establishments that employ over 40 million workers. When you read a headline that says the economy has created a certain number of jobs last month, that statistic is the change in the number of workers that businesses report having on their payrolls.

Because the BLS conducts two surveys of labor market conditions, it produces two measures of total employment. From the household survey, it obtains an estimate of the number of people who say they are working. From the establishment survey, it obtains an estimate of the number of workers firms have on their payrolls.

One might expect these two measures of employment to be identical, but that is not the case. Although they are positively correlated, the two measures can diverge, especially over short periods of time. A particularly large divergence occurred in the early 2000s, as the economy recovered from the recession of 2001. From November 2001 to August 2003, the establishment survey showed a decline in employment of 1.0 million, while the household survey showed an increase of 1.4 million. Some commentators said the economy was experiencing a "jobless recovery," but this description applied only to the establishment data, not to the household data.

Why might these two measures of employment diverge? Part of the explanation is that the surveys measure different things. For example, a person who runs his or her own business is self-employed. The household survey counts that person as working, whereas the establishment survey does not, because that person does not show up on any firm's payroll. As another example, a person who holds two jobs is counted as one employed person in the household survey, but is counted twice in the establishment survey, because that person would show up on the payroll of two firms.

Another part of the explanation for the divergence is that surveys are imperfect. For example, when new firms start up, it may take some time before those firms are included in the establishment survey. The BLS tries to estimate employment at start-ups, but the model it uses to produce these estimates is one possible source of error. A different problem arises from how the household survey extrapolates employment among the surveyed households to the entire population. If the BLS uses incorrect estimates of the size of the population, these errors will be reflected in its estimates of household employment. One possible source of incorrect population estimates is changes in the rate of immigration, both legal and illegal.

In the end, the divergence between the household and establishment surveys from 2001 to 2003 remains a mystery. Some economists believe that the establishment survey is the more accurate one because it has a larger sample. Yet one recent study suggests that the best measure of employment is an average of the two surveys.[5]

---

[5] George Perry, "Gauging Employment: Is the Professional Wisdom Wrong?," *Brookings Papers on Economic Activity* (2005): 2.

More important than the specifics of these surveys or this episode, however, is the broader lesson: all economic statistics are imperfect. Although they contain valuable information about what is happening in the economy, each one should be interpreted with a healthy dose of caution and a bit of skepticism.

2-4 Conclusion: From Economic Statistics to Economic Models

The three statistics discussed in this chapter—gross domestic product, the consumer price index, and the unemployment rate—quantify the performance of the economy. Public and private decisionmakers use these statistics to monitor changes in the economy and to formulate appropriate policies. Economists use these statistics to develop and test theories about how the economy works.

In the chapters that follow, we examine some of these theories. That is, we build models that explain how these variables are determined and how economic policy affects them. Having learned how to measure economic performance, we are now ready to learn how to explain it.

Summary

1. Gross domestic product (GDP) measures the income of everyone in the economy and, equivalently, the total expenditure on the economy's output of goods and services.
2. Nominal GDP values goods and services at current prices. Real GDP values goods and services at constant prices. Real GDP rises only when the amount of goods and services has increased, whereas nominal GDP can rise either because output has increased or because prices have increased.
3. GDP is the sum of four categories of expenditure: consumption, investment, government purchases, and net exports.
4. The consumer price index (CPI) measures the price of a fixed basket of goods and services purchased by a typical consumer. Like the GDP deflator, which is the ratio of nominal GDP to real GDP, the CPI measures the overall level of prices.
5. The labor-force participation rate shows the fraction of adults who are working or want to work. The unemployment rate shows what fraction of those who would like to work do not have a job.

KEY CONCEPTS

Gross domestic product (GDP)
Consumer price index (CPI)
Unemployment rate
National income accounting
Stocks and flows
Value added
Imputed value
Nominal versus real GDP
GDP deflator
National income accounts identity
Consumption
Investment
Government purchases
Net exports
Labor force
Labor-force participation rate

QUESTIONS FOR REVIEW

1. List the two things that GDP measures. How can GDP measure two things at once?
2. What does the consumer price index measure?
3. List the three categories used by the Bureau of Labor Statistics to classify everyone in the economy. How does the Bureau compute the unemployment rate?
4. Explain the two ways the Bureau of Labor Statistics measures total employment.

PROBLEMS AND APPLICATIONS

1. Look at the newspapers for the past few days. What new economic statistics have been released? How do you interpret these statistics?
2. A farmer grows a bushel of wheat and sells it to a miller for $1.00. The miller turns the wheat into flour and then sells the flour to a baker for $3.00. The baker uses the flour to make bread and sells the bread to an engineer for $6.00. The engineer eats the bread. What is the value added by each person? What is GDP?
3. Suppose a woman marries her butler. After they are married, her husband continues to wait on her as before, and she continues to support him as before (but as a husband rather than as an employee). How does the marriage affect GDP? How should it affect GDP?
4. Place each of the following transactions in one of the four components of expenditure: consumption, investment, government purchases, and net exports.

   a. Boeing sells an airplane to the Air Force.

   b. Boeing sells an airplane to American Airlines.

   c. Boeing sells an airplane to Air France.

   d. Boeing sells an airplane to Amelia Earhart.

   e. Boeing builds an airplane to be sold next year.
5. Find data on GDP and its components, and compute the percentage of GDP for the following components for 1950, 1980, and 2005.

   a. Personal consumption expenditures

   b. Gross private domestic investment

   c. Government purchases

   d. Net exports

   e. National defense purchases

   f. State and local purchases

   g. Imports

   Do you see any stable relationships in the data? Do you see any trends? (*Hint:* A good place to look for data is the statistical appendices of the *Economic Report of the President*, which is written each year by the Council of Economic Advisers. Alternatively, you can go to www.bea.doc.gov, which is the Web site of the Bureau of Economic Analysis.)
6. Consider an economy that produces and consumes bread and automobiles. In the following table are data for two different years.

	Year 2000	Year 2010
Price of an automobile	$50,000	$60,000
Price of a loaf of bread	$10	$20
Number of automobiles produced	100 cars	120 cars
Number of loaves of bread produced	500,000 loaves	400,000 loaves

a. Using the year 2000 as the base year, compute the following statistics for each year: nominal GDP, real GDP, the implicit price deflator for GDP, and a fixed-weight price index such as the CPI.

b. How much have prices risen between year 2000 and year 2010? Compare the answers given by the Laspeyres and Paasche price indices. Explain the difference.

c. Suppose you are a senator writing a bill to index Social Security and federal pensions. That is, your bill will adjust these benefits to offset changes in the cost of living. Will you use the GDP deflator or the CPI? Why?

7. Abby consumes only apples. In year 1, red apples cost $1 each, green apples cost $2 each, and Abby buys 10 red apples. In year 2, red apples cost $2, green apples cost $1, and Abby buys 10 green apples.

a. Compute a consumer price index for apples for each year. Assume that year 1 is the base year in which the consumer basket is fixed. How does your index change from year 1 to year 2?

b. Compute Abby's nominal spending on apples in each year. How does it change from year 1 to year 2?

c. Using year 1 as the base year, compute Abby's real spending on apples in each year. How does it change from year 1 to year 2?

d. Defining the implicit price deflator as nominal spending divided by real spending, compute the deflator for each year. How does the deflator change from year 1 to year 2?

e. Suppose that Abby is equally happy eating red or green apples. How much has the true cost of living increased for Abby? Compare this answer to your answers to parts (a) and (d). What does this example tell you about Laspeyres and Paasche price indices?

8. Consider how each of the following events is likely to affect real GDP. Do you think the change in real GDP reflects a similar change in economic well-being?

a. A hurricane in Florida forces Disney World to shut down for a month.

b. The discovery of a new, easy-to-grow strain of wheat increases farm harvests.

c. Increased hostility between unions and management sparks a rash of strikes.

d. Firms throughout the economy experience falling demand, causing them to lay off workers.

e. Congress passes new environmental laws that prohibit firms from using production methods that emit large quantities of pollution.

f. More high-school students drop out of school to take jobs mowing lawns.

g. Fathers around the country reduce their workweeks to spend more time with their children.

9. In a speech that Senator Robert Kennedy gave when he was running for president in 1968, he said the following about GDP:

> [It] does not allow for the health of our children, the quality of their education, or the joy of their play. It does not include the beauty of our poetry or the strength of our marriages, the intelligence of our public debate or the integrity of our public officials. It measures neither our courage, nor our wisdom, nor our devotion to our country. It measures everything, in short, except that which makes life worthwhile, and it can tell us everything about America except why we are proud that we are Americans.

Was Robert Kennedy right? If so, why do we care about GDP?

PART II

Classical Theory: The Economy in the Long Run

CHAPTER 3

National Income: Where It Comes From and Where It Goes

A large income is the best recipe for happiness I ever heard of.

— *Jane Austen*

The most important macroeconomic variable is gross domestic product (GDP). As we have seen, GDP measures both a nation's total output of goods and services and its total income. To appreciate the significance of GDP, one need only take a quick look at international data: compared with their poorer counterparts, nations with a high level of GDP per person have everything from better childhood nutrition to more televisions per household. A large GDP does not ensure that all of a nation's citizens are happy, but it may be the best recipe for happiness that macroeconomists have to offer.

This chapter addresses four groups of questions about the sources and uses of a nation's GDP:

- How much do the firms in the economy produce? What determines a nation's total income?
- Who gets the income from production? How much goes to compensate workers, and how much goes to compensate owners of capital?
- Who buys the output of the economy? How much do households purchase for consumption, how much do households and firms purchase for investment, and how much does the government buy for public purposes?
- What equilibrates the demand for and supply of goods and services? What ensures that desired spending on consumption, investment, and government purchases equals the level of production?

To answer these questions, we must examine how the various parts of the economy interact.

A good place to start is the circular flow diagram. In Chapter 2 we traced the circular flow of dollars in a hypothetical economy that produced one product, bread, from labor services. Figure 3-1 more accurately reflects how real

FIGURE 3-1

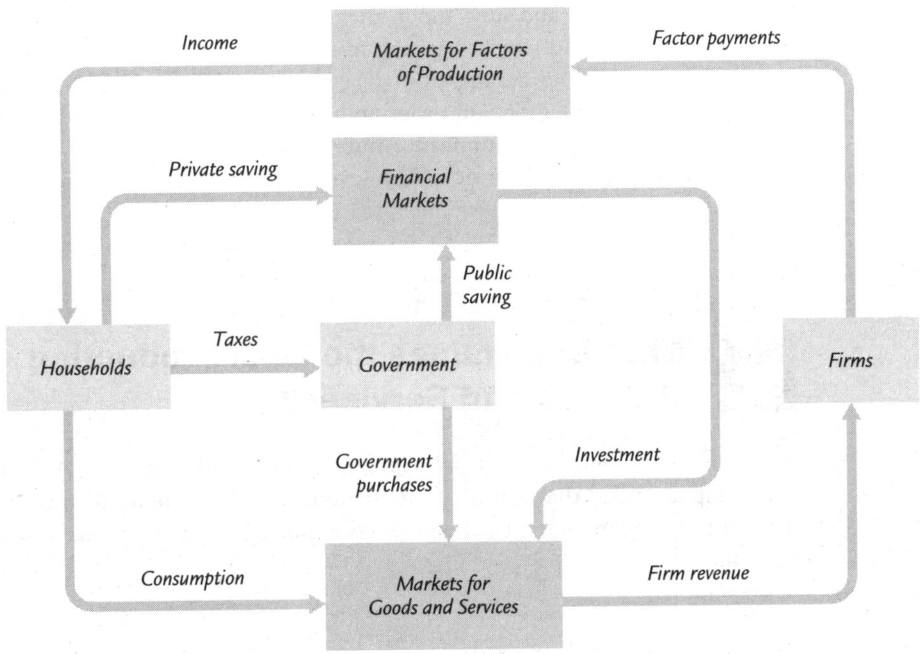

The Circular Flow of Dollars Through the Economy This figure is a more realistic version of the circular flow diagram found in Chapter 2. Each yellow box represents an economic actor—households, firms, and the government. Each blue box represents a type of market—the markets for goods and services, the markets for the factors of production, and financial markets. The green arrows show the flow of dollars among the economic actors through the three types of markets.

economies function. It shows the linkages among the economic actors—households, firms, and the government—and how dollars flow among them through the various markets in the economy.

Let's look at the flow of dollars from the viewpoints of these economic actors. Households receive income and use it to pay taxes to the government, to consume goods and services, and to save through the financial markets. Firms receive revenue from the sale of goods and services and use it to pay for the factors of production. Households and firms borrow in financial markets to buy investment goods, such as houses and factories. The government receives revenue from taxes and uses it to pay for government purchases. Any excess of tax revenue over government spending is called *public saving,* which can be either positive (a *budget surplus*) or negative (a *budget deficit*).

In this chapter we develop a basic classical model to explain the economic interactions depicted in Figure 3-1. We begin with firms and look at what determines their level of production (and, thus, the level of national income). Then we examine how the markets for the factors of production distribute this income to households. Next, we consider how much of this income households consume and how much they save. In addition to discussing the demand for goods and services arising from the consumption of households, we discuss the demand arising from investment and government purchases. Finally, we come full circle and examine how the demand for goods and services (the sum of consumption, investment, and government purchases) and the supply of goods and services (the level of production) are brought into balance.

3-1 What Determines the Total Production of Goods and Services?

An economy's output of goods and services—its GDP—depends on (1) its quantity of inputs, called the factors of production, and (2) its ability to turn inputs into output, as represented by the production function. We discuss each of these in turn.

The Factors of Production

Factors of production are the inputs used to produce goods and services. The two most important factors of production are capital and labor. Capital is the set of tools that workers use: the construction worker's crane, the accountant's calculator, and this author's personal computer. Labor is the time people spend working. We use the symbol K to denote the amount of capital and the symbol L to denote the amount of labor.

In this chapter we take the economy's factors of production as given. In other words, we assume that the economy has a fixed amount of capital and a fixed amount of labor. We write

$$K = \bar{K}.$$

$$L = \bar{L}.$$

The overbar means that each variable is fixed at some level. In Chapter 7 we examine what happens when the factors of production change over time, as they do in the real world. For now, to keep our analysis simple, we assume fixed amounts of capital and labor.

We also assume here that the factors of production are fully utilized—that is, that no resources are wasted. Again, in the real world, part of the labor force is unemployed, and some capital lies idle. In Chapter 6 we examine the reasons for unemployment, but for now we assume that capital and labor are fully employed.

The Production Function

The available production technology determines how much output is produced from given amounts of capital and labor. Economists express the available technology using a **production function.** Letting Y denote the amount of output, we write the production function as

$$Y = F(K, L).$$

This equation states that output is a function of the amount of capital and the amount of labor.

The production function reflects the available technology for turning capital and labor into output. If someone invents a better way to produce a good, the result is more output from the same amounts of capital and labor. Thus, technological change alters the production function.

Many production functions have a property called **constant returns to scale.** A production function has constant returns to scale if an increase of an equal percentage in all factors of production causes an increase in output of the same percentage. If the production function has constant returns to scale, then we get 10 percent more output when we increase both capital and labor by 10 percent. Mathematically, a production function has constant returns to scale if

$$zY = F(zK, zL)$$

for any positive number z. This equation says that if we multiply both the amount of capital and the amount of labor by some number z, output is also multiplied by z. In the next section we see that the assumption of constant returns to scale has an important implication for how the income from production is distributed.

As an example of a production function, consider production at a bakery. The kitchen and its equipment are the bakery's capital, the workers hired to make the bread are its labor, and the loaves of bread are its output. The bakery's production function shows that the number of loaves produced depends on the amount of equipment and the number of workers. If the production function has constant returns to scale, then doubling the amount of equipment and the number of workers doubles the amount of bread produced.

The Supply of Goods and Services

We can now see that the factors of production and the production function together determine the quantity of goods and services supplied, which in turn equals the economy's output. To express this mathematically, we write

$$\begin{aligned} Y &= F(\bar{K}, \bar{L}) \\ &= \bar{Y}. \end{aligned}$$

In this chapter, because we assume that the supplies of capital and labor and the technology are fixed, output is also fixed (at a level denoted here as $\bar{Y}$). When we discuss economic growth in Chapters 7 and 8, we will examine how increases in capital and labor and improvements in the production technology lead to growth in the economy's output.

3-2 How Is National Income Distributed to the Factors of Production?

As we discussed in Chapter 2, the total output of an economy equals its total income. Because the factors of production and the production function together determine the total output of goods and services, they also determine national income. The circular flow diagram in Figure 3-1 shows that this national income flows from firms to households through the markets for the factors of production.

In this section we continue developing our model of the economy by discussing how these factor markets work. Economists have long studied factor markets to understand the distribution of income. For example, Karl Marx, the noted nineteenth-century economist, spent much time trying to explain the incomes of capital and labor. The political philosophy of communism was in part based on Marx's now-discredited theory.

Here we examine the modern theory of how national income is divided among the factors of production. It is based on the classical (eighteenth-century) idea that prices adjust to balance supply and demand, applied here to the markets for the factors of production, together with the more recent (nineteenth-century) idea that the demand for each factor of production depends on the marginal productivity of that factor. This theory, called the *neoclassical theory of distribution,* is accepted by most economists today as the best place to start in understanding how the economy's income is distributed from firms to households.

Factor Prices

The distribution of national income is determined by factor prices. **Factor prices** are the amounts paid to the factors of production. In an economy where the two factors of production are capital and labor, the two factor prices are the wage workers earn and the rent the owners of capital collect.

As Figure 3-2 illustrates, the price each factor of production receives for its services is in turn determined by the supply and demand for that factor. Because we have assumed that the economy's factors of production are fixed, the factor supply curve in Figure 3-2 is vertical. Regardless of the factor price, the quantity of the factor supplied to the market is the same. The intersection of the downward-sloping factor demand curve and the vertical supply curve determines the equilibrium factor price.

To understand factor prices and the distribution of income, we must examine the demand for the factors of production. Because factor demand arises from the

FIGURE 3-2

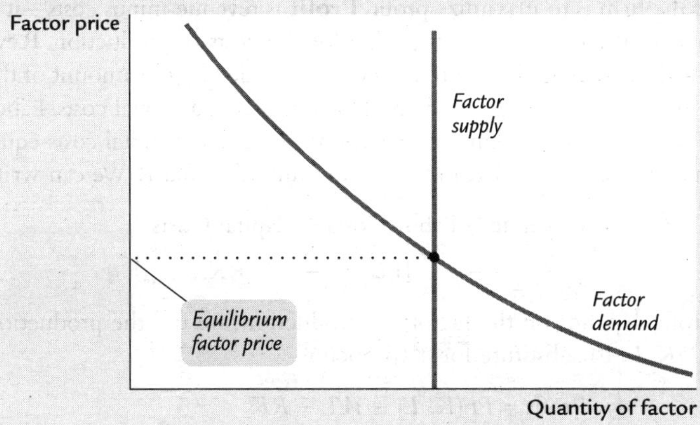

How a Factor of Production Is Compensated The price paid to any factor of production depends on the supply and demand for that factor's services. Because we have assumed that supply is fixed, the supply curve is vertical. The demand curve is downward sloping. The intersection of supply and demand determines the equilibrium factor price.

thousands of firms that use capital and labor, we now look at the decisions faced by a typical firm about how much of these factors to employ.

The Decisions Facing the Competitive Firm

The simplest assumption to make about a typical firm is that it is competitive. A **competitive firm** is small relative to the markets in which it trades, so it has little influence on market prices. For example, our firm produces a good and sells it at the market price. Because many firms produce this good, our firm can sell as much as it wants without causing the price of the good to fall, or it can stop selling altogether without causing the price of the good to rise. Similarly, our firm cannot influence the wages of the workers it employs because many other local firms also employ workers. The firm has no reason to pay more than the market wage, and if it tried to pay less, its workers would take jobs elsewhere. Therefore, the competitive firm takes the prices of its output and its inputs as given by market conditions.

To make its product, the firm needs two factors of production, capital and labor. As we did for the aggregate economy, we represent the firm's production technology with the production function

$$Y = F(K, L),$$

where Y is the number of units produced (the firm's output), K the number of machines used (the amount of capital), and L the number of hours worked by the firm's employees (the amount of labor). The firm produces more output if it uses more machines or if its employees work more hours.

The firm sells its output at a price P, hires workers at a wage W, and rents capital at a rate R. Notice that when we speak of firms renting capital, we are assuming that households own the economy's stock of capital. In this analysis, households rent out their capital, just as they sell their labor. The firm obtains both factors of production from the households that own them.[1]

The goal of the firm is to maximize profit. **Profit** is revenue minus costs—it is what the owners of the firm keep after paying for the costs of production. Revenue equals $P \times Y$, the selling price of the good P multiplied by the amount of the good the firm produces Y. Costs include both labor costs and capital costs. Labor costs equal $W \times L$, the wage W times the amount of labor L. Capital costs equal $R \times K$, the rental price of capital R times the amount of capital K. We can write

$$\begin{aligned} \text{Profit} &= \text{Revenue} - \text{Labor Costs} - \text{Capital Costs} \\ &= PY - WL - RK. \end{aligned}$$

To see how profit depends on the factors of production, we use the production function $Y = F(K, L)$ to substitute for Y to obtain

$$\text{Profit} = PF(K, L) - WL - RK.$$

This equation shows that profit depends on the product price P, the factor prices W and R, and the factor quantities L and K. The competitive firm takes the product price and the factor prices as given and chooses the amounts of labor and capital that maximize profit.

The Firm's Demand for Factors

We now know that our firm will hire labor and rent capital in the quantities that maximize profit. But what are those profit-maximizing quantities? To answer this question, we first consider the quantity of labor and then the quantity of capital.

The Marginal Product of Labor The more labor the firm employs, the more output it produces. The **marginal product of labor *(MPL)*** is the extra amount of output the firm gets from one extra unit of labor, holding the amount of capital fixed. We can express this using the production function:

$$MPL = F(K, L + 1) - F(K, L).$$

The first term on the right-hand side is the amount of output produced with K units of capital and $L + 1$ units of labor; the second term is the amount of output produced with K units of capital and L units of labor. This equation states that the marginal product of labor is the difference between the amount of output produced with $L + 1$ units of labor and the amount produced with only L units of labor.

Most production functions have the property of **diminishing marginal product:** holding the amount of capital fixed, the marginal product of labor

---

[1] This is a simplification. In the real world, the ownership of capital is indirect because firms own capital and households own the firms. That is, real firms have two functions: owning capital and producing output. To help us understand how the factors of production are compensated, however, we assume that firms only produce output and that households own capital directly.

decreases as the amount of labor increases. Consider again the production of bread at a bakery. As a bakery hires more labor, it produces more bread. The *MPL* is the amount of extra bread produced when an extra unit of labor is hired. As more labor is added to a fixed amount of capital, however, the *MPL* falls. Fewer additional loaves are produced because workers are less productive when the kitchen is more crowded. In other words, holding the size of the kitchen fixed, each additional worker adds fewer loaves of bread to the bakery's output.

Figure 3-3 graphs the production function. It illustrates what happens to the amount of output when we hold the amount of capital constant and vary the amount of labor. This figure shows that the marginal product of labor is the slope of the production function. As the amount of labor increases, the production function becomes flatter, indicating diminishing marginal product.

From the Marginal Product of Labor to Labor Demand When the competitive, profit-maximizing firm is deciding whether to hire an additional unit of labor, it considers how that decision would affect profits. It therefore compares the extra revenue from the increased production that results from the added labor to the extra cost of higher spending on wages. The increase in revenue from an additional unit of labor depends on two variables: the marginal product of labor and the price of the output. Because an extra unit of labor produces *MPL* units of output and each unit of output sells for *P* dollars, the extra revenue is

FIGURE 3-3

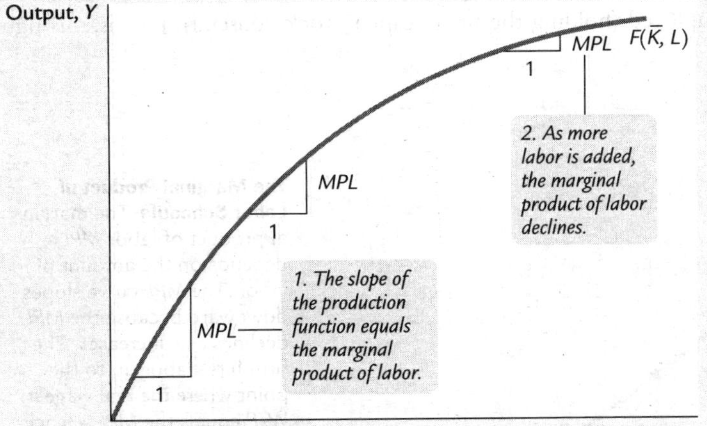

The Production Function This curve shows how output depends on labor input, holding the amount of capital constant. The marginal product of labor *MPL* is the change in output when the labor input is increased by 1 unit. As the amount of labor increases, the production function becomes flatter, indicating diminishing marginal product.

$P \times MPL$. The extra cost of hiring one more unit of labor is the wage W. Thus, the change in profit from hiring an additional unit of labor is

$$\Delta\text{Profit} = \Delta\text{Revenue} - \Delta\text{Cost}$$
$$= (P \times MPL) - W.$$

The symbol Δ (called *delta*) denotes the change in a variable.

We can now answer the question we asked at the beginning of this section: how much labor does the firm hire? The firm's manager knows that if the extra revenue $P \times MPL$ exceeds the wage W, an extra unit of labor increases profit. Therefore, the manager continues to hire labor until the next unit would no longer be profitable—that is, until the MPL falls to the point where the extra revenue equals the wage. The competitive firm's demand for labor is determined by

$$P \times MPL = W.$$

We can also write this as

$$MPL = W/P.$$

W/P is the **real wage**—the payment to labor measured in units of output rather than in dollars. To maximize profit, the firm hires up to the point at which the marginal product of labor equals the real wage.

For example, again consider a bakery. Suppose the price of bread P is \$2 per loaf, and a worker earns a wage W of \$20 per hour. The real wage W/P is 10 loaves per hour. In this example, the firm keeps hiring workers as long as the additional worker would produce at least 10 loaves per hour. When the MPL falls to 10 loaves per hour or less, hiring additional workers is no longer profitable.

Figure 3-4 shows how the marginal product of labor depends on the amount of labor employed (holding the firm's capital stock constant). That is, this figure

FIGURE 3-4

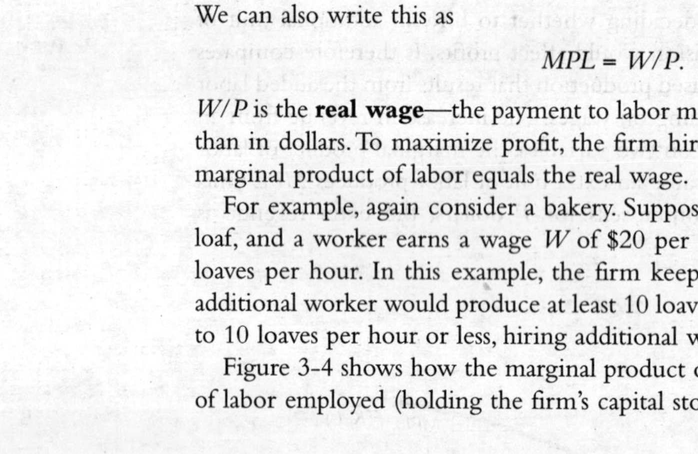

The Marginal Product of Labor Schedule The marginal product of labor MPL depends on the amount of labor. The MPL curve slopes downward because the MPL declines as L increases. The firm hires labor up to the point where the real wage W/P equals the MPL. Hence, this schedule is also the firm's labor demand curve.

graphs the *MPL* schedule. Because the *MPL* diminishes as the amount of labor increases, this curve slopes downward. For any given real wage, the firm hires up to the point at which the *MPL* equals the real wage. Hence, the *MPL* schedule is also the firm's labor demand curve.

The Marginal Product of Capital and Capital Demand The firm decides how much capital to rent in the same way it decides how much labor to hire. The **marginal product of capital (*MPK*)** is the amount of extra output the firm gets from an extra unit of capital, holding the amount of labor constant:

$$MPK = F(K + 1, L) - F(K, L).$$

Thus, the marginal product of capital is the difference between the amount of output produced with $K + 1$ units of capital and that produced with only K units of capital.

Like labor, capital is subject to diminishing marginal product. Once again consider the production of bread at a bakery. The first several ovens installed in the kitchen will be very productive. However, if the bakery installs more and more ovens, while holding its labor force constant, it will eventually contain more ovens than its employees can effectively operate. Hence, the marginal product of the last few ovens is lower than that of the first few.

The increase in profit from renting an additional machine is the extra revenue from selling the output of that machine minus the machine's rental price:

$$\begin{aligned} \Delta\text{Profit} &= \Delta\text{Revenue} - \Delta\text{Cost} \\ &= (P \times MPK) - R. \end{aligned}$$

To maximize profit, the firm continues to rent more capital until the *MPK* falls to equal the real rental price:

$$MPK = R/P.$$

The **real rental price of capital** is the rental price measured in units of goods rather than in dollars.

To sum up, the competitive, profit-maximizing firm follows a simple rule about how much labor to hire and how much capital to rent. *The firm demands each factor of production until that factor's marginal product falls to equal its real factor price.*

The Division of National Income

Having analyzed how a firm decides how much of each factor to employ, we can now explain how the markets for the factors of production distribute the economy's total income. If all firms in the economy are competitive and profit maximizing, then each factor of production is paid its marginal contribution to the production process. The real wage paid to each worker equals the *MPL*, and the real rental price paid to each owner of capital equals the *MPK*. The total real wages paid to labor are therefore $MPL \times L$, and the total real return paid to capital owners is $MPK \times K$.

The income that remains after the firms have paid the factors of production is the **economic profit** of the owners of the firms. Real economic profit is

$$\text{Economic Profit} = Y - (MPL \times L) - (MPK \times K).$$

Because we want to examine the distribution of national income, we rearrange the terms as follows:

$$Y = (MPL \times L) + (MPK \times K) + \text{Economic Profit}.$$

Total income is divided among the return to labor, the return to capital, and economic profit.

How large is economic profit? The answer is surprising: if the production function has the property of constant returns to scale, as is often thought to be the case, then economic profit must be zero. That is, nothing is left after the factors of production are paid. This conclusion follows from a famous mathematical result called *Euler's theorem,*[2] which states that if the production function has constant returns to scale, then

$$F(K, L) = (MPK \times K) + (MPL \times L).$$

If each factor of production is paid its marginal product, then the sum of these factor payments equals total output. In other words, constant returns to scale, profit maximization, and competition together imply that economic profit is zero.

If economic profit is zero, how can we explain the existence of "profit" in the economy? The answer is that the term "profit" as normally used is different from economic profit. We have been assuming that there are three types of agents: workers, owners of capital, and owners of firms. Total income is divided among wages, return to capital, and economic profit. In the real world, however, most firms own rather than rent the capital they use. Because firm owners and capital owners are the same people, economic profit and the return to capital are often lumped together. If we call this alternative definition **accounting profit,** we can say that

$$\text{Accounting Profit} = \text{Economic Profit} + (MPK \times K).$$

Under our assumptions—constant returns to scale, profit maximization, and competition—economic profit is zero. If these assumptions approximately describe the world, then the "profit" in the national income accounts must be mostly the return to capital.

We can now answer the question posed at the beginning of this chapter about how the income of the economy is distributed from firms to households. Each factor of production is paid its marginal product, and these factor payments exhaust total output. *Total output is divided between the payments to capital and the payments to labor, depending on their marginal productivities.*

CASE STUDY

The Black Death and Factor Prices

According to the neoclassical theory of distribution, factor prices equal the marginal products of the factors of production. Because the marginal products depend on the quantities of the factors, a change in the quantity of any one fac-

[2] *Mathematical note:* To prove Euler's theorem, begin with the definition of constant returns to scale: $zY = F(zK, zL)$. Now differentiate with respect to z and then evaluate at $z = 1$.

tor alters the marginal products of all the factors. Therefore, a change in the supply of a factor alters equilibrium factor prices and the distribution of income.

Fourteenth-century Europe provides a grisly natural experiment to study how factor quantities affect factor prices. The outbreak of the bubonic plague—the Black Death—in 1348 reduced the population of Europe by about one-third within a few years. Because the marginal product of labor increases as the amount of labor falls, this massive reduction in the labor force should have raised the marginal product of labor and equilibrium real wages. (That is, the economy should have moved to the left along the curves in Figures 3-3 and 3-4.) The evidence confirms the theory: real wages approximately doubled during the plague years. The peasants who were fortunate enough to survive the plague enjoyed economic prosperity.

The reduction in the labor force caused by the plague should also have affected the return to land, the other major factor of production in medieval Europe. With fewer workers available to farm the land, an additional unit of land would have produced less additional output, and so land rents should have fallen. Once again, the theory is confirmed: real rents fell 50 percent or more during this period. While the peasant classes prospered, the landed classes suffered reduced incomes.[3]

The Cobb-Douglas Production Function

What production function describes how actual economies turn capital and labor into GDP? One answer to this question came from a historic collaboration between a U.S. senator and a mathematician.

Paul Douglas was a U.S. senator from Illinois from 1949 to 1966. In 1927, however, when he was still a professor of economics, he noticed a surprising fact: the division of national income between capital and labor had been roughly constant over a long period. In other words, as the economy grew more prosperous over time, the total income of workers and the total income of capital owners grew at almost exactly the same rate. This observation caused Douglas to wonder what conditions might lead to constant factor shares.

Douglas asked Charles Cobb, a mathematician, what production function, if any, would produce constant factor shares if factors always earned their marginal products. The production function would need to have the property that

$$\text{Capital Income} = MPK \times K = \alpha Y,$$

and

$$\text{Labor Income} = MPL \times L = (1 - \alpha)\, Y,$$

where α is a constant between zero and one that measures capital's share of income. That is, α determines what share of income goes to capital and what share goes to labor. Cobb showed that the function with this property is

$$F(K,L) = A\, K^{\alpha} L^{1-\alpha},$$

[3] Carlo M. Cipolla, *Before the Industrial Revolution: European Society and Economy, 1000–1700*, 2d ed. (New York: Norton, 1980), 200-202.

where A is a parameter greater than zero that measures the productivity of the available technology. This function became known as the **Cobb-Douglas production function.**

Let's take a closer look at some of the properties of this production function. First, the Cobb-Douglas production function has constant returns to scale. That is, if capital and labor are increased by the same proportion, then output increases by that proportion as well.[4]

Next, consider the marginal products for the Cobb-Douglas production function. The marginal product of labor is[5]

$$MPL = (1 - \alpha)\, A\, K^{\alpha} L^{-\alpha}$$

and the marginal product of capital is

$$MPK = \alpha\, A\, K^{\alpha-1} L^{1-\alpha}.$$

From these equations, recalling that α is between zero and one, we can see what causes the marginal products of the two factors to change. An increase in the amount of capital raises the *MPL* and reduces the *MPK*. Similarly, an increase in the amount of labor reduces the *MPL* and raises the *MPK*. A technological advance that increases the parameter A raises the marginal product of both factors proportionately.

The marginal products for the Cobb-Douglas production function can also be written as[6]

$$MPL = (1 - \alpha)Y/L.$$

$$MPK = \alpha Y/K.$$

---

[4] *Mathematical note:* To prove that the Cobb-Douglas production function has constant returns to scale, examine what happens when we multiply capital and labor by a constant z:

$$F(zK, zL) = A(zK)^{\alpha}(zL)^{1-\alpha}.$$

Expanding terms on the right,

$$F(zK, zL) = Az^{\alpha} K^{\alpha} z^{1-\alpha} L^{1-\alpha}.$$

Rearranging to bring like terms together, we get

$$F(zK, zL) = Az^{\alpha} z^{1-\alpha} K^{\alpha} L^{1-\alpha}.$$

Since $z^{\alpha} z^{1-\alpha} = z$, our function becomes

$$F(zK, zL) = z\, A\, K^{\alpha} L^{1-\alpha}.$$

But $A\, K^{\alpha} L^{1-\alpha} = F(K, L)$. Thus,

$$F(zK, zL) = zF(K, L) = zY.$$

Hence, the amount of output Y increases by the same factor z, which implies that this production function has constant returns to scale.

[5] *Mathematical note:* Obtaining the formulas for the marginal products from the production function requires a bit of calculus. To find the *MPL*, differentiate the production function with respect to L. This is done by multiplying by the exponent $(1 - \alpha)$, and then subtracting 1 from the old exponent to obtain the new exponent, $-\alpha$. Similarly, to obtain the MPK, differentiate the production function with respect to K.

[6] *Mathematical note:* To check these expressions for the marginal products, substitute in the production function for Y to show that these expressions are equivalent to the earlier formulas for the marginal products.

The *MPL* is proportional to output per worker, and the *MPK* is proportional to output per unit of capital. Y/L is called *average labor productivity,* and Y/K is called *average capital productivity*. If the production function is Cobb-Douglas, then the marginal productivity of a factor is proportional to its average productivity.

We can now verify that if factors earn their marginal products, then the parameter α indeed tells us how much income goes to labor and how much goes to capital. The total amount paid to labor, which we have seen is $MPL \times L$, is simply $(1 - \alpha)Y$. Therefore, $(1 - \alpha)$ is labor's share of output. Similarly, the total amount paid to capital, $MPK \times K$, is αY, and α is capital's share of output. The ratio of labor income to capital income is a constant, $(1 - \alpha)/\alpha$, just as Douglas observed. The factor shares depend only on the parameter α, not on the amounts of capital or labor or on the state of technology as measured by the parameter A.

More recent U.S. data are also consistent with the Cobb-Douglas production function. Figure 3-5 shows the ratio of labor income to total income in the United States from 1960 to 2004. Despite the many changes in the economy

FIGURE 3-5

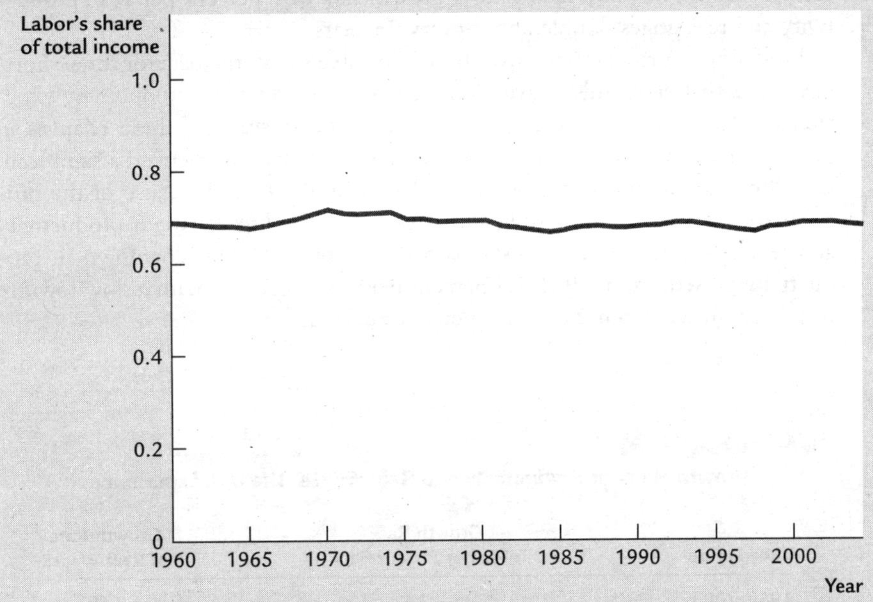

The Ratio of Labor Income to Total Income Labor income has remained about 0.7 of total income over a long period of time. This approximate constancy of factor shares is consistent with the Cobb-Douglas production function.

Source: U.S. Department of Commerce. This figure is produced from U.S. national income accounts data. Labor income is compensation of employees. Total income is the sum of labor income, corporate profits, net interest, rental income, and depreciation. Proprietors' income is excluded from these calculations, because it is a combination of labor income and capital income.

over the past four decades, this ratio has remained about 0.7. This division of income is easily explained by a Cobb-Douglas production function in which the parameter α is about 0.3.

The Cobb-Douglas production function is not the last word in explaining the economy's production of goods and services or the distribution of national income between capital and labor. It is, however, a good place to start.

CASE STUDY

Labor Productivity as the Key Determinant of Real Wages

The neoclassical theory of distribution tells us that the real wage W/P equals the marginal product of labor. The Cobb-Douglas production function tells us that the marginal product of labor is proportional to average labor productivity Y/L. If this theory is right, then workers should enjoy rapidly rising living standards when labor productivity is growing robustly. Is this true?

Table 3-1 presents some data on growth in productivity and real wages for the U.S. economy. From 1959 to 2003, productivity as measured by output per hour of work grew about 2.1 percent per year. Real wages grew at 2.0 percent—almost exactly the same rate. With a growth rate of 2 percent per year, productivity and real wages double about every 35 years.

Productivity growth varies over time. The table shows the data for three shorter periods that economists have identified as having different productivity experiences. (Case studies in Chapter 8 examine the reasons for these changes in productivity growth.) Around 1973, the U.S. economy experienced a significant slowdown in productivity growth that lasted until 1995. The cause of the productivity slowdown is not well understood, but the link between productivity and real wages was exactly as standard theory predicts. The slowdown in productivity growth from 2.9 to 1.4 percent per year coincided with a slowdown in real wage growth from 2.8 to 1.2 percent per year.

TABLE 3-1

Growth in Labor Productivity and Real Wages: The U.S. Experience

Time Period	Growth Rate of Labor Productivity	Growth Rate of Real Wages
1959–2003	2.1%	2.0%
1959–1973	2.9	2.8
1973–1995	1.4	1.2
1995–2003	3.0	3.0

Source: Economic Report of the President 2005, Table B-49. Growth in labor productivity is measured here as the annualized rate of change in output per hour in the nonfarm business sector. Growth in real wages is measured as the annualized change in compensation per hour in the nonfarm business sector divided by the implicit price deflator for that sector.

Productivity growth picked up again around 1995, and many observers hailed the arrival of the "new economy." This productivity acceleration is often attributed to the spread of computers and information technology. As theory predicts, growth in real wages picked up as well. From 1995 to 2003, both productivity and real wages grew by 3.0 percent per year.

Theory and history both confirm the close link between labor productivity and real wages. This lesson is the key to understanding why workers today are better off than workers in previous generations.

3-3 What Determines the Demand for Goods and Services?

We have seen what determines the level of production and how the income from production is distributed to workers and owners of capital. We now continue our tour of the circular flow diagram, Figure 3-1, and examine how the output from production is used.

In Chapter 2 we identified the four components of GDP:

- Consumption (C)
- Investment (I)
- Government purchases (G)
- Net exports (NX).

The circular flow diagram contains only the first three components. For now, to simplify the analysis, we assume our economy is a *closed economy*—a country that does not trade with other countries. Thus, net exports are always zero. (We examine the macroeconomics of *open economies* in Chapter 5.)

A closed economy has three uses for the goods and services it produces. These three components of GDP are expressed in the national income accounts identity:

$$Y = C + I + G.$$

Households consume some of the economy's output; firms and households use some of the output for investment; and the government buys some of the output for public purposes. We want to see how GDP is allocated among these three uses.

Consumption

When we eat food, wear clothing, or go to a movie, we are consuming some of the output of the economy. All forms of consumption together make up two-thirds of GDP. Because consumption is so large, macroeconomists have devoted much energy to studying how households decide how much to consume.

Chapter 16 examines this work in detail. Here we consider the simplest story of consumer behavior.

Households receive income from their labor and their ownership of capital, pay taxes to the government, and then decide how much of their after-tax income to consume and how much to save. As we discussed in Section 3-2, the income that households receive equals the output of the economy Y. The government then taxes households an amount T. (Although the government imposes many kinds of taxes, such as personal and corporate income taxes and sales taxes, for our purposes we can lump all these taxes together.) We define income after the payment of all taxes, $Y - T$, as **disposable income.** Households divide their disposable income between consumption and saving.

We assume that the level of consumption depends directly on the level of disposable income. The higher is disposable income, the greater is consumption. Thus,

$$C = C(Y - T).$$

This equation states that consumption is a function of disposable income. The relationship between consumption and disposable income is called the **consumption function.**

The **marginal propensity to consume (MPC)** is the amount by which consumption changes when disposable income increases by one dollar. The *MPC* is between zero and one: an extra dollar of income increases consumption, but by less than one dollar. Thus, if households obtain an extra dollar of income, they save a portion of it. For example, if the *MPC* is 0.7, then households spend 70 cents of each additional dollar of disposable income on consumer goods and services and save 30 cents.

Figure 3-6 illustrates the consumption function. The slope of the consumption function tells us how much consumption increases when disposable income increases by one dollar. That is, the slope of the consumption function is the *MPC*.

FIGURE 3-6

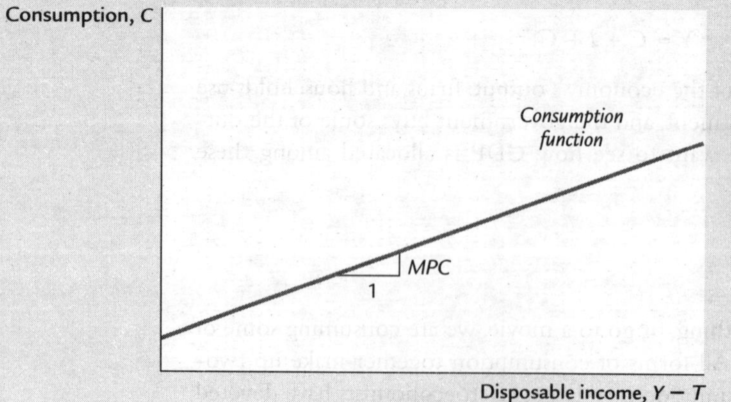

The Consumption Function The consumption function relates consumption C to disposable income $Y - T$. The marginal propensity to consume *MPC* is the amount by which consumption increases when disposable income increases by one dollar.

Investment

Both firms and households purchase investment goods. Firms buy investment goods to add to their stock of capital and to replace existing capital as it wears out. Households buy new houses, which are also part of investment. Total investment in the United States averages about 15 percent of GDP.

The quantity of investment goods demanded depends on the **interest rate,** which measures the cost of the funds used to finance investment. For an investment project to be profitable, its return (the revenue from increased future production of goods and services) must exceed its cost (the payments for borrowed funds). If the interest rate rises, fewer investment projects are profitable, and the quantity of investment goods demanded falls.

For example, suppose a firm is considering whether it should build a $1 million factory that would yield a return of $100,000 per year, or 10 percent. The firm compares this return to the cost of borrowing the $1 million. If the interest rate is below 10 percent, the firm borrows the money in financial markets and makes the investment. If the interest rate is above 10 percent, the firm forgoes the investment opportunity and does not build the factory.

The firm makes the same investment decision even if it does not have to borrow the $1 million but rather uses its own funds. The firm can always deposit this money in a bank or a money market fund and earn interest on it. Building the factory is more profitable than the deposit if and only if the interest rate is less than the 10 percent return on the factory.

A person wanting to buy a new house faces a similar decision. The higher the interest rate, the greater the cost of carrying a mortgage. A $100,000 mortgage costs $8,000 per year if the interest rate is 8 percent and $10,000 per year if the interest rate is 10 percent. As the interest rate rises, the cost of owning a home rises, and the demand for new homes falls.

When studying the role of interest rates in the economy, economists distinguish between the nominal interest rate and the real interest rate. This distinction is relevant when the overall level of prices is changing. The **nominal interest rate** is the interest rate as usually reported: it is the rate of interest that investors pay to borrow money. The **real interest rate** is the nominal interest rate corrected for the effects of inflation. If the nominal interest rate is 8 percent and the inflation rate is 3 percent, then the real interest rate is 5 percent. In Chapter 4 we discuss the relation between nominal and real interest rates in detail. Here it is sufficient to note that the real interest rate measures the true cost of borrowing and, thus, determines the quantity of investment.

We can summarize this discussion with an equation relating investment I to the real interest rate r:

$$I = I(r).$$

Figure 3-7 shows this investment function. It slopes downward, because as the interest rate rises, the quantity of investment demanded falls.

FIGURE 3-7

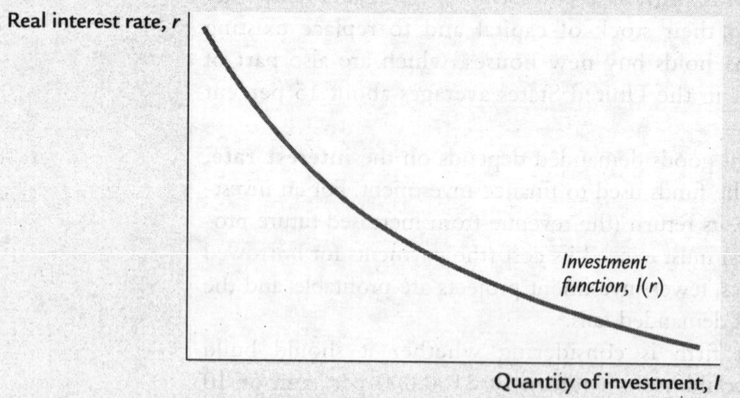

The Investment Function The investment function relates the quantity of investment I to the real interest rate r. Investment depends on the real interest rate because the interest rate is the cost of borrowing. The investment function slopes downward: when the interest rate rises, fewer investment projects are profitable.

Government Purchases

Government purchases are the third component of the demand for goods and services. The federal government buys guns, missiles, and the services of government employees. Local governments buy library books, build schools, and hire teachers. Governments at all levels build roads and other public works. All these transactions make up government purchases of goods and services, which account for about 20 percent of GDP in the United States.

These purchases are only one type of government spending. The other type is transfer payments to households, such as welfare for the poor and Social Security payments for the elderly. Unlike government purchases, transfer payments are not made in exchange for some of the economy's output of goods and services. Therefore, they are not included in the variable G.

Transfer payments do affect the demand for goods and services indirectly. Transfer payments are the opposite of taxes: they increase households' disposable income, just as taxes reduce disposable income. Thus, an increase in transfer payments financed by an increase in taxes leaves disposable income unchanged. We can now revise our definition of T to equal taxes minus transfer payments. Disposable income, $Y - T$, includes both the negative impact of taxes and the positive impact of transfer payments.

If government purchases equal taxes minus transfers, then $G = T$ and the government has a *balanced budget*. If G exceeds T, the government runs a *budget deficit,* which it funds by issuing government debt—that is, by borrowing in the financial markets. If G is less than T, the government runs a *budget surplus,* which it can use to repay some of its outstanding debt.

Here we do not try to explain the political process that leads to a particular fiscal policy—that is, to the level of government purchases and taxes. Instead, we take government purchases and taxes as exogenous variables. To denote that these variables are fixed outside of our model of national income, we write

$$G = \bar{G}.$$
$$T = \bar{T}.$$

FYI The Many Different Interest Rates

If you look in the business section of a newspaper, you will find many different interest rates reported. By contrast, throughout this book, we will talk about "the" interest rate, as if there were only one interest rate in the economy. The only distinction we will make is between the nominal interest rate (which is not corrected for inflation) and the real interest rate (which is corrected for inflation). Almost all of the interest rates reported in the newspaper are nominal.

Why does the newspaper report so many interest rates? The various interest rates differ in three ways:

- *Term*. Some loans in the economy are for short periods of time, even as short as overnight. Other loans are for thirty years or even longer. The interest rate on a loan depends on its term. Long-term interest rates are usually, but not always, higher than short-term interest rates.
- *Credit risk*. In deciding whether to make a loan, a lender must take into account the probability that the borrower will repay. The law allows borrowers to default on their loans by declaring bankruptcy. The higher the perceived probability of default, the higher the interest rate. Because the safest credit risk is the government, government bonds tend to pay a low interest rate. At the other extreme, financially shaky corporations can raise funds only by issuing *junk bonds,* which pay a high interest rate to compensate for the high risk of default.
- *Tax treatment*. The interest on different types of bonds is taxed differently. Most important, when state and local governments issue bonds, called *municipal bonds,* the holders of the bonds do not pay federal income tax on the interest income. Because of this tax advantage, municipal bonds pay a lower interest rate.

When you see two different interest rates in the newspaper, you can almost always explain the difference by considering the term, the credit risk, and the tax treatment of the loan.

Although there are many different interest rates in the economy, macroeconomists can usually ignore these distinctions. The various interest rates tend to move up and down together. The assumption that there is only one interest rate is, for our purposes, a useful simplification.

We do, however, want to examine the impact of fiscal policy on the variables determined within the model, the endogenous variables. The endogenous variables here are consumption, investment, and the interest rate.

To see how the exogenous variables affect the endogenous variables, we must complete the model. This is the subject of the next section.

3-4 What Brings the Supply and Demand for Goods and Services Into Equilibrium?

We have now come full circle in the circular flow diagram, Figure 3-1. We began by examining the supply of goods and services, and we have just discussed the demand for them. How can we be certain that all these flows balance? In other words, what ensures that the sum of consumption, investment, and government purchases equals the amount of output produced? We will see that in this classical model, the interest rate is the price that has the crucial role of equilibrating supply and demand.

There are two ways to think about the role of the interest rate in the economy. We can consider how the interest rate affects the supply and demand for goods or services. Or we can consider how the interest rate affects the supply and demand for loanable funds. As we will see, these two approaches are two sides of the same coin.

Equilibrium in the Market for Goods and Services: The Supply and Demand for the Economy's Output

The following equations summarize the discussion of the demand for goods and services in Section 3-3:

$$Y = C + I + G.$$

$$C = C(Y - T).$$

$$I = I(r).$$

$$G = \overline{G}.$$

$$T = \overline{T}.$$

The demand for the economy's output comes from consumption, investment, and government purchases. Consumption depends on disposable income; investment depends on the real interest rate; and government purchases and taxes are the exogenous variables set by fiscal policymakers.

To this analysis, let's add what we learned about the supply of goods and services in Section 3-1. There we saw that the factors of production and the production function determine the quantity of output supplied to the economy:

$$Y = F(\overline{K}, \overline{L})$$

$$= \overline{Y}.$$

Now let's combine these equations describing the supply and demand for output. If we substitute the consumption function and the investment function into the national income accounts identity, we obtain

$$Y = C(Y - T) + I(r) + G.$$

Because the variables G and T are fixed by policy, and the level of output Y is fixed by the factors of production and the production function, we can write

$$\overline{Y} = C(\overline{Y} - \overline{T}) + I(r) + \overline{G}.$$

This equation states that the supply of output equals its demand, which is the sum of consumption, investment, and government purchases.

Notice that the interest rate r is the only variable not already determined in the last equation. This is because the interest rate still has a key role to play: it must adjust to ensure that the demand for goods equals the supply. The greater the interest rate, the lower the level of investment, and thus the lower the demand for goods and services, $C + I + G$. If the interest rate is too high, investment is too low, and the demand for output falls short of the supply. If the interest rate is too low, investment is too high, and the demand exceeds the supply. *At the equilibrium interest rate, the demand for goods and services equals the supply.*

This conclusion may seem somewhat mysterious: how does the interest rate get to the level that balances the supply and demand for goods and services? The best way to answer this question is to consider how financial markets fit into the story.

Equilibrium in the Financial Markets: The Supply and Demand for Loanable Funds

Because the interest rate is the cost of borrowing and the return to lending in financial markets, we can better understand the role of the interest rate in the economy by thinking about the financial markets. To do this, rewrite the national income accounts identity as

$$Y - C - G = I.$$

The term $Y - C - G$ is the output that remains after the demands of consumers and the government have been satisfied; it is called **national saving** or simply **saving** (S). In this form, the national income accounts identity shows that saving equals investment.

To understand this identity more fully, we can split national saving into two parts—one part representing the saving of the private sector and the other representing the saving of the government:

$$S = (Y - T - C) + (T - G) = I.$$

The term $(Y - T - C)$ is disposable income minus consumption, which is **private saving**. The term $(T - G)$ is government revenue minus government spending, which is **public saving**. (If government spending exceeds government revenue, the government runs a budget deficit, and public saving is negative.) National saving is the sum of private and public saving. The circular flow diagram in Figure 3-1 reveals an interpretation of this equation: this equation states that the flows into the financial markets (private and public saving) must balance the flows out of the financial markets (investment).

To see how the interest rate brings financial markets into equilibrium, substitute the consumption function and the investment function into the national income accounts identity:

$$Y - C(Y - T) - G = I(r).$$

Next, note that G and T are fixed by policy and Y is fixed by the factors of production and the production function:

$$\bar{Y} - C(\bar{Y} - \bar{T}) - \bar{G} = I(r)$$
$$\bar{S} = I(r).$$

The left-hand side of this equation shows that national saving depends on income Y and the fiscal policy variables G and T. For fixed values of Y, G, and

T, national saving *S* is also fixed. The right-hand side of the equation shows that investment depends on the interest rate.

Figure 3-8 graphs saving and investment as a function of the interest rate. The saving function is a vertical line because in this model saving does not depend on the interest rate (we relax this assumption later). The investment function slopes downward: the higher the interest rate, the fewer investment projects are profitable.

From a quick glance at Figure 3-8, one might think it was a supply-and-demand diagram for a particular good. In fact, saving and investment can be interpreted in terms of supply and demand. In this case, the "good" is **loanable funds,** and its "price" is the interest rate. Saving is the supply of loanable funds—households lend their saving to investors or deposit their saving in a bank that then loans the funds out. Investment is the demand for loanable funds—investors borrow from the public directly by selling bonds or indirectly by borrowing from banks. Because investment depends on the interest rate, the quantity of loanable funds demanded also depends on the interest rate.

The interest rate adjusts until the amount that firms want to invest equals the amount that households want to save. If the interest rate is too low, investors want more of the economy's output than households want to save. Equivalently, the quantity of loanable funds demanded exceeds the quantity supplied. When this happens, the interest rate rises. Conversely, if the interest rate is too high, households want to save more than firms want to invest; because the quantity of loanable funds supplied is greater than the quantity demanded, the interest rate falls. The equilibrium interest rate is found where the two curves cross. *At the equilibrium interest rate, households' desire to save balances firms' desire to invest, and the quantity of loanable funds supplied equals the quantity demanded.*

FIGURE 3-8

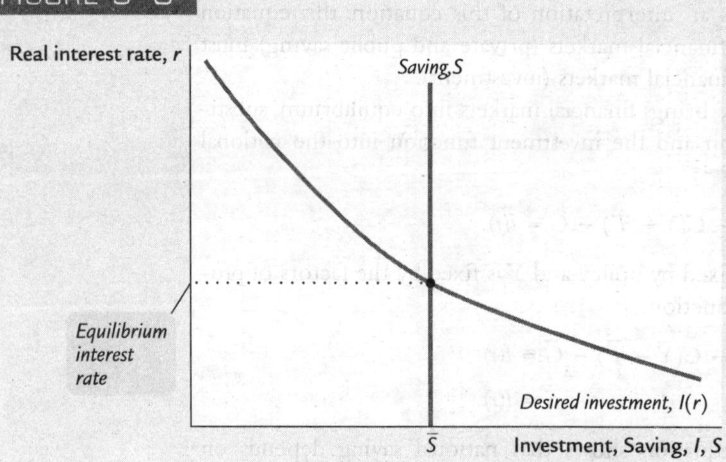

Saving, Investment, and the Interest Rate The interest rate adjusts to bring saving and investment into balance. The vertical line represents saving—the supply of loanable funds. The downward-sloping line represents investment—the demand for loanable funds. The intersection of these two curves determines the equilibrium interest rate.

Changes in Saving: The Effects of Fiscal Policy

We can use our model to show how fiscal policy affects the economy. When the government changes its spending or the level of taxes, it affects the demand for the economy's output of goods and services and alters national saving, investment, and the equilibrium interest rate.

An Increase in Government Purchases Consider first the effects of an increase in government purchases by an amount ΔG. The immediate impact is to increase the demand for goods and services by ΔG. But since total output is fixed by the factors of production, the increase in government purchases must be met by a decrease in some other category of demand. Because disposable income $Y - T$ is unchanged, consumption C is unchanged. The increase in government purchases must be met by an equal decrease in investment.

To induce investment to fall, the interest rate must rise. Hence, the increase in government purchases causes the interest rate to increase and investment to decrease. Government purchases are said to **crowd out** investment.

To grasp the effects of an increase in government purchases, consider the impact on the market for loanable funds. Because the increase in government purchases is not accompanied by an increase in taxes, the government finances the additional spending by borrowing—that is, by reducing public saving. With private saving unchanged, this government borrowing reduces national saving. As Figure 3-9 shows, a reduction in national saving is represented by a leftward shift in the supply of loanable funds available for investment. At the initial interest rate, the demand for loanable funds exceeds the supply. The equilibrium interest rate rises to the point where the investment schedule crosses the new saving schedule. Thus, an increase in government purchases causes the interest rate to rise from r_1 to r_2.

FIGURE 3-9

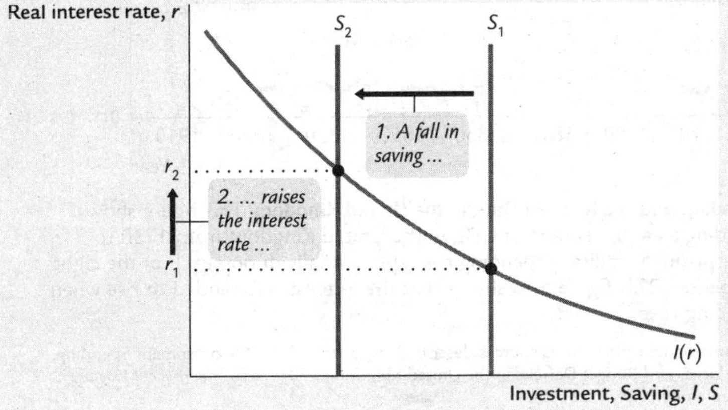

A Reduction in Saving A reduction in saving, possibly the result of a change in fiscal policy, shifts the saving schedule to the left. The new equilibrium is the point at which the new saving schedule crosses the investment schedule. A reduction in saving lowers the amount of investment and raises the interest rate. Fiscal-policy actions that reduce saving are said to crowd out investment.

CASE STUDY

Wars and Interest Rates in the United Kingdom, 1730–1920

Wars are traumatic—both for those who fight them and for a nation's economy. Because the economic changes accompanying them are often large, wars provide a natural experiment with which economists can test their theories. We can learn about the economy by seeing how in wartime the endogenous variables respond to the major changes in the exogenous variables.

One exogenous variable that changes substantially in wartime is the level of government purchases. Figure 3-10 shows military spending as a percentage of GDP for the United Kingdom from 1730 to 1919. This graph shows, as one would expect, that government purchases rose suddenly and dramatically during the eight wars of this period.

Our model predicts that this wartime increase in government purchases—and the increase in government borrowing to finance the wars—should have raised

FIGURE 3-10

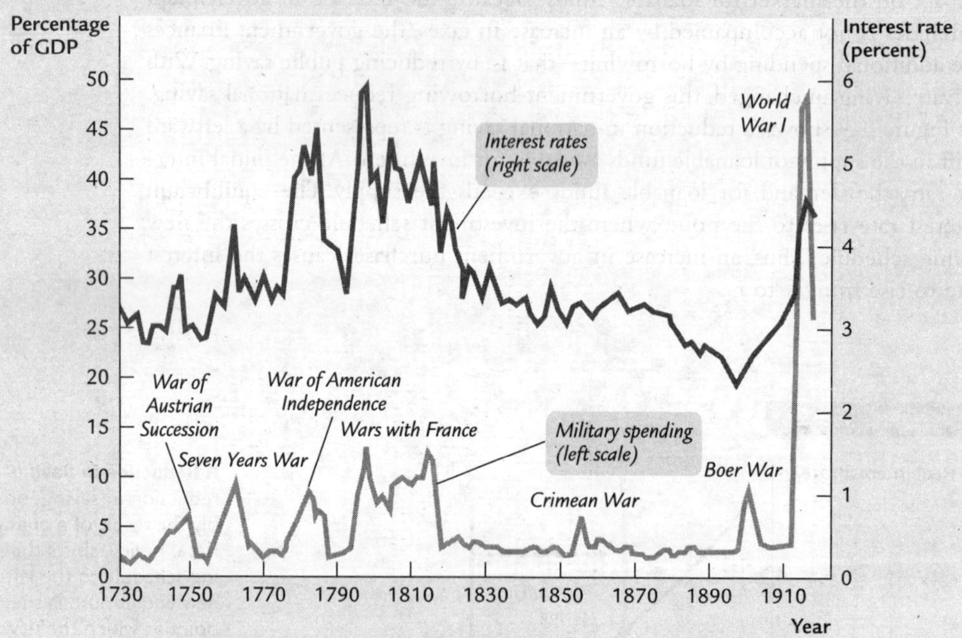

Military Spending and the Interest Rate in the United Kingdom This figure shows military spending as a percentage of GDP in the United Kingdom from 1730 to 1919. Not surprisingly, military spending rose substantially during each of the eight wars of this period. This figure also shows that the interest rate tended to rise when military spending rose.

Source: Series constructed from various sources described in Robert J. Barro, "Government Spending, Interest Rates, Prices, and Budget Deficits in the United Kingdom, 1701-1918," *Journal of Monetary Economics* 20 (September 1987): 221-248.

the demand for goods and services, reduced the supply of loanable funds, and raised the interest rate. To test this prediction, Figure 3-10 also shows the interest rate on long-term government bonds, called *consols* in the United Kingdom. A positive association between military purchases and interest rates is apparent in this figure. These data support the model's prediction: interest rates do tend to rise when government purchases increase.[7]

One problem with using wars to test theories is that many economic changes may be occurring at the same time. For example, in World War II, while government purchases increased dramatically, rationing also restricted consumption of many goods. In addition, the risk of defeat in the war and default by the government on its debt presumably increases the interest rate the government must pay. Economic models predict what happens when one exogenous variable changes and all the other exogenous variables remain constant. In the real world, however, many exogenous variables may change at once. Unlike controlled laboratory experiments, the natural experiments on which economists must rely are not always easy to interpret.

A Decrease in Taxes Now consider a reduction in taxes of ΔT. The immediate impact of the tax cut is to raise disposable income and thus to raise consumption. Disposable income rises by ΔT, and consumption rises by an amount equal to ΔT times the marginal propensity to consume *MPC*. The higher the *MPC*, the greater the impact of the tax cut on consumption.

Because the economy's output is fixed by the factors of production and the level of government purchases is fixed by the government, the increase in consumption must be met by a decrease in investment. For investment to fall, the interest rate must rise. Hence, a reduction in taxes, like an increase in government purchases, crowds out investment and raises the interest rate.

We can also analyze the effect of a tax cut by looking at saving and investment. Because the tax cut raises disposable income by ΔT, consumption goes up by $MPC \times \Delta T$. National saving S, which equals Y-C-G, falls by the same amount as consumption rises. As in Figure 3-9, the reduction in saving shifts the supply of loanable funds to the left, which increases the equilibrium interest rate and crowds out investment.

Changes in Investment Demand

So far, we have discussed how fiscal policy can change national saving. We can also use our model to examine the other side of the market—the demand for investment. In this section we look at the causes and effects of changes in investment demand.

[7] Daniel K. Benjamin and Levis A. Kochin, "War, Prices, and Interest Rates: A Martial Solution to Gibson's Paradox," in M. D. Bordo and A. J. Schwartz, eds., *A Retrospective on the Classical Gold Standard, 1821–1931* (Chicago: University of Chicago Press, 1984), 587-612; Robert J. Barro, "Government Spending, Interest Rates, Prices, and Budget Deficits in the United Kingdom, 1701-1918," *Journal of Monetary Economics* 20 (September 1987): 221-248.

One reason investment demand might increase is technological innovation. Suppose, for example, that someone invents a new technology, such as the railroad or the computer. Before a firm or household can take advantage of the innovation, it must buy investment goods. The invention of the railroad had no value until railroad cars were produced and tracks were laid. The idea of the computer was not productive until computers were manufactured. Thus, technological innovation leads to an increase in investment demand.

Investment demand may also change because the government encourages or discourages investment through the tax laws. For example, suppose that the government increases personal income taxes and uses the extra revenue to provide tax cuts for those who invest in new capital. Such a change in the tax laws makes more investment projects profitable and, like a technological innovation, increases the demand for investment goods.

Figure 3-11 shows the effects of an increase in investment demand. At any given interest rate, the demand for investment goods (and also for loanable funds) is higher. This increase in demand is represented by a shift in the investment schedule to the right. The economy moves from the old equilibrium, point A, to the new equilibrium, point B.

The surprising implication of Figure 3-11 is that the equilibrium amount of investment is unchanged. Under our assumptions, the fixed level of saving determines the amount of investment; in other words, there is a fixed supply of loanable funds. An increase in investment demand merely raises the equilibrium interest rate.

We would reach a different conclusion, however, if we modified our simple consumption function and allowed consumption (and its flip side, saving) to depend on the interest rate. Because the interest rate is the return to saving (as well as the cost of borrowing), a higher interest rate might reduce consumption and increase saving. If so, the saving schedule would be upward sloping rather than vertical.

FIGURE 3-11

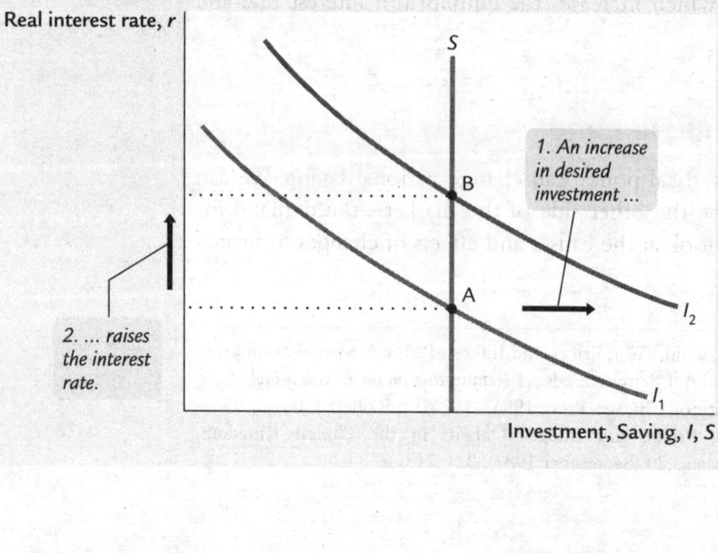

An Increase in the Demand for Investment An increase in the demand for investment goods shifts the investment schedule to the right. At any given interest rate, the amount of investment is greater. The equilibrium moves from point A to point B. Because the amount of saving is fixed, the increase in investment demand raises the interest rate while leaving the equilibrium amount of investment unchanged.

FIGURE 3-12

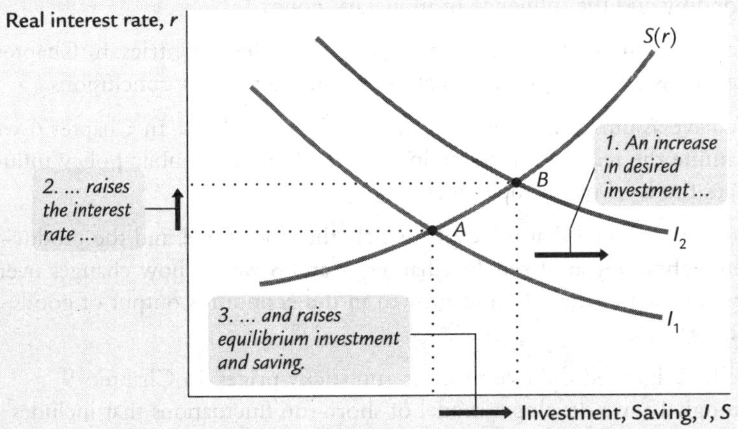

An Increase in Investment Demand When Saving Depends on the Interest Rate When saving is positively related to the interest rate, a rightward shift in the investment schedule increases the interest rate and the amount of investment. The higher interest rate induces people to increase saving, which in turn allows investment to increase.

With an upward-sloping saving schedule, an increase in investment demand would raise both the equilibrium interest rate and the equilibrium quantity of investment. Figure 3-12 shows such a change. The increase in the interest rate causes households to consume less and save more. The decrease in consumption frees resources for investment.

3-5 Conclusion

In this chapter we have developed a model that explains the production, distribution, and allocation of the economy's output of goods and services. The model relies on the classical assumption that prices adjust to equilibrate supply and demand. In this model, factor prices equilibrate factor markets, and the interest rate equilibrates the supply and demand for goods and services (or, equivalently, the supply and demand for loanable funds). Because the model incorporates all the interactions illustrated in the circular flow diagram in Figure 3-1, it is sometimes called a *general equilibrium model.*

Throughout the chapter, we have discussed various applications of the model. The model can explain how income is divided among the factors of production and how factor prices depend on factor supplies. We have also used the model to discuss how fiscal policy alters the allocation of output among its alternative uses—consumption, investment, and government purchases—and how it affects the equilibrium interest rate.

At this point it is useful to review some of the simplifying assumptions we have made in this chapter. In the following chapters we relax some of these assumptions to address a greater range of questions.

- We have ignored the role of money, the asset with which goods and services are bought and sold. In Chapter 4 we discuss how money affects the economy and the influence of monetary policy.
- We have assumed that there is no trade with other countries. In Chapter 5 we consider how international interactions affect our conclusions.
- We have assumed that the labor force is fully employed. In Chapter 6 we examine the reasons for unemployment and see how public policy influences the level of unemployment.
- We have assumed that the capital stock, the labor force, and the production technology are fixed. In Chapters 7 and 8 we see how changes over time in each of these lead to growth in the economy's output of goods and services.
- We have ignored the role of short-run sticky prices. In Chapters 9 through 13, we develop a model of short-run fluctuations that includes sticky prices. We then discuss how the model of short-run fluctuations relates to the model of national income developed in this chapter.

Before going on to these chapters, go back to the beginning of this one and make sure you can answer the four groups of questions about national income that begin the chapter.

Summary

1. The factors of production and the production technology determine the economy's output of goods and services. An increase in one of the factors of production or a technological advance raises output.
2. Competitive, profit-maximizing firms hire labor until the marginal product of labor equals the real wage. Similarly, these firms rent capital until the marginal product of capital equals the real rental price. Therefore, each factor of production is paid its marginal product. If the production function has constant returns to scale, all output is used to compensate the inputs.
3. The economy's output is used for consumption, investment, and government purchases. Consumption depends positively on disposable income. Investment depends negatively on the real interest rate. Government purchases and taxes are the exogenous variables of fiscal policy.
4. The real interest rate adjusts to equilibrate the supply and demand for the economy's output—or, equivalently, to equilibrate the supply of loanable funds (saving) and the demand for loanable funds (investment). A decrease in national saving, perhaps because of an increase in government purchases or a decrease in taxes, reduces the equilibrium amount of investment and raises the interest rate. An increase in investment demand, perhaps because of a

technological innovation or a tax incentive for investment, also raises the interest rate. An increase in investment demand increases the quantity of investment only if higher interest rates stimulate additional saving.

KEY CONCEPTS

Factors of production
Production function
Constant returns to scale
Factor prices
Competition
Profit
Marginal product of labor (*MPL*)
Diminishing marginal product
Real wage
Marginal product of capital (*MPK*)
Real rental price of capital
Economic profit versus accounting profit
Cobb-Douglas production function
Disposable income
Consumption function
Marginal propensity to consume (*MPC*)
Interest rate
Nominal interest rate
Real interest rate
National saving (saving)
Private saving
Public saving
Loanable funds
Crowding out

QUESTIONS FOR REVIEW

1. What determines the amount of output an economy produces?
2. Explain how a competitive, profit-maximizing firm decides how much of each factor of production to demand.
3. What is the role of constant returns to scale in the distribution of income?
4. Write down a Cobb-Douglas production function for which capital earns one-fourth of total income.
5. What determines consumption and investment?
6. Explain the difference between government purchases and transfer payments. Give two examples of each.
7. What makes the demand for the economy's output of goods and services equal the supply?
8. Explain what happens to consumption, investment, and the interest rate when the government increases taxes.

PROBLEMS AND APPLICATIONS

1. Use the neoclassical theory of distribution to predict the impact on the real wage and the real rental price of capital of each of the following events:
   a. A wave of immigration increases the labor force.
   b. An earthquake destroys some of the capital stock.
   c. A technological advance improves the production function.
2. If a 10-percent increase in both capital and labor causes output to increase by less than 10 percent, the production function is said to exhibit *decreasing returns to scale*. If it causes output to increase by more than 10 percent, the production function is said to exhibit *increasing returns to scale*. Why might a production function exhibit decreasing or increasing returns to scale?
3. Suppose that an economy's production function is Cobb-Douglas with parameter $\alpha = 0.3$.
   a. What fractions of income do capital and labor receive?

b. Suppose that immigration raises the labor force by 10 percent. What happens to total output (in percent)? The rental price of capital? The real wage?

c. Suppose that a gift of capital from abroad raises the capital stock by 10 percent. What happens to total output (in percent)? The rental price of capital? The real wage?

d. Suppose that a technological advance raises the value of the parameter A by 10 percent. What happens to total output (in percent)? The rental price of capital? The real wage?

4. Figure 3-5 shows that in U.S. data, labor's share of total income is approximately a constant over time. Table 3-1 shows that the trend in the real wage closely tracks the trend in labor productivity. How are these facts related? Could the first fact be true without the second also being true?

5. According to the neoclassical theory of distribution, the real wage earned by any worker equals that worker's marginal productivity. Let's use this insight to examine the incomes of two groups of workers: farmers and barbers.

a. Over the past century, the productivity of farmers has risen substantially because of technological progress. According to the neoclassical theory, what should have happened to their real wage?

b. In what units is the real wage discussed in part (a) measured?

c. Over the same period, the productivity of barbers has remained constant. What should have happened to their real wage?

d. In what units is the real wage in part (c) measured?

e. Suppose workers can move freely between being farmers and being barbers. What does this mobility imply for the wages of farmers and barbers?

f. What do your previous answers imply for the price of haircuts relative to the price of food?

g. Who benefits from technological progress in farming—farmers or barbers?

6. (This problem requires the use of calculus.) Consider a Cobb-Douglas production function with three inputs. K is capital (the number of machines), L is labor (the number of workers), and H is human capital (the number of college degrees among the workers). The production function is

$$Y = K^{1/3}L^{1/3}H^{1/3}.$$

a. Derive an expression for the marginal product of labor. How does an increase in the amount of human capital affect the marginal product of labor?

b. Derive an expression for the marginal product of human capital. How does an increase in the amount of human capital affect the marginal product of human capital?

c. What is the income share paid to labor? What is the income share paid to human capital? In the national income accounts of this economy, what share of total income do you think workers would appear to receive? (*Hint:* Consider where the return to human capital shows up.)

d. An unskilled worker earns the marginal product of labor, whereas a skilled worker earns the marginal product of labor plus the marginal product of human capital. Using your answers to (a) and (b), find the ratio of the skilled wage to the unskilled wage. How does an increase in the amount of human capital affect this ratio? Explain.

e. Some people advocate government funding of college scholarships as a way of creating a more egalitarian society. Others argue that scholarships help only those who are able to go to college. Do your answers to the preceding questions shed light on this debate?

7. The government raises taxes by \$100 billion. If the marginal propensity to consume is 0.6, what happens to the following? Do they rise or fall? By what amounts?

a. Public saving.

b. Private saving.

c. National saving.

d. Investment.

8. Suppose that an increase in consumer confidence raises consumers' expectations about their future income and thus increases the amount they want to consume today. This might be interpreted as an upward shift in the consumption function.

How does this shift affect investment and the interest rate?

9. Consider an economy described by the following equations:

$$Y = C + I + G$$
$$Y = 5{,}000$$
$$G = 1{,}000$$
$$T = 1{,}000$$
$$C = 250 + 0.75(Y - T)$$
$$I = 1{,}000 - 50\ r.$$

a. In this economy, compute private saving, public saving, and national saving.

b. Find the equilibrium interest rate.

c. Now suppose that G rises to 1,250. Compute private saving, public saving, and national saving.

d. Find the new equilibrium interest rate.

10. Suppose that the government increases taxes and government purchases by equal amounts. What happens to the interest rate and investment in response to this balanced budget change? Does your answer depend on the marginal propensity to consume?

11. When the government subsidizes investment, such as with an investment tax credit, the subsidy often applies to only some types of investment. This question asks you to consider the effect of such a change. Suppose there are two types of investment in the economy: business investment and residential investment. And suppose that the government institutes an investment tax credit only for business investment.

a. How does this policy affect the demand curve for business investment? The demand curve for residential investment?

b. Draw the economy's supply and demand for loanable funds. How does this policy affect the supply and demand for loanable funds? What happens to the equilibrium interest rate?

c. Compare the old and the new equilibrium. How does this policy affect the total quantity of investment? The quantity of business investment? The quantity of residential investment?

12. If consumption depended on the interest rate, how would that affect the conclusions reached in this chapter about the effects of fiscal policy?

13. Macroeconomic data do not show a strong correlation between investment and interest rates. Let's examine why this might be so. Use our model in which the interest rate adjusts to equilibrate the supply of loanable funds (which is upward sloping) and the demand for loanable funds (which is downward sloping).

a. Suppose the demand for loanable funds were stable but the supply fluctuated from year to year. What might cause these fluctuations in supply? In this case, what correlation between investment and interest rates would you find?

b. Suppose the supply of loanable funds were stable but the demand fluctuated from year to year. What might cause these fluctuations in demand? In this case, what correlation between investment and interest rates would you find now?

c. Suppose that both supply and demand in this market fluctuated over time. If you were to construct a scatterplot of investment and the interest rate, what would you find?

d. Which of the above three cases seems most empirically realistic to you?

CHAPTER

4 Money and Inflation

Lenin is said to have declared that the best way to destroy the Capitalist System was to debauch the currency. . . . Lenin was certainly right. There is no subtler, no surer means of overturning the existing basis of society than to debauch the currency. The process engages all the hidden forces of economic law on the side of destruction, and does it in a manner which not one man in a million is able to diagnose.

— John Maynard Keynes

In 1970 the *New York Times* cost 15 cents, the median price of a single-family home was $23,400, and the average wage in manufacturing was $3.36 per hour. In 2004 the *Times* cost $1.00, the price of a home was $221,000, and the average wage was $16.15 per hour. This overall increase in prices is called **inflation**, and it is the subject of this chapter.

The rate of inflation—the percentage change in the overall level of prices—varies greatly over time and across countries. In the United States, according to the consumer price index, prices rose an average of 2.4 percent per year in the 1960s, 7.1 percent per year in the 1970s, 5.5 percent per year in the 1980s, and 3.0 percent per year in the 1990s. Even when the U.S inflation problem became severe during the 1970s, however, it was nothing compared to the episodes of extraordinarily high inflation, called **hyperinflation**, that other countries have experienced from time to time. A classic example is Germany in 1923, when prices increased an average of 500 percent *per month*.

In this chapter we examine the classical theory of the causes, effects, and social costs of inflation. The theory is "classical" in the sense that it assumes that prices are flexible. As we first discussed in Chapter 1, most economists believe this assumption describes the behavior of the economy in the long run. By contrast, many prices are thought to be sticky in the short run, and beginning in Chapter 9, we incorporate this fact into our analysis. Yet, for now, we ignore short-run price stickiness. As we will see, the classical theory of inflation not only provides a good description of the long run, it also provides a useful foundation for the short-run analysis we develop later.

The "hidden forces of economic law" that lead to inflation are not as mysterious as Keynes claims in the quotation that opens this chapter. Inflation is simply an increase in the average level of prices, and a *price* is the rate at which money is exchanged for a good or a service. To understand inflation, therefore, we must understand money—what it is, what affects its supply and demand, and what influence it has on the economy. Thus, Section 4-1 begins our analysis of inflation by discussing the economist's concept of "money" and how, in most modern economies, the government controls the quantity of money in the hands of the public. Section 4-2 shows that the quantity of money determines the price level and that the rate of growth in the quantity of money determines the rate of inflation.

Inflation in turn has numerous effects of its own on the economy. Section 4-3 discusses the revenue that the government raises by printing money, sometimes called the *inflation tax*. Section 4-4 examines how inflation affects the nominal interest rate. Section 4-5 discusses how the nominal interest rate in turn affects the quantity of money people wish to hold and, thereby, the price level.

After completing our analysis of the causes and effects of inflation, in Section 4-6 we address what is perhaps the most important question about inflation: Is it a major social problem? Does inflation amount to "overturning the existing basis of society," as the chapter's opening quotation suggests?

Finally, in Section 4-7, we discuss the dramatic case of hyperinflation. Hyperinflations are interesting to examine because they show clearly the causes, effects, and costs of inflation. Just as seismologists learn much by studying earthquakes, economists learn much by studying how hyperinflations begin and end.

4-1 What Is Money?

When we say that a person has a lot of money, we usually mean that he or she is wealthy. By contrast, economists use the term *money* in a more specialized way. To an economist, money does not refer to all wealth but only to one type of it: **money** is the stock of assets that can be readily used to make transactions. Roughly speaking, the dollars in the hands of the public make up the nation's stock of money.

The Functions of Money

Money has three purposes. It is a store of value, a unit of account, and a medium of exchange.

As a **store of value**, money is a way to transfer purchasing power from the present to the future. If I work today and earn $100, I can hold the money and spend it tomorrow, next week, or next month. Of course, money is an imperfect store of value: if prices are rising, the amount you can buy with any given quantity of money is falling. Even so, people hold money because they can trade the money for goods and services at some time in the future.

As a **unit of account**, money provides the terms in which prices are quoted and debts are recorded. Microeconomics teaches us that resources are allocated according to relative prices—the prices of goods relative to other goods—yet stores post their prices in dollars and cents. A car dealer tells you that a car costs $20,000, not 400 shirts (even though it may amount to the same thing). Similarly, most debts require the debtor to deliver a specified number of dollars in the future, not a specified amount of some commodity. Money is the yardstick with which we measure economic transactions.

As a **medium of exchange**, money is what we use to buy goods and services. "This note is legal tender for all debts, public and private" is printed on the U.S. dollar. When we walk into stores, we are confident that the shopkeepers will accept our money in exchange for the items they are selling. The ease with which money is converted into other things—goods and services—is sometimes called money's *liquidity*.

To better understand the functions of money, try to imagine an economy without it: a barter economy. In such a world, trade requires the *double coincidence of wants*—the unlikely happenstance of two people each having a good that the other wants at the right time and place to make an exchange. A barter economy permits only simple transactions.

Money makes more indirect transactions possible. A professor uses her salary to buy books; the book publisher uses its revenue from the sale of books to buy paper; the paper company uses its revenue from the sale of paper to pay the lumberjack; the lumberjack uses his income to send his child to college; and the college uses its tuition receipts to pay the salary of the professor. In a complex, modern economy, trade is usually indirect and requires the use of money.

The Types of Money

Money takes many forms. In the U.S. economy we make transactions with an item whose sole function is to act as money: dollar bills. These pieces of green paper with small portraits of famous Americans would have little value if they were not widely accepted as money. Money that has no intrinsic value is called **fiat money** because it is established as money by government decree, or fiat.

"And how would you like your funny money?"

Drawing by Bernard Schoenbaum; © 1979 The New Yorker Magazine, Inc.

Although fiat money is the norm in most economies today, most societies in the past have used for money a commodity with some intrinsic value. Money of this sort is called **commodity money**. The most widespread example of commodity money is gold. When people use gold as money (or use paper money that is redeemable for gold), the economy is said to be on a **gold standard**. Gold is a form of commodity money because it can be used for various purposes—jewelry, dental fillings, and so on—as well as for transactions. The gold standard was common throughout the world during the late nineteenth century.

CASE STUDY

Money in a POW Camp

An unusual form of commodity money developed in some Nazi prisoner of war (POW) camps during World War II. The Red Cross supplied the prisoners with various goods—food, clothing, cigarettes, and so on. Yet these rations were allocated without close attention to personal preferences, so the allocations were often inefficient. One prisoner may have preferred chocolate, while another may have preferred cheese, and a third may have wanted a new shirt. The differing tastes and endowments of the prisoners led them to trade with one another.

Barter proved to be an inconvenient way to allocate these resources, however, because it required the double coincidence of wants. In other words, a barter system was not the easiest way to ensure that each prisoner received the goods he valued most. Even the limited economy of the POW camp needed some form of money to facilitate transactions.

Eventually, cigarettes became the established "currency" in which prices were quoted and with which trades were made. A shirt, for example, cost about 80 cigarettes. Services were also quoted in cigarettes: some prisoners offered to do other prisoners' laundry for 2 cigarettes per garment. Even nonsmokers were happy to accept cigarettes in exchange, knowing they could trade the cigarettes in the future for some good they did enjoy. Within the POW camp the cigarette became the store of value, the unit of account, and the medium of exchange.[1]

How Fiat Money Evolves

It is not surprising that some form of commodity money arises to facilitate exchange: people are willing to accept a commodity currency such as gold because it has intrinsic value. The development of fiat money, however, is more perplexing. What would make people begin to value something that is intrinsically useless?

To understand how the evolution from commodity money to fiat money takes place, imagine an economy in which people carry around bags of gold. When a purchase is made, the buyer measures out the appropriate amount of gold. If the seller is convinced that the weight and purity of the gold are right, the buyer and seller make the exchange.

The government might first get involved in the monetary system to help people reduce transaction costs. Using raw gold as money is costly because it takes

[1] R.A. Radford, "The Economic Organisation of a P.O.W. Camp," *Economica* (November 1945): 189-201. The use of cigarettes as money is not limited to this example. In the Soviet Union in the late 1980s, packs of Marlboros were preferred to the ruble in the large underground economy.

time to verify the purity of the gold and to measure the correct quantity. To reduce these costs, the government can mint gold coins of known purity and weight. The coins are easier to use than gold bullion because their values are widely recognized.

The next step is for the government to accept gold from the public in exchange for gold certificates—pieces of paper that can be redeemed for a certain quantity of gold. If people believe the government's promise to redeem the paper bills for gold, the bills are just as valuable as the gold itself. In addition, because the bills are lighter than gold (and gold coins), they are easier to use in transactions. Eventually, no one carries gold around at all, and these gold-backed government bills become the monetary standard.

Finally, the gold backing becomes irrelevant. If no one ever bothers to redeem the bills for gold, no one cares if the option is abandoned. As long as everyone continues to accept the paper bills in exchange, they will have value and serve as money. Thus, the system of commodity money evolves into a system of fiat money. Notice that in the end the use of money in exchange is a social convention: everyone values fiat money because they expect everyone else to value it.

CASE STUDY

Money and Social Conventions on the Island of Yap

The economy of Yap, a small island in the Pacific, once had a type of money that was something between commodity and fiat money. The traditional medium of exchange in Yap was *fei*, stone wheels up to 12 feet in diameter. These stones had holes in the center so that they could be carried on poles and used for exchange.

Large stone wheels are not a convenient form of money. The stones were heavy, so it took substantial effort for a new owner to take his *fei* home after completing a transaction. Although the monetary system facilitated exchange, it did so at great cost.

Eventually, it became common practice for the new owner of the *fei* not to bother to take physical possession of the stone. Instead, the new owner accepted a claim to the *fei* without moving it. In future bargains, he traded this claim for goods that he wanted. Having physical possession of the stone became less important than having legal claim to it.

This practice was put to a test when a valuable stone was lost at sea during a storm. Because the owner lost his money by accident rather than through negligence, everyone agreed that his claim to the *fei* remained valid. Even generations later, when no one alive had ever seen this stone, the claim to this *fei* was still valued in exchange.[2]

[2] Norman Angell, *The Story of Money* (New York: Frederick A. Stokes Company, 1929), 88-89.

How the Quantity of Money Is Controlled

The quantity of money available in an economy is called the **money supply**. For commodity money, the money supply is simply the quantity of that commodity. In an economy that uses fiat money, such as most economies today, the government controls the supply of money: legal restrictions give the government a monopoly on the printing of money. Just as the level of taxation and the level of government purchases are policy instruments of the government, so is the supply of money. The control over the money supply is called **monetary policy**.

In the United States and many other countries, monetary policy is delegated to a partially independent institution called the **central bank**. The central bank of the United States is the **Federal Reserve**—often called *the Fed*. If you look at a U.S. dollar bill, you will see that it is called a *Federal Reserve Note.* Decisions over monetary policy are made by the Federal Open Market Committee. This committee is made up of members of the Federal Reserve Board, who are appointed by the president and confirmed by Congress, together with the presidents of the regional Federal Reserve Banks. The Federal Open Market Committee meets about every six weeks to discuss and set monetary policy.

The primary way in which the Fed controls the supply of money is through **open-market operations**—the purchase and sale of government bonds. When the Fed wants to increase the money supply, it uses some of the dollars it has to buy government bonds from the public. Because these dollars leave the Fed and enter into the hands of the public, the purchase increases the quantity of money in circulation. Conversely, when the Fed wants to decrease the money supply, it sells some government bonds from its own portfolio. This open-market sale of bonds takes some dollars out of the hands of the public and, thus, decreases the quantity of money in circulation.

In Chapter 18 we discuss in detail how the Fed controls the supply of money. For our current discussion, these details are not crucial. It is sufficient to assume that the Fed (or any other central bank) directly controls the supply of money.

How the Quantity of Money Is Measured

One goal of this chapter is to determine how the money supply affects the economy; we turn to that topic in the next section. As a background for that analysis, let's first discuss how economists measure the quantity of money.

Because money is the stock of assets used for transactions, the quantity of money is the quantity of those assets. In simple economies, this quantity is easy to measure. In the POW camp, the quantity of money was the quantity of cigarettes in the camp. But how can we measure the quantity of money in more complex economies? The answer is not obvious, because no single asset is used for all transactions. People can use various assets, such as cash in their wallets or deposits in their checking accounts, to make transactions, although some assets are more convenient than others.

The most obvious asset to include in the quantity of money is **currency**, the sum of outstanding paper money and coins. Most day-to-day transactions use currency as the medium of exchange.

A second type of asset used for transactions is **demand deposits**, the funds people hold in their checking accounts. If most sellers accept personal checks, assets in a checking account are almost as convenient as currency. In both cases, the assets are in a form ready to facilitate a transaction. Demand deposits are therefore added to currency when measuring the quantity of money.

Once we admit the logic of including demand deposits in the measured money stock, many other assets become candidates for inclusion. Funds in savings accounts, for example, can be easily transferred into checking accounts; these assets are almost as convenient for transactions. Money market mutual funds allow investors to write checks against their accounts, although restrictions sometimes apply with regard to the size of the check or the number of checks written. Because these assets can be easily used for transactions, they should arguably be included in the quantity of money.

Because it is hard to judge which assets should be included in the money stock, various measures are available. Table 4-1 presents the four measures of the money stock that the Federal Reserve calculates for the U.S. economy, together with a list of which assets are included in each measure. From the smallest to the largest, they are designated *C*, *M*1, *M*2, and *M*3. The most common measures for studying the effects of money on the economy are *M*1 and *M*2. There is no consensus, however, about which measure of the money stock is best. Disagreements about monetary policy sometimes arise because different measures of money are moving in different directions.

TABLE 4-1

The Measures of Money

Symbol	Assets Included	Amount in September 2005 (billions of dollars)
C	Currency	715.4
*M*1	Currency plus demand deposits, traveler's checks, and other checkable deposits	1363.4
*M*2	*M*1 plus retail money market mutual fund balances, saving deposits (including money market deposit accounts), and small time deposits	6587.9
*M*3	*M*2 plus large time deposits, repurchase agreements, Eurodollars, and institution-only money market mutual fund balances	9976.2

Source: Federal Reserve

FYI How Do Credit Cards and Debit Cards Fit into the Monetary System?

Many people use credit or debit cards to make purchases. Because money is the medium of exchange, one might naturally wonder how these cards fit into the measurement and analysis of money.

Let's start with credit cards. Although one might guess that credit cards are part of the economy's stock of money, in fact measures of the quantity of money do not take credit cards into account. Credit cards are not really a method of payment but a method of *deferring* payment. When you buy an item with a credit card, the bank that issued the card pays the store what it is due. Later, you will have to repay the bank. When the time comes to pay your credit card bill, you will likely do so by writing a check against your checking account. The balance in this checking account is part of the economy's stock of money.

The story is different with debit cards, which automatically withdraw funds from a bank account to pay for items bought. Rather than allowing users to postpone payment for their purchases, a debit card allows users immediate access to deposits in their bank accounts. Using a debit card is similar to writing a check. The account balances that lie behind debit cards are included in measures of the quantity of money.

Even though credit cards are not a form of money, they are still important for analyzing the monetary system. Because people with credit cards can pay many of their bills all at once at the end of the month, rather than sporadically as they make purchases, they may hold less money on average than people without credit cards. Thus, the increased popularity of credit cards may reduce the amount of money that people choose to hold. In other words, credit cards are not part of the supply of money, but they may affect the demand for money.

4-2 The Quantity Theory of Money

Having defined what money is and described how it is controlled and measured, we can now examine how the quantity of money affects the economy. To do this, we need a theory of how the quantity of money is related to other economic variables, such as prices and incomes. The theory we will now develop, called the *quantity theory of money*, has its roots in the work of the early monetary theorists, including the philosopher and economist David Hume (1711–1776). It remains the leading explanation for how money affects the economy in the long run.

Transactions and the Quantity Equation

People hold money to buy goods and services. The more money they need for such transactions, the more money they hold. Thus, the quantity of money in the economy is related to the number of dollars exchanged in transactions.

The link between transactions and money is expressed in the following equation, called the **quantity equation**:

$$\text{Money} \times \text{Velocity} = \text{Price} \times \text{Transactions}$$

$$M \times V = P \times T.$$

Let's examine each of the four variables in this equation.

The right-hand side of the quantity equation tells us about transactions. T represents the total number of transactions during some period of time, say, a year. In other words, T is the number of times in a year that goods or services are exchanged for money. P is the price of a typical transaction—the number of dollars exchanged. The product of the price of a transaction and the number of transactions, PT, equals the number of dollars exchanged in a year.

The left-hand side of the quantity equation tells us about the money used to make the transactions. M is the quantity of money. V is called the **transactions velocity of money** and measures the rate at which money circulates in the economy. In other words, velocity tells us the number of times a dollar bill changes hands in a given period of time.

For example, suppose that 60 loaves of bread are sold in a given year at \$0.50 per loaf. Then T equals 60 loaves per year, and P equals \$0.50 per loaf. The total number of dollars exchanged is

$$PT = \$0.50/\text{loaf} \times 60\ \text{loaves/year} = \$30/\text{year}.$$

The right-hand side of the quantity equation equals \$30 per year, which is the dollar value of all transactions.

Suppose further that the quantity of money in the economy is \$10. By rearranging the quantity equation, we can compute velocity as

$$\begin{aligned} V &= PT/M \\ &= (\$30/\text{year})/(\$10) \\ &= 3 \text{ times per year.} \end{aligned}$$

That is, for \$30 of transactions per year to take place with \$10 of money, each dollar must change hands 3 times per year.

The quantity equation is an *identity*: the definitions of the four variables make it true. The equation is useful because it shows that if one of the variables changes, one or more of the others must also change to maintain the equality. For example, if the quantity of money increases and the velocity of money remains unchanged, then either the price or the number of transactions must rise.

From Transactions to Income

When studying the role of money in the economy, economists usually use a slightly different version of the quantity equation than the one just introduced. The problem with the first equation is that the number of transactions is difficult to measure. To solve this problem, the number of transactions T is replaced by the total output of the economy Y.

Transactions and output are related, because the more the economy produces, the more goods are bought and sold. They are not the same, however. When one person sells a used car to another person, for example, they make a transaction using money, even though the used car is not part of current output. Nonetheless, the dollar value of transactions is roughly proportional to the dollar value of output.

If Y denotes the amount of output and P denotes the price of one unit of output, then the dollar value of output is PY. We encountered measures for these variables when we discussed the national income accounts in Chapter 2: Y is real GDP, P the GDP deflator, and PY nominal GDP. The quantity equation becomes

$$\text{Money} \times \text{Velocity} = \text{Price} \times \text{Output}$$

$$M \times V = P \times Y.$$

Because Y is also total income, V in this version of the quantity equation is called the **income velocity of money**. The income velocity of money tells us the number of times a dollar bill enters someone's income in a given period of time. This version of the quantity equation is the most common, and it is the one we use from now on.

The Money Demand Function and the Quantity Equation

When we analyze how money affects the economy, it is often useful to express the quantity of money in terms of the quantity of goods and services it can buy. This amount, M/P, is called **real money balances**.

Real money balances measure the purchasing power of the stock of money. For example, consider an economy that produces only bread. If the quantity of money is \$10, and the price of a loaf is \$0.50, then real money balances are 20 loaves of bread. That is, at current prices, the stock of money in the economy is able to buy 20 loaves.

A **money demand function** is an equation that shows the determinants of the quantity of real money balances people wish to hold. A simple money demand function is

$$(M/P)^d = kY,$$

where k is a constant that tells us how much money people want to hold for every dollar of income. This equation states that the quantity of real money balances demanded is proportional to real income.

The money demand function is like the demand function for a particular good. Here the "good" is the convenience of holding real money balances. Just as owning an automobile makes it easier for a person to travel, holding money makes it easier to make transactions. Therefore, just as higher income leads to a greater demand for automobiles, higher income also leads to a greater demand for real money balances.

This money demand function offers another way to view the quantity equation. To see this, add to the money demand function the condition that the demand for real money balances $(M/P)^d$ must equal the supply M/P. Therefore,

$$M/P = kY.$$

A simple rearrangement of terms changes this equation into

$$M(1/k) = PY,$$

which can be written as

$$MV = PY,$$

where $V = 1/k$. These few steps of simple mathematics show the link between the demand for money and the velocity of money. When people want to hold a lot of money for each dollar of income (k is large), money changes hands infrequently (V is small). Conversely, when people want to hold only a little money (k is small), money changes hands frequently (V is large). In other words, the money demand parameter k and the velocity of money V are opposite sides of the same coin.

The Assumption of Constant Velocity

The quantity equation can be viewed as a definition: it defines velocity V as the ratio of nominal GDP, PY, to the quantity of money M. Yet if we make the additional assumption that the velocity of money is constant, then the quantity equation becomes a useful theory about the effects of money, called the **quantity theory of money**.

As with many of the assumptions in economics, the assumption of constant velocity is only an approximation to reality. Velocity does change if the money demand function changes. For example, when automatic teller machines were introduced, people could reduce their average money holdings, which meant a fall in the money demand parameter k and an increase in velocity V. Nonetheless, experience shows that the assumption of constant velocity is a useful one in many situations. Let's therefore assume that velocity is constant and see what this assumption implies about the effects of the money supply on the economy.

Once we assume that velocity is constant, the quantity equation can be seen as a theory of what determines nominal GDP. The quantity equation says

$$M\bar{V} = PY,$$

where the bar over V means that velocity is fixed. Therefore, a change in the quantity of money (M) must cause a proportionate change in nominal GDP (PY). That is, if velocity is fixed, the quantity of money determines the dollar value of the economy's output.

Money, Prices, and Inflation

We now have a theory to explain what determines the economy's overall level of prices. The theory has three building blocks:

1. The factors of production and the production function determine the level of output Y. We borrow this conclusion from Chapter 3.

2. The money supply M determines the nominal value of output PY. This conclusion follows from the quantity equation and the assumption that the velocity of money is fixed.

3. The price level P is then the ratio of the nominal value of output PY to the level of output Y.

In other words, the productive capability of the economy determines real GDP, the quantity of money determines nominal GDP, and the GDP deflator is the ratio of nominal GDP to real GDP.

This theory explains what happens when the central bank changes the supply of money. Because velocity is fixed, any change in the supply of money leads to a proportionate change in nominal GDP. Because the factors of production and the production function have already determined real GDP, the change in nominal GDP must represent a change in the price level. Hence, the quantity theory implies that the price level is proportional to the money supply.

Because the inflation rate is the percentage change in the price level, this theory of the price level is also a theory of the inflation rate. The quantity equation, written in percentage-change form, is

$$\% \text{ Change in } M + \% \text{ Change in } V = \% \text{ Change in } P + \% \text{ Change in } Y.$$

Consider each of these four terms. First, the percentage change in the quantity of money M is under the control of the central bank. Second, the percentage change in velocity V reflects shifts in money demand; we have assumed that velocity is constant, so the percentage change in velocity is zero. Third, the percentage change in the price level P is the rate of inflation; this is the variable in the equation that we would like to explain. Fourth, the percentage change in output Y depends on growth in the factors of production and on technological progress, which for our present purposes we are taking as given. This analysis tells us that (except for a constant that depends on exogenous growth in output) the growth in the money supply determines the rate of inflation.

Thus, the quantity theory of money states that the central bank, which controls the money supply, has ultimate control over the rate of inflation. If the central bank keeps the money supply stable, the price level will be stable. If the central bank increases the money supply rapidly, the price level will rise rapidly.

CASE STUDY

Inflation and Money Growth

"Inflation is always and everywhere a monetary phenomenon." So wrote Milton Friedman, the great economist who won the Nobel Prize for economics in 1976. The quantity theory of money leads us to agree that the growth in the quantity of money is the primary determinant of the inflation rate. Yet Friedman's claim is empirical, not theoretical. To evaluate his claim, and to judge the usefulness of our theory, we need to look at data on money and prices.

Friedman, together with fellow economist Anna Schwartz, wrote two treatises on monetary history that documented the sources and effects of changes in the quantity of money over the past century.[3] Figure 4-1 uses some of their data and plots the average rate of money growth and the average rate of inflation in the United States over each decade since the 1870s. The data verify the link between inflation and growth in the quantity of money. Decades with high money growth (such as the 1970s) tend to have high inflation, and decades with low money growth (such as the 1930s) tend to have low inflation.

Figure 4-2 examines the same question using international data. It shows the average rate of inflation and the average rate of money growth in 119 countries plus the Euro Area during the period from 1996 to 2004. Again, the link between

FIGURE 4-1

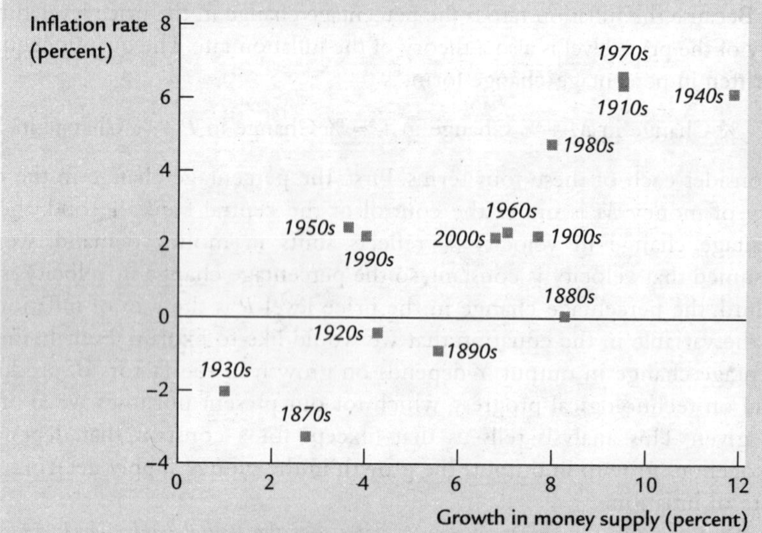

Historical Data on U.S. Inflation and Money Growth In this scatterplot of money growth and inflation, each point represents a decade. The horizontal axis shows the average growth in the money supply (as measured by *M2*) over the decade, and the vertical axis shows the average rate of inflation (as measured by the GDP deflator). The positive correlation between money growth and inflation is evidence for the quantity theory's prediction that high money growth leads to high inflation.

Source: For the data through the 1960s: Milton Friedman and Anna J. Schwartz, *Monetary Trends in the United States and the United Kingdom: Their Relation to Income, Prices, and Interest Rates 1867-1975* (Chicago: University of Chicago Press, 1982). For recent data: U.S. Department of Commerce, Federal Reserve Board. The data point for the 2000s includes only the first half of the decade.

[3] Milton Friedman and Anna J. Schwartz, *A Monetary History of the United States, 1867–1960* (Princeton, NJ: Princeton University Press, 1963); Milton Friedman and Anna J. Schwartz, *Monetary Trends in the United States and the United Kingdom: Their Relation to Income, Prices, and Interest Rates, 1867–1975* (Chicago: University of Chicago Press, 1982).

FIGURE 4-2

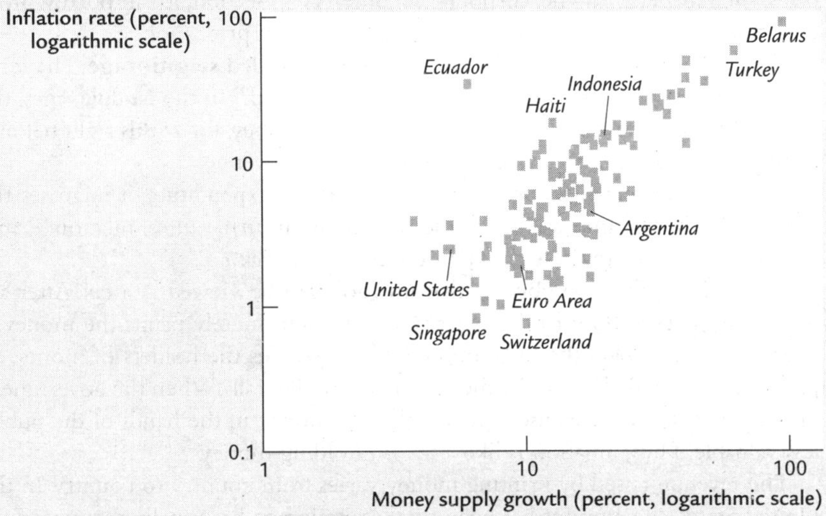

International Data on Inflation and Money Growth In this scatterplot, each point represents a country. The horizontal axis shows the average growth in the money supply (as measured by currency plus demand deposits) during the period 1996 to 2004, and the vertical axis shows the average rate of inflation (as measured by the CPI). Once again, the positive correlation is evidence for the quantity theory's prediction that high money growth leads to high inflation.

Source: International Financial Statistics.

money growth and inflation is clear. Countries with high money growth (such as Turkey) tend to have high inflation, and countries with low money growth (such as Singapore) tend to have low inflation.

If we looked at monthly data on money growth and inflation, rather than data for ten-year periods, we would not see as close a connection between these two variables. This theory of inflation works best in the long run, not in the short run. We examine the short-run impact of changes in the quantity of money when we turn to economic fluctuations in Part Four of this book.

4-3 Seigniorage: The Revenue From Printing Money

So far, we have seen how growth in the money supply causes inflation. With inflation as a consequence, what would ever induce a central bank to increase the money supply so much? Here we examine one answer to this question.

Let's start with an indisputable fact: all governments spend money. Some of this spending is to buy goods and services (such as roads and police), and some is to provide transfer payments (for the poor and elderly, for example). A government can finance its spending in three ways. First, it can raise revenue through taxes, such as personal and corporate income taxes. Second, it can borrow from the public by selling government bonds. Third, it can print money.

The revenue raised by the printing of money is called **seigniorage**. The term comes from *seigneur,* the French word for "feudal lord." In the Middle Ages, the lord had the exclusive right on his manor to coin money. Today this right belongs to the central government, and it is one source of revenue.

When the government prints money to finance expenditure, it increases the money supply. The increase in the money supply, in turn, causes inflation. Printing money to raise revenue is like imposing an *inflation tax*.

At first it may not be obvious that inflation can be viewed as a tax. After all, no one receives a bill for this tax—the government merely prints the money it needs. Who then pays the inflation tax? The answer is the holders of money. As prices rise, the real value of the money in your wallet falls. When the government prints new money for its use, it makes the old money in the hands of the public less valuable. Thus, inflation is like a tax on holding money.

The revenue raised by printing money varies from country to country. In the United States, the amount has been small: seigniorage has usually accounted for less than 3 percent of government revenue. In Italy and Greece, seigniorage has often been more than 10 percent of government revenue.[4] In countries experiencing hyperinflation, seigniorage is often the government's chief source of revenue—indeed, the need to print money to finance expenditure is a primary cause of hyperinflation.

CASE STUDY

Paying for the American Revolution

Although seigniorage has not been a major source of revenue for the U.S. government in recent history, the situation was very different two centuries ago. Beginning in 1775 the Continental Congress needed to find a way to finance the Revolution, but it had limited ability to raise revenue through taxation. It therefore relied on the printing of fiat money to help pay for the war.

The Continental Congress's reliance on seigniorage increased over time. In 1775 new issues of continental currency were about \$6 million. This amount increased to \$19 million in 1776, \$13 million in 1777, \$63 million in 1778, and \$125 million in 1779.

Not surprisingly, this rapid growth in the money supply led to massive inflation. At the end of the war, the price of gold measured in continental dollars was more than 100 times its level of only a few years earlier. The large quantity of the continental currency made the continental dollar nearly worthless. This experience also gave birth to a once-popular expression: people used to say something was "not worth a continental" to mean that the item had little real value.

[4] Stanley Fischer, "Seigniorage and the Case for a National Money," *Journal of Political Economy* 90 (April 1982): 295–313.

When the new nation won its independence, there was a natural skepticism about fiat money. Upon the recommendation of the first Secretary of Treasury, Alexander Hamilton, the Congress passed the Mint Act of 1792, which established gold and silver as the basis for a new system of commodity money.

4-4 Inflation and Interest Rates

As we first discussed in Chapter 3, interest rates are among the most important macroeconomic variables. In essence, they are the prices that link the present and the future. Here we discuss the relationship between inflation and interest rates.

Two Interest Rates: Real and Nominal

Suppose you deposit your savings in a bank account that pays 8 percent interest annually. Next year, you withdraw your savings and the accumulated interest. Are you 8 percent richer than you were when you made the deposit a year earlier?

The answer depends on what "richer" means. Certainly, you have 8 percent more dollars than you had before. But if prices have risen, each dollar buys less, and your purchasing power has not risen by 8 percent. If the inflation rate was 5 percent over the year, then the amount of goods you can buy has increased by only 3 percent. And if the inflation rate was 10 percent, then your purchasing power has fallen by 2 percent.

Economists call the interest rate that the bank pays the **nominal interest rate** and the increase in your purchasing power the **real interest rate**. If i denotes the nominal interest rate, r the real interest rate, and π the rate of inflation, then the relationship among these three variables can be written as

$$r = i - \pi.$$

The real interest rate is the difference between the nominal interest rate and the rate of inflation.[5]

The Fisher Effect

Rearranging terms in our equation for the real interest rate, we can show that the nominal interest rate is the sum of the real interest rate and the inflation rate:

$$i = r + \pi.$$

The equation written in this way is called the **Fisher equation**, after economist Irving Fisher (1867–1947). It shows that the nominal interest rate can change for two reasons: because the real interest rate changes or because the inflation rate changes.

[5] *Mathematical note:* This equation relating the real interest rate, nominal interest rate, and inflation rate is only an approximation. The exact formula is $(1 + r) = (1 + i)/(1 + \pi)$. The approximation in the text is reasonably accurate as long as r, i, and π are relatively small (say, less than 20 percent per year).

Once we separate the nominal interest rate into these two parts, we can use this equation to develop a theory that explains the nominal interest rate. Chapter 3 showed that the real interest rate adjusts to equilibrate saving and investment. The quantity theory of money shows that the rate of money growth determines the rate of inflation. The Fisher equation then tells us to add the real interest rate and the inflation rate together to determine the nominal interest rate.

The quantity theory and the Fisher equation together tell us how money growth affects the nominal interest rate. *According to the quantity theory, an increase in the rate of money growth of 1 percent causes a 1 percent increase in the rate of inflation. According to the Fisher equation, a 1 percent increase in the rate of inflation in turn causes a 1 percent increase in the nominal interest rate.* The one-for-one relation between the inflation rate and the nominal interest rate is called the **Fisher effect**.

CASE STUDY

Inflation and Nominal Interest Rates

How useful is the Fisher effect in explaining interest rates? To answer this question we look at two types of data on inflation and nominal interest rates.

FIGURE 4-3

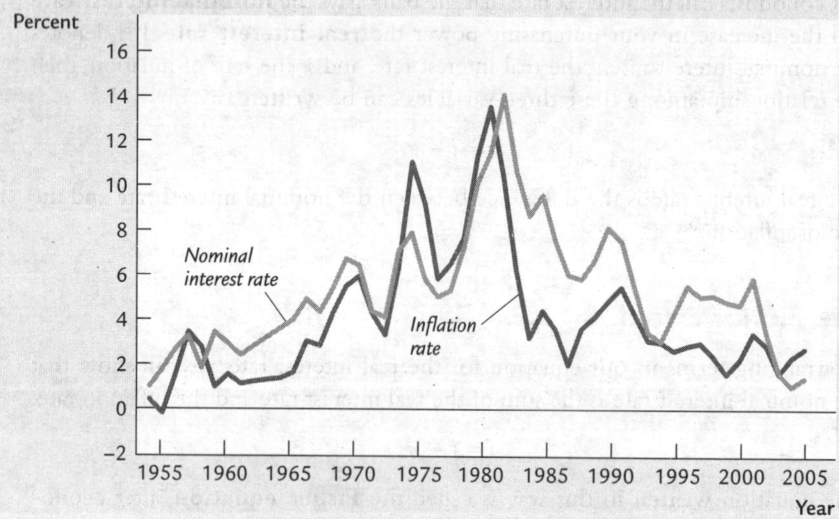

Inflation and Nominal Interest Rates Over Time This figure plots the nominal interest rate (on three-month Treasury bills) and the inflation rate (as measured by the CPI) in the United States since 1954. It shows the Fisher effect: higher inflation leads to a higher nominal interest rate.

Source: Federal Reserve and U.S. Department of Labor.

Figure 4-3 shows the variation over time in the nominal interest rate and the inflation rate in the United States. You can see that the Fisher effect has done a good job explaining fluctuations in the nominal interest rate over the past 50 years. When inflation is high, nominal interest rates are typically high, and when inflation is low, nominal interest rates are typically low as well.

Similar support for the Fisher effect comes from examining the variation across countries. As Figure 4-4 shows, a nation's inflation rate and its nominal interest rate are related. Countries with high inflation tend to have high nominal interest rates as well, and countries with low inflation tend to have low nominal interest rates.

FIGURE 4-4

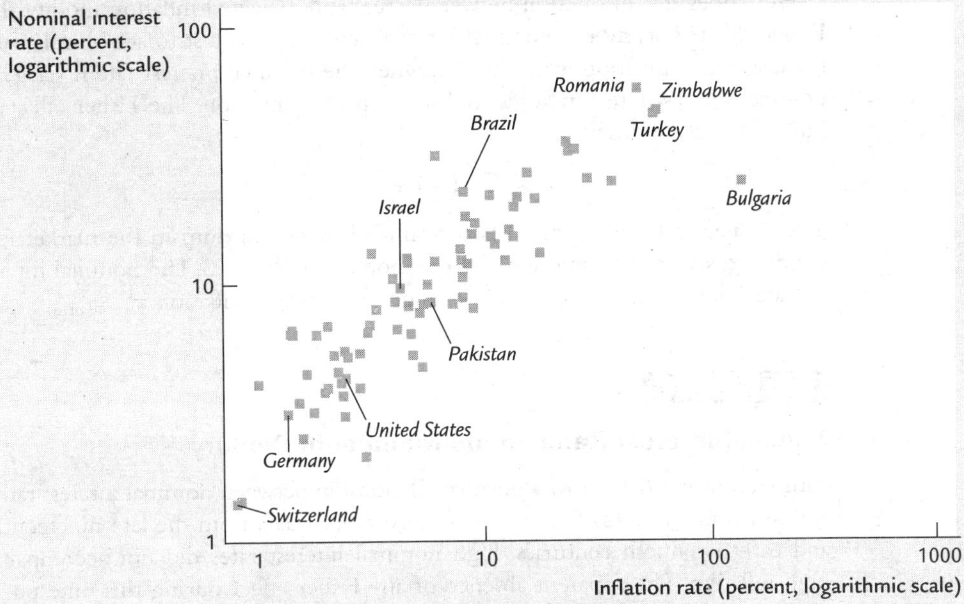

Inflation and Nominal Interest Rates Across Countries This scatterplot shows the average nominal interest rate on short-term Treasury bills and the average inflation rate in 77 countries during the period 1996 to 2004. The positive correlation between the inflation rate and the nominal interest rate is evidence for the Fisher effect.

Source: International Financial Statistics.

The link between inflation and interest rates is well known to Wall Street investment firms. Because bond prices move inversely with interest rates, one can get rich by predicting correctly the direction in which interest rates will move. Many Wall Street firms hire *Fed watchers* to monitor monetary policy and news about inflation to anticipate changes in interest rates.

Two Real Interest Rates: *Ex Ante* and *Ex Post*

When a borrower and lender agree on a nominal interest rate, they do not know what the inflation rate over the term of the loan will be. Therefore, we must distinguish between two concepts of the real interest rate: the real interest rate the borrower and lender expect when the loan is made, called the ***ex ante* real interest rate**, and the real interest rate actually realized, called the ***ex post* real interest rate**.

Although borrowers and lenders cannot predict future inflation with certainty, they do have some expectation about what the inflation rate will be. Let π denote actual future inflation and π^e the expectation of future inflation. The *ex ante* real interest rate is $i - \pi^e$, and the *ex post* real interest rate is $i - \pi$. The two real interest rates differ when actual inflation π differs from expected inflation π^e.

How does this distinction between actual and expected inflation modify the Fisher effect? Clearly, the nominal interest rate cannot adjust to actual inflation, because actual inflation is not known when the nominal interest rate is set. The nominal interest rate can adjust only to expected inflation. The Fisher effect is more precisely written as

$$i = r + \pi^e.$$

The *ex ante* real interest rate r is determined by equilibrium in the market for goods and services, as described by the model in Chapter 3. The nominal interest rate i moves one-for-one with changes in expected inflation π^e.

CASE STUDY

Nominal Interest Rates in the Nineteenth Century

Although recent data show a positive relationship between nominal interest rates and inflation rates, this finding is not universal. In data from the late nineteenth and early twentieth centuries, high nominal interest rates did not accompany high inflation. The apparent absence of any Fisher effect during this time puzzled Irving Fisher. He suggested that inflation "caught merchants napping."

How should we interpret the absence of an apparent Fisher effect in nineteenth-century data? Does this period of history provide evidence against the adjustment of nominal interest rates to inflation? Recent research suggests that this period has little to tell us about the validity of the Fisher effect. The reason is that the Fisher effect relates the nominal interest rate to *expected* inflation and, according to this research, inflation at this time was largely unexpected.

Although expectations are not observable, we can draw inferences about them by examining the persistence of inflation. In recent experience, inflation has been very persistent: when it is high one year, it tends to be high the next year as well. Therefore, when people have observed high inflation, it has been rational for them to expect high inflation in the future. By contrast, during the nineteenth century, when the gold standard was in effect, inflation had little persistence.

High inflation in one year was just as likely to be followed the next year by low inflation as by high inflation. Therefore, high inflation did not imply high expected inflation and did not lead to high nominal interest rates. So, in a sense, Fisher was right to say that inflation "caught merchants napping."[6]

4-5 The Nominal Interest Rate and the Demand for Money

The quantity theory is based on a simple money demand function: it assumes that the demand for real money balances is proportional to income. Although the quantity theory is a good place to start when analyzing the effects of money on the economy, it is not the whole story. Here we add another determinant of the quantity of money demanded—the nominal interest rate.

The Cost of Holding Money

The money you hold in your wallet does not earn interest. If, instead of holding that money, you used it to buy government bonds or deposited it in a savings account, you would earn the nominal interest rate. The nominal interest rate is the opportunity cost of holding money: it is what you give up by holding money rather than bonds.

Another way to see that the cost of holding money equals the nominal interest rate is by comparing the real returns on alternative assets. Assets other than money, such as government bonds, earn the real return r. Money earns an expected real return of $-\pi^e$, because its real value declines at the rate of inflation. When you hold money, you give up the difference between these two returns. Thus, the cost of holding money is $r - (-\pi^e)$, which the Fisher equation tells us is the nominal interest rate i.

Just as the quantity of bread demanded depends on the price of bread, the quantity of money demanded depends on the price of holding money. Hence, the demand for real money balances depends both on the level of income and on the nominal interest rate. We write the general money demand function as

$$(M/P)^d = L(i, Y).$$

The letter L is used to denote money demand because money is the economy's most liquid asset (the asset most easily used to make transactions). This equation states that the demand for the liquidity of real money balances is a function of income and the nominal interest rate. The higher the level of income Y, the greater the demand for real money balances. The higher the nominal interest rate i, the lower the demand for real money balances.

[6] Robert B. Barsky, "The Fisher Effect and the Forecastability and Persistence of Inflation," *Journal of Monetary Economics* 19 (January 1987): 3–24.

Future Money and Current Prices

Money, prices, and interest rates are now related in several ways. Figure 4-5 illustrates the linkages we have discussed. As the quantity theory of money explains, money supply and money demand together determine the equilibrium price level. Changes in the price level are, by definition, the rate of inflation. Inflation, in turn, affects the nominal interest rate through the Fisher effect. But now, because the nominal interest rate is the cost of holding money, the nominal interest rate feeds back to affect the demand for money.

Consider how the introduction of this last link affects our theory of the price level. First, equate the supply of real money balances M/P to the demand $L(i, Y)$:

$$M/P = L(i,\ Y).$$

Next, use the Fisher equation to write the nominal interest rate as the sum of the real interest rate and expected inflation:

$$M/P = L(r + \pi^e,\ Y).$$

This equation states that the level of real money balances depends on the expected rate of inflation.

The last equation tells a more sophisticated story about the determination of the price level than does the quantity theory. The quantity theory of money says that today's money supply determines today's price level. This conclusion remains partly true: if the nominal interest rate and the level of output are held constant, the price level moves proportionately with the money supply. Yet the nominal

FIGURE 4-5

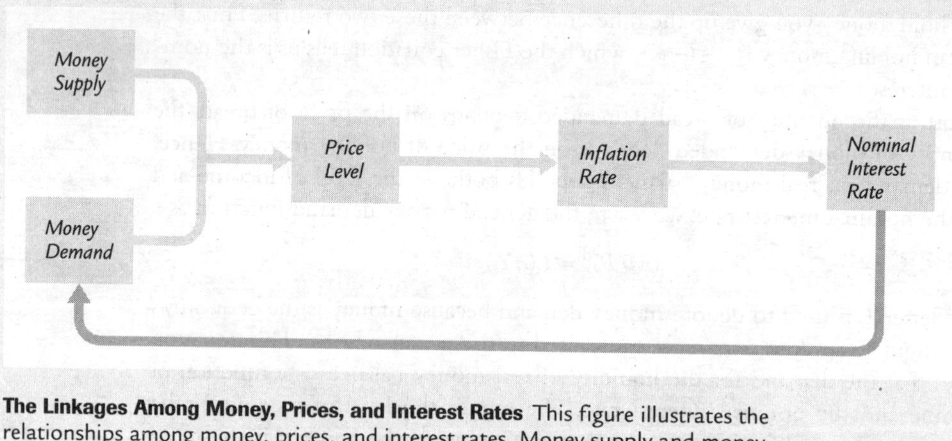

The Linkages Among Money, Prices, and Interest Rates This figure illustrates the relationships among money, prices, and interest rates. Money supply and money demand determine the price level. Changes in the price level determine the inflation rate. The inflation rate influences the nominal interest rate. Because the nominal interest rate is the cost of holding money, it may affect money demand. This last link (shown as a blue line) is omitted from the basic quantity theory of money.

interest rate is not constant; it depends on expected inflation, which in turn depends on growth in the money supply. The presence of the nominal interest rate in the money demand function yields an additional channel through which money supply affects the price level.

This general money-demand equation implies that the price level depends not only on today's money supply but also on the money supply expected in the future. To see why, suppose the Fed announces that it will increase the money supply in the future, but it does not change the money supply today. This announcement causes people to expect higher money growth and higher inflation. Through the Fisher effect, this increase in expected inflation raises the nominal interest rate. The higher nominal interest rate increases the cost of holding money and therefore reduces the demand for real money balances. Because the Fed has not changed the quantity of money available today, the reduced demand for real money balances leads to a higher price level. Hence, higher expected money growth in the future leads to a higher price level today.

The effect of money on prices is complex. The appendix to this chapter presents the *Cagan model*, which shows how the price level is related to current and future money. The conclusion of the analysis is that the price level depends on a weighted average of the current money supply and the money supply expected to prevail in the future.

4-6 The Social Costs of Inflation

Our discussion of the causes and effects of inflation does not tell us much about the social problems that result from inflation. We turn to those problems now.

The Layman's View and the Classical Response

If you ask the average person why inflation is a social problem, he will probably answer that inflation makes him poorer. "Each year my boss gives me a raise, but prices go up and that takes some of my raise away from me." The implicit assumption in this statement is that if there were no inflation, he would get the same raise and be able to buy more goods.

This complaint about inflation is a common fallacy. As we know from Chapter 3, the purchasing power of labor—the real wage—depends on the marginal productivity of labor, not on how much money the government chooses to print. If the central bank reduces inflation by slowing the rate of money growth, workers will not see their real wage increasing more rapidly. Instead, when inflation slows, firms will increase the prices of their products less each year and, as a result, will give their workers smaller raises.

According to the classical theory of money, a change in the overall price level is like a change in the units of measurement. It is as if we switched from measuring distances in feet to measuring them in inches: numbers get larger, but nothing really changes. Imagine that tomorrow morning you wake up and find that, for some reason, all dollar figures in the economy have been multiplied by ten. The price of everything you buy has increased tenfold, but so have your wage and the value of your savings. What difference would such a price increase make to your life? All numbers would have an extra zero at the end, but nothing else would change. Your economic well-being depends on relative prices, not the overall price level.

Why, then, is a persistent increase in the price level a social problem? It turns out that the costs of inflation are subtle. Indeed, economists disagree about the size of the social costs. To the surprise of many laymen, some economists argue that the costs of inflation are small—at least for the moderate rates of inflation that most countries have experienced in recent years.[7]

CASE STUDY

What Economists and the Public Say About Inflation

As we have been discussing, laymen and economists hold very different views about the costs of inflation. Economist Robert Shiller has documented this difference of opinion in a survey of the two groups. The survey results are striking, for they show how the study of economics changes a person's attitudes.

In one question, Shiller asked people whether their "biggest gripe about inflation" was that "inflation hurts my real buying power, it makes me poorer." Of the general public, 77 percent agreed with this statement, compared to only 12 percent of economists. Shiller also asked people whether they agreed with the following statement: "When I see projections about how many times more a college education will cost, or how many times more the cost of living will be in coming decades, I feel a sense of uneasiness; these inflation projections really make me worry that my own income will not rise as much as such costs will." Among the general public, 66 percent said they fully agreed with this statement, whereas only 5 percent of economists agreed with it.

Survey respondents were asked to judge the seriousness of inflation as a policy problem: "Do you agree that preventing high inflation is an important national priority, as important as preventing drug abuse or preventing deterioration in the quality of our schools?" Fifty-two percent of laymen, but only 18 percent of economists, fully agreed with this view. Apparently, inflation worries the public much more than it does the economics profession.

The public's distaste for inflation may be psychological. Shiller asked those surveyed if they agreed with the following statement: "I think that if my pay went up I would feel more satisfaction in my job, more sense of fulfillment, even if prices went up just as much." Of the public, 49 percent fully or partly agreed with this statement, compared to 8 percent of economists.

---

[7] See, for example, Chapter 2 of Alan Blinder, *Hard Heads, Soft Hearts: Tough-Minded Economics for a Just Society* (Reading, MA: Addison Wesley, 1987).

Do these survey results mean that laymen are wrong and economists are right about the costs of inflation? Not necessarily. But economists do have the advantage of having given the issue more thought. So let's now consider what some of the costs of inflation might be.[8]

The Costs of Expected Inflation

Consider first the case of expected inflation. Suppose that every month the price level rose by 1 percent. What would be the social costs of such a steady and predictable 12 percent annual inflation?

One cost is the distortion of the inflation tax on the amount of money people hold. As we have already discussed, a higher inflation rate leads to a higher nominal interest rate, which in turn leads to lower real money balances. If people are to hold lower money balances on average, they must make more frequent trips to the bank to withdraw money—for example, they might withdraw $50 twice a week rather than $100 once a week. The inconvenience of reducing money holding is metaphorically called the **shoeleather cost** of inflation, because walking to the bank more often causes one's shoes to wear out more quickly.

A second cost of inflation arises because high inflation induces firms to change their posted prices more often. Changing prices is sometimes costly: for example, it may require printing and distributing a new catalog. These costs are called **menu costs**, because the higher the rate of inflation, the more often restaurants have to print new menus.

A third cost of inflation arises because firms facing menu costs change prices infrequently; therefore, the higher the rate of inflation, the greater the variability in relative prices. For example, suppose a firm issues a new catalog every January. If there is no inflation, then the firm's prices relative to the overall price level are constant over the year. Yet if inflation is 1 percent per month, then from the beginning to the end of the year the firm's relative prices fall by 12 percent. Sales from this catalog will tend to be low early in the year (when its prices are relatively high) and high later in the year (when its prices are relatively low). Hence, when inflation induces variability in relative prices, it leads to microeconomic inefficiencies in the allocation of resources.

A fourth cost of inflation results from the tax laws. Many provisions of the tax code do not take into account the effects of inflation. Inflation can alter individuals' tax liability, often in ways that lawmakers did not intend.

One example of the failure of the tax code to deal with inflation is the tax treatment of capital gains. Suppose you buy some stock today and sell it a year from now at the same real price. It would seem reasonable for the government not to levy a tax, because you have earned no real income from this investment. Indeed, if there is no inflation, a zero tax liability would be the outcome. But

[8] Robert J. Shiller, "Why Do People Dislike Inflation?" in Christina D. Romer and David H. Romer, eds., *Reducing Inflation: Motivation and Strategy* (Chicago: University of Chicago Press, 1997).

suppose the rate of inflation is 12 percent and you initially paid $100 per share for the stock; for the real price to be the same a year later, you must sell the stock for $112 per share. In this case the tax code, which ignores the effects of inflation, says that you have earned $12 per share in income, and the government taxes you on this capital gain. The problem, of course, is that the tax code measures income as the nominal rather than the real capital gain. In this example, and in many others, inflation distorts how taxes are levied.

A fifth cost of inflation is the inconvenience of living in a world with a changing price level. Money is the yardstick with which we measure economic transactions. When there is inflation, that yardstick is changing in length. To continue the analogy, suppose that Congress passed a law specifying that a yard would equal 36 inches in 2006, 35 inches in 2007, 34 inches in 2008, and so on. Although the law would result in no ambiguity, it would be highly inconvenient. When someone measured a distance in yards, it would be necessary to specify whether the measurement was in 2006 yards or 2007 yards; to compare distances measured in different years, one would need to make an "inflation" correction. Similarly, the dollar is a less useful measure when its value is always changing. The changing value of the dollar requires that we correct for inflation when comparing dollar figures from different times.

For example, a changing price level complicates personal financial planning. One important decision that all households face is how much of their income to consume today and how much to save for retirement. A dollar saved today and invested at a fixed nominal interest rate will yield a fixed dollar amount in the future. Yet the real value of that dollar amount—which will determine the retiree's living standard—depends on the future price level. Deciding how much to save would be much simpler if people could count on the price level in 30 years being similar to its level today.

The Costs of Unexpected Inflation

Unexpected inflation has an effect that is more pernicious than any of the costs of steady, anticipated inflation: it arbitrarily redistributes wealth among individuals. You can see how this works by examining long-term loans. Most loan agreements specify a nominal interest rate, which is based on the rate of inflation expected at the time of the agreement. If inflation turns out differently from what was expected, the *ex post* real return that the debtor pays to the creditor differs from what both parties anticipated. On the one hand, if inflation turns out to be higher than expected, the debtor wins and the creditor loses because the debtor repays the loan with less valuable dollars. On the other hand, if inflation turns out to be lower than expected, the creditor wins and the debtor loses because the repayment is worth more than the two parties anticipated.

Consider, for example, a person taking out a mortgage in 1960. At the time, a 30-year mortgage had an interest rate of about 6 percent per year. This rate was based on a low rate of expected inflation—inflation over the previous decade had averaged only 2.5 percent. The creditor probably expected to receive a real return of about 3.5 percent, and the debtor expected to pay this real return. In fact, over the life of the mortgage, the inflation rate averaged 5 percent, so the *ex post* real return was only 1 percent. This unanticipated inflation benefited the debtor at the expense of the creditor.

Unanticipated inflation also hurts individuals on fixed pensions. Workers and firms often agree on a fixed nominal pension when the worker retires (or even earlier). Because the pension is deferred earnings, the worker is essentially providing the firm a loan: the worker provides labor services to the firm while young but does not get fully paid until old age. Like any creditor, the worker is hurt when inflation is higher than anticipated. Like any debtor, the firm is hurt when inflation is lower than anticipated.

These situations provide a clear argument against variable inflation. The more variable the rate of inflation, the greater the uncertainty that both debtors and creditors face. Because most people are *risk averse*—they dislike uncertainty—the unpredictability caused by highly variable inflation hurts almost everyone.

Given these effects of uncertain inflation, it is puzzling that nominal contracts are so prevalent. One might expect debtors and creditors to protect themselves from this uncertainty by writing contracts in real terms—that is, by indexing to some measure of the price level. In economies with high and variable inflation, indexation is often widespread; sometimes this indexation takes the form of writing contracts using a more stable foreign currency. In economies with moderate inflation, such as the United States, indexation is less common. Yet even in the United States, some long-term obligations are indexed. For example, Social Security benefits for the elderly are adjusted annually in response to changes in the consumer price index. And in 1997, the U.S. federal government issued inflation-indexed bonds for the first time.

Finally, in thinking about the costs of inflation, it is important to note a widely documented but little understood fact: high inflation is variable inflation. That is, countries with high average inflation also tend to have inflation rates that change greatly from year to year. The implication is that if a country decides to pursue a high-inflation monetary policy, it will likely have to accept highly variable inflation as well. As we have just discussed, highly variable inflation increases uncertainty for both creditors and debtors by subjecting them to arbitrary and potentially large redistributions of wealth.

CASE STUDY

The Free Silver Movement, the Election of 1896, and the Wizard of Oz

The redistributions of wealth caused by unexpected changes in the price level are often a source of political turmoil, as evidenced by the Free Silver movement in the late nineteenth century. From 1880 to 1896 the price level in the United States fell 23 percent. This deflation was good for creditors, primarily the bankers of the Northeast, but it was bad for debtors, primarily the farmers of the South and West. One proposed solution to this problem was to replace the gold standard with a bimetallic standard, under which both gold and silver could be minted into coin. The move to a bimetallic standard would increase the money supply and stop the deflation.

The silver issue dominated the presidential election of 1896. William McKinley, the Republican nominee, campaigned on a platform of preserving the gold standard. William Jennings Bryan, the Democratic nominee, supported the bimetallic standard. In a famous speech, Bryan proclaimed, "You shall not press down upon the brow of labor this crown of thorns, you shall not crucify mankind upon a cross of gold." Not surprisingly, McKinley was the candidate of the conservative Eastern establishment, whereas Bryan was the candidate of the Southern and Western populists.

This debate over silver found its most memorable expression in a children's book, *The Wizard of Oz*. Written by a Midwestern journalist, L. Frank Baum, just after the 1896 election, it tells the story of Dorothy, a girl lost in a strange land far from her home in Kansas. Dorothy (representing traditional American values) makes three friends: a scarecrow (the farmer), a tin woodman (the industrial worker), and a lion whose roar exceeds his might (William Jennings Bryan). Together, the four of them make their way along a perilous yellow brick road (the gold standard), hoping to find the Wizard who will help Dorothy return home. Eventually they arrive in Oz (Washington), where everyone sees the world through green glasses (money). The Wizard (William McKinley) tries to be all things to all people but turns out to be a fraud. Dorothy's problem is solved only when she learns about the magical power of her silver slippers.[9]

Although the Republicans won the election of 1896 and the United States stayed on a gold standard, the Free Silver advocates got the inflation that they wanted. Around the time of the election, gold was discovered in Alaska, Australia, and South Africa. In addition, gold refiners devised the cyanide process, which facilitated the extraction of gold from ore. These developments led to increases in the money supply and in prices. From 1896 to 1910 the price level rose 35 percent.

One Benefit of Inflation

So far, we have discussed the many costs of inflation. These costs lead many economists to conclude that monetary policymakers should aim for zero inflation. Yet there is another side to the story. Some economists believe that a little bit of inflation—say, 2 or 3 percent per year—can be a good thing.

The argument for moderate inflation starts with the observation that cuts in nominal wages are rare: firms are reluctant to cut their workers' nominal wages,

[9] The movie made forty years later hid much of the allegory by changing Dorothy's slippers from silver to ruby. For more on this topic, see Henry M. Littlefield, "The Wizard of Oz: Parable on Populism," *American Quarterly* 16 (Spring 1964): 47–58; and Hugh Rockoff, "The Wizard of Oz as a Monetary Allegory," *Journal of Political Economy* 98 (August 1990): 739–760. It should be noted that there is no direct evidence that Baum intended his work as a monetary allegory, so some people believe that the parallels are the work of economic historians' overactive imaginations.

and workers are reluctant to accept such cuts. A 2-percent wage cut in a zero-inflation world is, in real terms, the same as a 3-percent raise with 5-percent inflation, but workers do not always see it that way. The 2-percent wage cut may seem like an insult, whereas the 3-percent raise is, after all, still a raise. Empirical studies confirm that nominal wages rarely fall.

This finding suggests that some inflation may make labor markets work better. The supply and demand for different kinds of labor are always changing. Sometimes an increase in supply or decrease in demand leads to a fall in the equilibrium real wage for a group of workers. If nominal wages can't be cut, then the only way to cut real wages is to allow inflation to do the job. Without inflation, the real wage will be stuck above the equilibrium level, resulting in higher unemployment.

For this reason, some economists argue that inflation "greases the wheels" of labor markets. Only a little inflation is needed: an inflation rate of 2 percent lets real wages fall by 2 percent per year, or 20 percent per decade, without cuts in nominal wages. Such automatic reductions in real wages are impossible with zero inflation.[10]

4-7 Hyperinflation

Hyperinflation is often defined as inflation that exceeds 50 percent per month, which is just over 1 percent per day. Compounded over many months, this rate of inflation leads to very large increases in the price level. An inflation rate of 50 percent per month implies a more than 100-fold increase in the price level over a year, and a more than 2-million-fold increase over three years. Here we consider the costs and causes of such extreme inflation.

The Costs of Hyperinflation

Although economists debate whether the costs of moderate inflation are large or small, no one doubts that hyperinflation extracts a high toll on society. The costs are qualitatively the same as those we discussed earlier. When inflation reaches extreme levels, however, these costs are more apparent because they are so severe.

The shoeleather costs associated with reduced money holding, for instance, are serious under hyperinflation. Business executives devote much time and energy to cash management when cash loses its value quickly. By diverting this time and energy from more socially valuable activities, such as production and investment decisions, hyperinflation makes the economy run less efficiently.

---

[10] For a recent paper examining this benefit of inflation, see George A. Akerlof, William T. Dickens, and George L. Perry, "The Macroeconomics of Low Inflation," *Brookings Papers on Economic Activity,* 1996:1, pp. 1–76.

Menu costs also become larger under hyperinflation. Firms have to change prices so often that normal business practices, such as printing and distributing catalogs with fixed prices, become impossible. In one restaurant during the German hyperinflation of the 1920s, a waiter would stand up on a table every 30 minutes to call out the new prices.

Similarly, relative prices do not do a good job of reflecting true scarcity during hyperinflations. When prices change frequently by large amounts, it is hard for customers to shop around for the best price. Highly volatile and rapidly rising prices can alter behavior in many ways. According to one report, when patrons entered a pub during the German hyperinflation, they would often buy two pitchers of beer. Although the second pitcher would lose value by getting warm over time, it would lose value less rapidly than the money left sitting in the patron's wallet.

Tax systems are also distorted by hyperinflation—but in ways that are different from the distortions of moderate inflation. In most tax systems there is a delay between the time a tax is levied and the time the tax is paid to the government. In the United States, for example, taxpayers are required to make estimated income tax payments every three months. This short delay does not matter much under low inflation. By contrast, during hyperinflation, even a short delay greatly reduces real tax revenue. By the time the government gets the money it is due, the money has fallen in value. As a result, once hyperinflations start, the real tax revenue of the government often falls substantially.

Finally, no one should underestimate the sheer inconvenience of living with hyperinflation. When carrying money to the grocery store is as burdensome as carrying the groceries back home, the monetary system is not doing its best to facilitate exchange. The government tries to overcome this problem by adding more and more zeros to the paper currency, but often it cannot keep up with the exploding price level.

Eventually, these costs of hyperinflation become intolerable. Over time, money loses its role as a store of value, unit of account, and medium of exchange. Barter becomes more common. And more stable unofficial monies—cigarettes or the U.S. dollar—start to replace the official money.

CASE STUDY

Life During the Bolivian Hyperinflation

The following article from the *Wall Street Journal* shows what life was like during the Bolivian hyperinflation of 1985. What costs of inflation does this article emphasize?

Precarious Peso - Amid Wild Inflation, Bolivians Concentrate on Swapping Currency

LA PAZ, Bolivia—When Edgar Miranda gets his monthly teacher's pay of 25 million pesos, he hasn't a moment to lose. Every hour, pesos drop in value. So, while his wife rushes to market to lay in a month's supply of rice and noodles, he is off with the rest of the pesos to change them into black-market dollars.

Mr. Miranda is practicing the First Rule of Survival amid the most out-of-control inflation in the world today. Bolivia is a case study of how runaway inflation undermines a society. Price increases are so huge that the figures build up almost beyond comprehension. In one six-month period, for example, prices soared at an annual rate of 38,000%. By official count, however, last year's inflation reached 2,000%, and this year's is expected to hit 8,000%—though other estimates range many times higher. In any event, Bolivia's rate dwarfs Israel's 370% and Argentina's 1,100%—two other cases of severe inflation.

It is easier to comprehend what happens to the 38-year-old Mr. Miranda's pay if he doesn't quickly change it into dollars. The day he was paid 25 million pesos, a dollar cost 500,000 pesos. So he received $50. Just days later, with the rate at 900,000 pesos, he would have received $27.

"We think only about today and converting every peso into dollars," says Ronald MacLean, the manager of a gold-mining firm. "We have become myopic."

And intent on survival. Civil servants won't hand out a form without a bribe. Lawyers, accountants, hairdressers, even prostitutes have almost given up working to become money-changers in the streets. Workers stage repeated strikes and steal from their bosses. The bosses smuggle production abroad, take out phony loans, duck taxes—anything to get dollars for speculation.

The production at the state mines, for example, dropped to 12,000 tons last year from 18,000. The miners pad their wages by smuggling out the richest ore in their lunch pails, and the ore goes by a contraband network into neighboring Peru. Without a major tin mine, Peru now exports some 4,000 metric tons of tin a year.

"We don't produce anything. We are all currency speculators," a heavy-equipment dealer in La Paz says. "People don't know what's good and bad anymore. We have become an amoral society. . . ."

It is an open secret that practically all of the black-market dollars come from the illegal cocaine trade with the U.S. Cocaine traffickers earn an estimated $1 billion a year. . .

But meanwhile the country is suffering from inflation largely because the government's revenues cover a mere 15% of its expenditures and its deficit has widened to nearly 25% of the country's total annual output. The revenues are hurt by a lag in tax payments, and taxes aren't being collected largely because of widespread theft and bribery.

Source: Reprinted by permission of the *Wall Street Journal.* © August 13, 1985, page 1, Dow Jones & Company, Inc. All rights reserved worldwide.

The Causes of Hyperinflation

Why do hyperinflations start, and how do they end? This question can be answered at different levels.

The most obvious answer is that hyperinflations are due to excessive growth in the supply of money. When the central bank prints money, the price level rises. When it prints money rapidly enough, the result is hyperinflation. To stop the hyperinflation, the central bank must reduce the rate of money growth.

This answer is incomplete, however, for it leaves open the question of why central banks in hyperinflating economies choose to print so much money. To address this deeper question, we must turn our attention from monetary to fiscal policy. Most hyperinflations begin when the government has inadequate tax revenue to pay for its spending. Although the government might prefer to

"I told you the Fed should have tightened."

finance this budget deficit by issuing debt, it may find itself unable to borrow, perhaps because lenders view the government as a bad credit risk. To cover the deficit, the government turns to the only mechanism at its disposal—the printing press. The result is rapid money growth and hyperinflation.

Once the hyperinflation is under way, the fiscal problems become even more severe. Because of the delay in collecting tax payments, real tax revenue falls as inflation rises. Thus, the government's need to rely on seigniorage is self-reinforcing. Rapid money creation leads to hyperinflation, which leads to a larger budget deficit, which leads to even more rapid money creation.

The ends of hyperinflations almost always coincide with fiscal reforms. Once the magnitude of the problem becomes apparent, the government musters the political will to reduce government spending and increase taxes. These fiscal reforms reduce the need for seigniorage, which allows a reduction in money growth. Hence, even if inflation is always and everywhere a monetary phenomenon, the end of hyperinflation is often a fiscal phenomenon as well.[11]

CASE STUDY

Hyperinflation in Interwar Germany

After World War I, Germany experienced one of history's most spectacular examples of hyperinflation. At the war's end, the Allies demanded that Germany pay substantial reparations. These payments led to fiscal deficits in Germany, which the German government eventually financed by printing large quantities of money.

Panel (a) of Figure 4-6 shows the quantity of money and the general price level in Germany from January 1922 to December 1924. During this period both money and prices rose at an amazing rate. For example, the price of a daily newspaper rose from 0.30 marks in January 1921 to 1 mark in May 1922, to 8 marks in October 1922, to 100 marks in February 1923, and to 1,000 marks in September 1923. Then, in the fall of 1923, prices took off: the

[11] For more on these issues, see Thomas J. Sargent, "The End of Four Big Inflations," in Robert Hall, ed., *Inflation* (Chicago: University of Chicago Press, 1983), 41–98; and Rudiger Dornbusch and Stanley Fischer, "Stopping Hyperinflations: Past and Present," *Weltwirtschaftliches Archiv* 122 (April 1986): 1–47.

FIGURE 4-6

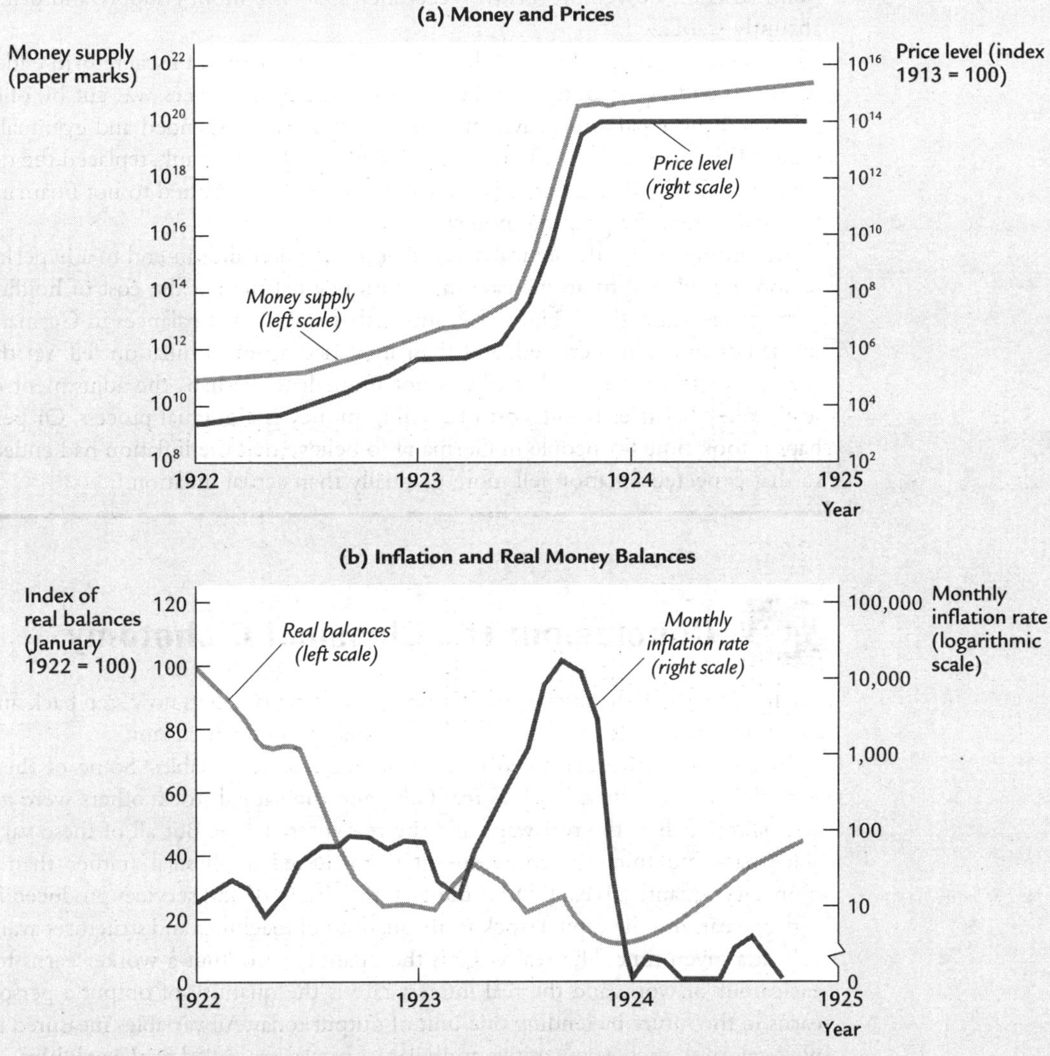

Money and Prices in Interwar Germany Panel (a) shows the money supply and the price level in Germany from January 1922 to December 1924. The immense increases in the money supply and the price level provide a dramatic illustration of the effects of printing large amounts of money. Panel (b) shows inflation and real money balances. As inflation rose, real money balances fell. When the inflation ended at the end of 1923, real money balances rose.

Source: Adapted from Thomas J. Sargent, "The End of Four Big Inflations," in Robert Hall, ed., *Inflation* (Chicago: University of Chicago Press, 1983): 41-98.

newspaper sold for 2,000 marks on October 1, 20,000 marks on October 15, 1 million marks on October 29, 15 million marks on November 9, and 70 million marks on November 17. In December 1923 the money supply and prices abruptly stabilized.[12]

Just as fiscal problems caused the German hyperinflation, a fiscal reform ended it. At the end of 1923, the number of government employees was cut by one-third, and the reparations payments were temporarily suspended and eventually reduced. At the same time, a new central bank, the Rentenbank, replaced the old central bank, the Reichsbank. The Rentenbank was committed to not financing the government by printing money.

According to our theoretical analysis of money demand, an end to a hyperinflation should lead to an increase in real money balances as the cost of holding money falls. Panel (b) of Figure 4-6 shows that real money balances in Germany did fall as inflation increased, and then increased again as inflation fell. Yet the increase in real money balances was not immediate. Perhaps the adjustment of real money balances to the cost of holding money is a gradual process. Or perhaps it took time for people in Germany to believe that the inflation had ended, so that expected inflation fell more gradually than actual inflation.

4-8 Conclusion: The Classical Dichotomy

We have finished our discussion of money and inflation. Let's now step back and examine a key assumption that has been implicit in our discussion.

In Chapter 3, we explained many macroeconomic variables. Some of these variables were *quantities,* such as real GDP and the capital stock; others were *relative prices,* such as the real wage and the real interest rate. But all of these variables had one thing in common—they measured a physical (rather than a monetary) quantity. Real GDP is the quantity of goods and services produced in a given year, and the capital stock is the quantity of machines and structures available at a given time. The real wage is the quantity of output a worker earns for each hour of work, and the real interest rate is the quantity of output a person earns in the future by lending one unit of output today. All variables measured in physical units, such as quantities and relative prices, are called **real variables**.

In this chapter we examined **nominal variables**—variables expressed in terms of money. The economy has many nominal variables, such as the price level, the inflation rate, and the dollar wage a person earns.

At first it may seem surprising that we were able to explain real variables without introducing nominal variables or the existence of money. In Chapter 3 we

[12] The data on newspaper prices are from Michael Mussa, "Sticky Individual Prices and the Dynamics of the General Price Level," *Carnegie-Rochester Conference on Public Policy* 15 (Autumn 1981): 261–296.

studied the level and allocation of the economy's output without mentioning the price level or the rate of inflation. Our theory of the labor market explained the real wage without explaining the nominal wage.

Economists call this theoretical separation of real and nominal variables the **classical dichotomy**. It is the hallmark of classical macroeconomic theory. The classical dichotomy is an important insight because it simplifies economic theory. In particular, it allows us to examine real variables, as we have done, while ignoring nominal variables. The classical dichotomy arises because, in classical economic theory, changes in the money supply do not influence real variables. This irrelevance of money for real variables is called **monetary neutrality**. For many purposes—in particular for studying long-run issues—monetary neutrality is approximately correct.

Yet monetary neutrality does not fully describe the world in which we live. Beginning in Chapter 9, we discuss departures from the classical model and monetary neutrality. These departures are crucial for understanding many macroeconomic phenomena, such as short-run economic fluctuations.

Summary

1. Money is the stock of assets used for transactions. It serves as a store of value, a unit of account, and a medium of exchange. Different sorts of assets are used as money: commodity money systems use an asset with intrinsic value, whereas fiat money systems use an asset whose sole function is to serve as money. In modern economies, a central bank such as the Federal Reserve is responsible for controlling the supply of money.

2. The quantity theory of money assumes that the velocity of money is stable and concludes that nominal GDP is proportional to the stock of money. Because the factors of production and the production function determine real GDP, the quantity theory implies that the price level is proportional to the quantity of money. Therefore, the rate of growth in the quantity of money determines the inflation rate.

3. Seigniorage is the revenue that the government raises by printing money. It is a tax on money holding. Although seigniorage is quantitatively small in most economies, it is often a major source of government revenue in economies experiencing hyperinflation.

4. The nominal interest rate is the sum of the real interest rate and the inflation rate. The Fisher effect says that the nominal interest rate moves one-for-one with expected inflation.

5. The nominal interest rate is the opportunity cost of holding money. Thus, one might expect the demand for money to depend on the nominal interest rate. If it does, then the price level depends on both the current quantity of money and the quantities of money expected in the future.

6. The costs of expected inflation include shoeleather costs, menu costs, the cost of relative price variability, tax distortions, and the inconvenience of making inflation corrections. In addition, unexpected inflation causes arbitrary redistributions of wealth between debtors and creditors. One possible benefit of inflation is that it improves the functioning of labor markets by allowing real wages to reach equilibrium levels without cuts in nominal wages.
7. During hyperinflations, most of the costs of inflation become severe. Hyperinflations typically begin when governments finance large budget deficits by printing money. They end when fiscal reforms eliminate the need for seigniorage.
8. According to classical economic theory, money is neutral: the money supply does not affect real variables. Therefore, classical theory allows us to study how real variables are determined without any reference to the money supply. The equilibrium in the money market then determines the price level and, as a result, all other nominal variables. This theoretical separation of real and nominal variables is called the classical dichotomy.

KEY CONCEPTS

Inflation
Hyperinflation
Money
Store of value
Unit of account
Medium of exchange
Fiat money
Commodity money
Gold standard
Money supply
Monetary policy
Central bank
Federal Reserve
Open-market operations
Currency
Demand deposits
Quantity equation
Transactions velocity of money
Income velocity of money
Real money balances
Money demand function
Quantity theory of money
Seigniorage
Nominal and real interest rates
Fisher equation and Fisher effect
Ex ante and *ex post* real interest rates
Shoeleather costs
Menu costs
Real and nominal variables
Classical dichotomy
Monetary neutrality

QUESTIONS FOR REVIEW

1. Describe the functions of money.
2. What is fiat money? What is commodity money?
3. Who controls the money supply and how?
4. Write the quantity equation and explain it.
5. What does the assumption of constant velocity imply?
6. Who pays the inflation tax?
7. If inflation rises from 6 to 8 percent, what happens to real and nominal interest rates according to the Fisher effect?
8. List all the costs of inflation you can think of, and rank them according to how important you think they are.
9. Explain the roles of monetary and fiscal policy in causing and ending hyperinflations.
10. Define the terms *real variable* and *nominal variable,* and give an example of each.

PROBLEMS AND APPLICATIONS

1. What are the three functions of money? Which of the functions do the following items satisfy? Which do they not satisfy?
   a. A credit card
   b. A painting by Rembrandt
   c. A subway token
2. In the country of Wiknam, the velocity of money is constant. Real GDP grows by 5 percent per year, the money stock grows by 14 percent per year, and the nominal interest rate is 11 percent. What is the real interest rate?
3. A newspaper article once reported that the U.S. economy was experiencing a low rate of inflation. It said that "low inflation has a downside: 45 million recipients of Social Security and other benefits will see their checks go up by just 2.8 percent next year."
   a. Why does inflation affect the increase in Social Security and other benefits?
   b. Is this effect a cost of inflation as the article suggests? Why or why not?
4. Suppose you are advising a small country (such as Bermuda) on whether to print its own money or to use the money of its larger neighbor (such as the United States). What are the costs and benefits of a national money? Does the relative political stability of the two countries have any role in this decision?
5. During World War II, both Germany and England had plans for a paper weapon: they each printed the other's currency, with the intention of dropping large quantities by airplane. Why might this have been an effective weapon?
6. Calvin Coolidge once said that "inflation is repudiation." What might he have meant by this? Do you agree? Why or why not? Does it matter whether the inflation is expected or unexpected?
7. Some economic historians have noted that during the period of the gold standard, gold discoveries were most likely to occur after a long deflation. (The discoveries of 1896 are an example.) Why might this be true?
8. Suppose that consumption depends on the level of real money balances (on the grounds that real money balances are part of wealth). Show that if real money balances depend on the nominal interest rate, then an increase in the rate of money growth affects consumption, investment, and the real interest rate. Does the nominal interest rate adjust more than one-for-one or less than one-for-one to expected inflation?

   This deviation from the classical dichotomy and the Fisher effect is called the *Mundell-Tobin effect*. How might you decide whether the Mundell-Tobin effect is important in practice?
9. Use the Internet to identify a country that has had high inflation over the past year and another country that has had low inflation. (*Hint*: One useful website is http://www.economist.com/markets/indicators/) For these two countries, find the rate of money growth and the current level of the nominal interest rate. Relate your findings to the theories presented in this chapter.

The Cagan Model: How Current and Future Money Affect the Price Level

In this chapter we showed that if the quantity of real money balances demanded depends on the cost of holding money, the price level depends on both the current money supply and the future money supply. This appendix develops the *Cagan model* to show more explicitly how this works.[13]

To keep the math as simple as possible, we posit a money demand function that is linear in the natural logarithms of all the variables. The money demand function is

$$m_t - p_t = -\gamma(p_{t+1} - p_t), \tag{A1}$$

where m_t is the log of the quantity of money at time t, p_t is the log of the price level at time t, and γ is a parameter that governs the sensitivity of money demand to the rate of inflation. By the property of logarithms, $m_t - p_t$ is the log of real money balances, and $p_{t+1} - p_t$ is the inflation rate between period t and period $t + 1$. This equation states that if inflation goes up by 1 percentage point, real money balances fall by γ percent.

We have made a number of assumptions in writing the money demand function in this way. First, by excluding the level of output as a determinant of money demand, we are implicitly assuming that it is constant. Second, by including the rate of inflation rather than the nominal interest rate, we are assuming that the real interest rate is constant. Third, by including actual inflation rather than expected inflation, we are assuming perfect foresight. All of these assumptions are to keep the analysis as simple as possible.

We want to solve Equation A1 to express the price level as a function of current and future money. To do this, note that Equation A1 can be rewritten as

$$p_t = \left(\frac{1}{1+\gamma}\right) m_t + \left(\frac{\gamma}{1+\gamma}\right) p_{t+1}. \tag{A2}$$

This equation states that the current price level p_t is a weighted average of the current money supply m_t and the next period's price level p_{t+1}. The next period's price level will be determined the same way as this period's price level:

$$p_{t+1} = \left(\frac{1}{1+\gamma}\right) m_{t+1} + \left(\frac{\gamma}{1+\gamma}\right) p_{t+2}. \tag{A3}$$

Now substitute Equation A3 for p_{t+1} in Equation A2 to obtain

$$p_t = \frac{1}{1+\gamma} m_t + \frac{\gamma}{(1+\gamma)^2} m_{t+1} + \frac{\gamma^2}{(1+\gamma)^2} p_{t+2}. \tag{A4}$$

[13] This model is derived from Phillip Cagan, "The Monetary Dynamics of Hyperinflation," in Milton Friedman, ed., *Studies in the Quantity Theory of Money* (Chicago: University of Chicago Press, 1956).

Equation A4 states that the current price level is a weighted average of the current money supply, the next period's money supply, and the following period's price level. Once again, the price level in $t + 2$ is determined as in Equation A2:

$$p_{t+2} = \left(\frac{1}{1+\gamma}\right) m_{t+2} + \left(\frac{\gamma}{1+\gamma}\right) p_{t+3}. \tag{A5}$$

Now substitute Equation A5 into Equation A4 to obtain

$$p_t = \frac{1}{1+\gamma} m_t + \frac{\gamma}{(1+\gamma)^2} m_{t+1} + \frac{\gamma^2}{(1+\gamma)^3} m_{t+2} + \frac{\gamma^3}{(1+\gamma)^3} p_{t+3}. \tag{A6}$$

By now you see the pattern. We can continue to use Equation A2 to substitute for the future price level. If we do this an infinite number of times, we find

$$p_t = \left(\frac{1}{1+\gamma}\right)\left[m_t + \left(\frac{\gamma}{1+\gamma}\right) m_{t+1} + \left(\frac{\gamma}{1+\gamma}\right)^2 m_{t+2} + \left(\frac{\gamma}{1+\gamma}\right)^3 m_{t+3} + \cdots\right], \tag{A7}$$

where "..." indicates an infinite number of analogous terms. According to Equation A7, the current price level is a weighted average of the current money supply and all future money supplies.

Note the importance of γ, the parameter governing the sensitivity of real money balances to inflation. The weights on the future money supplies decline geometrically at rate $\gamma/(1 + \gamma)$. If γ is small, then $\gamma/(1 + \gamma)$ is small, and the weights decline quickly. In this case, the current money supply is the primary determinant of the price level. (Indeed, if γ equals zero, then we obtain the quantity theory of money: the price level is proportional to the current money supply, and the future money supplies do not matter at all.) If γ is large, then $\gamma/(1 + \gamma)$ is close to 1, and the weights decline slowly. In this case, the future money supplies play a key role in determining today's price level.

Finally, let's relax the assumption of perfect foresight. If the future is not known with certainty, then we should write the money demand function as

$$m_t - p_t = -\gamma(Ep_{t+1} - p_t), \tag{A8}$$

where Ep_{t+1} is the expected price level. Equation A8 states that real money balances depend on expected inflation. By following steps similar to those above, we can show that

$$p_t = \left(\frac{1}{1+\gamma}\right)\left[m_t + \left(\frac{\gamma}{1+\gamma}\right) Em_{t+1} + \left(\frac{\gamma}{1+\gamma}\right)^2 Em_{t+2} + \left(\frac{\gamma}{1+\gamma}\right)^3 Em_{t+3} + \cdots\right]. \tag{A9}$$

Equation A9 states that the price level depends on the current money supply and expected future money supplies.

Some economists use this model to argue that *credibility* is important for ending hyperinflation. Because the price level depends on both current and expected future money, inflation depends on both current and expected future money growth. Therefore, to end high inflation, both money growth and expected money growth must fall. Expectations, in turn, depend on credibility—the perception that the central bank is committed to a new, more stable policy.

How can a central bank achieve credibility in the midst of hyperinflation? Credibility is often achieved by removing the underlying cause of the hyperinflation—the need for seigniorage. Thus, a credible fiscal reform is often necessary for a credible change in monetary policy. This fiscal reform might take the form of reducing government spending and making the central bank more independent from the government. Reduced spending decreases the need for seigniorage, while increased independence allows the central bank to resist government demands for seigniorage.

MORE PROBLEMS AND APPLICATIONS

1. In the Cagan model, if the money supply is expected to grow at some constant rate μ (so that $Em_{t+s} = m_t + s\mu$), then Equation A9 can be shown to imply that $p_t = m_t + \gamma\mu$.
   a. Interpret this result.
   b. What happens to the price level p_t when the money supply m_t changes, holding the money growth rate μ constant?
   c. What happens to the price level p_t when the money growth rate μ changes, holding the current money supply m_t constant?
   d. If a central bank is about to reduce the rate of money growth μ but wants to hold the price level p_t constant, what should it do with m_t? Can you see any practical problems that might arise in following such a policy?
   e. How do your previous answers change in the special case where money demand does not depend on the expected rate of inflation (so that $\gamma = 0$)?

CHAPTER

5

The Open Economy

No nation was ever ruined by trade.

— *Benjamin Franklin*

Even if you never leave your home town, you are an active participant in a global economy. When you go to the grocery store, for instance, you might choose between apples grown locally and grapes grown in Chile. When you make a deposit into your local bank, the bank might lend those funds to your next door neighbor or to a Japanese company building a factory outside Tokyo. Because our economy is integrated with many others around the world, consumers have more goods and services from which to choose, and savers have more opportunities to invest their wealth.

In previous chapters we simplified our analysis by assuming a closed economy. In actuality, however, most economies are open: they export goods and services abroad, they import goods and services from abroad, and they borrow and lend in world financial markets. Figure 5-1 gives some sense of the importance of these international interactions by showing imports and exports as a percentage of GDP for seven major industrial countries. As the figure shows, imports and exports in the United States are more than 10 percent of GDP. Trade is even more important for many other countries—in Canada and Germany, for instance, imports and exports are more than a third of GDP. In these countries, international trade is central to analyzing economic developments and formulating economic policies.

This chapter begins our study of open-economy macroeconomics. We begin in Section 5-1 with questions of measurement. To understand how an open economy works, we must understand the key macroeconomic variables that measure the interactions among countries. Accounting identities reveal a key insight: the flow of goods and services across national borders is always matched by an equivalent flow of funds to finance capital accumulation.

In Section 5-2 we examine the determinants of these international flows. We develop a model of the small open economy that corresponds to our model of the closed economy in Chapter 3. The model shows the factors that determine whether a country is a borrower or a lender in world markets, and how policies at home and abroad affect the flows of capital and goods.

In Section 5-3 we extend the model to discuss the prices at which a country makes exchanges in world markets. We examine what determines the price of domestic goods relative to foreign goods. We also examine what determines the rate at which the domestic currency trades for foreign currencies. Our model

FIGURE 5-1

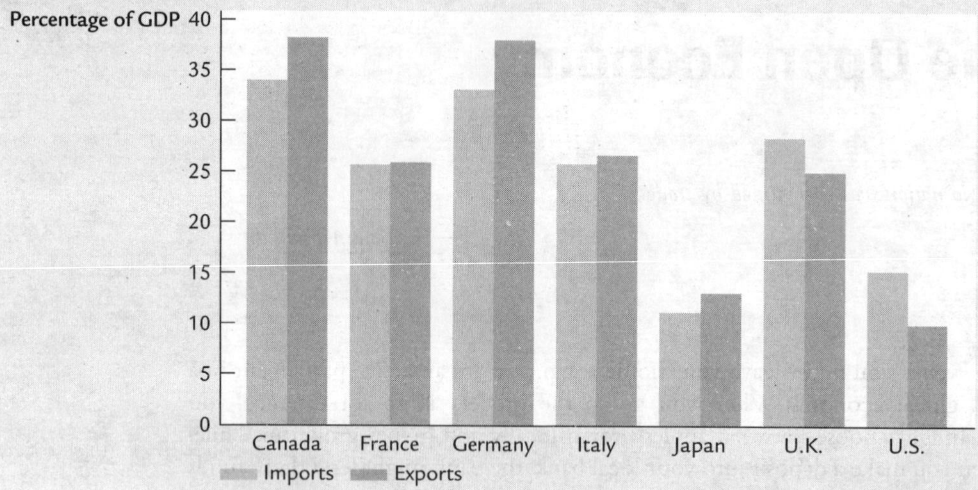

Imports and Exports as a Percentage of Output: 2004 While international trade is important for the United States, it is even more vital for other countries.

Source: International Financial Statistics.

shows how protectionist trade policies—policies designed to protect domestic industries from foreign competition—influence the amount of international trade and the exchange rate.

5-1 The International Flows of Capital and Goods

The key macroeconomic difference between open and closed economies is that, in an open economy, a country's spending in any given year need not equal its output of goods and services. A country can spend more than it produces by borrowing from abroad, or it can spend less than it produces and lend the difference to foreigners. To understand this more fully, let's take another look at national income accounting, which we first discussed in Chapter 2.

The Role of Net Exports

Consider the expenditure on an economy's output of goods and services. In a closed economy, all output is sold domestically, and expenditure is divided into three components: consumption, investment, and government purchases. In an open economy, some output is sold domestically and some is exported to be sold abroad. We can divide expenditure on an open economy's output Y into four components:

- C^d, consumption of domestic goods and services,
- I^d, investment in domestic goods and services,
- G^d, government purchases of domestic goods and services,
- EX, exports of domestic goods and services.

The division of expenditure into these components is expressed in the identity

$$Y = C^d + I^d + G^d + EX.$$

The sum of the first three terms, $C^d + I^d + G^d$, is domestic spending on domestic goods and services. The fourth term, EX, is foreign spending on domestic goods and services.

A bit of manipulation can make this identity more useful. Note that domestic spending on *all* goods and services equals domestic spending on *domestic* goods and services and domestic spending on *foreign* goods and services. Hence, total consumption C equals consumption of domestic goods and services C^d plus consumption of foreign goods and services C^f; total investment I equals investment in domestic goods and services I^d plus investment in foreign goods and services I^f; and total government purchases G equals government purchases of domestic goods and services G^d plus government purchases of foreign goods and services G^f. Thus,

$$C = C^d + C^f,$$

$$I = I^d + I^f,$$

$$G = G^d + G^f.$$

We substitute these three equations into the identity above:

$$Y = (C - C^f) + (I - I^f) + (G - G^f) + EX.$$

We can rearrange to obtain

$$Y = C + I + G + EX - (C^f + I^f + G^f).$$

The sum of domestic spending on foreign goods and services $(C^f + I^f + G^f)$ is expenditure on imports (IM). We can thus write the national income accounts identity as

$$Y = C + I + G + EX - IM.$$

Because spending on imports is included in domestic spending $(C + I + G)$, and because goods and services imported from abroad are not part of a country's output, this equation subtracts spending on imports. Defining **net exports** to be exports minus imports $(NX = EX - IM)$, the identity becomes

$$Y = C + I + G + NX.$$

This equation states that expenditure on domestic output is the sum of consumption, investment, government purchases, and net exports. This is the most common form of the national income accounts identity; it should be familiar from Chapter 2.

The national income accounts identity shows how domestic output, domestic spending, and net exports are related. In particular,

$$NX = Y - (C + I + G)$$

$$\text{Net Exports} = \text{Output} - \text{Domestic Spending}.$$

This equation shows that in an open economy, domestic spending need not equal the output of goods and services. *If output exceeds domestic spending, we export the difference: net exports are positive. If output falls short of domestic spending, we import the difference: net exports are negative.*

International Capital Flows and the Trade Balance

In an open economy, as in the closed economy we discussed in Chapter 3, financial markets and goods markets are closely related. To see the relationship, we must rewrite the national income accounts identity in terms of saving and investment. Begin with the identity

$$Y = C + I + G + NX.$$

Subtract C and G from both sides to obtain

$$Y - C - G = I + NX.$$

Recall from Chapter 3 that $Y - C - G$ is national saving S, the sum of private saving, $Y - T - C$, and public saving, $T - G$, where T stands for taxes. Therefore,

$$S = I + NX.$$

Subtracting I from both sides of the equation, we can write the national income accounts identity as

$$S - I = NX.$$

This form of the national income accounts identity shows that an economy's net exports must always equal the difference between its saving and its investment.

Let's look more closely at each part of this identity. The easy part is the right-hand side, NX, the net export of goods and services. Another name for net exports is the **trade balance**, because it tells us how our trade in goods and services departs from the benchmark of equal imports and exports.

The left-hand side of the identity is the difference between domestic saving and domestic investment, $S - I$, which we'll call **net capital outflow**. (It's sometimes called *net foreign investment.*) Net capital outflow equals the amount that domestic residents are lending abroad minus the amount that foreigners are lending to us. If net capital outflow is positive, the economy's saving exceeds its investment, and it is lending the excess to foreigners. If the net capital outflow is negative, the economy is experiencing a capital inflow: investment exceeds saving, and the economy is financing this extra investment by borrowing from abroad. Thus, net capital outflow reflects the international flow of funds to finance capital accumulation.

The national income accounts identity shows that net capital outflow always equals the trade balance. That is,

$$\begin{aligned} \text{Net Capital Outflow} &= \text{Trade Balance} \\ S - I &= NX. \end{aligned}$$

If $S - I$ and NX are positive, we have a **trade surplus**. In this case, we are net lenders in world financial markets, and we are exporting more goods than we are importing. If $S - I$ and NX are negative, we have a **trade deficit**. In this case, we are net borrowers in world financial markets, and we are importing more goods than we are exporting. If $S - I$ and NX are exactly zero, we are said to have **balanced trade** because the value of imports equals the value of exports.

The national income accounts identity shows that the international flow of funds to finance capital accumulation and the international flow of goods and services are two sides of the same coin. If domestic saving exceeds domestic investment, the surplus saving is used to make loans to foreigners. Foreigners require these loans because we are providing them with more goods and services than they are providing us. That is, we are running a trade surplus. If investment exceeds saving, the extra investment must be financed by borrowing from abroad. These foreign loans enable us to import more goods and services than we export. That is, we are running a trade deficit. Table 5-1 summarizes these lessons.

Note that the international flow of capital can take many forms. It is easiest to assume—as we have done so far—that when we run a trade deficit, foreigners make loans to us. This happens, for example, when the Japanese buy the debt issued by U.S. corporations or by the U.S. government. But the flow of capital can also take the form of foreigners buying domestic assets, such as when a citizen of Germany buys stock from an American on the New York Stock

TABLE 5-1

International Flows of Goods and Capital: Summary

This table shows the three outcomes that an open economy can experience.

Trade Surplus	Balanced Trade	Trade Deficit
Exports > Imports	Exports = Imports	Exports < Imports
Net Exports > 0	Net Exports = 0	Net Exports < 0
$Y > C + I + G$	$Y = C + I + G$	$Y < C + I + G$
Saving > Investment	Saving = Investment	Saving < Investment
Net Capital Outflow > 0	Net Capital Outflow = 0	Net Capital Outflow < 0

Exchange. Whether foreigners buy domestically issued debt or domestically owned assets, they obtain a claim to the future returns to domestic capital. In both cases, foreigners end up owning some of the domestic capital stock.

International Flows of Goods and Capital: An Example

The equality of net exports and net capital outflow is an identity: it must hold by the way the variables are defined and the numbers are added up. But it is easy to miss the intuition behind this important relationship. The best way to understand it is to consider an example.

Imagine that Bill Gates sells a copy of the Windows operating system to a Japanese consumer for 5,000 yen. Because Mr. Gates is a U.S. resident, the sale represents an export of the United States. Other things equal, U.S. net exports rise. What else happens to make the identity hold? It depends on what Mr. Gates does with the 5,000 yen.

FYI The Irrelevance of Bilateral Trade Balances

The trade balance we have been discussing measures the difference between a nation's exports and its imports with the rest of the world. Sometimes you might hear in the media a report on a nation's trade balance with a specific other nation. This is called a *bilateral* trade balance. For example, the U.S. bilateral trade balance with China equals exports that the United States sells to China minus imports that the United States buys from China.

The overall trade balance is, as we have seen, inextricably linked to a nation's saving and investment. That is not true of a bilateral trade balance. Indeed, a nation can have large trade deficits and surpluses with specific trading partners, while having balanced trade overall.

For example, suppose the world has three countries: the United States, China, and Australia. The United States sells $100 billion in machine tools to Australia, Australia sells $100 billion in wheat to China, and China sells $100 billion in toys to the United States. In this case, the United States has a bilateral trade deficit with China, China has a bilateral trade deficit with Australia, and Australia has a bilateral trade deficit with the United States. But each of the three nations has balanced trade overall, exporting and importing $100 billion in goods.

Bilateral trade deficits receive more attention in the political arena than they deserve. This is in part because international relations are conducted country to country, so politicians and diplomats are naturally drawn to statistics measuring country-to-country economic transactions. Most economists, however, believe that bilateral trade balances are not very meaningful. From a macroeconomic standpoint, it is a nation's trade balance with all foreign nations put together that matters.

The same lesson applies to individuals as it does to nations. Your own personal trade balance is the difference between your income and your spending, and you may be concerned if these two variables are out of line. But you should not be concerned with the difference between your income and spending with a particular person or firm. Economist Robert Solow once explained the irrelevance of bilateral trade balances as follows: "I have a chronic deficit with my barber, who doesn't buy a darned thing from me." But that doesn't stop Mr. Solow from living within his means, or getting a haircut when he needs it.

Suppose Mr. Gates decides to stuff the 5,000 yen in his mattress. In this case, Mr. Gates has allocated some of his saving to an investment in the Japanese economy (in the form of the Japanese currency) rather than to an investment in the U.S. economy. Thus, U.S. saving exceeds U.S. investment. The rise in U.S. net exports is matched by a rise in the U.S. net capital outflow.

If Mr. Gates wants to invest in Japan, however, he is unlikely to make currency his asset of choice. He might use the 5,000 yen to buy some stock in, say, the Sony Corporation, or he might buy a bond issued by the Japanese government. In either case, some of U.S. saving is flowing abroad. Once again, the U.S. net capital outflow exactly balances U.S. net exports.

The opposite situation occurs in Japan. When the Japanese consumer buys a copy of the Windows operating system, Japan's purchases of goods and services ($C + I + G$) rise, but there is no change in what Japan has produced (Y). The transaction reduces Japan's saving ($S = Y - C - G$) for a given level of investment (I). While the U.S. experiences a net capital outflow, Japan experiences a net capital inflow.

Now let's change the example. Suppose that instead of investing his 5,000 yen in a Japanese asset, Mr. Gates uses it to buy something made in Japan, such as a Sony Walkman. In this case, imports into the United States rise. Together, the Windows export and the Walkman import represent balanced trade between Japan and the United States. Because exports and imports rise equally, net exports and net capital outflow are both unchanged.

A final possibility is that Mr. Gates exchanges his 5,000 yen for U.S. dollars at a local bank. But this doesn't change the situation: the bank now has to do something with the 5,000 yen. It can buy Japanese assets (a U.S. net capital outflow); it can buy a Japanese good (a U.S. import); or it can sell the yen to another American who wants to make such a transaction. If you follow the money, you can see that, in the end, U.S. net exports must equal U.S. net capital outflow.

5-2 Saving and Investment in a Small Open Economy

So far in our discussion of the international flows of goods and capital, we have rearranged accounting identities. That is, we have defined some of the variables that measure transactions in an open economy, and we have shown the links among these variables that follow from their definitions. Our next step is to develop a model that explains the behavior of these variables. We can then use the model to answer questions such as how the trade balance responds to changes in policy.

Capital Mobility and the World Interest Rate

In a moment we present a model of the international flows of capital and goods. Because the trade balance equals the net capital outflow, which in turn equals saving minus investment, our model focuses on saving and investment.

To develop this model, we use some elements that should be familiar from Chapter 3, but in contrast to the Chapter 3 model, we do not assume that the real interest rate equilibrates saving and investment. Instead, we allow the economy to run a trade deficit and borrow from other countries, or to run a trade surplus and lend to other countries.

If the real interest rate does not adjust to equilibrate saving and investment in this model, what *does* determine the real interest rate? We answer this question here by considering the simple case of a **small open economy** with perfect capital mobility. By "small" we mean that this economy is a small part of the world market and thus, by itself, can have only a negligible effect on the world interest rate. By "perfect capital mobility" we mean that residents of the country have full access to world financial markets. In particular, the government does not impede international borrowing or lending.

Because of this assumption of perfect capital mobility, the interest rate in our small open economy, r, must equal the **world interest rate** r^*, the real interest rate prevailing in world financial markets:

$$r = r^*.$$

Residents of the small open economy need never borrow at any interest rate above r^*, because they can always get a loan at r^* from abroad. Similarly, residents of this economy need never lend at any interest rate below r^* because they can always earn r^* by lending abroad. Thus, the world interest rate determines the interest rate in our small open economy.

Let us discuss for a moment what determines the world real interest rate. In a closed economy, the equilibrium of domestic saving and domestic investment determines the interest rate. Barring interplanetary trade, the world economy is a closed economy. Therefore, the equilibrium of world saving and world investment determines the world interest rate. Our small open economy has a negligible effect on the world real interest rate because, being a small part of the world, it has a negligible effect on world saving and world investment. Hence, our small open economy takes the world interest rate as exogenously given.

Why Assume a Small Open Economy?

The analysis in the body of this chapter assumes that the nation being studied is a small open economy. (The same approach is taken in Chapter 12, which examines short-run fluctuations in an open economy.) This assumption raises some questions.

Q: Is the United States well described by the assumption of a small open economy?

A: No, it is not, at least not completely. The United States does borrow and lend in world financial markets, and these markets exert a strong influence over the U.S. real interest rate, but it would be an exaggeration to say that the U.S. real interest rate is determined solely by world financial markets.

Q: So why are we assuming a small open economy?

A: Some nations, such as Canada and Netherlands, are better described by the assumption of a small open economy. Yet the main reason for making this assumption is to develop understanding and intuition for the macroeconomics of open economies. Remember from Chapter 1 that economic models are built with simplifying assumptions. An assumption need not be realistic to be useful. Assuming a small open economy simplifies the analysis greatly and, therefore, will help clarify our thinking.

Q: Can we relax this assumption and make the model more realistic?

A: Yes, we can, and we will. The appendix to this chapter (and the appendix to Chapter 12) considers the more realistic and more complicated case of a large open economy. Some instructors skip directly to this material when teaching these topics because the approach is more realistic for economies such as the United States. Others think that students should walk before they run and, therefore, begin with the simplifying assumption of a small open economy.

The Model

To build the model of the small open economy, we take three assumptions from Chapter 3:

- The economy's output Y is fixed by the factors of production and the production function. We write this as

$$Y = \bar{Y} = F(\bar{K}, \bar{L}).$$

- Consumption C is positively related to disposable income $Y - T$. We write the consumption function as

$$C = C(Y - T).$$

- Investment I is negatively related to the real interest rate r. We write the investment function as

$$I = I(r).$$

These are the three key parts of our model. If you do not understand these relationships, review Chapter 3 before continuing.

We can now return to the accounting identity and write it as

$$NX = (Y - C - G) - I$$

$$NX = S - I.$$

Substituting the Chapter 3 assumptions recapped above and the assumption that the interest rate equals the world interest rate, we obtain

$$NX = [\bar{Y} - C(\bar{Y} - T) - G] - I(r^*)$$

$$= \qquad \bar{S} \qquad - I(r^*).$$

This equation shows that the trade balance NX depends on those variables that determine saving S and investment I. Because saving depends on fiscal policy (lower government purchases G or higher taxes T raise national saving) and investment depends on the world real interest rate r^* (a higher interest rate makes some investment projects unprofitable), the trade balance depends on these variables as well.

FIGURE 5-2

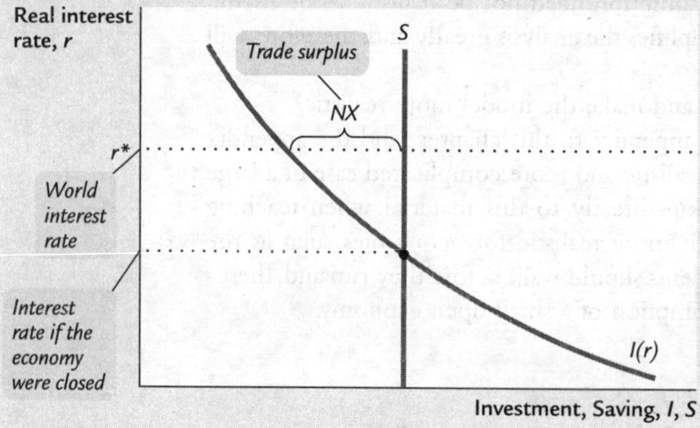

Saving and Investment in a Small Open Economy In a closed economy, the real interest rate adjusts to equilibrate saving and investment. In a small open economy, the interest rate is determined in world financial markets. The difference between saving and investment determines the trade balance. Here there is a trade surplus, because at the world interest rate, saving exceeds investment.

In Chapter 3 we graphed saving and investment as in Figure 5-2. In the closed economy studied in that chapter, the real interest rate adjusts to equilibrate saving and investment—that is, the real interest rate is found where the saving and investment curves cross. In the small open economy, however, the real interest rate equals the world real interest rate. *The trade balance is determined by the difference between saving and investment at the world interest rate.*

At this point, you might wonder about the mechanism that causes the trade balance to equal the net capital outflow. The determinants of the capital flows are easy to understand. When saving falls short of investment, investors borrow from abroad; when saving exceeds investment, the excess is lent to other countries. But what causes those who import and export to behave in a way that ensures that the international flow of goods exactly balances this international flow of capital? For now we leave this question unanswered, but we return to it in Section 5-3 when we discuss the determination of exchange rates.

How Policies Influence the Trade Balance

Suppose that the economy begins in a position of balanced trade. That is, at the world interest rate, investment I equals saving S, and net exports NX equal zero. Let's use our model to predict the effects of government policies at home and abroad.

Fiscal Policy at Home Consider first what happens to the small open economy if the government expands domestic spending by increasing government purchases. The increase in G reduces national saving, because $S = Y - C - G$. With an unchanged world real interest rate, investment remains the same. Therefore, saving falls below investment, and some investment must now be financed by borrowing from abroad. Because $NX = S - I$, the fall in S implies a fall in NX. The economy now runs a trade deficit.

The same logic applies to a decrease in taxes. A tax cut lowers T, raises disposable income $Y - T$, stimulates consumption, and reduces national saving.

FIGURE 5-3

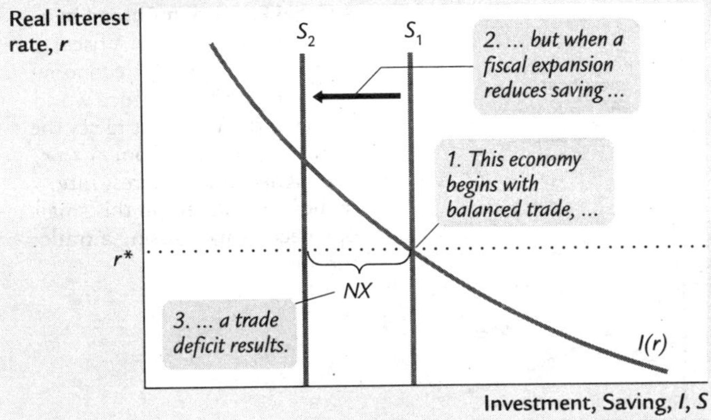

A Fiscal Expansion at Home in a Small Open Economy An increase in government purchases or a reduction in taxes reduces national saving and thus shifts the saving schedule to the left, from S_1 to S_2. The result is a trade deficit.

(Even though some of the tax cut finds its way into private saving, public saving falls by the full amount of the tax cut; in total, saving falls.) Because $NX = S - I$, the reduction in national saving in turn lowers NX.

Figure 5-3 illustrates these effects. A fiscal policy change that increases private consumption C or public consumption G reduces national saving ($Y - C - G$) and, therefore, shifts the vertical line that represents saving from S_1 to S_2. Because NX is the distance between the saving schedule and the investment schedule at the world interest rate, this shift reduces NX. *Hence, starting from balanced trade, a change in fiscal policy that reduces national saving leads to a trade deficit.*

Fiscal Policy Abroad Consider now what happens to a small open economy when foreign governments increase their government purchases. If these foreign countries are a small part of the world economy, then their fiscal change has a negligible impact on other countries. But if these foreign countries are a large part of the world economy, their increase in government purchases reduces world saving. The decrease in world saving causes the world interest rate to rise, just as we saw in our closed economy model (remember, Earth is a closed economy).

The increase in the world interest rate raises the cost of borrowing and, thus, reduces investment in our small open economy. Because there has been no change in domestic saving, saving S now exceeds investment I, and some of our saving begins to flow abroad. Because $NX = S - I$, the reduction in I must also increase NX. Hence, reduced saving abroad leads to a trade surplus at home.

Figure 5-4 illustrates how a small open economy starting from balanced trade responds to a foreign fiscal expansion. Because the policy change is occurring abroad, the domestic saving and investment schedules remain the same. The only change is an increase in the world interest rate from r_1^* to r_2^*. The trade balance is the difference between the saving and investment

FIGURE 5-4

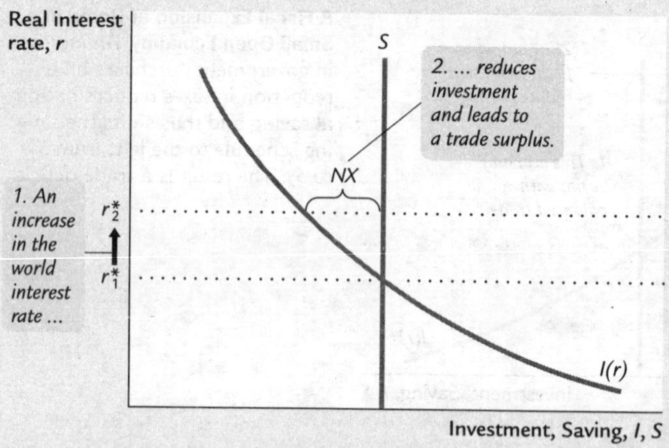

A Fiscal Expansion Abroad in a Small Open Economy A fiscal expansion in a foreign economy large enough to influence world saving and investment raises the world interest rate from r_1^* to r_2^*. The higher world interest rate reduces investment in this small open economy, causing a trade surplus.

schedules; because saving exceeds investment at r_2^*, there is a trade surplus. *Hence, starting from balanced trade, an increase in the world interest rate due to a fiscal expansion abroad leads to a trade surplus.*

Shifts in Investment Demand Consider what happens to our small open economy if its investment schedule shifts outward—that is, if the demand for investment goods at every interest rate increases. This shift would occur if, for example, the government changed the tax laws to encourage investment by providing an investment tax credit. Figure 5-5 illustrates the impact of a shift in the

FIGURE 5-5

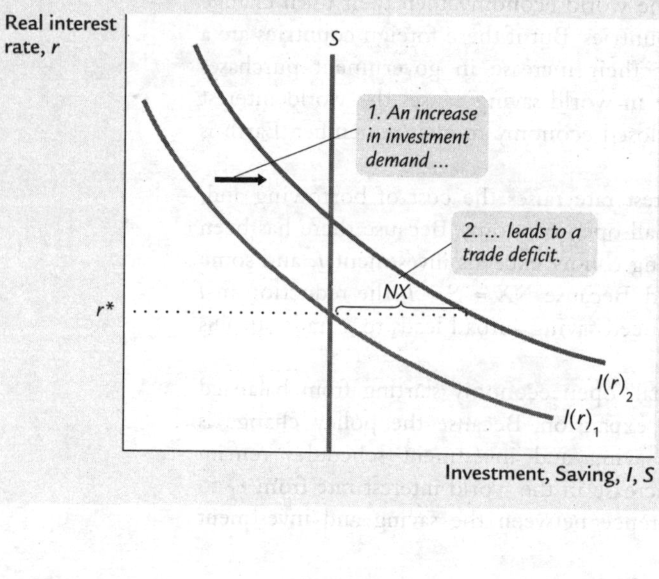

A Shift in the Investment Schedule in a Small Open Economy An outward shift in the investment schedule from $I(r)_1$ to $I(r)_2$ increases the amount of investment at the world interest rate r^*. As a result, investment now exceeds saving, which means the economy is borrowing from abroad and running a trade deficit.

investment schedule. At a given world interest rate, investment is now higher. Because saving is unchanged, some investment must now be financed by borrowing from abroad. Capital flows into the economy to finance the increased investment, so that the net capital outflow is negative. Put differently, because $NX = S - I$, the increase in I implies a decrease in NX. *Hence, starting from balanced trade, an outward shift in the investment schedule causes a trade deficit.*

Evaluating Economic Policy

Our model of the open economy shows that the flow of goods and services measured by the trade balance is inextricably connected to the international flow of funds for capital accumulation. The net capital outflow is the difference between domestic saving and domestic investment. Thus, the impact of economic policies on the trade balance can always be found by examining their impact on domestic saving and domestic investment. Policies that increase investment or decrease saving tend to cause a trade deficit, and policies that decrease investment or increase saving tend to cause a trade surplus.

Our analysis of the open economy has been positive, not normative. That is, our analysis of how economic policies influence the international flows of capital and goods has not told us whether these policies are desirable. Evaluating economic policies and their impact on the open economy is a frequent topic of debate among economists and policymakers.

When a country runs a trade deficit, policymakers must confront the question of whether it represents a national problem. Most economists view a trade deficit not as a problem in itself, but perhaps as a symptom of a problem. A trade deficit could be a reflection of low saving. In a closed economy, low saving leads to low investment and a smaller future capital stock. In an open economy, low saving leads to a trade deficit and a growing foreign debt, which eventually must be repaid. In both cases, high current consumption leads to lower future consumption, implying that future generations bear the burden of low national saving.

Yet trade deficits are not always a reflection of economic malady. When poor rural economies develop into modern industrial economies, they sometimes finance their high levels of investment with foreign borrowing. In these cases, trade deficits are a sign of economic development. For example, South Korea ran large trade deficits throughout the 1970s, and it became one of the success stories of economic growth. The lesson is that one cannot judge economic performance from the trade balance alone. Instead, one must look at the underlying causes of the international flows.

CASE STUDY

The U.S. Trade Deficit

During the 1980s, 1990s, and early 2000s, the United States ran large trade deficits. Panel (a) of Figure 5-6 documents this experience by showing net exports as a percentage of GDP. The exact size of the trade deficit fluctuated over

FIGURE 5-6

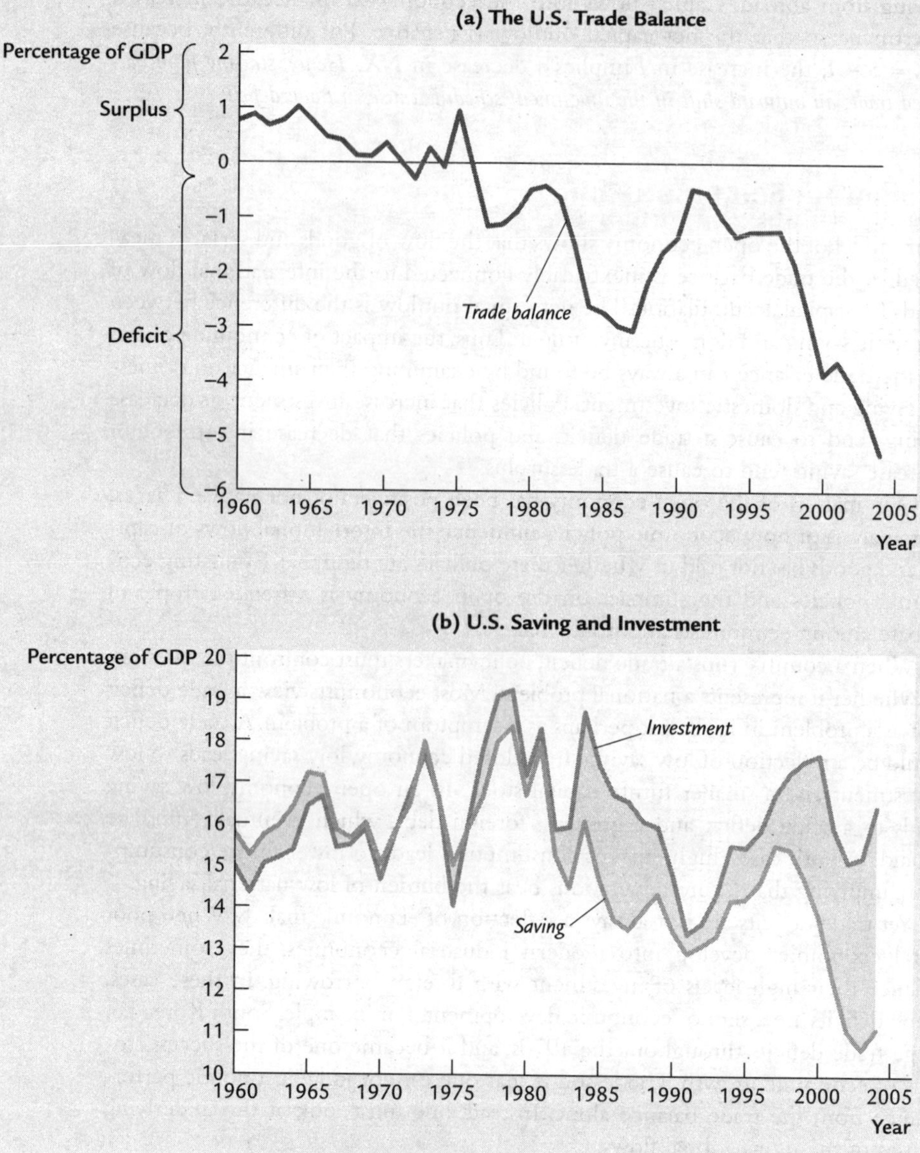

The Trade Balance, Saving, and Investment: The U.S. Experience Panel (a) shows the trade balance as a percentage of GDP. Positive numbers represent a surplus, and negative numbers represent a deficit. Panel (b) shows national saving and investment as a percentage of GDP since 1960. The trade balance equals saving minus investment.

Source: U.S. Department of Commerce.

time, but it was large throughout these two and a half decades. In 2004, the trade deficit was $624 billion, or 5.3 percent of GDP. As accounting identities require, this trade deficit had to be financed by borrowing from abroad (or, equivalently, by selling U.S. assets abroad). During this period, the United States went from being the world's largest creditor to the world's largest debtor.

What caused the U.S. trade deficit? There is no single explanation. But to understand some of the forces at work, it helps to look at national saving and domestic investment, as shown in panel (b) of the figure. Keep in mind that the trade deficit is the difference between saving and investment.

The start of the trade deficit coincided with a fall in national saving. This development can be explained by the expansionary fiscal policy in the 1980s. With the support of President Reagan, the U.S. Congress passed legislation in 1981 that substantially cut personal income taxes over the next three years. Because these tax cuts were not met with equal cuts in government spending, the federal budget went into deficit. These budget deficits were among the largest ever experienced in a period of peace and prosperity, and they continued long after Reagan left office. According to our model, such a policy should reduce national saving, thereby causing a trade deficit. And, in fact, that is exactly what happened. Because the government budget and trade balance went into deficit at roughly the same time, these shortfalls were called the *twin deficits*.

Things started to change in the 1990s, when the U.S. federal government got its fiscal house in order. The first President Bush and President Clinton both signed tax increases, while Congress kept a lid on spending. In addition to these policy changes, rapid productivity growth in the late 1990s raised incomes and, thus, further increased tax revenue. These developments moved the U.S. federal budget from deficit to surplus, which in turn caused national saving to rise.

In contrast to what our model predicts, the increase in national saving did not coincide with a shrinking trade deficit, because domestic investment rose at the same time. The likely explanation is that the boom in information technology caused an expansionary shift in the U.S. investment function. Even though fiscal policy was pushing the trade deficit toward surplus, the investment boom was an even stronger force pushing the trade balance toward deficit.

In the early 2000s, fiscal policy once again put downward pressure on national saving. With the second President Bush in the White House, tax cuts were signed into law in 2001 and 2003, while the war on terror led to substantial increases in government spending. The federal government was again running budget deficits. National saving fell to historic lows, and the trade deficit reached historic highs.

The history of the U.S. trade deficit shows that this statistic, by itself, does not tell us much about what is happening in the economy. We have to look deeper at saving, investment, and the policies and events that cause them to change over time.[1]

[1] For more on this topic, see Catherine L. Mann, *Is the U.S. Trade Deficit Sustainable?* Institute for International Economics, 1999.

CASE STUDY

Why Doesn't Capital Flow to Poor Countries?

The U.S. trade deficit discussed in the previous case study represents a flow of capital into the United States from the rest of the world. What countries were the source of these capital flows? Because the world is a closed economy, the capital must be coming from those countries that were running trade surpluses. In 2005, this group included many nations that were far poorer than the United States, such as Russia, South Korea, and China. In these nations, saving exceeded investment in domestic capital. These countries were sending funds abroad to countries like the United States, where investment in domestic capital exceeded saving.

From one perspective, the direction of international capital flows is a paradox. Recall our discussion of production functions in Chapter 3. There, we established that an empirically realistic production function is the Cobb-Douglas form:

$$F(K,L) = A\,K^{\alpha}L^{1-\alpha},$$

where K is capital, L is labor, A is a variable representing the state of technology, and α is a parameter that determines capital's share of total income. For this production function, the marginal product of capital is

$$MPK = \alpha\,A\,(K/L)^{\alpha-1}.$$

The marginal product of capital tells us how much extra output an extra unit of capital would produce. Because α is capital's share, it must be less than 1, so $\alpha - 1 < 0$. This means that an increase in K/L decreases MPK. In other words, holding other variables constant, the more capital a nation has, the less valuable an extra unit of capital is. This phenomenon of diminishing marginal product says that capital should be more valuable where capital is scarce.

This prediction, however, seems at odds with the international flow of capital represented by trade imbalances. Capital does not seem to flow to those nations where it should be most valuable. Instead of capital-rich countries like the United States lending to capital-poor countries, we often observe the opposite. Why is that?

One reason is that there are important differences among nations other than their accumulation of capital. Poor nations have not only lower levels of capital accumulation (represented by K/L) but also inferior production capabilities (represented by the variable A). For example, compared to rich nations, poor nations may have less access to advanced technologies, lower levels of education (or *human capital*), or less efficient economic policies. Such differences could mean less output for given inputs of capital and labor; in the Cobb-Douglas production function, this is translated into a lower value of the parameter A. If so, then capital need not be more valuable in poor nations, even though capital is scarce.

A second reason why capital might not flow to poor nations is that property rights are often not enforced. Corruption is typically much higher; revolutions, coups, and expropriation of wealth are more common; and governments often default on their debts. So even if capital is more valuable in poor nations, foreigners may avoid investing their wealth there simply because they are afraid of losing it. Moreover, local investors face similar incentives. Imagine that you lived in a poor nation and you happened to be lucky enough to have some wealth to invest; you might well decide that putting it in a safe country like the United States was your best option, even if capital is less valuable there than in your home country.

Whichever of these two reasons is correct, the challenge for poor nations is to find ways to reverse the situation. If these nations offered the same production efficiency and legal protections as the U.S. economy, the direction of international capital flows would likely reverse. The U.S. trade deficit would become a trade surplus, and capital would flow to these emerging nations. Such a change would help the poor of the world escape poverty.[2]

5-3 Exchange Rates

Having examined the international flows of capital and of goods and services, we now extend the analysis by considering the prices that apply to these transactions. The *exchange rate* between two countries is the price at which residents of those countries trade with each other. In this section we first examine precisely what the exchange rate measures, and we then discuss how exchange rates are determined.

Nominal and Real Exchange Rates

Economists distinguish between two exchange rates: the nominal exchange rate and the real exchange rate. Let's discuss each in turn and see how they are related.

The Nominal Exchange Rate The **nominal exchange rate** is the relative price of the currency of two countries. For example, if the exchange rate between the U.S. dollar and the Japanese yen is 120 yen per dollar, then you can exchange one dollar for 120 yen in world markets for foreign currency. A Japanese who wants to obtain dollars would pay 120 yen for each dollar he bought. An American who wants to obtain yen would get 120 yen for each dollar he paid. When people refer to "the exchange rate" between two countries, they usually mean the nominal exchange rate.

[2] For more on this topic, see Robert E. Lucas, "Why Doesn't Capital Flow from Rich to Poor Countries?" *American Economic Review* 80 (May 1990): 92–96.

FYI

How Newspapers Report the Exchange Rate

You can find nominal exchange rates reported daily in many newspapers. Here's how they are reported in the *Wall Street Journal*.

Notice that each exchange rate is reported in two ways. On this Tuesday, one dollar bought 115.62 yen, and one yen bought 0.008649 dollars. We can say the exchange rate is 115.62 yen per dollar, or we can say the exchange rate is 0.008649 dollars per yen. Because 0.008649 equals 1/115.62, these two ways of expressing the exchange rate are equivalent. This book always expresses the exchange rate in units of foreign currency per dollar.

The exchange rate on this Tuesday of 115.62 yen per dollar was up from 114.92 yen per dollar on Monday. Such a rise in the exchange rate is called an *appreciation* of the dollar; a fall in the exchange rate is called a *depreciation*. When the domestic currency appreciates, it buys more of the foreign currency; when it depreciates, it buys less. An appreciation is sometimes called a *strengthening* of the currency, and a depreciation is sometimes called a *weakening* of the currency.

EXCHANGE RATES

October 18, 2005

EXCHANGE RATES

The foreign exchange mid-range rates below apply to trading among banks in amounts of $1 million and more, as quoted at 4 p.m. Eastern time by Reuters and other sources. Retail transactions provide fewer units of foreign currency per dollar.

	U.S. $ EQUIV.		CURRENCY PER U.S. $	
Country	**Tue**	**Mon**	**Tue**	**Mon**
Argentina (Peso) - y	.3368	.3368	2.9691	2.9691
Australia (Dollar)	.7481	.7490	1.3367	1.3351
Bahrain (Dinar)	2.6526	2.6527	.3770	.3770
Brazil (Real)	.4447	.4474	2.2487	2.2351
Canada (Dollar	.8486	.8481	1.1784	1.1791
1-month forward	.8494	.8488	1.1773	1.1781
3-months forward	.8509	.8504	1.1752	1.1759
6-months forward	.8529	.8526	1.1725	1.1729
Chile (Peso)	.001872	.001872	534.19	534.19
China (Renminbi)	.1237	.1236	8.0869	8.0896
Colombia (Peso)	.0004381	.0004348	2282.58	2299.91
Czech. Rep. (Koruna)				
Commercial rate	.04024	.04039	24.851	24.759
Denmark (Krone)	.1603	.1611	6.2383	6.2073
Ecuador (US Dolalr)	1.0000	1.0000	1.0000	1.0000
Egypt (Pound) - y	.1735	.1734	5.7630	5.7663
Hong Kong (Dollar)	.1289	.1289	7.7588	7.7571
Hungary (Forint)	.004733	.004770	211.28	209.64
India (Rupee)	.02218	.02232	45.086	44.803
Indonesia (Rupiah)	.0000991	.0000990	10091	10101
Israel (Shekel)	.2155	.2155	4.6404	4.6404
Japan (Yen)	.008649	.008702	115.62	114.92
1-month forward	.008680	.008733	115.21	114.51
3-months forward	.008741	.008793	114.40	113.73
6-months forward	.008837	.008891	113.16	112.47
Jordan (Dinar)	1.4098	1.4098	0.7093	0.7093
Kuwair (Dinar)	3.4239	3.4245	0.2921	0.2920
Lebanon (Pound)	.0006653	.0006649	1503.08	1503.99
Malaysia (Ringgit) - b	.2650	.2650	3.7736	3.7736
Malta (Lira)	2.7859	2.8013	0.3590	0.3570
Mexico (Peso)				
Floating rate	.0921	.0922	10.8578	10.8483
New Zealand (Dollar)	.6964	.6966	1.4360	1.4355
Norway (Krone)	.1529	.1541	6.5402	6.4893
Pakistan (Rupee)	.01671	.01674	59.844	59.737
Peru (new Sol)	.2952	.2952	3.3875	3.3875
Philippines (Peso)	.01795	.01791	55.710	55.835
Poland (Zloty)	.3079	.3084	3.2478	3.2425
Russia (Ruble) - a	.03494	.03994	28.621	28.580
Saudi Arabia (Riyal)	.2666	.2666	3.7509	3.7509
Singapore (Dollar)	.5901	.5909	1.6946	1.6923
Slovak Rep. (Koruna)	0.03066	.03094	32.616	.32.321
South Africa (Rand)	.1519	.1530	6.5833	6.5359
South Korea (Won)	.0009492	.0009537	1053.52	1048.55
Sweden (Krona)	.1266	.1271	7.8989	7.8678
Switzerland (Franc)	.7700	.7742	1.2987	1.2917
1-month forward	.7722	.7765	1.2950	1.2878
3-months forward	.7766	.7808	1.2877	1.2807
6-months forward	.7834	.7876	1.2765	1.2697
Taiwan (Dollar)	.02978	.02989	33.580	33.456
Thailand (Baht)	.02447	.02446	40.866	40.883
Turkey (New Lira) - d	.7299	.7348	1.3700	1.3610
U.K. (Pound)	1.7505	1.7542	0.5713	0.5701
1-month forward	1.7497	1.7533	0.5715	0.5704
3-months forward	1.7491	1.7527	0.5717	0.5705
6-months forward	1.7494	1.7529	0.5716	0.5705
United Arab (Dirham)	.2723	.2723	3.6724	3.6724
Uruguay (Peso)				
Financial	.04270	.04270	23.419	23.419
Venezuela (Bolivar)	.000466	.000466	2145.92	2145.92
SDR	1.4390	1.4456	0.6949	0.6918
Euro	1.1962	1.2026	0.8360	0.8315

Special Drawing Rights (SDR) are based on exchange rates for the U.S., British, and Japanese currencies. Source: International Monetary Fund.

a-Russian Central Bank rate. b-Government rate. d-Rebased as of Jan. 1, 2005. y-Floating rate.

Source: *Wall Street Journal*, October 18, 2005. Reprinted by permission of the *Wall Street Journal*,

The Real Exchange Rate The **real exchange rate** is the relative price of the goods of two countries. That is, the real exchange rate tells us the rate at which we can trade the goods of one country for the goods of another. The real exchange rate is sometimes called the *terms of trade.*

To see the relation between the real and nominal exchange rates, consider a single good produced in many countries: cars. Suppose an American car costs $10,000 and a similar Japanese car costs 2,400,000 yen. To compare the prices of the two cars, we must convert them into a common currency. If a dollar is worth 120 yen, then the American car costs 1,200,000 yen. Comparing the price of the American car (1,200,000 yen) and the price of the Japanese car (2,400,000 yen), we conclude that the American car costs one-half of what the Japanese car costs. In other words, at current prices, we can exchange 2 American cars for 1 Japanese car.

We can summarize our calculation as follows:

$$\text{Real Exchange Rate} = \frac{(120 \text{ yen/dollar}) \times (10{,}000 \text{ dollars/American Car})}{(2{,}400{,}000 \text{ yen/Japanese Car})}$$

$$= 0.5 \frac{\text{Japanese Car}}{\text{American Car}}.$$

At these prices and this exchange rate, we obtain one-half of a Japanese car per American car. More generally, we can write this calculation as

$$\text{Real Exchange Rate} = \frac{\text{Nominal Exchange Rate} \times \text{Price of Domestic Good}}{\text{Price of Foreign Good}}.$$

The rate at which we exchange foreign and domestic goods depends on the prices of the goods in the local currencies and on the rate at which the currencies are exchanged.

This calculation of the real exchange rate for a single good suggests how we should define the real exchange rate for a broader basket of goods. Let e be the nominal exchange rate (the number of yen per dollar), P be the price level in the United States (measured in dollars), and P^* be the price level in Japan (measured in yen). Then the real exchange rate ϵ is

$$\text{Real Exchange Rate} = \text{Nominal Exchange Rate} \times \text{Ratio of Price Levels}$$

$$\epsilon = e \times (P/P^*).$$

The real exchange rate between two countries is computed from the nominal exchange rate and the price levels in the two countries. *If the real exchange rate is high, foreign goods are relatively cheap, and domestic goods are relatively expensive. If the real exchange rate is low, foreign goods are relatively expensive, and domestic goods are relatively cheap.*

The Real Exchange Rate and the Trade Balance

What macroeconomic influence does the real exchange rate exert? To answer this question, remember that the real exchange rate is nothing more than a relative price. Just as the relative price of hamburgers and pizza determines which you choose for lunch, the relative price of domestic and foreign goods affects the demand for these goods.

"How about Nebraska? The dollar's still strong in Nebraska."

Suppose first that the real exchange rate is low. In this case, because domestic goods are relatively cheap, domestic residents will want to purchase fewer imported goods: they will buy Fords rather than Toyotas, drink Coors rather than Heineken, and vacation in Florida rather than Italy. For the same reason, foreigners will want to buy many of our goods. As a result of both of these actions, the quantity of our net exports demanded will be high.

The opposite occurs if the real exchange rate is high. Because domestic goods are expensive relative to foreign goods, domestic residents will want to buy many imported goods, and foreigners will want to buy few of our goods. Therefore, the quantity of our net exports demanded will be low.

We write this relationship between the real exchange rate and net exports as

$$NX = NX(\epsilon).$$

This equation states that net exports are a function of the real exchange rate. Figure 5-7 illustrates the negative relationship between the trade balance and the real exchange rate.

FIGURE 5-7

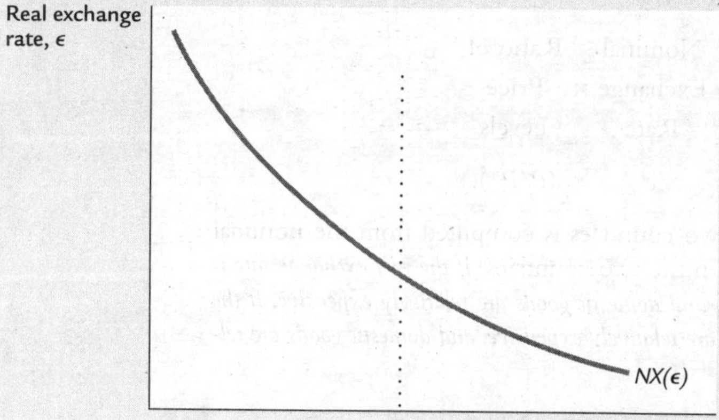

Net Exports and the Real Exchange Rate The figure shows the relationship between the real exchange rate and net exports: the lower the real exchange rate, the less expensive are domestic goods relative to foreign goods, and thus the greater are our net exports. Note that a portion of the horizontal axis measures negative values of NX: because imports can exceed exports, net exports can be less than zero.

The Determinants of the Real Exchange Rate

We now have all the pieces needed to construct a model that explains what factors determine the real exchange rate. In particular, we combine the relationship between net exports and the real exchange rate we just discussed with the model of the trade balance we developed earlier in the chapter. We can summarize the analysis as follows:

- The real exchange rate is related to net exports. When the real exchange rate is lower, domestic goods are less expensive relative to foreign goods, and net exports are greater.
- The trade balance (net exports) must equal the net capital outflow, which in turn equals saving minus investment. Saving is fixed by the consumption function and fiscal policy; investment is fixed by the investment function and the world interest rate.

Figure 5-8 illustrates these two conditions. The line showing the relationship between net exports and the real exchange rate slopes downward because a low real exchange rate makes domestic goods relatively inexpensive. The line representing the excess of saving over investment, $S - I$, is vertical because neither saving nor investment depends on the real exchange rate. The crossing of these two lines determines the equilibrium exchange rate.

Figure 5-8 looks like an ordinary supply-and-demand diagram. In fact, you can think of this diagram as representing the supply and demand for foreign-currency exchange. The vertical line, $S - I$, represents the net capital outflow and thus the supply of dollars to be exchanged into foreign currency and invested abroad. The downward-sloping line, NX, represents the net demand for dollars coming from foreigners who want dollars to buy our goods. *At the equilibrium real exchange rate, the supply of dollars available from the net capital outflow balances the demand for dollars by foreigners buying our net exports.*

FIGURE 5-8

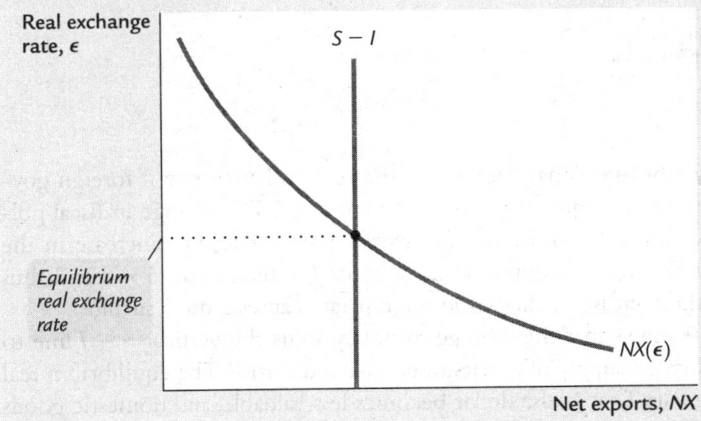

How the Real Exchange Rate is Determined The real exchange rate is determined by the intersection of the vertical line representing saving minus investment and the downward-sloping net-exports schedule. At this intersection, the quantity of dollars supplied for the flow of capital abroad equals the quantity of dollars demanded for the net export of goods and services.

How Policies Influence the Real Exchange Rate

We can use this model to show how the changes in economic policy we discussed earlier affect the real exchange rate.

Fiscal Policy at Home What happens to the real exchange rate if the government reduces national saving by increasing government purchases or cutting taxes? As we discussed earlier, this reduction in saving lowers $S - I$ and thus NX. That is, the reduction in saving causes a trade deficit.

Figure 5-9 shows how the equilibrium real exchange rate adjusts to ensure that NX falls. The change in policy shifts the vertical $S - I$ line to the left, lowering the supply of dollars to be invested abroad. The lower supply causes the equilibrium real exchange rate to rise from ϵ_1 to ϵ_2—that is, the dollar becomes more valuable. Because of the rise in the value of the dollar, domestic goods become more expensive relative to foreign goods, which causes exports to fall and imports to rise. The change in exports and the change in imports both act to reduce net exports.

FIGURE 5-9

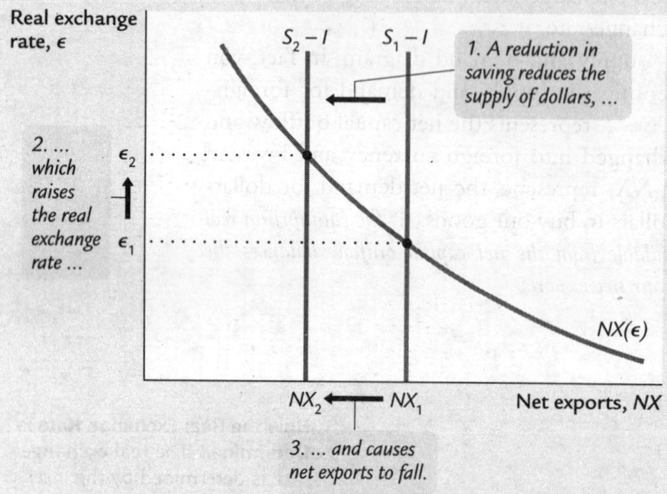

The Impact of Expansionary Fiscal Policy at Home on the Real Exchange Rate Expansionary fiscal policy at home, such as an increase in government purchases or a cut in taxes, reduces national saving. The fall in saving reduces the supply of dollars to be exchanged into foreign currency, from $S_1 - I$ to $S_2 - I$. This shift raises the equilibrium real exchange rate from ϵ_1 to ϵ_2.

Fiscal Policy Abroad What happens to the real exchange rate if foreign governments increase government purchases or cut taxes? This change in fiscal policy reduces world saving and raises the world interest rate. The increase in the world interest rate reduces domestic investment I, which raises $S - I$ and thus NX. That is, the increase in the world interest rate causes a trade surplus.

Figure 5-10 shows that this change in policy shifts the vertical $S - I$ line to the right, raising the supply of dollars to be invested abroad. The equilibrium real exchange rate falls. That is, the dollar becomes less valuable, and domestic goods become less expensive relative to foreign goods.

FIGURE 5-10

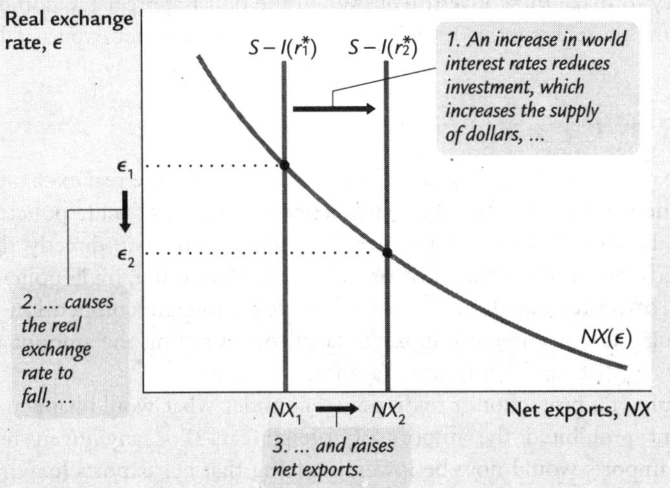

The Impact of Expansionary Fiscal Policy Abroad on the Real Exchange Rate Expansionary fiscal policy abroad reduces world saving and raises the world interest rate from r_1^* to r_2^*. The increase in the world interest rate reduces investment at home, which in turn raises the supply of dollars to be exchanged into foreign currencies. As a result, the equilibrium real exchange rate falls from ϵ_1 to ϵ_2.

Shifts in Investment Demand What happens to the real exchange rate if investment demand at home increases, perhaps because Congress passes an investment tax credit? At the given world interest rate, the increase in investment demand leads to higher investment. A higher value of I means lower values of $S - I$ and NX. That is, the increase in investment demand causes a trade deficit.

Figure 5-11 shows that the increase in investment demand shifts the vertical $S - I$ line to the left, reducing the supply of dollars to be invested abroad. The

FIGURE 5-11

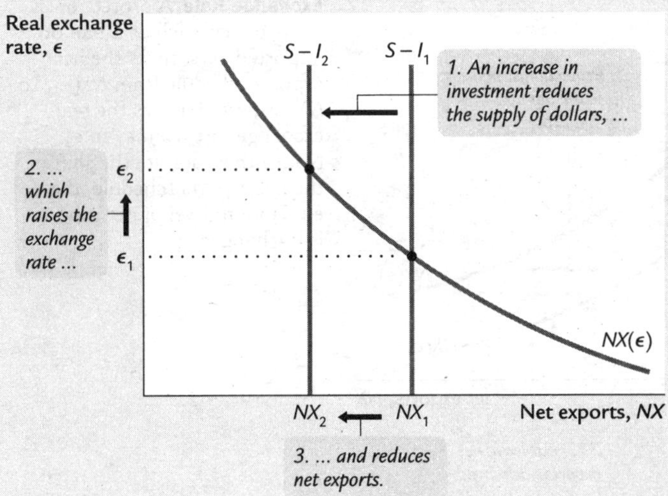

The Impact of an Increase in Investment Demand on the Real Exchange Rate An increase in investment demand raises the quantity of domestic investment from I_1 to I_2. As a result, the supply of dollars to be exchanged into foreign currencies falls from $S - I_1$ to $S - I_2$. This fall in supply raises the equilibrium real exchange rate from ϵ_1 to ϵ_2.

equilibrium real exchange rate rises. Hence, when the investment tax credit makes investing in the United States more attractive, it also increases the value of the U.S. dollars necessary to make these investments. When the dollar appreciates, domestic goods become more expensive relative to foreign goods, and net exports fall.

The Effects of Trade Policies

Now that we have a model that explains the trade balance and the real exchange rate, we have the tools to examine the macroeconomic effects of trade policies. Trade policies, broadly defined, are policies designed to influence directly the amount of goods and services exported or imported. Most often, trade policies take the form of protecting domestic industries from foreign competition—either by placing a tax on foreign imports (a tariff) or restricting the amount of goods and services that can be imported (a quota).

As an example of a protectionist trade policy, consider what would happen if the government prohibited the import of foreign cars. For any given real exchange rate, imports would now be lower, implying that net exports (exports minus imports) would be higher. Thus, the net-exports schedule shifts outward, as in Figure 5-12. To see the effects of the policy, we compare the old equilibrium and the new equilibrium. In the new equilibrium, the real exchange rate is higher, and net exports are unchanged. Despite the shift in the net-exports schedule, the equilibrium level of net exports remains the same, because the protectionist policy does not alter either saving or investment.

FIGURE 5-12

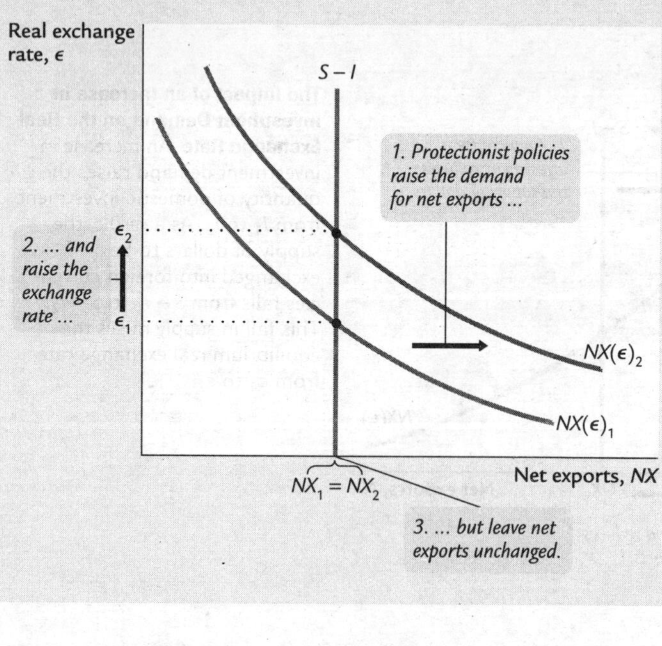

The Impact of Protectionist Trade Policies on the Real Exchange Rate A protectionist trade policy, such as a ban on imported cars, shifts the net exports schedule from $NX(\epsilon)_1$ to $NX(\epsilon)_2$, which raises the real exchange rate from ϵ_1 to ϵ_2. Notice that, despite the shift in the net-exports schedule, the equilibrium level of net exports is unchanged.

This analysis shows that protectionist trade policies do not affect the trade balance. This surprising conclusion is often overlooked in the popular debate over trade policies. Because a trade deficit reflects an excess of imports over exports, one might guess that reducing imports—such as by prohibiting the import of foreign cars—would reduce a trade deficit. Yet our model shows that protectionist policies lead only to an appreciation of the real exchange rate. The increase in the price of domestic goods relative to foreign goods tends to lower net exports by stimulating imports and depressing exports. Thus, the appreciation offsets the increase in net exports that is directly attributable to the trade restriction.

Although protectionist trade policies do not alter the trade balance, they do affect the amount of trade. As we have seen, because the real exchange rate appreciates, the goods and services we produce become more expensive relative to foreign goods and services. We therefore export less in the new equilibrium. Because net exports are unchanged, we must import less as well. (The appreciation of the exchange rate does stimulate imports to some extent, but this only partly offsets the decrease in imports due to the trade restriction.) Thus, protectionist policies reduce both the quantity of imports and the quantity of exports.

This fall in the total amount of trade is the reason economists almost always oppose protectionist policies. International trade benefits all countries by allowing each country to specialize in what it produces best and by providing each country with a greater variety of goods and services. Protectionist policies diminish these gains from trade. Although these policies benefit certain groups within society—for example, a ban on imported cars helps domestic car producers—society on average is worse off when policies reduce the amount of international trade.

The Determinants of the Nominal Exchange Rate

Having seen what determines the real exchange rate, we now turn our attention to the nominal exchange rate—the rate at which the currencies of two countries trade. Recall the relationship between the real and the nominal exchange rate:

$$\begin{array}{ccccc} \text{Real} & & \text{Nominal} & & \text{Ratio of} \\ \text{Exchange} & = & \text{Exchange} & \times & \text{Price} \\ \text{Rate} & & \text{Rate} & & \text{Levels} \\ \epsilon & = & e & \times & (P/P^*). \end{array}$$

We can write the nominal exchange rate as

$$e = \epsilon \times (P^*/P).$$

This equation shows that the nominal exchange rate depends on the real exchange rate and the price levels in the two countries. Given the value of the real exchange rate, if the domestic price level P rises, then the nominal exchange rate e will fall: because a dollar is worth less, a dollar will buy fewer yen. However, if the Japanese price level P^* rises, then the nominal exchange rate will increase: because the yen is worth less, a dollar will buy more yen.

It is instructive to consider changes in exchange rates over time. The exchange rate equation can be written

$$\% \text{ Change in } e = \% \text{ Change in } \epsilon + \% \text{ Change in } P^* - \% \text{ Change in } P.$$

The percentage change in ϵ is the change in the real exchange rate. The percentage change in P is the domestic inflation rate π, and the percentage change in P^* is the foreign country's inflation rate π^*. Thus, the percentage change in the nominal exchange rate is

$$\% \text{ Change in } e = \% \text{ Change in } \epsilon \qquad + (\pi^* - \pi)$$

$$\begin{matrix}\text{Percentage Change in} \\ \text{Nominal Exchange Rate}\end{matrix} = \begin{matrix}\text{Percentage Change in} \\ \text{Real Exchange Rate}\end{matrix} + \begin{matrix}\text{Difference in} \\ \text{Inflation Rates.}\end{matrix}$$

This equation states that the percentage change in the nominal exchange rate between the currencies of two countries equals the percentage change in the real exchange rate plus the difference in their inflation rates. *If a country has a high rate of inflation relative to the United States, a dollar will buy an increasing amount of the foreign currency over time. If a country has a low rate of inflation relative to the United States, a dollar will buy a decreasing amount of the foreign currency over time.*

This analysis shows how monetary policy affects the nominal exchange rate. We know from Chapter 4 that high growth in the money supply leads to high inflation. Here, we have just seen that one consequence of high inflation is a depreciating currency: high π implies falling e. In other words, just as growth in the amount of money raises the price of goods measured in terms of money, it also tends to raise the price of foreign currencies measured in terms of the domestic currency.

CASE STUDY

Inflation and Nominal Exchange Rates

If we look at data on exchange rates and price levels of different countries, we quickly see the importance of inflation for explaining changes in the nominal exchange rate. The most dramatic examples come from periods of very high inflation. For example, the price level in Mexico rose by 2,300 percent from 1983 to 1988. Because of this inflation, the number of pesos a person could buy with a U.S. dollar rose from 144 in 1983 to 2,281 in 1988.

The same relationship holds true for countries with more moderate inflation. Figure 5-13 is a scatterplot showing the relationship between inflation and the exchange rate for 15 countries. On the horizontal axis is the difference between each country's average inflation rate and the average inflation rate of the United States ($\pi^* - \pi$). On the vertical axis is the average percentage change in the exchange rate between each country's currency and the U.S. dollar (% change in e). The positive relationship between these two variables is clear in this figure. Countries with relatively high inflation tend to have depreciating currencies (you can buy more of them with your dollars over time), and countries with relatively low inflation tend to have appreciating currencies (you can buy less of them with your dollars over time).

FIGURE 5-13

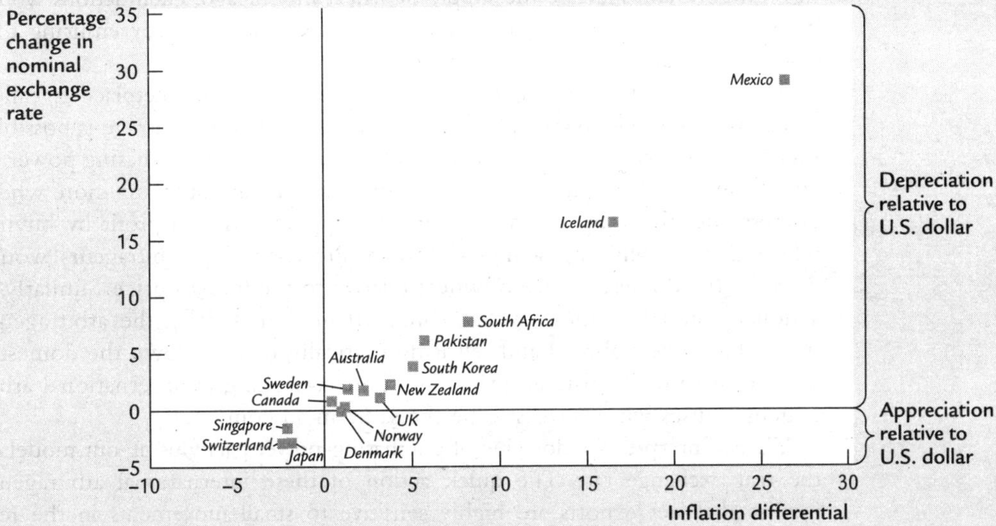

Inflation Differentials and the Exchange Rate This scatterplot shows the relationship between inflation and the nominal exchange rate. The horizontal axis shows the country's average inflation rate minus the U.S. average inflation rate over the period 1972-2004. The vertical axis is the average percentage change in the country's exchange rate (per U.S. dollar) over that period. This figure shows that countries with relatively high inflation tend to have depreciating currencies, and that countries with relatively low inflation tend to have appreciating currencies.

Source: International Financial Statistics.

As an example, consider the exchange rate between Swiss francs and U.S. dollars. Both Switzerland and the United States have experienced inflation over the past thirty years, so both the franc and the dollar buy fewer goods than they once did. But, as Figure 5-13 shows, inflation in Switzerland has been lower than inflation in the United States. This means that the value of the franc has fallen less than the value of the dollar. Therefore, the number of Swiss francs you can buy with a U.S. dollar has been falling over time.

The Special Case of Purchasing-Power Parity

A famous hypothesis in economics, called the *law of one price,* states that the same good cannot sell for different prices in different locations at the same time. If a bushel of wheat sold for less in New York than in Chicago, it would be profitable to buy wheat in New York and then sell it in Chicago. This profit opportunity would become quickly apparent to astute *arbitrageurs*—people who specialize in "buying low" in one market and "selling high" in another. As the arbitrageurs took advantage of this opportunity, they would increase the demand for wheat in New York and increase the supply of wheat in Chicago. Their actions would drive the price up in New York and down in Chicago, thereby ensuring that prices are equalized in the two markets.

The law of one price applied to the international marketplace is called **purchasing-power parity**. It states that if international arbitrage is possible, then a dollar (or any other currency) must have the same purchasing power in every country. The argument goes as follows. If a dollar could buy more wheat domestically than abroad, there would be opportunities to profit by buying wheat domestically and selling it abroad. Profit-seeking arbitrageurs would drive up the domestic price of wheat relative to the foreign price. Similarly, if a dollar could buy more wheat abroad than domestically, the arbitrageurs would buy wheat abroad and sell it domestically, driving down the domestic price relative to the foreign price. Thus, profit-seeking by international arbitrageurs causes wheat prices to be the same in all countries.

We can interpret the doctrine of purchasing-power parity using our model of the real exchange rate. The quick action of these international arbitrageurs implies that net exports are highly sensitive to small movements in the real exchange rate. A small decrease in the price of domestic goods relative to foreign goods—that is, a small decrease in the real exchange rate—causes arbitrageurs to buy goods domestically and sell them abroad. Similarly, a small increase in the relative price of domestic goods causes arbitrageurs to import goods from abroad. Therefore, as in Figure 5-14, the net-exports schedule is very flat at the real exchange rate that equalizes purchasing power among countries: any small movement in the real exchange rate leads to a large change in net exports. This extreme sensitivity of net exports guarantees that the equilibrium real exchange rate is always close to the level that ensures purchasing-power parity.

Purchasing-power parity has two important implications. First, because the net-exports schedule is flat, changes in saving or investment do not influence the

FIGURE 5-14

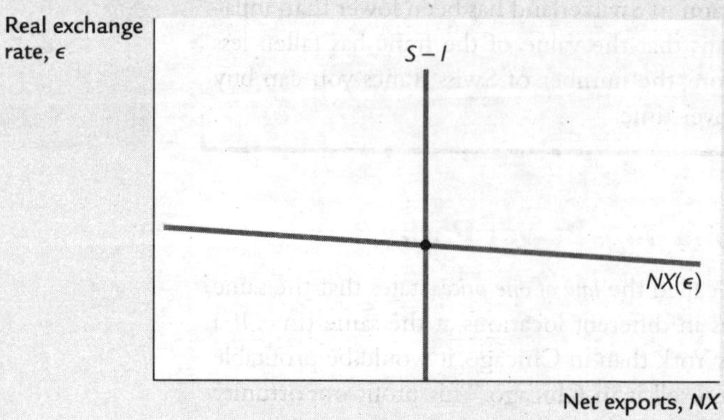

Purchasing-Power Parity The law of one price applied to the international marketplace suggests that net exports are highly sensitive to small movements in the real exchange rate. This high sensitivity is reflected here with a very flat net-exports schedule.

real or nominal exchange rate. Second, because the real exchange rate is fixed, all changes in the nominal exchange rate result from changes in price levels.

Is this doctrine of purchasing-power parity realistic? Most economists believe that, despite its appealing logic, purchasing-power parity does not provide a completely accurate description of the world. First, many goods are not easily traded. A haircut can be more expensive in Tokyo than in New York, yet there is no room for international arbitrage because it is impossible to transport haircuts. Second, even tradable goods are not always perfect substitutes. Some consumers prefer Toyotas, and others prefer Fords. Thus, the relative price of Toyotas and Fords can vary to some extent without leaving any profit opportunities. For these reasons, real exchange rates do in fact vary over time.

Although the doctrine of purchasing-power parity does not describe the world perfectly, it does provide a reason why movement in the real exchange rate will be limited. There is much validity to its underlying logic: the farther the real exchange rate drifts from the level predicted by purchasing-power parity, the greater the incentive for individuals to engage in international arbitrage in goods. Although we cannot rely on purchasing-power parity to eliminate all changes in the real exchange rate, this doctrine does provide a reason to expect that fluctuations in the real exchange rate will typically be small or temporary.[3]

CASE STUDY

The Big Mac Around the World

The doctrine of purchasing-power parity says that after we adjust for exchange rates, we should find that goods sell for the same price everywhere. Conversely, it says that the exchange rate between two currencies should depend on the price levels in the two countries.

To see how well this doctrine works, *The Economist,* an international newsmagazine, regularly collects data on the price of a good sold in many countries: the McDonald's Big Mac hamburger. According to purchasing-power parity, the price of a Big Mac should be closely related to the country's nominal exchange rate. The higher the price of a Big Mac in the local currency, the higher the exchange rate (measured in units of local currency per U.S. dollar) should be.

Table 5-2 presents the international prices in 2005, when a Big Mac sold for $3.06 in the United States (this was the average price in New York, San Francisco, Chicago, and Atlanta). With these data we can use the doctrine of purchasing-power parity to predict nominal exchange rates. For example, because a Big Mac cost 28 pesos in Mexico, we would predict that the exchange rate between the dollar and the peso was 28/3.06, or around 9.15, pesos per dollar. At this exchange rate, a Big Mac would have cost the same in Mexico and the United States.

[3] To learn more about purchasing-power parity, see Kenneth A. Froot and Kenneth Rogoff, "Perspectives on PPP and Long-Run Real Exchange Rates," in Gene M. Grossman and Kenneth Rogoff, eds., *Handbook of International Economics,* vol. 3 (Amsterdam: North-Holland, 1995).

TABLE 5-2

Big Mac Prices and the Exchange Rate: An Application of Purchasing-Power Parity

Country	Currency	Price of a Big Mac	Exchange Rate (per U.S. dollar) Predicted	Actual
Indonesia	Rupiah	14,770	4,771	9,654
South Korea	Won	2,498	817	1,003
Chile	Peso	1,496	490	591
Hungary	Forint	532	173	205
Japan	Yen	252	81.7	108
Taiwan	Dollar	75.4	24.5	31.3
Thailand	Baht	60.2	19.6	40.7
Czech Rep.	Koruna	56.6	18.4	24.6
Russia	Ruble	42.1	13.7	28.4
Sweden	Krona	31.4	10.1	7.53
Mexico	Peso	28.1	9.15	10.9
Denmark	Krone	27.9	9.07	6.10
South Africa	Rand	14.2	4.56	6.76
China	Yuan	10.5	3.43	8.28
Egypt	Pound	8.99	2.94	5.80
Poland	Zloty	6.49	2.12	3.31
Switzerland	Franc	6.34	2.06	1.25
Brazil	Real	5.95	1.93	2.49
Malaysia	Ringgit	5.24	1.72	3.80
Argentina	Peso	4.75	1.55	2.90
New Zealand	Dollar	4.45	1.45	1.40
Singapore	Dollar	3.61	1.18	1.66
Canada	Dollar	3.30	1.07	1.26
Australia	Dollar	3.26	1.06	1.30
United States	Dollar	3.06	1.00	1.00
Euro Area	Euro	2.93	0.95	0.82
United Kingdom	Pound	1.89	0.61	0.55

Note: The predicted exchange rate is the exchange rate that would make the price of a Big Mac in that country equal to its price in the United States.
Source: The Economist, June 9, 2005.

Table 5-2 shows the predicted and actual exchange rates for 27 countries, ranked by the predicted exchange rate. You can see that the evidence on purchasing-power parity is mixed. As the last two columns show, the actual and predicted exchange rates are usually in the same ballpark. Our theory predicts, for instance, that a U.S. dollar should buy the greatest number of Indonesian rupiahs and fewest British pounds, and this turns out to be true. In the case of Mexico, the predicted exchange rate of 9.15 pesos per dollar is close to the actual exchange rate of 10.9. Yet the theory's predictions are far from exact and, in many cases, are off by 30 percent or more. Hence, although the theory of purchasing-power parity provides a rough guide to the level of exchange rates, it does not explain exchange rates completely.

5-4 Conclusion: The United States as a Large Open Economy

In this chapter we have seen how a small open economy works. We have examined the determinants of the international flow of funds for capital accumulation and the international flow of goods and services. We have also examined the determinants of a country's real and nominal exchange rates. Our analysis shows how various policies—monetary policies, fiscal policies, and trade policies—affect the trade balance and the exchange rate.

The economy we have studied is "small" in the sense that its interest rate is fixed by world financial markets. That is, we have assumed that this economy does not affect the world interest rate, and that the economy can borrow and lend at the world interest rate in unlimited amounts. This assumption contrasts with the assumption we made when we studied the closed economy in Chapter 3. In the closed economy, the domestic interest rate equilibrates domestic saving and domestic investment, implying that policies that influence saving or investment alter the equilibrium interest rate.

Which of these analyses should we apply to an economy such as the United States? The answer is a little of both. The United States is neither so large nor so isolated that it is immune to developments occurring abroad. The large trade deficits of the 1980s, 1990s, and 2000s show the importance of international financial markets for funding U.S. investment. Hence, the closed-economy analysis of Chapter 3 cannot by itself fully explain the impact of policies on the U.S. economy.

Yet the U.S. economy is not so small and so open that the analysis of this chapter applies perfectly either. First, the United States is large enough that it can influence world financial markets. For example, large U.S. budget deficits were often blamed for the high real interest rates that prevailed throughout the world in the 1980s. Second, capital may not be perfectly mobile across countries. If individuals prefer holding their wealth in domestic rather than foreign assets, funds for capital accumulation will not flow freely to equate interest rates in all countries. For these two reasons, we cannot directly apply our model of the small open economy to the United States.

When analyzing policy for a country such as the United States, we need to combine the closed-economy logic of Chapter 3 and the small-open-economy logic of this chapter. The appendix to this chapter builds a model of an economy between these two extremes. In this intermediate case, there is international borrowing and lending, but the interest rate is not fixed by world financial markets. Instead, the more the economy borrows from abroad, the higher the interest rate it must offer foreign investors. The results, not surprisingly, are a mixture of the two polar cases we have already examined.

Consider, for example, a reduction in national saving due to a fiscal expansion. As in the closed economy, this policy raises the real interest rate and crowds out domestic investment. As in the small open economy, it also reduces the net capital outflow, leading to a trade deficit and an appreciation of the exchange rate. Hence, although the model of the small open economy examined here does not precisely describe an economy such as the United States, it does provide approximately the right answer to how policies affect the trade balance and the exchange rate.

Summary

1. Net exports are the difference between exports and imports. They are equal to the difference between what we produce and what we demand for consumption, investment, and government purchases.
2. The net capital outflow is the excess of domestic saving over domestic investment. The trade balance is the amount received for our net exports of goods and services. The national income accounts identity shows that the net capital outflow always equals the trade balance.
3. The impact of any policy on the trade balance can be determined by examining its impact on saving and investment. Policies that raise saving or lower investment lead to a trade surplus, and policies that lower saving or raise investment lead to a trade deficit.
4. The nominal exchange rate is the rate at which people trade the currency of one country for the currency of another country. The real exchange rate is the rate at which people trade the goods produced by the two countries. The real exchange rate equals the nominal exchange rate multiplied by the ratio of the price levels in the two countries.
5. Because the real exchange rate is the price of domestic goods relative to foreign goods, an appreciation of the real exchange rate tends to reduce net exports. The equilibrium real exchange rate is the rate at which the quantity of net exports demanded equals the net capital outflow.
6. The nominal exchange rate is determined by the real exchange rate and the price levels in the two countries. Other things equal, a high rate of inflation leads to a depreciating currency.

KEY CONCEPTS

Net exports
Trade balance
Net capital outflow
Trade surplus and trade deficit
Balanced trade
Small open economy
World interest rate
Nominal exchange rate
Real exchange rate
Purchasing-power parity

QUESTIONS FOR REVIEW

1. What are the net capital outflow and the trade balance? Explain how they are related.
2. Define the nominal exchange rate and the real exchange rate.
3. If a small open economy cuts defense spending, what happens to saving, investment, the trade balance, the interest rate, and the exchange rate?
4. If a small open economy bans the import of Japanese VCRs, what happens to saving, investment, the trade balance, the interest rate, and the exchange rate?
5. If Japan has low inflation and Mexico has high inflation, what will happen to the exchange rate between the Japanese yen and the Mexican peso?

PROBLEMS AND APPLICATIONS

1. Use the model of the small open economy to predict what would happen to the trade balance, the real exchange rate, and the nominal exchange rate in response to each of the following events.
   a. A fall in consumer confidence about the future induces consumers to spend less and save more.
   b. The introduction of a stylish line of Toyotas makes some consumers prefer foreign cars over domestic cars.
   c. The introduction of automatic teller machines reduces the demand for money.
2. Consider an economy described by the following equations:

$$Y = C + I + G + NX,$$
$$Y = 5{,}000,$$
$$G = 1{,}000,$$
$$T = 1{,}000,$$
$$C = 250 + 0.75(Y - T),$$
$$I = 1{,}000 - 50r,$$
$$NX = 500 - 500\epsilon,$$
$$r = r^* = 5.$$

   a. In this economy, solve for national saving, investment, the trade balance, and the equilibrium exchange rate.
   b. Suppose now that G rises to 1,250. Solve for national saving, investment, the trade balance, and the equilibrium exchange rate. Explain what you find.
   c. Now suppose that the world interest rate rises from 5 to 10 percent. (G is again 1,000). Solve for national saving, investment, the trade balance, and the equilibrium exchange rate. Explain what you find.
3. The country of Leverett is a small open economy. Suddenly, a change in world fashions makes the exports of Leverett unpopular.
   a. What happens in Leverett to saving, investment, net exports, the interest rate, and the exchange rate?
   b. The citizens of Leverett like to travel abroad. How will this change in the exchange rate affect them?
   c. The fiscal policymakers of Leverett want to adjust taxes to maintain the exchange rate at its previous level. What should they do? If they do this, what are the overall effects on saving, investment, net exports, and the interest rate?
4. In 2005, Federal Reserve Governor Ben Bernanke said in a speech: "Over the past decade a combination of diverse forces has created a significant increase in the global supply of saving—a global saving glut—which helps to explain both the increase in the U.S. current account deficit [a broad measure of the trade deficit] and the relatively low level of long-term real interest rates in the world today." Is this statement consistent with the models you have learned? Explain.
5. What will happen to the trade balance and the real exchange rate of a small open economy when government purchases increase, such as during a

war? Does your answer depend on whether this is a local war or a world war?

6. A case study in this chapter concludes that if poor nations offered better production efficiency and legal protections, the trade balance in rich nations such as the United States would move toward surplus. Let's consider why this might be the case.

   a. If the world's poor nations offer better production efficiency and legal protection, what would happen to the investment demand function in those countries?

   b. How would the change you describe in part (a) affect the demand for loanable funds in world financial markets?

   c. How would the change you describe in part (b) affect the world interest rate?

   d. How would the change in the world interest rate you describe in part (c) affect the trade balance in rich nations?

7. The president is considering placing a tariff on the import of Japanese luxury cars. Discuss the economics and politics of such a policy. In particular, how would the policy affect the U.S. trade deficit? How would it affect the exchange rate? Who would be hurt by such a policy? Who would benefit?

8. Suppose that some foreign countries begin to subsidize investment by instituting an investment tax credit.

   a. What happens to world investment demand as a function of the world interest rate?

   b. What happens to the world interest rate?

   c. What happens to investment in our small open economy?

   d. What happens to our trade balance?

   e. What happens to our real exchange rate?

9. "Traveling in Mexico is much cheaper now than it was ten years ago," says a friend. "Ten years ago, a dollar bought 10 pesos; this year, a dollar buys 15 pesos."

   Is your friend right or wrong? Given that total inflation over this period was 25 percent in the United States and 100 percent in Mexico, has it become more or less expensive to travel in Mexico? Write your answer using a concrete example—such as an American hot dog versus a Mexican taco—that will convince your friend.

10. You read in a newspaper that the nominal interest rate is 12 percent per year in Canada and 8 percent per year in the United States. Suppose that the real interest rates are equalized in the two countries and that purchasing-power parity holds.

    a. Using the Fisher equation (discussed in Chapter 4), what can you infer about expected inflation in Canada and in the United States?

    b. What can you infer about the expected change in the exchange rate between the Canadian dollar and the U.S. dollar?

    c. A friend proposes a get-rich-quick scheme: borrow from a U.S. bank at 8 percent, deposit the money in a Canadian bank at 12 percent, and make a 4 percent profit. What's wrong with this scheme?

The Large Open Economy

When analyzing policy for a country such as the United States, we need to combine the closed-economy logic of Chapter 3 and the small-open-economy logic of this chapter. This appendix presents a model of an economy between these two extremes, called the *large open economy.*

Net Capital Outflow

The key difference between the small and large open economies is the behavior of the net capital outflow. In the model of the small open economy, capital flows freely into or out of the economy at a fixed world interest rate r^*. The model of the large open economy makes a different assumption about international capital flows. To understand this assumption, keep in mind that the net capital outflow is the amount that domestic investors lend abroad minus the amount that foreign investors lend here.

Imagine that you are a domestic investor—such as the portfolio manager of a university endowment—deciding where to invest your funds. You could invest domestically (for example, by making loans to U.S. companies), or you could invest abroad (by making loans to foreign companies). Many factors may affect your decision, but surely one of them is the interest rate you can earn. The higher the interest rate you can earn domestically, the less attractive you would find foreign investment.

Investors abroad face a similar decision. They have a choice between investing in their home country and lending to someone in the United States. The higher the interest rate in the United States, the more willing foreigners are to lend to U.S. companies and to buy U.S. assets.

Thus, because of the behavior of both domestic and foreign investors, the net flow of capital to other countries, which we'll denote as CF, is negatively related to the domestic real interest rate r. As the interest rate rises, less of our saving flows abroad, and more funds for capital accumulation flow in from other countries. We write this as

$$CF = CF(r).$$

FIGURE 5-15

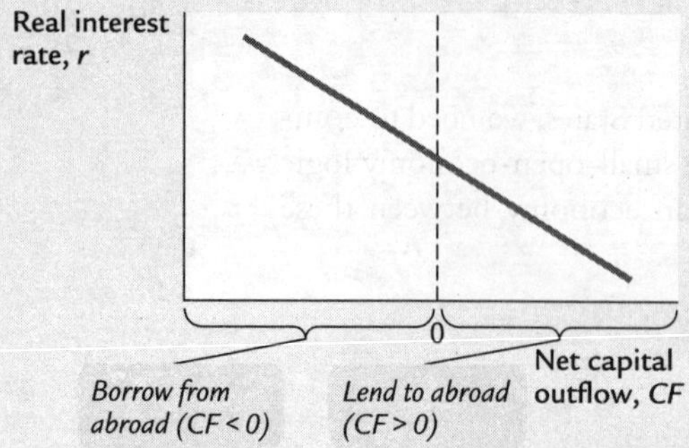

How the Net Capital Outflow Depends on the Interest Rate A higher domestic interest rate discourages domestic investors from lending abroad and encourages foreign investors to lend here. Therefore, net capital outflow CF is negatively related to the interest rate.

This equation states that the net capital outflow is a function of the domestic interest rate. Figure 5-15 illustrates this relationship. Notice that *CF* can be either positive or negative, depending on whether the economy is a lender or borrower in world financial markets.

To see how this *CF* function relates to our previous models, consider Figure 5-16. This figure shows two special cases: a vertical *CF* function and a horizontal *CF* function.

The closed economy is the special case shown in panel (a) of Figure 5-16. In the closed economy, there is no international borrowing or lending, and the interest rate adjusts to equilibrate domestic saving and investment. This means that $CF = 0$ at all interest rates. This situation would arise if investors here and

FIGURE 5-16

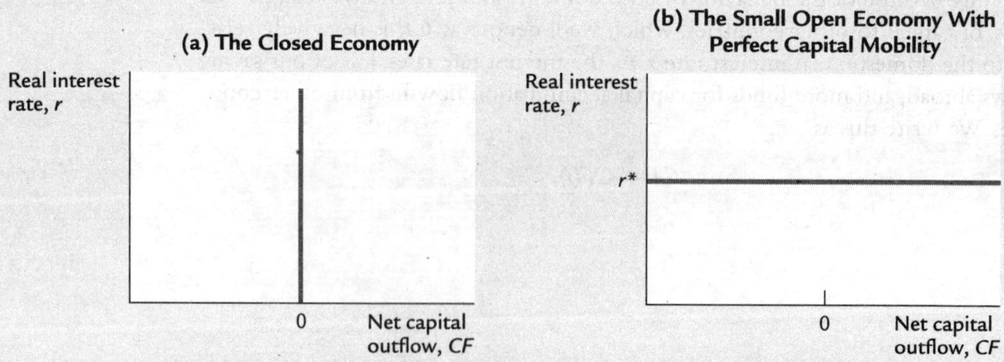

Two Special Cases In the closed economy, shown in panel (a), the net capital outflow is zero for all interest rates. In the small open economy with perfect capital mobility, shown in panel (b), the net capital outflow is perfectly elastic at the world interest rate r^*.

abroad were unwilling to hold foreign assets, regardless of the return. It might also arise if the government prohibited its citizens from transacting in foreign financial markets, as some governments do.

The small open economy with perfect capital mobility is the special case shown in panel (b) of Figure 5-16. In this case, capital flows freely into and out of the country at the fixed world interest rate r^*. This situation would arise if investors here and abroad bought whatever asset yielded the highest return, and if this economy were too small to affect the world interest rate. The economy's interest rate would be fixed at the interest rate prevailing in world financial markets.

Why isn't the interest rate of a large open economy such as the United States fixed by the world interest rate? There are two reasons. The first is that the United States is large enough to influence world financial markets. The more the United States lends abroad, the greater is the supply of loans in the world economy, and the lower interest rates become around the world. The more the United States borrows from abroad (that is, the more negative CF becomes), the higher are world interest rates. We use the label "large open economy" because this model applies to an economy large enough to affect world interest rates.

There is, however, a second reason the interest rate in an economy may not be fixed by the world interest rate: capital may not be perfectly mobile. That is, investors here and abroad may prefer to hold their wealth in domestic rather than foreign assets. Such a preference for domestic assets could arise because of imperfect information about foreign assets or because of government impediments to international borrowing and lending. In either case, funds for capital accumulation will not flow freely to equalize interest rates in all countries. Instead, the net capital outflow will depend on domestic interest rates relative to foreign interest rates. U.S. investors will lend abroad only if U.S. interest rates are comparatively low, and foreign investors will lend in the United States only if U.S. interest rates are comparatively high. The large-open-economy model, therefore, may apply even to a small economy if capital does not flow freely into and out of the economy.

Hence, either because the large open economy affects world interest rates, or because capital is imperfectly mobile, or perhaps for both reasons, the CF function slopes downward. Except for this new downward-sloping CF function, the model of the large open economy resembles the model of the small open economy. We put all the pieces together in the next section.

The Model

To understand how the large open economy works, we need to consider two key markets: the market for loanable funds (where the interest rate is determined) and the market for foreign exchange (where the exchange rate is determined). The interest rate and the exchange rate are two prices that guide the allocation of resources.

The Market for Loanable Funds An open economy's saving S is used in two ways: to finance domestic investment I and to finance the net capital outflow CF. We can write

$$S = I + CF.$$

FIGURE 5-17

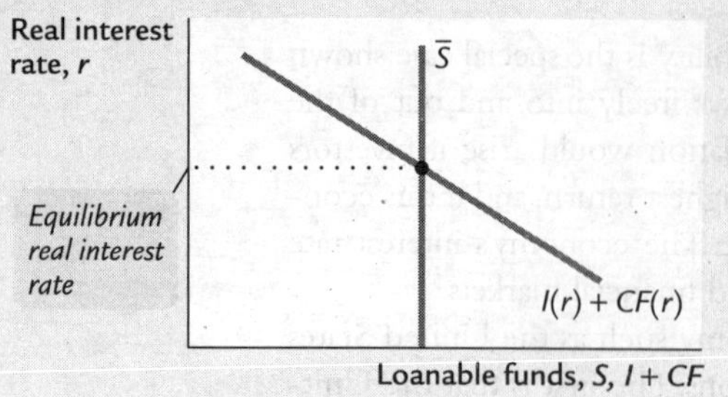

The Market for Loanable Funds in the Large Open Economy At the equilibrium interest rate, the supply of loanable funds from saving S balances the demand for loanable funds from domestic investment I and capital investments abroad CF.

Consider how these three variables are determined. National saving is fixed by the level of output, fiscal policy, and the consumption function. Investment and net capital outflow both depend on the domestic real interest rate. We can write

$$\bar{S} = I(r) + CF(r).$$

Figure 5-17 shows the market for loanable funds. The supply of loanable funds is national saving. The demand for loanable funds is the sum of the demand for domestic investment and the demand for foreign investment (net capital outflow). The interest rate adjusts to equilibrate supply and demand.

The Market for Foreign Exchange Next, consider the relationship between the net capital outflow and the trade balance. The national income accounts identity tells us

$$NX = S - I.$$

Because NX is a function of the real exchange rate, and because $CF = S - I$, we can write

$$NX(\epsilon) = CF.$$

Figure 5-18 shows the equilibrium in the market for foreign exchange. Once again, the real exchange rate is the price that equilibrates the trade balance and the net capital outflow.

FIGURE 5-18

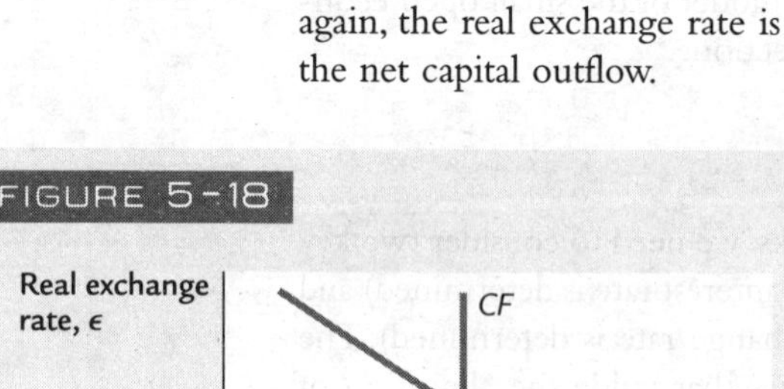

The Market for Foreign Currency Exchange in the Large Open Economy At the equilibrium exchange rate, the supply of dollars from the net capital outflow, CF, balances the demand for dollars from our net exports of goods and services, NX.

The last variable we should consider is the nominal exchange rate. As before, the nominal exchange rate is the real exchange rate times the ratio of the price levels:

$$e = \epsilon \times (P^*/P).$$

The real exchange rate is determined as in Figure 5-18, and the price levels are determined by monetary policies here and abroad, as we discussed in Chapter 4. Forces that move the real exchange rate or the price levels also move the nominal exchange rate.

Policies in the Large Open Economy

We can now consider how economic policies influence the large open economy. Figure 5-19 shows the three diagrams we need for the analysis. Panel (a) shows the equilibrium in the market for loanable funds; panel (b) shows the relationship between the equilibrium interest rate and the net capital outflow; and panel (c) shows the equilibrium in the market for foreign exchange.

Fiscal Policy at Home Consider the effects of expansionary fiscal policy—an increase in government purchases or a decrease in taxes. Figure 5-20 shows what happens. The policy reduces national saving S, thereby reducing the supply of

FIGURE 5-19

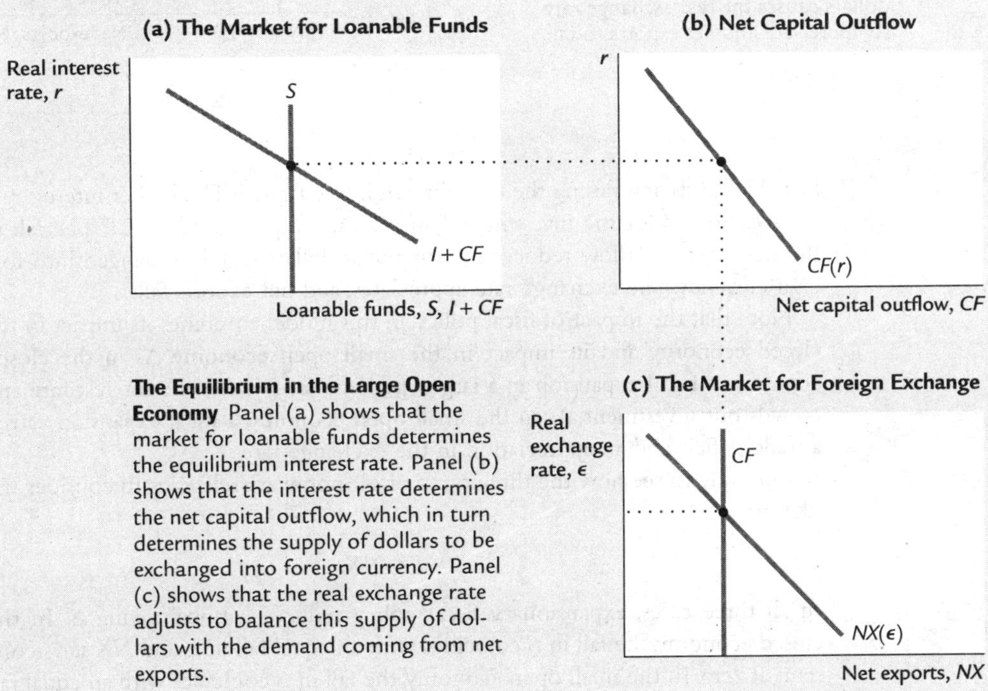

The Equilibrium in the Large Open Economy Panel (a) shows that the market for loanable funds determines the equilibrium interest rate. Panel (b) shows that the interest rate determines the net capital outflow, which in turn determines the supply of dollars to be exchanged into foreign currency. Panel (c) shows that the real exchange rate adjusts to balance this supply of dollars with the demand coming from net exports.

FIGURE 5-20

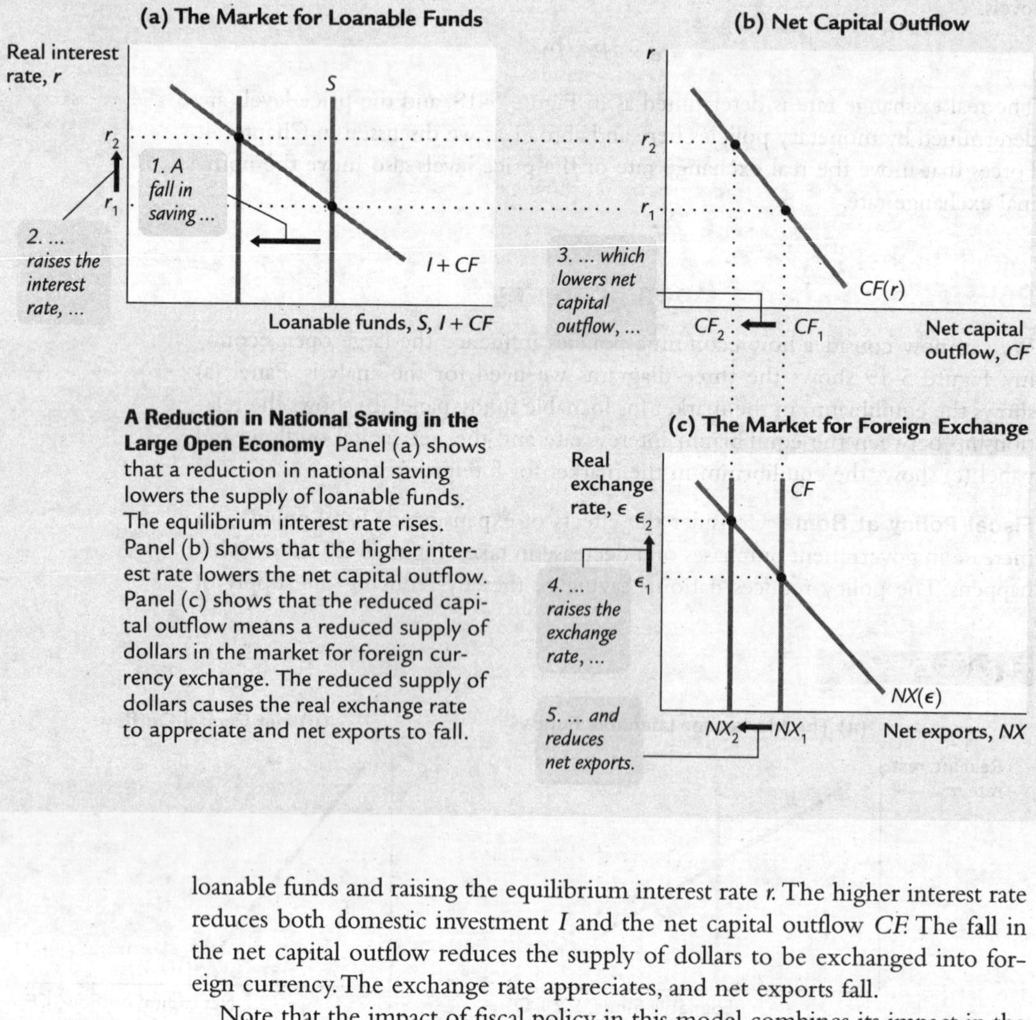

A Reduction in National Saving in the Large Open Economy Panel (a) shows that a reduction in national saving lowers the supply of loanable funds. The equilibrium interest rate rises. Panel (b) shows that the higher interest rate lowers the net capital outflow. Panel (c) shows that the reduced capital outflow means a reduced supply of dollars in the market for foreign currency exchange. The reduced supply of dollars causes the real exchange rate to appreciate and net exports to fall.

loanable funds and raising the equilibrium interest rate *r*. The higher interest rate reduces both domestic investment *I* and the net capital outflow *CF*. The fall in the net capital outflow reduces the supply of dollars to be exchanged into foreign currency. The exchange rate appreciates, and net exports fall.

Note that the impact of fiscal policy in this model combines its impact in the closed economy and its impact in the small open economy. As in the closed economy, a fiscal expansion in a large open economy raises the interest rate and crowds out investment. As in the small open economy, a fiscal expansion causes a trade deficit and an appreciation in the exchange rate.

One way to see how the three types of economy are related is to consider the identity

$$S = I + NX.$$

In all three cases, expansionary fiscal policy reduces national saving *S*. In the closed economy, the fall in *S* coincides with an equal fall in *I*, and *NX* stays constant at zero. In the small open economy, the fall in *S* coincides with an equal fall in *NX*, and *I* remains constant at the level fixed by the world interest rate. The large open economy is the intermediate case: both I and NX fall, each by less than the fall in S.

Shifts in Investment Demand Suppose that the investment demand schedule shifts outward, perhaps because Congress passes an investment tax credit. Figure 5-21 shows the effect. The demand for loanable funds rises, raising the equilibrium interest rate. The higher interest rate reduces the net capital outflow: Americans make fewer loans abroad, and foreigners make more loans to Americans. The fall in the net capital outflow reduces the supply of dollars in the market for foreign exchange. The exchange rate appreciates, and net exports fall.

FIGURE 5-21

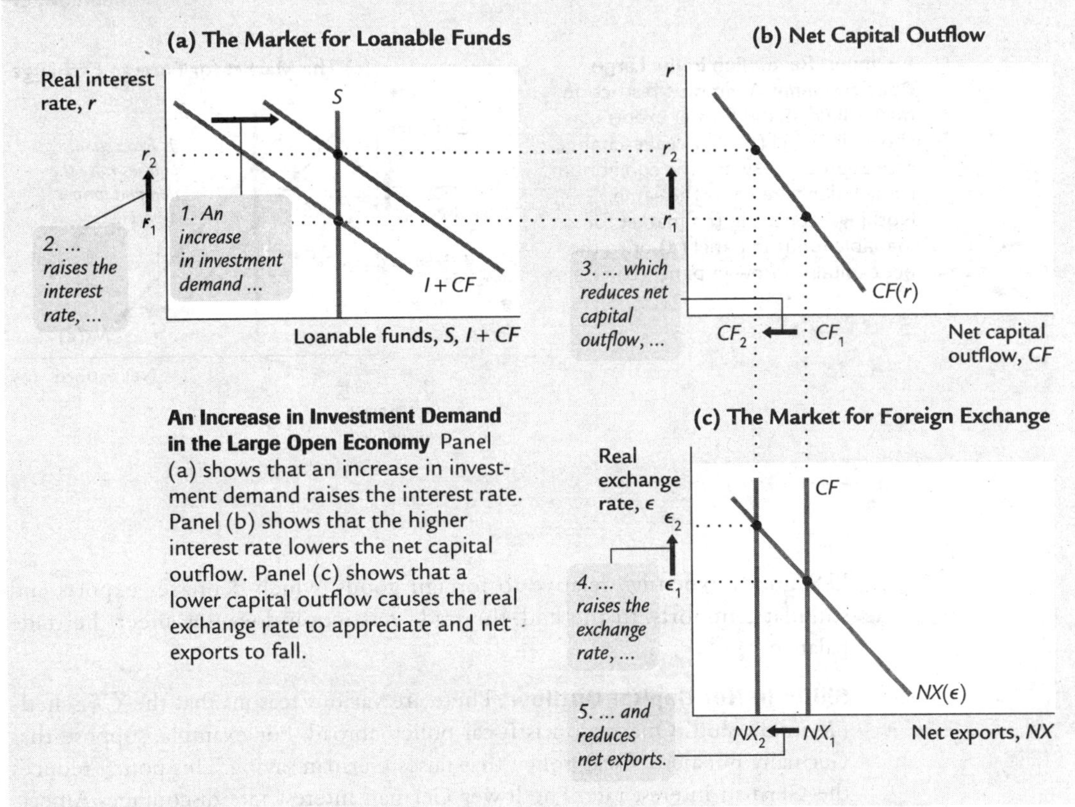

An Increase in Investment Demand in the Large Open Economy Panel (a) shows that an increase in investment demand raises the interest rate. Panel (b) shows that the higher interest rate lowers the net capital outflow. Panel (c) shows that a lower capital outflow causes the real exchange rate to appreciate and net exports to fall.

Trade Policies Figure 5-22 shows the effect of a trade restriction, such as an import quota. The reduced demand for imports shifts the net exports schedule outward in panel (c). Because nothing has changed in the market for loanable funds, the interest rate remains the same, which in turn implies that the net capital outflow remains the same. The shift in the net exports schedule causes the exchange rate to appreciate. The rise in the exchange rate makes

FIGURE 5-22

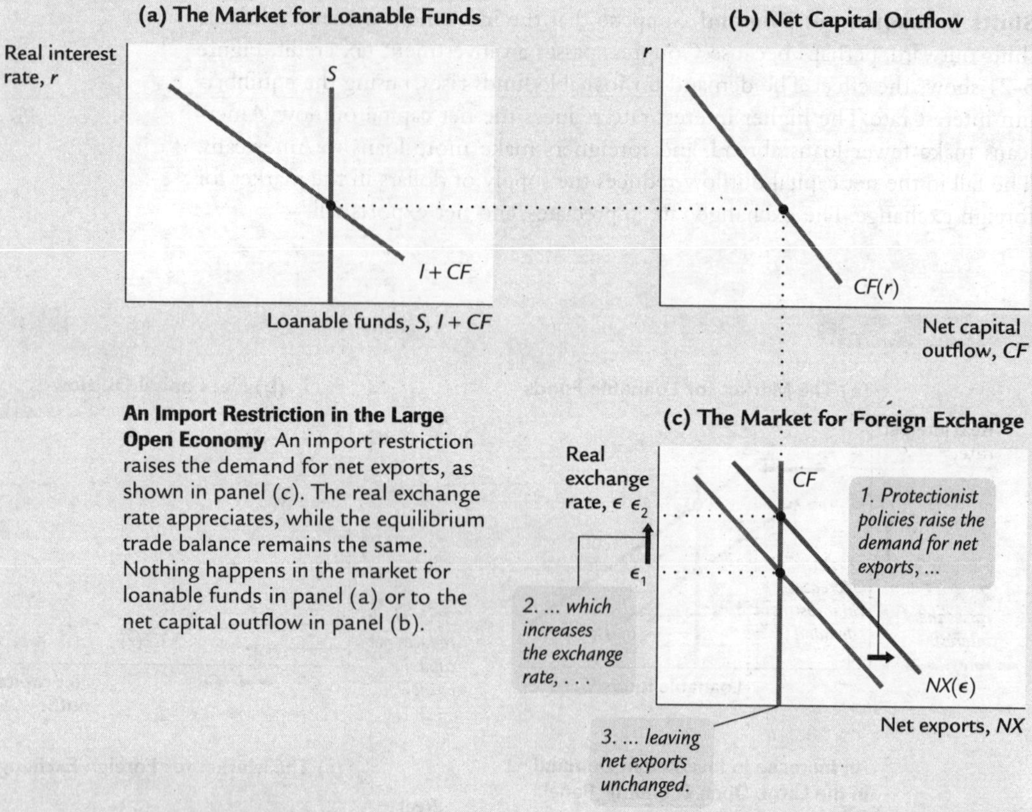

An Import Restriction in the Large Open Economy An import restriction raises the demand for net exports, as shown in panel (c). The real exchange rate appreciates, while the equilibrium trade balance remains the same. Nothing happens in the market for loanable funds in panel (a) or to the net capital outflow in panel (b).

U.S. goods expensive relative to foreign goods, which depresses exports and stimulates imports. In the end, the trade restriction does not affect the trade balance.

Shifts in Net Capital Outflow There are various reasons that the *CF* schedule might shift. One reason is fiscal policy abroad. For example, suppose that Germany pursues a fiscal policy that raises German saving. This policy reduces the German interest rate. The lower German interest rate discourages American investors from lending in Germany and encourages German investors to lend in the United States. For any given U.S. interest rate, the U.S. net capital outflow falls.

Another reason the *CF* schedule might shift is political instability abroad. Suppose that a war or revolution breaks out in another country. Investors around the world will try to withdraw their assets from that country and seek a "safe haven" in a stable country such as the United States. The result is a reduction in the U.S. net capital outflow.

FIGURE 5-23

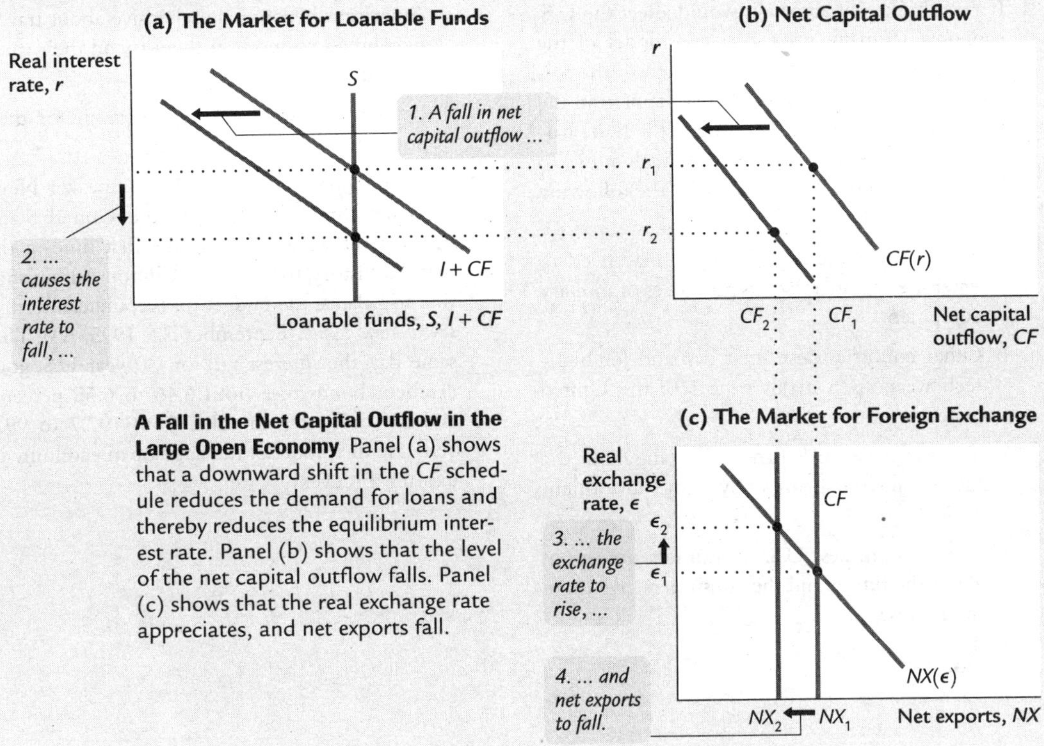

A Fall in the Net Capital Outflow in the Large Open Economy Panel (a) shows that a downward shift in the *CF* schedule reduces the demand for loans and thereby reduces the equilibrium interest rate. Panel (b) shows that the level of the net capital outflow falls. Panel (c) shows that the real exchange rate appreciates, and net exports fall.

Figure 5-23 shows the impact of a leftward shift in the *CF* schedule. The reduced demand for loanable funds lowers the equilibrium interest rate. The lower interest rate tends to raise net capital outflow, but because this only partly mitigates the shift in the *CF* schedule, *CF* still falls. The reduced level of net capital outflow reduces the supply of dollars in the market for foreign exchange. The exchange rate appreciates, and net exports fall.

Conclusion

How different are large and small open economies? Certainly, policies affect the interest rate in a large open economy, unlike in a small open economy. But, in other ways, the two models yield similar conclusions. In both large and small open economies, policies that raise saving or lower investment lead to trade surpluses. Similarly, policies that lower saving or raise investment lead to trade deficits. In both economies, protectionist trade policies cause the exchange rate to appreciate and do not influence the trade balance. Because the results are so similar, for most questions one can use the simpler model of the small open economy, even if the economy being examined is not really small.

MORE PROBLEMS AND APPLICATIONS

1. If a war broke out abroad, it would affect the U.S. economy in many ways. Use the model of the large open economy to examine each of the following effects of such a war. What happens in the United States to saving, investment, the trade balance, the interest rate, and the exchange rate? (To keep things simple, consider each of the following effects separately.)
   a. The U.S. government, fearing it may need to enter the war, increases its purchases of military equipment.
   b. Other countries raise their demand for high-tech weapons, a major export of the United States.
   c. The war makes U.S. firms uncertain about the future, and the firms delay some investment projects.
   d. The war makes U.S. consumers uncertain about the future, and the consumers save more in response.
   e. Americans become apprehensive about traveling abroad, so more of them spend their vacations in the United States.
   f. Foreign investors seek a safe haven for their portfolios in the United States.

2. On September 21, 1995, "House Speaker Newt Gingrich threatened to send the United States into default on its debt for the first time in the nation's history, to force the Clinton Administration to balance the budget on Republican terms" (*New York Times,* September 22, 1995, A1). That same day, the interest rate on 30-year U.S. government bonds rose from 6.46 to 6.55 percent, and the dollar fell in value from 102.7 to 99.0 yen. Use the model of the large open economy to explain this event.

CHAPTER

6

Unemployment

A man willing to work, and unable to find work, is perhaps the saddest sight that fortune's inequality exhibits under the sun.

— *Thomas Carlyle*

Unemployment is the macroeconomic problem that affects people most directly and severely. For most people, the loss of a job means a reduced living standard and psychological distress. It is no surprise that unemployment is a frequent topic of political debate and that politicians often claim that their proposed policies would help create jobs.

Economists study unemployment to identify its causes and to help improve the public policies that affect the unemployed. Some of these policies, such as job-training programs, help people find employment. Others, such as unemployment insurance, alleviate some of the hardships that the unemployed face. Still other policies affect the prevalence of unemployment inadvertently. Laws mandating a high minimum wage, for instance, are widely thought to raise unemployment among the least skilled and experienced members of the labor force.

Our discussions of the labor market so far have ignored unemployment. In particular, the model of national income in Chapter 3 was built with the assumption that the economy was always at full employment. In reality, of course, not everyone in the labor force has a job all the time: all free-market economies experience some unemployment.

Figure 6-1 shows the rate of unemployment—the percentage of the labor force unemployed—in the United States since 1952. Although the rate of unemployment fluctuates from year to year, it never gets even close to zero. The average is between 5 and 6 percent, meaning that about 1 out of every 18 people wanting a job does not have one.

In this chapter we begin our study of unemployment by discussing why there is always some unemployment and what determines its level. We do not study what determines the year-to-year fluctuations in the rate of unemployment until Part Four of this book, which examines short-run economic fluctuations. Here we examine the determinants of the **natural rate of unemployment**—the average rate of unemployment around which the economy fluctuates. The natural rate is

FIGURE 6-1

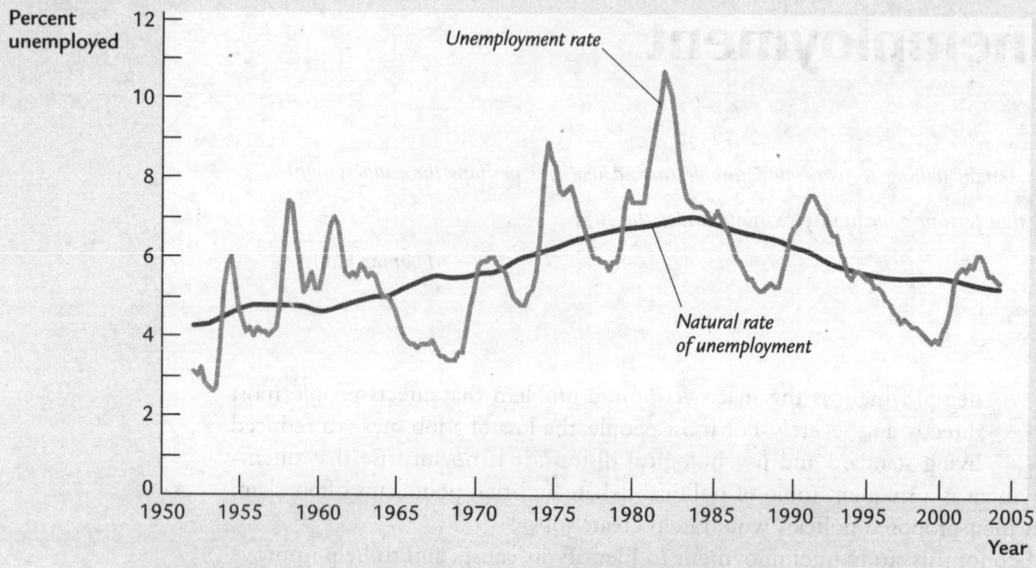

The Unemployment Rate and the Natural Rate of Unemployment in the United States There is always some unemployment. The natural rate of unemployment is the average level around which the unemployment rate fluctuates. (The natural rate of unemployment for any particular quarter is estimated here by averaging all the unemployment rates from ten years earlier to ten years later. Future unemployment rates are set at 5.5 percent.)

Source: Bureau of Labor Statistics.

the rate of unemployment toward which the economy gravitates in the long run, given all the labor-market imperfections that impede workers from instantly finding jobs.

6-1 Job Loss, Job Finding, and the Natural Rate of Unemployment

Every day some workers lose or quit their jobs, and some unemployed workers are hired. This perpetual ebb and flow determines the fraction of the labor force that is unemployed. In this section we develop a model of labor-force dynamics that shows what determines the natural rate of unemployment.[1]

We start with some notation. Let L denote the labor force, E the number of employed workers, and U the number of unemployed workers. Because every

[1] Robert E. Hall, "A Theory of the Natural Rate of Unemployment and the Duration of Unemployment," *Journal of Monetary Economics* 5 (April 1979): 153–169.

worker is either employed or unemployed, the labor force is the sum of the employed and the unemployed:

$$L = E + U.$$

In this notation, the rate of unemployment is U/L.

To see what factors determine the unemployment rate, we assume that the labor force L is fixed and focus on the transition of individuals in the labor force between employment E and unemployment U. This is illustrated in Figure 6-2. Let s denote the *rate of job separation,* the fraction of employed individuals who lose their job each month. Let f denote the *rate of job finding,* the fraction of unemployed individuals who find a job each month. Together, the rate of job separation s and the rate of job finding f determine the rate of unemployment.

If the unemployment rate is neither rising nor falling—that is, if the labor market is in a steady state—then the number of people finding jobs must equal the number of people losing jobs. The number of people finding jobs is fU and the number of people losing jobs is sE, so we can write the steady-state condition as

$$fU = sE.$$

We can use this equation to find the steady-state unemployment rate. From our definition of the labor force, we know that $E = L - U$; that is, the number of employed equals the labor force minus the number of unemployed. If we substitute $(L - U)$ for E in the steady-state condition, we find

$$fU = s(L - U).$$

FIGURE 6-2

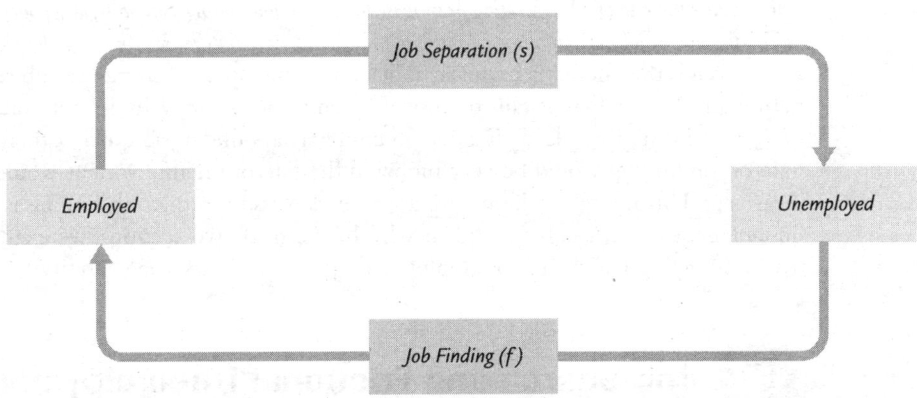

The Transitions Between Employment and Unemployment In every period, a fraction s of the employed lose their jobs, and a fraction f of the unemployed find jobs. The rates of job separation and job finding determine the rate of unemployment.

To get closer to solving for the unemployment rate, divide both sides of this equation by L to obtain

$$f\frac{U}{L} = s\left(1 - \frac{U}{L}\right).$$

Now we can solve for U/L to find

$$\frac{U}{L} = \frac{s}{s + f}.$$

This can also be written as

$$\frac{U}{L} = \frac{1}{1 + f/s}.$$

This equation shows that the steady-state rate of unemployment U/L depends on the rates of job separation s and job finding f. The higher the rate of job separation, the higher the unemployment rate. The higher the rate of job finding, the lower the unemployment rate.

Here's a numerical example. Suppose that 1 percent of the employed lose their jobs each month ($s = 0.01$). This means that on average jobs last 100 months, or about 8 years. Suppose further that 20 percent of the unemployed find a job each month ($f = 0.20$), so that spells of unemployment last 5 months on average. Then the steady-state rate of unemployment is

$$\frac{U}{L} = \frac{0.01}{0.01 + 0.20}$$

$$= 0.0476.$$

The rate of unemployment in this example is about 5 percent.

This simple model of the natural rate of unemployment has an important implication for public policy. *Any policy aimed at lowering the natural rate of unemployment must either reduce the rate of job separation or increase the rate of job finding. Similarly, any policy that affects the rate of job separation or job finding also changes the natural rate of unemployment.*

Although this model is useful in relating the unemployment rate to job separation and job finding, it fails to answer a central question: Why is there unemployment in the first place? If a person could always find a job quickly, then the rate of job finding would be very high and the rate of unemployment would be near zero. This model of the unemployment rate assumes that job finding is not instantaneous, but it fails to explain why. In the next two sections, we examine two underlying reasons for unemployment: job search and wage rigidity.

6-2 Job Search and Frictional Unemployment

One reason for unemployment is that it takes time to match workers and jobs. The equilibrium model of the aggregate labor market discussed in Chapter 3 assumes that all workers and all jobs are identical, and therefore that all workers are equally well suited for all jobs. If this were true and the labor market were in equilibrium, then a job loss would not cause unemployment: a laid-off worker would immediately find a new job at the market wage.

In fact, workers have different preferences and abilities, and jobs have different attributes. Furthermore, the flow of information about job candidates and job vacancies is imperfect, and the geographic mobility of workers is not instantaneous. For all these reasons, searching for an appropriate job takes time and effort, and this tends to reduce the rate of job finding. Indeed, because different jobs require different skills and pay different wages, unemployed workers may not accept the first job offer they receive. The unemployment caused by the time it takes workers to search for a job is called **frictional unemployment**.

Some frictional unemployment is inevitable in a changing economy. For many reasons, the types of goods that firms and households demand vary over time. As the demand for goods shifts, so does the demand for the labor that produces those goods. The invention of the personal computer, for example, reduced the demand for typewriters and, as a result, for labor by typewriter manufacturers. At the same time, it increased the demand for labor in the electronics industry. Similarly, because different regions produce different goods, the demand for labor may be rising in one part of the country and falling in another. An increase in the price of oil may cause the demand for labor to rise in oil-producing states such as Texas, but because expensive oil makes driving less attractive, it decreases the demand for labor in auto-producing states such as Michigan. Economists call a change in the composition of demand among industries or regions a **sectoral shift**. Because sectoral shifts are always occurring, and because it takes time for workers to change sectors, there is always frictional unemployment.

Sectoral shifts are not the only cause of job separation and frictional unemployment. In addition, workers find themselves unexpectedly out of work when their firms fail, when their job performance is deemed unacceptable, or when their particular skills are no longer needed. Workers also may quit their jobs to change careers or to move to different parts of the country. Regardless of the cause of the job separation, it will take time and effort for the worker to find a new job. As long as the supply and demand for labor among firms is changing, frictional unemployment is unavoidable.

Public Policy and Frictional Unemployment

Many public policies seek to decrease the natural rate of unemployment by reducing frictional unemployment. Government employment agencies disseminate information about job vacancies in order to match jobs and workers more efficiently. Publicly funded retraining programs are designed to ease the transition of workers from declining to growing industries. If these programs succeed at increasing the rate of job finding, they decrease the natural rate of unemployment.

Other government programs inadvertently increase the amount of frictional unemployment. One of these is **unemployment insurance**. Under this program, unemployed workers can collect a fraction of their wages for a certain period after losing their jobs. Although the precise terms of the program differ from year to year and from state to state, a typical worker covered by unemployment insurance in the United States receives 50 percent of his or her former wages for 26 weeks. In many European countries, unemployment-insurance programs are significantly more generous.

By softening the economic hardship of unemployment, unemployment insurance increases the amount of frictional unemployment and raises the natural rate. The unemployed who receive unemployment-insurance benefits are less pressed to search for new employment and are more likely to turn down unattractive job offers. Both of these changes in behavior reduce the rate of job finding. In addition, because workers know that their incomes are partially protected by unemployment insurance, they are less likely to seek jobs with stable employment prospects and are less likely to bargain for guarantees of job security. These behavioral changes raise the rate of job separation.

That unemployment insurance raises the natural rate of unemployment does not necessarily imply that the policy is ill-advised. The program has the benefit of reducing workers' uncertainty about their incomes. Moreover, inducing workers to reject unattractive job offers may lead to a better matching between workers and jobs. Evaluating the costs and benefits of different systems of unemployment insurance is a difficult task that continues to be a topic of much research.

Economists who study unemployment insurance often propose reforms that would reduce the amount of unemployment. One common proposal is to require a firm that lays off a worker to bear the full cost of that worker's unemployment benefits. Such a system is called *100 percent experience rated,* because the rate that each firm pays into the unemployment-insurance system fully reflects the unemployment experience of its own workers. Most current programs are *partially experience rated*. Under this system, when a firm lays off a worker, it is charged for only part of the worker's unemployment benefits; the remainder comes from the program's general revenue. Because a firm pays only a fraction of the cost of the unemployment it causes, it has an incentive to lay off workers when its demand for labor is temporarily low. By reducing that incentive, the proposed reform may reduce the prevalence of temporary layoffs.

CASE STUDY

Unemployment Insurance and the Rate of Job Finding

Many studies have examined the effect of unemployment insurance on job search. The most persuasive studies use data on the experiences of unemployed individuals, rather than economy-wide rates of unemployment. Individual data often yield sharp results that are open to few alternative explanations.

One study followed the experience of individual workers as they used up their eligibility for unemployment-insurance benefits. It found that when unemployed workers become ineligible for benefits, they are more likely to find jobs. In particular, the probability of a person finding a job more than doubles when his or her benefits run out. One possible explanation is that an absence of benefits increases the search effort of unemployed workers. Another possibility is that workers without benefits are more likely to accept job offers that would otherwise be declined because of low wages or poor working conditions.[2]

Additional evidence on how economic incentives affect job search comes from an experiment that the state of Illinois ran in 1985. Randomly selected new claimants for unemployment insurance were each offered a $500 bonus if they found employment within 11 weeks. The subsequent experience of this group was compared to that of a control group not offered the incentive. The average duration of unemployment for the group offered the $500 bonus was 17.0 weeks, compared to 18.3 weeks for the control group. Thus, the bonus reduced the average spell of unemployment by 7 percent, suggesting that more effort was devoted to job search. This experiment shows clearly that the incentives provided by the unemployment-insurance system affect the rate of job finding.[3]

6-3 Real-Wage Rigidity and Structural Unemployment

A second reason for unemployment is **wage rigidity**—the failure of wages to adjust to a level at which labor supply equals labor demand. In the equilibrium model of the labor market, as outlined in Chapter 3, the real wage adjusts to equilibrate labor supply and labor demand. Yet wages are not always flexible. Sometimes the real wage is stuck above the market-clearing level.

Figure 6-3 shows why wage rigidity leads to unemployment. When the real wage is above the level that equilibrates supply and demand, the quantity of labor supplied exceeds the quantity demanded. Firms must in some way ration the scarce jobs among workers. Real-wage rigidity reduces the rate of job finding and raises the level of unemployment.

The unemployment resulting from wage rigidity and job rationing is sometimes called **structural unemployment**. Workers are unemployed not because they are actively searching for the jobs that best suit their individual skills but because there is a fundamental mismatch between the number of people who want to work and the number of jobs that are available. At the going wage, the quantity of labor supplied exceeds the quantity of labor demanded, so many workers are simply waiting for jobs to open up.

To understand wage rigidity and structural unemployment, we must examine why the labor market does not clear. When the real wage exceeds the equilibrium level and the supply of workers exceeds the demand, we might expect firms to lower the wages they pay. Structural unemployment arises because firms fail

[2] Lawrence F. Katz and Bruce D. Meyer, "Unemployment Insurance, Recall Expectations, and Unemployment Outcomes," *Quarterly Journal of Economics* 105 (November 1990): 973–1002.

[3] Stephen A. Woodbury and Robert G. Spiegelman, "Bonuses to Workers and Employers to Reduce Unemployment: Randomized Trials in Illinois," *American Economic Review* 77 (September 1987): 513–530.

FIGURE 6-3

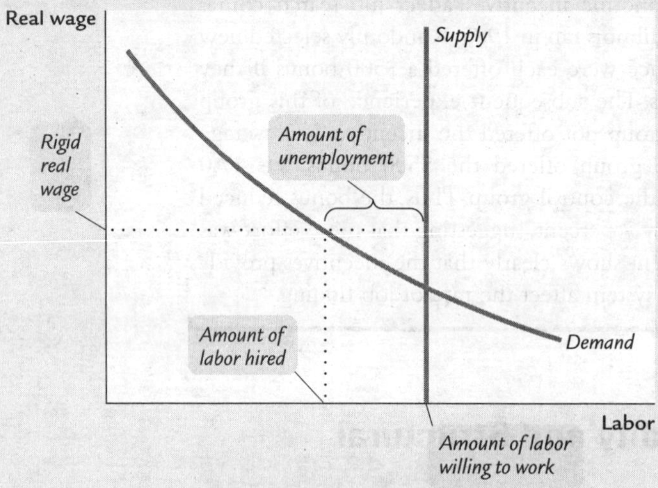

Real-Wage Rigidity Leads to Job Rationing If the real wage is stuck above the equilibrium level, then the supply of labor exceeds the demand. The result is unemployment.

to reduce wages despite an excess supply of labor. We now turn to three causes of this wage rigidity: minimum-wage laws, the monopoly power of unions, and efficiency wages.

Minimum-Wage Laws

The government causes wage rigidity when it prevents wages from falling to equilibrium levels. Minimum-wage laws set a legal minimum on the wages that firms pay their employees. Since the passage of the Fair Labor Standards Act of 1938, the U.S. federal government has enforced a minimum wage that usually has been between 30 and 50 percent of the average wage in manufacturing. For most workers, then, this minimum wage is not binding, because they earn well above the minimum. Yet for some workers, especially the unskilled and inexperienced, the minimum wage raises their wage above its equilibrium level and, therefore, reduces the quantity of their labor that firms demand.

Economists believe that the minimum wage has its greatest impact on teenage unemployment. The equilibrium wages of teenagers tend to be low for two reasons. First, because teenagers are among the least skilled and least experienced members of the labor force, they tend to have low marginal productivity. Second, teenagers often take some of their "compensation" in the form of on-the-job training rather than direct pay. An apprenticeship is a classic example of training offered in place of wages. For both these reasons, the wage at which the supply of teenage workers equals the demand is low. The minimum wage is therefore more often binding for teenagers than for others in the labor force.

Many economists have studied the impact of the minimum wage on teenage employment. These researchers compare the variation in the minimum wage over time with the variation in the number of teenagers with jobs. These studies find that a 10 percent increase in the minimum wage reduces teenage employment by 1 to 3 percent.[4]

The minimum wage is a perennial source of political debate. Advocates of a higher minimum wage view it as a means of raising the income of the working poor. Certainly, the minimum wage provides only a meager standard of living: in the United States, two adults working full time at minimum-wage jobs would just exceed the official poverty level for a family of four. Although minimum-wage advocates often admit that the policy causes unemployment for some workers, they argue that this cost is worth bearing to raise others out of poverty.

Opponents of a higher minimum wage claim that it is not the best way to help the working poor. They contend not only that the increased labor costs would raise unemployment but also that the minimum wage is poorly targeted. Many minimum-wage earners are teenagers from middle-class homes working for discretionary spending money, rather than heads of households working to support their families.

Many economists and policymakers believe that tax credits are a better way to increase the incomes of the working poor. The *earned income tax credit* is an amount that poor working families are allowed to subtract from the taxes they owe. For a family with very low income, the credit exceeds its taxes, and the family receives a payment from the government. Unlike the minimum wage, the earned income tax credit does not raise labor costs to firms and, therefore, does not reduce the quantity of labor that firms demand. It has the disadvantage, however, of reducing the government's tax revenue.

CASE STUDY

The Characteristics of Minimum-Wage Workers

Who earns the minimum wage? The question can be answered using the Current Population Survey—the labor market survey used to calculate the unemployment rate and many other statistics. In 2005, the Bureau of Labor Statistics released a report describing the workers who earned at or below the minimum wage in 2004, when the minimum was $5.15 per hour. Here is a summary:

- About 74 million American workers are paid hourly, representing 60 percent of all wage and salary workers. Of these workers, 520,000 report earning exactly $5.15 per hour, and another 1.5 million report earning

---

[4] Charles Brown, "Minimum Wage Laws: Are They Overrated?" *Journal of Economic Perspectives* 2 (Summer 1988): 133–146. Brown presents the mainstream view of the effects of minimum wages, but it should be noted that the magnitude of employment effects is controversial. For research suggesting negligible employment effects, see David Card and Alan Krueger, *Myth and Measurement: The New Economics of the Minimum Wage* (Princeton, NJ: Princeton University Press, 1995); and Lawrence Katz and Alan Krueger, "The Effects of the Minimum Wage on the Fast-Food Industry," *Industrial and Labor Relations Review* 46 (October 1992): 6–21. For research suggesting the opposite conclusion, see David Neumark and William Wascher, "Employment Effects of Minimum and Subminimum Wages: Panel Data on State Minimum Wage Laws," *Industrial and Labor Relations Review* 46 (October 1992): 55–81.

less. A reported wage below the minimum is possible because some workers are exempt from the statute (newspaper delivery workers, for example), because enforcement is imperfect, and because some workers round down to $5.00 when reporting their wages on surveys.

- Minimum-wage workers are more likely to be women than men. About 2 percent of men and 4 percent of women reported wages at or below the prevailing federal minimum.
- Minimum-wage workers tend to be young. About half of all hourly-paid workers earning $5.15 or less were under age 25, and about one-fourth were age 16–19. Among teenagers, about 9 percent earned $5.15 or less, compared with about 2 percent of workers age 25 and over.
- Minimum-wage workers tend to be less educated. Among hourly-paid workers age 16 and over, about 2 percent of those who had only a high-school diploma earned $5.15 or less, compared with about 1 percent for those who had obtained a college degree.
- Minimum-wage workers are more likely to be working part-time. Among part-time workers (those who usually work less than 35 hours per week), 7 percent were paid $5.15 or less, compared to 1 percent of full-time workers.
- The industry with the highest proportion of workers with reported hourly wages at or below $5.15 was leisure and hospitality (about 15 percent). About three-fifths of all workers paid at or below the minimum wage were employed in this industry, primarily in food services and drinking places. For many of these workers, tips supplement the hourly wages received.

These facts by themselves do not tell us whether the minimum wage is a good or bad policy, or whether it is too high or too low. But when evaluating any public policy, it is useful to keep in mind those individuals who are affected by it.[5]

Unions and Collective Bargaining

A second cause of wage rigidity is the monopoly power of unions. Table 6-1 shows the importance of unions in several major countries. In the United States, only 18 percent of workers have their wages set through collective bargaining. In most European countries, unions play a much larger role.

The wages of unionized workers are determined not by the equilibrium of supply and demand but by bargaining between union leaders and firm management. Often, the final agreement raises the wage above the equilibrium level and allows the firm to decide how many workers to employ. The result is a reduction

[5] The figures reported here are from the website of the Bureau of Labor Statistics. The link is http://www.bls.gov/cps/minwage2004.htm

TABLE 6-1

Percent of Workers Covered by Collective Bargaining

Country	Percent
United States	18%
Japan	23
Canada	38
United Kingdom	47
Switzerland	53
New Zealand	67
Spain	68
Netherlands	71
Norway	75
Portugal	79
Australia	80
Sweden	83
Belgium	90
Germany	90
France	92
Finland	95
Austria	98

Source: OECD Employment Outlook 2004, as reported in Alberto Alesina, Edward Glaeser, and Bruce Sacerdote, "Work and Leisure in the U.S. and Europe: Why So Different?" *NBER Macroeconomics Annual* 2005.

in the number of workers hired, a lower rate of job finding, and an increase in structural unemployment.

Unions can also influence the wages paid by firms whose workforces are not unionized because the threat of unionization can keep wages above the equilibrium level. Most firms dislike unions. Unions not only raise wages but also increase the bargaining power of labor on many other issues, such as hours of employment and working conditions. A firm may choose to pay its workers high wages to keep them happy and discourage them from forming a union.

The unemployment caused by unions and by the threat of unionization is an instance of conflict between different groups of workers—**insiders** and **outsiders**. Those workers already employed by a firm, the insiders, typically try to keep their firm's wages high. The unemployed, the outsiders, bear part of the cost of higher wages because at a lower wage they might be hired. These two groups inevitably have conflicting interests. The effect of any bargaining process on wages and employment depends crucially on the relative influence of each group.

The conflict between insiders and outsiders is resolved differently in different countries. In some countries, such as the United States, wage bargaining takes place at the level of the firm or plant. In other countries, such as Sweden, wage bargaining takes place at the national level—with the government often playing a key role. Despite a highly unionized labor force, Sweden has not experienced extraordinarily high unemployment throughout its history. One possible explanation is that the centralization of wage bargaining and the role of the government in the bargaining process give more influence to the outsiders, which keeps wages closer to the equilibrium level.

Efficiency Wages

Efficiency-wage theories propose a third cause of wage rigidity in addition to minimum-wage laws and unionization. These theories hold that high wages make workers more productive. The influence of wages on worker efficiency may explain the failure of firms to cut wages despite an excess supply of labor. Even though a wage reduction would lower a firm's wage bill, it would also—if these theories are correct—lower worker productivity and the firm's profits.

Economists have proposed various theories to explain how wages affect worker productivity. One efficiency-wage theory, which is applied mostly to poorer countries, holds that wages influence nutrition. Better-paid workers can afford a more nutritious diet, and healthier workers are more productive. A firm may decide to pay a wage above the equilibrium level to maintain a healthy work force. Obviously, this consideration is not important for employers in wealthier countries, such as the United States and most of Europe, because the equilibrium wage is well above the level necessary to maintain good health.

A second efficiency-wage theory, which is more relevant for developed countries, holds that high wages reduce labor turnover. Workers quit jobs for many reasons—to accept better positions at other firms, to change careers, or to move to other parts of the country. The more a firm pays its workers, the greater is their incentive to stay with the firm. By paying a high wage, a firm reduces the frequency at which its workers quit, thereby decreasing the time and money spent hiring and training new workers.

A third efficiency-wage theory holds that the average quality of a firm's work force depends on the wage it pays its employees. If a firm reduces its wage, the best employees may take jobs elsewhere, leaving the firm with inferior employees who have fewer alternative opportunities. Economists recognize this unfavorable sorting as an example of *adverse selection*—the tendency of people with more information (in this case, the workers, who know their own outside opportunities) to self-select in a way that disadvantages people with less information (the firm). By paying a wage above the equilibrium level, the firm may reduce adverse selection, improve the average quality of its work force, and thereby increase productivity.

A fourth efficiency-wage theory holds that a high wage improves worker effort. This theory posits that firms cannot perfectly monitor their employees' work effort, and that employees must themselves decide how hard to work. Workers can choose to work hard, or they can choose to shirk and risk getting caught and fired. Economists recognize this possibility as an example of *moral hazard*—the tendency of people to behave inappropriately when their behavior is imperfectly monitored. The firm can reduce the problem of moral hazard by paying a high wage. The higher the wage, the greater the cost to the worker of getting fired. By paying a higher wage, a firm induces more of its employees not to shirk and thus increases their productivity.

Although these four efficiency-wage theories differ in detail, they share a common theme: because a firm operates more efficiently if it pays its workers a high wage, the firm may find it profitable to keep wages above the level that balances supply and demand. The result of this higher-than-equilibrium wage is a lower rate of job finding and greater unemployment.[6]

CASE STUDY

Henry Ford's $5 Workday

In 1914 the Ford Motor Company started paying its workers $5 per day. The prevailing wage at the time was between $2 and $3 per day, so Ford's wage was well above the equilibrium level, Not surprisingly, long lines of job seekers waited outside the Ford plant gates hoping for a chance to earn this high wage.

What was Ford's motive? Henry Ford later wrote, "We wanted to pay these wages so that the business would be on a lasting foundation. We were building for the future. A low wage business is always insecure. . . . The payment of five dollars a day for an eight hour day was one of the finest cost cutting moves we ever made."

From the standpoint of traditional economic theory, Ford's explanation seems peculiar. He was suggesting that *high* wages imply *low* costs. But perhaps Ford had discovered efficiency-wage theory. Perhaps he was using the high wage to increase worker productivity.

Evidence suggests that paying such a high wage did benefit the company. According to an engineering report written at the time, "The Ford high wage does away with all the inertia and living force resistance. . . . The workingmen are absolutely docile, and it is safe to say that since the last day of 1913, every single day has seen major reductions in Ford shops' labor costs." Absenteeism fell by 75 percent, suggesting a large increase in worker effort. Alan Nevins, a historian who studied the early Ford Motor Company, wrote, "Ford and his associates freely declared on many occasions that the high wage policy had turned out to be good business. By this they meant that it had improved the discipline of the workers, given them a more loyal interest in the institution, and raised their personal efficiency."[7]

[6] For more extended discussions of efficiency wages, see Janet Yellen, "Efficiency Wage Models of Unemployment," *American Economic Review Papers and Proceedings* (May 1984): 200–205; and Lawrence Katz, "Efficiency Wages: A Partial Evaluation," *NBER Macroeconomics Annual* (1986): 235–276.

[7] Jeremy I. Bulow and Lawrence H. Summers, "A Theory of Dual Labor Markets With Application to Industrial Policy, Discrimination, and Keynesian Unemployment," *Journal of Labor Economics* 4 (July 1986): 376–414; Daniel M. G. Raff and Lawrence H. Summers, "Did Henry Ford Pay Efficiency Wages?" *Journal of Labor Economics* 5 (October 1987, Part 2): S57–S86.

6-4 Labor Market Experience: The United States

So far we have developed the theory behind the natural rate of unemployment. We began by showing that the economy's steady-state unemployment rate depends on the rates of job separation and job finding. Then we discussed two reasons why job finding is not instantaneous: the process of job search (which leads to frictional unemployment) and wage rigidity (which leads to structural unemployment). Wage rigidity, in turn, arises from minimum-wage laws, unionization, and efficiency wages.

With these theories as background, we now examine some additional facts about unemployment, focusing at first on the case of American labor markets. These facts will help us to evaluate our theories and assess public policies aimed at reducing unemployment.

The Duration of Unemployment

When a person becomes unemployed, is the spell of unemployment likely to be short or long? The answer to this question is important because it indicates the reasons for the unemployment and what policy response is appropriate. On the one hand, if most unemployment is short-term, one might argue that it is frictional and perhaps unavoidable. Unemployed workers may need some time to search for the job that is best suited to their skills and tastes. On the other hand, long-term unemployment cannot easily be attributed to the time it takes to match jobs and workers: we would not expect this matching process to take many months. Long-term unemployment is more likely to be structural unemployment, representing a mismatch between the number of jobs available and the number of people who want to work. Thus, data on the duration of unemployment can affect our view about the reasons for unemployment.

The answer to our question turns out to be subtle. The data show that most spells of unemployment are short but that most weeks of unemployment are attributable to the long-term unemployed. Consider the data for a typical year, 1974, during which the unemployment rate was 5.6 percent. In that year, 60 percent of the spells of unemployment ended within one month, yet 69 percent of the weeks of unemployment occurred in spells that lasted two or more months.[8]

To see how both these facts can be true, consider the following example. Suppose that 10 people are unemployed for part of a given year. Of these 10 people, 8 are unemployed for 1 month, and 2 are unemployed for 12 months, totaling 32 months of unemployment. In this example, most spells of unemployment are short: 8 of the 10 unemployment spells, or 80 percent, end in 1 month. Yet most months of unemployment are attributable to the long-term unemployed: 24 of the 32 months of unemployment, or 75 percent, are experienced by the 2 work-

[8] Kim B. Clark and Lawrence H. Summers, "Labor Market Dynamics and Unemployment: A Reconsideration," *Brookings Papers on Economic Activity* (1979:1): 13–72.

ers who are unemployed for 12 months. Depending on whether we look at spells of unemployment or months of unemployment, most unemployment can appear to be short-term or long-term.

This evidence on the duration of unemployment has an important implication for public policy. If the goal is to lower substantially the natural rate of unemployment, policies must aim at the long-term unemployed, because these individuals account for a large amount of unemployment. Yet policies must be carefully targeted, because the long-term unemployed constitute a small minority of those who become unemployed. Most people who become unemployed find work within a short time.

Variation in the Unemployment Rate Across Demographic Groups

The rate of unemployment varies substantially across different groups within the population. Table 6-2 presents the U.S. unemployment rates for different demographic groups in 2004, when the overall unemployment rate was 5.5 percent.

This table shows that younger workers have much higher unemployment rates than older ones. To explain this difference, recall our model of the natural rate of unemployment. The model isolates two possible causes for a high rate of unemployment: a low rate of job finding and a high rate of job separation. When economists study data on the transition of individuals between employment and unemployment, they find that those groups with high unemployment tend to have high rates of job separation. They find less variation across groups in the rate of job finding. For example, an employed white male is four times more likely to become unemployed if he is a teenager than if he is middle-aged; once unemployed, his rate of job finding is not closely related to his age.

These findings help explain the higher unemployment rates for younger workers. Younger workers have only recently entered the labor market, and they are often uncertain about their career plans. It may be best for them to try different types of jobs before making a long-term commitment to a specific occupation. If so, we should expect a higher rate of job separation and a higher rate of frictional unemployment for this group.

Another fact that stands out from Table 6-2 is that unemployment rates are much higher for blacks than for whites. This phenomenon is not well understood.

TABLE 6-2

Unemployment Rate by Demographic Group: 2004

Age	White Men	White Women	Black Men	Black Women
16-19	16.4	13.7	35.6	27.6
20 and over	4.4	4.2	9.9	8.9

Source: U.S. Department of Labor.

Data on transitions between employment and unemployment show that the higher unemployment rates for blacks, and especially for black teenagers, arise because of both higher rates of job separation and lower rates of job finding. Possible reasons for the lower rates of job finding include less access to informal job-finding networks and discrimination by employers.

Trends in Unemployment

Over the past half century, the natural rate of unemployment in the United States has not been stable. If you look back at Figure 6-1, you will see that unemployment averaged below 5 percent in the 1950s and 1960s, rose to over 6 percent in the 1970s and 1980s, and then drifted back below 5 percent in the 1990s. Although economists do not have a conclusive explanation for these changes, they have proposed several hypotheses.

Demographics One explanation stresses the changing composition of the U.S. labor force. After World War II, birthrates rose dramatically: the number of births rose from 2.9 million in 1945 to a peak of 4.3 million in 1957, before falling back to 3.1 million in 1973. This rise in births in the 1950s led to a rise in the number of young workers in the 1970s. Younger workers have higher unemployment rates, however, so when the baby-boom generation entered the labor force, they increased the average level of unemployment. Then as the baby-boom workers aged, the average age of the labor force increased, lowering the average unemployment rate in the 1990s.

This demographic change, however, cannot fully explain the trends in unemployment because similar trends are apparent for fixed demographic groups. For example, for men between the ages of 25 and 54, the average unemployment rate rose from 3.0 percent in the 1960s to 6.1 percent in the 1980s. Thus, although demographic changes may be part of the story of rising unemployment over this period, there must be other explanations of the long-term trend as well.

Sectoral Shifts A second explanation is based on changes in the prevalence of sectoral shifts. The greater the amount of reallocation among regions and industries, the greater the rate of job separation and the higher the level of frictional unemployment. One source of sectoral shifts during the 1970s and early 1980s was the great volatility in oil prices caused by OPEC, the international oil cartel. These large changes in oil prices may have required reallocating labor between more-energy-intensive and less-energy-intensive sectors. If so, oil-price volatility may have increased unemployment during this period. The increase in oil-price volatility in the early 2000s, however, did not cause a similar rise in the natural rate of unemployment, but this may be because the economy is now significantly less oil-intensive (as measured by oil consumption per unit of GDP) than it was three decades ago.

Productivity A third explanation for the trends in unemployment emphasizes the link between unemployment and productivity. As Chapter 8 discusses more fully, the 1970s experienced a slowdown in productivity growth, and the 1990s experienced a pickup in productivity growth. These productivity changes roughly coincide with changes in unemployment. Perhaps slowing productivity during the 1970s raised the natural rate of unemployment, and accelerating productivity during the 1990s lowered it.

Why such an effect would occur, however, is not obvious. In standard theories of the labor market, higher productivity means greater labor demand and thus higher real wages, but unemployment is unchanged. This prediction is consistent with the long-term data, which show consistent upward trends in productivity and real wages but no trend in unemployment. Yet suppose that workers are slow to catch on to news about productivity. When productivity changes, workers may only gradually alter the real wages they ask from their employers, making real wages sluggish in response to labor demand. An acceleration in productivity growth, such as that experienced during the 1990s, will increase labor demand and, with a sluggish real wage, reduce the amount of unemployment.

In the end, the trends in the unemployment rate remain a mystery. The proposed explanations are plausible, but none seems conclusive on its own. Perhaps there is no single answer. The upward drift in the unemployment rate in the 1970s and 1980s and the downward drift in the 1990s may be the result of several unrelated developments.[9]

Transitions Into and Out of the Labor Force

So far we have ignored an important aspect of labor-market dynamics: the movement of individuals into and out of the labor force. Our model of the natural rate of unemployment assumes that the labor force is fixed. In this case, the sole reason for unemployment is job separation, and the sole reason for leaving unemployment is job finding.

In fact, movements into and out of the labor force are important. About one-third of the unemployed have only recently entered the labor force. Some of these entrants are young workers still looking for their first jobs; others have worked before but had temporarily left the labor force. In addition, not all unemployment ends with job finding: almost half of all spells of unemployment end in the unemployed person's withdrawal from the labor market.

Individuals entering and leaving the labor force make unemployment statistics more difficult to interpret. On the one hand, some individuals calling themselves unemployed may not be seriously looking for jobs and perhaps should best be viewed as out of the labor force. Their "unemployment" may not represent a social problem. On the other hand, some individuals may want jobs but, after unsuccess-

[9] On the role of demographics, see Robert Shimer, "Why Is the U.S. Unemployment Rate So Much Lower?" *NBER Macroeconomics Annual* 13 (1998). On the role of sectoral shifts, see David M. Lilien, "Sectoral Shifts and Cyclical Unemployment," *Journal of Political Economy* 90 (August 1982): 777–793. On the role of productivity, see Laurence Ball and Robert Moffitt, "Productivity Growth and the Phillips Curve," in Alan B. Krueger and Robert M. Solow, eds., *The Roaring Nineties: Can Full Employment Be Sustained?* (New York: Russell Sage Foundation and Century Foundation Press, 2002).

ful searches, have given up looking. These **discouraged workers** are counted as being out of the labor force and do not show up in unemployment statistics. Even though their joblessness is unmeasured, it may nonetheless be a social problem.

Because of these and many other issues that complicate the interpretation of the unemployment data, the Bureau of Labor Statistics calculates several measures of labor underutilization. Table 6-3 gives the definitions and their values as of October 2005. The measures range from 1.7 to 8.7 percent, depending on the characteristics one uses to classify a worker as not fully employed.

TABLE 6-3

Alternative Measures of Labor Underutilization

Variable	Description	Rate
U-1	Persons unemployed 15 weeks or longer, as a percent of the civilian labor force (includes only very long-term unemployed)	1.7 %
U-2	Job losers and persons who have completed temporary jobs, as a percent of the civilian labor force (excludes job leavers)	2.3
U-3	Total unemployed, as a percentage of the civilian labor force (official unemployment rate)	5.0
U-4	Total unemployed, plus discouraged workers, as a percent of the civilian labor force plus discouraged workers	5.2
U-5	Total unemployed plus all marginally attached workers, as a percent of the civilian labor force plus all marginally attached workers	5.8
U-6	Total unemployed, plus all marginally attached workers, plus total employed part-time for economic reasons, as a percent of the civilian labor force plus all marginally attached workers	8.7

Note: Marginally attached workers are persons who currently are neither working nor looking for work but indicate that they want and are available for a job and have looked for work sometime in the recent past. *Discouraged workers,* a subset of the marginally attached, have given a job-market related reason for not currently looking for a job. *Persons employed part time for economic reasons* are those who want and are available for full-time work but have had to settle for a part-time schedule.
Source: U.S. Department of Labor. Data are for October 2005.

6-5 Labor Market Experience: Europe

Although our discussion has focused largely on the United States, many fascinating and sometimes puzzling phenomena become apparent when economists compare the experiences of Americans in the labor market with those of Europeans.

The Rise in European Unemployment

Figure 6-4 shows the rate of unemployment in the four largest European countries—France, Germany, Italy, and the United Kingdom. As you can see, the rate of unemployment in these countries has risen substantially. For France and Germany, the change is particularly pronounced: unemployment averaged about 2 percent in the 1960s and about 10 percent in recent years.

FIGURE 6-4

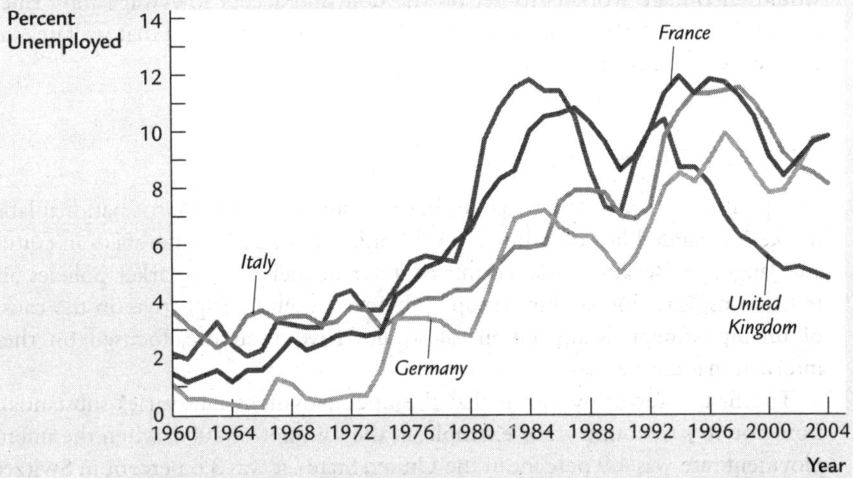

Unemployment in Europe This figure shows the unemployment rate in the four largest nations in Europe. The figure shows that the European unemployment rate has risen substantially over time, especially in France and Germany.

Source: Bureau of Labor Statistics.

What is the cause of rising European unemployment? No one knows for sure, but there is a leading theory. Many economists believe that the problem can be traced to the interaction between a long-standing policy and a recent shock. The long-standing policy is generous benefits for unemployed workers. The recent shock is a technologically driven fall in the demand for unskilled workers relative to skilled workers.

There is no question that most European countries have generous programs for those without jobs. These programs go by various names: social insurance, the welfare state, or simply "the dole." Many countries allow the unemployed to collect benefits for years, rather than for only a short period of time as in the United States. In some sense, those living on the dole are really out of the labor force: given the employment opportunities available, taking a job is less attractive than remaining without work. Yet these people are often counted as unemployed in government statistics.

There is also no question that the demand for unskilled workers has fallen relative to the demand for skilled workers. This change in demand is probably due to changes in technology: computers, for example, increase the demand for workers who can use them and reduce the demand for those who cannot. In the United States, this change in demand has been reflected in wages rather than unemployment: over the past two decades, the wages of unskilled workers have fallen substantially relative to the wages of skilled workers. In Europe, however, the welfare state provides unskilled workers with an alternative to working for low wages. As the wages of unskilled workers fall, more workers view the dole as their best available option. The result is higher unemployment.

This diagnosis of high European unemployment does not suggest an easy remedy. Reducing the magnitude of government benefits for the unemployed would encourage workers to get off the dole and accept low-wage jobs. But it would also exacerbate economic inequality—the very problem that welfare-state policies were designed to address.[10]

Unemployment Variation Within Europe

Europe is not a single labor market but is, instead, a collection of national labor markets, separated not only by national borders but also by differences in culture and language. Because these countries differ in their labor-market policies and institutions, variation within Europe provides a useful perspective on the causes of unemployment. Many empirical studies have, therefore, focused on these international differences.

The first noteworthy fact is that the unemployment rate varies substantially from country to country. For example, in the summer of 2005, when the unemployment rate was 4.9 percent in the United States, it was 3.6 percent in Switzerland and 11.6 percent in Germany. Although in recent years average unemployment has been higher in Europe than in the United States, about a third of Europeans have been living in nations with unemployment rates lower than the U.S. rate.

A second notable fact is that much of the variation in unemployment rates is attributable to the long-term unemployed. The unemployment rate can be separated into two pieces—the percentage of the labor force that has been unemployed for less than a year and the percentage of the labor force that has been unemployed for more than a year. The long-term unemployment rate exhibits more variability from country to country than does the short-term unemployment rate.

National unemployment rates are correlated with a variety of labor-market policies. Unemployment rates are higher in nations with more generous unemployment insurance, as measured by the replacement rate—the percentage of previous wages that is replaced when a worker loses a job. In addition, nations tend to have higher unemployment, especially higher long-term unemployment, if benefits can be collected for longer periods of time.

Although government spending on unemployment insurance seems to raise unemployment, spending on "active" labor-market policies appears to decrease it. These active labor-market policies include job training, assistance with job search, and subsidized employment. Spain, for instance, has historically had a high rate of unemployment, a fact that can be explained by the combination of generous payments to the unemployed with minimal assistance at helping them find new jobs.

The role of unions also varies from country to country, as we saw in Table 6-1. This fact also helps explain differences in labor-market outcomes. National

[10] For more discussion of these issues, see Paul Krugman, "Past and Prospective Causes of High Unemployment," in *Reducing Unemployment: Current Issues and Policy Options,* Federal Reserve Bank of Kansas City, August 1994.

unemployment rates are positively correlated with the percentage of the labor force whose wages are set by collective bargaining with unions. The adverse impact of unions on unemployment is smaller, however, in nations where there is substantial coordination among employers in bargaining with unions, perhaps because coordination may moderate the upward pressure on wages.

A word of warning: Correlation does not imply causation, so empirical results such as these should be interpreted with caution. But they do suggest that a nation's unemployment rate, rather than being immutable, is instead a function of the choices a nation makes.[11]

CASE STUDY

The Secrets to Happiness

Why are some people more satisfied with their lives than others? This is a deep and difficult question, most often left to philosophers, psychologists, and self-help gurus. But part of the answer is macroeconomic. Recent research has shown that people are happier when they are living in a country with low inflation and low unemployment.

From 1975 to 1991, a survey called the Euro-Barometer Survey Series asked 264,710 people living in 12 European countries about their happiness and overall satisfaction with life. One question asked, "On the whole, are you very satisfied, fairly satisfied, not very satisfied, or not at all satisfied with the life you lead?" To see what determines happiness, the answers to this question were correlated with individual and macroeconomic variables. Other things equal, people are more satisfied with their lives if they are rich, educated, married, in school, self-employed, retired, female, and young or old (as opposed to middle aged). They are less satisfied if they are unemployed, divorced, or living with adolescent children. (Some of these correlations may reflect the effects, rather than causes, of happiness: for example, a happy person may find it easier than an unhappy one to keep a job and a spouse.)

Beyond these individual characteristics, the economy's overall rates of unemployment and inflation also play a significant role in explaining reported happiness. An increase in the unemployment rate of 4 percentage points is large enough to move 11 percent of the population down from one life-satisfaction category to another. The overall unemployment rate reduces satisfaction even after controlling for an individual's employment status. That is, the employed in a high-unemployment nation are less happy than their counterparts in a low-unemployment nation, perhaps because they are more worried about job loss or perhaps out of sympathy with their fellow citizens.

High inflation is also associated with lower life satisfaction, although the effect is not as large. A 1.7 percentage point increase in inflation reduces happiness by about as much as a 1 percentage point increase in unemployment.

[11] Stephen Nickell, "Unemployment and Labor Market Rigidities: Europe versus North America," *Journal of Economic Perspectives* 11 (September 1997): 55–74.

The commonly cited "misery index," which is the sum of the inflation and unemployment rates, apparently gives too much weight to inflation relative to unemployment.[12]

The Rise of European Leisure

Not only are Europeans more likely to be unemployed than Americans, but those who have jobs typically work fewer hours than do their American counterparts. Figure 6-5 presents some data on how many hours a typical employed person works in four major countries. In the 1960s, the number of hours worked was about the same in each of these countries, and it was declining gradually on both sides of the Atlantic. But around 1980, hours worked settled at a plateau in the United States, while it continued to decline in Europe. Today, the typical American works about 20 percent more hours than does the typical resident of western Europe.

Economists have proposed several hypotheses to explain this difference.

FIGURE 6-5

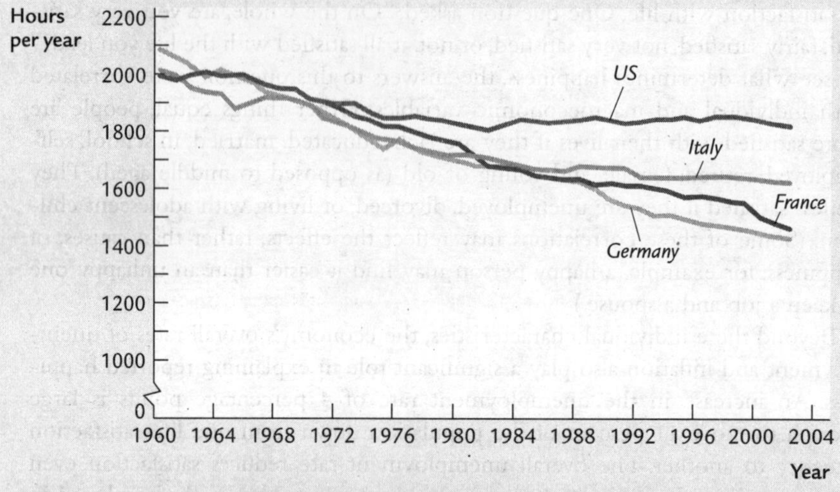

Annual Hours Worked per Employed Person Over time, European workers have reduced the number of hours they work.

Source: OECD. Annual hours are equivalent to 52 times usual weekly hours minus holidays, vacations, sick leave. Computations from Alberto Alesina, Edward Glaeser, and Bruce Sacerdote, "Work and Leisure in the U.S. and Europe: Why So Different?" *NBER Macroeconomics Annual* 2005.

[12] Rafael Di Tella, Robert J. MacCulloch, and Andrew J. Oswald, "Preferences over Inflation and Unemployment: Evidence from Surveys of Happiness," *American Economic Review* 91 (March 2001): 335–341.

Edward Prescott, the 2004 winner of the Nobel Prize in economics, has concluded that "virtually all of the large differences between U.S. labor supply and those of Germany and France are due to differences in tax systems." This hypothesis is consistent with the two facts: (1) Europeans face higher tax rates than Americans, and (2) European tax rates have risen significantly over the past several decades. Some economists take these facts as powerful evidence for the impact of taxes on work effort. Yet others are skeptical, arguing that to explain the differences in hours worked by tax rates alone requires an implausibly large elasticity of labor supply.

A related hypothesis is that the difference in observed work effort may be attributable to the underground economy. When tax rates are high, people have a greater incentive to work "off the books" in order to evade taxes. For obvious reasons, data on the underground economy are hard to come by. But economists who study the subject believe the underground economy is larger in Europe than it is in the United States. This fact suggests that the difference in actual hours worked, including work in the underground economy, may be smaller than the difference in measured hours worked.

Another hypothesis stresses the role of unions. As we have seen, collective bargaining is more important in European than in U.S. labor markets. Unions often push for shorter workweeks in contract negotiations, and they lobby the government for a variety of labor-market regulations, such as official holidays. Economists Alberto Alesina, Edward Glaeser, and Bruce Sacerdote conclude that "mandated holidays can explain 80 percent of the difference in weeks worked between the U.S. and Europe and 30 percent of the difference in total labor supply between the two regions." They suggest that Prescott may overstate the role of taxes because, looking across countries, tax rates and unionization rates are positively correlated; as a result, the effects of high taxes and the effects of widespread unionization are hard to disentangle.

A final hypothesis emphasizes the possibility of different preferences. As technological advance and economic growth have made all advanced countries richer, people around the world must decide whether to take the greater prosperity in the form of increased consumption of goods and services or increased leisure. According to economist Olivier Blanchard, "the main difference [between the continents] is that Europe has used some of the increase in productivity to increase leisure rather than income, while the U.S. has done the opposite." Blanchard believes that Europeans simply have more taste for leisure than do Americans. (As a French economist working in the United States, he may have special insight into this phenomenon.) If Blanchard is right, this raises the even harder question of why tastes vary by geography.

Economists continue to debate the merits of these alternative hypotheses. In the end, there may be some truth to all of them.[13]

[13] To read more about this topic, see Edward C. Prescott "Why Do Americans Work So Much More Than Europeans?" *Federal Reserve Bank of Minneapolis Quarterly Review*, Vol. 28, No. 1 (July 2004): 2–13; Alberto Alesina, Edward Glaeser, and Bruce Sacerdote, "Work and Leisure in the U.S. and Europe: Why So Different?" *NBER Macroeconomics Annual* 2005; Olivier Blanchard, "The Economic Future of Europe" NBER Working Paper No. 10310, 2004, forthcoming in the *Journal of Economic Perspectives*.

6-6 Conclusion

Unemployment represents wasted resources. Unemployed workers have the potential to contribute to national income but are not doing so. Those searching for jobs to suit their skills are happy when the search is over, and those waiting for jobs in firms that pay above-equilibrium wages are happy when positions open up.

Unfortunately, neither frictional unemployment nor structural unemployment can be easily reduced. The government cannot make job search instantaneous, and it cannot easily bring wages closer to equilibrium levels. Zero unemployment is not a plausible goal for free-market economies.

Yet public policy is not powerless in the fight to reduce unemployment. Job-training programs, the unemployment-insurance system, the minimum wage, and the laws governing collective bargaining are often topics of political debate. The policies we choose are likely to have important effects on the economy's natural rate of unemployment.

Summary

1. The natural rate of unemployment is the steady-state rate of unemployment. It depends on the rate of job separation and the rate of job finding.
2. Because it takes time for workers to search for the job that best suits their individual skills and tastes, some frictional unemployment is inevitable. Various government policies, such as unemployment insurance, alter the amount of frictional unemployment.
3. Structural unemployment results when the real wage remains above the level that equilibrates labor supply and labor demand. Minimum-wage legislation is one cause of wage rigidity. Unions and the threat of unionization are another. Finally, efficiency-wage theories suggest that, for various reasons, firms may find it profitable to keep wages high despite an excess supply of labor.
4. Whether we conclude that most unemployment is short-term or long-term depends on how we look at the data. Most spells of unemployment are short. Yet most weeks of unemployment are attributable to the small number of long-term unemployed.
5. The unemployment rates among demographic groups differ substantially. In particular, the unemployment rates for younger workers are much higher than for older workers. This results from a difference in the rate of job separation rather than from a difference in the rate of job finding.
6. The natural rate of unemployment in the United States has exhibited long-term trends. In particular, it rose from the 1950s to the 1970s and then started drifting downward again in the 1990s and early 2000s. Various

explanations have been proposed, including the changing demographic composition of the labor force, changes in the prevalence of sectoral shifts, and changes in the rate of productivity growth.

7. Individuals who have recently entered the labor force, including both new entrants and reentrants, make up about one-third of the unemployed. Transitions into and out of the labor force make unemployment statistics more difficult to interpret.

8. American and European labor markets exhibit some significant differences. In recent years, Europe has experienced significantly more unemployment than the United States, and employed Europeans work fewer hours than employed Americans.

KEY CONCEPTS

Natural rate of unemployment	Unemployment insurance	Insiders versus outsiders
Frictional unemployment	Wage rigidity	Efficiency wages
Sectoral shift	Structural unemployment	Discouraged workers

QUESTIONS FOR REVIEW

1. What determines the natural rate of unemployment?
2. Describe the difference between frictional unemployment and structural unemployment.
3. Give three explanations why the real wage may remain above the level that equilibrates labor supply and labor demand.
4. Is most unemployment long-term or short-term? Explain your answer.
5. How do economists explain the high natural rate of unemployment in the 1970s and 1980s? How do they explain the fall in the natural rate in the 1990s and early 2000s?

PROBLEMS AND APPLICATIONS

1. Answer the following questions about your own experience in the labor force:
   a. When you or one of your friends is looking for a part-time job, how many weeks does it typically take? After you find a job, how many weeks does it typically last?
   b. From your estimates, calculate (in a rate per week) your rate of job finding f and your rate of job separation s. (*Hint:* If f is the rate of job finding, then the average spell of unemployment is $1/f$.)
   c. What is the natural rate of unemployment for the population you represent?
2. In this chapter we saw that the steady-state rate of unemployment is $U/L = s/(s + f)$. Suppose that the unemployment rate does not begin at this level. Show that unemployment will evolve over time and reach this steady state. (*Hint:* Express the change in the number of unemployed as a function of s, f, and U. Then show that if unemployment is above the natural rate, unemployment falls, and if unemployment is below the natural rate, unemployment rises.)

3. The residents of a certain dormitory have collected the following data: People who live in the dorm can be classified as either involved in a relationship or uninvolved. Among involved people, 10 percent experience a breakup of their relationship every month. Among uninvolved people, 5 percent will enter into a relationship every month. What is the steady-state fraction of residents who are uninvolved?

4. Suppose that Congress passes legislation making it more difficult for firms to fire workers. (An example is a law requiring severance pay for fired workers.) If this legislation reduces the rate of job separation without affecting the rate of job finding, how would the natural rate of unemployment change? Do you think that it is plausible that the legislation would not affect the rate of job finding? Why or why not?

5. Consider an economy with the following Cobb-Douglas production function:

$$Y = K^{1/3}L^{2/3}.$$

The economy has 1,000 units of capital and a labor force of 1,000 workers.

a. Derive the equation describing labor demand in this economy as a function of the real wage and the capital stock. (*Hint:* Review Chapter 3.)

b. If the real wage can adjust to equilibrate labor supply and labor demand, what is the real wage? In this equilibrium, what is employment, output, and the total amount earned by workers?

c. Now suppose that Congress, concerned about the welfare of the working class, passes a law requiring firms to pay workers a real wage of 1 unit of output. How does this wage compare to the equilibrium wage?

d. Congress cannot dictate how many workers firms hire at the mandated wage. Given this fact, what are the effects of this law? Specifically, what happens to employment, output, and the total amount earned by workers?

e. Will Congress succeed in its goal of helping the working class? Explain.

f. Do you think that this analysis provides a good way of thinking about a minimum-wage law? Why or why not?

6. Suppose that a country experiences a reduction in productivity—that is, an adverse shock to the production function.

a. What happens to the labor demand curve?

b. How would this change in productivity affect the labor market—that is, employment, unemployment, and real wages—if the labor market were always in equilibrium?

c. How would this change in productivity affect the labor market if unions prevented real wages from falling?

7. When workers' wages rise, their decision on how much time to spend working is affected in two conflicting ways—as you may have learned in courses in microeconomics. The *income effect* is the impulse to work less, because greater incomes mean workers can afford to consume more leisure. The *substitution effect* is the impulse to work more, because the reward to working an additional hour has risen (equivalently, the opportunity cost of leisure has gone up). Apply these concepts to Blanchard's hypothesis about American and European tastes for leisure. On which side of the Atlantic do income effects appear larger than substitution effects? On which side do the two effects approximately cancel? Do you think it is a reasonable hypothesis that tastes for leisure vary by geography? Why or why not?

8. In any city at any time, some of the stock of usable office space is vacant. This vacant office space is unemployed capital. How would you explain this phenomenon? Is it a social problem?

PART III

Growth Theory: The Economy in the Very Long Run

CHAPTER

7

Economic Growth I: Capital Accumulation and Population Growth

The question of growth is nothing new but a new disguise for an age-old issue, one which has always intrigued and preoccupied economics: the present versus the future.

— *James Tobin*

If you have ever spoken with your grandparents about what their lives were like when they were young, most likely you learned an important lesson about economic growth: material standards of living have improved substantially over time for most families in most countries. This advance comes from rising incomes, which have allowed people to consume greater quantities of goods and services.

To measure economic growth, economists use data on gross domestic product, which measures the total income of everyone in the economy. The real GDP of the United States today is more than three times its 1950 level, and real GDP per person is more than twice its 1950 level. In any given year, we also observe large differences in the standard of living among countries. Table 7-1 shows income per person in 2004 of the world's 14 most populous countries. The United States tops the list with an income of $39,710 per person. Nigeria has an income per person of only $930—less than 3 percent of the figure for the United States.

Our goal in this part of the book is to understand what causes these differences in income over time and across countries. In Chapter 3 we identified the factors of production—capital and labor—and the production technology as the sources of the economy's output and, thus, of its total income. Differences in income, then, must come from differences in capital, labor, and technology.

Our primary task in this chapter and the next is to develop a theory of economic growth called the **Solow growth model**. Our analysis in Chapter 3 enabled us to describe how the economy produces and uses its output at one point in time. The analysis was static—a snapshot of the economy. To explain why our national income grows, and why some economies grow faster than others, we must broaden our analysis so that it describes changes in the economy over time. By developing such a model, we make our analysis dynamic—more like a movie than a photograph. The Solow growth model shows how saving, population growth, and

TABLE 7-1

International Differences in the Standard of Living

Country	Income per Person (2004, in U.S. dollars)	Country	Income per Person (2004, in U.S. dollars)
United States	$39,710	Philippines	4,890
Japan	30,040	Indonesia	3,460
Germany	27,950	India	3,100
Russia	9,620	Vietnam	2,700
Mexico	9,590	Pakistan	2,160
Brazil	8,020	Bangladesh	1,980
China	5,530	Nigeria	930

Source: World Bank.

technological progress affect the level of an economy's output and its growth over time. In this chapter we analyze the roles of saving and population growth. In the next chapter we introduce technological progress.[1]

7-1 The Accumulation of Capital

The Solow growth model is designed to show how growth in the capital stock, growth in the labor force, and advances in technology interact in an economy, and how they affect a nation's total output of goods and services. We will build this model in a series of steps. Our first step is to examine how the supply and demand for goods determine the accumulation of capital. In this first step, we assume that the labor force and technology are fixed. We then relax these assumptions by introducing changes in the labor force later in this chapter and by introducing changes in technology in the next.

The Supply and Demand for Goods

The supply and demand for goods played a central role in our static model of the closed economy in Chapter 3. The same is true for the Solow model. By considering the supply and demand for goods, we can see what determines how much output is produced at any given time and how this output is allocated among alternative uses.

[1] The Solow growth model is named after economist Robert Solow and was developed in the 1950s and 1960s. In 1987 Solow won the Nobel Prize in economics for his work in economic growth. The model was introduced in Robert M. Solow, "A Contribution to the Theory of Economic Growth," *Quarterly Journal of Economics* (February 1956): 65–94.

The Supply of Goods and the Production Function The supply of goods in the Solow model is based on the production function, which states that output depends on the capital stock and the labor force:

$$Y = F(K, L).$$

The Solow growth model assumes that the production function has constant returns to scale. This assumption is often considered realistic, and as we will see shortly, it helps simplify the analysis. Recall that a production function has constant returns to scale if

$$zY = F(zK, zL)$$

for any positive number z. That is, if both capital and labor are multiplied by z, the amount of output is also multiplied by z.

Production functions with constant returns to scale allow us to analyze all quantities in the economy relative to the size of the labor force. To see that this is true, set $z = 1/L$ in the preceding equation to obtain

$$Y/L = F(K/L, 1).$$

This equation shows that the amount of output per worker Y/L is a function of the amount of capital per worker K/L. (The number "1" is constant and thus can be ignored.) The assumption of constant returns to scale implies that the size of the economy—as measured by the number of workers—does not affect the relationship between output per worker and capital per worker.

Because the size of the economy does not matter, it will prove convenient to denote all quantities in per worker terms. We designate quantities per worker with lowercase letters, so $y = Y/L$ is output per worker, and $k = K/L$ is capital per worker. We can then write the production function as

$$y = f(k),$$

where we define $f(k) = F(k, 1)$. Figure 7-1 illustrates this production function.

The slope of this production function shows how much extra output a worker produces when given an extra unit of capital. This amount is the marginal product of capital MPK. Mathematically, we write

$$MPK = f(k + 1) - f(k).$$

Note that in Figure 7-1, as the amount of capital increases, the production function becomes flatter, indicating that the production function exhibits diminishing marginal product of capital. When k is low, the average worker has only a little capital to work with, so an extra unit of capital is very useful and produces a lot of additional output. When k is high, the average worker has a lot of capital, so an extra unit increases production only slightly.

The Demand for Goods and the Consumption Function The demand for goods in the Solow model comes from consumption and investment. In other words, output per worker y is divided between consumption per worker c and investment per worker i:

FIGURE 7-1

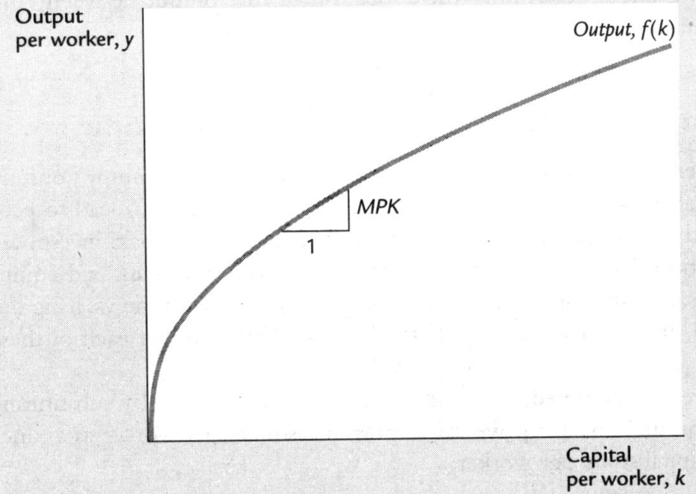

The Production Function The production function shows how the amount of capital per worker k determines the amount of output per worker $y = f(k)$. The slope of the production function is the marginal product of capital: if k increases by 1 unit, y increases by MPK units. The production function becomes flatter as k increases, indicating diminishing marginal product of capital.

$$y = c + i.$$

This equation is the per worker version of the national income accounts identity for an economy. Notice that it omits government purchases (which for present purposes we can ignore) and net exports (because we are assuming a closed economy).

The Solow model assumes that each year people save a fraction s of their income and consume a fraction $(1 - s)$. We can express this idea with the following consumption function:

$$c = (1 - s)y,$$

where s, the saving rate, is a number between zero and one. Keep in mind that various government policies can potentially influence a nation's saving rate, so one of our goals is to find what saving rate is desirable. For now, however, we just take the saving rate s as given.

To see what this consumption function implies for investment, substitute $(1 - s)y$ for c in the national income accounts identity:

$$y = (1 - s)y + i.$$

Rearrange the terms to obtain

$$i = sy.$$

This equation shows that investment equals saving, as we first saw in Chapter 3. Thus, the rate of saving s is also the fraction of output devoted to investment.

We have now introduced the two main ingredients of the Solow model—the production function and the consumption function—which describe the economy at any moment in time. For any given capital stock k, the production function $y = f(k)$ determines how much output the economy produces, and the saving rate s determines the allocation of that output between consumption and investment.

Growth in the Capital Stock and the Steady State

At any moment, the capital stock is a key determinant of the economy's output, but the capital stock can change over time, and those changes can lead to economic growth. In particular, two forces influence the capital stock: investment and depreciation. *Investment* refers to the expenditure on new plant and equipment, and it causes the capital stock to rise. *Depreciation* refers to the wearing out of old capital, and it causes the capital stock to fall. Let's consider each of these in turn.

As we have already noted, investment per worker i equals sy. By substituting the production function for y, we can express investment per worker as a function of the capital stock per worker:

$$i = sf(k).$$

This equation relates the existing stock of capital k to the accumulation of new capital i. Figure 7-2 shows this relationship. This figure illustrates how, for any value of k, the amount of output is determined by the production function $f(k)$, and the allocation of that output between consumption and saving is determined by the saving rate s.

To incorporate depreciation into the model, we assume that a certain fraction δ of the capital stock wears out each year. Here δ (the lowercase Greek letter

FIGURE 7-2

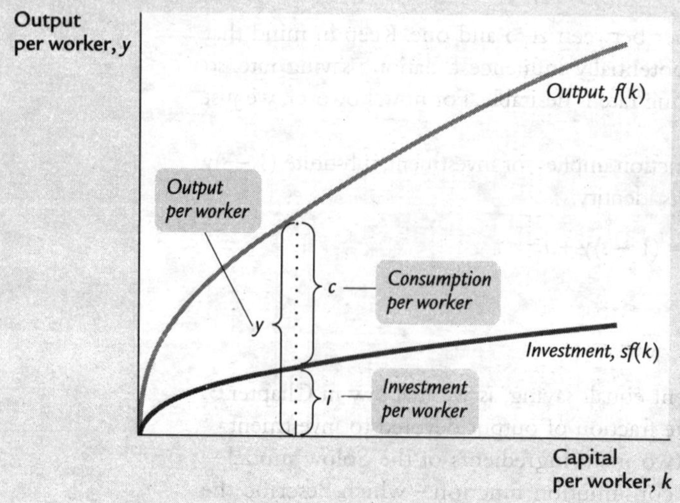

Output, Consumption, and Investment The saving rate s determines the allocation of output between consumption and investment. For any level of capital k, output is $f(k)$, investment is $sf(k)$, and consumption is $f(k) - sf(k)$.

FIGURE 7-3

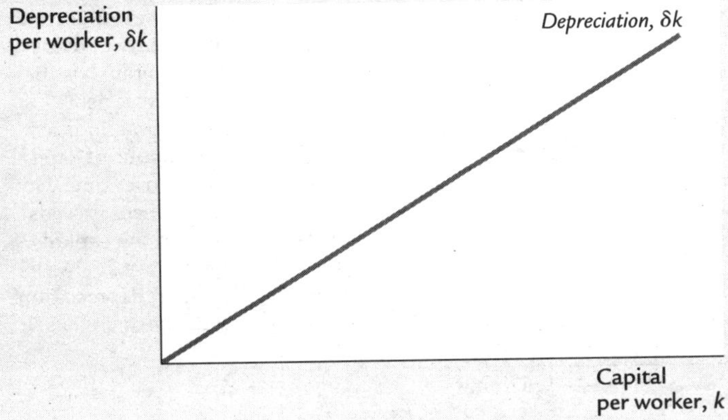

Depreciation A constant fraction δ of the capital stock wears out every year. Depreciation is therefore proportional to the capital stock.

delta) is called the *depreciation rate.* For example, if capital lasts an average of 25 years, then the depreciation rate is 4 percent per year ($\delta = 0.04$). The amount of capital that depreciates each year is δk. Figure 7-3 shows how the amount of depreciation depends on the capital stock.

We can express the impact of investment and depreciation on the capital stock with this equation:

$$\begin{array}{ccccc} \text{Change in Capital Stock} & = & \text{Investment} & - & \text{Depreciation} \\ \Delta k & = & i & - & \delta k, \end{array}$$

where Δk is the change in the capital stock between one year and the next. Because investment i equals $sf(k)$, we can write this as

$$\Delta k = sf(k) - \delta k.$$

Figure 7-4 graphs the terms of this equation—investment and depreciation—for different levels of the capital stock k. The higher the capital stock, the greater the amounts of output and investment. Yet the higher the capital stock, the greater also the amount of depreciation.

As Figure 7-4 shows, there is a single capital stock k^* at which the amount of investment equals the amount of depreciation. If the economy finds itself at this level of the capital stock, the capital stock will not change because the two forces acting on it—investment and depreciation—just balance. That is, at k^*, $\Delta k = 0$, so the capital stock k and output $f(k)$ are steady over time (rather than growing or shrinking). We therefore call k^* the **steady-state** level of capital.

The steady state is significant for two reasons. As we have just seen, an economy at the steady state will stay there. In addition, and just as important, an economy *not* at the steady state will go there. That is, regardless of the level of capital with which the economy begins, it ends up with the steady-state level of capital. In this sense, *the steady state represents the long-run equilibrium of the economy.*

FIGURE 7-4

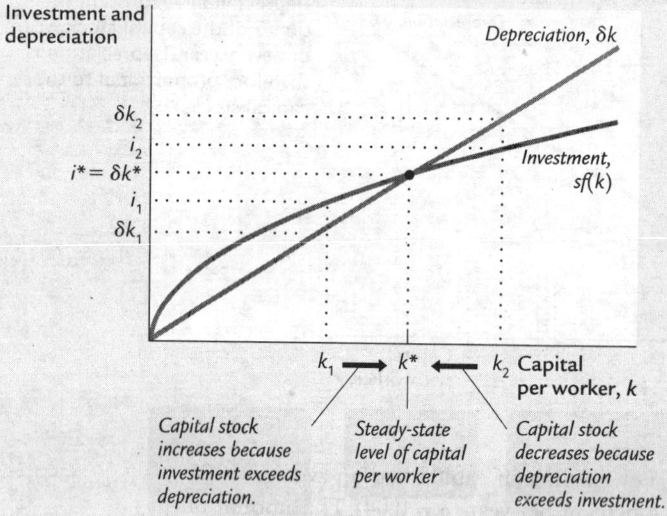

Investment, Depreciation, and the Steady State The steady-state level of capital k^* is the level at which investment equals depreciation, indicating that the amount of capital will not change over time. Below k^* investment exceeds depreciation, so the capital stock grows. Above k^* investment is less than depreciation, so the capital stock shrinks.

To see why an economy always ends up at the steady state, suppose that the economy starts with less than the steady-state level of capital, such as level k_1 in Figure 7-4. In this case, the level of investment exceeds the amount of depreciation. Over time, the capital stock will rise and will continue to rise—along with output $f(k)$—until it approaches the steady state k^*.

Similarly, suppose that the economy starts with more than the steady-state level of capital, such as level k_2. In this case, investment is less than depreciation: capital is wearing out faster than it is being replaced. The capital stock will fall, again approaching the steady-state level. Once the capital stock reaches the steady state, investment equals depreciation, and there is no pressure for the capital stock to either increase or decrease.

Approaching the Steady State: A Numerical Example

Let's use a numerical example to see how the Solow model works and how the economy approaches the steady state. For this example, we assume that the production function is

$$Y = K^{1/2}L^{1/2}.$$

From Chapter 3, you will recognize this as the Cobb-Douglas production function with the capital-share parameter α equal to 1/2. To derive the per-worker production function $f(k)$, divide both sides of the production function by the labor force L:

$$\frac{Y}{L} = \frac{K^{1/2}L^{1/2}}{L}.$$

Rearrange to obtain

$$\frac{Y}{L} = \left(\frac{K}{L}\right)^{1/2}.$$

Because $y = Y/L$ and $k = K/L$, this equation becomes

$$y = k^{1/2},$$

which can also be written as

$$y = \sqrt{k}.$$

This form of the production function states that output per worker is equal to the square root of the amount of capital per worker.

To complete the example, let's assume that 30 percent of output is saved ($s = 0.3$), that 10 percent of the capital stock depreciates every year ($\delta = 0.1$), and that the economy starts off with 4 units of capital per worker ($k = 4$). Given these numbers, we can now examine what happens to this economy over time.

We begin by looking at the production and allocation of output in the first year, when the economy has 4 units of capital. Here are the steps we follow.

- According to the production function $y = \sqrt{k}$, the 4 units of capital per worker k produce 2 units of output per worker y.
- Because 30 percent of output is saved and invested and 70 percent is consumed, $i = 0.6$ and $c = 1.4$.
- Because 10 percent of the capital stock depreciates, $\delta k = 0.4$.
- With investment of 0.6 and depreciation of 0.4, the change in the capital stock is $\Delta k = 0.2$.

Thus, the economy begins its second year with 4.2 units of capital per worker.

We can do the same calculations for each subsequent year. Table 7-2 shows how the economy progresses. Every year, because investment exceeds depreciation, new capital is added and output grows. Over many years, the economy approaches a steady state with 9 units of capital per worker. In this steady state, investment of 0.9 exactly offsets depreciation of 0.9, so that the capital stock and output are no longer growing.

Following the progress of the economy for many years is one way to find the steady-state capital stock, but there is another way that requires fewer calculations. Recall that

$$\Delta k = sf(k) - \delta k.$$

This equation shows how k evolves over time. Because the steady state is (by definition) the value of k at which $\Delta k = 0$, we know that

$$0 = sf(k^*) - \delta k^*,$$

or, equivalently,

$$\frac{k^*}{f(k^*)} = \frac{s}{\delta}.$$

TABLE 7-2

Approaching the Steady State: A Numerical Example

Assumptions: $y = \sqrt{k}$; $s = 0.3$; $\delta = 0.1$; initial $k = 4.0$

Year	k	y	c	i	δk	Δk
1	4.000	2.000	1.400	0.600	0.400	0.200
2	4.200	2.049	1.435	0.615	0.420	0.195
3	4.395	2.096	1.467	0.629	0.440	0.189
4	4.584	2.141	1.499	0.642	0.458	0.184
5	4.768	2.184	1.529	0.655	0.477	0.178
⋮						
10	5.602	2.367	1.657	0.710	0.560	0.150
⋮						
25	7.321	2.706	1.894	0.812	0.732	0.080
⋮						
100	8.962	2.994	2.096	0.898	0.896	0.002
⋮						
∞	9.000	3.000	2.100	0.900	0.900	0.000

This equation provides a way of finding the steady-state level of capital per worker, k^*. Substituting in the numbers and production function from our example, we obtain

$$\frac{k^*}{\sqrt{k^*}} = \frac{0.3}{0.1}.$$

Now square both sides of this equation to find

$$k^* = 9.$$

The steady-state capital stock is 9 units per worker. This result confirms the calculation of the steady state in Table 7-2.

CASE STUDY

The Miracle of Japanese and German Growth

Japan and Germany are two success stories of economic growth. Although today they are economic superpowers, in 1945 the economies of both countries were in shambles. World War II had destroyed much of their capital stocks. In the decades after the war, however, these two countries experienced some of the most rapid growth rates on record. Between 1948 and 1972, output per person grew at 8.2 percent per year in Japan and 5.7 percent per year in Germany, compared to only 2.2 percent per year in the United States.

Are the postwar experiences of Japan and Germany so surprising from the standpoint of the Solow growth model? Consider an economy in steady state. Now suppose that a war destroys some of the capital stock. (That is, suppose the capital stock drops from k^* to k_1 in Figure 7-4.) Not surprisingly, the level of output falls immediately. But if the saving rate—the fraction of output devoted to saving and investment—is unchanged, the economy will then experience a period of high growth. Output grows because, at the lower capital stock, more capital is added by investment than is removed by depreciation. This high growth continues until the economy approaches its former steady state. Hence, although destroying part of the capital stock immediately reduces output, it is followed by higher-than-normal growth. The "miracle" of rapid growth in Japan and Germany, as it is often described in the business press, is what the Solow model predicts for countries in which war has greatly reduced the capital stock.

How Saving Affects Growth

The explanation of Japanese and German growth after World War II is not quite as simple as suggested in the preceding case study. Another relevant fact is that both Japan and Germany save and invest a higher fraction of their output than does the United States. To understand more fully the international differences in economic performance, we must consider the effects of different saving rates.

Consider what happens to an economy when its saving rate increases. Figure 7-5 shows such a change. The economy is assumed to begin in a steady state with saving rate s_1 and capital stock k_1^*. When the saving rate increases from s_1 to s_2, the $sf(k)$ curve shifts upward. At the initial saving rate s_1 and the initial capital stock k_1^*, the amount of investment just offsets the amount of depreciation. Immediately after the saving rate rises, investment is higher, but the capital stock and depreciation are unchanged. Therefore, investment exceeds depreciation. The capital stock will gradually rise until the economy reaches the new steady state k_2^*, which has a higher capital stock and a higher level of output than the old steady state.

The Solow model shows that the saving rate is a key determinant of the steady-state capital stock. *If the saving rate is high, the economy will have a large capital stock and a high level of output in the steady state. If the saving rate is low, the economy will have a small capital stock and a low level of output in the steady state.* This conclusion sheds light on many discussions of fiscal policy. As we saw in Chapter 3, a government budget deficit can reduce national saving and crowd out investment. Now we can see that the long-run consequences of a reduced saving rate are a lower capital stock and lower national income. This is why many economists are critical of persistent budget deficits.

What does the Solow model say about the relationship between saving and economic growth? Higher saving leads to faster growth in the Solow model, but only temporarily. An increase in the rate of saving raises growth only until the

FIGURE 7-5

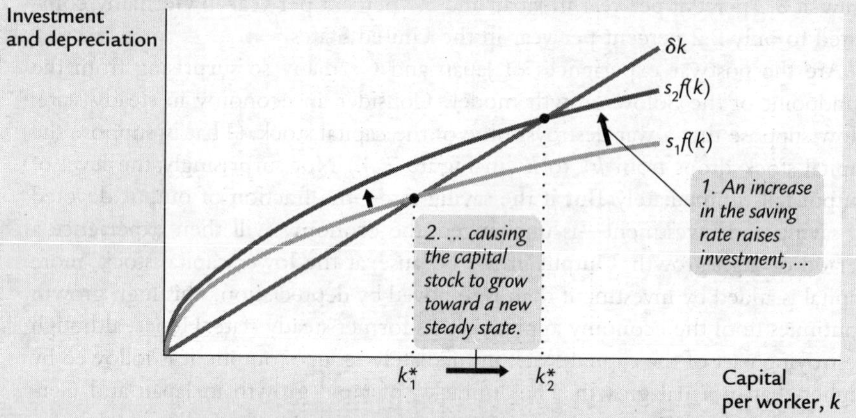

An Increase in the Saving Rate An increase in the saving rate s implies that the amount of investment for any given capital stock is higher. It therefore shifts the saving function upward. At the initial steady state k_1^*, investment now exceeds depreciation. The capital stock rises until the economy reaches a new steady state k_2^* with more capital and output.

economy reaches the new steady state. If the economy maintains a high saving rate, it will maintain a large capital stock and a high level of output, but it will not maintain a high rate of growth forever. Policies that alter the steady-state growth rate of income per person are said to have a *growth effect;* we will see examples of such policies in the next chapter. By contrast, a higher saving rate is said to have a *level effect,* because only the level of income per person—and not its growth rate—is influenced by the saving rate in the steady state.

Now that we understand how saving and growth interact, we can more fully explain the impressive economic performance of Germany and Japan after World War II. Not only were their initial capital stocks low because of the war, but their steady-state capital stocks were high because of their high saving rates. Both of these facts help explain the rapid growth of these two countries in the 1950s and 1960s.

CASE STUDY

Saving and Investment Around the World

We started this chapter with an important question: Why are some countries so rich while others are mired in poverty? Our analysis has taken us a step closer to the answer. According to the Solow model, if a nation devotes a large fraction of its income to saving and investment, it will have a high steady-state capital stock and a high level of income. If a nation saves and invests only a small fraction of its income, its steady-state capital and income will be low.

FIGURE 7-6

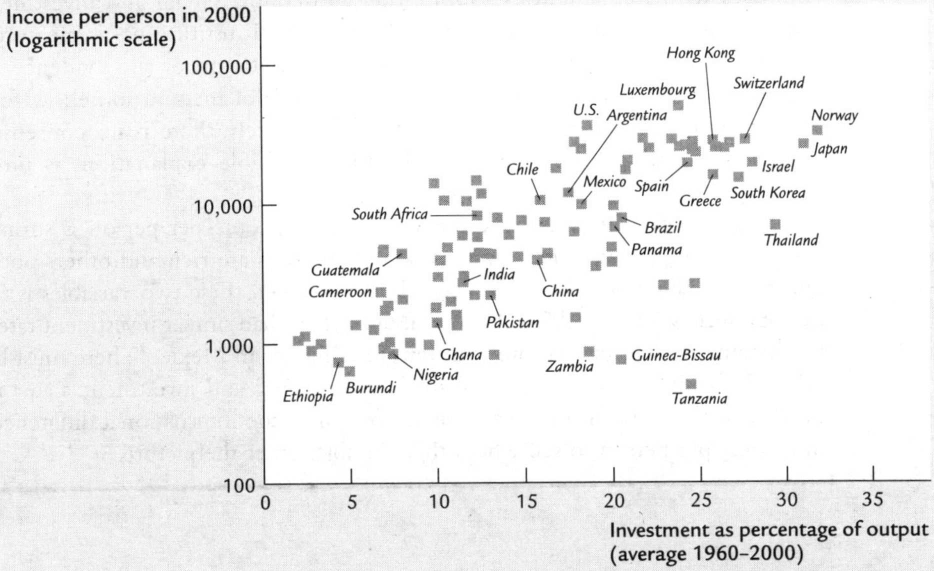

International Evidence on Investment Rates and Income per Person This scatterplot shows the experience of 96 countries, each represented by a single point. The horizontal axis shows the country's rate of investment, and the vertical axis shows the country's income per person. High investment is associated with high income per person, as the Solow model predicts.

Source: Alan Heston, Robert Summers and Bettina Aten, Penn World Table Version 6.1, Center for International Comparisons at the University of Pennsylvania (CICUP), October 2002.

Let's now look at some data to see if this theoretical result in fact helps explain the large international variation in standards of living. Figure 7-6 is a scatterplot of data from 96 countries. (The figure includes most of the world's economies. It excludes major oil-producing countries and countries that were communist during much of this period, because their experiences are explained by their special circumstances.) The data show a positive relationship between the fraction of output devoted to investment and the level of income per person. That is, countries with high rates of investment, such as the United States and Japan, usually have high incomes, whereas countries with low rates of investment, such as Ethiopia and Burundi, have low incomes. Thus, the data are consistent with the Solow model's prediction that the investment rate is a key determinant of whether a country is rich or poor.

The strong correlation shown in this figure is an important fact, but it raises as many questions as it resolves. One might naturally ask, why do rates of saving and investment vary so much from country to country? There are many potential answers, such as tax policy, retirement patterns, the development of financial markets, and cultural differences. In addition, political stability may play a role: not surprisingly, rates of saving and investment tend to be low in countries with frequent wars, revolutions, and coups. Saving and investment also tend to be low in countries with poor political institutions, as measured by estimates of official corruption. A final interpretation of the evidence in Figure 7-6 is reverse causation: perhaps high levels of income somehow foster high rates of saving and investment. Unfortunately, there is no consensus among economists about which of the many possible explanations is most important.

The association between investment rates and income per person is strong, and it is an important clue as to why some countries are rich and others poor, but it is not the whole story. The correlation between these two variables is far from perfect. Mexico and Zambia, for instance, have had similar investment rates, but income per person is more than ten times higher in Mexico. There must be other determinants of living standards beyond saving and investment. Later in this chapter and also in the next one, we return to the international differences in income per person to see what other variables enter the picture.

7-2 The Golden Rule Level of Capital

So far, we have used the Solow model to examine how an economy's rate of saving and investment determines its steady-state levels of capital and income. This analysis might lead you to think that higher saving is always a good thing, for it always leads to greater income. Yet suppose a nation had a saving rate of 100 percent. That would lead to the largest possible capital stock and the largest possible income. But if all of this income is saved and none is ever consumed, what good is it?

This section uses the Solow model to discuss the optimal amount of capital accumulation from the standpoint of economic well-being. In the next chapter, we discuss how government policies influence a nation's saving rate. But first, in this section, we present the theory behind these policy decisions.

Comparing Steady States

To keep our analysis simple, let's assume that a policymaker can set the economy's saving rate at any level. By setting the saving rate, the policymaker determines the economy's steady state. What steady state should the policymaker choose?

When choosing a steady state, the policymaker's goal is to maximize the well-being of the individuals who make up the society. Individuals themselves do not care about the amount of capital in the economy, or even the amount of output. They care about the amount of goods and services they can consume. Thus, a benevolent policymaker would want to choose the steady state with the highest level of consumption. The steady-state value of k that maximizes consumption is called the **Golden Rule level of capital** and is denoted k^*_{gold}.[2]

How can we tell whether an economy is at the Golden Rule level? To answer this question, we must first determine steady-state consumption per worker. Then we can see which steady state provides the most consumption.

To find steady-state consumption per worker, we begin with the national income accounts identity

$$y = c + i$$

and rearrange it as

$$c = y - i.$$

Consumption is simply output minus investment. Because we want to find steady-state consumption, we substitute steady-state values for output and investment. Steady-state output per worker is $f(k^*)$, where k^* is the steady-state capital stock per worker. Furthermore, because the capital stock is not changing in the steady state, investment is equal to depreciation δk^*. Substituting $f(k^*)$ for y and δk^* for i, we can write steady-state consumption per worker as

$$c^* = f(k^*) - \delta k^*.$$

According to this equation, steady-state consumption is what's left of steady-state output after paying for steady-state depreciation. This equation shows that an increase in steady-state capital has two opposing effects on steady-state consumption. On the one hand, more capital means more output. On the other hand, more capital also means that more output must be used to replace capital that is wearing out.

Figure 7-7 graphs steady-state output and steady-state depreciation as a function of the steady-state capital stock. Steady-state consumption is the gap between output and depreciation. This figure shows that there is one level of the capital stock—the Golden Rule level k^*_{gold}—that maximizes consumption.

When comparing steady states, we must keep in mind that higher levels of capital affect both output and depreciation. If the capital stock is below the Golden Rule level, an increase in the capital stock raises output more than depreciation, so that consumption rises. In this case, the production function is steeper than the δk^* line, so the gap between these two curves—which equals consumption—grows as k^* rises. By contrast, if the capital stock is above the Golden Rule level, an increase in the capital stock reduces consumption,

[2] Edmund Phelps, "The Golden Rule of Accumulation: A Fable for Growthmen," *American Economic Review* 51 (September 1961): 638–643.

FIGURE 7-7

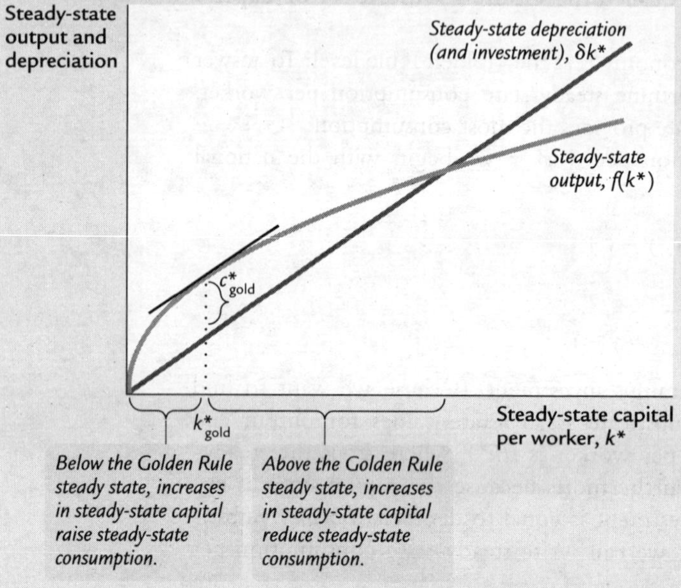

Steady-State Consumption The economy's output is used for consumption or investment. In the steady state, investment equals depreciation. Therefore, steady-state consumption is the difference between output $f(k^*)$ and depreciation δk^*. Steady-state consumption is maximized at the Golden Rule steady state. The Golden Rule capital stock is denoted k^*_{gold}, and the Golden Rule consumption is denoted c^*_{gold}.

because the increase in output is smaller than the increase in depreciation. In this case, the production function is flatter than the δk^* line, so the gap between the curves—consumption—shrinks as k^* rises. At the Golden Rule level of capital, the production function and the δk^* line have the same slope, and consumption is at its greatest level.

We can now derive a simple condition that characterizes the Golden Rule level of capital. Recall that the slope of the production function is the marginal product of capital *MPK*. The slope of the δk^* line is δ. Because these two slopes are equal at k^*_{gold}, the Golden Rule is described by the equation

$$MPK = \delta.$$

At the Golden Rule level of capital, the marginal product of capital equals the depreciation rate.

To make the point somewhat differently, suppose that the economy starts at some steady-state capital stock k^* and that the policymaker is considering increasing the capital stock to $k^* + 1$. The amount of extra output from this increase in capital would be $f(k^* + 1) - f(k^*)$, the marginal product of capital *MPK*. The amount of extra depreciation from having one more unit of capital is the depreciation rate δ. Thus, the net effect of this extra unit of capital on consumption is $MPK - \delta$. If $MPK - \delta > 0$, then increases in capital increase consumption, so k^* must be below the Golden Rule level. If $MPK - \delta < 0$, then increases in capital decrease consumption, so k^* must be above the Golden Rule level. Therefore, the following condition describes the Golden Rule:

$$MPK - \delta = 0.$$

At the Golden Rule level of capital, the marginal product of capital net of depreciation ($MPK - \delta$) equals zero. As we will see, a policymaker can use this condition to find the Golden Rule capital stock for an economy.[3]

Keep in mind that the economy does not automatically gravitate toward the Golden Rule steady state. If we want any particular steady-state capital stock, such as the Golden Rule, we need a particular saving rate to support it. Figure 7-8 shows the steady state if the saving rate is set to produce the Golden Rule level of capital. If the saving rate is higher than the one used in this figure, the steady-state capital stock will be too high. If the saving rate is lower, the steady-state capital stock will be too low. In either case, steady-state consumption will be lower than it is at the Golden Rule steady state.

FIGURE 7-8

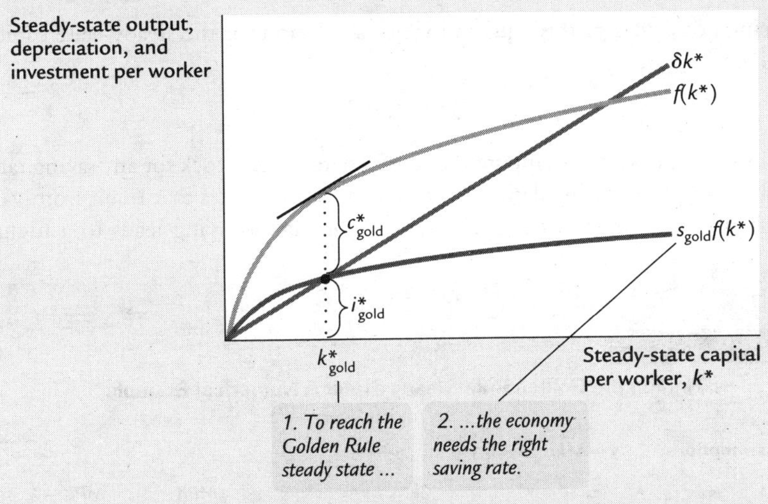

The Saving Rate and the Golden Rule There is only one saving rate that produces the Golden Rule level of capital k^*_{gold}. Any change in the saving rate would shift the $sf(k)$ curve and would move the economy to a steady state with a lower level of consumption.

---

[3] *Mathematical note*: Another way to derive the condition for the Golden Rule uses a bit of calculus. Recall that $c^* = f(k^*) - \delta k^*$. To find the k^* that maximizes c^*, differentiate to find $dc^*/dk^* = f'(k^*) - \delta$ and set this derivative equal to zero. Noting that $f'(k^*)$ is the marginal product of capital, we obtain the Golden Rule condition in the text.

Finding the Golden Rule Steady State: A Numerical Example

Consider the decision of a policymaker choosing a steady state in the following economy. The production function is the same as in our earlier example:

$$y = \sqrt{k}.$$

Output per worker is the square root of capital per worker. Depreciation δ is again 10 percent of capital. This time, the policymaker chooses the saving rate s and thus the economy's steady state.

To see the outcomes available to the policymaker, recall that the following equation holds in the steady state:

$$\frac{k^*}{f(k^*)} = \frac{s}{\delta}.$$

In this economy, this equation becomes

$$\frac{k^*}{\sqrt{k^*}} = \frac{s}{0.1}.$$

Squaring both sides of this equation yields a solution for the steady-state capital stock. We find

$$k^* = 100s^2.$$

Using this result, we can compute the steady-state capital stock for any saving rate.

Table 7-3 presents calculations showing the steady states that result from various saving rates in this economy. We see that higher saving leads to a higher

TABLE 7-3

Finding the Golden Rule Steady State: A Numerical Example

Assumptions: $y = \sqrt{k}$; $\delta = 0.1$

s	k^*	y^*	δk^*	c^*	MPK	$MPK - \delta$
0.0	0.0	0.0	0.0	0.0	∞	∞
0.1	1.0	1.0	0.1	0.9	0.500	0.400
0.2	4.0	2.0	0.4	1.6	0.250	0.150
0.3	9.0	3.0	0.9	2.1	0.167	0.067
0.4	16.0	4.0	1.6	2.4	0.125	0.025
0.5	**25.0**	**5.0**	**2.5**	**2.5**	**0.100**	**0.000**
0.6	36.0	6.0	3.6	2.4	0.083	−0.017
0.7	49.0	7.0	4.9	2.1	0.071	−0.029
0.8	64.0	8.0	6.4	1.6	0.062	−0.038
0.9	81.0	9.0	8.1	0.9	0.056	−0.044
1.0	100.0	10.0	10.0	0.0	0.050	−0.050

capital stock, which in turn leads to higher output and higher depreciation. Steady-state consumption, the difference between output and depreciation, first rises with higher saving rates and then declines. Consumption is highest when the saving rate is 0.5. Hence, a saving rate of 0.5 produces the Golden Rule steady state.

Recall that another way to identify the Golden Rule steady state is to find the capital stock at which the net marginal product of capital ($MPK - \delta$) equals zero. For this production function, the marginal product is[4]

$$MPK = \frac{1}{2\sqrt{k}}.$$

Using this formula, the last two columns of Table 7-3 present the values of MPK and $MPK - \delta$ in the different steady states. Note that the net marginal product of capital is exactly zero when the saving rate is at its Golden Rule value of 0.5. Because of diminishing marginal product, the net marginal product of capital is greater than zero whenever the economy saves less than this amount, and it is less than zero whenever the economy saves more.

This numerical example confirms that the two ways of finding the Golden Rule steady state—looking at steady-state consumption or looking at the marginal product of capital—give the same answer. If we want to know whether an actual economy is currently at, above, or below its Golden Rule capital stock, the second method is usually more convenient, because it is relatively straightforward to estimate the marginal product of capital. By contrast, evaluating an economy with the first method requires estimates of steady-state consumption at many different saving rates; such information is harder to obtain. Thus, when we apply this kind of analysis to the U.S. economy in the next chapter, we will evaluate U.S. saving by examining the marginal product of capital. Before engaging in that policy analysis, however, we need to proceed further in our development and understanding of the Solow model.

The Transition to the Golden Rule Steady State

Let's now make our policymaker's problem more realistic. So far, we have been assuming that the policymaker can simply choose the economy's steady state and jump there immediately. In this case, the policymaker would choose the steady state with highest consumption—the Golden Rule steady state. But now suppose that the economy has reached a steady state other than the Golden Rule. What happens to consumption, investment, and capital when the economy makes the transition between steady states? Might the impact of the transition deter the policymaker from trying to achieve the Golden Rule?

We must consider two cases: the economy might begin with more capital than in the Golden Rule steady state, or with less. It turns out that the two cases offer

[4] *Mathematical note:* To derive this formula, note that the marginal product of capital is the derivative of the production function with respect to k.

very different problems for policymakers. (As we will see in the next chapter, the second case—too little capital—describes most actual economies, including that of the United States.)

Starting With Too Much Capital We first consider the case in which the economy begins at a steady state with more capital than it would have in the Golden Rule steady state. In this case, the policymaker should pursue policies aimed at reducing the rate of saving in order to reduce the capital stock. Suppose that these policies succeed and that at some point—call it time t_0—the saving rate falls to the level that will eventually lead to the Golden Rule steady state.

Figure 7-9 shows what happens to output, consumption, and investment when the saving rate falls. The reduction in the saving rate causes an immediate increase in consumption and a decrease in investment. Because investment and depreciation were equal in the initial steady state, investment will now be less than depreciation, which means the economy is no longer in a steady state. Gradually, the capital stock falls, leading to reductions in output, consumption, and investment. These variables continue to fall until the economy reaches the new steady state. Because we are assuming that the new steady state is the Golden Rule steady state, consumption must be higher than it was before the change in the saving rate, even though output and investment are lower.

Note that, compared to the old steady state, consumption is higher not only in the new steady state but also along the entire path to it. When the capital stock exceeds the Golden Rule level, reducing saving is clearly a good policy, for it increases consumption at every point in time.

FIGURE 7-9

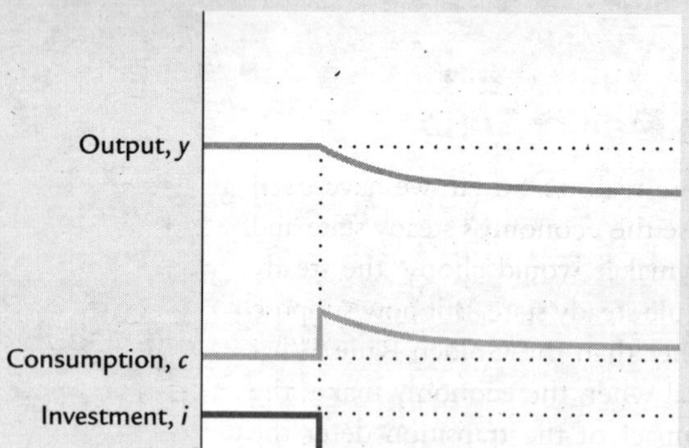

Reducing Saving When Starting With More Capital Than in the Golden Rule Steady State This figure shows what happens over time to output, consumption, and investment when the economy begins with more capital than the Golden Rule level and the saving rate is reduced. The reduction in the saving rate (at time t_0) causes an immediate increase in consumption and an equal decrease in investment. Over time, as the capital stock falls, output, consumption, and investment fall together. Because the economy began with too much capital, the new steady state has a higher level of consumption than the initial steady state.

Starting With Too Little Capital When the economy begins with less capital than in the Golden Rule steady state, the policymaker must raise the saving rate to reach the Golden Rule. Figure 7-10 shows what happens. The increase in the saving rate at time t_0 causes an immediate fall in consumption and a rise in investment. Over time, higher investment causes the capital stock to rise. As capital accumulates, output, consumption, and investment gradually increase, eventually approaching the new steady-state levels. Because the initial steady state was below the Golden Rule, the increase in saving eventually leads to a higher level of consumption than that which prevailed initially.

Does the increase in saving that leads to the Golden Rule steady state raise economic welfare? Eventually it does, because the new steady-state level of consumption is higher than the initial level. But achieving that new steady state requires an initial period of reduced consumption. Note the contrast to the case in which the economy begins above the Golden Rule. *When the economy begins above the Golden Rule, reaching the Golden Rule produces higher consumption at all points in time. When the economy begins below the Golden Rule, reaching the Golden Rule requires initially reducing consumption to increase consumption in the future.*

When deciding whether to try to reach the Golden Rule steady state, policymakers have to take into account that current consumers and future consumers are not always the same people. Reaching the Golden Rule achieves the highest steady-state level of consumption and thus benefits future generations. But when the economy is initially below the Golden Rule, reaching the Golden Rule requires raising investment and thus lowering the consumption of current generations. Thus, when choosing whether to increase capital accumulation, the policymaker faces a tradeoff among the welfare of different generations. A policymaker

FIGURE 7-10

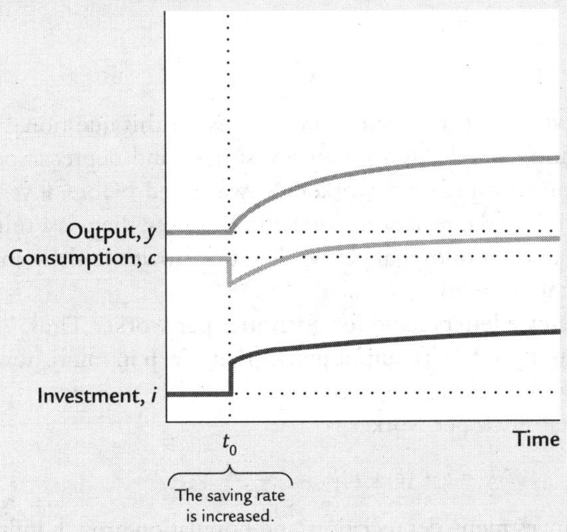

Increasing Saving When Starting With Less Capital Than in the Golden Rule Steady State This figure shows what happens over time to output, consumption, and investment when the economy begins with less capital than the Golden Rule, and the saving rate is increased. The increase in the saving rate (at time t_0) causes an immediate drop in consumption and an equal jump in investment. Over time, as the capital stock grows, output, consumption, and investment increase together. Because the economy began with less capital than the Golden Rule, the new steady state has a higher level of consumption than the initial steady state.

who cares more about current generations than about future generations may decide not to pursue policies to reach the Golden Rule steady state. By contrast, a policymaker who cares about all generations equally will choose to reach the Golden Rule. Even though current generations will consume less, an infinite number of future generations will benefit by moving to the Golden Rule.

Thus, optimal capital accumulation depends crucially on how we weigh the interests of current and future generations. The biblical Golden Rule tells us, "do unto others as you would have them do unto you." If we heed this advice, we give all generations equal weight. In this case, it is optimal to reach the Golden Rule level of capital—which is why it is called the "Golden Rule."

7-3 Population Growth

The basic Solow model shows that capital accumulation, by itself, cannot explain sustained economic growth: high rates of saving lead to high growth temporarily, but the economy eventually approaches a steady state in which capital and output are constant. To explain the sustained economic growth that we observe in most parts of the world, we must expand the Solow model to incorporate the other two sources of economic growth—population growth and technological progress. In this section we add population growth to the model.

Instead of assuming that the population is fixed, as we did in Sections 7-1 and 7-2, we now suppose that the population and the labor force grow at a constant rate n. For example, the U.S. population grows about 1 percent per year, so $n = 0.01$. This means that if 150 million people are working one year, then 151.5 million (1.01×150) are working the next year, and 153.015 million (1.01×151.5) the year after that, and so on.

The Steady State With Population Growth

How does population growth affect the steady state? To answer this question, we must discuss how population growth, along with investment and depreciation, influences the accumulation of capital per worker. As we noted before, investment raises the capital stock, and depreciation reduces it. But now there is a third force acting to change the amount of capital per worker: the growth in the number of workers causes capital per worker to fall.

We continue to let lowercase letters stand for quantities per worker. Thus, $k = K/L$ is capital per worker, and $y = Y/L$ is output per worker. Keep in mind, however, that the number of workers is growing over time.

The change in the capital stock per worker is

$$\Delta k = i - (\delta + n)k.$$

This equation shows how investment, depreciation, and population growth influence the per-worker capital stock. Investment increases k, whereas depreciation and population growth decrease k. We saw this equation earlier in this chapter for the special case of a constant population ($n = 0$).

We can think of the term $(\delta + n)k$ as defining *break-even investment*—the amount of investment necessary to keep the capital stock per worker constant. Break-even investment includes the depreciation of existing capital, which equals δk. It also includes the amount of investment necessary to provide new workers with capital. The amount of investment necessary for this purpose is nk, because there are n new workers for each existing worker, and because k is the amount of capital for each worker. The equation shows that population growth reduces the accumulation of capital per worker much the way depreciation does. Depreciation reduces k by wearing out the capital stock, whereas population growth reduces k by spreading the capital stock more thinly among a larger population of workers.[5]

Our analysis with population growth now proceeds much as it did previously. First, we substitute $sf(k)$ for i. The equation can then be written as

$$\Delta k = sf(k) - (\delta + n)k.$$

To see what determines the steady-state level of capital per worker, we use Figure 7-11, which extends the analysis of Figure 7-4 to include the effects of population growth. An economy is in a steady state if capital per worker k is

FIGURE 7-11

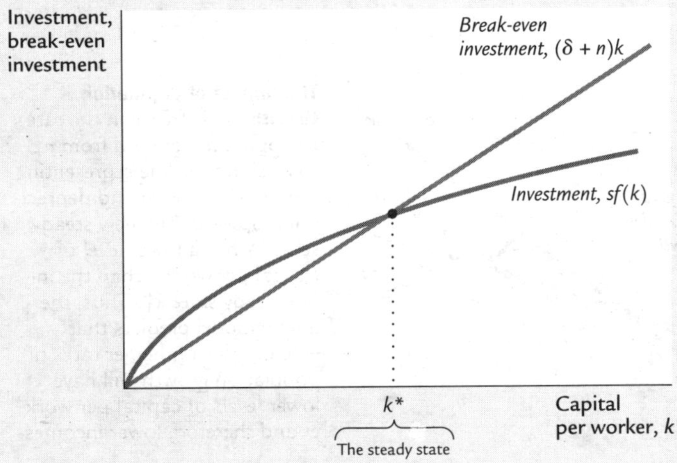

Population Growth in the Solow Model Depreciation and population growth are two reasons the capital stock per worker shrinks. If n is the rate of population growth and δ is the rate of depreciation, then $(\delta + n)k$ is *break-even investment*—the amount of investment necessary to keep constant the capital stock per worker k. For the economy to be in a steady state, investment $sf(k)$ must offset the effects of depreciation and population growth $(\delta + n)k$. This is represented by the crossing of the two curves.

[5] *Mathematical note:* Formally deriving the equation for the change in k requires a bit of calculus. Note that the change in k per unit of time is $dk/dt = d(K/L)/dt$. After applying the chain rule, we can write this as $dk/dt = (1/L)(dK/dt) - (K/L^2)(dL/dt)$. Now use the following facts to substitute in this equation: $dK/dt = I - \delta K$ and $(dL/dt)/L = n$. After a bit of manipulation, this produces the equation in the text.

unchanging. As before, we designate the steady-state value of k as k^*. If k is less than k^*, investment is greater than break-even investment, so k rises. If k is greater than k^*, investment is less than break-even investment, so k falls.

In the steady state, the positive effect of investment on the capital stock per worker exactly balances the negative effects of depreciation and population growth. That is, at k^*, $\Delta k = 0$ and $i^* = \delta k^* + nk^*$. Once the economy is in the steady state, investment has two purposes. Some of it (δk^*) replaces the depreciated capital, and the rest (nk^*) provides the new workers with the steady-state amount of capital.

The Effects of Population Growth

Population growth alters the basic Solow model in three ways. First, it brings us closer to explaining sustained economic growth. In the steady state with population growth, capital per worker and output per worker are constant. Because the number of workers is growing at rate n, however, *total* capital and *total* output must also be growing at rate n. Hence, although population growth cannot explain sustained growth in the standard of living (because output per worker is constant in the steady state), it can help explain sustained growth in total output.

Second, population growth gives us another explanation for why some countries are rich and others are poor. Consider the effects of an increase in population growth. Figure 7-12 shows that an increase in the rate of population growth from n_1 to n_2 reduces the steady-state level of capital per worker from k_1^* to k_2^*. Because

FIGURE 7-12

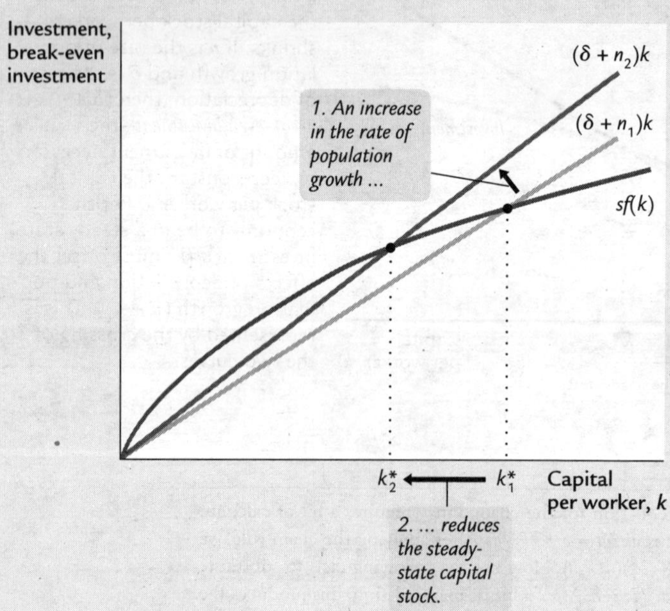

The Impact of Population Growth An increase in the rate of population growth from n_1 to n_2 shifts the line representing population growth and depreciation upward. The new steady state k_2^* has a lower level of capital per worker than the initial steady state k_1^*. Thus, the Solow model predicts that economies with higher rates of population growth will have lower levels of capital per worker and therefore lower incomes.

k^* is lower, and because $y^* = f(k^*)$, the level of output per worker y^* is also lower. Thus, the Solow model predicts that countries with higher population growth will have lower levels of GDP per person. Notice that a change in the population growth rate, like a change in the saving rate, has a level effect on income per person, but does not affect the steady-state growth rate of income per person.

Finally, population growth affects our criterion for determining the Golden Rule (consumption-maximizing) level of capital. To see how this criterion changes, note that consumption per worker is

$$c = y - i.$$

Because steady-state output is $f(k^*)$ and steady-state investment is $(\delta + n)k^*$, we can express steady-state consumption as

$$c^* = f(k^*) - (\delta + n)k^*.$$

Using an argument largely the same as before, we conclude that the level of k^* that maximizes consumption is the one at which

$$MPK = \delta + n,$$

or equivalently,

$$MPK - \delta = n.$$

In the Golden Rule steady state, the marginal product of capital net of depreciation equals the rate of population growth.

CASE STUDY

Population Growth Around the World

Let's return now to the question of why standards of living vary so much around the world. The analysis we have just completed suggests that population growth may be one of the answers. According to the Solow model, a nation with a high rate of population growth will have a low steady-state capital stock per worker and thus also a low level of income per worker. In other words, high population growth tends to impoverish a country because it is hard to maintain a high level of capital per worker when the number of workers is growing quickly. To see whether the evidence supports this conclusion, we again look at cross-country data.

Figure 7-13 is a scatterplot of data for the same 96 countries examined in the previous case study (and in Figure 7-6). The figure shows that countries with high rates of population growth tend to have low levels of income per person. The international evidence is consistent with our model's prediction that the rate of population growth is one determinant of a country's standard of living.

This conclusion is not lost on policymakers. Those trying to pull the world's poorest nations out of poverty, such as the advisers sent to developing nations by the World Bank, often advocate reducing fertility by increasing education about birth-control methods and expanding women's job opportunities. Toward the same end, China has followed the totalitarian policy of allowing only one child

FIGURE 7-13

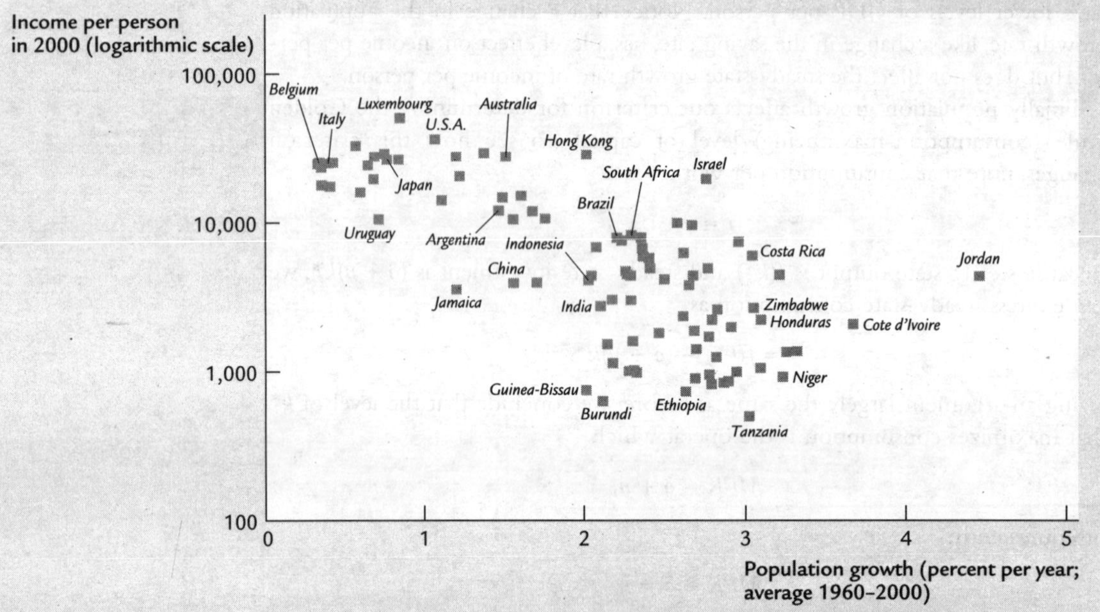

International Evidence on Population Growth and Income per Person This figure is a scatterplot of data from 96 countries. It shows that countries with high rates of population growth tend to have low levels of income per person, as the Solow model predicts.

Source: Alan Heston, Robert Summers and Bettina Aten, Penn World Table Version 6.1, Center for International Comparisons at the University of Pennsylvania (CICUP), October 2002.

per couple. These policies to reduce population growth should, if the Solow model is right, raise income per person in the long run.

In interpreting the cross-country data, however, it is important to keep in mind that correlation does not imply causation. The data show that low population growth is typically associated with high levels of income per person, and the Solow model offers one possible explanation for this fact, but other explanations are also possible. It is conceivable that high income encourages low population growth, perhaps because birth-control techniques are more readily available in richer countries. The international data can help us evaluate a theory of growth, such as the Solow model, because they show us whether the theory's predictions are borne out in the world. But often more than one theory can explain the same facts.

Alternative Perspectives on Population Growth

The Solow growth model highlights the interaction between population growth and capital accumulation. In this model, high population growth reduces output per worker because rapid growth in the number of workers forces the capital stock to be spread more thinly, so in the steady state, each worker is equipped with less capital. The model omits some other potential effects of population growth. Here we consider two—one emphasizing the interaction of population with natural resources, the other emphasizing the interaction of population with technology.

The Malthusian Model In his book *An Essay on the Principle of Population as It Affects the Future Improvement of Society,* the early economist Thomas Robert Malthus (1766–1834) offered what may be history's most chilling forecast. Malthus argued that an ever increasing population would continually strain society's ability to provide for itself. Mankind, he predicted, would forever live in poverty.

Malthus began by noting that "food is necessary to the existence of man" and that "the passion between the sexes is necessary and will remain nearly in its present state." He concluded that "the power of population is infinitely greater than the power in the earth to produce subsistence for man." According to Malthus, the only check on population growth was "misery and vice." Attempts by charities or governments to alleviate poverty were counterproductive, he argued, because they merely allowed the poor to have more children, placing even greater strains on society's productive capabilities.

Although the Malthusian model may have described the world when Malthus lived, its prediction that mankind would remain in poverty forever has proven very wrong. The world population has increased about sixfold over the past two centuries, but average living standards are much higher. Because of economic growth, chronic hunger and malnutrition are less common now than they were in Malthus's day. Famines occur from time to time, but they are more often the result of an unequal income distribution or political instability than an inadequate production of food.

Malthus failed to see that growth in mankind's ingenuity would more than offset the effects of a larger population. Pesticides, fertilizers, mechanized farm equipment, new crop varieties, and other technological advances that Malthus never imagined have allowed each farmer to feed ever greater numbers of people. Even with more mouths to feed, few farmers are necessary because each farmer is so productive. Today, fewer than 2 percent of Americans work on farms, producing enough food to feed the nation and some excess to export as well.

In addition, although the "passion between the sexes" is just as strong now as it was in Malthus's day, the link between passion and population growth that Malthus assumed has been broken by modern birth control. Many advanced nations, such as those in Western Europe, are now experiencing fertility below replacement rates. Over the next century, shrinking populations may be more likely than rapidly expanding ones. There is now little reason to think that an ever expanding population will overwhelm food production and doom mankind to poverty.[6]

The Kremerian Model While Malthus saw population growth as a threat to rising living standards, economist Michael Kremer has suggested that world population growth is a key driver of advancing economic prosperity. If there are more

---

[6] For modern analyses of the Malthusian model, see Oded Galor and David N. Weil, "Population, Technology, and Growth: From Malthusian Stagnation to the Demographic Transition and Beyond," *American Economic Review* 90 (September 2000): 806–828; and Gary D. Hansen and Edward C. Prescott, "Malthus to Solow," *American Economic Review* 92 (September 2002): 1205–1217.

people, Kremer argues, then there are more scientists, inventors, and engineers to contribute to innovation and technological progress.

As evidence for this hypothesis, Kremer begins by noting that over the broad span of human history, world growth rates have increased together with world population. For example, world growth was more rapid when the world population was 1 billion (which occurred around the year 1800) than it was when the population was only 100 million (around 500 B.C.). This fact is consistent with the hypothesis that having more people induces more technological progress.

Kremer's second, more compelling piece of evidence comes from comparing regions of the world. The melting of the polar ice caps at the end of the ice age around 10,000 B.C. flooded the land bridges and separated the world into several distinct regions that could not communicate with one another for thousands of years. If technological progress is more rapid when there are more people to discover things, then the more populous regions should have experienced more rapid growth.

And, indeed, they did. The most successful region of the world in 1500 (when Columbus reestablished technological contact) included the "Old World" civilizations of the large Eurasia-Africa region. Next in technological development were the Aztec and Mayan civilizations in the Americas, followed by the hunter-gatherers of Australia, and then the primitive people of Tasmania, who lacked even fire-making and most stone and bone tools. The least populous isolated region was Flinders Island, a tiny island between Tasmania and Australia. With few people to contribute new innovations, Flinders Island had the least technological advance and, in fact, seemed to regress. Around 3000 B.C., human society on Flinders Island died out completely.

Kremer concludes from this evidence that a large population is a prerequisite for technological advance.[7]

7-4 Conclusion

This chapter has started the process of building the Solow growth model. The model as developed so far shows how saving and population growth determine the economy's steady-state capital stock and its steady-state level of income per person. As we have seen, it sheds light on many features of actual growth experiences—why Germany and Japan grew so rapidly after being devastated by World War II, why countries that save and invest a high fraction of their output are richer than countries that save and invest a smaller fraction, and why countries with high rates of population growth are poorer than countries with low rates of population growth.

What the model cannot do, however, is explain the persistent growth in living standards we observe in most countries. In the model we now have, when

[7] Michael Kremer, "Population Growth and Technological Change: One Million B.C. to 1990," *Quarterly Journal of Economics* 108 (August 1993): 681–716.

the economy reaches its steady state, output per worker stops growing. To explain persistent growth, we need to introduce technological progress into the model. That is our first job in the next chapter.

Summary

1. The Solow growth model shows that in the long run, an economy's rate of saving determines the size of its capital stock and thus its level of production. The higher the rate of saving, the higher the stock of capital and the higher the level of output.
2. In the Solow model, an increase in the rate of saving has a level effect on income per person: it causes a period of rapid growth, but eventually that growth slows as the new steady state is reached. Thus, although a high saving rate yields a high steady-state level of output, saving by itself cannot generate persistent economic growth.
3. The level of capital that maximizes steady-state consumption is called the Golden Rule level. If an economy has more capital than in the Golden Rule steady state, then reducing saving will increase consumption at all points in time. By contrast, if the economy has less capital than in the Golden Rule steady state, then reaching the Golden Rule requires increased investment and thus lower consumption for current generations.
4. The Solow model shows that an economy's rate of population growth is another long-run determinant of the standard of living. According to the Solow model, the higher the rate of population growth, the lower the steady-state levels of capital per worker and output per worker. Other theories highlight other effects of population growth. Malthus suggested that population growth will strain the natural resources necessary to produce food; Kremer suggested that a large population may promote technological progress.

KEY CONCEPTS

Solow growth model

Steady state

Golden Rule level of capital

QUESTIONS FOR REVIEW

1. In the Solow model, how does the saving rate affect the steady-state level of income? How does it affect the steady-state rate of growth?
2. Why might an economic policymaker choose the Golden Rule level of capital?
3. Might a policymaker choose a steady state with more capital than in the Golden Rule steady state? With less capital than in the Golden Rule steady state? Explain your answers.
4. In the Solow model, how does the rate of population growth affect the steady-state level of income? How does it affect the steady-state rate of growth?

PROBLEMS AND APPLICATIONS

1. Country A and country B both have the production function

$$Y = F(K, L) = K^{1/2}L^{1/2}.$$

   a. Does this production function have constant returns to scale? Explain.

   b. What is the per-worker production function, $y = f(k)$?

   c. Assume that neither country experiences population growth or technological progress and that 5 percent of capital depreciates each year. Assume further that country A saves 10 percent of output each year and country B saves 20 percent of output each year. Using your answer from part (b) and the steady-state condition that investment equals depreciation, find the steady-state level of capital per worker for each country. Then find the steady-state levels of income per worker and consumption per worker.

   d. Suppose that both countries start off with a capital stock per worker of 2. What are the levels of income per worker and consumption per worker? Remembering that the change in the capital stock is investment less depreciation, use a calculator or a computer spreadsheet to show how the capital stock per worker will evolve over time in both countries. For each year, calculate income per worker and consumption per worker. How many years will it be before the consumption in country B is higher than the consumption in country A?

2. In the discussion of German and Japanese postwar growth, the text describes what happens when part of the capital stock is destroyed in a war. By contrast, suppose that a war does not directly affect the capital stock, but that casualties reduce the labor force.

   a. What is the immediate impact on total output and on output per person?

   b. Assuming that the saving rate is unchanged and that the economy was in a steady state before the war, what happens subsequently to output per worker in the postwar economy? Is the growth rate of output per worker after the war smaller or greater than normal?

3. Consider an economy described by the production function: $Y = F(K, L) = K^{0.3}L^{0.7}$.

   a. What is the per-worker production function?

   b. Assuming no population growth or technological progress, find the steady-state capital stock per worker, output per worker, and consumption per worker as a function of the saving rate and the depreciation rate.

   c. Assume that the depreciation rate is 10 percent per year. Make a table showing steady-state capital per worker, output per worker, and consumption per worker for saving rates of 0 percent, 10 percent, 20 percent, 30 percent, and so on. (You will need a calculator with an exponent key for this.) What saving rate maximizes output per worker? What saving rate maximizes consumption per worker?

   d. (Harder) Use calculus to find the marginal product of capital. Add to your table the marginal product of capital net of depreciation for each of the saving rates. What does your table show?

4. "Devoting a larger share of national output to investment would help restore rapid productivity growth and rising living standards." Do you agree with this claim? Explain.

5. One view of the consumption function is that workers have high propensities to consume and capitalists have low propensities to consume. To explore the implications of this view, suppose that an economy consumes all wage income and saves all capital income. Show that if the factors of production earn their marginal product, this economy reaches the Golden Rule level of capital. (*Hint:* Begin with the identity that saving equals investment. Then use the steady-state condition that investment is just enough to keep up with depreciation and population growth, and the fact that saving equals capital income in this economy.)

6. Many demographers predict that the United States will have zero population growth in the twenty-first century, in contrast to average population growth of about 1 percent per year in the twentieth century. Use the Solow model to forecast the effect of this slowdown in population growth on the growth of total output and the

growth of output per person. Consider the effects both in the steady state and in the transition between steady states.

7. In the Solow model, population growth leads to steady-state growth in total output, but not in output per worker. Do you think this would still be true if the production function exhibited increasing or decreasing returns to scale? Explain. (For the definitions of increasing and decreasing returns to scale, see Chapter 3, "Problems and Applications," Problem 2.)

8. Consider how unemployment would affect the Solow growth model. Suppose that output is produced according to the production function $Y = K^{\alpha}[(1 - u)L]^{1-\alpha}$, where K is capital, L is the labor force, and u is the natural rate of unemployment. The national saving rate is s, the labor force grows at rate n, and capital depreciates at rate δ.

   a. Express output per worker ($y = Y/L$) as a function of capital per worker ($k = K/L$) and the natural rate of unemployment. Describe the steady state of this economy.

   b. Suppose that some change in government policy reduces the natural rate of unemployment. Describe how this change affects output both immediately and over time. Is the steady-state effect on output larger or smaller than the immediate effect? Explain.

9. Choose two countries that interest you—one rich and one poor. What is the income per person in each country? Find some data on country characteristics that might help explain the difference in income: investment rates, population growth rates, educational attainment, and so on. (*Hint:* The Web site of the World Bank, www.worldbank.org, is one place to find such data.) How might you figure out which of these factors is most responsible for the observed income difference?

CHAPTER

8

Economic Growth II: Technology, Empirics, and Policy

Is there some action a government of India could take that would lead the Indian economy to grow like Indonesia's or Egypt's? If so, what, exactly? If not, what is it about the "nature of India" that makes it so? The consequences for human welfare involved in questions like these are simply staggering: Once one starts to think about them, it is hard to think about anything else.

— Robert E. Lucas, Jr.

This chapter continues our analysis of the forces governing long-run economic growth. With the basic version of the Solow growth model as our starting point, we take on four new tasks.

Our first task is to make the Solow model more general and more realistic. In Chapter 3 we saw that capital, labor, and technology are the key determinants of a nation's production of goods and services. In Chapter 7 we developed the Solow model to show how changes in capital (saving and investment) and changes in the labor force (population growth) affect the economy's output. We are now ready to add the third source of growth—changes in technology—into the mix. The Solow model does not explain technological progress but, instead, takes it as exogenously given and shows how it interacts with other variables in the process of economic growth.

Our second task is to move from theory to empirics. That is, we consider how well the Solow model fits the facts. Over the past two decades, a large literature has examined the predictions of the Solow model and other models of economic growth. It turns out that the glass is both half full and half empty. The Solow model can shed much light on international growth experiences, but it is far from the last word on the subject.

Our third task is to examine how a nation's public policies can influence the level and growth of its citizens' standard of living. In particular, we address five questions: Should our society save more or save less? How can policy influence the rate of saving? Are there some types of investment that policy should especially encourage? What institutions ensure that the economy's resources are put to their best use? How can policy increase the rate of technological progress? The Solow growth model provides the theoretical framework within which we consider these policy issues.

Our fourth and final task is to consider what the Solow model leaves out. As we have discussed previously, models help us understand the world by simplifying it. After completing an analysis of a model, therefore, it is important to consider whether we have oversimplified matters. In the last section, we examine a new set of theories, called *endogenous growth theories*, that hope to explain the technological progress that the Solow model takes as exogenous.

8-1 Technological Progress in the Solow Model

So far, our presentation of the Solow model has assumed an unchanging relationship between the inputs of capital and labor and the output of goods and services. Yet the model can be modified to include exogenous technological progress, which over time expands society's ability to produce.

The Efficiency of Labor

To incorporate technological progress, we must return to the production function that relates total capital K and total labor L to total output Y. Thus far, the production function has been

$$Y = F(K, L).$$

We now write the production function as

$$Y = F(K, L \times E),$$

where E is a new (and somewhat abstract) variable called the **efficiency of labor**. The efficiency of labor is meant to reflect society's knowledge about production methods: as the available technology improves, the efficiency of labor rises. For instance, the efficiency of labor rose when assembly-line production transformed manufacturing in the early twentieth century, and it rose again when computerization was introduced in the late twentieth century. The efficiency of labor also rises when there are improvements in the health, education, or skills of the labor force.

The term $L \times E$ measures the *effective number of workers*. It takes into account the number of workers L and the efficiency of each worker E. This new production function states that total output Y depends on the inputs of capital K and effective workers $L \times E$.

The essence of this approach to modeling technological progress is that increases in the efficiency of labor E are analogous to increases in the labor force

L. Suppose, for example, that an advance in production methods makes the efficiency of labor E double between 1980 and 2010. This means that a single worker in 2010 is, *in effect*, as productive as two workers were in 1980. That is, even if the actual number of workers (L) stays the same from 1980 to 2010, the effective number of workers ($L \times E$) doubles, and the economy will benefit from the increased production of goods and services.

The simplest assumption about technological progress is that it causes the efficiency of labor E to grow at some constant rate g. For example, if $g = 0.02$, then each unit of labor becomes 2 percent more efficient each year: output increases as if the labor force had increased by an additional 2 percent. This form of technological progress is called *labor augmenting*, and g is called the rate of **labor-augmenting technological progress**. Because the labor force L is growing at rate n, and the efficiency of each unit of labor E is growing at rate g, the effective number of workers $L \times E$ is growing at rate $n + g$.

The Steady State With Technological Progress

Because technological progress is modeled here as labor augmenting, it has effects similar to those of population growth. Although technological progress does not cause the actual number of workers to increase, each worker in effect comes with more units of labor over time. Thus, technological progress causes the effective number of workers to increase. The analytic tools we used in Chapter 7 to study the Solow model with population growth are easily adapted to studying the Solow model with labor-augmenting technological progress.

We begin by reconsidering our notation. Previously, we analyzed the economy in terms of quantities per worker; now we analyze the economy in terms of quantities per effective worker. We now let $k = K/(L \times E)$ stand for capital per effective worker, and $y = Y/(L \times E)$ stand for output per effective worker. With these definitions, we can again write $y = f(k)$.

Our analysis of the economy proceeds just as it did when we examined population growth. The equation showing the evolution of k over time now changes to

$$\Delta k = sf(k) - (\delta + n + g)k.$$

As before, the change in the capital stock Δk equals investment $sf(k)$ minus break-even investment $(\delta + n + g)k$. Now, however, because $k = K/(L \times E)$, break-even investment includes three terms: to keep k constant, δk is needed to replace depreciating capital, nk is needed to provide capital for new workers, and gk is needed to provide capital for the new "effective workers" created by technological progress.[1]

[1] *Mathematical note:* This model with technological progress is a strict generalization of the model analyzed in Chapter 7. In particular, if the efficiency of labor is constant at $E = 1$, then $g = 0$, and the definitions of k and y reduce to our previous definitions. In this case, the more general model considered here simplifies precisely to the Chapter 7 version of the Solow model.

FIGURE 8-1

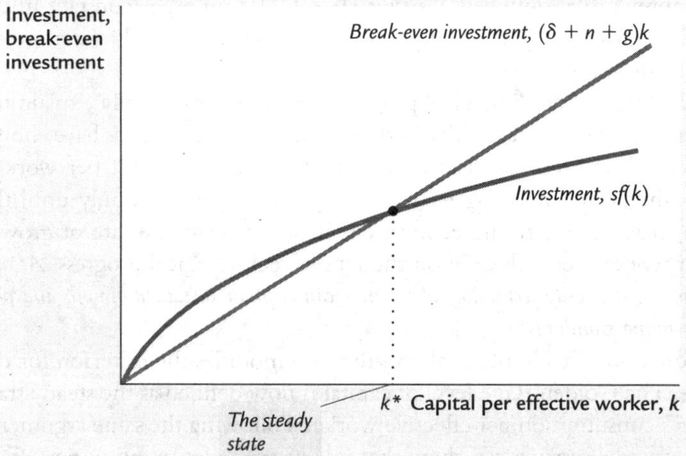

Technological Progress and the Solow Growth Model Labor-augmenting technological progress at rate g enters our analysis of the Solow growth model in much the same way as did population growth at rate n. Now that k is defined as the amount of capital per effective worker, increases in the effective number of workers because of technological progress tend to decrease k. In the steady state, investment $sf(k)$ exactly offsets the reductions in k attributable to depreciation, population growth, and technological progress.

As shown in Figure 8-1, the inclusion of technological progress does not substantially alter our analysis of the steady state. There is one level of k, denoted k^*, at which capital per effective worker and output per effective worker are constant. As before, this steady state represents the long-run equilibrium of the economy.

The Effects of Technological Progress

Table 8-1 shows how four key variables behave in the steady state with technological progress. As we have just seen, capital per effective worker k is constant in the steady state. Because $y = f(k)$, output per effective worker is also constant. It is these quantities per effective worker that are steady in the steady state.

From this information, we can also infer what's happening to other variables, those not expressed per effective worker. For instance, consider output per actual

TABLE 8-1

Steady-State Growth Rates in the Solow Model With Technological Progress

Variable	Symbol	Steady-State Growth Rate
Capital per effective worker	$k = K/(E \times L)$	0
Output per effective worker	$y = Y/(E \times L) = f(k)$	0
Output per worker	$Y/L = y \times E$	g
Total output	$Y = y \times (E \times L)$	$n + g$

worker $Y/L = y \times E$. Because y is constant in the steady state and E is growing at rate g, output per worker must also be growing at rate g in the steady state. Similarly, the economy's total output is $Y = y \times (E \times L)$. Because y is constant in the steady state, E is growing at rate g, and L is growing at rate n, total output grows at rate $n + g$ in the steady state.

With the addition of technological progress, our model can finally explain the sustained increases in standards of living that we observe. That is, we have shown that technological progress can lead to sustained growth in output per worker. By contrast, a high rate of saving leads to a high rate of growth only until the steady state is reached. Once the economy is in steady state, the rate of growth of output per worker depends only on the rate of technological progress. *According to the Solow model, only technological progress can explain sustained growth and persistently rising living standards.*

The introduction of technological progress also modifies the criterion for the Golden Rule. The Golden Rule level of capital is now defined as the steady state that maximizes consumption per effective worker. Following the same arguments that we have used before, we can show that steady-state consumption per effective worker is

$$c^* = f(k^*) - (\delta + n + g)k^*.$$

Steady-state consumption is maximized if

$$MPK = \delta + n + g,$$

or

$$MPK - \delta = n + g.$$

That is, at the Golden Rule level of capital, the net marginal product of capital, $MPK - \delta$, equals the rate of growth of total output, $n + g$. Because actual economies experience both population growth and technological progress, we must use this criterion to evaluate whether they have more or less capital than they would at the Golden Rule steady state.

8-2 From Growth Theory to Growth Empirics

So far in this chapter we have introduced exogenous technological progress into the Solow model to explain sustained growth in standards of living. Let's now discuss what happens when the theory is forced to confront the facts.

Balanced Growth

According to the Solow model, technological progress causes the values of many variables to rise together in the steady state. This property, called *balanced growth*, does a good job of describing the long-run data for the U.S. economy.

Consider first output per worker Y/L and the capital stock per worker K/L. According to the Solow model, in the steady state, both of these variables grow at g, the rate of technological progress. U.S. data for the past half-century show that output per worker and the capital stock per worker have in fact grown at approximately the same rate—about 2 percent per year. To put it another way, the capital-output ratio has remained approximately constant over time.

Technological progress also affects factor prices. Problem 3(d) at the end of the chapter asks you to show that, in the steady state, the real wage grows at the rate of technological progress. The real rental price of capital, however, is constant over time. Again, these predictions hold true for the United States. Over the past 50 years, the real wage has increased about 2 percent per year; it has increased by about the same amount as real GDP per worker. Yet the real rental price of capital (measured as real capital income divided by the capital stock) has remained about the same.

The Solow model's prediction about factor prices—and the success of this prediction—is especially noteworthy when contrasted with Karl Marx's theory of the development of capitalist economies. Marx predicted that the return to capital would decline over time and that this would lead to economic and political crisis. Economic history has not supported Marx's prediction, which partly explains why we now study Solow's theory of growth rather than Marx's.

Convergence

If you travel around the world, you will see tremendous variation in living standards. The world's poor countries have average levels of income per person that are less than one-tenth the average levels in the world's rich countries. These differences in income are reflected in almost every measure of the quality of life—from the number of televisions and telephones per household to the infant mortality rate and life expectancy.

Much research has been devoted to the question of whether economies converge over time to one another. In particular, do economies that start off poor subsequently grow faster than economies that start off rich? If they do, then the world's poor economies will tend to catch up with the world's rich economies. This property of catch up is called *convergence*. If there is not convergence, then countries that start off behind are likely to remain poor.

The Solow model makes clear predictions about when convergence should occur. According to the model, whether two economies will converge depends on why they differ in the first place. On the one hand, suppose two economies happen by historical accident to start off with different capital stocks, but they have the same steady state, as determined by their saving rates, population growth rates, and the efficiency of labor. In this case, we should expect the two economies to converge; the poorer economy with the smaller capital stock will naturally grow more quickly to reach the steady state. (In a case study in Chapter 7, we applied this logic to explain rapid growth in Germany and Japan after World War II.) On the other hand, if two economies have different steady states, perhaps because the economies have different rates of saving, then we should not expect convergence. Instead, each economy will approach its own steady state.

Experience is consistent with this analysis. In samples of economies with similar cultures and policies, studies find that economies converge to one another at a rate of about 2 percent per year. That is, the gap between rich and poor economies closes by about 2 percent each year. An example is the economies of individual American states. For historical reasons, such as the Civil War of the 1860s, income levels varied greatly among states a century ago. Yet these differences have slowly disappeared over time.

In international data, a more complex picture emerges. When researchers examine only data on income per person, they find little evidence of convergence: countries that start off poor do not grow faster on average than countries that start off rich. This finding suggests that different countries have different steady states. If statistical techniques are used to control for some of the determinants of the steady state, such as saving rates, population growth rates, and accumulation of human capital (education), then once again the data show convergence at a rate of about 2 percent per year. In other words, the economies of the world exhibit *conditional convergence*: they appear to be converging to their own steady states, which in turn are determined by such variables as saving, population growth, and human capital.[2]

Factor Accumulation Versus Production Efficiency

As a matter of accounting, international differences in income per person can be attributed to either (1) differences in the factors of production, such as the quantities of physical and human capital, or (2) differences in the efficiency with which economies use their factors of production. That is, a worker in a poor country may be poor because he lacks tools and skills or because the tools and skills he has are not being put to their best use. To describe this issue in terms of the Solow model, the question is whether the large gap between rich and poor is explained by differences in capital accumulation (including human capital) or differences in the production function.

Much research has attempted to estimate the relative importance of these two sources of income disparities. The exact answer varies from study to study, but both factor accumulation and production efficiency appear important. Moreover, a common finding is that they are positively correlated: nations with high levels of physical and human capital also tend to use those factors efficiently.[3]

---

[2] Robert Barro and Xavier Sala-i-Martin, "Convergence Across States and Regions," *Brookings Papers on Economic Activity* 1 (1991): 107–182; N. Gregory Mankiw, David Romer, and David N. Weil, "A Contribution to the Empirics of Economic Growth," *Quarterly Journal of Economics* (May 1992): 407–437.

[3] Robert E. Hall and Charles I. Jones, "Why Do Some Countries Produce So Much More Output per Worker Than Others?" *Quarterly Journal of Economics* 114 (February 1999): 83–116; Peter J. Klenow and Andres Rodriguez-Clare, "The Neoclassical Revival in Growth Economics: Has It Gone Too Far?" *NBER Macroeconomics Annual* (1997): 73–103.

There are several ways to interpret this positive correlation. One hypothesis is that an efficient economy may encourage capital accumulation. For example, a person in a well-functioning economy may have greater resources and incentive to stay in school and accumulate human capital. Another hypothesis is that capital accumulation may induce greater efficiency. If there are positive externalities to physical and human capital, then countries that save and invest more will appear to have better production functions (unless the research study accounts for these externalities, which is hard to do). Thus, greater production efficiency may cause greater factor accumulation, or the other way around.

A final hypothesis is that both factor accumulation and production efficiency are driven by a common third variable. Perhaps the common third variable is the quality of the nation's institutions, including the government's policymaking process. As one economist put it, when governments screw up, they screw up big time. Bad policies, such as high inflation, excessive budget deficits, widespread market interference, and rampant corruption, often go hand in hand. We should not be surprised that economies exhibiting these maladies both accumulate less capital and fail to use the capital they have as efficiently as they might.

CASE STUDY

Is Free Trade Good for Economic Growth?

At least since Adam Smith, economists have advocated free trade as a policy that promotes national prosperity. Here is how Smith put the argument in his 1776 classic, *The Wealth of Nations:*

> "It is a maxim of every prudent master of a family, never to attempt to make at home what it will cost him more to make than to buy. The tailor does not attempt to make his own shoes, but buys them of the shoemaker. The shoemaker does not attempt to make his own clothes but employs a tailor. . . .
>
> What is prudence in the conduct of every private family can scarce be folly in that of a great kingdom. If a foreign country can supply us with a commodity cheaper than we ourselves can make it, better buy it of them with some part of the produce of our own industry employed in a way in which we have some advantage."

Today, economists make the case with greater rigor, relying on David Ricardo's theory of comparative advantage as well as more modern theories of international trade. According to these theories, a nation open to trade can achieve greater production efficiency and a higher standard of living by specializing in those goods for which it has a comparative advantage.

A skeptic might point out that this is just theory. What about the evidence? Do nations that permit free trade in fact enjoy greater prosperity? A large literature addresses precisely this question.

One approach is to look at international data to see if countries that are open to trade typically enjoy greater prosperity. The fact is that they do. Economists Andrew Warner and Jeffrey Sachs studied the period from 1970 to 1989. They report that among developed nations, the open economies grew at 2.3 percent per year, while the closed economies grew at 0.7 percent per year. Among developing nations, the open economies grew at 4.5 percent per year, while the closed economies again grew at 0.7 percent per year. These findings are consistent with Smith's view that trade enhances prosperity, but they are not conclusive. Correlation does not prove causation. Perhaps being closed to trade is correlated with various other restrictive government policies, and it is those other policies that retard growth.

A second approach is to look at what happens when closed economies remove their trade restrictions. Once again, Smith's hypothesis fares well. Throughout history, when nations open themselves up to the world economy, the typical result is a subsequent increase in economic growth. This occurred in Japan in the 1850s, South Korea in the 1960s, and Vietnam in the 1990s. But once again, correlation does not prove causation. Trade liberalization is often accompanied by other reforms, and it is hard to disentangle the effects of trade from the effects of the other reforms.

A third approach to measuring the impact of trade on growth, proposed by economists Jeffrey Frankel and David Romer, is to look at the impact of geography. Some countries trade less simply because they are geographically disadvantaged. For example, New Zealand is disadvantaged compared to Belgium because it is farther from other populous countries. Similarly, landlocked countries are disadvantaged compared to countries with their own seaports. Because these geographical characteristics are correlated with trade, but arguably uncorrelated with other determinants of economic prosperity, they can be used to identify the causal impact of trade on income. (The statistical technique, which you may have studied in an econometrics course, is called *instrumental variables*.) After analyzing the data, Frankel and Romer conclude that "a rise of one percentage point in the ratio of trade to GDP increases income per person by at least one-half percentage point. Trade appears to raise income by spurring the accumulation of human and physical capital and by increasing output for given levels of capital."

The overwhelming weight of the evidence from this body of research is that Adam Smith was right. Openness to international trade is good for economic growth.[4]

8-3 Policies to Promote Growth

So far we have used the Solow model to uncover the theoretical relationships among the different sources of economic growth, and we have discussed some of the empirical work that describes actual growth experiences. We can now use the theory and evidence to help guide our thinking about economic policy.

[4] Jeffrey D. Sachs and Andrew Warner, "Economic Reform and the Process of Global Integration." *Brookings Papers on Economic Activity* (1995): 1–95; Jeffrey A. Frankel and David Romer, "Does Trade Cause Growth?" *American Economic Review* 89 (June 1999): 379–399.

Evaluating the Rate of Saving

According to the Solow growth model, how much a nation saves and invests is a key determinant of its citizens' standard of living. So let's begin our policy discussion with a natural question: Is the rate of saving in the U.S. economy too low, too high, or about right?

As we have seen, the saving rate determines the steady-state levels of capital and output. One particular saving rate produces the Golden Rule steady state, which maximizes consumption per worker and thus economic well-being. The Golden Rule provides the benchmark against which we can compare the U.S. economy.

To decide whether the U.S. economy is at, above, or below the Golden Rule steady state, we need to compare the marginal product of capital net of depreciation ($MPK - \delta$) with the growth rate of total output ($n + g$). As we established in Section 8-1, at the Golden Rule steady state, $MPK - \delta = n + g$. If the economy is operating with less capital than in the Golden Rule steady state, then diminishing marginal product tells us that $MPK - \delta > n + g$. In this case, increasing the rate of saving will increase capital accumulation and economic growth and, eventually, lead to a steady state with higher consumption (although consumption will be lower for part of the transition to the new steady state). On the other hand, if the economy has more capital than in the Golden Rule steady state, then $MPK - \delta < n + g$. In this case, capital accumulation is excessive: reducing the rate of saving would lead to higher consumption both immediately and in the long run.

To make this comparison for a real economy, such as the U.S. economy, we need an estimate of the growth rate of output ($n + g$) and an estimate of the net marginal product of capital ($MPK - \delta$). Real GDP in the United States grows an average of 3 percent per year, so $n + g = 0.03$. We can estimate the net marginal product of capital from the following three facts:

1. The capital stock is about 2.5 times one year's GDP.
2. Depreciation of capital is about 10 percent of GDP.
3. Capital income is about 30 percent of GDP.

Using the notation of our model (and the result from Chapter 3 that capital owners earn income of *MPK* for each unit of capital), we can write these facts as

1. $k = 2.5y$.
2. $\delta k = 0.1y$.
3. $MPK \times k = 0.3y$.

We solve for the rate of depreciation δ by dividing equation 2 by equation 1:

$$\delta k/k = (0.1y)/(2.5y)$$
$$\delta = 0.04.$$

And we solve for the marginal product of capital *MPK* by dividing equation 3 by equation 1:

$$(MPK \times k)/k = (0.3y)/(2.5y)$$
$$MPK = 0.12.$$

Thus, about 4 percent of the capital stock depreciates each year, and the marginal product of capital is about 12 percent per year. The net marginal product of capital, $MPK - \delta$, is about 8 percent per year.

We can now see that the return to capital ($MPK - \delta = 8$ percent per year) is well in excess of the economy's average growth rate ($n + g = 3$ percent per year). This fact, together with our previous analysis, indicates that the capital stock in the U.S. economy is well below the Golden Rule level. In other words, if the United States saved and invested a higher fraction of its income, it would grow more rapidly and eventually reach a steady state with higher consumption.

This conclusion is not unique to the U.S. economy. When calculations similar to those above are done for other economies, the results are similar. The possibility of excessive saving and capital accumulation beyond the Golden Rule level is intriguing as a matter of theory, but it appears not to be a problem that actual economies face. In practice, economists are more often concerned with insufficient saving. It is this kind of calculation that provides the intellectual foundation for this concern.[5]

Changing the Rate of Saving

The preceding calculations show that to move the U.S. economy toward the Golden Rule steady state, policymakers should increase national saving. But how can they do that? We saw in Chapter 3 that, as a matter of sheer accounting, higher national saving means higher public saving, higher private saving, or some combination of the two. Much of the debate over policies to increase growth centers on which of these options is likely to be most effective.

The most direct way in which the government affects national saving is through public saving—the difference between what the government receives in tax revenue and what it spends. When the government's spending exceeds its revenue, the government runs a *budget deficit*, which represents negative public saving. As we saw in Chapter 3, a budget deficit raises interest rates and crowds out investment; the resulting reduction in the capital stock is part of the burden of the national debt on future generations. Conversely, if the government spends less than it raises in revenue, it runs a *budget surplus*, which it can use to retire some of the national debt and stimulate investment.

The government also affects national saving by influencing private saving—the saving done by households and firms. In particular, how much people decide to save depends on the incentives they face, and these incentives are altered by a variety of public policies. Many economists argue that high tax rates on capital—including the corporate income tax, the federal income tax, the estate tax, and many state income and estate taxes—discourage private saving by reducing the rate of return that savers earn. On the other hand, tax-exempt retirement

[5] For more on this topic and some international evidence, see Andrew B. Abel, N. Gregory Mankiw, Lawrence H. Summers, and Richard J. Zeckhauser, "Assessing Dynamic Efficiency: Theory and Evidence," *Review of Economic Studies* 56 (1989): 1–19.

accounts, such as IRAs, are designed to encourage private saving by giving preferential treatment to income saved in these accounts. Some economists have proposed increasing the incentive to save by replacing the current system of income taxation with a system of consumption taxation.

Many disagreements over public policy are rooted in different views about how much private saving responds to incentives. For example, suppose that the government were to increase the amount that people can put into tax-exempt retirement accounts. Would people respond to the increased incentive to save by saving more? Or would people merely transfer saving done in other forms into these accounts—reducing tax revenue and thus public saving without any stimulus to private saving? The desirability of the policy depends on the answers to these questions. Unfortunately, despite much research on this issue, no consensus has emerged.

Allocating the Economy's Investment

The Solow model makes the simplifying assumption that there is only one type of capital. In the world, of course, there are many types. Private businesses invest in traditional types of capital, such as bulldozers and steel plants, and newer types of capital, such as computers and robots. The government invests in various forms of public capital, called *infrastructure*, such as roads, bridges, and sewer systems.

In addition, there is *human capital*—the knowledge and skills that workers acquire through education, from early childhood programs such as Head Start to on-the-job training for adults in the labor force. Although the capital variable in the Solow model is usually interpreted as including only physical capital, in many ways human capital is analogous to physical capital. Like physical capital, human capital raises our ability to produce goods and services. Raising the level of human capital requires investment in the form of teachers, libraries, and student time. Recent research on economic growth has emphasized that human capital is at least as important as physical capital in explaining international differences in standards of living. One way of modeling this fact is to give the variable we call "capital" a broader definition that includes both human and physical capital.[6]

Policymakers trying to stimulate economic growth must confront the issue of what kinds of capital the economy needs most. In other words, what kinds of capital yield the highest marginal products? To a large extent, policymakers can rely on the marketplace to allocate the pool of saving to alternative types of investment. Those industries with the highest marginal products of capital will naturally be most willing to borrow at market interest rates to finance new investment. Many economists advocate that the government should merely create a "level

---

[6] Earlier in this chapter, when we were interpreting K as only physical capital, human capital was folded into the efficiency-of-labor parameter E. The alternative approach suggested here is to include human capital as part of K instead, so E represents technology but not human capital. If K is given this broader interpretation, then much of what we call labor income is really the return to human capital. As a result, the true capital share is much larger than the traditional Cobb–Douglas value of about 1/3. For more on this topic, see N. Gregory Mankiw, David Romer, and David N. Weil, "A Contribution to the Empirics of Economic Growth," *Quarterly Journal of Economics* (May 1992): 407–437.

playing field" for different types of capital—for example, by ensuring that the tax system treats all forms of capital equally. The government can then rely on the market to allocate capital efficiently.

Other economists have suggested that the government should actively encourage particular forms of capital. Suppose, for instance, that technological advance occurs as a by-product of certain economic activities. This would happen if new and improved production processes are devised during the process of building capital (a phenomenon called *learning by doing*) and if these ideas become part of society's pool of knowledge. Such a by-product is called a *technological externality* (or a *knowledge spillover*). In the presence of such externalities, the social returns to capital exceed the private returns, and the benefits of increased capital accumulation to society are greater than the Solow model suggests.[7] Moreover, some types of capital accumulation may yield greater externalities than others. If, for example, installing robots yields greater technological externalities than building a new steel mill, then perhaps the government should use the tax laws to encourage investment in robots. The success of such an *industrial policy*, as it is sometimes called, requires that the government be able to measure accurately the externalities of different economic activities so it can give the correct incentive to each activity.

Most economists are skeptical about industrial policies for two reasons. First, measuring the externalities from different sectors is so difficult as to be virtually impossible. If policy is based on poor measurements, its effects might be close to random and, thus, worse than no policy at all. Second, the political process is far from perfect. Once the government gets in the business of rewarding specific industries with subsidies and tax breaks, the rewards are as likely to be based on political clout as on the magnitude of externalities.

One type of capital that necessarily involves the government is public capital. Local, state, and federal governments are always deciding whether to borrow to finance new roads, bridges, and transit systems. During his first presidential campaign, Bill Clinton argued that the United States had been investing too little in infrastructure. He claimed that a higher level of infrastructure investment would make the economy substantially more productive. Among economists, this claim had both defenders and critics. Yet all of them agree that measuring the marginal product of public capital is difficult. Private capital generates an easily measured rate of profit for the firm owning the capital, whereas the benefits of public capital are more diffuse. Moreover, while private capital investment is made by investors spending their own money, the allocation of resources for public capital involves the political process and taxpayer funding. It is all too common to see "bridges to nowhere" being built simply because the local senator or congressman has the political muscle to get funds approved.[8]

---

[7] Paul Romer, "Crazy Explanations for the Productivity Slowdown," *NBER Macroeconomics Annual* 2 (1987): 163–201.

[8] Example: "Ground hasn't been broken yet, but the infamous 'bridge to nowhere' that would connect Ketchikan, Alaska, to an offshore island where only 50 people live, appears to be indestructible. The [federal] highway bill allots $223 million for that project." *USA Today*, October 23, 2005.

Establishing the Right Institutions

As we discussed earlier, economists who study international differences in the standard of living attribute some of these differences to the inputs of physical and human capital and some to the productivity with which these inputs are used. One reason that nations may have different levels of production efficiency is that they have different institutions that guide the allocation of scarce resources. Creating the right institutions is important for ensuring that resources are allocated to their best use.

A nation's legal tradition is an example of such an institution. Some countries, such as the United States, Australia, India, and Singapore, are former colonies of the United Kingdom and, therefore, have English-style common-law systems. Other nations, such as Italy, Spain, and most of Latin America, have legal traditions that derive from the French Napoleonic Codes. Studies have found that legal protections for shareholders and creditors are stronger in the English-style legal systems than in the French-style systems. As a result, the English-style countries have better developed capital markets. Nations with more developed capital markets, in turn, experience more rapid growth because it is easier for small and start-up companies to finance investment projects, leading to a more efficient allocation of the nation's capital.[9]

Another important institutional difference across countries is the quality of government itself. Ideally, governments should provide a "helping hand" to the market system, protecting property rights, enforcing contracts, promoting competition, prosecuting fraud, and so on. Yet governments sometimes diverge from this ideal and act more like a "grabbing hand," using the authority of the state to enrich a few powerful individuals at the expense of the broader community. Empirical studies have shown that the extent of corruption in a nation is indeed a significant determinant of economic growth.[10]

Adam Smith, the great eighteenth-century economist, was well aware of the role of institutions in economic growth. He once wrote, "Little else is requisite to carry a state to the highest degree of opulence from the lowest barbarism but peace, easy taxes, and a tolerable administration of justice: all the rest being brought about by the natural course of things." Sadly, many nations do not enjoy these three simple advantages.

CASE STUDY

The Colonial Origins of Modern Institutions

International data show a remarkable correlation between latitude and economic prosperity: nations closer to the equator typically have lower levels of income per person than nations farther from the equator. This fact is true in both the northern and southern hemispheres.

---

[9] Rafael La Porta, Florencio Lopez-de-Silanes, Andrei Shleifer, and Robert Vishny, "Law and Finance," *Journal of Political Economy* 106 (1998): 1113–1155; Ross Levine and Robert G. King, "Finance and Growth: Schumpeter Might Be Right," *Quarterly Journal of Economics* 108 (1993): 717–737.

[10] Paulo Mauro, "Corruption and Growth," *Quarterly Journal of Economics* 110 (1995): 681–712.

What explains the correlation? Some economists have suggested that the tropical climates near the equator have a direct negative impact on productivity. In the heat of the tropics, agriculture is more difficult, and disease is more prevalent. This makes the production of goods and services more difficult.

Although the direct impact of geography is one reason tropical nations tend to be poor, it is not the whole story. Recent research by Daron Acemoglu, Simon Johnson, and James Robinson has suggested an indirect mechanism—the impact of geography on institutions. Here is their explanation, presented in several steps:

1. In the seventeenth, eighteenth, and nineteenth centuries, tropical climates presented European settlers with an increased risk of disease, especially from malaria and yellow fever. As a result, when Europeans were colonizing much of the rest of the world, they avoided settling in tropical areas, such as much of Africa and Central America. The European settlers preferred areas with more moderate climates and better health conditions, such as the United States, Canada, and New Zealand.
2. In those areas where Europeans settled in large numbers, the settlers established European-like institutions that protected individual property rights and limited the power of government. By contrast, in tropical climates, the colonial powers often set up "extractive" institutions, including authoritarian governments, so they could take advantage of the area's natural resources. These institutions enriched the colonizers, but they did little to foster economic growth.
3. Although the era of colonial rule is now long over, the early institutions that the European colonizers established are strongly correlated with the modern institutions in the former colonies. In tropical nations, where the colonial powers set up extractive institutions, there is typically less protection of property rights even today. When the colonizers left, the extractive institutions remained and were simply taken over by new ruling elites.
4. The quality of institutions is a key determinant of economic performance. Where property rights are well protected, people have more incentive to make the investments that lead to economic growth. Where property rights are less respected, as is typically the case in tropical nations, investment and growth lag behind.

This research suggests much of the international variation in living standards that we observe today is a result of the long reach of history.[11]

Encouraging Technological Progress

The Solow model shows that sustained growth in income per worker must come from technological progress. The Solow model, however, takes technological progress as exogenous; it does not explain it. Unfortunately, the determinants of technological progress are not well understood.

[11] Daron Acemoglu, Simon Johnson, and James A. Robinson, "The Colonial Origins of Comparative Development: An Empirical Investigation," *American Economic Review* 91 (December 2001): 1369–1401.

Despite this limited understanding, many public policies are designed to stimulate technological progress. Most of these policies encourage the private sector to devote resources to technological innovation. For example, the patent system gives a temporary monopoly to inventors of new products; the tax code offers tax breaks for firms engaging in research and development; and government agencies, such as the National Science Foundation, directly subsidize basic research in universities. In addition, as discussed above, proponents of industrial policy argue that the government should take a more active role in promoting specific industries that are key for rapid technological advance.

In recent years, the encouragement of technological progress has taken on an international dimension. Many of the companies that engage in research to advance technology are located in the United States and other developed nations. Developing nations such as China have an incentive to "free ride" on this research by not strictly enforcing intellectual property rights. That is, Chinese companies often use the ideas developed abroad without compensating the patent holders. The United States has strenuously objected to this practice, and China has promised to step up enforcement. If intellectual property rights were better enforced around the world, firms would have more incentive to engage in research, and this would promote worldwide technological progress.

CASE STUDY

The Worldwide Slowdown in Economic Growth: 1972–1995

Beginning in the early 1970s, and lasting until the mid-1990s, world policymakers faced a perplexing problem: a global slowdown in economic growth. Table 8-2 presents data on the growth in real GDP per person for the seven major world economies. Growth in the United States fell from 2.2 percent before 1972 to 1.5

TABLE 8-2

Growth Around the World

	GROWTH IN OUTPUT PER PERSON (PERCENT PER YEAR)		
Country	**1948–1972**	**1972–1995**	**1995–2004**
Canada	2.9	1.8	2.4
France	4.3	1.6	1.7
West Germany	5.7	2.0	
Germany			1.2
Italy	4.9	2.3	1.5
Japan	8.2	2.6	1.2
United Kingdom	2.4	1.8	2.5
United States	2.2	1.5	2.2

Source: Angus Maddison, *Phases of Capitalist Development* (Oxford: Oxford University Press, 1982); *OECD National Accounts;* and *World Bank: World Development Indicators.*

percent from 1972 to 1995. Other countries experienced similar or more severe declines. Accumulated over many years, even a small change in the rate of growth has a large effect on economic well-being. Real income in the United States today is almost 20 percent lower than it would have been had growth remained at its previous level.

Why did this slowdown occur? Studies have shown that it was attributable to a fall in the rate at which the production function was improving over time. The appendix to this chapter explains how economists measure changes in the production function with a variable called *total factor productivity*, which is closely related to the efficiency of labor in the Solow model. There are, however, many hypotheses to explain this fall in productivity growth. Here are four of them.

Measurement Problems One possibility is that the productivity slowdown did not really occur and that it shows up in the data because the data are flawed. As you may recall from Chapter 2, one problem in measuring inflation is correcting for changes in the quality of goods and services. The same issue arises when measuring output and productivity. For instance, if technological advance leads to *more* computers being built, then the increase in output and productivity is easy to measure. But if technological advance leads to *faster* computers being built, then output and productivity have increased, but that increase is more subtle and harder to measure. Government statisticians try to correct for changes in quality, but despite their best efforts, the resulting data are far from perfect.

Unmeasured quality improvements mean that our standard of living is rising more rapidly than the official data indicate. This issue should make us suspicious of the data, but by itself it cannot explain the productivity slowdown. To explain a *slowdown* in growth, one must argue that the measurement problems got *worse*. There is some indication that this might be so. As history passes, fewer people work in industries with tangible and easily measured output, such as agriculture, and more work in industries with intangible and less easily measured output, such as medical services. Yet few economists believe that measurement problems were the full story.

Oil Prices When the productivity slowdown began around 1973, the obvious hypothesis to explain it was the large increase in oil prices caused by the actions of the OPEC oil cartel. The primary piece of evidence was the timing: productivity growth slowed at the same time that oil prices skyrocketed. Over time, however, this explanation has appeared less likely. One reason is that the accumulated shortfall in productivity seems too large to be explained by an increase in oil prices—petroleum-based products are not that large a fraction of the typical firm's costs. In addition, if this explanation were right, productivity should have sped up when political turmoil in OPEC caused oil prices to plummet in 1986. Unfortunately, that did not happen.

Worker Quality Some economists suggest that the productivity slowdown might have been caused by changes in the labor force. In the early 1970s, the large baby-boom generation started leaving school and taking jobs. At the same time, changing social norms encouraged many women to leave full-time housework and enter the labor force. Both of these developments lowered the average level of experience among workers, which in turn lowered average productivity.

Other economists point to changes in worker quality as gauged by human capital. Although the educational attainment of the labor force continued to rise throughout this period, it was not increasing as rapidly as it did in the past. Moreover, declining performance on some standardized tests suggests that the quality of education was declining. If so, this could explain slowing productivity growth.

The Depletion of Ideas Still other economists suggest that the world started to run out of new ideas about how to produce in the early 1970s, pushing the economy into an age of slower technological progress. These economists often argue that the anomaly is not the period since 1970 but the preceding two decades. In the late 1940s, the economy had a large backlog of ideas that had not been fully implemented because of the Great Depression of the 1930s and World War II in the first half of the 1940s. After the economy used up this backlog, the argument goes, a slowdown in productivity growth was likely. Indeed, although the growth rates in the 1970s, 1980s, and early 1990s were disappointing compared to those of the 1950s and 1960s, they were not lower than average growth rates from 1870 to 1950.

Which of these suspects is the culprit? All of them are plausible, but it is difficult to prove beyond a reasonable doubt that any one of them is guilty. The worldwide slowdown in economic growth that began in the mid-1970s remains a mystery.[12]

CASE STUDY

Information Technology and the New Economy: 1995-????

As any good doctor will tell you, sometimes a patient's illness goes away on its own, even if the doctor has failed to come up with a convincing diagnosis and remedy. This seems to be the outcome with the productivity slowdown discussed in the previous case study. Economists have not yet figured it out, but beginning in the middle of the 1990s, the problem disappeared. Economic growth took off, as shown in the third column of Table 8-2. In the United States, output per person accelerated from 1.5 back to 2.2 percent per year. Commentators proclaimed we were living in a "new economy."

As with the slowdown in economic growth in the 1970s, the acceleration in the 1990s is hard to explain definitively. But part of the credit goes to advances in computer and information technology, including the Internet.

Observers of the computer industry often cite Moore's law, which states that computer processing power doubles about every 18 months. This is not an inevitable law of nature but an empirical regularity describing the rapid technological progress this industry has enjoyed. In the 1980s and early 1990s, economists

[12] For various views on the growth slowdown, see "Symposium: The Slowdown in Productivity Growth," *The Journal of Economic Perspectives* 2 (Fall 1988): 3–98.

were surprised that the rapid progress in computing did not have a larger effect on the overall economy. Economist Robert Solow once quipped that "we can see the computer age everywhere but in the productivity statistics."

There are two reasons why the macroeconomic effects of the computer revolution might not have shown up until the mid-1990s. One is that the computer industry was previously a smaller part of the economy. Business spending on computer hardware and software rose from 6 percent of nonresidential investment in 1980 to 24 percent in 2004. As computers made up a larger part of the economy, technological advance in that sector had a greater overall effect.

The second reason why the productivity benefits of computers may have been delayed is that it took time for firms to figure out how best to use the technology. Whenever firms change their production systems and train workers to use a technology, they disrupt the existing means of production. Measured productivity can fall for a while before the economy reaps the benefits. Indeed, some economists even suggest that the spread of computers can help explain the productivity slowdown that began in the 1970s.

Economic history provides some support for the idea that new technologies influence growth with a long lag. The electric light bulb was invented in 1879. But it took several decades before electricity had a big economic impact. For businesses to reap large productivity gains, they had to do more than just replace steam engines with electric motors; they had to rethink the entire organization of factories. Similarly, replacing the typewriters on desks with computers and word processing programs, as was common in the 1980s, may have had small productivity effects. Only later, when the Internet and other advanced applications were invented, did the computers yield large economic gains.

Eventually, advances in technology should show up in economic growth, as was the case in the second half of the 1990s. This extra growth occurs through three channels. First, because the computer industry is part of the economy, productivity growth in that industry directly affects overall productivity growth. Second, because computers are a type of capital good, falling computer prices allow firms to accumulate more computing capital for every dollar of investment spending; the resulting increase in capital accumulation raises growth in all sectors that use computers as a factor of production. Third, the innovations in the computer industry may induce other industries to reevaluate their own production methods, and this reevaluation in turn leads to productivity growth in those industries.

The big, open question is how long the computer industry will remain an engine of growth. Will Moore's law describe the future as well as it has described the past? Will the technological advances of the next decade be as profound as the Internet was during the last decade? Stay tuned.[13]

---

[13] For more on this topic, see the symposium on "Computers and Productivity" in the Fall 2000 issue of *The Journal of Economic Perspectives*. On the parallel between electricity and computers, see Paul A. David, "The Dynamo and the Computer: A Historical Perspective on the Modern Productivity Paradox," *American Economic Review* 80, no. 2 (May 1990): 355–361.

8-4 Beyond the Solow Model: Endogenous Growth Theory

A chemist, a physicist, and an economist are all trapped on a desert island, trying to figure out how to open a can of food.

"Let's heat the can over the fire until it explodes," says the chemist.

"No, no," says the physicist, "Let's drop the can onto the rocks from the top of a high tree."

"I have an idea," says the economist. "First, we assume a can opener. . . ."

This old joke takes aim at how economists use assumptions to simplify—and sometimes oversimplify—the problems they face. It is particularly apt when evaluating the theory of economic growth. One goal of growth theory is to explain the persistent rise in living standards that we observe in most parts of the world. The Solow growth model shows that such persistent growth must come from technological progress. But where does technological progress come from? In the Solow model, it is just assumed!

The preceding two Case Studies on the productivity slowdown of the 1970s and speed-up of the 1990s suggest that changes in the pace of technological progress are tremendously important. To understand fully the process of economic growth, we need to go beyond the Solow model and develop models that explain technological advance. Models that do this often go by the label **endogenous growth theory** because they reject the Solow model's assumption of exogenous technological change. Although the field of endogenous growth theory is large and sometimes complex, here we get a quick taste of this modern research.[14]

The Basic Model

To illustrate the idea behind endogenous growth theory, let's start with a particularly simple production function:

$$Y = AK,$$

where Y is output, K is the capital stock, and A is a constant measuring the amount of output produced for each unit of capital. Notice that this production function does not exhibit the property of diminishing returns to capital. One extra unit of capital produces A extra units of output, regardless of how much capital there is. This absence of diminishing returns to capital is the key difference between this endogenous growth model and the Solow model.

---

[14] This section provides a brief introduction to the large and fascinating literature on endogenous growth theory. Early and important contributions to this literature include Paul M. Romer, "Increasing Returns and Long-Run Growth," *Journal of Political Economy* 94 (October 1986): 1002–1037; and Robert E. Lucas, Jr., "On the Mechanics of Economic Development," *Journal of Monetary Economics* 22 (1988): 3–42. The reader can learn more about this topic in the undergraduate textbooks by Charles I. Jones, *Introduction to Economic Growth*, 2nd ed., (New York: Norton, 2002) or David N. Weil, *Economic Growth* (Pearson, 2005).

Now let's see what this production function says about economic growth. As before, we assume a fraction s of income is saved and invested. We therefore describe capital accumulation with an equation similar to those we used previously:

$$\Delta K = sY - \delta K.$$

This equation states that the change in the capital stock (ΔK) equals investment (sY) minus depreciation (δK). Combining this equation with the $Y = AK$ production function, we obtain after a bit of manipulation

$$\Delta Y/Y = \Delta K/K = sA - \delta.$$

This equation shows what determines the growth rate of output $\Delta Y/Y$. Notice that, as long as $sA > \delta$, the economy's income grows forever, even without the assumption of exogenous technological progress.

Thus, a simple change in the production function can alter dramatically the predictions about economic growth. In the Solow model, saving leads to growth temporarily, but diminishing returns to capital eventually force the economy to approach a steady state in which growth depends only on exogenous technological progress. By contrast, in this endogenous growth model, saving and investment can lead to persistent growth.

But is it reasonable to abandon the assumption of diminishing returns to capital? The answer depends on how we interpret the variable K in the production function $Y = AK$. If we take the traditional view that K includes only the economy's stock of plants and equipment, then it is natural to assume diminishing returns. Giving 10 computers to each worker does not make the worker 10 times as productive as he or she is with one computer.

Advocates of endogenous growth theory, however, argue that the assumption of constant (rather than diminishing) returns to capital is more palatable if K is interpreted more broadly. Perhaps the best case for the endogenous growth model is to view knowledge as a type of capital. Clearly, knowledge is an important input into the economy's production—both its production of goods and services and its production of new knowledge. Compared to other forms of capital, however, it is less natural to assume that knowledge exhibits the property of diminishing returns. (Indeed, the increasing pace of scientific and technological innovation over the past few centuries has led some economists to argue that there are increasing returns to knowledge.) If we accept the view that knowledge is a type of capital, then this endogenous growth model with its assumption of constant returns to capital becomes a more plausible description of long-run economic growth.

A Two-Sector Model

Although the $Y = AK$ model is the simplest example of endogenous growth, the theory has gone well beyond this. One line of research has tried to develop models with more than one sector of production in order to offer a better description of the forces that govern technological progress. To see what we might learn from such models, let's sketch out an example.

The economy has two sectors, which we can call manufacturing firms and research universities. Firms produce goods and services, which are used for consumption and investment in physical capital. Universities produce a factor of production called "knowledge," which is then freely used in both sectors. The economy is described by the production function for firms, the production function for universities, and the capital-accumulation equation:

$$Y = F[K,(1 - u)LE] \quad \text{(production function in manufacturing firms)},$$

$$\Delta E = g(u)E \quad \text{(production function in research universities)},$$

$$\Delta K = sY - \delta K \quad \text{(capital accumulation)},$$

where u is the fraction of the labor force in universities (and $1 - u$ is the fraction in manufacturing), E is the stock of knowledge (which in turn determines the efficiency of labor), and g is a function that shows how the growth in knowledge depends on the fraction of the labor force in universities. The rest of the notation is standard. As usual, the production function for the manufacturing firms is assumed to have constant returns to scale: if we double both the amount of physical capital (K) and the effective number of workers in manufacturing [$(1 - u)LE$], we double the output of goods and services (Y).

This model is a cousin of the $Y = AK$ model. Most important, this economy exhibits constant (rather than diminishing) returns to capital, as long as capital is broadly defined to include knowledge. In particular, if we double both physical capital K and knowledge E, then we double the output of both sectors in the economy. As a result, like the $Y = AK$ model, this model can generate persistent growth without the assumption of exogenous shifts in the production function. Here persistent growth arises endogenously because the creation of knowledge in universities never slows down.

At the same time, however, this model is also a cousin of the Solow growth model. If u, the fraction of the labor force in universities, is held constant, then the efficiency of labor E grows at the constant rate $g(u)$. This result of constant growth in the efficiency of labor at rate g is precisely the assumption made in the Solow model with technological progress. Moreover, the rest of the model—the manufacturing production function and the capital-accumulation equation—also resembles the rest of the Solow model. As a result, for any given value of u, this endogenous-growth model works just like the Solow model.

There are two key decision variables in this model. As in the Solow model, the fraction of output used for saving and investment, s, determines the steady-state stock of physical capital. In addition, the fraction of labor in universities, u, determines the growth in the stock of knowledge. Both s and u affect the level of income, although only u affects the steady-state growth rate of income. Thus, this model of endogenous growth takes a small step in the direction of showing which societal decisions determine the rate of technological change.

The Microeconomics of Research and Development

The two-sector endogenous growth model just presented takes us closer to understanding technological progress, but it still tells only a rudimentary story about the creation of knowledge. If one thinks about the process of research and development for even a moment, three facts become apparent. First, although knowledge is largely a public good (that is, a good freely available to everyone), much research is done in firms that are driven by the profit motive. Second, research is profitable because innovations give firms temporary monopolies, either because of the patent system or because there is an advantage to being the first firm on the market with a new product. Third, when one firm innovates, other firms build on that innovation to produce the next generation of innovations. These (essentially microeconomic) facts are not easily connected with the (essentially macroeconomic) growth models we have discussed so far.

Some endogenous growth models try to incorporate these facts about research and development. Doing this requires modeling the decisions that firms face as they engage in research, and modeling the interactions among firms that have some degree of monopoly power over their innovations. Going into more detail about these models is beyond the scope of this book. But it should be clear already that one virtue of these endogenous growth models is that they offer a more complete description of the process of technological innovation.

One question these models are designed to address is whether, from the standpoint of society as a whole, private profit-maximizing firms tend to engage in too little or too much research. In other words, is the social return to research (which is what society cares about) greater or smaller than the private return (which is what motivates individual firms)? It turns out that, as a theoretical matter, there are effects in both directions. On the one hand, when a firm creates a new technology, it makes other firms better off by giving them a base of knowledge on which to build in future research. As Isaac Newton famously remarked, "If I have seen farther than others, it is because I was standing on the shoulders of giants." On the other hand, when one firm invests in research, it can also make other firms worse off by merely being first to discover a technology that another firm would have invented. This duplication of research effort has been called the "stepping on toes" effect. Whether firms left to their own devices do too little or too much research depends on whether the positive "standing on shoulders" externality or the negative "stepping on toes" externality is more prevalent.

Although theory alone is ambiguous about whether research effort is more or less than optimal, the empirical work in this area is usually less so. Many studies have suggested the "standing on shoulders" externality is important and, as a result, the social return to research is large—often in excess of 40 percent per year. This is an impressive rate of return, especially when compared to the return to physical capital, which we earlier estimated to be about 8 percent per year. In the judgment of some economists, this finding justifies substantial government subsidies to research.[15]

[15] For an overview of the empirical literature on the effects of research, see Zvi Griliches, "The Search for R&D Spillovers," *Scandinavian Journal of Economics* 94 (1991): 29–47.

CASE STUDY

Economic Growth as a Process of Creative Destruction

In his 1942 book, *Capitalism, Socialism, and Democracy*, economist Joseph Schumpeter suggested that economic progress comes through a process of "creative destruction." According to Schumpeter, the driving force behind progress is the entrepreneur with an idea for a new product, a new way to produce an old product, or some other innovation. When the entrepreneur's firm enters the market, it has some degree of monopoly power over its innovation; indeed, it is the prospect of monopoly profits that motivates the entrepreneur. The entry of the new firm is good for consumers, who now have an expanded range of choices, but it is often bad for incumbent producers, who may find it hard to compete with the entrant. If the new product is sufficiently better than old ones, the incumbents may even be driven out of business. Over time, the process keeps renewing itself. The entrepreneur's firm becomes an incumbent, enjoying high profitability until its product is displaced by another entrepreneur with the next generation of innovation.

History confirms Schumpeter's thesis that there are winners and losers from technological progress. For example, in England in the early nineteenth century, an important innovation was the invention and spread of machines that could produce textiles using unskilled workers at low cost. This technological advance was good for consumers who could clothe themselves more cheaply. Yet skilled knitters in England saw their jobs threatened by new technology, and they responded by organizing violent revolts. The rioting workers, called Luddites, smashed the weaving machines used in the wool and cotton mills and set the homes of the mill owners on fire (a less than creative form of destruction). Today, the term "Luddite" refers to anyone who opposes technological progress.

A more recent example of creative destruction entails the retailing giant Wal-Mart. Although retailing may seem a relatively static activity, in fact it is a sector that has seen sizable rates of technological progress over the past several decades. Through better inventory-control, marketing, and personnel-management techniques, for example, Wal-Mart has found ways to bring goods to consumers at lower cost than traditional retailers. These changes benefit consumers, who can buy goods at lower prices, and the stockholders of Wal-Mart, who share in its profitability. But they adversely affect small mom-and-pop stores, who find it hard to compete when a Wal-Mart opens nearby.

Faced with the prospect of being the victims of creative destruction, incumbent producers often look to the political process to stop the entry of new, more efficient competitors. The original Luddites wanted the British government to save their jobs by restricting the spread of the new textile technology; instead, the Parliament sent troops to suppress the Luddite riots. Similarly, in recent years, local retailers have sometimes tried to use local land-use regulations to stop Wal-Mart from entering their market. The cost of such entry restrictions, however, is to slow the pace of technological progress. In Europe, where entry regulations are stricter than they are in the United States, the economies have not seen the emergence of retailing giants like Wal-Mart; as a result, productivity growth in retailing has been much lower.[16]

Schumpeter's vision of how capitalist economies work has merit as a matter of economic history. Moreover, it has inspired some recent work in the theory of economic growth. One line of endogenous growth theory, pioneered by economists Philippe Aghion and Peter Howitt, builds on Schumpeter's insights by modeling technological advance as a process of entrepreneurial innovation and creative destruction.[17]

8-5 Conclusion

Long-run economic growth is the single most important determinant of the economic well-being of a nation's citizens. Everything else that macroeconomists study—unemployment, inflation, trade deficits, and so on—pales in comparison.

Fortunately, economists know quite a lot about the forces that govern economic growth. The Solow growth model and the more recent endogenous growth models show how saving, population growth, and technological progress interact in determining the level and growth of a nation's standard of living. Although these theories offer no magic recipe to ensure an economy achieves rapid growth, they do offer much insight, and they provide the intellectual framework for much of the debate over public policy aimed at promoting long-run economic growth.

Summary

1. In the steady state of the Solow growth model, the growth rate of income per person is determined solely by the exogenous rate of technological progress.
2. Many empirical studies have examined to what extent the Solow model can help explain long-run economic growth. The model can explain much of what we see in the data, such as balanced growth and conditional convergence. Recent studies have also found that international variation in standards

[16] Robert J. Gordon, "Why was Europe Left at the Station When America's Productivity Locomotive Departed?" *NBER Working Paper* No. 10661, 2004.

[17] Philippe Aghion and Peter Howitt, "A Model of Growth Through Creative Destruction," *Econometrica* 60 (1992): 323–351.

of living is attributable to a combination of capital accumulation and the efficiency with which capital is used.

3. In the Solow model with population growth and technological progress, the Golden Rule (consumption-maximizing) steady state is characterized by equality between the net marginal product of capital ($MPK - \delta$) and the steady-state growth rate of total income ($n + g$). In the U.S. economy, the net marginal product of capital is well in excess of the growth rate, indicating that the U.S. economy has much less capital than it would have in the Golden Rule steady state.
4. Policymakers in the United States and other countries often claim that their nations should devote a larger percentage of their output to saving and investment. Increased public saving and tax incentives for private saving are two ways to encourage capital accumulation. Policymakers can also promote economic growth by setting up the right legal and financial institutions so resources are allocated efficiently and by ensuring proper incentives to encourage research and technological progress.
5. In the early 1970s, the rate of growth of income per person fell substantially in most industrialized countries, including the United States. The cause of this slowdown is not well understood. In the mid-1990s, the U.S. growth rate increased, most likely because of advances in information technology.
6. Modern theories of endogenous growth attempt to explain the rate of technological progress, which the Solow model takes as exogenous. These models try to explain the decisions that determine the creation of knowledge through research and development.

KEY CONCEPTS

Efficiency of labor

Labor-augmenting technological progress

Endogenous growth theory

QUESTIONS FOR REVIEW

1. In the Solow model, what determines the steady-state rate of growth of income per worker?
2. In the steady state of the Solow model, at what rate does output per person grow? At what rate does capital per person grow? How does this compare with the U.S. experience?
3. What data would you need to determine whether an economy has more or less capital than in the Golden Rule steady state?
4. How can policymakers influence a nation's saving rate?
5. What has happened to the rate of productivity growth over the past 40 years? How might you explain this phenomenon?
6. How does endogenous growth theory explain persistent growth without the assumption of exogenous technological progress? How does this differ from the Solow model?

PROBLEMS AND APPLICATIONS

1. An economy described by the Solow growth model has the following production function:

$$y = \sqrt{k}.$$

   a. Solve for the steady-state value of y as a function of s, n, g, and δ.

   b. A developed country has a saving rate of 28 percent and a population growth rate of 1 percent per year. A less-developed country has a saving rate of 10 percent and a population growth rate of 4 percent per year. In both countries, $g = 0.02$ and $\delta = 0.04$. Find the steady-state value of y for each country.

   c. What policies might the less-developed country pursue to raise its level of income?

2. In the United States, the capital share of GDP is about 30 percent; the average growth in output is about 3 percent per year; the depreciation rate is about 4 percent per year; and the capital-output ratio is about 2.5. Suppose that the production function is Cobb-Douglas, so that the capital share in output is constant, and that the United States has been in a steady state. (For a discussion of the Cobb-Douglas production function, see Chapter 3.)

   a. What must the saving rate be in the initial steady state? [*Hint:* Use the steady-state relationship, $sy = (\delta + n + g)k$.]

   b. What is the marginal product of capital in the initial steady state?

   c. Suppose that public policy raises the saving rate so that the economy reaches the Golden Rule level of capital. What will the marginal product of capital be at the Golden Rule steady state? Compare the marginal product at the Golden Rule steady state to the marginal product in the initial steady state. Explain.

   d. What will the capital-output ratio be at the Golden Rule steady state? (*Hint:* For the Cobb-Douglas production function, the capital-output ratio is related to the marginal product of capital.)

   e. What must the saving rate be to reach the Golden Rule steady state?

3. Prove each of the following statements about the steady state of the Solow model with population growth and technological progress.

   a. The capital-output ratio is constant.

   b. Capital and labor each earn a constant share of an economy's income. [*Hint:* Recall the definition $MPK = f(k + 1) - f(k)$.]

   c. Total capital income and total labor income both grow at the rate of population growth plus the rate of technological progress, $n + g$.

   d. The real rental price of capital is constant, and the real wage grows at the rate of technological progress g. (*Hint:* The real rental price of capital equals total capital income divided by the capital stock, and the real wage equals total labor income divided by the labor force.)

4. Two countries, Richland and Poorland, are described by the Solow growth model. They have the same Cobb-Douglas production function, $F(K,L) = A\,K^{\alpha}L^{1-\alpha}$, but with different quantities of capital and labor. Richland saves 32 percent of its income, while Poorland saves 10 percent. Richland has population growth of 1 percent per year, while Poorland has population growth of 3 percent. (The numbers in this problem are chosen to be approximately realistic descriptions of rich and poor nations.) Both nations have technological progress at a rate of 2 percent per year and depreciation at a rate of 5 percent per year.

   a. What is the per worker production function $f(k)$?

   b. Solve for the ratio of Richland's steady-state income per worker to Poorland's. (*Hint:* The parameter α will play a role in your answer.)

   c. If the Cobb-Douglas parameter α takes the conventional value of about 1/3, how much higher should income per worker be in Richland compared to Poorland?

   d. Income per worker in Richland is actually 16 times income per worker in Poorland. Can you explain this fact by changing the value of the parameter α? What must it be? Can you think of any way of justifying such a value for this parameter? How else might you explain the large difference in income between Richland and Poorland?

5. The amount of education the typical person receives varies substantially among countries. Suppose you were to compare a country with a highly educated labor force and a country with a less educated labor force. Assume that education affects only the level of the efficiency of labor. Also assume that the countries are otherwise the same: they have the same saving rate, the same depreciation rate, the same population growth rate, and the same rate of technological progress. Both countries are described by the Solow model and are in their steady states. What would you predict for the following variables?

   a. The rate of growth of total income.

   b. The level of income per worker.

   c. The real rental price of capital.

   d. The real wage.

6. This question asks you to analyze in more detail the two-sector endogenous growth model presented in the text.

   a. Rewrite the production function for manufactured goods in terms of output per effective worker and capital per effective worker.

   b. In this economy, what is break-even investment (the amount of investment needed to keep capital per effective worker constant)?

   c. Write down the equation of motion for k, which shows Δk as saving minus break-even investment. Use this equation to draw a graph showing the determination of steady-state k. (*Hint:* This graph will look much like those we used to analyze the Solow model.)

   d. In this economy, what is the steady-state growth rate of output per worker Y/L? How do the saving rate s and the fraction of the labor force in universities u affect this steady-state growth rate?

   e. Using your graph, show the impact of an increase in u. (*Hint:* This change affects both curves.) Describe both the immediate and the steady-state effects.

   f. Based on your analysis, is an increase in u an unambiguously good thing for the economy? Explain.

Accounting for the Sources of Economic Growth

Real GDP in the United States has grown more than 3 percent per year over the past half century. What explains this growth? In Chapter 3 we linked the output of the economy to the factors of production—capital and labor—and to the production technology. Here we develop a technique called *growth accounting* that divides the growth in output into three different sources: increases in capital, increases in labor, and advances in technology. This breakdown provides us with a measure of the rate of technological change.

Increases in the Factors of Production

We first examine how increases in the factors of production contribute to increases in output. To do this, we start by assuming there is no technological change, so the production function relating output Y to capital K and labor L is constant over time:

$$Y = F(K, L).$$

In this case, the amount of output changes only because the amount of capital or labor changes.

Increases in Capital First, consider changes in capital. If the amount of capital increases by ΔK units, by how much does the amount of output increase? To answer this question, we need to recall the definition of the marginal product of capital MPK:

$$MPK = F(K + 1, L) - F(K, L).$$

The marginal product of capital tells us how much output increases when capital increases by 1 unit. Therefore, when capital increases by ΔK units, output increases by approximately $MPK \times \Delta K$.[18]

For example, suppose that the marginal product of capital is 1/5; that is, an additional unit of capital increases the amount of output produced by one-fifth of a unit. If we increase the amount of capital by 10 units, we can compute the amount of additional output as follows:

[18] Note the word "approximately" here. This answer is only an approximation because the marginal product of capital varies: it falls as the amount of capital increases. An exact answer would take into account that each unit of capital has a different marginal product. If the change in K is not too large, however, the approximation of a constant marginal product is very accurate.

$$\begin{aligned}\Delta Y &= \quad MPK \quad \times \quad \Delta K \\ &= 1/5 \frac{\text{units of output}}{\text{unit of capital}} \times 10 \text{ units of capital} \\ &= 2 \text{ units of output.}\end{aligned}$$

By increasing capital by 10 units, we obtain 2 more units of output. Thus, we use the marginal product of capital to convert changes in capital into changes in output.

Increases in Labor Next, consider changes in labor. If the amount of labor increases by ΔL units, by how much does output increase? We answer this question the same way we answered the question about capital. The marginal product of labor *MPL* tells us how much output changes when labor increases by 1 unit—that is,

$$MPL = F(K, L + 1) - F(K, L).$$

Therefore, when the amount of labor increases by ΔL units, output increases by approximately $MPL \times \Delta L$.

For example, suppose that the marginal product of labor is 2; that is, an additional unit of labor increases the amount of output produced by 2 units. If we increase the amount of labor by 10 units, we can compute the amount of additional output as follows:

$$\begin{aligned}\Delta Y &= \quad MPL \quad \times \quad \Delta L \\ &= 2 \frac{\text{units of output}}{\text{unit of labor}} \times 10 \text{ units of labor} \\ &= 20 \text{ units of output.}\end{aligned}$$

By increasing labor by 10 units, we obtain 20 more units of output. Thus, we use the marginal product of labor to convert changes in labor into changes in output.

Increases in Capital and Labor Finally, let's consider the more realistic case in which both factors of production change. Suppose that the amount of capital increases by ΔK and the amount of labor increases by ΔL. The increase in output then comes from two sources: more capital and more labor. We can divide this increase into the two sources using the marginal products of the two inputs:

$$\Delta Y = (MPK \times \Delta K) + (MPL \times \Delta L).$$

The first term in parentheses is the increase in output resulting from the increase in capital, and the second term in parentheses is the increase in output resulting from the increase in labor. This equation shows us how to attribute growth to each factor of production.

We now want to convert this last equation into a form that is easier to interpret and apply to the available data. First, with some algebraic rearrangement, the equation becomes[19]

$$\frac{\Delta Y}{Y} = \left(\frac{MPK \times K}{Y}\right)\frac{\Delta K}{K} + \left(\frac{MPL \times L}{Y}\right)\frac{\Delta L}{L}.$$

This form of the equation relates the growth rate of output, $\Delta Y/Y$, to the growth rate of capital, $\Delta K/K$, and the growth rate of labor, $\Delta L/L$.

Next, we need to find some way to measure the terms in parentheses in the last equation. In Chapter 3 we showed that the marginal product of capital equals its real rental price. Therefore, $MPK \times K$ is the total return to capital, and $(MPK \times K)/Y$ is capital's share of output. Similarly, the marginal product of labor equals the real wage. Therefore, $MPL \times L$ is the total compensation that labor receives, and $(MPL \times L)/Y$ is labor's share of output. Under the assumption that the production function has constant returns to scale, Euler's theorem (which we discussed in Chapter 3) tells us that these two shares sum to 1. In this case, we can write

$$\frac{\Delta Y}{Y} = \alpha\frac{\Delta K}{K} + (1 - \alpha)\frac{\Delta L}{L},$$

where α is capital's share and $(1 - \alpha)$ is labor's share.

This last equation gives us a simple formula for showing how changes in inputs lead to changes in output. In particular, we must weight the growth rates of the inputs by the factor shares. As we discussed in Chapter 3, capital's share in the United States is about 30 percent, that is, $\alpha = 0.30$. Therefore, a 10 percent increase in the amount of capital ($\Delta K/K = 0.10$) leads to a 3 percent increase in the amount of output ($\Delta Y/Y = 0.03$). Similarly, a 10 percent increase in the amount of labor ($\Delta L/L = 0.10$) leads to a 7 percent increase in the amount of output ($\Delta Y/Y = 0.07$).

Technological Progress

So far in our analysis of the sources of growth, we have been assuming that the production function does not change over time. In practice, of course, technological progress improves the production function. For any given amount of inputs, we get more output today than we did in the past. We now extend the analysis to allow for technological progress.

We include the effects of the changing technology by writing the production function as

$$Y = AF(K, L),$$

[19] *Mathematical note:* To see that this is equivalent to the previous equation, note that we can multiply both sides of this equation by Y and thereby cancel Y from three places in which it appears. We can cancel the K in the top and bottom of the first term on the right-hand side and the L in the top and bottom of the second term on the right-hand side. These algebraic manipulations turn this equation into the previous one.

where A is a measure of the current level of technology called *total factor productivity*. Output now increases not only because of increases in capital and labor but also because of increases in total factor productivity. If total factor productivity increases by 1 percent and if the inputs are unchanged, then output increases by 1 percent.

Allowing for a changing technology adds another term to our equation accounting for economic growth:

$$\frac{\Delta Y}{Y} = \alpha\frac{\Delta K}{K} + (1-\alpha)\frac{\Delta L}{L} + \frac{\Delta A}{A}$$

$$\begin{matrix}\text{Growth in} \\ \text{Output}\end{matrix} = \begin{matrix}\text{Contribution} \\ \text{of Capital}\end{matrix} + \begin{matrix}\text{Contribution} \\ \text{of Labor}\end{matrix} + \begin{matrix}\text{Growth in Total} \\ \text{Factor Productivity}\end{matrix}.$$

This is the key equation of growth accounting. It identifies and allows us to measure the three sources of growth: changes in the amount of capital, changes in the amount of labor, and changes in total factor productivity.

Because total factor productivity is not observable directly, it is measured indirectly. We have data on the growth in output, capital, and labor; we also have data on capital's share of output. From these data and the growth-accounting equation, we can compute the growth in total factor productivity to make sure that everything adds up:

$$\frac{\Delta A}{A} = \frac{\Delta Y}{Y} - \alpha\frac{\Delta K}{K} - (1-\alpha)\frac{\Delta L}{L}.$$

$\Delta A/A$ is the change in output that cannot be explained by changes in inputs. Thus, the growth in total factor productivity is computed as a residual—that is, as the amount of output growth that remains after we have accounted for the determinants of growth that we can measure directly. Indeed, $\Delta A/A$ is sometimes called the *Solow residual*, after Robert Solow, who first showed how to compute it.[20]

Total factor productivity can change for many reasons. Changes most often arise because of increased knowledge about production methods, and the Solow residual is often used as a measure of technological progress. Yet other factors, such as education and government regulation, can affect total factor productivity as well. For example, if higher public spending raises the quality of education, then workers may become more productive and output may rise, which implies higher total factor productivity. As another example, if government regulations require firms to purchase capital to reduce pollution or increase worker safety, then the capital stock may rise without any increase in measured output, which implies lower total factor productivity. *Total factor productivity captures anything that changes the relation between measured inputs and measured output.*

[20] Robert M. Solow, "Technical Change and the Aggregate Production Function," *Review of Economics and Statistics* 39 (1957): 312–320. It is natural to ask how growth in labor efficiency E relates to growth in total factor productivity. One can show that $\Delta A/A = (1-\alpha)\Delta E/E$, where α is capital's share. Thus, technological change as measured by growth in the efficiency of labor is proportional to technological change as measured by the Solow residual.

The Sources of Growth in the United States

Having learned how to measure the sources of economic growth, we now look at the data. Table 8-3 uses U.S. data to measure the contributions of the three sources of growth between 1948 and 2002.

This table shows that output in the non-farm business sector has grown an average of 3.6 percent per year during this time. Of this 3.6 percent, 1.2 percent is attributable to increases in the capital stock, 1.2 percent to increases in the labor input, and 1.2 percent to increases in total factor productivity. These data show that increases in capital, labor, and productivity have contributed almost equally to economic growth in the United States.

Table 8-3 also shows that the growth in total factor productivity slowed substantially around 1972. In a case study in this chapter, we discussed some hypotheses to explain this productivity slowdown.

TABLE 8-3

Accounting for Economic Growth in the United States

Years	Output Growth $\Delta Y/Y$	=	Capital $\alpha\Delta K/K$	+	Labor $(1-\alpha)\Delta L/L$	+	Total Factor Productivity $\Delta A/A$
			SOURCE OF GROWTH				
			(average percentage increase per year)				
1948–2002	3.6		1.2		1.2		1.2
1948–1972	4.0		1.2		1.0		1.8
1972–1995	3.2		1.3		1.4		0.5
1995–2002	3.7		1.7		0.9		1.1

Source: U.S. Department of Labor. Data are for the non-farm business sector.

CASE STUDY

Growth in the East Asian Tigers

Perhaps the most spectacular growth experiences in recent history have been those of the "Tigers" of East Asia: Hong Kong, Singapore, South Korea, and Taiwan. From 1966 to 1990, while real income per person was growing about 2 percent per year in the United States, it grew more than 7 percent per year in each of these countries. In the course of a single generation, real income per person increased fivefold, moving the Tigers from among the world's poorest countries to among the richest. (In the late 1990s, a period of pronounced financial turmoil tarnished the reputation of some of these economies. But this short-run problem, which we examine in a case study in Chapter 12, doesn't come close to reversing the spectacular long-run growth performance that the Asian Tigers have experienced.)

What accounts for these growth miracles? Some commentators have argued that the success of these four countries is hard to reconcile with basic growth theory, such as the Solow growth model, which takes technology as growing at a constant, exogenous rate. They have suggested that these countries' rapid growth is explained by their ability to imitate foreign technologies. By adopting technology developed abroad, the argument goes, these countries managed to improve their production functions substantially in a relatively short period of time. If this argument is correct, these countries should have experienced unusually rapid growth in total factor productivity.

One recent study shed light on this issue by examining in detail the data from these four countries. The study found that their exceptional growth can be traced to large increases in measured factor inputs: increases in labor-force participation, increases in the capital stock, and increases in educational attainment. In South Korea, for example, the investment-GDP ratio rose from about 5 percent in the 1950s to about 30 percent in the 1980s; the percentage of the working population with at least a high-school education went from 26 percent in 1966 to 75 percent in 1991.

Once we account for growth in labor, capital, and human capital, little of the growth in output is left to explain. None of these four countries experienced unusually rapid growth in total factor productivity. Indeed, the average growth in total factor productivity in the East Asian Tigers was almost exactly the same as in the United States. Thus, although these countries' rapid growth has been truly impressive, it is easy to explain using the tools of basic growth theory.[21]

MORE PROBLEMS AND APPLICATIONS

1. In the economy of Solovia, the owners of capital get two-thirds of national income, and the workers receive one-third.
   a. The men of Solovia stay at home performing household chores, while the women work in factories. If some of the men started working outside the home so that the labor force increased by 5 percent, what would happen to the measured output of the economy? Does labor productivity—defined as output per worker—increase, decrease, or stay the same? Does total factor productivity increase, decrease, or stay the same?
   b. In year 1, the capital stock was 6, the labor input was 3, and output was 12. In year 2, the capital stock was 7, the labor input was 4, and output was 14. What happened to total factor productivity between the two years?
2. Labor productivity is defined as Y/L, the amount of output divided by the amount of labor input. Start with the growth-accounting equation and show that the growth in labor productivity

[21] Alwyn Young, "The Tyranny of Numbers: Confronting the Statistical Realities of the East Asian Growth Experience," *Quarterly Journal of Economics* 101 (August 1995): 641–680.

depends on growth in total factor productivity and growth in the capital-labor ratio. In particular, show that

$$\frac{\Delta(Y/L)}{Y/L} = \frac{\Delta A}{A} + \alpha\frac{\Delta(K/L)}{K/L}.$$

Hint: You may find the following mathematical trick helpful. If $z = wx$, then the growth rate of z is approximately the growth rate of w plus the growth rate of x. That is,

$$\Delta z/z \approx \Delta w/w + \Delta x/x.$$

3. Suppose an economy described by the Solow model is in a steady state with population growth n of 1.8 percent per year and technological progress g of 1.8 percent per year. Total output and total capital grow at 3.6 percent per year. Suppose further that the capital share of output is 1/3. If you used the growth-accounting equation to divide output growth into three sources—capital, labor, and total factor productivity—how much would you attribute to each source? Compare your results to the figures we found for the United States in Table 8-3.

PART IV

Business Cycle Theory: The Economy in the Short Run

CHAPTER

9

Introduction to Economic Fluctuations

The modern world regards business cycles much as the ancient Egyptians regarded the overflowing of the Nile. The phenomenon recurs at intervals, it is of great importance to everyone, and natural causes of it are not in sight.

— *John Bates Clark, 1898*

Economic fluctuations present a recurring problem for economists and policymakers. On average, the real GDP of the U.S. grows about 3.5 percent per year. But this long-run average hides the fact that the economy's output of goods and services does not grow smoothly. Growth is higher in some years than in others; sometimes the economy loses ground, and growth turns negative. These fluctuations in the economy's output are closely associated with fluctuations in employment. When the economy experiences a period of falling output and rising unemployment, the economy is said to be in *recession.*

A recent recession occurred in 2001. In the first and third quarters of that year, real GDP fell from the previous quarter, indicating a decline in the economy's production of goods and services. Although the recession was officially over by the end of the year, the economy was slow to recover. From the fourth quarter of 2000 to the fourth quarter of 2002, growth averaged only 1.2 percent. The unemployment rate rose from 3.9 percent in December 2000 to 6.3 percent in June 2003. The recession and its aftermath dominated the economic news of the time—and this recession was mild by historical standards.

Economists call these short-run fluctuations in output and employment the *business cycle.* Although this term suggests that economic fluctuations are regular and predictable, they are not. Recessions are as irregular as they are common. Sometimes they are close together, and sometimes they are far apart. In 1982, only two years after the previous recession, the economy experienced another one. By the end of that year, the unemployment rate reached 10.8 percent—the highest level since the Great Depression of the 1930s. But after the 1982 recession, it was eight years before the economy experienced another one.

These historical events raise a variety of related questions: What causes short-run fluctuations? What model should we use to explain them? Can policymakers avoid recessions? If so, what policy levers should they use?

In Parts Two and Three of this book, we developed theories to explain how the economy behaves in the long run. Here, in Part Four, we see how economists explain these short-run fluctuations. We begin in this chapter with three tasks. First, we examine the data that describe short-run economic fluctuations. Second, we discuss the key differences between how the economy behaves in the long run and how it behaves in the short run. Third, we introduce the model of aggregate supply and aggregate demand, which most economists use to explain short-run fluctuations. Developing this model in more detail will be our primary job in the chapters that follow.

Just as Egypt now controls the flooding of the Nile Valley with the Aswan Dam, modern society tries to control the business cycle with appropriate economic policies. The model we develop over the next several chapters shows how monetary and fiscal policies influence the business cycle. We will see that these policies can potentially stabilize the economy or, if poorly conducted, make the problem of economic instability even worse.

9-1 The Facts about the Business Cycle

Before thinking about the theory of business cycles, let's look at some of the facts that describe short-run fluctuations in economic activity.

GDP and Its Components

The economy's gross domestic product measures total income and total expenditure in the economy. Because GDP is the broadest gauge of overall economic conditions, it is the natural place to start in analyzing the business cycle. Figure 9-1 shows the growth of real GDP since 1970. The horizontal line shows the average growth rate of 3.5 percent per year. You can see that economic growth is not at all steady and that, occasionally, it turns negative.

The shaded areas in the figure indicate periods of recession. The official arbiter of when recessions begin and end is the National Bureau of Economic Research, a nonprofit economic research group. The NBER's Business Cycle Dating Committee (of which the author of this book was once a member) decides when recessions begin and end. According to an old rule of thumb, a recession is a period of at least two consecutive quarters of declining real GDP. This rule, however, does not always hold. In the most recently revised data, for example, the recession

"Well, so long Eddie, the recession's over."

FIGURE 9-1

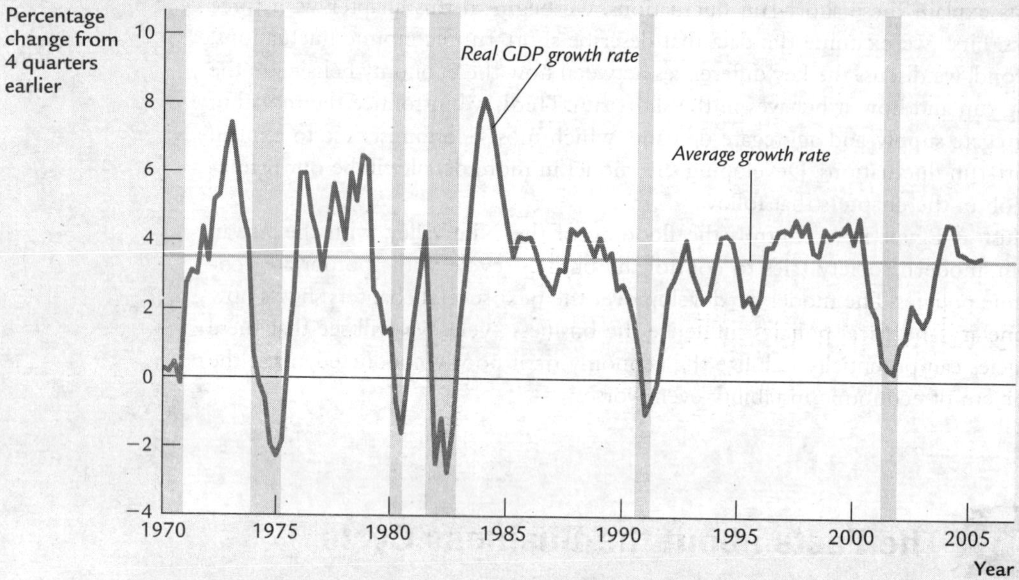

Real GDP Growth in the United States Growth in real GDP averages about 3.5 percent per year, but there are substantial fluctuations around this average. The shaded areas represent periods of recession.

Source: U.S. Department of Commerce.

of 2001 had two quarters of negative growth, but those quarters were not consecutive. In fact, the NBER's Business Cycle Dating Committee does not follow any fixed rule but, instead, looks at a variety of economic time series and uses its judgment when picking the starting and ending dates of recessions.[1]

Figure 9-2 shows the growth in two major components of GDP—consumption in panel (a) and investment in panel (b). Growth in both of these variables declines during recessions. Take note, however, of the scales for the vertical axes. Investment is far more volatile than consumption over the business cycle. When the economy heads into a recession, households respond to the fall in their incomes by consuming less, but the decline in spending on business equipment, structures, new housing, and inventories is even more substantial.

[1] Note that Figure 9-1 plots growth in real GDP from four quarters earlier, rather than from the immediately preceding quarter. During the 2001 recession, this measure declined but never turned negative.

FIGURE 9-2

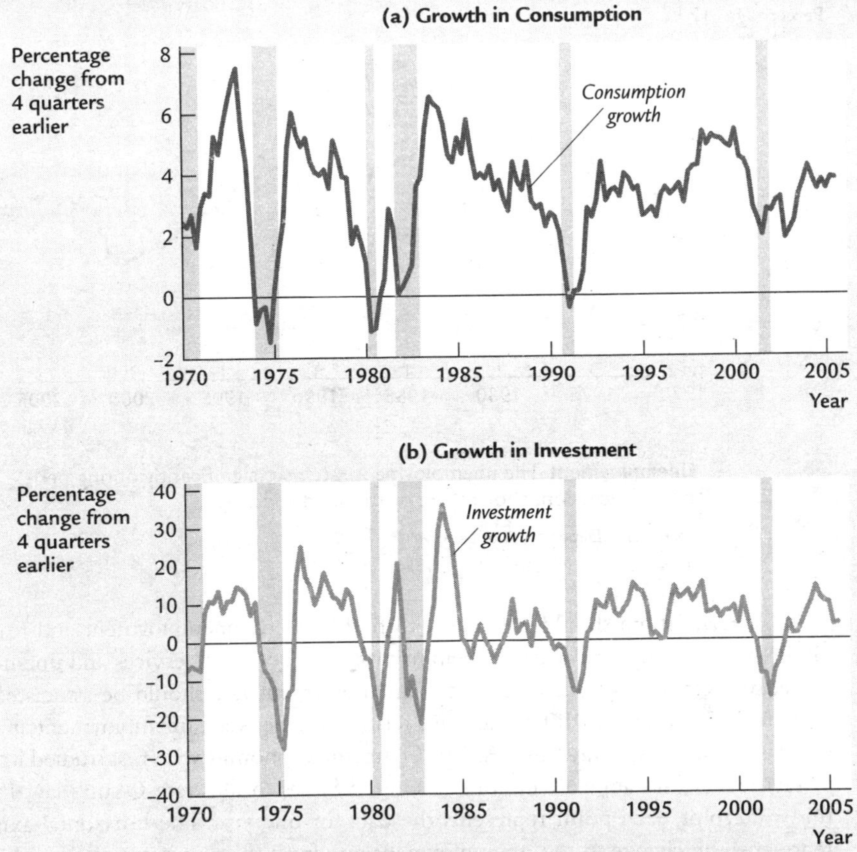

Growth in Consumption and Investment When the economy heads into a recession, growth in real consumption and investment spending both decline. Investment spending shown in panel (b) is considerably more volatile than consumption spending shown in panel (a). The shaded areas represent periods of recession.

Source: U.S. Department of Commerce.

Unemployment and Okun's Law

The business cycle is apparent not only in data from the national income accounts but also in data that describe conditions in the labor market. Figure 9-3 shows the unemployment rate since 1970, again with the shaded areas representing periods of recession. You can see that unemployment rises in each recession. Other labor-market measures tell a similar story. For example, job vacancies, as measured by the number of help-wanted ads in newspapers, decline during recessions. Put simply, when the economy heads into an economic downturn, jobs are harder to find.

FIGURE 9-3

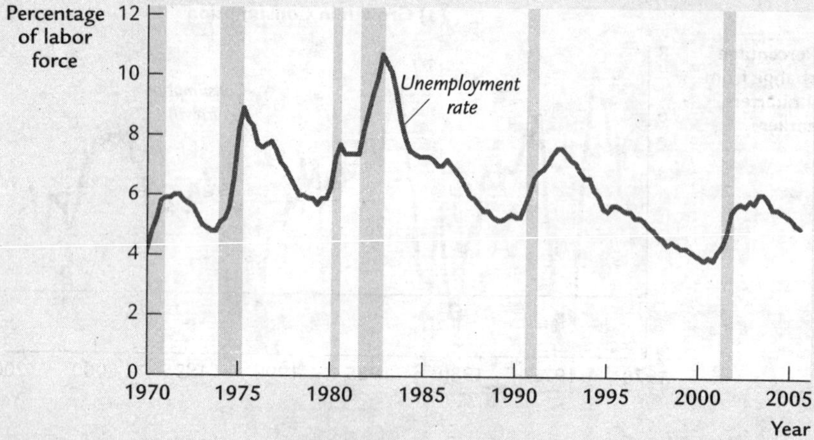

Unemployment The unemployment rate rises significantly during periods of recession, shown here by the shaded areas.

Source: U.S. Department of Labor.

What relationship should we expect to find between unemployment and real GDP? Because employed workers help to produce goods and services and unemployed workers do not, increases in the unemployment rate should be associated with decreases in real GDP. This negative relationship between unemployment and GDP is called **Okun's law**, after Arthur Okun, the economist who first studied it.[2]

Figure 9-4 uses annual data for the United States to illustrate Okun's law. In this scatterplot, each point represents the data for one year. The horizontal axis represents the change in the unemployment rate from the previous year, and the vertical axis represents the percentage change in GDP. This figure shows clearly that year-to-year changes in the unemployment rate are closely associated with year-to-year changes in real GDP.

We can be more precise about the magnitude of the Okun's law relationship. The line drawn through the scatter of points tells us that

$$\text{Percentage Change in Real GDP} \\ = 3.5\% - 2 \times \text{Change in the Unemployment Rate.}$$

If the unemployment rate remains the same, real GDP grows by about 3.5 percent; this normal growth in the production of goods and services is due to growth in the labor force, capital accumulation, and technological progress. In

[2] Arthur M. Okun, "Potential GNP: Its Measurement and Significance," in *Proceedings of the Business and Economics Statistics Section, American Statistical Association* (Washington, D.C.: American Statistical Association, 1962): 98–103; reprinted in Arthur M. Okun, *Economics for Policymaking* (Cambridge, MA: MIT Press, 1983), 145–158.

FIGURE 9-4

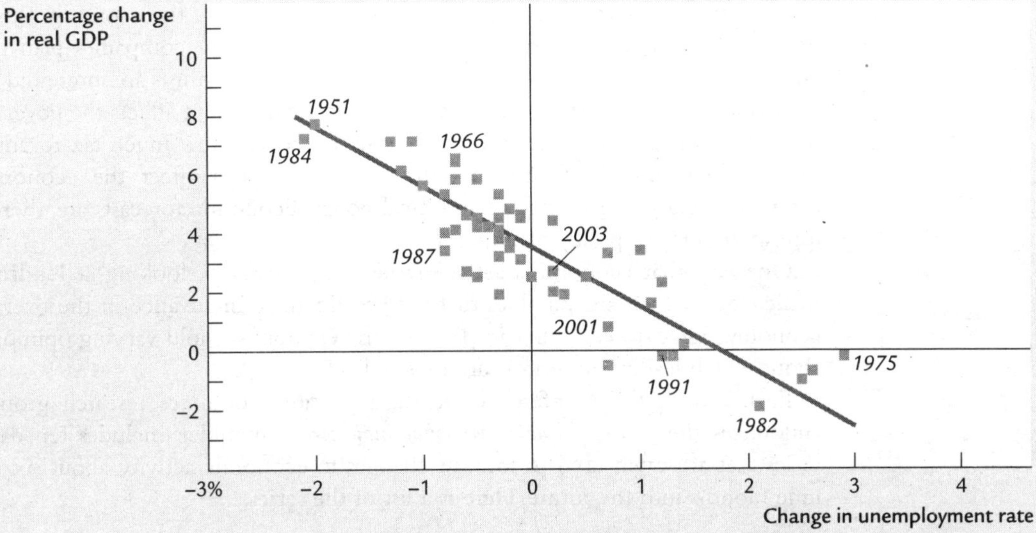

Okun's Law This figure is a scatterplot of the change in the unemployment rate on the horizontal axis and the percentage change in real GDP on the vertical axis, using data on the U.S economy. Each point represents one year. The negative correlation between these variables shows that increases in unemployment tend to be associated with lower-than-normal growth in real GDP.

Source: U.S. Department of Commerce, U.S. Department of Labor.

addition, for every percentage point the unemployment rate rises, real GDP growth typically falls by 2 percent. Hence, if the unemployment rate rises from 5 to 8 percent, then real GDP growth would be

$$\text{Percentage Change in Real GDP} = 3.5\% - 2 \times (8\% - 5\%)$$
$$= -2.5\%.$$

In this case, Okun's law says that GDP would fall by 2.5 percent, indicating that the economy is in a recession.

Okun's law is a reminder that the forces that govern the short-run business cycle are very different from those that shape long-run economic growth. As we saw in Chapters 7 and 8, long-run growth in GDP is determined primarily by technological progress. The long-run trend leading to higher standards of living from generation to generation is not associated with any long-run trend in the rate of unemployment. By contrast, short-run movements in GDP are highly correlated with the utilization of the economy's labor force. The declines in the production of goods and services that occur during recessions are always associated with increases in joblessness.

Leading Economic Indicators

Many economists, particularly those working in business and government, are engaged in the task of forecasting short-run fluctuations in the economy. Business economists are interested in forecasting to help their companies plan for changes in the economic environment. Government economists are interested in forecasting for two reasons. First, the economic environment affects the government; for example, the state of the economy influences how much tax revenue the government collects. Second, the government can affect the economy through its choice of monetary and fiscal policy. Economic forecasts are, therefore, an input into policy planning.

One way that economists arrive at their forecasts is by looking at **leading indicators**, which are variables that tend to fluctuate in advance of the overall economy. Forecasts can differ in part because economists hold varying opinions about which leading indicators are most reliable.

Each month the Conference Board, a private economics research group, announces the *index of leading economic indicators.* This index includes ten data series that are often used to forecast changes in economic activity about six to nine months into the future. Here is a list of the series.

- *Average workweek of production workers in manufacturing.* Because businesses often adjust the work hours of existing employees before making new hires or laying off workers, average weekly hours is a leading indicator of employment changes. A longer workweek indicates that firms are asking their employees to work long hours because they are experiencing strong demand for their products; it thus indicates that firms are likely to increase hiring and production in the future. A shorter workweek indicates weak demand, suggesting that firms are more likely to lay off workers and cut back production,

- *Average initial weekly claims for unemployment insurance.* The number of people making new claims on the unemployment insurance system is one of the most quickly available indicators of conditions in the labor market. This series is inverted in computing the index of leading indicators, so that an increase in the series lowers the index. An increase in the number of people making new claims for unemployment insurance indicates that firms are laying off workers and cutting back production, which will soon show up in data on employment and production.

- *New orders for consumer goods and materials, adjusted for inflation.* This is a very direct measure of the demand that firms are experiencing. Because an increase in orders depletes a firm's inventories, it typically predicts subsequent increases in production and employment.

- *New orders, nondefense capital goods.* This is the counterpart to the above series, but for investment goods rather than consumer goods, and it tells a similar story.

- *Vendor performance.* This is a measure of the number of companies receiving slower deliveries from suppliers. Vendor performance is a leading indicator because deliveries slow down when companies are experiencing increased demand for their products. Slower deliveries therefore indicate a future increase in economic activity.
- *New building permits issued.* Construction of new buildings is part of investment—a particularly volatile component of GDP. An increase in building permits means that builders are planning to increase construction, which indicates a rise in overall economic activity.
- *Index of stock prices.* The stock market reflects expectations about future economic conditions because stock-market investors bid up prices when they expect companies to be profitable. An increase in stock prices indicates that investors expect the economy to grow rapidly, and a decrease in stock prices indicates that investors expect an economic slowdown.
- *Money supply (M2), adjusted for inflation.* Because the money supply is related to total spending, more money predicts increased spending, which in turn means higher production and employment.
- *Interest rate spread: the yield spread between 10-year Treasury notes and 3-month Treasury bills.* This spread, sometimes called the slope of the yield curve, reflects the market's expectation about future interest rates, which in turn reflect the condition of the economy. A large spread means that interest rates are expected to rise, which typically occurs when economic activity increases.
- *Index of consumer expectations.* This is a direct measure of expectations, based on a survey conducted by the University of Michigan's Survey Research Center. Increased optimism about future economic conditions among consumers suggests increased consumer demand for goods and services, which in turn will encourage businesses to expand production and employment to meet the demand.

The index of leading indicators is far from a precise predictor of the future, but it is one input into planning by both businesses and the government.

9-2 Time Horizons in Macroeconomics

Now that we have some sense about the facts that describe short-run economic fluctuations, we can turn to our basic task in this part of the book: building a theory to explain these fluctuations. That job, it turns out, is not a simple one. It will take us not only the rest of this chapter but also the next four chapters to develop the model of short-run fluctuations in its entirety.

Before we start building the model, however, let's step back and ask a fundamental question: Why do economists need different models for different time horizons? Why can't we stop the course here and be content with the classical models developed in Chapters 3 through 8? The answer, as this book has consistently reminded its reader, is that classical macroeconomic theory applies to the long run but not to the short run. But why is this so?

How the Short Run and Long Run Differ

Most macroeconomists believe that the key difference between the short run and the long run is the behavior of prices. *In the long run, prices are flexible and can respond to changes in supply or demand. In the short run, many prices are "sticky" at some predetermined level.* Because prices behave differently in the short run than in the long run, various economic events and policies have different effects over different time horizons.

To see how the short run and the long run differ, consider the effects of a change in monetary policy. Suppose that the Federal Reserve suddenly reduces the money supply by 5 percent. According to the classical model, which almost all economists agree describes the economy in the long run, the money supply affects nominal variables—variables measured in terms of money—but not real variables. In the long run, a 5-percent reduction in the money supply lowers all prices (including nominal wages) by 5 percent while output, employment, and other real variables remain the same. Thus, in the long run, changes in the money supply do not cause fluctuations in output and employment.

In the short run, however, many prices do not respond to changes in monetary policy. A reduction in the money supply does not immediately cause all firms to cut the wages they pay, all stores to change the price tags on their goods, all mail-order firms to issue new catalogs, and all restaurants to print new menus. Instead, there is little immediate change in many prices; that is, many prices are sticky. This short-run price stickiness implies that the short-run impact of a change in the money supply is not the same as the long-run impact.

A model of economic fluctuations must take into account this short-run price stickiness. We will see that the failure of prices to adjust quickly and completely means that, in the short run, real variables such as output and employment must do some of the adjusting instead. In other words, during the time horizon over which prices are sticky, the classical dichotomy no longer holds: nominal variables can influence real variables, and the economy can deviate from the equilibrium predicted by the classical model.

CASE STUDY

The Puzzle of Sticky Magazine Prices

How sticky are prices? The answer to this question depends on what price we consider. Some commodities, such as wheat, soybeans, and pork bellies, are traded on organized exchanges, and their prices change every minute. No one would call these prices sticky. Yet the prices of most goods and services change much less frequently. One survey found that 39 percent of firms change their prices once a year, and another 10 percent change their prices less than once a year.[3]

The reasons for price stickiness are not always apparent. Consider, for example, the market for magazines. A study has documented that magazines change their newsstand prices very infrequently. The typical magazine allows inflation to erode its real price by about 25 percent before it raises its nominal price. When inflation is 4 percent per year, the typical magazine changes its price about every 6 years.[4]

Why do magazines keep their prices the same for so long? Economists do not have a definitive answer. The question is puzzling because it would seem that for magazines, the cost of a price change is small. To change prices, a mail-order firm must issue a new catalog and a restaurant must print a new menu, but a magazine publisher can simply print a new price on the cover of the next issue. Perhaps the cost to the publisher of charging the wrong price is also small. Or maybe customers would find it inconvenient if the price of their favorite magazine changed every month.

As the magazine example shows, explaining at the microeconomic level why prices are sticky is sometimes hard. The cause of price stickiness is, therefore, an active area of research, which we discuss more fully in Chapter 19. In this chapter, however, we simply assume that prices are sticky so we can start developing the link between sticky prices and the business cycle. Although not yet fully explained, short-run price stickiness is widely believed to be crucial for understanding short-run economic fluctuations.

The Model of Aggregate Supply and Aggregate Demand

How does the introduction of sticky prices change our view of how the economy works? We can answer this question by considering economists' two favorite words—supply and demand.

In classical macroeconomic theory, the amount of output depends on the economy's ability to *supply* goods and services, which in turn depends on the supplies of capital and labor and on the available production technology. This is the essence of the basic classical model in Chapter 3, as well as of the Solow growth model in Chapters 7 and 8. Flexible prices are a crucial

[3] Alan S. Blinder, "On Sticky Prices: Academic Theories Meet the Real World," in N. G. Mankiw, ed., *Monetary Policy* (Chicago: University of Chicago Press, 1994), 117–154. A case study in Chapter 19 discusses this survey in more detail.

[4] Stephen G. Cecchetti, "The Frequency of Price Adjustment: A Study of the Newsstand Prices of Magazines," *Journal of Econometrics* 31 (1986): 255–274.

assumption of classical theory. The theory posits, sometimes implicitly, that prices adjust to ensure that the quantity of output demanded equals the quantity supplied.

The economy works quite differently when prices are sticky. In this case, as we will see, output also depends on the economy's *demand* for goods and services. Demand, in turn, depends on a variety of factors: consumers' confidence about their economic prospects, firms' perceptions about the profitability of new investments, and monetary and fiscal policy. Because monetary and fiscal policy can influence demand, and demand in turn can influence the economy's output over the time horizon when prices are sticky, price stickiness provides a rationale for why these policies may be useful in stabilizing the economy in the short run.

In the rest of this chapter, we start developing a model that makes these ideas more precise. The model of supply and demand, which we used in Chapter 1 to discuss the market for pizza, offers some of the most fundamental insights in economics. This model shows how the supply and demand for any good jointly determine the good's price and the quantity sold, and how shifts in supply and demand affect the price and quantity. We now introduce the "economy-size" version of this model—*the model of aggregate supply and aggregate demand.* This macroeconomic model allows us to study how the aggregate price level and the quantity of aggregate output are determined in the short run. It also provides a way to contrast how the economy behaves in the long run and how it behaves in the short run.

Although the model of aggregate supply and aggregate demand resembles the model of supply and demand for a single good, the analogy is not exact. The model of supply and demand for a single good considers only one good within a large economy. By contrast, as we will see in the coming chapters, the model of aggregate supply and aggregate demand is a sophisticated model that incorporates the interactions among many markets. In the remainder of this chapter we get a first glimpse at those interactions by examining the model in its most simplified form. Our goal here is not to explain the model fully but, instead, to introduce the model's key elements and illustrate how it can help explain short-run economic fluctuations.

9-3 Aggregate Demand

Aggregate demand (*AD*) is the relationship between the quantity of output demanded and the aggregate price level. In other words, the aggregate demand curve tells us the quantity of goods and services people want to buy at any given level of prices. We examine the theory of aggregate demand in detail in Chapters 10 through 12. Here we use the quantity theory of money to provide a simple, although incomplete, derivation of the aggregate demand curve.

The Quantity Equation as Aggregate Demand

Recall from Chapter 4 that the quantity theory says that

$$MV = PY,$$

where M is the money supply, V is the velocity of money, P is the price level, and Y is the amount of output. If the velocity of money is constant, then this equation states that the money supply determines the nominal value of output, which in turn is the product of the price level and the amount of output.

When interpreting this equation, it is useful to recall that the quantity equation can be rewritten in terms of the supply and demand for real money balances:

$$M/P = (M/P)^{d} = kY,$$

where $k = 1/V$ is a parameter determining how much money people want to hold for every dollar of income. In this form, the quantity equation states that the supply of real money balances M/P equals the demand for real money balances $(M/P)^{d}$ and that the demand is proportional to output Y. The velocity of money V is the "flip side" of the money demand parameter k. The assumption of constant velocity is equivalent to the assumption of a constant demand for real money balances per unit of output.

If we assume that velocity V is constant and the money supply M is fixed by the central bank, then the quantity equation yields a negative relationship between the price level P and output Y. Figure 9-5 graphs the combinations of P and Y that satisfy the quantity equation holding M and V constant. This downward-sloping curve is called the aggregate demand curve.

FIGURE 9-5

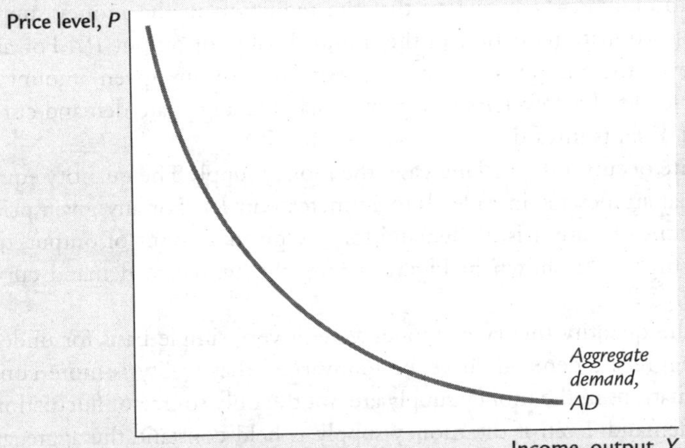

The Aggregate Demand Curve The aggregate demand curve AD shows the relationship between the price level P and the quantity of goods and services demanded Y. It is drawn for a given value of the money supply M. The aggregate demand curve slopes downward: the higher the price level P, the lower the level of real balances M/P, and therefore the lower the quantity of goods and services demanded Y.

Why the Aggregate Demand Curve Slopes Downward

As a strictly mathematical matter, the quantity equation explains the downward slope of the aggregate demand curve very simply. The money supply M and the velocity of money V determine the nominal value of output PY. Once PY is fixed, if P goes up, Y must go down.

What is the economics that lies behind this mathematical relationship? For a complete explanation of the downward slope of the aggregate demand curve, we have to wait for a couple of chapters. For now, however, consider the following logic: Because we have assumed the velocity of money is fixed, the money supply determines the dollar value of all transactions in the economy. (This conclusion should be familiar from Chapter 4.) If the price level rises, each transaction requires more dollars, so the number of transactions and thus the quantity of goods and services purchased must fall.

We can also explain the downward slope of the aggregate demand curve by thinking about the supply and demand for real money balances. If output is higher, people engage in more transactions and need higher real balances M/P. For a fixed money supply M, higher real balances imply a lower price level. Conversely, if the price level is lower, real money balances are higher; the higher level of real balances allows a greater volume of transactions, which means a greater quantity of output is demanded.

Shifts in the Aggregate Demand Curve

The aggregate demand curve is drawn for a fixed value of the money supply. In other words, it tells us the possible combinations of P and Y for a given value of M. If the Fed changes the money supply, then the possible combinations of P and Y change, which means the aggregate demand curve shifts.

For example, consider what happens if the Fed reduces the money supply. The quantity equation, $MV = PY$, tells us that the reduction in the money supply leads to a proportionate reduction in the nominal value of output PY. For any given price level, the amount of output is lower, and for any given amount of output, the price level is lower. As in Figure 9-6(a), the aggregate demand curve relating P and Y shifts inward.

The opposite occurs if the Fed increases the money supply. The quantity equation tells us that an increase in M leads to an increase in PY. For any given price level, the amount of output is higher, and for any given amount of output, the price level is higher. As shown in Figure 9-6(b), the aggregate demand curve shifts outward.

Although the quantity theory of money gives a very simple basis for understanding the aggregate demand curve, be forewarned that reality is more complicated. Fluctuations in the money supply are not the only source of fluctuations in aggregate demand. Even if the money supply is held constant, the aggregate demand curve shifts if some event causes a change in the velocity of money. Over the next two chapters, we develop a more general model of aggregate demand, called the *IS-LM model,* which will allow us to consider many possible reasons for shifts in the aggregate demand curve.

FIGURE 9-6

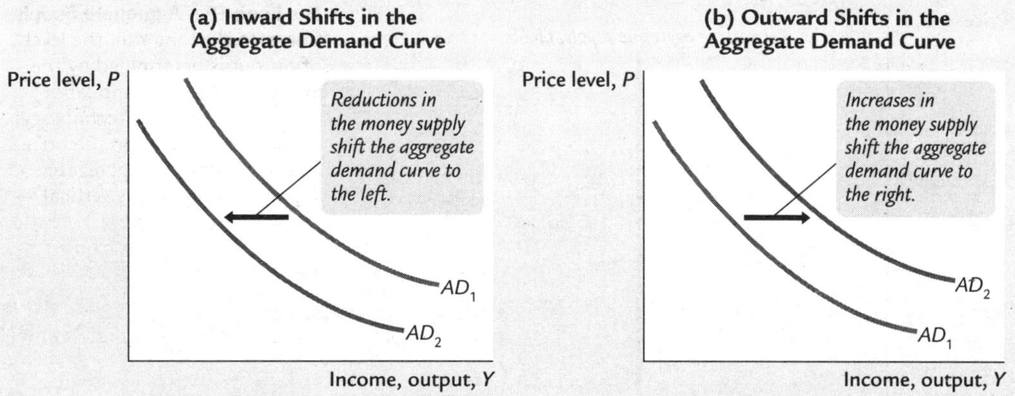

Shifts in the Aggregate Demand Curve Changes in the money supply shift the aggregate demand curve. In panel (a), a decrease in the money supply M reduces the nominal value of output PY. For any given price level P, output Y is lower. Thus, a decrease in the money supply shifts the aggregate demand curve inward from AD_1 to AD_2. In panel (b), an increase in the money supply M raises the nominal value of output PY. For any given price level P, output Y is higher. Thus, an increase in the money supply shifts the aggregate demand curve outward from AD_1 to AD_2.

9-4 Aggregate Supply

By itself, the aggregate demand curve does not tell us the price level or the amount of output that will prevail in the economy; it merely gives a relationship between these two variables. To accompany the aggregate demand curve, we need another relationship between P and Y that crosses the aggregate demand curve—an aggregate supply curve. The aggregate demand and aggregate supply curves together pin down the economy's price level and quantity of output.

Aggregate supply (*AS*) is the relationship between the quantity of goods and services supplied and the price level. Because the firms that supply goods and services have flexible prices in the long run but sticky prices in the short run, the aggregate supply relationship depends on the time horizon. We need to discuss two different aggregate supply curves: the long-run aggregate supply curve *LRAS* and the short-run aggregate supply curve *SRAS*. We also need to discuss how the economy makes the transition from the short run to the long run.

The Long Run: The Vertical Aggregate Supply Curve

Because the classical model describes how the economy behaves in the long run, we derive the long-run aggregate supply curve from the classical model. Recall from Chapter 3 that the amount of output produced depends on the fixed amounts of capital and labor and on the available technology. To show this, we write

$$\begin{aligned} Y &= F(\bar{K}, \bar{L}) \\ &= \bar{Y}. \end{aligned}$$

FIGURE 9-7

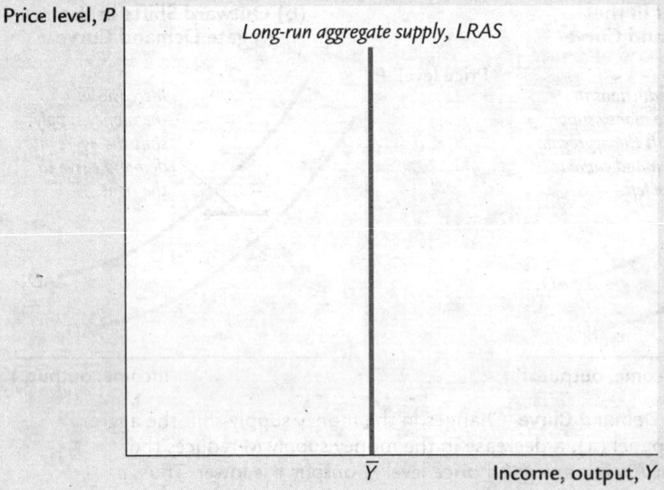

The Long-Run Aggregate Supply Curve In the long run, the level of output is determined by the amounts of capital and labor and by the available technology; it does not depend on the price level. The long-run aggregate supply curve, *LRAS*, is vertical.

According to the classical model, output does not depend on the price level. To show that output is fixed at this level, regardless of the price level, we draw a vertical aggregate supply curve, as in Figure 9-7. In the long run, the intersection of the aggregate demand curve with this vertical aggregate supply curve determines the price level.

If the aggregate supply curve is vertical, then changes in aggregate demand affect prices but not output. For example, if the money supply falls, the aggregate demand curve shifts downward, as in Figure 9-8. The economy moves from the

FIGURE 9-8

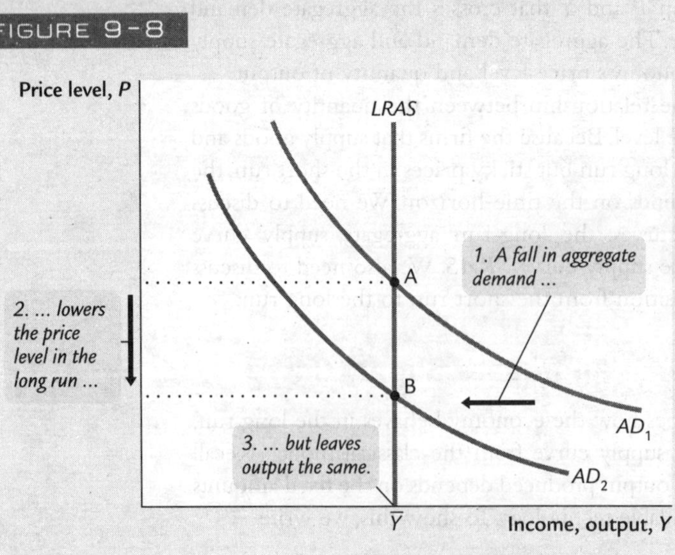

Shifts in Aggregate Demand in the Long Run A reduction in the money supply shifts the aggregate demand curve downward from AD_1 to AD_2. The equilibrium for the economy moves from point A to point B. Because the aggregate supply curve is vertical in the long run, the reduction in aggregate demand affects the price level but not the level of output.

old intersection of aggregate supply and aggregate demand, point A, to the new intersection, point B. The shift in aggregate demand affects only prices.

The vertical aggregate supply curve satisfies the classical dichotomy, because it implies that the level of output is independent of the money supply. This long-run level of output, $\bar{Y}$, is called the *full-employment*, or *natural*, level of output. It is the level of output at which the economy's resources are fully employed or, more realistically, at which unemployment is at its natural rate.

The Short Run: The Horizontal Aggregate Supply Curve

The classical model and the vertical aggregate supply curve apply only in the long run. In the short run, some prices are sticky and, therefore, do not adjust to changes in demand. Because of this price stickiness, the short-run aggregate supply curve is not vertical.

In this chapter, we will simplify things by assuming an extreme example. Suppose that all firms have issued price catalogs and that it is too costly for them to issue new ones. Thus, all prices are stuck at predetermined levels. At these prices, firms are willing to sell as much as their customers are willing to buy, and they hire just enough labor to produce the amount demanded. Because the price level is fixed, we represent this situation in Figure 9-9 with a horizontal aggregate supply curve.

The short-run equilibrium of the economy is the intersection of the aggregate demand curve and this horizontal short-run aggregate supply curve. In this case, changes in aggregate demand do affect the level of output. For example, if the Fed suddenly reduces the money supply, the aggregate demand curve shifts inward, as in Figure 9-10. The economy moves from the old intersection of aggregate demand and aggregate supply, point A, to the new intersection, point B. The movement from point A to point B represents a decline in output at a fixed price level.

Thus, a fall in aggregate demand reduces output in the short run because prices do not adjust instantly. After the sudden fall in aggregate demand, firms

FIGURE 9-9

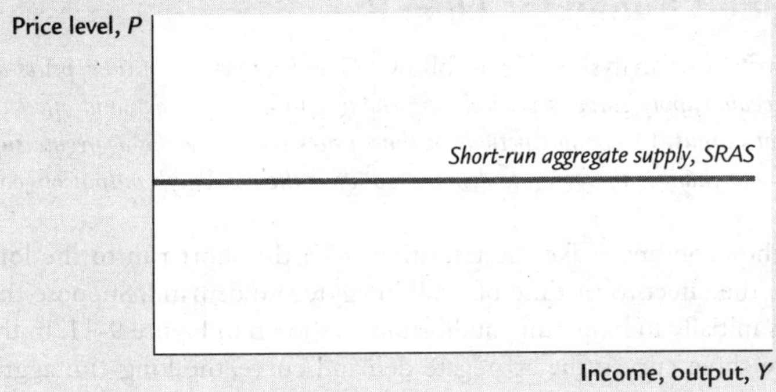

The Short-Run Aggregate Supply Curve In this extreme example, all prices are fixed in the short run. Therefore, the short-run aggregate supply curve, *SRAS*, is horizontal.

FIGURE 9-10

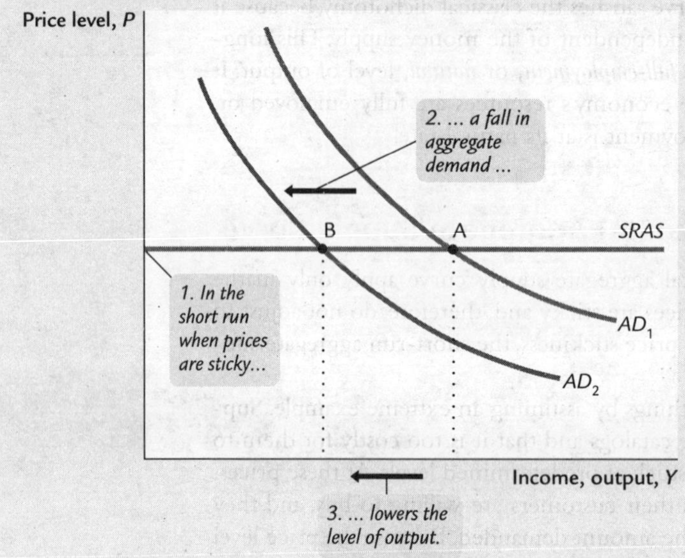

Shifts in Aggregate Demand in the Short Run A reduction in the money supply shifts the aggregate demand curve downward from AD_1 to AD_2. The equilibrium for the economy moves from point A to point B. Because the aggregate supply curve is horizontal in the short run, the reduction in aggregate demand reduces the level of output.

are stuck with prices that are too high. With demand low and prices high, firms sell less of their product, so they reduce production and lay off workers. The economy experiences a recession.

Once again, be forewarned that reality is a bit more complicated than illustrated here. Although many prices are sticky in the short run, some prices are able to respond quickly to changing circumstances. As we will see in Chapter 13, in an economy with some sticky prices and some flexible prices, the short-run aggregate supply curve is upward sloping rather than horizontal. Figure 9-10 illustrates the extreme case in which all prices are stuck. Because this case is simpler, it is a useful starting point for thinking about short-run aggregate supply.

From the Short Run to the Long Run

We can summarize our analysis so far as follows: *Over long periods of time, prices are flexible, the aggregate supply curve is vertical, and changes in aggregate demand affect the price level but not output. Over short periods of time, prices are sticky, the aggregate supply curve is flat, and changes in aggregate demand do affect the economy's output of goods and services.*

How does the economy make the transition from the short run to the long run? Let's trace the effects over time of a fall in aggregate demand. Suppose that the economy is initially in long-run equilibrium, as shown in Figure 9-11. In this figure, there are three curves: the aggregate demand curve, the long-run aggregate supply curve, and the short-run aggregate supply curve. The long-run equi-

FIGURE 9-11

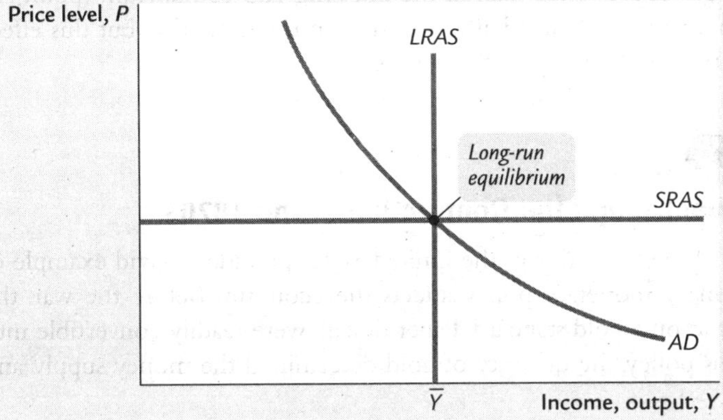

Long-Run Equilibrium In the long run, the economy finds itself at the intersection of the long-run aggregate supply curve and the aggregate demand curve. Because prices have adjusted to this level, the short-run aggregate supply curve crosses this point as well.

librium is the point at which aggregate demand crosses the long-run aggregate supply curve. Prices have adjusted to reach this equilibrium. Therefore, when the economy is in its long-run equilibrium, the short-run aggregate supply curve must cross this point as well.

Now suppose that the Fed reduces the money supply and the aggregate demand curve shifts downward, as in Figure 9-12. In the short run, prices are sticky, so the economy moves from point A to point B. Output and employment fall below their natural levels, which means the economy is in a recession. Over time, in response to the low demand, wages and prices fall. The gradual reduction in the price level moves the economy downward along the aggregate

FIGURE 9-12

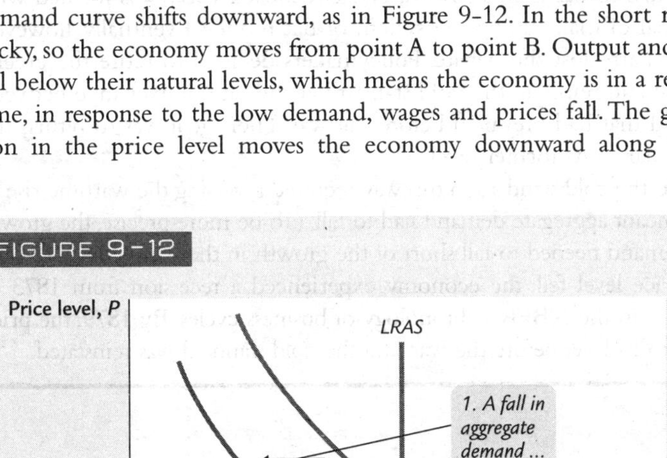

A Reduction in Aggregate Demand The economy begins in long-run equilibrium at point A. A reduction in aggregate demand, perhaps caused by a decrease in the money supply, moves the economy from point A to point B, where output is below its natural level. As prices fall, the economy gradually recovers from the recession, moving from point B to point C.

demand curve to point C, which is the new long-run equilibrium. In the new long-run equilibrium (point C), output and employment are back to their natural levels, but prices are lower than in the old long-run equilibrium (point A). Thus, a shift in aggregate demand affects output in the short run, but this effect dissipates over time as firms adjust their prices.

CASE STUDY

Gold, Greenbacks, and the Contraction of the 1870s

The aftermath of the Civil War in the United States provides a vivid example of how contractionary monetary policy affects the economy. Before the war, the United States was on a gold standard. Paper dollars were readily convertible into gold. Under this policy, the quantity of gold determined the money supply and the price level.

In 1862, after the Civil War broke out, the Treasury announced that it would no longer redeem dollars for gold. In essence, this act replaced the gold standard with a system of fiat money. Over the next few years, the government printed large quantities of paper currency—called *greenbacks* for their color—and used the seigniorage to finance wartime expenditure. Because of this increase in the money supply, the price level approximately doubled during the war.

When the war was over, much political debate centered on the question of whether to return to the gold standard. The Greenback Party was formed with the primary goal of maintaining the system of fiat money. Eventually, however, the Greenback Party lost the debate. Policymakers decided to retire the greenbacks over time and reinstate the gold standard at the rate of exchange between dollars and gold that had prevailed before the war. Their goal was to return the value of the dollar to its former level.

Returning to the gold standard in this way required reversing the wartime rise in prices, which meant aggregate demand had to fall. (To be more precise, the growth in aggregate demand needed to fall short of the growth in the natural level of output.) As the price level fell, the economy experienced a recession from 1873 to 1879, the longest in the NBER's chronology of business cycles. By 1879, the price level was back to its level before the war, and the gold standard was reinstated.

9-5 Stabilization Policy

Fluctuations in the economy as a whole come from changes in aggregate supply or aggregate demand. Economists call exogenous events that shift these curves **shocks** to the economy. A shock that shifts the aggregate demand curve is called a **demand shock**, and a shock that shifts the aggregate supply curve is called a **supply shock**. These shocks disrupt the economy by pushing output and employment away from their natural levels. One goal of the model of aggregate supply and aggregate demand is to show how shocks cause economic fluctuations.

Another goal of the model is to evaluate how macroeconomic policy can respond to these shocks. Economists use the term **stabilization policy** to refer to policy actions aimed at reducing the severity of short-run economic fluctuations. Because output and employment fluctuate around their long-run natural levels, stabilization policy dampens the business cycle by keeping output and employment as close to their natural levels as possible.

In the coming chapters, we examine in detail how stabilization policy works and what practical problems arise in its use. Here we begin our analysis of stabilization policy using our simplified version of the model of aggregate demand and aggregate supply. In particular, we examine how monetary policy might respond to shocks. Monetary policy is an important component of stabilization policy because, as we have seen, the money supply has a powerful impact on aggregate demand.

Shocks to Aggregate Demand

Consider an example of a demand shock: the introduction and expanded availability of credit cards. Because credit cards are often a more convenient way to make purchases than using cash, they reduce the quantity of money that people choose to hold. This reduction in money demand is equivalent to an increase in the velocity of money. When each person holds less money, the money demand parameter k falls. This means that each dollar of money moves from hand to hand more quickly, so velocity V (= $1/k$) rises.

If the money supply is held constant, the increase in velocity causes nominal spending to rise and the aggregate demand curve to shift outward, as in Figure 9-13. In the short run, the increase in demand raises the output of the

FIGURE 9-13

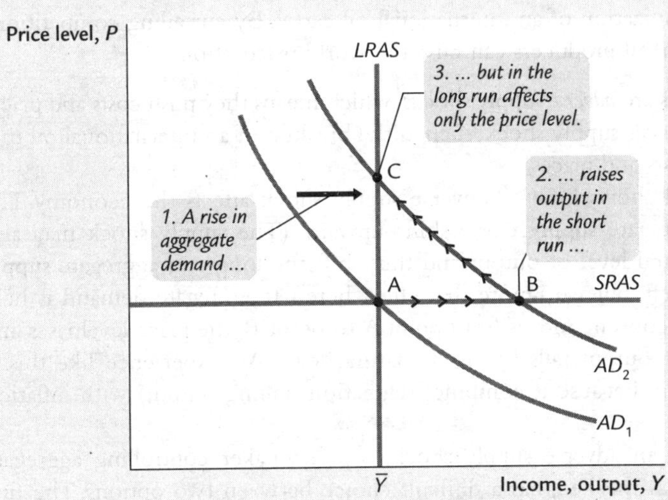

An Increase in Aggregate Demand The economy begins in long-run equilibrium at point A. An increase in aggregate demand, perhaps due to an increase in the velocity of money, moves the economy from point A to point B, where output is above its natural level. As prices rise, output gradually returns to its natural level, and the economy moves from point B to point C.

economy—it causes an economic boom. At the old prices, firms now sell more output. Therefore, they hire more workers, ask their existing workers to work longer hours, and make greater use of their factories and equipment.

Over time, the high level of aggregate demand pulls up wages and prices. As the price level rises, the quantity of output demanded declines, and the economy gradually approaches the natural level of production. But during the transition to the higher price level, the economy's output is higher than its natural level.

What can the Fed do to dampen this boom and keep output closer to the natural level? The Fed might reduce the money supply to offset the increase in velocity. Offsetting the change in velocity would stabilize aggregate demand. Thus, the Fed can reduce or even eliminate the impact of demand shocks on output and employment if it can skillfully control the money supply. Whether the Fed in fact has the necessary skill is a more difficult question, which we take up in Chapter 14.

Shocks to Aggregate Supply

Shocks to aggregate supply, as well as shocks to aggregate demand, can cause economic fluctuations. A supply shock is a shock to the economy that alters the cost of producing goods and services and, as a result, the prices that firms charge. Because supply shocks have a direct impact on the price level, they are sometimes called *price shocks.* Here are some examples:

- A drought that destroys crops. The reduction in food supply pushes up food prices.
- A new environmental protection law that requires firms to reduce their emissions of pollutants. Firms pass on the added costs to customers in the form of higher prices.
- An increase in union aggressiveness. This pushes up wages and the prices of the goods produced by union workers.
- The organization of an international oil cartel. By curtailing competition, the major oil producers can raise the world price of oil.

All these events are *adverse* supply shocks, which means they push costs and prices upward. A *favorable* supply shock, such as the breakup of an international oil cartel, reduces costs and prices.

Figure 9-14 shows how an adverse supply shock affects the economy. The short-run aggregate supply curve shifts upward. (The supply shock may also lower the natural level of output and thus shift the long-run aggregate supply curve to the left, but we ignore that effect here.) If aggregate demand is held constant, the economy moves from point A to point B: the price level rises and the amount of output falls below its natural level. An experience like this is called *stagflation,* because it combines stagnation (falling output) with inflation (rising prices).

Faced with an adverse supply shock, a policymaker controlling aggregate demand, such as the Fed, has a difficult choice between two options. The first option, implicit in Figure 9-14, is to hold aggregate demand constant. In this

FIGURE 9-14

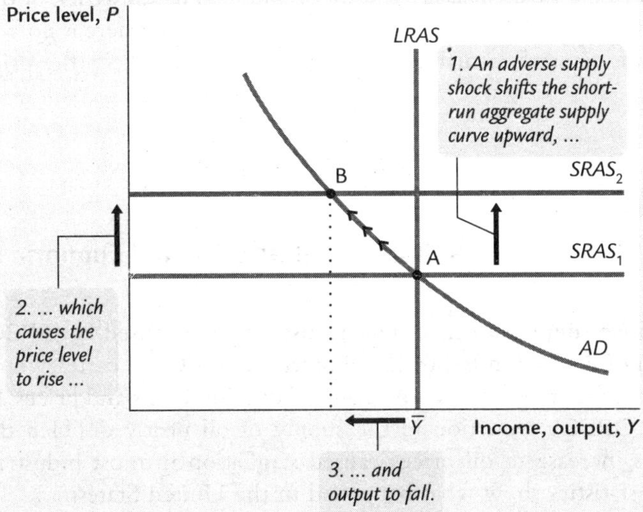

An Adverse Supply Shock An adverse supply shock pushes up costs and thus prices. If aggregate demand is held constant, the economy moves from point A to point B, leading to stagflation—a combination of increasing prices and falling output. Eventually, as prices fall, the economy returns to the natural level of output, point A.

case, output and employment are lower than the natural level. Eventually, prices will fall to restore full employment at the old price level (point A), but the cost of this adjustment process is a painful recession.

The second option, illustrated in Figure 9-15, is to expand aggregate demand to bring the economy toward the natural level of output more

FIGURE 9-15

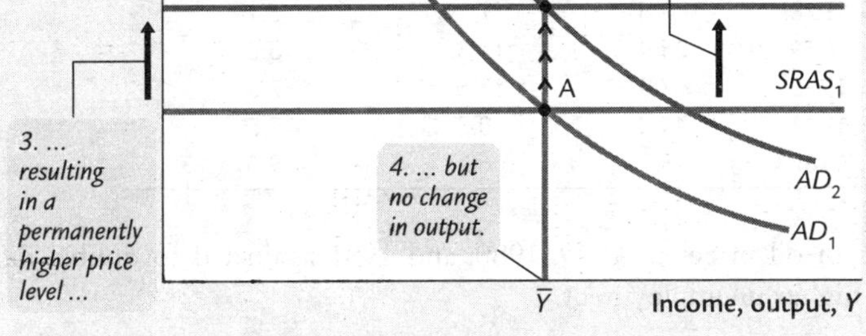

Accommodating an Adverse Supply Shock In response to an adverse supply shock, the Fed can increase aggregate demand to prevent a reduction in output. The economy moves from point A to point C. The cost of this policy is a permanently higher level of prices.

quickly. If the increase in aggregate demand coincides with the shock to aggregate supply, the economy goes immediately from point A to point C. In this case, the Fed is said to *accommodate* the supply shock. The drawback of this option, of course, is that the price level is permanently higher. There is no way to adjust aggregate demand to maintain full employment and keep the price level stable.

CASE STUDY

How OPEC Helped Cause Stagflation in the 1970s and Euphoria in the 1980s

The most disruptive supply shocks in recent history were caused by OPEC, the Organization of Petroleum Exporting Countries. OPEC is a cartel, which is an organization of suppliers that coordinate production levels and prices. In the early 1970s, OPEC's reduction in the supply of oil nearly doubled the world price. This increase in oil prices caused stagflation in most industrial countries. These statistics show what happened in the United States:

Year	Change in Oil Prices	Inflation Rate (CPI)	Unemployment Rate
1973	11.0%	6.2%	4.9%
1974	68.0	11.0	5.6
1975	16.0	9.1	8.5
1976	3.3	5.8	7.7
1977	8.1	6.5	7.1

The 68-percent increase in the price of oil in 1974 was an adverse supply shock of major proportions. As one would have expected, this shock led to both higher inflation and higher unemployment.

A few years later, when the world economy had nearly recovered from the first OPEC recession, almost the same thing happened again. OPEC raised oil prices, causing further stagflation. Here are the statistics for the United States:

Year	Change in Oil Prices	Inflation Rate (CPI)	Unemployment Rate
1978	9.4%	7.7%	6.1%
1979	25.4	11.3	5.8
1980	47.8	13.5	7.0
1981	44.4	10.3	7.5
1982	−8.7	6.1	9.5

The increases in oil prices in 1979, 1980, and 1981 again led to double-digit inflation and higher unemployment.

In the mid-1980s, political turmoil among the Arab countries weakened OPEC's ability to restrain supplies of oil. Oil prices fell, reversing the stagflation of the 1970s and the early 1980s. Here's what happened:

Year	Change in Oil Prices	Inflation Rate (CPI)	Unemployment Rate
1983	−7.1%	3.2%	9.5%
1984	−1.7	4.3	7.4
1985	−7.5	3.6	7.1
1986	−44.5	1.9	6.9
1987	18.3	3.6	6.1

In 1986 oil prices fell by nearly half. This favorable supply shock led to one of the lowest inflation rates experienced in recent U.S. history and to falling unemployment.

More recently, OPEC has not been a major cause of economic fluctuations. There are two reasons for the cartel's diminished macroeconomic influence.

First, OPEC has been less successful at raising the price of oil. Although world oil prices have fluctuated, the changes have not been as large as those experienced during the 1970s, and the real price of oil has never returned to the peaks reached in the early 1980s. Measured in 2006 dollars, oil reached about $100 a barrel in the early 1980s. By comparison, from 2003 to 2005, oil prices were a source of much concern, as the Iraq war and other events pushed oil prices higher. But oil prices during this time period stayed below $70 a barrel.

Second, conservation efforts and technological changes have made the U.S. economy less susceptible to oil shocks. The economy today is more service-based and less manufacturing-based, and services typically use less energy to produce than do manufactured goods. The amount of oil consumed per unit of real GDP has fallen about 40 percent over the past three decades. This fact suggests that even if oil prices were again to reach $100 per barrel, the macroeconomic impact would be much smaller today. In other words, it would take a much larger oil price change to have the impact on the economy that we observed in the 1970s and 1980s.

But we should not be too sanguine. Events in the Middle East are still a potential source of shocks to economies around the world. If the rise in oil prices were ever large enough, the economic result could well resemble the stagflation of the 1970s.[5]

[5] Some economists have suggested that changes in oil prices played a major role in economic fluctuations even before the 1970s. See James D. Hamilton, "Oil and the Macroeconomy Since World War II," *Journal of Political Economy* 91 (April 1983): 228–248.

9-6 Conclusion

This chapter introduced a framework to study economic fluctuations: the model of aggregate supply and aggregate demand. The model is built on the assumption that prices are sticky in the short run and flexible in the long run. It shows how shocks to the economy cause output to deviate temporarily from the level implied by the classical model.

The model also highlights the role of monetary policy. On the one hand, poor monetary policy can be a source of destabilizing shocks to the economy. On the other hand, a well-run monetary policy can respond to shocks and stabilize the economy.

In the chapters that follow, we refine our understanding of this model and our analysis of stabilization policy. Chapters 10 through 12 go beyond the quantity equation to refine our theory of aggregate demand. Chapter 13 examines aggregate supply in more detail. Chapter 14 examines the debate over the virtues and limits of stabilization policy.

Summary

1. Economies experience short-run fluctuations in economic activity, measured most broadly by real GDP. These fluctuations are associated with movement in many macroeconomic variables. In particular, when GDP growth declines, consumption growth falls (typically by a smaller amount), investment growth falls (typically by a larger amount), and unemployment rises. Although economists look at various leading indicators to predict these fluctuations, these fluctuations are largely unpredictable.
2. The crucial difference between how the economy works in the long run and how it works in the short run is that prices are flexible in the long run but sticky in the short run. The model of aggregate supply and aggregate demand provides a framework to analyze economic fluctuations and see how the impact of policies and events varies over different time horizons.
3. The aggregate demand curve slopes downward. It tells us that the lower the price level, the greater the aggregate quantity of goods and services demanded.
4. In the long run, the aggregate supply curve is vertical because output is determined by the amounts of capital and labor and by the available technology, but not by the level of prices. Therefore, shifts in aggregate demand affect the price level but not output or employment.
5. In the short run, the aggregate supply curve is horizontal, because wages and prices are sticky at predetermined levels. Therefore, shifts in aggregate demand affect output and employment.
6. Shocks to aggregate demand and aggregate supply cause economic fluctuations. Because the Fed can shift the aggregate demand curve, it can attempt to offset these shocks to maintain output and employment at their natural levels.

KEY CONCEPTS

Okun's Law
Leading indicators
Aggregate demand
Aggregate supply
Shocks
Demand shocks
Supply shocks
Stabilization policy

QUESTIONS FOR REVIEW

1. When real GDP declines during a recession, what typically happens to consumption, investment, and the unemployment rate?
2. Give an example of a price that is sticky in the short run and flexible in the long run.
3. Why does the aggregate demand curve slope downward?
4. Explain the impact of an increase in the money supply in the short run and in the long run
5. Why is it easier for the Fed to deal with demand shocks than with supply shocks?

PROBLEMS AND APPLICATIONS

1. Suppose that a change in government regulations allows banks to start paying interest on checking accounts. Recall that the money stock is the sum of currency and demand deposits, including checking accounts, so this regulatory change makes holding money more attractive.
   a. How does this change affect the demand for money?
   b. What happens to the velocity of money?
   c. If the Fed keeps the money supply constant, what will happen to output and prices in the short run and in the long run?
   d. Should the Fed keep the money supply constant in response to this regulatory change? Why or why not?
2. Suppose the Fed reduces the money supply by 5 percent.
   a. What happens to the aggregate demand curve?
   b. What happens to the level of output and the price level in the short run and in the long run?
   c. According to Okun's law, what happens to unemployment in the short run and in the long run?
   d. What happens to the real interest rate in the short run and in the long run? (*Hint:* Use the model of the real interest rate in Chapter 3 to see what happens when output changes.)
3. Let's examine how the goals of the Fed influence its response to shocks. Suppose Fed A cares only about keeping the price level stable, and Fed B cares only about keeping output and employment at their natural levels. Explain how each Fed would respond to
   a. An exogenous decrease in the velocity of money.
   b. An exogenous increase in the price of oil.
4. The official arbiter of when recessions begin and end is the National Bureau of Economic Research, a nonprofit economics research group. Go to the NBER's Web site (www.nber.org) and find the latest turning point in the business cycle. When did it occur? Was this a switch from expansion to contraction or the other way around? List all the recessions (contractions) that have occurred during your lifetime and the dates when they began and ended.

CHAPTER 10

Aggregate Demand I: Building the *IS-LM* Model

I shall argue that the postulates of the classical theory are applicable to a special case only and not to the general case. . . . Moreover, the characteristics of the special case assumed by the classical theory happen not to be those of the economic society in which we actually live, with the result that its teaching is misleading and disastrous if we attempt to apply it to the facts of experience.

— *John Maynard Keynes,* The General Theory

Of all the economic fluctuations in world history, the one that stands out as particularly large, painful, and intellectually significant is the Great Depression of the 1930s. During this time, the United States and many other countries experienced massive unemployment and greatly reduced incomes. In the worst year, 1933, one-fourth of the U.S. labor force was unemployed, and real GDP was 30 percent below its 1929 level.

This devastating episode caused many economists to question the validity of classical economic theory—the theory we examined in Chapters 3 through 6. Classical theory seemed incapable of explaining the Depression. According to that theory, national income depends on factor supplies and the available technology, neither of which changed substantially from 1929 to 1933. After the onset of the Depression, many economists believed that a new model was needed to explain such a large and sudden economic downturn and to suggest government policies that might reduce the economic hardship so many people faced.

In 1936 the British economist John Maynard Keynes revolutionized economics with his book *The General Theory of Employment, Interest, and Money.* Keynes proposed a new way to analyze the economy, which he presented as an alternative to classical theory. His vision of how the economy works quickly became a center of controversy. Yet, as economists debated *The General Theory,* a new understanding of economic fluctuations gradually developed.

Keynes proposed that low aggregate demand is responsible for the low income and high unemployment that characterize economic downturns. He criticized classical theory for assuming that aggregate supply alone—capital, labor, and technology—determines national income. Economists today reconcile these two views with the model of aggregate demand and aggregate supply introduced in Chapter 9. In the long run, prices are flexible, and aggregate supply determines income. But in the short run, prices are sticky, so changes in aggregate demand influence income.

In this chapter and the next, we continue our study of economic fluctuations by looking more closely at aggregate demand. Our goal is to identify the variables that shift the aggregate demand curve, causing fluctuations in national income. We also examine more fully the tools policymakers can use to influence aggregate demand. In Chapter 9 we derived the aggregate demand curve from the quantity theory of money, and we showed that monetary policy can shift the aggregate demand curve. In this chapter we see that the government can influence aggregate demand with both monetary and fiscal policy.

The model of aggregate demand developed in this chapter, called the ***IS-LM* model**, is the leading interpretation of Keynes's theory. The goal of the model is to show what determines national income for a given price level. There are two ways to view this exercise. We can view the *IS-LM* model as showing what causes income to change in the short run when the price level is fixed because all prices are sticky. Or we can view the model as showing what causes the aggregate demand curve to shift. These two views of the model are equivalent: as Figure 10-1 shows, in the short run when the price level is fixed, shifts in the aggregate demand curve lead to changes in the equilibrium level of national income.

The two parts of the *IS-LM* model are, not surprisingly, the ***IS* curve** and the ***LM* curve**. *IS* stands for "investment" and "saving," and the *IS* curve represents what's going on in the market for goods and services (which we first

FIGURE 10-1

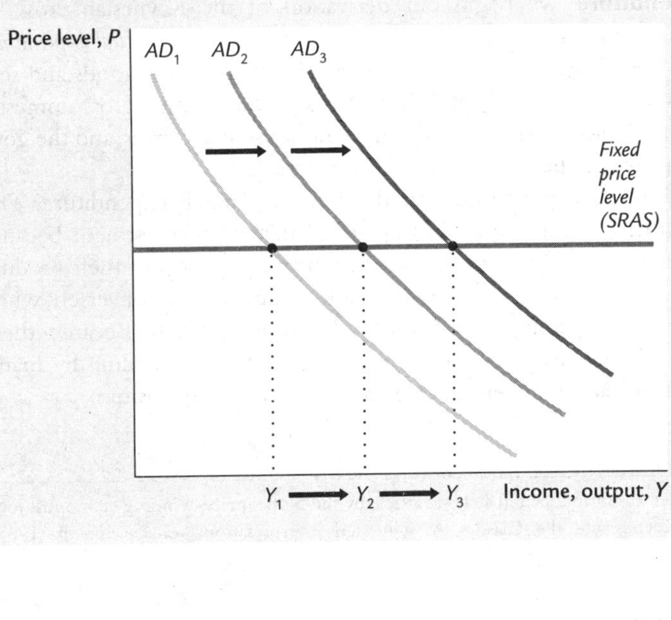

Shifts in Aggregate Demand For a given price level, national income fluctuates because of shifts in the aggregate demand curve. The *IS-LM* model takes the price level as given and shows what causes income to change. The model therefore shows what causes aggregate demand to shift.

discussed in Chapter 3). *LM* stands for "liquidity" and "money," and the *LM* curve represents what's happening to the supply and demand for money (which we first discussed in Chapter 4). Because the interest rate influences both investment and money demand, it is the variable that links the two halves of the *IS-LM* model. The model shows how interactions between the goods and money markets determine the position and slope of the aggregate demand curve and, therefore, the level of national income in the short run.[1]

10-1 The Goods Market and the *IS* Curve

The *IS* curve plots the relationship between the interest rate and the level of income that arises in the market for goods and services. To develop this relationship, we start with a basic model called the **Keynesian cross**. This model is the simplest interpretation of Keynes's theory of national income and is a building block for the more complex and realistic *IS-LM* model.

The Keynesian Cross

In *The General Theory* Keynes proposed that an economy's total income was, in the short run, determined largely by the spending plans of households, businesses, and government. The more people want to spend, the more goods and services firms can sell. The more firms can sell, the more output they will choose to produce and the more workers they will choose to hire. Keynes believed that the problem during recessions and depressions was inadequate spending. The Keynesian cross is an attempt to model this insight.

Planned Expenditure We begin our derivation of the Keynesian cross by drawing a distinction between actual and planned expenditure. *Actual expenditure* is the amount households, firms, and the government spend on goods and services, and as we first saw in Chapter 2, it equals the economy's gross domestic product (GDP). *Planned expenditure* is the amount households, firms, and the government would like to spend on goods and services.

Why would actual expenditure ever differ from planned expenditure? The answer is that firms might engage in unplanned inventory investment because their sales do not meet their expectations. When firms sell less of their product than they planned, their stock of inventories automatically rises; conversely, when firms sell more than planned, their stock of inventories falls. Because these unplanned changes in inventory are counted as investment spending by firms, actual expenditure can be either above or below planned expenditure.

---

[1] The *IS-LM* model was introduced in a classic article by the Nobel prize-winning economist John R. Hicks, "Mr. Keynes and the Classics: A Suggested Interpretation," *Econometrica* 5 (1937): 147–159.

Now consider the determinants of planned expenditure. Assuming that the economy is closed, so that net exports are zero, we write planned expenditure E as the sum of consumption C, planned investment I, and government purchases G:

$$E = C + I + G.$$

To this equation, we add the consumption function

$$C = C(Y - T).$$

This equation states that consumption depends on disposable income $(Y - T)$, which is total income Y minus taxes T. To keep things simple, for now we take planned investment as exogenously fixed:

$$I = \bar{I}.$$

Finally, as in Chapter 3, we assume that fiscal policy—the levels of government purchases and taxes—is fixed:

$$G = \bar{G},$$
$$T = \bar{T}.$$

Combining these five equations, we obtain

$$E = C(Y - \bar{T}) + \bar{I} + \bar{G}.$$

This equation shows that planned expenditure is a function of income Y, the level of planned investment $\bar{I}$, and the fiscal policy variables $\bar{G}$ and $\bar{T}$.

Figure 10-2 graphs planned expenditure as a function of the level of income. This line slopes upward because higher income leads to higher consumption and thus higher planned expenditure. The slope of this line is the marginal propensity to consume, the *MPC:* it shows how much planned expenditure increases when income rises by \$1. This planned-expenditure function is the first piece of the model called the Keynesian cross.

FIGURE 10-2

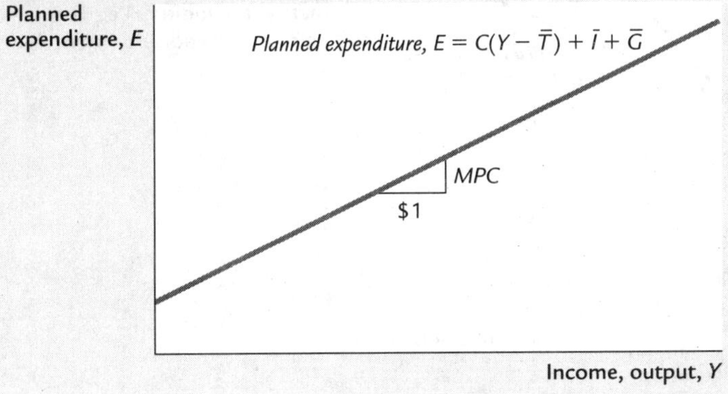

Planned Expenditure as a Function of Income Planned expenditure depends on income because higher income leads to higher consumption, which is part of planned expenditure. The slope of the planned-expenditure function is the marginal propensity to consume, *MPC*.

The Economy in Equilibrium The next piece of the Keynesian cross is the assumption that the economy is in equilibrium when actual expenditure equals planned expenditure. This assumption is based on the idea that when people's plans have been realized, they have no reason to change what they are doing. Recalling that Y as GDP equals not only total income but also total actual expenditure on goods and services, we can write this equilibrium condition as

$$\text{Actual Expenditure} = \text{Planned Expenditure}$$
$$Y = E.$$

The 45-degree line in Figure 10-3 plots the points where this condition holds. With the addition of the planned-expenditure function, this diagram becomes the Keynesian cross. The equilibrium of this economy is at point A, where the planned-expenditure function crosses the 45-degree line.

How does the economy get to equilibrium? In this model, inventories play an important role in the adjustment process. Whenever an economy is not in equilibrium, firms experience unplanned changes in inventories, and this induces them to change production levels. Changes in production in turn influence total income and expenditure, moving the economy toward equilibrium.

For example, suppose the economy finds itself with GDP at a level greater than the equilibrium level, such as the level Y_1 in Figure 10-4. In this case, planned expenditure E_1 is less than production Y_1, so firms are selling less than they are producing. Firms add the unsold goods to their stock of inventories. This unplanned rise in inventories induces firms to lay off workers and reduce production; these actions in turn reduce GDP. This process of unintended inventory accumulation and falling income continues until income Y falls to the equilibrium level.

FIGURE 10-3

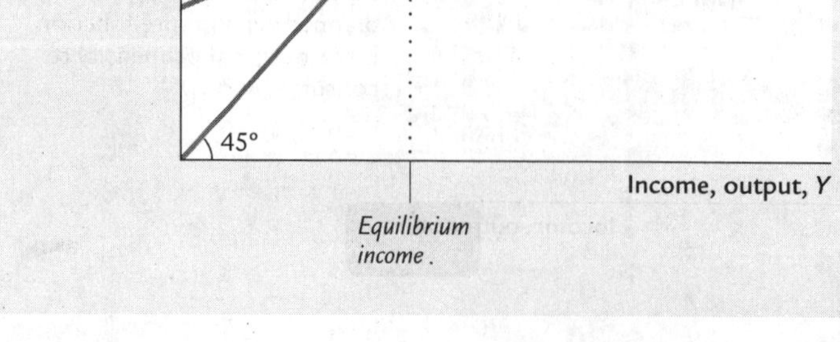

The Keynesian Cross The equilibrium in the Keynesian cross is the point at which income (actual expenditure) equals planned expenditure (point A).

FIGURE 10-4

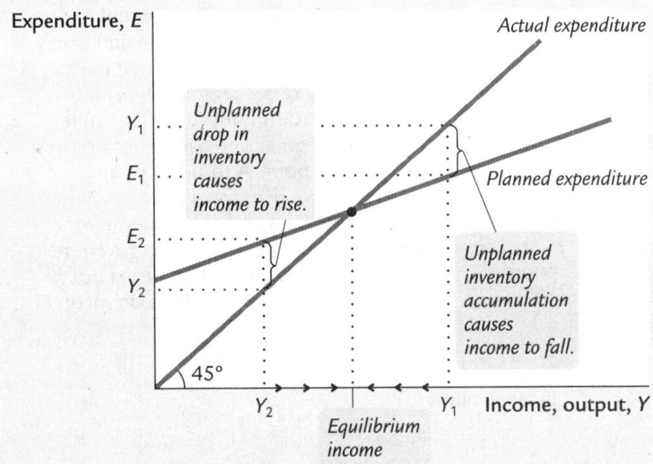

The Adjustment to Equilibrium in the Keynesian Cross If firms are producing at level Y_1, then planned expenditure E_1 falls short of production, and firms accumulate inventories. This inventory accumulation induces firms to decrease production. Similarly, if firms are producing at level Y_2, then planned expenditure E_2 exceeds production, and firms run down their inventories. This fall in inventories induces firms to increase production. In both cases, the firms' decisions drive the economy toward equilibrium.

Similarly, suppose GDP is at a level lower than the equilibrium level, such as the level Y_2 in Figure 10-4. In this case, planned expenditure E_2 is greater than production Y_2. Firms meet the high level of sales by drawing down their inventories. But when firms see their stock of inventories dwindle, they hire more workers and increase production. GDP rises, and the economy approaches the equilibrium.

In summary, the Keynesian cross shows how income Y is determined for given levels of planned investment I and fiscal policy G and T. We can use this model to show how income changes when one of these exogenous variables changes.

Fiscal Policy and the Multiplier: Government Purchases Consider how changes in government purchases affect the economy. Because government purchases are one component of expenditure, higher government purchases result in higher planned expenditure for any given level of income. If government purchases rise by ΔG, then the planned-expenditure schedule shifts upward by ΔG, as in Figure 10-5. The equilibrium of the economy moves from point A to point B.

This graph shows that an increase in government purchases leads to an even greater increase in income. That is, ΔY is larger than ΔG. The ratio $\Delta Y/\Delta G$ is called the **government-purchases multiplier**;

"Your Majesty, my voyage will not only forge a new route to the spices of the East but also create over three thousand new jobs."

FIGURE 10-5

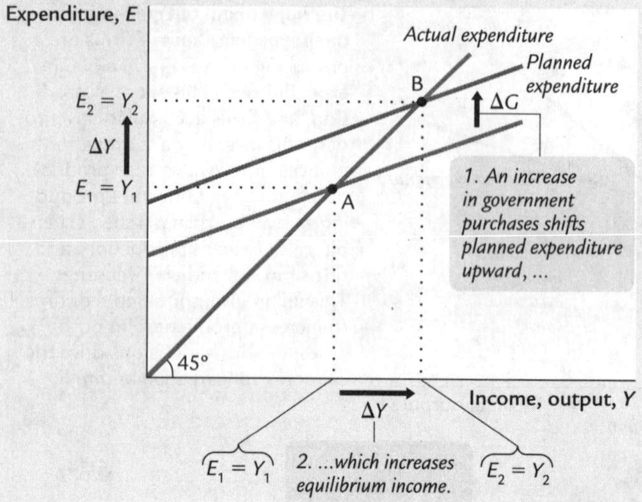

An Increase in Government Purchases in the Keynesian Cross An increase in government purchases of ΔG raises planned expenditure by that amount for any given level of income. The equilibrium moves from point A to point B, and income rises from Y_1 to Y_2. Note that the increase in income ΔY exceeds the increase in government purchases ΔG. Thus, fiscal policy has a multiplied effect on income.

it tells us how much income rises in response to a $1 increase in government purchases. An implication of the Keynesian cross is that the government-purchases multiplier is larger than 1.

Why does fiscal policy have a multiplied effect on income? The reason is that, according to the consumption function $C = C(Y - T)$, higher income causes higher consumption. When an increase in government purchases raises income, it also raises consumption, which further raises income, which further raises consumption, and so on. Therefore, in this model, an increase in government purchases causes a greater increase in income.

How big is the multiplier? To answer this question, we trace through each step of the change in income. The process begins when expenditure rises by ΔG, which implies that income rises by ΔG as well. This increase in income in turn raises consumption by $MPC \times \Delta G$, where MPC is the marginal propensity to consume. This increase in consumption raises expenditure and income once again. This second increase in income of $MPC \times \Delta G$ again raises consumption, this time by $MPC \times (MPC \times \Delta G)$, which again raises expenditure and income, and so on. This feedback from consumption to income to consumption continues indefinitely. The total effect on income is

$$
\begin{aligned}
&\text{Initial Change in Government Purchases} = && \Delta G \\
&\text{First Change in Consumption} && = MPC \times \Delta G \\
&\text{Second Change in Consumption} && = MPC^2 \times \Delta G \\
&\text{Third Change in Consumption} && = MPC^3 \times \Delta G \\
&\quad\vdots && \quad\vdots
\end{aligned}
$$

$$\Delta Y = (1 + MPC + MPC^2 + MPC^3 + \cdots)\Delta G.$$

The government-purchases multiplier is

$$\Delta Y/\Delta G = 1 + MPC + MPC^2 + MPC^3 + \cdots$$

This expression for the multiplier is an example of an *infinite geometric series.* A result from algebra allows us to write the multiplier as[2]

$$\Delta Y/\Delta G = 1/(1 - MPC).$$

For example, if the marginal propensity to consume is 0.6, the multiplier is

$$\begin{aligned} \Delta Y/\Delta G &= 1 + 0.6 + 0.6^2 + 0.6^3 + \cdots \\ &= 1/(1 - 0.6) \\ &= 2.5. \end{aligned}$$

In this case, a \$1.00 increase in government purchases raises equilibrium income by \$2.50.[3]

Fiscal Policy and the Multiplier: Taxes Consider now how changes in taxes affect equilibrium income. A decrease in taxes of ΔT immediately raises disposable income $Y - T$ by ΔT and, therefore, increases consumption by $MPC \times \Delta T$. For any given level of income Y, planned expenditure is now higher. As Figure 10-6 shows, the planned-expenditure schedule shifts upward by $MPC \times \Delta T$. The equilibrium of the economy moves from point A to point B.

---

[2] *Mathematical note:* We prove this algebraic result as follows. For $|x| < 1$, let

$$z = 1 + x + x^2 + \cdots.$$

Multiply both sides of this equation by x:

$$xz = x + x^2 + x^3 + \cdots.$$

Subtract the second equation from the first:

$$z - xz = 1.$$

Rearrange this last equation to obtain

$$z(1 - x) = 1,$$

which implies

$$z = 1/(1 - x).$$

This completes the proof.

[3] *Mathematical note:* The government-purchases multiplier is most easily derived using a little calculus. Begin with the equation

$$Y = C(Y - T) + I + G.$$

Holding T and I fixed, differentiate to obtain

$$dY = C'dY + dG,$$

and then rearrange to find

$$dY/dG = 1/(1 - C').$$

This is the same as the equation in the text.

FIGURE 10-6

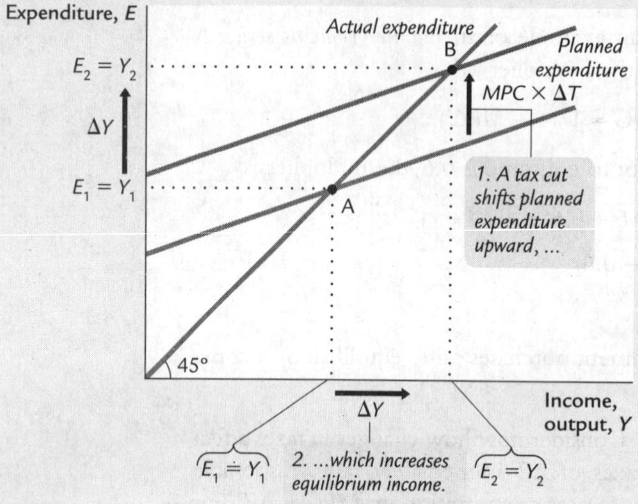

A Decrease in Taxes in the Keynesian Cross A decrease in taxes of ΔT raises planned expenditure by $MPC \times \Delta T$ for any given level of income. The equilibrium moves from point A to point B, and income rises from Y_1 to Y_2. Again, fiscal policy has a multiplied effect on income.

Just as an increase in government purchases has a multiplied effect on income, so does a decrease in taxes. As before, the initial change in expenditure, now $MPC \times \Delta T$, is multiplied by $1/(1 - MPC)$. The overall effect on income of the change in taxes is

$$\Delta Y/\Delta T = -MPC/(1 - MPC).$$

This expression is the **tax multiplier**, the amount income changes in response to a \$1 change in taxes. (The negative sign indicates that income moves in the opposite direction as taxes.) For example, if the marginal propensity to consume is 0.6, then the tax multiplier is

$$\Delta Y/\Delta T = -0.6/(1 - 0.6) = -1.5.$$

In this example, a \$1.00 cut in taxes raises equilibrium income by \$1.50.[4]

---

[4] *Mathematical note:* As before, the multiplier is most easily derived using a little calculus. Begin with the equation

$$Y = C(Y - T) + I + G.$$

Holding I and G fixed, differentiate to obtain

$$dY = C'(dY - dT),$$

and then rearrange to find

$$dY/dT = -C'/(1 - C').$$

This is the same as the equation in the text.

CASE STUDY

Cutting Taxes to Stimulate the Economy: The Kennedy and Bush Tax Cuts

When John F. Kennedy became president of the United States in 1961, he brought to Washington some of the brightest young economists of the day to work on his Council of Economic Advisers. These economists, who had been schooled in the economics of Keynes, brought Keynesian ideas to discussions of economic policy at the highest level.

One of the council's first proposals was to expand national income by reducing taxes. This eventually led to a substantial cut in personal and corporate income taxes in 1964. The tax cut was intended to stimulate expenditure on consumption and investment and lead to higher levels of income and employment. When a reporter asked Kennedy why he advocated a tax cut, Kennedy replied, "To stimulate the economy. Don't you remember your Economics 101?"

As Kennedy's economic advisers predicted, the passage of the tax cut was followed by an economic boom. Growth in real GDP was 5.3 percent in 1964 and 6.0 percent in 1965. The unemployment rate fell from 5.7 percent in 1963 to 5.2 percent in 1964 and then to 4.5 percent in 1965.

Economists continue to debate the source of this rapid growth in the early 1960s. A group called *supply-siders* argues that the economic boom resulted from the incentive effects of the cut in income tax rates. According to supply-siders, when workers are allowed to keep a higher fraction of their earnings, they supply substantially more labor and expand the aggregate supply of goods and services. Keynesians, however, emphasize the impact of tax cuts on aggregate demand. Most likely, both views have some truth: *Tax cuts stimulate aggregate supply by improving workers' incentives and expand aggregate demand by raising households' disposable income.*

When George W. Bush was elected president in 2000, a major element of his platform was a cut in income taxes. Bush and his advisors used both supply-side and Keynesian rhetoric to make the case for their policy. (Full disclosure: The author of this textbook was one of Bush's economic advisers from 2003 to 2005.) During the campaign, when the economy was doing fine, they argued that lower marginal tax rates would improve work incentives. But when the economy started to slow, and unemployment started to rise, the argument shifted to emphasize that the tax cut would stimulate spending and help the economy recover from the recession.

Congress passed major tax cuts in 2001 and 2003. After the second tax cut, the weak recovery from the 2001 recession turned into a robust one. Growth in real GDP was 4.4 percent in 2004. The unemployment rate fell from its peak of 6.3 percent in June 2003 to 5.4 percent in December 2004.

When President Bush signed the 2003 tax bill, he explained the measure using the logic of aggregate demand: "When people have more money, they can spend it on goods and services. And in our society, when they demand an additional good or a service, somebody will produce the good or a service. And when somebody produces that good or a service, it means somebody is more likely to be able to find a job." The explanation could have come from an exam in Economics 101.

The Interest Rate, Investment, and the *IS* Curve

The Keynesian cross is only a stepping stone on our path to the *IS-LM* model, which explains the economy's aggregate demand curve. The Keynesian cross is useful because it shows how the spending plans of households, firms, and the government determine the economy's income. Yet it makes the simplifying assumption that the level of planned investment I is fixed. As we discussed in Chapter 3, an important macroeconomic relationship is that planned investment depends on the interest rate r.

To add this relationship between the interest rate and investment to our model, we write the level of planned investment as

$$I = I(r).$$

This investment function is graphed in panel (a) of Figure 10-7. Because the interest rate is the cost of borrowing to finance investment projects, an increase

FIGURE 10-7

Deriving the *IS* Curve Panel (a) shows the investment function: an increase in the interest rate from r_1 to r_2 reduces planned investment from $I(r_1)$ to $I(r_2)$. Panel (b) shows the Keynesian cross: a decrease in planned investment from $I(r_1)$ to $I(r_2)$ shifts the planned-expenditure function downward and thereby reduces income from Y_1 to Y_2. Panel (c) shows the *IS* curve summarizing this relationship between the interest rate and income: the higher the interest rate, the lower the level of income.

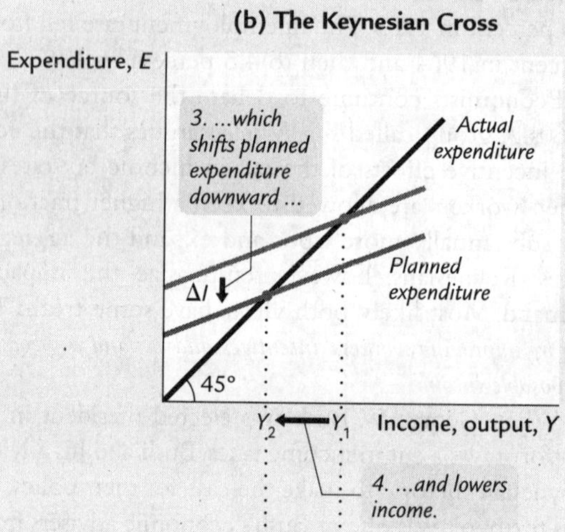

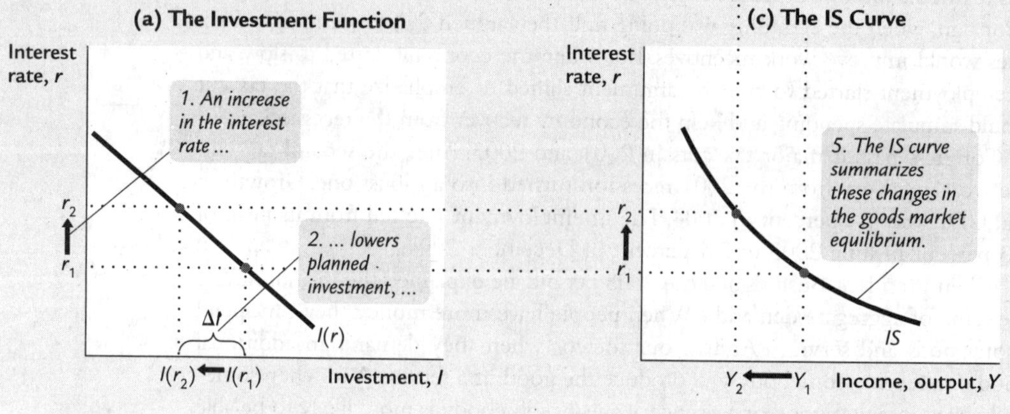

in the interest rate reduces planned investment. As a result, the investment function slopes downward.

To determine how income changes when the interest rate changes, we can combine the investment function with the Keynesian-cross diagram. Because investment is inversely related to the interest rate, an increase in the interest rate from r_1 to r_2 reduces the quantity of investment from $I(r_1)$ to $I(r_2)$. The reduction in planned investment, in turn, shifts the planned-expenditure function downward, as in panel (b) of Figure 10-7. The shift in the planned-expenditure function causes the level of income to fall from Y_1 to Y_2. Hence, an increase in the interest rate lowers income.

The *IS* curve, shown in panel (c) of Figure 10-7, summarizes this relationship between the interest rate and the level of income. In essence, the *IS* curve combines the interaction between r and I expressed by the investment function and the interaction between I and Y demonstrated by the Keynesian cross. Each point on the *IS* curve represents equilibrium in the goods market, and the curve illustrates how the equilibrium level of income depends on the interest rate. Because an increase in the interest rate causes planned investment to fall, which in turn causes equilibrium income to fall, the *IS* curve slopes downward.

How Fiscal Policy Shifts the *IS* Curve

The *IS* curve shows us, for any given interest rate, the level of income that brings the goods market into equilibrium. As we learned from the Keynesian cross, the equilibrium level of income also depends on government spending G and taxes T. The *IS* curve is drawn for a given fiscal policy; that is, when we construct the *IS* curve, we hold G and T fixed. When fiscal policy changes, the *IS* curve shifts.

Figure 10-8 uses the Keynesian cross to show how an increase in government purchases ΔG shifts the *IS* curve. This figure is drawn for a given interest rate $\bar{r}$ and thus for a given level of planned investment. The Keynesian cross shows that this change in fiscal policy raises planned expenditure and thereby increases equilibrium income from Y_1 to Y_2. Therefore, an increase in government purchases shifts the *IS* curve outward.

We can use the Keynesian cross to see how other changes in fiscal policy shift the *IS* curve. Because a decrease in taxes also expands expenditure and income, it too shifts the *IS* curve outward. A decrease in government purchases or an increase in taxes reduces income; therefore, such a change in fiscal policy shifts the *IS* curve inward.

In summary, the IS *curve shows the combinations of the interest rate and the level of income that are consistent with equilibrium in the market for goods and services. The* IS *curve is drawn for a given fiscal policy. Changes in fiscal policy that raise the demand for goods and services shift the* IS *curve to the right. Changes in fiscal policy that reduce the demand for goods and services shift the* IS *curve to the left.*

FIGURE 10-8

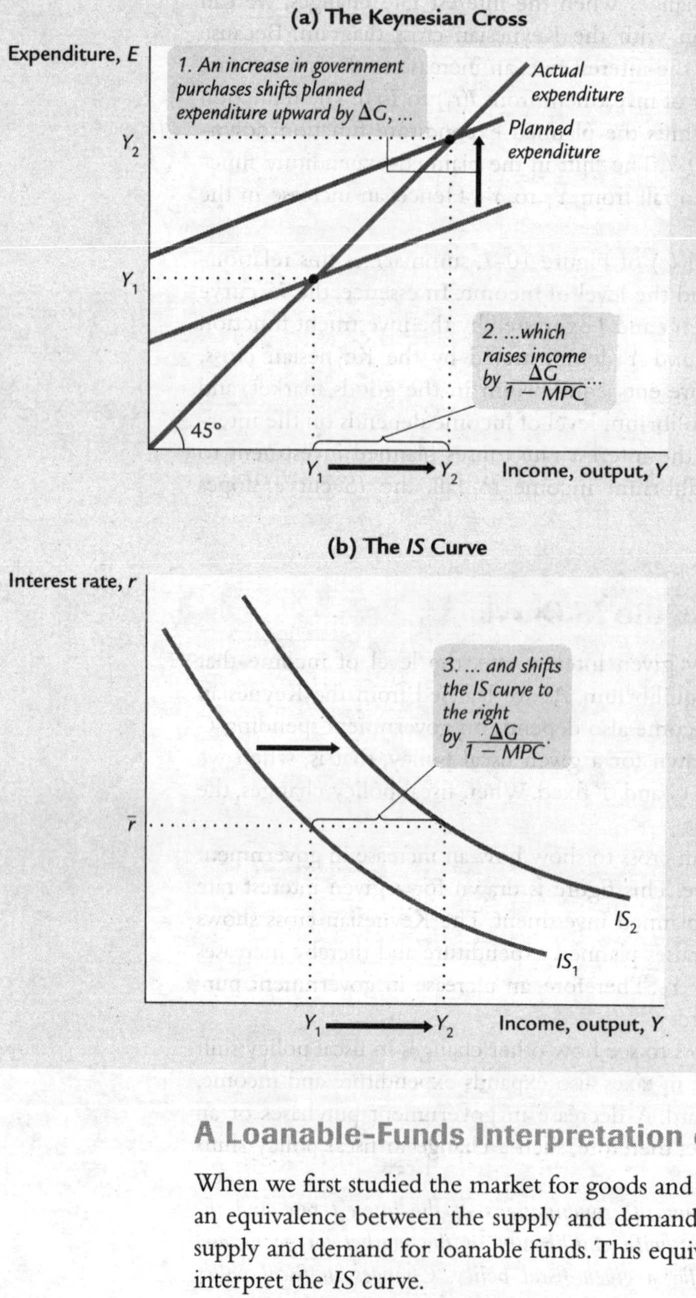

An Increase in Government Purchases Shifts the *IS* Curve Outward Panel (a) shows that an increase in government purchases raises planned expenditure. For any given interest rate, the upward shift in planned expenditure of ΔG leads to an increase in income Y of $\Delta G/(1 - MPC)$. Therefore, in panel (b), the *IS* curve shifts to the right by this amount.

A Loanable-Funds Interpretation of the *IS* Curve

When we first studied the market for goods and services in Chapter 3, we noted an equivalence between the supply and demand for goods and services and the supply and demand for loanable funds. This equivalence provides another way to interpret the *IS* curve.

Recall that the national income accounts identity can be written as

$$Y - C - G = I$$

$$S = I.$$

The left-hand side of this equation is national saving S, and the right-hand side is investment I. National saving represents the supply of loanable funds, and investment represents the demand for these funds.

To see how the market for loanable funds produces the *IS* curve, substitute the consumption function for C and the investment function for I:

$$Y - C(Y - T) - G = I(r).$$

The left-hand side of this equation shows that the supply of loanable funds depends on income and fiscal policy. The right-hand side shows that the demand for loanable funds depends on the interest rate. The interest rate adjusts to equilibrate the supply and demand for loans.

As Figure 10-9 illustrates, we can interpret the *IS* curve as showing the interest rate that equilibrates the market for loanable funds for any given level of income. When income rises from Y_1 to Y_2, national saving, which equals $Y - C - G$, increases. (Consumption rises by less than income, because the marginal propensity to consume is less than 1.) As panel (a) shows, the increased supply of loanable funds drives down the interest rate from r_1 to r_2. The *IS* curve in panel (b) summarizes this relationship: higher income implies higher saving, which in turn implies a lower equilibrium interest rate. For this reason, the *IS* curve slopes downward.

This alternative interpretation of the *IS* curve also explains why a change in fiscal policy shifts the *IS* curve. An increase in government purchases or a decrease in taxes reduces national saving for any given level of income. The reduced supply of loanable funds raises the interest rate that equilibrates the market. Because the interest rate is now higher for any given level of

FIGURE 10-9

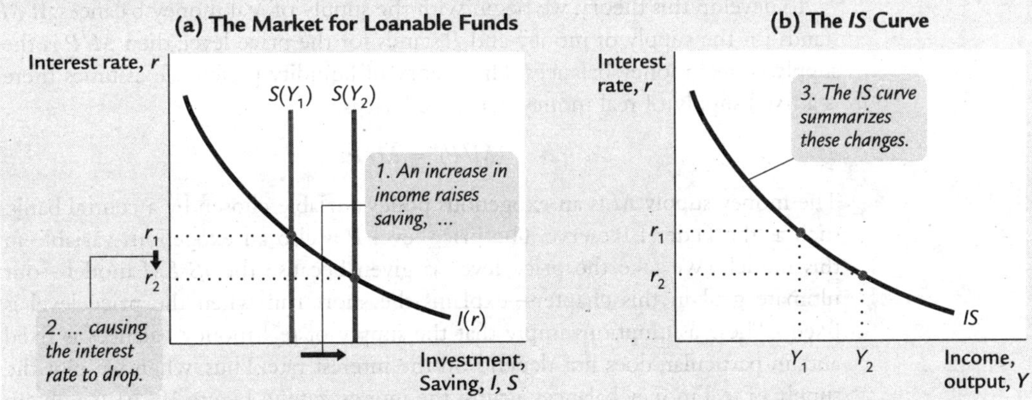

A Loanable-Funds Interpretation of the *IS* Curve Panel (a) shows that an increase in income from Y_1 to Y_2 raises saving and thus lowers the interest rate that equilibrates the supply and demand for loanable funds. The *IS* curve in panel (b) expresses this negative relationship between income and the interest rate.

income, the *IS* curve shifts upward in response to the expansionary change in fiscal policy.

Finally, note that the *IS* curve does not determine either income *Y* or the interest rate *r*—it describes only the relationship between *Y* and *r* that arises in the market for goods and services (or, equivalently, the market for loanable funds). Recall that our goal in this chapter is to understand aggregate demand; that is, we want to find what determines equilibrium income *Y* for a given price level *P*. The *IS* curve is just half the story. To complete the story, we need another relationship between *Y* and *r*, to which we now turn.

10-2 The Money Market and the *LM* Curve

The *LM* curve plots the relationship between the interest rate and the level of income that arises in the market for money balances. To understand this relationship, we begin by looking at a theory of the interest rate, called the **theory of liquidity preference**.

The Theory of Liquidity Preference

In his classic work *The General Theory*, Keynes offered his view of how the interest rate is determined in the short run. That explanation is called the theory of liquidity preference, because it posits that the interest rate adjusts to balance the supply and demand for the economy's most liquid asset—money. Just as the Keynesian cross is a building block for the *IS* curve, the theory of liquidity preference is a building block for the *LM* curve.

To develop this theory, we begin with the supply of real money balances. If *M* stands for the supply of money and *P* stands for the price level, then *M*/*P* is the supply of real money balances. The theory of liquidity preference assumes there is a fixed supply of real money balances. That is,

$$(M/P)^s = \bar{M}/\bar{P}.$$

The money supply *M* is an exogenous policy variable chosen by a central bank, such as the Federal Reserve. The price level *P* is also an exogenous variable in this model. (We take the price level as given because the *IS-LM* model—our ultimate goal in this chapter—explains the short run when the price level is fixed.) These assumptions imply that the supply of real money balances is fixed and, in particular, does not depend on the interest rate. Thus, when we plot the supply of real money balances against the interest rate in Figure 10-10, we obtain a vertical supply curve.

Next, consider the demand for real money balances. The theory of liquidity preference posits that the interest rate is one determinant of how much

FIGURE 10-10

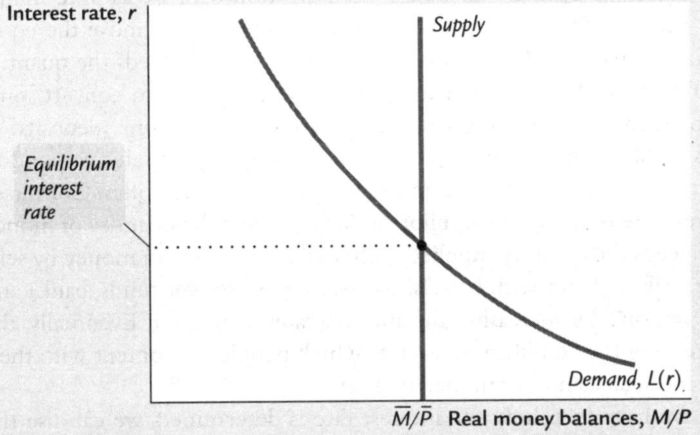

The Theory of Liquidity Preference The supply and demand for real money balances determine the interest rate. The supply curve for real money balances is vertical because the supply does not depend on the interest rate. The demand curve is downward-sloping because a higher interest rate raises the cost of holding money and thus lowers the quantity demanded. At the equilibrium interest rate, the quantity of real money balances demanded equals the quantity supplied.

money people choose to hold. The reason is that the interest rate is the opportunity cost of holding money: it is what you forgo by holding some of your assets as money, which does not bear interest, instead of as interest-bearing bank deposits or bonds. When the interest rate rises, people want to hold less of their wealth in the form of money. We can write the demand for real money balances as

$$(M/P)^d = L(r),$$

where the function $L(\ )$ shows that the quantity of money demanded depends on the interest rate. The demand curve in Figure 10-10 slopes downward because higher interest rates reduce the quantity of real money balances demanded.[5]

According to the theory of liquidity preference, the supply and demand for real money balances determine what interest rate prevails in the economy. That is, the interest rate adjusts to equilibrate the money market. As the figure shows, at the equilibrium interest rate, the quantity of real money balances demanded equals the quantity supplied.

[5] Note that r is being used to denote the interest rate here, as it was in our discussion of the *IS* curve. More accurately, it is the nominal interest rate that determines money demand and the real interest rate that determines investment. To keep things simple, we are ignoring expected inflation, which creates the difference between the real and nominal interest rates. For short-run analysis, it is often realistic to assume that expected inflation is constant, in which case real and nominal interest rates move together. The role of expected inflation in the *IS-LM* model is explored in Chapter 11.

How does the interest rate get to this equilibrium of money supply and money demand? The adjustment occurs because whenever the money market is not in equilibrium, people try to adjust their portfolios of assets and, in the process, alter the interest rate. For instance, if the interest rate is above the equilibrium level, the quantity of real money balances supplied exceeds the quantity demanded. Individuals holding the excess supply of money try to convert some of their non-interest-bearing money into interest-bearing bank deposits or bonds. Banks and bond issuers, who prefer to pay lower interest rates, respond to this excess supply of money by lowering the interest rates they offer. Conversely, if the interest rate is below the equilibrium level, so that the quantity of money demanded exceeds the quantity supplied, individuals try to obtain money by selling bonds or making bank withdrawals. To attract now scarcer funds, banks and bond issuers respond by increasing the interest rates they offer. Eventually, the interest rate reaches the equilibrium level, at which people are content with their portfolios of monetary and nonmonetary assets.

Now that we have seen how the interest rate is determined, we can use the theory of liquidity preference to show how the interest rate responds to changes in the supply of money. Suppose, for instance, that the Fed suddenly decreases the money supply. A fall in M reduces M/P, because P is fixed in the model. The supply of real money balances shifts to the left, as in Figure 10-11. The equilibrium interest rate rises from r_1 to r_2, and the higher interest rate makes people satisfied to hold the smaller quantity of real money balances. The opposite would occur if the Fed had suddenly increased the money supply. Thus, according to the theory of liquidity preference, a decrease in the money supply raises the interest rate, and an increase in the money supply lowers the interest rate.

FIGURE 10-11

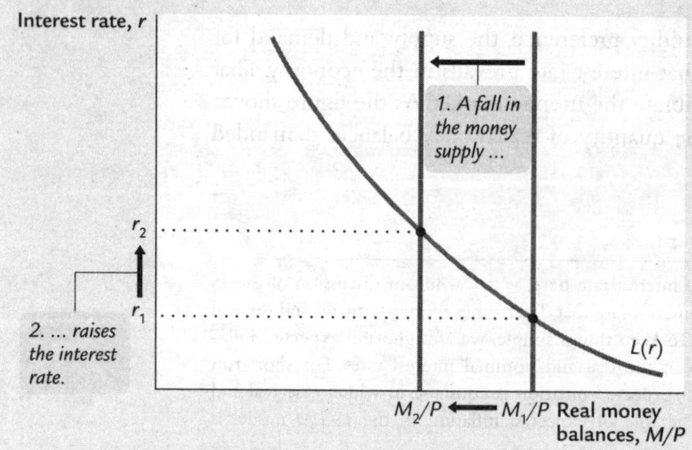

A Reduction in the Money Supply in the Theory of Liquidity Preference If the price level is fixed, a reduction in the money supply from M_1 to M_2 reduces the supply of real money balances. The equilibrium interest rate therefore rises from r_1 to r_2.

CASE STUDY

Does a Monetary Tightening Raise or Lower Interest Rates?

How does a tightening of monetary policy influence nominal interest rates? According to the theories we have been developing, the answer depends on the time horizon. Our analysis of the Fisher effect in Chapter 4 suggests that, in the long run when prices are flexible, a reduction in money growth would lower inflation, and this in turn would lead to lower nominal interest rates. Yet the theory of liquidity preference predicts that, in the short run when prices are sticky, anti-inflationary monetary policy would lead to falling real money balances and higher interest rates.

Both conclusions are consistent with experience. A good illustration occurred during the early 1980s, when the U.S. economy saw the largest and quickest reduction in inflation in recent history.

Here's the background: By the late 1970s inflation in the U.S. economy had reached the double-digit range and was a major national problem. In 1979 consumer prices were rising at a rate of 11.3 percent per year. In October of that year, only two months after becoming the chairman of the Federal Reserve, Paul Volcker decided that it was time to change course. He announced that monetary policy would aim to reduce the rate of inflation. This announcement began a period of tight money that, by 1983, brought the inflation rate down to about 3 percent.

Let's look at what happened to nominal interest rates. If we look immediately after the October 1979 announcement of tighter monetary policy, we see a fall in real money balances and a rise in the interest rate—just as the theory of liquidity preference predicts. Nominal interest rates on three-month Treasury bills rose from 10 percent just before the October 1979 announcement to 12 percent in 1980 and 14 percent in 1981. Yet these high interest rates were only temporary. As Volcker's change in monetary policy lowered inflation and expectations of inflation, nominal interest rates gradually fell, reaching 6 percent in 1986.

The lesson is that to understand the link between monetary policy and nominal interest rates, we need to keep in mind both the theory of liquidity preference and the Fisher effect. A monetary tightening leads to higher nominal interest rates in the short run and lower nominal interest rates in the long run.

Income, Money Demand, and the *LM* Curve

Having developed the theory of liquidity preference as an explanation for what determines the interest rate, we can now use the theory to derive the *LM* curve. We begin by considering the following question: how does a change in the economy's level of income Y affect the market for real money balances? The answer (which should be familiar from Chapter 4) is that the level of income affects the demand for money. When income is high, expenditure is high, so people engage in more transactions that require the use of money. Thus, greater income implies greater money demand. We can express these ideas by writing the money demand function as

$$(M/P)^d = L(r, Y).$$

The quantity of real money balances demanded is negatively related to the interest rate and positively related to income.

Using the theory of liquidity preference, we can figure out what happens to the equilibrium interest rate when the level of income changes. For example, consider what happens in Figure 10-12 when income increases from Y_1 to Y_2. As panel (a) illustrates, this increase in income shifts the money demand curve to the right. With the supply of real money balances unchanged, the interest rate must rise from r_1 to r_2 to equilibrate the money market. Therefore, according to the theory of liquidity preference, higher income leads to a higher interest rate.

The *LM* curve shown in panel (b) of Figure 10-12 summarizes this relationship between the level of income and the interest rate. Each point on the *LM* curve represents equilibrium in the money market, and the curve illustrates how the equilibrium interest rate depends on the level of income. The higher the level of income, the higher the demand for real money balances, and the higher the equilibrium interest rate. For this reason, the *LM* curve slopes upward.

FIGURE 10-12

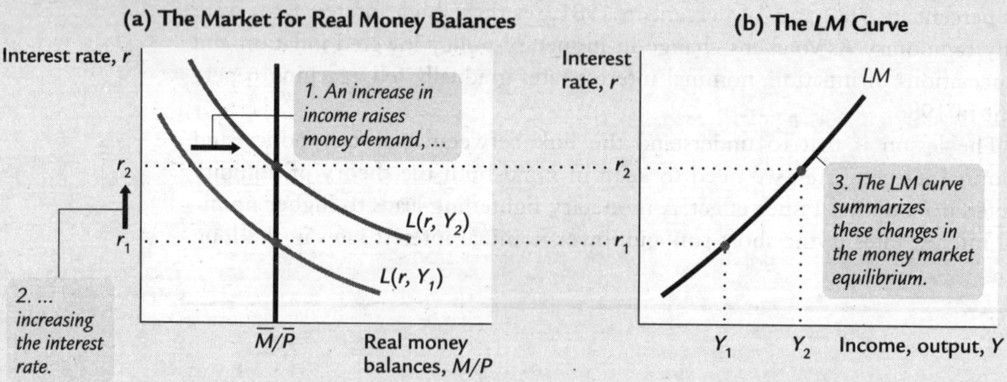

Deriving the *LM* Curve Panel (a) shows the market for real money balances: an increase in income from Y_1 to Y_2 raises the demand for money and thus raises the interest rate from r_1 to r_2. Panel (b) shows the *LM* curve summarizing this relationship between the interest rate and income: the higher the level of income, the higher the interest rate.

How Monetary Policy Shifts the *LM* Curve

The *LM* curve tells us the interest rate that equilibrates the money market at any level of income. Yet, as we saw earlier, the equilibrium interest rate also depends on the supply of real money balances, M/P. This means that the *LM* curve is drawn for a *given* supply of real money balances. If real money balances change—for example, if the Fed alters the money supply—the *LM* curve shifts.

We can use the theory of liquidity preference to understand how monetary policy shifts the *LM* curve. Suppose that the Fed decreases the money supply from M_1 to M_2, which causes the supply of real money balances to fall from M_1/P to M_2/P. Figure 10-13 shows what happens. Holding constant the amount of income and thus the demand curve for real money balances, we see that a reduction in the supply of real money balances raises the interest rate that equilibrates the money market. Hence, a decrease in the money supply shifts the *LM* curve upward.

In summary, the LM *curve shows the combinations of the interest rate and the level of income that are consistent with equilibrium in the market for real money balances. The* LM *curve is drawn for a given supply of real money balances. Decreases in the supply of real money balances shift the* LM *curve upward. Increases in the supply of real money balances shift the* LM *curve downward.*

FIGURE 10-13

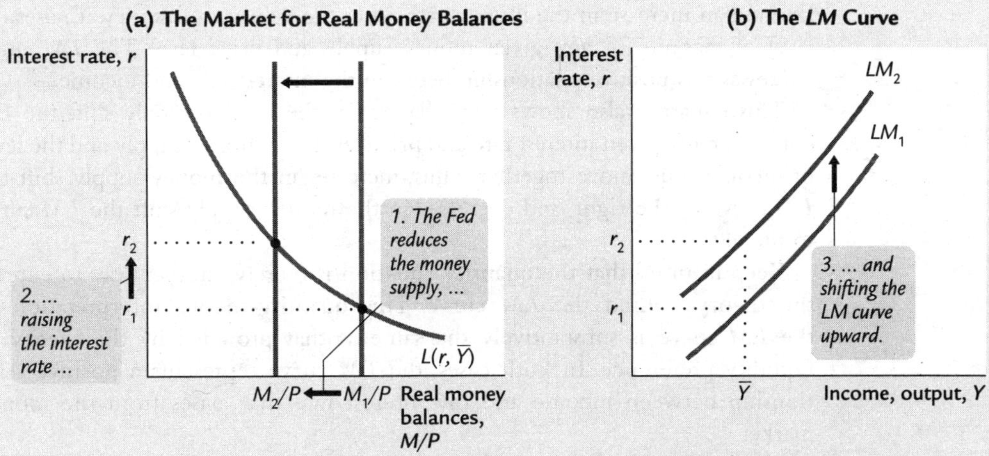

A Reduction in the Money Supply Shifts the *LM* Curve Upward Panel (a) shows that for any given level of income $\bar{Y}$, a reduction in the money supply raises the interest rate that equilibrates the money market. Therefore, the *LM* curve in panel (b) shifts upward.

A Quantity-Equation Interpretation of the *LM* Curve

When we first discussed aggregate demand and the short-run determination of income in Chapter 9, we derived the aggregate demand curve from the quantity theory of money. We described the money market with the quantity equation,

$$MV = PY,$$

and assumed that velocity V is constant. This assumption implies that, for any given price level P, the supply of money M by itself determines the level of income Y. Because the level of income does not depend on the interest rate, the quantity theory is equivalent to a vertical *LM* curve.

We can derive the more realistic upward-sloping *LM* curve from the quantity equation by relaxing the assumption that velocity is constant. The assumption of constant velocity is based on the assumption that the demand for real money balances depends only on the level of income. Yet, as we have noted in our discussion of the liquidity-preference model, the demand for real money balances also depends on the interest rate: a higher interest rate raises the cost of holding money and reduces money demand. When people respond to a higher interest rate by holding less money, each dollar they do hold must be used more often to support a given volume of transactions—that is, the velocity of money must increase. We can write this as

$$MV(r) = PY.$$

The velocity function $V(r)$ indicates that velocity is positively related to the interest rate.

This form of the quantity equation yields an *LM* curve that slopes upward. Because an increase in the interest rate raises the velocity of money, it raises the level of income for any given money supply and price level. The *LM* curve expresses this positive relationship between the interest rate and income.

This equation also shows why changes in the money supply shift the *LM* curve. For any given interest rate and price level, the money supply and the level of income must move together. Thus, increases in the money supply shift the *LM* curve to the right, and decreases in the money supply shift the *LM* curve to the left.

Keep in mind that the quantity equation is merely another way to express the theory behind the *LM* curve. This quantity-theory interpretation of the *LM* curve is substantively the same as that provided by the theory of liquidity preference. In both cases, the *LM* curve represents a positive relationship between income and the interest rate that arises from the money market.

Finally, remember that the *LM* curve by itself does not determine either income Y or the interest rate r that will prevail in the economy. Like the *IS* curve, the *LM* curve is only a relationship between these two endogenous variables. To understand the economy's overall equilibrium for a given price level, we must consider both equilibrium in the goods market and equilibrium in the money market. That is, we need to use the *IS* and *LM* curves together.

10-3 Conclusion: The Short-Run Equilibrium

We now have all the pieces of the *IS-LM* model. The two equations of this model are

$$Y = C(Y - T) + I(r) + G \qquad IS,$$

$$M/P = L(r, Y) \qquad LM.$$

The model takes fiscal policy, G and T, monetary policy M, and the price level P as exogenous. Given these exogenous variables, the *IS* curve provides the combinations of r and Y that satisfy the equation representing the goods market, and the *LM* curve provides the combinations of r and Y that satisfy the equation representing the money market. These two curves are shown together in Figure 10-14.

The equilibrium of the economy is the point at which the *IS* curve and the *LM* curve cross. This point gives the interest rate r and the level of income Y that satisfy conditions for equilibrium in both the goods market and the money market. In other words, at this intersection, actual expenditure equals planned expenditure, and the demand for real money balances equals the supply.

As we conclude this chapter, let's recall that our ultimate goal in developing the *IS-LM* model is to analyze short-run fluctuations in economic activity. Figure 10-15 illustrates how the different pieces of our theory fit together. In this chapter we developed the Keynesian cross and the theory of liquidity preference

FIGURE 10-14

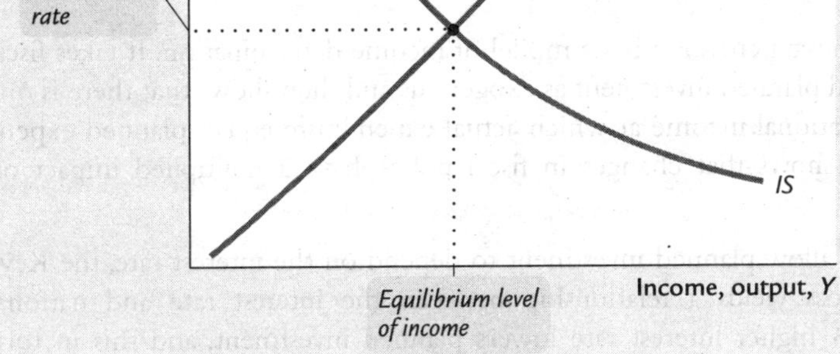

Equilibrium in the *IS-LM* Model The intersection of the *IS* and *LM* curves represents simultaneous equilibrium in the market for goods and services and in the market for real money balances for given values of government spending, taxes, the money supply, and the price level.

FIGURE 10-15

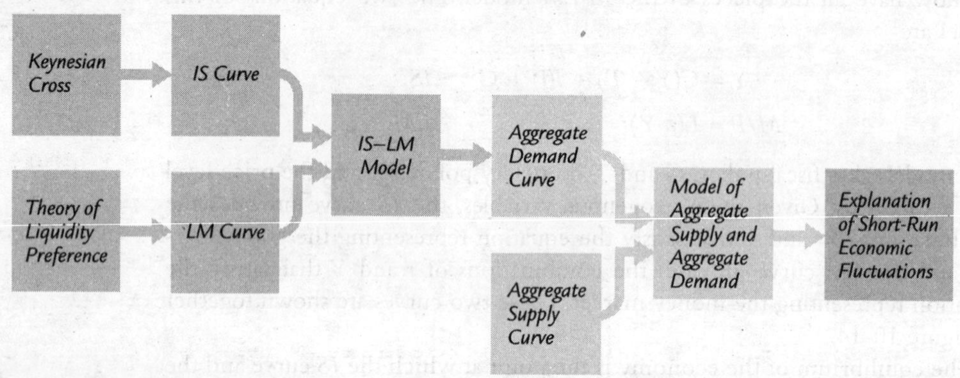

The Theory of Short-Run Fluctuations This schematic diagram shows how the different pieces of the theory of short-run fluctuations fit together. The Keynesian cross explains the *IS* curve, and the theory of liquidity preference explains the *LM* curve. The *IS* and *LM* curves together yield the *IS-LM* model, which explains the aggregate demand curve. The aggregate demand curve is part of the model of aggregate supply and aggregate demand, which economists use to explain short-run fluctuations in economic activity.

as building blocks for the *IS-LM* model. As we see more fully in the next chapter, the *IS-LM* model helps explain the position and slope of the aggregate demand curve. The aggregate demand curve, in turn, is a piece of the model of aggregate supply and aggregate demand, which economists use to explain the short-run effects of policy changes and other events on national income.

Summary

1. The Keynesian cross is a basic model of income determination. It takes fiscal policy and planned investment as exogenous and then shows that there is one level of national income at which actual expenditure equals planned expenditure. It shows that changes in fiscal policy have a multiplied impact on income.

2. Once we allow planned investment to depend on the interest rate, the Keynesian cross yields a relationship between the interest rate and national income. A higher interest rate lowers planned investment, and this in turn lowers national income. The downward-sloping *IS* curve summarizes this negative relationship between the interest rate and income.

3. The theory of liquidity preference is a basic model of the determination of the interest rate. It takes the money supply and the price level as exogenous and assumes that the interest rate adjusts to equilibrate the supply and demand for real money balances. The theory implies that increases in the money supply lower the interest rate.

4. Once we allow the demand for real money balances to depend on national income, the theory of liquidity preference yields a relationship between income and the interest rate. A higher level of income raises the demand for real money balances, and this in turn raises the interest rate. The upward-sloping *LM* curve summarizes this positive relationship between income and the interest rate.

5. The *IS-LM* model combines the elements of the Keynesian cross and the elements of the theory of liquidity preference. The *IS* curve shows the points that satisfy equilibrium in the goods market, and the *LM* curve shows the points that satisfy equilibrium in the money market. The intersection of the *IS* and *LM* curves shows the interest rate and income that satisfy equilibrium in both markets for a given price level.

KEY CONCEPTS

IS-LM model
IS curve
LM curve
Keynesian cross
Government-purchases multiplier
Tax multiplier
Theory of liquidity preference

QUESTIONS FOR REVIEW

1. Use the Keynesian cross to explain why fiscal policy has a multiplied effect on national income.
2. Use the theory of liquidity preference to explain why an increase in the money supply lowers the interest rate. What does this explanation assume about the price level?
3. Why does the *IS* curve slope downward?
4. Why does the *LM* curve slope upward?

PROBLEMS AND APPLICATIONS

1. Use the Keynesian cross to predict the impact of
   a. An increase in government purchases.
   b. An increase in taxes.
   c. An equal increase in government purchases and taxes.
2. In the Keynesian cross, assume that the consumption function is given by

$$C = 200 + 0.75\,(Y - T).$$

   Planned investment is 100; government purchases and taxes are both 100.
   a. Graph planned expenditure as a function of income.
   b. What is the equilibrium level of income?
   c. If government purchases increase to 125, what is the new equilibrium income?
   d. What level of government purchases is needed to achieve an income of 1,600?

3. Although our development of the Keynesian cross in this chapter assumes that taxes are a fixed amount, in many countries (including the United States) taxes depend on income. Let's represent the tax system by writing tax revenue as

$$T = \overline{T} + tY,$$

where $\overline{T}$ and t are parameters of the tax code. The parameter t is the marginal tax rate: if income rises by \$1, taxes rise by $t \times$ \$1.

a. How does this tax system change the way consumption responds to changes in GDP?

b. In the Keynesian cross, how does this tax system alter the government-purchases multiplier?

c. In the *IS-LM* model, how does this tax system alter the slope of the *IS* curve?

4. Consider the impact of an increase in thriftiness in the Keynesian cross. Suppose the consumption function is

$$C = \overline{C} + c(Y - T),$$

where $\overline{C}$ is a parameter called *autonomous consumption* and c is the marginal propensity to consume.

a. What happens to equilibrium income when the society becomes more thrifty, as represented by a decline in $\overline{C}$?

b. What happens to equilibrium saving?

c. Why do you suppose this result is called the *paradox of thrift*?

d. Does this paradox arise in the classical model of Chapter 3? Why or why not?

5. Suppose that the money demand function is

$$(M/P)^d = 1{,}000 - 100r,$$

where r is the interest rate in percent. The money supply M is 1,000 and the price level P is 2.

a. Graph the supply and demand for real money balances.

b. What is the equilibrium interest rate?

c. Assume that the price level is fixed. What happens to the equilibrium interest rate if the supply of money is raised from 1,000 to 1,200?

d. If the Fed wishes to raise the interest rate to 7 percent, what money supply should it set?

CHAPTER 11

Aggregate Demand II: Applying the *IS-LM* Model

Science is a parasite: the greater the patient population the better the advance in physiology and pathology; and out of pathology arises therapy. The year 1932 was the trough of the great depression, and from its rotten soil was belatedly begot a new subject that today we call macroeconomics.

— *Paul Samuelson*

In Chapter 10 we assembled the pieces of the *IS-LM* model as a step toward understanding short-run economic fluctuations. We saw that the *IS* curve represents the equilibrium in the market for goods and services, that the *LM* curve represents the equilibrium in the market for real money balances, and that the *IS* and *LM* curves together determine the interest rate and national income in the short run when the price level is fixed. Now we turn our attention to applying the *IS-LM* model to analyze three issues.

First, we examine the potential causes of fluctuations in national income. We use the *IS-LM* model to see how changes in the exogenous variables (government purchases, taxes, and the money supply) influence the endogenous variables (the interest rate and national income) for a given price level. We also examine how various shocks to the goods market (the *IS* curve) and the money market (the *LM* curve) affect the interest rate and national income in the short run.

Second, we discuss how the *IS-LM* model fits into the model of aggregate supply and aggregate demand we introduced in Chapter 9. In particular, we examine how the *IS-LM* model provides a theory to explain the slope and position of the aggregate demand curve. Here we relax the assumption that the price level is fixed and show that the *IS-LM* model implies a negative relationship between the price level and national income. The model can also tell us what events shift the aggregate demand curve and in what direction.

Third, we examine the Great Depression of the 1930s. As this chapter's opening quotation indicates, this episode gave birth to short-run macroeconomic theory, for it led Keynes and his many followers to think that aggregate demand was the key to understanding fluctuations in national income. With the benefit of hindsight, we can use the *IS-LM* model to discuss the various explanations of this traumatic economic downturn.

11-1 Explaining Fluctuations With the *IS-LM* Model

The intersection of the *IS* curve and the *LM* curve determines the level of national income. When one of these curves shifts, the short-run equilibrium of the economy changes, and national income fluctuates. In this section we examine how changes in policy and shocks to the economy can cause these curves to shift.

How Fiscal Policy Shifts the *IS* Curve and Changes the Short-Run Equilibrium

We begin by examining how changes in fiscal policy (government purchases and taxes) alter the economy's short-run equilibrium. Recall that changes in fiscal policy influence planned expenditure and thereby shift the *IS* curve. The *IS-LM* model shows how these shifts in the *IS* curve affect income and the interest rate.

Changes in Government Purchases Consider an increase in government purchases of ΔG. The government-purchases multiplier in the Keynesian cross tells us that this change in fiscal policy raises the level of income at any given interest rate by $\Delta G/(1 - MPC)$. Therefore, as Figure 11-1 shows, the *IS* curve shifts to the right by this amount. The equilibrium of the economy moves from point A to point B. The increase in government purchases raises both income and the interest rate.

To understand fully what's happening in Figure 11-1, it helps to keep in mind the building blocks for the *IS-LM* model from the preceding chapter—the Keynesian cross and the theory of liquidity preference. Here is the story.

FIGURE 11-1

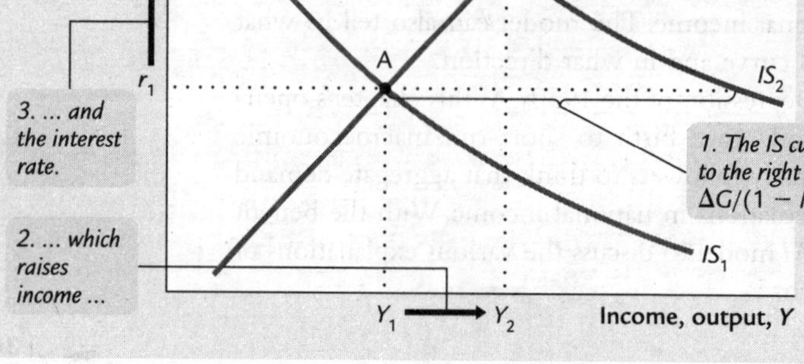

An Increase in Government Purchases in the *IS-LM* Model An increase in government purchases shifts the *IS* curve to the right. The equilibrium moves from point A to point B. Income rises from Y_1 to Y_2, and the interest rate rises from r_1 to r_2.

When the government increases its purchases of goods and services, the economy's planned expenditure rises. The increase in planned expenditure stimulates the production of goods and services, which causes total income Y to rise. These effects should be familiar from the Keynesian cross.

Now consider the money market, as described by the theory of liquidity preference. Because the economy's demand for money depends on income, the rise in total income increases the quantity of money demanded at every interest rate. The supply of money has not changed, however, so higher money demand causes the equilibrium interest rate r to rise.

The higher interest rate arising in the money market, in turn, has ramifications back in the goods market. When the interest rate rises, firms cut back on their investment plans. This fall in investment partially offsets the expansionary effect of the increase in government purchases. Thus, the increase in income in response to a fiscal expansion is smaller in the *IS-LM* model than it is in the Keynesian cross (where investment is assumed to be fixed). You can see this in Figure 11-1. The horizontal shift in the *IS* curve equals the rise in equilibrium income in the Keynesian cross. This amount is larger than the increase in equilibrium income here in the *IS-LM* model. The difference is explained by the crowding out of investment due to a higher interest rate.

Changes in Taxes In the *IS-LM* model, changes in taxes affect the economy much the same as changes in government purchases do, except that taxes affect expenditure through consumption. Consider, for instance, a decrease in taxes of ΔT. The tax cut encourages consumers to spend more and, therefore, increases planned expenditure. The tax multiplier in the Keynesian cross tells us that this change in policy raises the level of income at any given interest rate by $\Delta T \times MPC/(1 - MPC)$. Therefore, as Figure 11-2 illustrates, the *IS* curve shifts to the

FIGURE 11-2

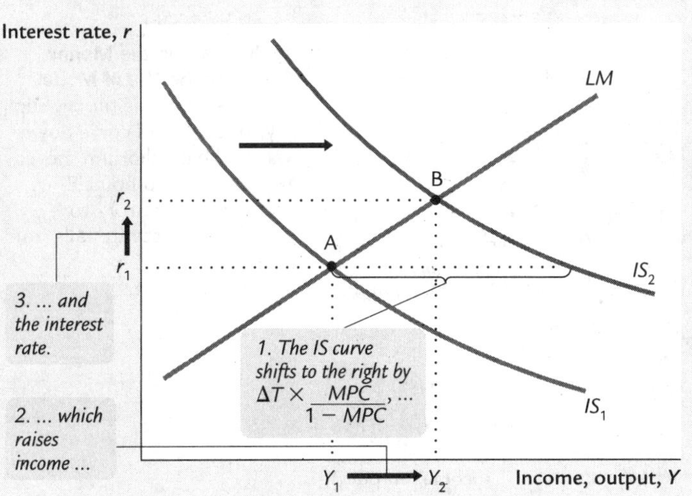

A Decrease in Taxes in the *IS-LM* Model A decrease in taxes shifts the *IS* curve to the right. The equilibrium moves from point A to point B. Income rises from Y_1 to Y_2, and the interest rate rises from r_1 to r_2.

right by this amount. The equilibrium of the economy moves from point A to point B. The tax cut raises both income and the interest rate. Once again, because the higher interest rate depresses investment, the increase in income is smaller in the *IS-LM* model than it is in the Keynesian cross.

How Monetary Policy Shifts the *LM* Curve and Changes the Short-Run Equilibrium

We now examine the effects of monetary policy. Recall that a change in the money supply alters the interest rate that equilibrates the money market for any given level of income and, thereby, shifts the *LM* curve. The *IS-LM* model shows how a shift in the *LM* curve affects income and the interest rate.

Consider an increase in the money supply. An increase in M leads to an increase in real money balances M/P, because the price level P is fixed in the short run. The theory of liquidity preference shows that for any given level of income, an increase in real money balances leads to a lower interest rate. Therefore, the *LM* curve shifts downward, as in Figure 11-3. The equilibrium moves from point A to point B. The increase in the money supply lowers the interest rate and raises the level of income.

Once again, to tell the story that explains the economy's adjustment from point A to point B, we rely on the building blocks of the *IS-LM* model—the Keynesian cross and the theory of liquidity preference. This time, we begin with the money market, where the monetary policy action occurs. When the Federal Reserve increases the supply of money, people have more money than they want to hold at the prevailing interest rate. As a result, they start depositing this extra money in banks or use it to buy bonds. The interest rate r then falls until people are willing to hold all the extra money that the Fed has created; this brings the

FIGURE 11-3

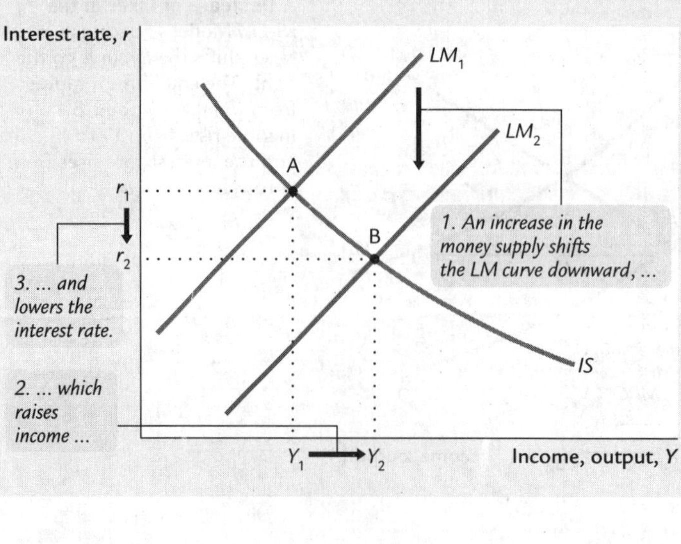

An Increase in the Money Supply in the *IS-LM* Model An increase in the money supply shifts the *LM* curve downward. The equilibrium moves from point A to point B. Income rises from Y_1 to Y_2, and the interest rate falls from r_1 to r_2.

money market to a new equilibrium. The lower interest rate, in turn, has ramifications for the goods market. A lower interest rate stimulates planned investment, which increases planned expenditure, production, and income *Y*.

Thus, the *IS-LM* model shows that monetary policy influences income by changing the interest rate. This conclusion sheds light on our analysis of monetary policy in Chapter 9. In that chapter we showed that in the short run, when prices are sticky, an expansion in the money supply raises income. But we did not discuss *how* a monetary expansion induces greater spending on goods and services—a process called the **monetary transmission mechanism**. The *IS-LM* model shows an important part of that mechanism: *an increase in the money supply lowers the interest rate, which stimulates investment and thereby expands the demand for goods and services.* The next chapter shows that in open economies, the exchange rate also has a role in the monetary transmission mechanism, but for large economies such as the United States, the interest rate has the leading role.

The Interaction Between Monetary and Fiscal Policy

When analyzing any change in monetary or fiscal policy, it is important to keep in mind that the policymakers who control these policy tools are aware of what the other policymakers are doing. A change in one policy, therefore, may influence the other, and this interdependence may alter the impact of a policy change.

For example, suppose Congress raises taxes. What effect will this policy have on the economy? According to the *IS-LM* model, the answer depends on how the Fed responds to the tax increase.

Figure 11-4 shows just three of the many possible outcomes. In panel (a), the Fed holds the money supply constant. The tax increase shifts the *IS* curve to the left. Income falls (because higher taxes reduce consumer spending), and the interest rate falls (because lower income reduces the demand for money). The fall in income indicates that the tax hike causes a recession.

In panel (b), the Fed wants to hold the interest rate constant. In this case, when the tax increase shifts the *IS* curve to the left, the Fed must decrease the money supply to keep the interest rate at its original level. This fall in the money supply shifts the *LM* curve upward. The interest rate does not fall, but income falls by a larger amount than if the Fed had held the money supply constant. Whereas in panel (a) the lower interest rate stimulated investment and partially offset the contractionary effect of the tax hike, in panel (b) the Fed deepens the recession by keeping the interest rate high.

In panel (c), the Fed wants to prevent the tax increase from lowering income. It must, therefore, raise the money supply and shift the *LM* curve downward enough to offset the shift in the *IS* curve. In this case, the tax increase does not cause a recession, but it does cause a large fall in the interest rate. Although the level of income is not changed, the combination of a tax increase and a monetary expansion does change the allocation of the economy's resources. The higher taxes depress consumption, while the lower interest rate stimulates investment. Income is not affected because these two effects exactly balance.

FIGURE 11-4

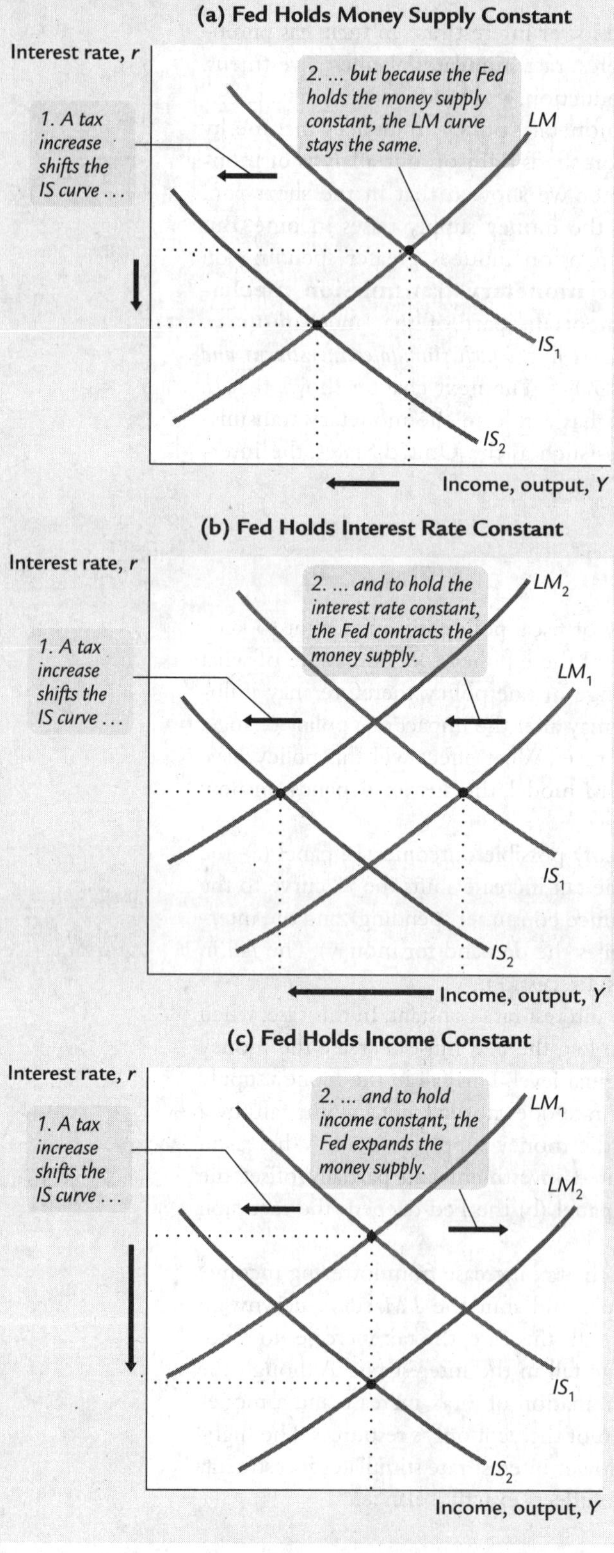

The Response of the Economy to a Tax Increase How the economy responds to a tax increase depends on how the central bank responds. In panel (a) the Fed holds the money supply constant. In panel (b) the Fed holds the interest rate constant by reducing the money supply. In panel (c) the Fed holds the level of income constant by raising the money supply.

From this example we can see that the impact of a change in fiscal policy depends on the policy the Fed pursues—that is, on whether it holds the money supply, the interest rate, or the level of income constant. More generally, whenever analyzing a change in one policy, we must make an assumption about its effect on the other policy. The most appropriate assumption depends on the case at hand and the many political considerations that lie behind economic policymaking.

CASE STUDY

Policy Analysis With Macroeconometric Models

The *IS-LM* model shows how monetary and fiscal policy influence the equilibrium level of income. The predictions of the model, however, are qualitative, not quantitative. The *IS-LM* model shows that increases in government purchases raise GDP and that increases in taxes lower GDP. But when economists analyze specific policy proposals, they need to know not only the direction of the effect but also the size. For example, if Congress increases taxes by $100 billion and if monetary policy is not altered, how much will GDP fall? To answer this question, economists need to go beyond the graphical representation of the *IS-LM* model.

Macroeconometric models of the economy provide one way to evaluate policy proposals. A *macroeconometric model* is a model that describes the economy quantitatively, rather than just qualitatively. Many of these models are essentially more complicated and more realistic versions of our *IS-LM* model. The economists who build macroeconometric models use historical data to estimate parameters such as the marginal propensity to consume, the sensitivity of investment to the interest rate, and the sensitivity of money demand to the interest rate. Once a model is built, economists can simulate the effects of alternative policies with the help of a computer.

Table 11-1 shows the fiscal-policy multipliers implied by one widely used macroeconometric model, the Data Resources Incorporated (DRI) model, named for the economic forecasting firm that developed it. The multipliers are given for two assumptions about how the Fed might respond to changes in fiscal policy.

One assumption about monetary policy is that the Fed keeps the nominal interest rate constant. That is, when fiscal policy shifts the *IS* curve to the right or to the left, the Fed adjusts the money supply to shift the *LM* curve in the same

TABLE 11-1

The Fiscal-Policy Multipliers in the DRI Model

	VALUE OF MULTIPLIERS	
Assumption About Monetary Policy	$\Delta Y/\Delta G$	$\Delta Y/\Delta T$
Nominal interest rate held constant	1.93	−1.19
Money supply held constant	0.60	−0.26

Note: This table gives the fiscal-policy multipliers for a sustained change in government purchases or in personal income taxes. These multipliers are for the fourth quarter after the policy change is made.

Source: Otto Eckstein, *The DRI Model of the U.S. Economy* (New York: McGraw-Hill, 1983), 169.

direction. Because there is no crowding out of investment due to a changing interest rate, the fiscal-policy multipliers are similar to those from the Keynesian cross. The DRI model indicates that, in this case, the government-purchases multiplier is 1.93, and the tax multiplier is −1.19. That is, a $100 billion increase in government purchases raises GDP by $193 billion, and a $100 billion increase in taxes lowers GDP by $119 billion.

The second assumption about monetary policy is that the Fed keeps the money supply constant so that the *LM* curve does not shift. In this case, the interest rate rises, and investment is crowded out, so the multipliers are much smaller. The government-purchases multiplier is only 0.60, and the tax multiplier is only −0.26. That is, a $100 billion increase in government purchases raises GDP by $60 billion, and a $100 billion increase in taxes lowers GDP by $26 billion.

Table 11-1 shows that the fiscal-policy multipliers are very different under the two assumptions about monetary policy. The impact of any change in fiscal policy depends crucially on how the Fed responds to that change.

Shocks in the *IS-LM* Model

Because the *IS-LM* model shows how national income is determined in the short run, we can use the model to examine how various economic disturbances affect income. So far we have seen how changes in fiscal policy shift the *IS* curve and how changes in monetary policy shift the *LM* curve. Similarly, we can group other disturbances into two categories: shocks to the *IS* curve and shocks to the *LM* curve.

Shocks to the *IS* curve are exogenous changes in the demand for goods and services. Some economists, including Keynes, have emphasized that such changes in demand can arise from investors' *animal spirits*—exogenous and perhaps self-fulfilling waves of optimism and pessimism. For example, suppose that firms become pessimistic about the future of the economy and that this pessimism causes them to build fewer new factories. This reduction in the demand for investment goods causes a contractionary shift in the investment function: at every interest rate, firms want to invest less. The fall in investment reduces planned expenditure and shifts the *IS* curve to the left, reducing income and employment. This fall in equilibrium income in part validates the firms' initial pessimism.

Shocks to the *IS* curve may also arise from changes in the demand for consumer goods. Suppose, for instance, that the election of a popular president increases consumer confidence in the economy. This induces consumers to save less for the future and consume more today. We can interpret this change as an upward shift in the consumption function. This shift in the consumption function increases planned expenditure and shifts the *IS* curve to the right, and this raises income.

Shocks to the *LM* curve arise from exogenous changes in the demand for money. For example, suppose that new restrictions on credit-card availability increase the amount of money people choose to hold. According to the theory of liquidity preference, when money demand rises, the interest rate necessary to equilibrate the money market is higher (for any given level of income and money supply). Hence, an increase in money demand shifts the *LM* curve upward, which tends to raise the interest rate and depress income.

In summary, several kinds of events can cause economic fluctuations by shifting the *IS* curve or the *LM* curve. Remember, however, that such fluctuations are not inevitable. Policymakers can try to use the tools of monetary and fiscal policy to offset exogenous shocks. If policymakers are sufficiently quick and skillful (admittedly, a big if), shocks to the *IS* or *LM* curves need not lead to fluctuations in income or employment.

CASE STUDY

The U.S. Recession of 2001

In 2001, the U.S. economy experienced a pronounced slowdown in economic activity. The unemployment rate rose from 3.9 percent in September 2000 to 4.9 percent in August 2001, and then to 6.3 percent in June 2003. In many ways, the slowdown looked like a typical recession driven by a fall in aggregate demand.

Three notable shocks explain this event. The first was a decline in the stock market. During the 1990s, the stock market experienced a boom of historic proportions, as investors became optimistic about the prospects of the new information technology. Some economists viewed the optimism as excessive at the time, and in hindsight this proved to be the case. When the optimism faded, average stock prices fell by about 25 percent from August 2000 to August 2001. The fall in the market reduced household wealth and thus consumer spending. In addition, the declining perceptions of the profitability of the new technologies led to a fall in investment spending. In the language of the *IS-LM* model, the *IS* curve shifted to the left.

The second shock was the terrorist attacks on New York and Washington on September 11, 2001. In the week after the attacks, the stock market fell another 12 percent, its biggest weekly loss since the Great Depression of the 1930s. Moreover, the attacks increased uncertainty about what the future would hold. Uncertainty can reduce spending because households and firms postpone some of their plans until the uncertainty is resolved. Thus, the terrorist attacks shifted the *IS* curve further to the left.

The third shock was a series of accounting scandals at some of the nation's most prominent corporations, including Enron and WorldCom. The result of these scandals was bankruptcy of some companies that had fraudulently represented themselves as more profitable than they truly were, criminal convictions for the executives who had been responsible for the fraud, and new laws aimed at regulating corporate accounting standards more thoroughly. These events further depressed stock prices and discouraged business investment—a third leftward shift in the *IS* curve.

Fiscal and monetary policymakers responded quickly to these events. Congress passed a major tax cut in 2001, including an immediate tax rebate, and a second major tax cut in 2003. One goal of these tax cuts was to stimulate consumer spending. (See the Case Study on cutting taxes in Chapter 10.) In addition, after the terrorist attacks, Congress increased government spending by appropriating funds to rebuild New York and to bail out the ailing airline industry. These fiscal measures shifted the *IS* curve to the right.

At the same time, the Federal Reserve pursued expansionary monetary policy, shifting the *LM* curve to the right. Money growth accelerated, and interest rates fell. The interest rate on three-month Treasury bills fell from 6.4 percent in November 2000 to 3.3 percent in August 2001 just before the terrorist attacks. After the attacks and corporate scandals hit the economy, the Fed increased its monetary stimulus, and the Treasury bill rate fell to 0.9 percent in July 2003—the lowest level in many decades.

Expansionary monetary and fiscal policy had the intended effects. Economic growth picked up in the second half of 2003 and was strong throughout 2004. By June 2005, the unemployment rate was back down to 5.0 percent.

What Is the Fed's Policy Instrument—The Money Supply or the Interest Rate?

Our analysis of monetary policy has been based on the assumption that the Fed influences the economy by controlling the money supply. By contrast, when the media report on changes in Fed policy, they often just say that the Fed has raised or lowered interest rates. Which is right? Even though these two views may seem different, both are correct, and it is important to understand why.

In recent years, the Fed has used the *federal funds rate*—the interest rate that banks charge one another for overnight loans—as its short-term policy instrument. When the Federal Open Market Committee meets every six weeks to set monetary policy, it votes on a target for this interest rate that will apply until the next meeting. After the meeting is over, the Fed's bond traders in New York are told to conduct the open-market operations necessary to hit that target. These open-market operations change the money supply and shift the *LM* curve so that the equilibrium interest rate (determined by the intersection of the *IS* and *LM* curves) equals the target interest rate that the Federal Open Market Committee has chosen.

As a result of this operating procedure, Fed policy is often discussed in terms of changing interest rates. Keep in mind, however, that behind these changes in interest rates are the necessary changes in the money supply. A newspaper might report, for instance, that "the Fed has lowered interest rates." To be more precise, we can translate this statement as meaning "the Federal Open Market Committee has instructed the Fed bond traders to buy bonds in open-market operations so as to increase the money supply, shift the *LM* curve, and reduce the equilibrium interest rate to hit a new lower target."

Why has the Fed chosen to use an interest rate, rather than the money supply, as its short-term policy instrument? One possible answer is that shocks to the *LM* curve are more prevalent than shocks to the *IS* curve. When the Fed targets interest rates, it automatically offsets *LM* shocks by adjusting the money supply, although this policy exacerbates *IS* shocks. If *LM* shocks are the more prevalent type, then a policy of targeting the interest rate leads to greater economic stability than a policy of targeting the money supply. (Problem 7 at the end of this chapter asks you to analyze this issue more fully.)

Another possible reason for using the interest rate as the short-term policy instrument is that interest rates are easier to measure than the money supply. As we saw in Chapter 4, the Fed has several different measures of money—*M*1, *M*2, and so on—which sometimes move in different directions. Rather than deciding which measure is best, the Fed avoids the question by using the federal funds rate as its policy instrument.

11-2 *IS-LM* as a Theory of Aggregate Demand

We have been using the *IS-LM* model to explain national income in the short run when the price level is fixed. To see how the *IS-LM* model fits into the model of aggregate supply and aggregate demand introduced in Chapter 9, we now examine what happens in the *IS-LM* model if the price level is allowed to change. By examining the effects of a changing the price level, we can finally deliver what was promised when we began our study of the *IS-LM* model: a theory to explain the position and slope of the aggregate demand curve.

From the *IS-LM* Model to the Aggregate Demand Curve

Recall from Chapter 9 that the aggregate demand curve describes a relationship between the price level and the level of national income. In Chapter 9 this relationship was derived from the quantity theory of money. The analysis showed that for a given money supply, a higher price level implies a lower level of income. Increases in the money supply shift the aggregate demand curve to the right, and decreases in the money supply shift the aggregate demand curve to the left.

To understand the determinants of aggregate demand more fully, we now use the *IS-LM* model, rather than the quantity theory, to derive the aggregate demand curve. First, we use the *IS-LM* model to show why national income falls as the price level rises—that is, why the aggregate demand curve is downward sloping. Second, we examine what causes the aggregate demand curve to shift.

To explain why the aggregate demand curve slopes downward, we examine what happens in the *IS-LM* model when the price level changes. This is done in Figure 11-5. For any given money supply *M*, a higher price level *P* reduces the supply of real money balances *M*/*P*. A lower supply of real money balances shifts the *LM* curve upward, which raises the equilibrium interest rate and lowers the equilibrium level of income, as shown in panel (a). Here the price level rises from P_1 to P_2, and

FIGURE 11-5

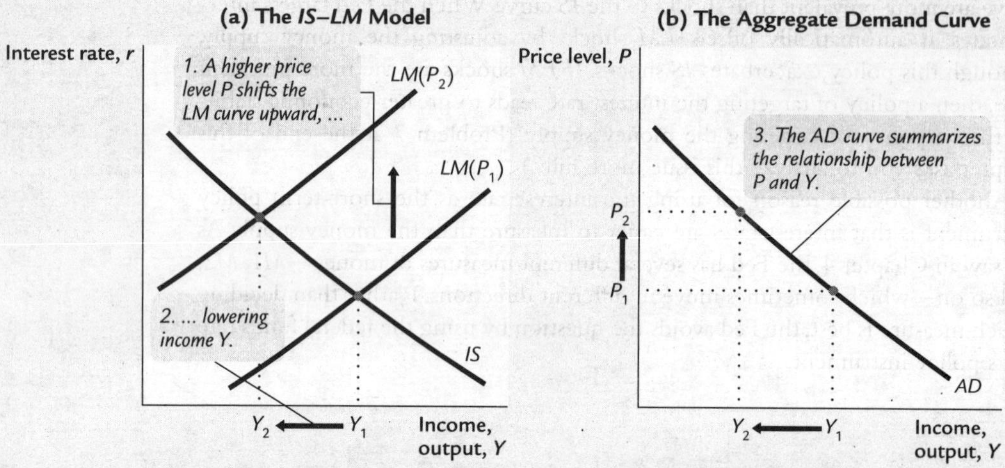

Deriving the Aggregate Demand Curve with the *IS-LM* Model Panel (a) shows the *IS-LM* model: an increase in the price level from P_1 to P_2 lowers real money balances and thus shifts the *LM* curve upward. The shift in the *LM* curve lowers income from Y_1 to Y_2. Panel (b) shows the aggregate demand curve summarizing this relationship between the price level and income: the higher the price level, the lower the level of income.

income falls from Y_1 to Y_2. The aggregate demand curve in panel (b) plots this negative relationship between national income and the price level. In other words, the aggregate demand curve shows the set of equilibrium points that arise in the *IS–LM* model as we vary the price level and see what happens to income.

What causes the aggregate demand curve to shift? Because the aggregate demand curve is merely a summary of results from the *IS-LM* model, events that shift the *IS* curve or the *LM* curve (for a given price level) cause the aggregate demand curve to shift. For instance, an increase in the money supply raises income in the *IS-LM* model for any given price level; it thus shifts the aggregate demand curve to the right, as shown in panel (a) of Figure 11-6. Similarly, an increase in government purchases or a decrease in taxes raises income in the *IS-LM* model for a given price level; it also shifts the aggregate demand curve to the right, as shown in panel (b) of Figure 11-6. Conversely, a decrease in the money supply, a decrease in government purchases, or an increase in taxes lowers income in the *IS-LM* model and shifts the aggregate demand curve to the left. Anything that changes income in the *IS-LM* model other than a change in the price level causes a shift in the aggregate demand curve. The factors shifting aggregate demand include not only monetary and fiscal policy but also shocks to the goods market (the *IS* curve) and shocks to the money market (the *LM* curve).

We can summarize these results as follows: *A change in income in the* IS–LM *model resulting from a change in the price level represents a movement along the aggregate demand curve. A change in income in the* IS–LM *model for a given price level represents a shift in the aggregate demand curve.*

FIGURE 11-6

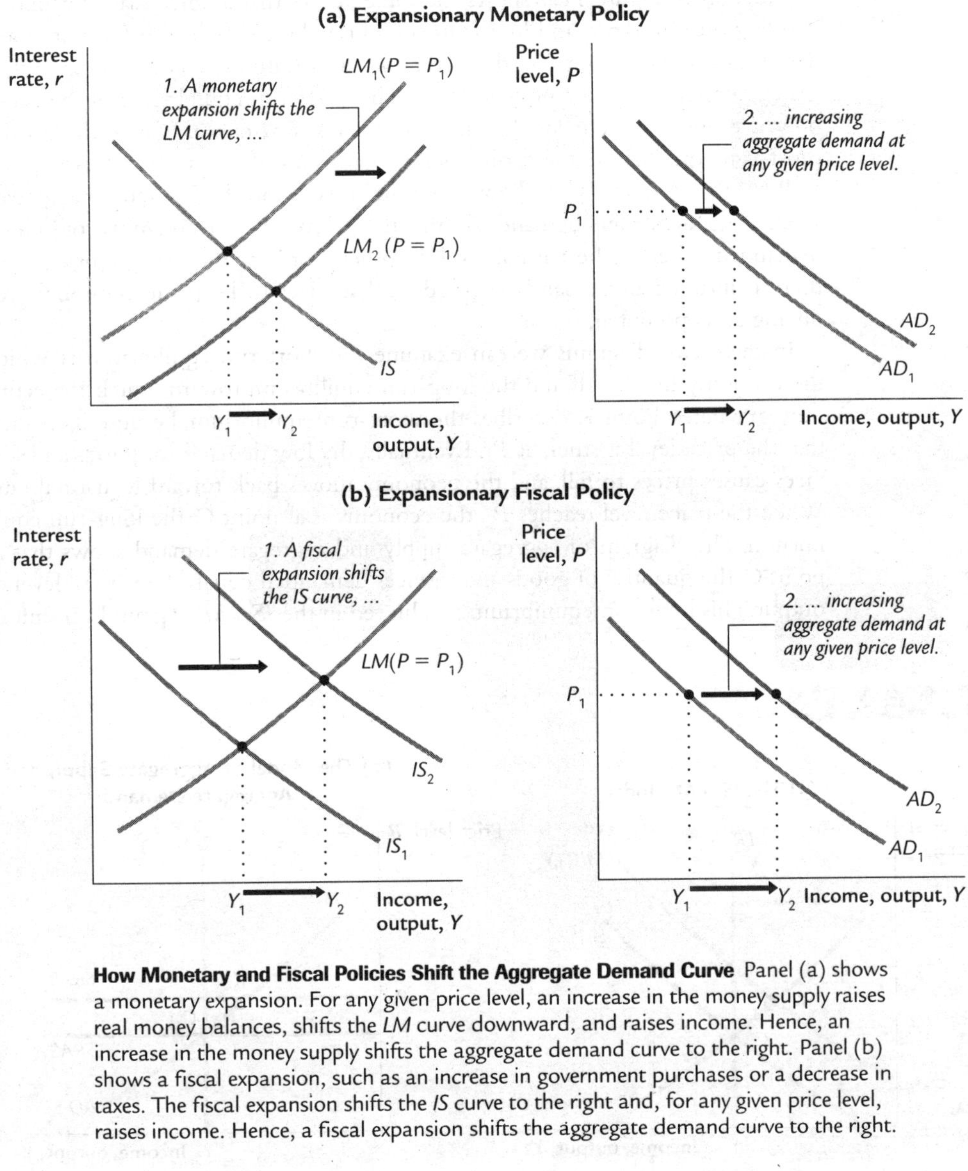

How Monetary and Fiscal Policies Shift the Aggregate Demand Curve Panel (a) shows a monetary expansion. For any given price level, an increase in the money supply raises real money balances, shifts the *LM* curve downward, and raises income. Hence, an increase in the money supply shifts the aggregate demand curve to the right. Panel (b) shows a fiscal expansion, such as an increase in government purchases or a decrease in taxes. The fiscal expansion shifts the *IS* curve to the right and, for any given price level, raises income. Hence, a fiscal expansion shifts the aggregate demand curve to the right.

The *IS-LM* Model in the Short Run and Long Run

The *IS-LM* model is designed to explain the economy in the short run when the price level is fixed. Yet, now that we have seen how a change in the price level influences the equilibrium in the *IS-LM* model, we can also use the model to describe the economy in the long run when the price level adjusts to ensure that the economy produces at its natural rate. By using the *IS-LM* model to describe the long run, we can show clearly how the

Keynesian model of income determination differs from the classical model of Chapter 3.

Panel (a) of Figure 11-7 shows the three curves that are necessary for understanding the short-run and long-run equilibria: the *IS* curve, the *LM* curve, and the vertical line representing the natural level of output $\bar{Y}$. The *LM* curve is, as always, drawn for a fixed price level, P_1. The short-run equilibrium of the economy is point K, where the *IS* curve crosses the *LM* curve. Notice that in this short-run equilibrium, the economy's income is less than its natural level.

Panel (b) of Figure 11-7 shows the same situation in the diagram of aggregate supply and aggregate demand. At the price level P_1, the quantity of output demanded is below the natural level. In other words, at the existing price level, there is insufficient demand for goods and services to keep the economy producing at its potential.

In these two diagrams we can examine the short-run equilibrium at which the economy finds itself and the long-run equilibrium toward which the economy gravitates. Point K describes the short-run equilibrium, because it assumes that the price level is stuck at P_1. Eventually, the low demand for goods and services causes prices to fall, and the economy moves back toward its natural rate. When the price level reaches P_2, the economy is at point C, the long-run equilibrium. The diagram of aggregate supply and aggregate demand shows that at point C, the quantity of goods and services demanded equals the natural level of output. This long-run equilibrium is achieved in the *IS-LM* diagram by a shift in

FIGURE 11-7

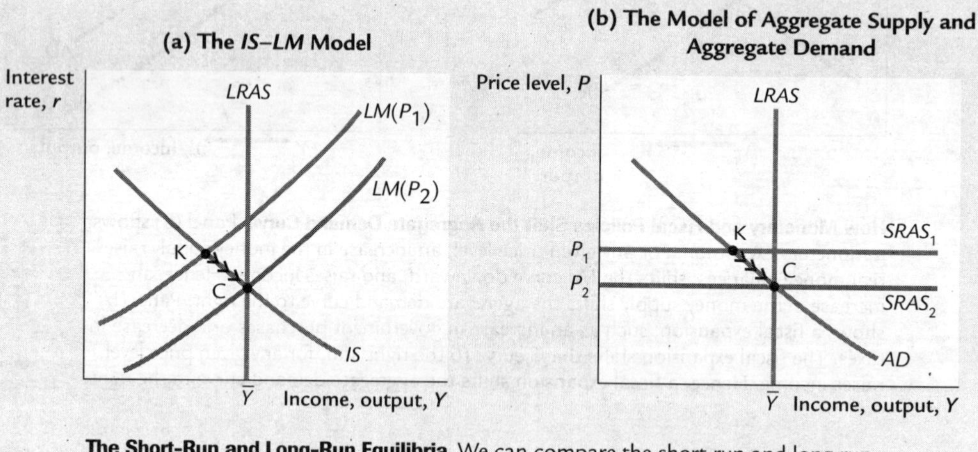

The Short-Run and Long-Run Equilibria We can compare the short-run and long-run equilibria using either the *IS-LM* diagram in panel (a) or the aggregate supply-aggregate demand diagram in panel (b). In the short run, the price level is stuck at P_1. The short-run equilibrium of the economy is therefore point K. In the long run, the price level adjusts so that the economy is at the natural level of output. The long-run equilibrium is therefore point C.

the *LM* curve: the fall in the price level raises real money balances and therefore shifts the *LM* curve to the right.

We can now see the key difference between Keynesian and classical approaches to the determination of national income. The Keynesian assumption (represented by point K) is that the price level is stuck. Depending on monetary policy, fiscal policy, and the other determinants of aggregate demand, output may deviate from its natural level. The classical assumption (represented by point C) is that the price level is fully flexible. The price level adjusts to ensure that national income is always at its natural level.

To make the same point somewhat differently, we can think of the economy as being described by three equations. The first two are the *IS* and *LM* equations:

$$Y = C(Y - T) + I(r) + G \qquad IS,$$

$$M/P = L(r, Y) \qquad LM.$$

The *IS* equation describes the equilibrium in the goods market, and the *LM* equation describes the equilibrium in the money market. These *two* equations contain *three* endogenous variables: Y, P, and r. To complete the system, we need a third equation. The Keynesian approach completes the model with the assumption of fixed prices, so the Keynesian third equation is

$$P = P_1.$$

This assumption implies that the remaining two variables r and Y must adjust to satisfy the remaining two equations *IS* and *LM*. The classical approach completes the model with the assumption that output reaches its natural level, so the classical third equation is

$$Y = \bar{Y}.$$

This assumption implies that the remaining two variables r and P must adjust to satisfy the remaining two equations *IS* and *LM*. Thus, the classical approach fixes output and allows the price level to adjust to satisfy the goods and money market equilibrium conditions, whereas the Keynesian approach fixes the price level and lets output move to satisfy the equilibrium conditions.

Which assumption is most appropriate? The answer depends on the time horizon. The classical assumption best describes the long run. Hence, our long-run analysis of national income in Chapter 3 and prices in Chapter 4 assumes that output equals its natural level. The Keynesian assumption best describes the short run. Therefore, our analysis of economic fluctuations relies on the assumption of a fixed price level.

11-3 The Great Depression

Now that we have developed the model of aggregate demand, let's use it to address the question that originally motivated Keynes: what caused the Great Depression? Even today, more than half a century after the event, economists

TABLE 11-2

What Happened During the Great Depression?

Year	Unemployment Rate (1)	Real GNP (2)	Consumption (2)	Investment (2)	Government Purchases (2)
1929	3.2	203.6	139.6	40.4	22.0
1930	8.9	183.5	130.4	27.4	24.3
1931	16.3	169.5	126.1	16.8	25.4
1932	24.1	144.2	114.8	4.7	24.2
1933	25.2	141.5	112.8	5.3	23.3
1934	22.0	154.3	118.1	9.4	26.6
1935	20.3	169.5	125.5	18.0	27.0
1936	17.0	193.2	138.4	24.0	31.8
1937	14.3	203.2	143.1	29.9	30.8
1938	19.1	192.9	140.2	17.0	33.9
1939	17.2	209.4	148.2	24.7	35.2
1940	14.6	227.2	155.7	33.0	36.4

Source: Historical Statistics of the United States, Colonial Times to 1970, Parts I and II (Washington, DC: U.S. Department of Commerce, Bureau of Census, 1975).

Note: (1) The unemployment rate is series D9. (2) Real GNP, consumption, investment, and government purchases are series F3, F48, F52, and F66, and are measured in billions of 1958 dollars. (3) The interest rate is the prime Commercial

continue to debate the cause of this major economic downturn. The Great Depression provides an extended case study to show how economists use the *IS-LM* model to analyze economic fluctuations.[1]

Before turning to the explanations economists have proposed, look at Table 11-2, which presents some statistics regarding the Depression. These statistics are the battlefield on which debate about the Depression takes place. What do you think happened? An *IS* shift? An *LM* shift? Or something else?

The Spending Hypothesis: Shocks to the *IS* Curve

Table 11-2 shows that the decline in income in the early 1930s coincided with falling interest rates. This fact has led some economists to suggest that the cause of the decline may have been a contractionary shift in the *IS* curve. This view is sometimes called the *spending hypothesis,* because it places primary blame for the Depression on an exogenous fall in spending on goods and services.

Economists have attempted to explain this decline in spending in several ways. Some argue that a downward shift in the consumption function caused

[1] For a flavor of the debate, see Milton Friedman and Anna J. Schwartz, *A Monetary History of the United States, 1867–1960* (Princeton, NJ: Princeton University Press, 1963); Peter Temin, *Did Monetary Forces Cause the Great Depression?* (New York: W. W. Norton, 1976); the essays in Karl Brunner, ed., *The Great Depression Revisited* (Boston: Martinus Nijhoff, 1981); and the symposium on the Great Depression in the Spring 1993 issue of the *Journal of Economic Perspectives.*

Year	Nominal Interest Rate (3)	Money Supply (4)	Price Level (5)	Inflation (6)	Real Money Balances (7)
1929	5.9	26.6	50.6	–	52.6
1930	3.6	25.8	49.3	−2.6	52.3
1931	2.6	24.1	44.8	−10.1	54.5
1932	2.7	21.1	40.2	−9.3	52.5
1933	1.7	19.9	39.3	−2.2	50.7
1934	1.0	21.9	42.2	7.4	51.8
1935	0.8	25.9	42.6	0.9	60.8
1936	0.8	29.6	42.7	0.2	62.9
1937	0.9	30.9	44.5	4.2	69.5
1938	0.8	30.5	43.9	−1.3	69.5
1939	0.6	34.2	43.2	−1.6	79.1
1940	0.6	39.7	43.9	1.6	90.3

Paper rate, 4–6 months, series x445. (4) The money supply is series x414, currency plus demand deposits, measured in billions of dollars. (5) The price level is the GNP deflator (1958 = 100), series E1. (6) The inflation rate is the percentage change in the price level series. (7) Real money balances, calculated by dividing the money supply by the price level and multiplying by 100, are in billions of 1958 dollars.

the contractionary shift in the *IS* curve. The stock market crash of 1929 may have been partly responsible for this shift: by reducing wealth and increasing uncertainty about the future prospects of the U.S. economy, the crash may have induced consumers to save more of their income rather than spend it.

Others explain the decline in spending by pointing to the large drop in investment in housing. Some economists believe that the residential investment boom of the 1920s was excessive and that once this "overbuilding" became apparent, the demand for residential investment declined drastically. Another possible explanation for the fall in residential investment is the reduction in immigration in the 1930s: a more slowly growing population demands less new housing.

Once the Depression began, several events occurred that could have reduced spending further. First, many banks failed in the early 1930s, in part because of inadequate bank regulation, and these bank failures may have exacerbated the fall in investment spending. Banks play the crucial role of getting the funds available for investment to those households and firms that can best use them. The closing of many banks in the early 1930s may have prevented some businesses from getting the funds they needed for capital investment and, therefore, may have led to a further contractionary shift in the investment function.[2]

In addition, the fiscal policy of the 1930s caused a contractionary shift in the *IS* curve. Politicians at that time were more concerned with balancing the budget

[2] Ben Bernanke, "Non-Monetary Effects of the Financial Crisis in the Propagation of the Great Depression," *American Economic Review* 73 (June 1983): 257–276.

than with using fiscal policy to keep production and employment at their natural levels. The Revenue Act of 1932 increased various taxes, especially those falling on lower- and middle-income consumers.[3] The Democratic platform of that year expressed concern about the budget deficit and advocated an "immediate and drastic reduction of governmental expenditures." In the midst of historically high unemployment, policymakers searched for ways to raise taxes and reduce government spending.

There are, therefore, several ways to explain a contractionary shift in the *IS* curve. Keep in mind that these different views may all be true. There may be no single explanation for the decline in spending. It is possible that all of these changes coincided and that together they led to a massive reduction in spending.

The Money Hypothesis: A Shock to the *LM* Curve

Table 11-2 shows that the money supply fell 25 percent from 1929 to 1933, during which time the unemployment rate rose from 3.2 percent to 25.2 percent. This fact provides the motivation and support for what is called the *money hypothesis,* which places primary blame for the Depression on the Federal Reserve for allowing the money supply to fall by such a large amount.[4] The best-known advocates of this interpretation are Milton Friedman and Anna Schwartz, who defend it in their treatise on U.S. monetary history. Friedman and Schwartz argue that contractions in the money supply have caused most economic downturns and that the Great Depression is a particularly vivid example.

Using the *IS-LM* model, we might interpret the money hypothesis as explaining the Depression by a contractionary shift in the *LM* curve. Seen in this way, however, the money hypothesis runs into two problems.

The first problem is the behavior of *real* money balances. Monetary policy leads to a contractionary shift in the *LM* curve only if real money balances fall. Yet from 1929 to 1931 real money balances rose slightly, because the fall in the money supply was accompanied by an even greater fall in the price level. Although the monetary contraction may be responsible for the rise in unemployment from 1931 to 1933, when real money balances did fall, it cannot easily explain the initial downturn from 1929 to 1931.

The second problem for the money hypothesis is the behavior of interest rates. If a contractionary shift in the *LM* curve triggered the Depression, we should have observed higher interest rates. Yet nominal interest rates fell continuously from 1929 to 1933.

These two reasons appear sufficient to reject the view that the Depression was instigated by a contractionary shift in the *LM* curve. But was the fall in

---

[3] E. Cary Brown, "Fiscal Policy in the 'Thirties: A Reappraisal," *American Economic Review* 46 (December 1956): 857–879.

[4] We discuss the reasons for this large decrease in the money supply in Chapter 18, where we examine the money supply process in more detail. In particular, see the Case Study "Bank Failures and the Money Supply in the 1930s."

the money stock irrelevant? Next, we turn to another mechanism through which monetary policy might have been responsible for the severity of the Depression—the deflation of the 1930s.

The Money Hypothesis Again: The Effects of Falling Prices

From 1929 to 1933 the price level fell 25 percent. Many economists blame this deflation for the severity of the Great Depression. They argue that the deflation may have turned what in 1931 was a typical economic downturn into an unprecedented period of high unemployment and depressed income. If correct, this argument gives new life to the money hypothesis. Because the falling money supply was, plausibly, responsible for the falling price level, it could have been responsible for the severity of the Depression. To evaluate this argument, we must discuss how changes in the price level affect income in the *IS-LM* model.

The Stabilizing Effects of Deflation In the *IS-LM* model we have developed so far, falling prices raise income. For any given supply of money M, a lower price level implies higher real money balances M/P. An increase in real money balances causes an expansionary shift in the *LM* curve, which leads to higher income.

Another channel through which falling prices expand income is called the **Pigou effect.** Arthur Pigou, a prominent classical economist in the 1930s, pointed out that real money balances are part of households' wealth. As prices fall and real money balances rise, consumers should feel wealthier and spend more. This increase in consumer spending should cause an expansionary shift in the *IS* curve, also leading to higher income.

These two reasons led some economists in the 1930s to believe that falling prices would help stabilize the economy. That is, they thought that a decline in the price level would automatically push the economy back toward full employment. Yet other economists were less confident in the economy's ability to correct itself. They pointed to other effects of falling prices, to which we now turn.

The Destabilizing Effects of Deflation Economists have proposed two theories to explain how falling prices could depress income rather than raise it. The first, called the **debt-deflation theory**, describes the effects of unexpected falls in the price level. The second explains the effects of expected deflation.

The debt-deflation theory begins with an observation from Chapter 4: unanticipated changes in the price level redistribute wealth between debtors and creditors. If a debtor owes a creditor \$1,000, then the real amount of this debt is \$1,000/P, where P is the price level. A fall in the price level raises the real amount of this debt—the amount of purchasing power the debtor must repay the creditor. Therefore, an unexpected deflation enriches creditors and impoverishes debtors.

The debt-deflation theory then posits that this redistribution of wealth affects spending on goods and services. In response to the redistribution from debtors to creditors, debtors spend less and creditors spend more. If these two groups have equal spending propensities, there is no aggregate impact. But it seems reasonable to assume that debtors have higher propensities to spend than creditors—perhaps that is why the debtors are in debt in the first place. In this case, debtors reduce their spending by more than creditors raise theirs. The net effect is a reduction in spending, a contractionary shift in the *IS* curve, and lower national income.

To understand how *expected* changes in prices can affect income, we need to add a new variable to the *IS-LM* model. Our discussion of the model so far has not distinguished between the nominal and real interest rates. Yet we know from previous chapters that investment depends on the real interest rate and that money demand depends on the nominal interest rate. If i is the nominal interest rate and π^e is expected inflation, then the *ex ante* real interest rate is $i - \pi^e$. We can now write the *IS-LM* model as

$$Y = C(Y - T) + I(i - \pi^e) + G \qquad IS,$$

$$M/P = L(i, Y) \qquad LM.$$

Expected inflation enters as a variable in the *IS* curve. Thus, changes in expected inflation shift the *IS* curve.

Let's use this extended *IS-LM* model to examine how changes in expected inflation influence the level of income. We begin by assuming that everyone expects the price level to remain the same. In this case, there is no expected inflation ($\pi^e = 0$), and these two equations produce the familiar *IS-LM* model. Figure 11-8 depicts this initial situation with the *LM* curve and the *IS* curve labeled IS_1. The intersection of these two curves determines the nominal and real interest rates, which for now are the same.

Now suppose that everyone suddenly expects that the price level will fall in the future, so that π^e becomes negative. The real interest rate is now higher at any given nominal interest rate. This increase in the real interest rate depresses

FIGURE 11-8

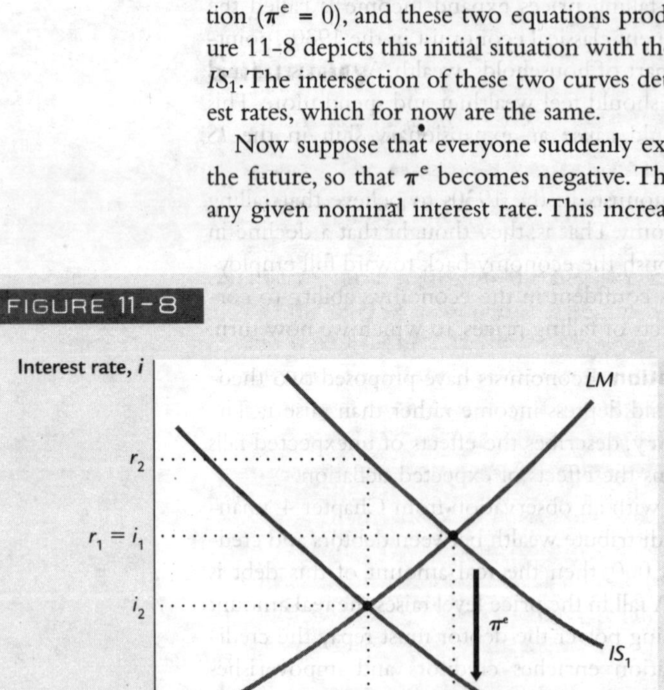

Expected Deflation in the *IS-LM* Model An expected deflation (a negative value of π^e) raises the real interest rate for any given nominal interest rate, and this depresses investment spending. The reduction in investment shifts the *IS* curve downward. The level of income falls from Y_1 to Y_2. The nominal interest rate falls from i_1 to i_2, and the real interest rate rises from r_1 to r_2.

planned investment spending, shifting the *IS* curve from IS_1 to IS_2. (The vertical distance of the downward shift exactly equals the expected deflation.) Thus, an expected deflation leads to a reduction in national income from Y_1 to Y_2. The nominal interest rate falls from i_1 to i_2, while the real interest rate rises from r_1 to r_2.

Here is the story behind this figure. When firms come to expect deflation, they become reluctant to borrow to buy investment goods because they believe they will have to repay these loans later in more valuable dollars. The fall in investment depresses planned expenditure, which in turn depresses income. The fall in income reduces the demand for money, and this reduces the nominal interest rate that equilibrates the money market. The nominal interest rate falls by less than the expected deflation, so the real interest rate rises.

Note that there is a common thread in these two stories of destabilizing deflation. In both, falling prices depress national income by causing a contractionary shift in the *IS* curve. Because a deflation of the size observed from 1929 to 1933 is unlikely except in the presence of a major contraction in the money supply, these two explanations give some of the responsibility for the Depression—especially its severity—to the Fed. In other words, if falling prices are destabilizing, then a contraction in the money supply can lead to a fall in income, even without a decrease in real money balances or a rise in nominal interest rates.

Could the Depression Happen Again?

Economists study the Depression both because of its intrinsic interest as a major economic event and to provide guidance to policymakers so that it will not happen again. To state with confidence whether this event could recur, we would need to know why it happened. Because there is not yet agreement on the causes of the Great Depression, it is impossible to rule out with certainty another depression of this magnitude.

Yet most economists believe that the mistakes that led to the Great Depression are unlikely to be repeated. The Fed seems unlikely to allow the money supply to fall by one-fourth. Many economists believe that the deflation of the early 1930s was responsible for the depth and length of the Depression. And it seems likely that such a prolonged deflation was possible only in the presence of a falling money supply.

The fiscal-policy mistakes of the Depression are also unlikely to be repeated. Fiscal policy in the 1930s not only failed to help but actually further depressed aggregate demand. Few economists today would advocate such a rigid adherence to a balanced budget in the face of massive unemployment.

In addition, there are many institutions today that would help prevent the events of the 1930s from recurring. The system of Federal Deposit Insurance makes widespread bank failures less likely. The income tax causes an automatic reduction in taxes when income falls, which stabilizes the economy. Finally, economists know more today than they did in the 1930s. Our knowledge of how the economy works, limited as it still is, should help policymakers formulate better policies to combat such widespread unemployment.

CASE STUDY

The Japanese Slump of the 1990s

After many years of rapid growth and enviable prosperity, the Japanese economy experienced a prolonged downturn during the 1990s. Real GDP grew at an average rate of only 1.3 percent over the decade, compared with 4.3 percent over the previous twenty years. Industrial production stagnated: after having risen by 50 percent from 1980 to 1991, it fell by 8 percent from 1991 to 2002. The unemployment rate, which had historically been very low in Japan, rose from 2.1 percent in 1991 to 5.4 percent in 2002, the highest rate since the government began compiling the statistic in 1953. After 2002, the Japanese economy started to recover, but only slowly. At the end of 2005, when this book was going to press, the unemployment rate had fallen to 4.5 percent.

Although the Japanese slump of the 1990s is not even close in magnitude to the Great Depression of the 1930s, the episodes are similar in several ways. First, both episodes are traced in part to a large decline in stock prices. In Japan, stock prices at the end of the 1990s were less than half the peak level they had reached about a decade earlier. Like the stock market, Japanese land prices had also skyrocketed in the 1980s before crashing in the 1990s. (At the peak of Japan's land bubble, it was said that the land under the Imperial Palace was worth more than the entire state of California.) When stock and land prices collapsed, Japanese citizens saw their wealth plummet. This decline in wealth, like that during the Great Depression, depressed consumer spending.

Second, during both episodes, banks ran into trouble and exacerbated the slump in economic activity. Japanese banks in the 1980s had made many loans that were backed by stock or land. When the value of this collateral fell, borrowers started defaulting on their loans. These defaults on the old loans reduced the banks' ability to make new loans. The resulting "credit crunch" made it harder for firms to finance investment projects and, thus, depressed investment spending.

Third, both episodes saw a fall in economic activity coincide with very low interest rates. In Japan in the 1990s, as in the United States in the 1930s, short-term nominal interest rates were less than 1 percent. This fact suggests that the cause of the slump was primarily a contractionary shift in the *IS* curve, because such a shift reduces both income and the interest rate. The obvious suspects to explain the *IS* shift are the crashes in stock and land prices and the problems in the banking system.

Finally, the policy debate in Japan mirrored the debate over the Great Depression. Some economists recommended that the Japanese government pass large tax cuts to encourage more consumer spending. Although this advice was followed to some extent, Japanese policymakers were reluctant to enact very large tax cuts because, like the U.S. policymakers in the 1930s, they wanted to avoid budget deficits. In Japan, this reluctance to increase government debt arose in part because the government was facing a large unfunded pension liability and a rapidly aging population.

Other economists recommended that the Bank of Japan expand the money supply more rapidly. Even if nominal interest rates could not go much lower, then perhaps more rapid money growth could raise expected inflation, lower real interest rates, and stimulate investment spending. Thus, although economists differed about whether fiscal or monetary policy was more likely to be effective, there was wide agreement that the solution to Japan's slump, like the solution to the Great Depression, rested in more aggressive expansion of aggregate demand.[5]

FYI The Liquidity Trap

In Japan in the 1990s and the United States in the 1930s, interest rates reached very low levels. As Table 11-2 shows, U.S. interest rates were well under 1 percent throughout the second half of the 1930s. The same was true in Japan during the second half of the 1990s. In 1999, Japanese short-term interest rates fell to about one-tenth of 1 percent.

Some economists describe this situation as a *liquidity trap*. According to the *IS-LM* model, expansionary monetary policy works by reducing interest rates and stimulating investment spending. But if interest rates have already fallen almost to zero, then perhaps monetary policy is no longer effective. Nominal interest rates cannot fall below zero: rather than making a loan at a negative nominal interest rate, a person would just hold cash. In this environment, expansionary monetary policy raises the supply of money, making the public's asset portfolio more liquid, but because interest rates can't fall any further, the extra liquidity might not have any effect. Aggregate demand, production, and employment may be "trapped" at low levels.

Other economists are skeptical about this argument. One response is that expansionary monetary policy might raise inflation expectations. Even if nominal interest rates cannot fall any further, higher expected inflation can lower real interest rates by making them negative, which would stimulate investment spending. A second response is that monetary expansion would cause the currency to lose value in the market for foreign-currency exchange. This depreciation would make the nation's goods cheaper abroad, stimulating export demand. This second argument goes beyond the closed-economy *IS-LM* model we have used in this chapter, but it has merit in the open-economy version of the model developed in the next chapter.

Is the liquidity trap something monetary policymakers need to worry about? Might the tools of monetary policy at times lose their power to influence the economy? There is no consensus about the answers. Skeptics say we shouldn't worry about the liquidity trap. But others say the possibility of a liquidity trap argues for a target rate of inflation greater than zero. Under zero inflation, the real interest rate, like the nominal interest, can never fall below zero. But if the normal rate of inflation is, say, 3 percent, then the central bank can easily push the real interest rate to negative 3 percent by lowering the nominal interest rate toward zero. Thus, moderate inflation gives monetary policymakers more room to stimulate the economy when needed, reducing the risk of falling into a liquidity trap.[6]

[5] To learn more about this episode, see Kenneth N. Kuttner and Adam S. Posen, "The Great Recession: Lessons for Macroeconomic Policy From Japan," *Brookings Papers on Economic Activity* 2 (2001): 93–160. Readers of this book will find Kuttner and Posen's conclusions reassuring: "[D]espite the persistent stagnation, and despite the seeming ineffectiveness of several well publicized announcements of policy changes (which proved to be more noise than action), the Japanese economy has behaved much as the textbooks would have predicted . . . In short, the basic lesson of Japan's Great Recession for policymakers is to trust what you learned in intermediate macroeconomics class: even under difficult economic circumstances, and even in institutional contexts far removed from those in which they were developed, the stabilization policy framework of the mainstream textbooks still applies."

[6] To read more about the liquidity trap, see Paul R. Krugman, "It's Baaack: Japan's Slump and the Return of the Liquidity Trap," *Brookings Panel on Economic Activity* 2 (1998): 137–205.

11-4 Conclusion

The purpose of this chapter and the previous one has been to deepen our understanding of aggregate demand. We now have the tools to analyze the effects of monetary and fiscal policy in the long run and in the short run. In the long run, prices are flexible, and we use the classical analysis of Parts Two and Three of this book. In the short run, prices are sticky, and we use the *IS–LM* model to examine how changes in policy influence the economy.

Although the model in this chapter provides the basic framework for analyzing the economy in the short run, it is not the whole story. In Chapter 12 we examine how international interactions affect our theory of aggregate demand, in Chapter 13 we examine the theory behind short-run aggregate supply, and in Chapter 14 we consider how this theoretical framework should be applied to the making of stabilization policy. In addition, in later chapters, we examine in more detail the elements of the *IS–LM* model, thereby refining our understanding of aggregate demand. In Chapter 16, for example, we study theories of consumption. Because the consumption function is a crucial piece of the *IS–LM* model, a deeper analysis of consumption may modify our view of the impact of monetary and fiscal policy on the economy. The simple *IS–LM* model presented in Chapters 10 and 11 provides the starting point for this further analysis.

Summary

1. The *IS–LM* model is a general theory of the aggregate demand for goods and services. The exogenous variables in the model are fiscal policy, monetary policy, and the price level. The model explains two endogenous variables: the interest rate and the level of national income.

2. The *IS* curve represents the negative relationship between the interest rate and the level of income that arises from equilibrium in the market for goods and services. The *LM* curve represents the positive relationship between the interest rate and the level of income that arises from equilibrium in the market for real money balances. Equilibrium in the *IS–LM* model—the intersection of the *IS* and *LM* curves—represents simultaneous equilibrium in the market for goods and services and in the market for real money balances.

3. The aggregate demand curve summarizes the results from the *IS–LM* model by showing equilibrium income at any given price level. The aggregate demand curve slopes downward because a lower price level increases real money balances, lowers the interest rate, stimulates investment spending, and thereby raises equilibrium income.

4. Expansionary fiscal policy—an increase in government purchases or a decrease in taxes—shifts the *IS* curve to the right. This shift in the *IS* curve increases the interest rate and income. The increase in income represents a

rightward shift in the aggregate demand curve. Similarly, contractionary fiscal policy shifts the *IS* curve to the left, lowers the interest rate and income, and shifts the aggregate demand curve to the left.

5. Expansionary monetary policy shifts the *LM* curve downward. This shift in the *LM* curve lowers the interest rate and raises income. The increase in income represents a rightward shift of the aggregate demand curve. Similarly, contractionary monetary policy shifts the *LM* curve upward, raises the interest rate, lowers income, and shifts the aggregate demand curve to the left.

KEY CONCEPTS

Monetary transmission mechanism

Pigou effect

Debt-deflation theory

QUESTIONS FOR REVIEW

1. Explain why the aggregate demand curve slopes downward.
2. What is the impact of an increase in taxes on the interest rate, income, consumption, and investment?
3. What is the impact of a decrease in the money supply on the interest rate, income, consumption, and investment?
4. Describe the possible effects of falling prices on equilibrium income.

PROBLEMS AND APPLICATIONS

1. According to the *IS-LM* model, what happens to the interest rate, income, consumption, and investment under the following circumstances?
   a. The central bank increases the money supply.
   b. The government increases government purchases.
   c. The government increases taxes.
   d. The government increases government purchases and taxes by equal amounts.
2. Use the *IS-LM* model to predict the effects of each of the following shocks on income, the interest rate, consumption, and investment. In each case, explain what the Fed should do to keep income at its initial level.
   a. After the invention of a new high-speed computer chip, many firms decide to upgrade their computer systems.
   b. A wave of credit-card fraud increases the frequency with which people make transactions in cash.
   c. A best-seller titled *Retire Rich* convinces the public to increase the percentage of their income devoted to saving.
3. Consider the economy of Hicksonia.
   a. The consumption function is given by

      $$C = 200 + 0.75(Y - T).$$

      The investment function is

      $$I = 200 - 25r.$$

      Government purchases and taxes are both 100. For this economy, graph the *IS* curve for r ranging from 0 to 8.
   b. The money demand function in Hicksonia is

      $$(M/P)^d = Y - 100r.$$

The money supply M is 1,000 and the price level P is 2. For this economy, graph the LM curve for r ranging from 0 to 8.

c. Find the equilibrium interest rate r and the equilibrium level of income Y.

d. Suppose that government purchases are raised from 100 to 150. How much does the IS curve shift? What are the new equilibrium interest rate and level of income?

e. Suppose instead that the money supply is raised from 1,000 to 1,200. How much does the LM curve shift? What are the new equilibrium interest rate and level of income?

f. With the initial values for monetary and fiscal policy, suppose that the price level rises from 2 to 4. What happens? What are the new equilibrium interest rate and level of income?

g. Derive and graph an equation for the aggregate demand curve. What happens to this aggregate demand curve if fiscal or monetary policy changes, as in parts (d) and (e)?

4. Explain why each of the following statements is true. Discuss the impact of monetary and fiscal policy in each of these special cases.

a. If investment does not depend on the interest rate, the *IS* curve is vertical.

b. If money demand does not depend on the interest rate, the *LM* curve is vertical.

c. If money demand does not depend on income, the *LM* curve is horizontal.

d. If money demand is extremely sensitive to the interest rate, the *LM* curve is horizontal.

5. Suppose that the government wants to raise investment but keep output constant. In the *IS-LM* model, what mix of monetary and fiscal policy will achieve this goal? In the early 1980s, the U.S. government cut taxes and ran a budget deficit while the Fed pursued a tight monetary policy. What effect should this policy mix have?

6. Use the *IS-LM* diagram to describe the short-run and long-run effects of the following changes on national income, the interest rate, the price level, consumption, investment, and real money balances.

a. An increase in the money supply.

b. An increase in government purchases.

c. An increase in taxes.

7. The Fed is considering two alternative monetary policies:

- holding the money supply constant and letting the interest rate adjust, or
- adjusting the money supply to hold the interest rate constant.

In the *IS-LM* model, which policy will better stabilize output under the following conditions?

a. All shocks to the economy arise from exogenous changes in the demand for goods and services.

b. All shocks to the economy arise from exogenous changes in the demand for money.

8. Suppose that the demand for real money balances depends on disposable income. That is, the money demand function is

$$M/P = L(r, Y - T).$$

Using the *IS-LM* model, discuss whether this change in the money demand function alters the following:

a. The analysis of changes in government purchases.

b. The analysis of changes in taxes.

The Simple Algebra of the *IS-LM* Model and the Aggregate Demand Curve

The chapter analyzes the *IS-LM* model with graphs of the *IS* and *LM* curves. Here we analyze the model with algebra. This alternative presentation offers additional insight into how monetary and fiscal policy influence aggregate demand.

The *IS* Curve

One way to think about the *IS* curve is that it describes the combinations of income Y and the interest rate r that satisfy an equation we first saw in Chapter 3:

$$Y = C(Y - T) + I(r) + G.$$

This equation combines the national income accounts identity, the consumption function, and the investment function. It states that the quantity of goods produced, Y, must equal the quantity of goods demanded, $C + I + G$.

We can learn more about the *IS* curve by considering the special case in which the consumption function and investment function are linear. That is, suppose that the consumption function is

$$C(Y - T) = a + b(Y - T),$$

where a and b are numbers greater than zero. The parameter b is the marginal propensity to consume, so we expect b to be between zero and one. The parameter a influences the level of consumption; it captures everything that affects consumer spending other than disposable income. Similarly, suppose the investment function is

$$I(r) = c - dr,$$

where c and d also are numbers greater than zero. The parameter d determines how much investment responds to the interest rate; because investment rises when the interest rate falls, there is a minus sign in front of d. The parameter c influences the level of investment; it captures everything that affects investment spending other than the interest rate.

We can now derive an algebraic expression for the *IS* curve and see what influences the *IS* curve's position and slope. If we substitute the consumption and investment functions into the goods-market equilibrium condition, we obtain

$$Y = [a + b(Y - T)] + (c - dr) + G.$$

Note that Y shows up on both sides of this equation. We can simplify this equation by bringing all the Y terms to the left-hand side and rearranging the terms on the right-hand side:

$$Y - bY = (a + c) + (G - bT) - dr.$$

We solve for Y to get

$$Y = \frac{a + c}{1 - b} + \frac{1}{1 - b}G + \frac{-b}{1 - b}T + \frac{-d}{1 - b}r.$$

This equation expresses the *IS* curve algebraically. It tells us the level of income Y for any given interest rate r and fiscal policy G and T. Holding fiscal policy fixed, the equation gives us a relationship between the interest rate and the level of income: the higher the interest rate, the lower the level of income. The *IS* curve graphs this equation for different values of Y and r given fixed values of G and T.

Using this last equation, we can verify our previous conclusions about the *IS* curve. First, because the coefficient of the interest rate is negative, the *IS* curve slopes downward: higher interest rates reduce income. Second, because the coefficient of government purchases is positive, an increase in government purchases shifts the *IS* curve to the right. Third, because the coefficient of taxes is negative, an increase in taxes shifts the *IS* curve to the left.

The coefficient of the interest rate, $-d/(1 - b)$, tells us what determines whether the *IS* curve is steep or flat. If investment is highly sensitive to the interest rate, then d is large, and income is highly sensitive to the interest rate as well. In this case, small changes in the interest rate lead to large changes in income: the *IS* curve is relatively flat. Conversely, if investment is not very sensitive to the interest rate, then d is small, and income is also not very sensitive to the interest rate. In this case, large changes in interest rates lead to small changes in income: the *IS* curve is relatively steep.

Similarly, the slope of the *IS* curve depends on the marginal propensity to consume b. The larger the marginal propensity to consume, the larger the change in income resulting from a given change in the interest rate. The reason is that a large marginal propensity to consume leads to a large multiplier for changes in investment. The larger the multiplier, the larger the impact of a change in investment on income, and the flatter the *IS* curve.

The marginal propensity to consume b also determines how much changes in fiscal policy shift the *IS* curve. The coefficient of G, $1/(1 - b)$, is the government-purchases multiplier in the Keynesian cross. Similarly, the coefficient of T, $-b/(1 - b)$, is the tax multiplier in the Keynesian cross. The larger the marginal propensity to consume, the greater the multiplier, and thus the greater the shift in the *IS* curve that arises from a change in fiscal policy.

The *LM* Curve

The *LM* curve describes the combinations of income Y and the interest rate r that satisfy the money-market equilibrium condition

$$M/P = L(r, Y).$$

This equation simply equates money supply and money demand.

We can learn more about the *LM* curve by considering the case in which the money demand function is linear—that is,

$$L(r, Y) = eY - fr,$$

where e and f are numbers greater than zero. The value of e determines how much the demand for money rises when income rises. The value of f determines how much the demand for money falls when the interest rate rises. There is a minus sign in front of the interest rate term because money demand is inversely related to the interest rate.

The equilibrium in the money market is now described by

$$M/P = eY - fr.$$

To see what this equation implies, rearrange the terms so that r is on the left-hand side. We obtain

$$r = (e/f)Y - (1/f)M/P.$$

This equation gives us the interest rate that equilibrates the money market for any values of income and real money balances. The *LM* curve graphs this equation for different values of Y and r given a fixed value of M/P.

From this last equation, we can verify some of our conclusions about the *LM* curve. First, because the coefficient of income is positive, the *LM* curve slopes upward: higher income requires a higher interest rate to equilibrate the money market. Second, because the coefficient of real money balances is negative, decreases in real balances shift the *LM* curve upward, and increases in real balances shift the *LM* curve downward.

From the coefficient of income, e/f, we can see what determines whether the *LM* curve is steep or flat. If money demand is not very sensitive to the level of income, then e is small. In this case, only a small change in the interest rate is necessary to offset the small increase in money demand caused by a change in income: the *LM* curve is relatively flat. Similarly, if the quantity of money demanded is not very sensitive to the interest rate, then f is small. In this case, a shift in money demand due to a change in income leads to a large change in the equilibrium interest rate: the *LM* curve is relatively steep.

The Aggregate Demand Curve

To find the aggregate demand equation, we must find the level of income that satisfies both the *IS* equation and the *LM* equation. To do this, substitute the *LM* equation for the interest rate r into the *IS* equation to obtain

$$Y = \frac{a + c}{1 - b} + \frac{1}{1 - b}G + \frac{-b}{1 - b}T + \frac{-d}{1 - b}\left(\frac{e}{f}Y - \frac{1}{f}\frac{M}{P}\right).$$

With some algebraic manipulation, we can solve for Y. The final equation for Y is

$$Y = \frac{z(a + c)}{1 - b} + \frac{z}{1 - b}G + \frac{-zb}{1 - b}T + \frac{d}{(1 - b)[f + de/(1 - b)]}\frac{M}{P},$$

where $z = f/[f + de/(1 - b)]$ is a composite of some of the parameters and is between zero and one.

This last equation expresses the aggregate demand curve algebraically. It says that income depends on fiscal policy, G and T, monetary policy M, and the price level P. The aggregate demand curve graphs this equation for different values of Y and P given fixed values of G, T, and M.

We can explain the slope and position of the aggregate demand curve with this equation. First, the aggregate demand curve slopes downward, because an increase in P lowers M/P and thus lowers Y. Second, increases in the money supply raise income and shift the aggregate demand curve to the right. Third, increases in government purchases or decreases in taxes also raise income and shift the aggregate demand curve to the right. Note that, because z is less than one, the multipliers for fiscal policy are smaller in the *IS-LM* model than in the Keynesian cross. Hence, the parameter z reflects the crowding out of investment discussed earlier.

Finally, this equation shows the relationship between the aggregate demand curve derived in this chapter from the *IS-LM* model and the aggregate demand curve derived in Chapter 9 from the quantity theory of money. The quantity theory assumes that the interest rate does not influence the quantity of real money balances demanded. Put differently, the quantity theory assumes that the parameter f equals zero. If f equals zero, then the composite parameter z also equals zero, so fiscal policy does not influence aggregate demand. Thus, the aggregate demand curve derived in Chapter 9 is a special case of the aggregate demand curve derived here.

CASE STUDY

The Effectiveness of Monetary and Fiscal Policy

Economists have long debated whether monetary or fiscal policy exerts a more powerful influence on aggregate demand. According to the *IS-LM* model, the answer to this question depends on the parameters of the *IS* and *LM* curves. Therefore, economists have spent much energy arguing about the size of these parameters. The most hotly contested parameters are those that describe the influence of the interest rate on economic decisions.

Those economists who believe that fiscal policy is more potent than monetary policy argue that the responsiveness of investment to the interest rate—measured by the parameter d—is small. If you look at the algebraic equation for aggregate demand, you will see that a small value of d implies a small effect of the money supply on income. The reason is that when d is small, the *IS* curve is nearly vertical, and shifts in the *LM* curve do not cause much of a change in income. In addition, a small value of d implies a large value of z, which in turn implies that fiscal policy has a large effect on income. The reason for this large effect is that when investment is not very responsive to the interest rate, there is little crowding out.

Those economists who believe that monetary policy is more potent than fiscal policy argue that the responsiveness of money demand to the interest rate—measured by the parameter f—is small. When f is small, z is small, and fiscal policy has a small effect on income; in this case, the *LM* curve is nearly vertical. In addition, when f is small, changes in the money supply have a large effect on income.

Few economists today endorse either of these extreme views. The evidence indicates that the interest rate affects both investment and money demand. This finding implies that both monetary and fiscal policy are important determinants of aggregate demand.

MORE PROBLEMS AND APPLICATIONS

1. Give an algebraic answer to each of the following questions. Then explain in words the economics that underlies your answer.
   a. How does the sensitivity of investment to the interest rate affect the slope of the aggregate demand curve?
   b. How does the sensitivity of money demand to the interest rate affect the slope of the aggregate demand curve?
   c. How does the marginal propensity to consume affect the response of aggregate demand to changes in government purchases?

CHAPTER 12

The Open Economy Revisited: The Mundell-Fleming Model and the Exchange-Rate Regime

The world is still a closed economy, but its regions and countries are becoming increasingly open. . . . The international economic climate has changed in the direction of financial integration, and this has important implications for economic policy.

— *Robert Mundell, 1963*

When conducting monetary and fiscal policy, policymakers often look beyond their own country's borders. Even if domestic prosperity is their sole objective, it is necessary for them to consider the rest of the world. The international flow of goods and services and the international flow of capital can affect an economy in profound ways. Policymakers ignore these effects at their peril.

In this chapter we extend our analysis of aggregate demand to include international trade and finance. The model developed in this chapter is called the **Mundell-Fleming model.** This model has been described as "the dominant policy paradigm for studying open-economy monetary and fiscal policy." In 1999, Robert Mundell was awarded the Nobel Prize for his work in open-economy macroeconomics, including this model.[1]

The Mundell-Fleming model is a close relative of the *IS-LM* model. Both models stress the interaction between the goods market and the money market. Both models assume that the price level is fixed and then show what causes short-run fluctuations in aggregate income (or, equivalently, shifts in the aggregate demand curve).

[1] The quotation is from Maurice Obstfeld and Kenneth Rogoff, *Foundations of International Finance* (Cambridge, MA: MIT Press, 1996)—a leading graduate-level textbook in open-economy macroeconomics. The Mundell-Fleming model was developed in the early 1960s. Mundell's contributions are collected in Robert A. Mundell, *International Economics* (New York: Macmillan, 1968). For Fleming's contribution, see J. Marcus Fleming, "Domestic Financial Policies Under Fixed and Under Floating Exchange Rates," *IMF Staff Papers* 9 (November 1962): 369–379. Fleming died in 1976, so he was not eligible to share in the Nobel award.

The key difference is that the *IS-LM* model assumes a closed economy, whereas the Mundell-Fleming model assumes an open economy. The Mundell-Fleming model extends the short-run model of national income from Chapters 10 and 11 by including the effects of international trade and finance discussed in Chapter 5.

The Mundell-Fleming model makes one important and extreme assumption: it assumes that the economy being studied is a small open economy with perfect capital mobility. That is, the economy can borrow or lend as much as it wants in world financial markets and, as a result, the economy's interest rate is determined by the world interest rate. Here is how Mundell himself explained, in his original 1963 article, why he made this assumption:

> In order to present my conclusions in the simplest possible way and to bring the implications for policy into sharpest relief, I assume the extreme degree of mobility that prevails when a country cannot maintain an interest rate different from the general level prevailing abroad. This assumption will overstate the case but it has the merit of posing a stereotype towards which international financial relations seem to be heading. At the same time it might be argued that the assumption is not far from the truth in those financial centers, of which Zurich, Amsterdam, and Brussels may be taken as examples, where the authorities already recognize their lessening ability to dominate money market conditions and insulate them from foreign influences. It should also have a high degree of relevance to a country like Canada whose financial markets are dominated to a great degree by the vast New York market.

As we will see, Mundell's assumption of a small open economy with perfect capital mobility will prove useful in developing a tractable and illuminating model.[2]

One lesson from the Mundell-Fleming model is that the behavior of an economy depends on the exchange-rate system it has adopted. Indeed, the model was first developed in large part to understand how alternative exchange-rate regimes work and how the choice of exchange-rate regime impinges on monetary and fiscal policy. We begin by assuming that the economy operates with a floating exchange rate. That is, we assume that the central bank allows the exchange rate to adjust to changing economic conditions. We then examine how the economy operates under a fixed exchange rate. After developing the model, we will be in a position to address an important policy question: What exchange-rate system should a nation adopt?

12-1 The Mundell-Fleming Model

In this section we construct the Mundell-Fleming model, and in the following sections we use the model to examine the impact of various policies. As you will see, the Mundell-Fleming model is built from components we have used in previous chapters. But these pieces are put together in a new way to address a new set of questions.

---

[2] This assumption—and thus the Mundell-Fleming model—does not apply exactly to a large open economy such as the United States. In the conclusion to this chapter (and more fully in the appendix), we consider what happens in the more complex case in which international capital mobility is less than perfect or a nation is so large that it can influence world financial markets.

The Key Assumption: Small Open Economy With Perfect Capital Mobility

Let's begin with the assumption of a small open economy with perfect capital mobility. As we saw in Chapter 5, this assumption means that the interest rate in this economy r is determined by the world interest rate r^*. Mathematically, we can write this assumption as

$$r = r^*.$$

This world interest rate is assumed to be exogenously fixed because the economy is sufficiently small relative to the world economy that it can borrow or lend as much as it wants in world financial markets without affecting the world interest rate.

Although the idea of perfect capital mobility is expressed with a simple equation, it is important not to lose sight of the sophisticated process that this equation represents. Imagine that some event were to occur that would normally raise the interest rate (such as a decline in domestic saving). In a small open economy, the domestic interest rate might rise by a little bit for a short time, but as soon as it did, foreigners would see the higher interest rate and start lending to this country (by, for instance, buying this country's bonds). The capital inflow would drive the domestic interest rate back toward r^*. Similarly, if any event were ever to start driving the domestic interest rate downward, capital would flow out of the country to earn a higher return abroad, and this capital outflow would drive the domestic interest rate back up to r^*. Hence, the $r = r^*$ equation represents the assumption that the international flow of capital is rapid enough to keep the domestic interest rate equal to the world interest rate.

The Goods Market and the *IS** Curve

The Mundell-Fleming model describes the market for goods and services much as the *IS-LM* model does, but it adds a new term for net exports. In particular, the goods market is represented with the following equation:

$$Y = C(Y - T) + I(r) + G + NX(e).$$

This equation states that aggregate income Y is the sum of consumption C, investment I, government purchases G, and net exports NX. Consumption depends positively on disposable income $Y - T$. Investment depends negatively on the interest rate. Net exports depend negatively on the exchange rate e. As before, we define the exchange rate e as the amount of foreign currency per unit of domestic currency—for example, e might be 100 yen per dollar.

You may recall that in Chapter 5 we related net exports to the real exchange rate (the relative price of goods at home and abroad) rather than the nominal exchange rate (the relative price of domestic and foreign currencies). If e is the nominal exchange rate, then the real exchange rate ϵ equals eP/P^*, where P is the domestic price level and P^* is the foreign price level. The Mundell-Fleming model, however, assumes that the price levels at home and abroad are fixed, so the real exchange rate is proportional to the nominal exchange rate. That is, when the nominal exchange rate appreciates (say, from 100 to 120 yen per dollar), foreign goods become cheaper compared to domestic goods, and this causes exports to fall and imports to rise.

The goods-market equilibrium condition above has two financial variables affecting expenditure on goods and services (the interest rate and the exchange rate), but the situation can be simplified using the assumption of perfect capital mobility, so $r = r^*$. We obtain

$$Y = C(Y - T) + I(r^*) + G + NX(e).$$

Let's call this the IS^* equation. (The asterisk reminds us that the equation holds the interest rate constant at the world interest rate r^*.) We can illustrate this equation on a graph in which income is on the horizontal axis and the exchange rate is on the vertical axis. This curve is shown in panel (c) of Figure 12-1.

FIGURE 12-1

The *IS Curve** The *IS** curve is derived from the net-exports schedule and the Keynesian cross. Panel (a) shows the net-exports schedule: an increase in the exchange rate from e_1 to e_2 lowers net exports from $NX(e_1)$ to $NX(e_2)$. Panel (b) shows the Keynesian cross: a decrease in net exports from $NX(e_1)$ to $NX(e_2)$ shifts the planned-expenditure schedule downward and reduces income from Y_1 to Y_2. Panel (c) shows the *IS** curve summarizing this relationship between the exchange rate and income: the higher the exchange rate, the lower the level of income.

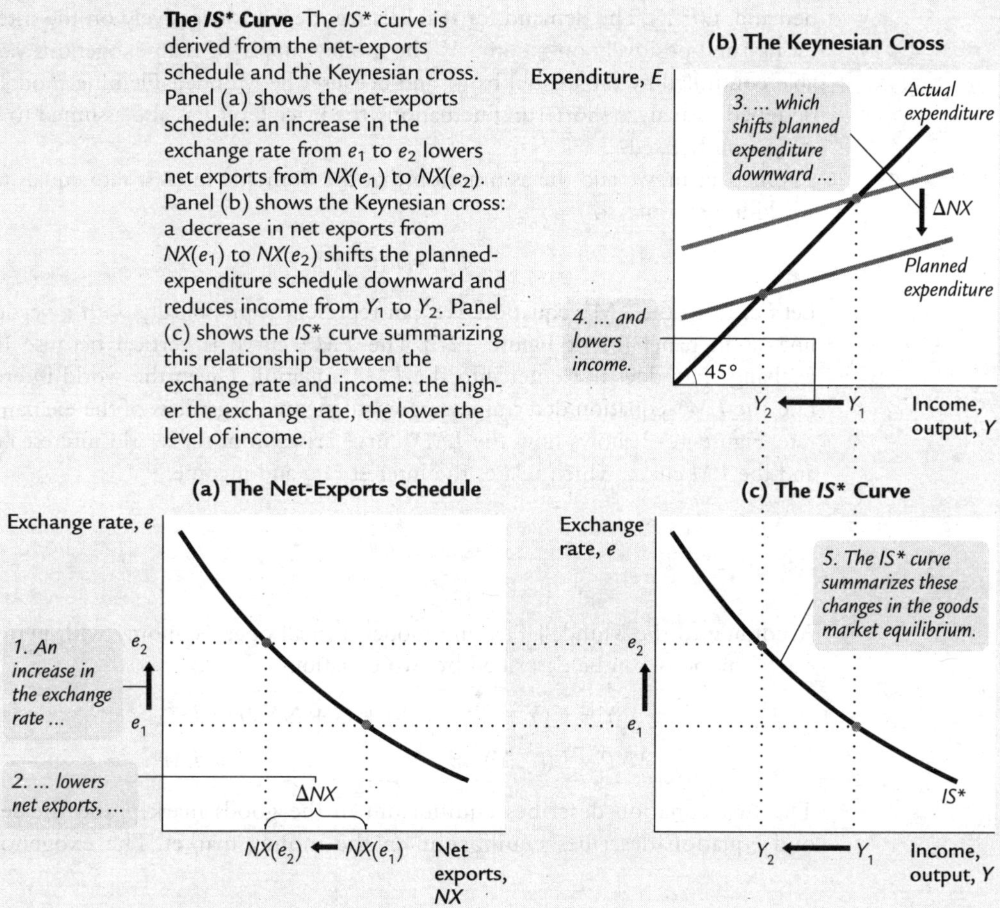

The IS^* curve slopes downward because a higher exchange rate reduces net exports, which in turn lowers aggregate income. To show how this works, the other panels of Figure 12-1 combine the net-exports schedule and the Keynesian cross to derive the IS^* curve. In panel (a), an increase in the exchange rate from e_1 to e_2 lowers net exports from $NX(e_1)$ to $NX(e_2)$. In panel (b), the reduction in net exports shifts the planned-expenditure schedule downward and thus lowers income from Y_1 to Y_2. The IS^* curve summarizes this relationship between the exchange rate e and income Y.

The Money Market and the *LM** Curve

The Mundell-Fleming model represents the money market with an equation that should be familiar from the *IS-LM* model:

$$M/P = L(r, Y).$$

This equation states that the supply of real money balances, M/P, equals the demand, $L(r, Y)$. The demand for real balances depends negatively on the interest rate and positively on income Y. The money supply M is an exogenous variable controlled by the central bank, and because the Mundell-Fleming model is designed to analyze short-run fluctuations, the price level P is also assumed to be exogenously fixed.

Once again, we add the assumption that the domestic interest rate equals the world interest rate, so $r = r^*$:

$$M/P = L(r^*, Y).$$

Let's call this the LM* equation. We can represent it graphically with a vertical line, as in panel (b) of Figure 12-2. The LM^* curve is vertical because the exchange rate does not enter into the LM^* equation. Given the world interest rate, the LM^* equation determines aggregate income, regardless of the exchange rate. Figure 12-2 shows how the LM^* curve arises from the world interest rate and the LM curve, which relates the interest rate and income.

Putting the Pieces Together

According to the Mundell-Fleming model, a small open economy with perfect capital mobility can be described by two equations:

$$Y = C(Y - T) + I(r^*) + G + NX(e) \qquad IS^*,$$

$$M/P = L(r^*, Y) \qquad LM^*.$$

The first equation describes equilibrium in the goods market, and the second equation describes equilibrium in the money market. The exogenous

FIGURE 12-2

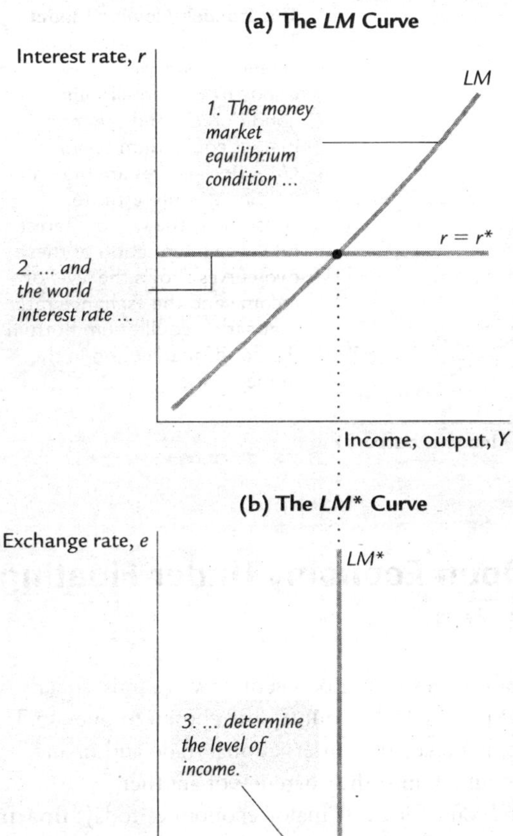

The LM^* Curve Panel (a) shows the standard LM curve [which graphs the equation $M/P = L(r,Y)$] together with a horizontal line representing the world interest rate r^*. The intersection of these two curves determines the level of income, regardless of the exchange rate. Therefore, as panel (b) shows, the LM^* curve is vertical.

variables are fiscal policy G and T, monetary policy M, the price level P, and the world interest rate r^*. The endogenous variables are income Y and the exchange rate e.

Figure 12-3 illustrates these two relationships. The equilibrium for the economy is found where the IS^* curve and the LM^* curve intersect. This intersection shows the exchange rate and the level of income at which the goods market and the money market are in equilibrium. With this diagram, we can use the Mundell-Fleming model to show how aggregate income Y and the exchange rate e respond to changes in policy.

FIGURE 12-3

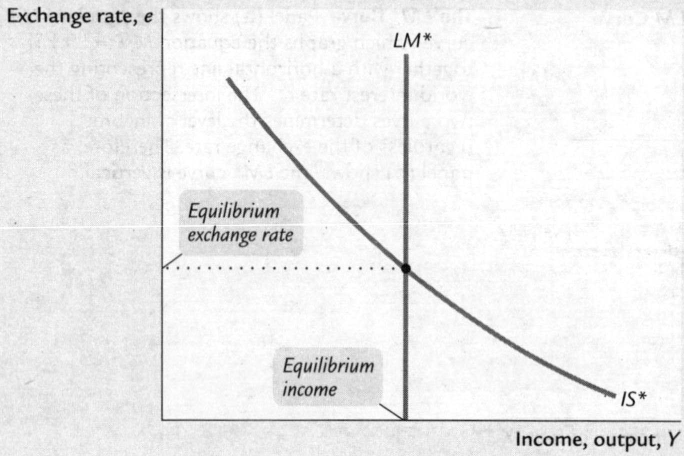

The Mundell-Fleming Model This graph of the Mundell-Fleming model plots the goods-market equilibrium condition IS^* and the money-market equilibrium condition LM^*. Both curves are drawn holding the interest rate constant at the world interest rate. The intersection of these two curves shows the level of income and the exchange rate that satisfy equilibrium both in the goods market and in the money market.

12-2 The Small Open Economy Under Floating Exchange Rates

Before analyzing the impact of policies in an open economy, we must specify the international monetary system in which the country has chosen to operate. That is, we must consider how people engaged in international trade and finance can convert the currency of one country into the currency of another.

We start with the system relevant for most major economies today: **floating exchange rates**. Under a system of floating exchange rates, the exchange rate is set by market forces and is allowed to fluctuate in response to changing economic conditions. In this case, the exchange rate e adjusts to achieve simultaneous equilibrium in the goods market and the money market. When something happens to change that equilibrium, the exchange rate is allowed to move to a new equilibrium value.

Let's now consider three policies that can change the equilibrium: fiscal policy, monetary policy, and trade policy. Our goal is to use the Mundell-Fleming model to show the impact of policy changes and to understand the economic forces at work as the economy moves from one equilibrium to another.

Fiscal Policy

Suppose that the government stimulates domestic spending by increasing government purchases or by cutting taxes. Because such expansionary fiscal policy increases planned expenditure, it shifts the IS^* curve to the right, as in Figure 12-4. As a result, the exchange rate appreciates, while the level of income remains the same.

FIGURE 12-4

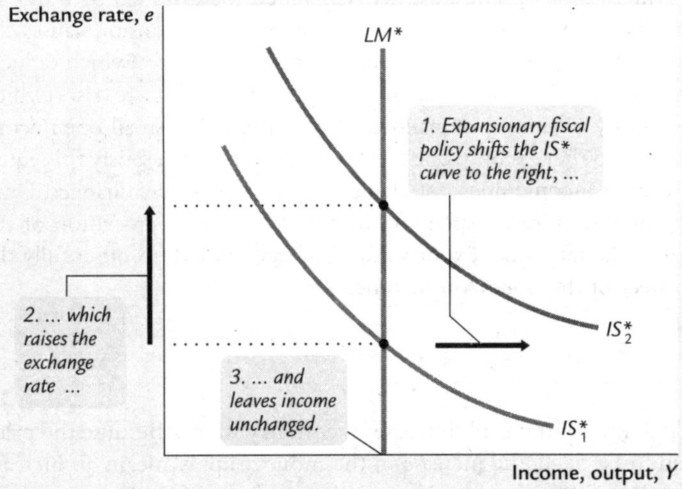

A Fiscal Expansion Under Floating Exchange Rates An increase in government purchases or a decrease in taxes shifts the IS^* curve to the right. This raises the exchange rate but has no effect on income.

Notice that fiscal policy has very different effects in a small open economy than it does in a closed economy. In the closed-economy *IS-LM* model, a fiscal expansion raises income, whereas in a small open economy with a floating exchange rate, a fiscal expansion leaves income at the same level. Mechanically, the difference arises because the LM^* curve is vertical, while the *LM* curve we used to study a closed economy is upward sloping. But this explanation is not very satisfying. What are the economic forces that lie behind the different outcomes? To answer this question, we must think through what is happening to the international flow of capital and the implications of these capital flows for the domestic economy.

The interest rate and the exchange rate are the key variables in the story. When income rises in a closed economy, the interest rate rises, because higher income increases the demand for money. That is not possible in a small open economy because, as soon as the interest rate starts to rise above the world interest rate r^*, capital quickly flows in from abroad to take advantage of the higher return. This capital inflow not only pushes the interest rate back to r^* but it also has another effect: because foreign investors need to buy the domestic currency to invest in the domestic economy, the capital inflow increases the demand for the domestic currency in the market for foreign-currency exchange, bidding up the value of the domestic currency. The appreciation of the domestic currency makes domestic goods expensive relative to foreign goods, reducing net exports. The fall in net exports exactly offsets the effects of the expansionary fiscal policy on income.

Why is the fall in net exports so great that it renders fiscal policy powerless to influence income? To answer this question, consider the equation that describes the money market:

$$M/P = L(r, Y).$$

In both closed and open economies, the quantity of real money balances supplied M/P is fixed by the central bank (which sets M) and the assumption of sticky prices (which fixes P). The quantity demanded (determined by r and Y) must equal this fixed supply. In a closed economy, a fiscal expansion causes the equilibrium interest rate to rise. This increase in the interest rate (which reduces the quantity of money demanded) allows equilibrium income to rise (which increases the quantity of money demanded). By contrast, in a small open economy, r is fixed at r^*, so there is only one level of income that can satisfy this equation, and this level of income does not change when fiscal policy changes. Thus, when the government increases spending or cuts taxes, the appreciation of the exchange rate and the fall in net exports must be large enough to offset fully the expansionary effect of the policy on income.

Monetary Policy

Suppose now that the central bank increases the money supply. Because the price level is assumed to be fixed, the increase in the money supply means an increase in real money balances. The increase in real balances shifts the LM^* curve to the right, as in Figure 12-5. Hence, an increase in the money supply raises income and lowers the exchange rate.

Although monetary policy influences income in an open economy, as it does in a closed economy, the monetary transmission mechanism is different. Recall that in a closed economy an increase in the money supply increases spending because it lowers the interest rate and stimulates investment. In a small open economy, this channel of monetary transmission is not available because the interest rate is fixed by the world interest rate. So how does monetary policy influence spending? To answer this question, once again we need

FIGURE 12-5

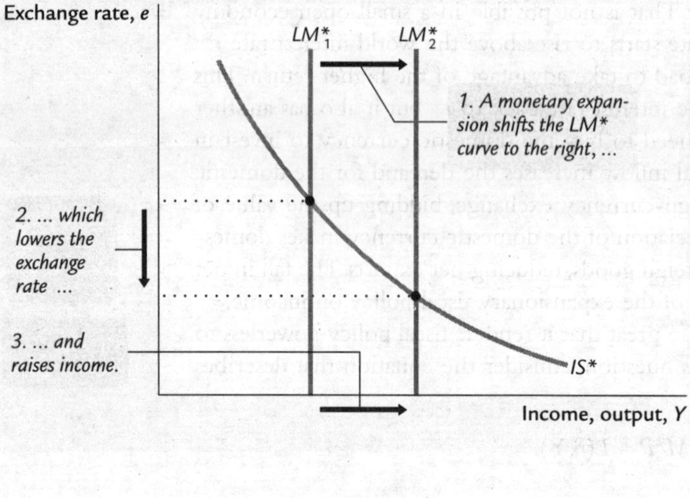

A Monetary Expansion Under Floating Exchange Rates An increase in the money supply shifts the LM^* curve to the right, lowering the exchange rate and raising income.

to think about the international flow of capital and its implications for the domestic economy.

The interest rate and the exchange rate are again the key variables. As soon as an increase in the money supply starts putting downward pressure on the domestic interest rate, capital flows out of the economy, as investors seek a higher return elsewhere. This capital outflow prevents the domestic interest rate from falling below the world interest rate r^*. It also has another effect: because investing abroad requires converting domestic currency into foreign currency, the capital outflow increases the supply of the domestic currency in the market for foreign-currency exchange, causing the domestic currency to depreciate in value. This depreciation makes domestic goods inexpensive relative to foreign goods, stimulating net exports. Hence, in a small open economy, monetary policy influences income by altering the exchange rate rather than the interest rate.

Trade Policy

Suppose that the government reduces the demand for imported goods by imposing an import quota or a tariff. What happens to aggregate income and the exchange rate? How does the economy reach its new equilibrium?

Because net exports equal exports minus imports, a reduction in imports means an increase in net exports. That is, the net-exports schedule shifts to the right, as in Figure 12-6. This shift in the net-exports schedule increases planned expenditure and thus moves the IS^* curve to the right. Because the LM^* curve is vertical, the trade restriction raises the exchange rate but does not affect income.

The economic forces behind this transition are similar to the case of expansionary fiscal policy. Because net exports are a component of GDP, the rightward shift in the net-exports schedule, other things equal, puts upward pressure on income Y; an increase in Y, in turn, increases money demand and puts upward pressure on the interest rate r. Foreign capital quickly responds by flowing into the domestic economy, pushing the interest rate back to the world interest rate r^* and causing the domestic currency to appreciate in value. Finally, the appreciation of the currency makes domestic goods more expensive relative to foreign goods, which decreases net exports NX and returns income Y to its initial level.

Often a stated goal of policies to restrict trade is to alter the trade balance NX. Yet, as we first saw in Chapter 5, such policies do not necessarily have that effect. The same conclusion holds in the Mundell-Fleming model under floating exchange rates. Recall that

$$NX(e) = Y - C(Y - T) - I(r^*) - G.$$

Because a trade restriction does not affect income, consumption, investment, or government purchases, it does not affect the trade balance. Although the shift in the net-exports schedule tends to raise NX, the increase in the exchange rate reduces NX by the same amount. The overall effect is simply *less trade*. The domestic economy imports less than it did before the trade restriction, but it exports less as well.

FIGURE 12-6

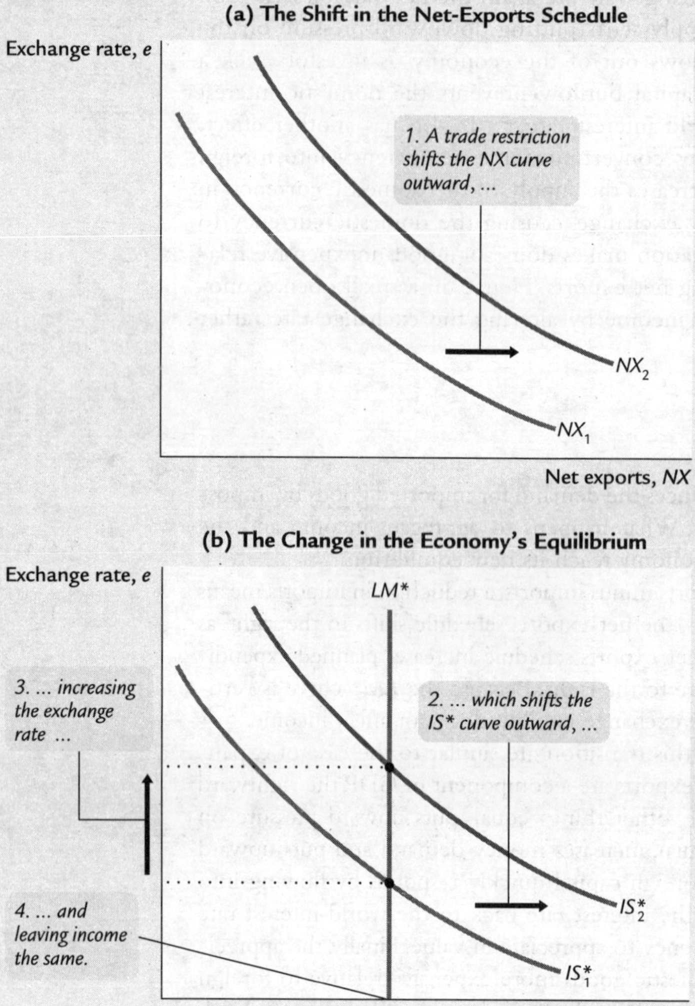

A Trade Restriction Under Floating Exchange Rates A tariff or an import quota shifts the net-exports schedule in panel (a) to the right. As a result, the IS^* curve in panel (b) shifts to the right, raising the exchange rate and leaving income unchanged.

12-3 The Small Open Economy Under Fixed Exchange Rates

We now turn to the second type of exchange-rate system: **fixed exchange rates**. Under a fixed exchange rate, the central bank announces a value for the exchange rate and stands ready to buy and sell the domestic currency to keep the exchange rate at its announced level. In the 1950s and 1960s, most of the world's major economies, including the United States, operated within the *Bretton Woods* *system*—an international monetary system under which most governments agreed to fix exchange rates. The world abandoned this system in the early 1970s, and most exchange rates were allowed to float. Yet fixed exchange rates are not merely of historical interest. More recently, China fixed the value of its currency against the U.S. dollar—a policy that, as we will see, was a source of some tension between the two countries.

In this section we discuss how such a system works, and we examine the impact of economic policies on an economy with a fixed exchange rate. Later in the chapter we examine the pros and cons of fixed exchange rates.

How a Fixed-Exchange-Rate System Works

Under a system of fixed exchange rates, a central bank stands ready to buy or sell the domestic currency for foreign currencies at a predetermined price. For example, suppose that the Fed announced that it was going to fix the exchange rate at 100 yen per dollar. It would then stand ready to give $1 in exchange for 100 yen or to give 100 yen in exchange for $1. To carry out this policy, the Fed would need a reserve of dollars (which it can print) and a reserve of yen (which it must have purchased previously).

A fixed exchange rate dedicates a country's monetary policy to the single goal of keeping the exchange rate at the announced level. In other words, the essence of a fixed-exchange-rate system is the commitment of the central bank to allow the money supply to adjust to whatever level will ensure that the equilibrium exchange rate in the market for foreign-currency exchange equals the announced exchange rate. Moreover, as long as the central bank stands ready to buy or sell foreign currency at the fixed exchange rate, the money supply adjusts automatically to the necessary level.

To see how fixing the exchange rate determines the money supply, consider the following example. Suppose that the Fed announces that it will fix the exchange rate at 100 yen per dollar, but, in the current equilibrium with the current money supply, the market exchange rate is 150 yen per dollar. This situation is illustrated in panel (a) of Figure 12-7. Notice that there is a profit opportunity: an arbitrageur could buy 300 yen in the foreign-exchange market for $2, and then sell the yen to the Fed for $3, making a $1 profit. When the Fed buys these yen from the arbitrageur, the dollars it pays for them automatically increase the money supply. The rise in the money supply shifts the LM^* curve to the right, lowering the equilibrium exchange rate. In this way, the money supply continues to rise until the equilibrium exchange rate falls to the announced level.

Conversely, suppose that when the Fed announces that it will fix the exchange rate at 100 yen per dollar, the equilibrium has a market exchange rate of 50 yen per dollar. Panel (b) of Figure 12-7 shows this situation. In this case, an arbitrageur could make a profit by buying 100 yen from the Fed for $1 and then selling the yen in the marketplace for $2. When the Fed sells these yen, the $1 it receives automatically reduces the money supply. The fall in the money supply shifts the LM^* curve to the left, raising the equilibrium exchange rate. The money supply continues to fall until the equilibrium exchange rate rises to the announced level.

FIGURE 12-7

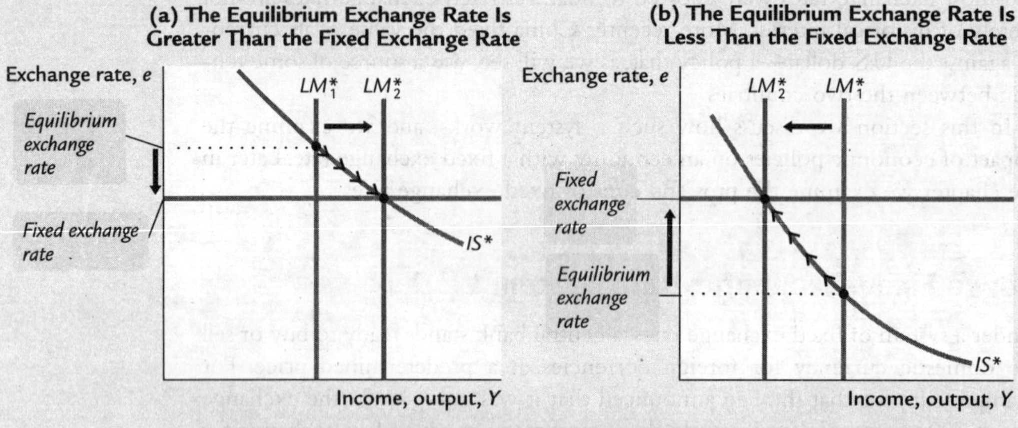

How a Fixed Exchange Rate Governs the Money Supply In panel (a), the equilibrium exchange rate initially exceeds the fixed level. Arbitrageurs will buy foreign currency in foreign-exchange markets and sell it to the Fed for a profit. This process automatically increases the money supply, shifting the *LM** curve to the right and lowering the exchange rate. In panel (b), the equilibrium exchange rate is initially below the fixed level. Arbitrageurs will buy dollars in foreign-exchange markets and use them to buy foreign currency from the Fed. This process automatically reduces the money supply, shifting the *LM** curve to the left and raising the exchange rate.

It is important to understand that this exchange-rate system fixes the *nominal* exchange rate. Whether it also fixes the real exchange rate depends on the time horizon under consideration. If prices are flexible, as they are in the long run, then the real exchange rate can change even while the nominal exchange rate is fixed. Therefore, in the long run described in Chapter 5, a policy to fix the nominal exchange rate would not influence any real variable, including the real exchange rate. A fixed nominal exchange rate would influence only the money supply and the price level. Yet in the short run described by the Mundell-Fleming model, prices are fixed, so a fixed nominal exchange rate implies a fixed real exchange rate as well.

CASE STUDY

The International Gold Standard

During the late nineteenth and early twentieth centuries, most of the world's major economies operated under a gold standard. Each country maintained a reserve of gold and agreed to exchange one unit of its currency for a specified amount of gold. Through the gold standard, the world's economies maintained a system of fixed exchange rates.

To see how an international gold standard fixes exchange rates, suppose that the U.S. Treasury stands ready to buy or sell 1 ounce of gold for $100, and the Bank of England stands ready to buy or sell 1 ounce of gold for 100 pounds. Together, these policies fix the rate of exchange between dollars and pounds: $1 must trade for 1 pound. Otherwise, the law of one price would be violated, and it would be profitable to buy gold in one country and sell it in the other.

For example, suppose that the market exchange rate were 2 pounds per dollar. In this case, an arbitrageur could buy 200 pounds for $100, use the pounds to buy 2 ounces of gold from the Bank of England, bring the gold to the United States, and sell it to the Treasury for $200—making a $100 profit. Moreover, by bringing the gold to the United States from England, the arbitrageur would increase the money supply in the United States and decrease the money supply in England.

Thus, during the era of the gold standard, the international transport of gold by arbitrageurs was an automatic mechanism adjusting the money supply and stabilizing exchange rates. This system did not completely fix exchange rates, because shipping gold across the Atlantic was costly. Yet the international gold standard did keep the exchange rate within a range dictated by transportation costs. It thereby prevented large and persistent movements in exchange rates.[3]

Fiscal Policy

Let's now examine how economic policies affect a small open economy with a fixed exchange rate. Suppose that the government stimulates domestic spending by increasing government purchases or by cutting taxes. This policy shifts the IS^* curve to the right, as in Figure 12-8, putting upward pressure on the market

FIGURE 12-8

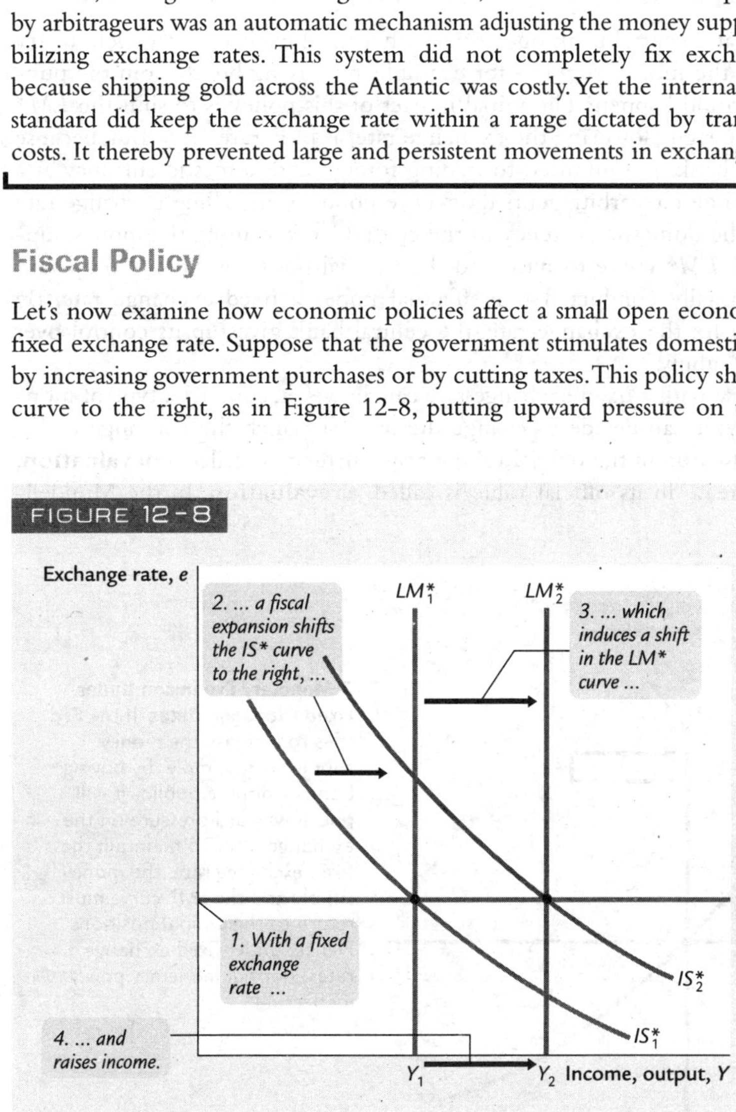

A Fiscal Expansion Under Fixed Exchange Rates A fiscal expansion shifts the IS^* curve to the right. To maintain the fixed exchange rate, the Fed must increase the money supply, thereby shifting the LM^* curve to the right. Hence, in contrast to the case of floating exchange rates, under fixed exchange rates a fiscal expansion raises income.

---

[3] For more on how the gold standard worked, see the essays in Barry Eichengreen, ed., *The Gold Standard in Theory and History* (New York: Methuen, 1985).

exchange rate. But because the central bank stands ready to trade foreign and domestic currency at the fixed exchange rate, arbitrageurs quickly respond to the rising exchange rate by selling foreign currency to the central bank, leading to an automatic monetary expansion. The rise in the money supply shifts the *LM** curve to the right. Thus, under a fixed exchange rate, a fiscal expansion raises aggregate income.

Monetary Policy

Imagine that a central bank operating with a fixed exchange rate were to try to increase the money supply—for example, by buying bonds from the public. What would happen? The initial impact of this policy is to shift the *LM** curve to the right, lowering the exchange rate, as in Figure 12-9. But, because the central bank is committed to trading foreign and domestic currency at a fixed exchange rate, arbitrageurs quickly respond to the falling exchange rate by selling the domestic currency to the central bank, causing the money supply and the *LM** curve to return to their initial positions. Hence, monetary policy as usually conducted is ineffectual under a fixed exchange rate. By agreeing to fix the exchange rate, the central bank gives up its control over the money supply.

A country with a fixed exchange rate can, however, conduct a type of monetary policy: it can decide to change the level at which the exchange rate is fixed. A reduction in the official value of the currency is called a **devaluation**, and an increase in its official value is called a **revaluation**. In the Mundell-

FIGURE 12-9

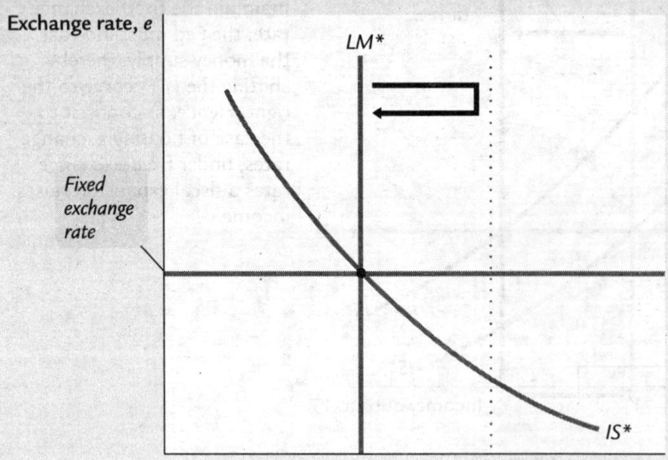

A Monetary Expansion Under Fixed Exchange Rates If the Fed tries to increase the money supply—for example, by buying bonds from the public—it will put downward pressure on the exchange rate. To maintain the fixed exchange rate, the money supply and the *LM** curve must return to their initial positions. Hence, under fixed exchange rates, normal monetary policy is ineffectual.

Fleming model, a devaluation shifts the LM^* curve to the right; it acts like an increase in the money supply under a floating exchange rate. A devaluation thus expands net exports and raises aggregate income. Conversely, a revaluation shifts the LM^* curve to the left, reduces net exports, and lowers aggregate income.

CASE STUDY

Devaluation and the Recovery From the Great Depression

The Great Depression of the 1930s was a global problem. Although events in the United States may have precipitated the downturn, all of the world's major economies experienced huge declines in production and employment. Yet not all governments responded to this calamity in the same way.

One key difference among governments was how committed they were to the fixed exchange rate set by the international gold standard. Some countries, such as France, Germany, Italy, and the Netherlands, maintained the old rate of exchange between gold and currency. Other countries, such as Denmark, Finland, Norway, Sweden, and the United Kingdom, reduced the amount of gold they would pay for each unit of currency by about 50 percent. By reducing the gold content of their currencies, these governments devalued their currencies relative to those of other countries.

The subsequent experience of these two groups of countries conforms to the prediction of the Mundell-Fleming model. Those countries that pursued a policy of devaluation recovered quickly from the Depression. The lower value of the currency raised the money supply, stimulated exports, and expanded production. By contrast, those countries that maintained the old exchange rate suffered longer with a depressed level of economic activity.[4]

Trade Policy

Suppose that the government reduces imports by imposing an import quota or a tariff. This policy shifts the net-exports schedule to the right and thus shifts the IS^* curve to the right, as in Figure 12-10. The shift in the IS^* curve tends to raise the exchange rate. To keep the exchange rate at the fixed level, the money supply must rise, shifting the LM^* curve to the right.

The result of a trade restriction under a fixed exchange rate is very different from that under a floating exchange rate. In both cases, a trade restriction shifts the net-exports schedule to the right, but only under a fixed exchange rate does a trade restriction increase net exports NX. The reason is that a trade

[4] Barry Eichengreen and Jeffrey Sachs, "Exchange Rates and Economic Recovery in the 1930s," *Journal of Economic History* 45 (December 1985): 925–946.

FIGURE 12-10

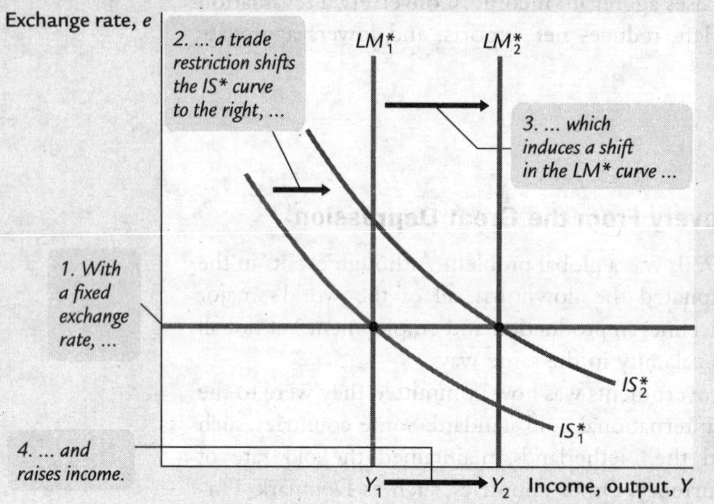

A Trade Restriction Under Fixed Exchange Rates A tariff or an import quota shifts the IS^* curve to the right. This induces an increase in the money supply to maintain the fixed exchange rate. Hence, aggregate income increases.

restriction under a fixed exchange rate induces monetary expansion rather than an appreciation of the exchange rate. The monetary expansion, in turn, raises aggregate income. Recall the accounting identity

$$NX = S - I.$$

When income rises, saving also rises, and this implies an increase in net exports.

Policy in the Mundell-Fleming Model: A Summary

The Mundell-Fleming model shows that the effect of almost any economic policy on a small open economy depends on whether the exchange rate is floating or fixed. Table 12-1 summarizes our analysis of the short-run effects of fiscal, monetary, and trade policies on income, the exchange rate, and the trade balance. What is most striking is that all of the results are different under floating and fixed exchange rates.

To be more specific, the Mundell-Fleming model shows that the power of monetary and fiscal policy to influence aggregate income depends on the exchange-rate regime. Under floating exchange rates, only monetary policy can affect income. The usual expansionary impact of fiscal policy is offset by a rise in the value of the currency and a decrease in net exports. Under fixed exchange rates, only fiscal policy can affect income. The normal potency of monetary policy is lost because the money supply is dedicated to maintaining the exchange rate at the announced level.

TABLE 12-1

The Mundell–Fleming Model: Summary of Policy Effects

	EXCHANGE-RATE REGIME					
	FLOATING			FIXED		
	IMPACT ON:					
Policy	Y	e	NX	Y	e	NX
Fiscal expansion	0	↑	↓	↑	0	0
Monetary expansion	↑	↓	↑	0	0	0
Import restriction	0	↑	0	↑	0	↑

Note: This table shows the direction of impact of various economic policies on income Y, the exchange rate e, and the trade balance NX. A "↑" indicates that the variable increases; a "↓" indicates that it decreases; a "0" indicates no effect. Remember that the exchange rate is defined as the amount of foreign currency per unit of domestic currency (for example, 100 yen per dollar).

12-4 Interest-Rate Differentials

So far, our analysis has assumed that the interest rate in a small open economy is equal to the world interest rate: $r = r^*$. To some extent, however, interest rates differ around the world. We now extend our analysis by considering the causes and effects of international interest-rate differentials.

Country Risk and Exchange-Rate Expectations

When we assumed earlier that the interest rate in our small open economy is determined by the world interest rate, we were applying the law of one price. We reasoned that if the domestic interest rate were above the world interest rate, people from abroad would lend to that country, driving the domestic interest rate down. And if the domestic interest rate were below the world interest rate, domestic residents would lend abroad to earn a higher return, driving the domestic interest rate up. In the end, the domestic interest rate would equal the world interest rate.

Why doesn't this logic always apply? There are two reasons.

One reason is country risk. When investors buy U.S. government bonds or make loans to U.S. corporations, they are fairly confident that they will be repaid with interest. By contrast, in some less developed countries, it is plausible to fear that a revolution or other political upheaval might lead to a default on loan repayments. Borrowers in such countries often have to pay higher interest rates to compensate lenders for this risk.

Another reason interest rates differ across countries is expected changes in the exchange rate. For example, suppose that people expect the Mexican peso to fall in value relative to the U.S. dollar. Then loans made in pesos will be repaid in a less valuable currency than loans made in dollars. To compensate for this expected fall in the Mexican currency, the interest rate in Mexico will be higher than the interest rate in the United States.

Thus, because of both country risk and expectations of future exchange-rate changes, the interest rate of a small open economy can differ from interest rates in other economies around the world. Let's now see how this fact affects our analysis.

Differentials in the Mundell-Fleming Model

To incorporate interest-rate differentials into the Mundell-Fleming model, we assume that the interest rate in our small open economy is determined by the world interest rate plus a risk premium θ:

$$r = r^* + \theta.$$

The risk premium is determined by the perceived political risk of making loans in a country and the expected change in the real exchange rate. For our purposes here, we can take the risk premium as exogenous in order to examine how changes in the risk premium affect the economy.

The model is largely the same as before. The two equations are

$$Y = C(Y - T) + I(r^* + \theta) + G + NX(e) \qquad IS^*,$$
$$M/P = L(r^* + \theta, Y) \qquad LM^*.$$

For any given fiscal policy, monetary policy, price level, and risk premium, these two equations determine the level of income and exchange rate that equilibrate the goods market and the money market. Holding constant the risk premium, the tools of monetary, fiscal, and trade policy work as we have already seen.

Now suppose that political turmoil causes the country's risk premium θ to rise. Because $r = r^* + \theta$, the most direct effect is that the domestic interest rate r rises. The higher interest rate, in turn, has two effects. First, the IS^* curve shifts to the left, because the higher interest rate reduces investment. Second, the LM^* curve shifts to the right, because the higher interest rate reduces the demand for money, and this allows a higher level of income for any given money supply. [Recall that Y must satisfy the equation $M/P = L(r^* + \theta, Y)$.] As Figure 12-11 shows, these two shifts cause income to rise and the currency to depreciate.

This analysis has an important implication: expectations about the exchange rate are partially self-fulfilling. For example, suppose that people come to believe that the Mexican peso will not be valuable in the future. Investors will place a larger risk premium on Mexican assets: θ will rise in Mexico. This expectation will drive up Mexican interest rates and, as we have just seen, will drive down the value of the Mexican currency. *Thus, the expectation that a currency will lose value in the future causes it to lose value today.*

One surprising—and perhaps inaccurate—prediction of this analysis is that an increase in country risk as measured by θ will cause the economy's income to increase. This occurs in Figure 12-11 because of the rightward shift in the LM^* curve. Although higher interest rates depress investment, the depreciation of the

FIGURE 12-11

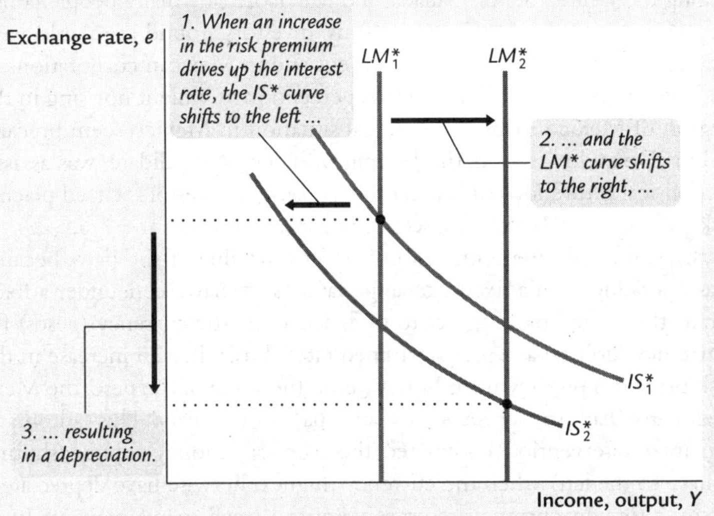

An Increase in the Risk Premium An increase in the risk premium associated with a country drives up its interest rate. Because the higher interest rate reduces investment, the *IS** curve shifts to the left. Because it also reduces money demand, the *LM** curve shifts to the right. Income rises, and the exchange rate depreciates.

currency stimulates net exports by an even greater amount. As a result, aggregate income rises.

There are three reasons why, in practice, such a boom in income does not occur. First, the central bank might want to avoid the large depreciation of the domestic currency and, therefore, may respond by decreasing the money supply M. Second, the depreciation of the domestic currency may suddenly increase the price of imported goods, causing an increase in the price level P. Third, when some event increases the country risk premium θ, residents of the country might respond to the same event by increasing their demand for money (for any given income and interest rate), because money is often the safest asset available. All three of these changes would tend to shift the *LM** curve toward the left, which mitigates the fall in the exchange rate but also tends to depress income.

Thus, increases in country risk are not desirable. In the short run, they typically lead to a depreciating currency and, through the three channels just described, falling aggregate income. In addition, because a higher interest rate reduces investment, the long-run implication is reduced capital accumulation and lower economic growth.

CASE STUDY

International Financial Crisis: Mexico 1994–1995

In August 1994, a Mexican peso was worth 30 cents. A year later, it was worth only 16 cents. What explains this massive fall in the value of the Mexican currency? Country risk is a large part of the story.

At the beginning of 1994, Mexico was a country on the rise. The recent passage of the North American Free Trade Agreement (NAFTA), which reduced trade barriers among the United States, Canada, and Mexico, made many people confident about the future of the Mexican economy. Investors around the world were eager to make loans to the Mexican government and to Mexican corporations.

Political developments soon changed that perception. A violent uprising in the Chiapas region of Mexico made the political situation in Mexico seem precarious. Then Luis Donaldo Colosio, the leading presidential candidate, was assassinated. The political future looked less certain, and many investors started placing a larger risk premium on Mexican assets.

At first, the rising risk premium did not affect the value of the peso, because Mexico was operating with a fixed exchange rate. As we have seen, under a fixed exchange rate, the central bank agrees to trade the domestic currency (pesos) for a foreign currency (dollars) at a predetermined rate. Thus, when an increase in the country risk premium put downward pressure on the value of the peso, the Mexican central bank had to accept pesos and pay out dollars. This automatic exchange-market intervention contracted the Mexican money supply (shifting the *LM** curve to the left) when the currency might otherwise have depreciated.

Yet Mexico's foreign-currency reserves were too small to maintain its fixed exchange rate. When Mexico ran out of dollars at the end of 1994, the Mexican government announced a devaluation of the peso. This decision had repercussions, however, because the government had repeatedly promised that it would not devalue. Investors became even more distrustful of Mexican policymakers and feared further Mexican devaluations.

Investors around the world (including those in Mexico) avoided buying Mexican assets. The country risk premium rose once again, adding to the upward pressure on interest rates and the downward pressure on the peso. The Mexican stock market plummeted. When the Mexican government needed to roll over some of its debt that was coming due, investors were unwilling to buy the new debt. Default appeared to be the government's only option. In just a few months, Mexico had gone from being a promising emerging economy to being a risky economy with a government on the verge of bankruptcy.

Then the United States stepped in. The U.S. government had three motives: to help its neighbor to the south, to prevent the massive illegal immigration that might follow government default and economic collapse, and to prevent the investor pessimism regarding Mexico from spreading to other developing countries. The U.S. government, together with the International Monetary Fund (IMF), led an international effort to bail out the Mexican government. In particular, the United States provided loan guarantees for Mexican government debt, which allowed the Mexican government to refinance the debt that was coming due. These loan guarantees helped restore confidence in the Mexican economy, thereby reducing to some extent the country risk premium.

Although the U.S. loan guarantees may well have stopped a bad situation from getting worse, they did not prevent the Mexican meltdown of 1994–1995 from being a painful experience for the Mexican people. Not only did the Mexican currency lose much of its value, but Mexico also went through a deep recession. Fortunately, by the late 1990s, the worst was over, and aggregate income was growing again. But the lesson from this experience is clear and could well apply again in the future: changes in perceived country risk, often attributable to political instability, are an important determinant of interest rates and exchange rates in small open economies.

CASE STUDY

International Financial Crisis: Asia 1997–1998

In 1997, as the Mexican economy was recovering from its financial crisis, a similar story started to unfold in several Asian economies, including Thailand, South Korea, and especially Indonesia. The symptoms were familiar: high interest rates, falling asset values, and a depreciating currency. In Indonesia, for instance, short-term nominal interest rates rose above 50 percent, the stock market lost about 90 percent of its value (measured in U.S. dollars), and the rupiah fell against the dollar by more than 80 percent. The crisis led to rising inflation in these countries (because the depreciating currency made imports more expensive) and to falling GDP (because high interest rates and reduced confidence depressed spending). Real GDP in Indonesia fell about 13 percent in 1998, making the downturn larger than any U.S. recession since the Great Depression of the 1930s.

What sparked this firestorm? The problem began in the Asian banking systems. For many years, the governments in the Asian nations had been more involved in managing the allocation of resources—in particular, financial resources—than is true in the United States and other developed countries. Some commentators had applauded this "partnership" between government and private enterprise and had even suggested that the United States should follow the example. Over time, however, it became clear that many Asian banks had been extending loans to those with the most political clout rather than to those with the most profitable investment projects. Once rising default rates started to expose this "crony capitalism," as it was then called, international investors started to lose confidence in the future of these economies. The risk premiums for Asian assets rose, causing interest rates to skyrocket and currencies to collapse.

International crises of confidence often involve a vicious circle that can amplify the problem. Here is one story about what happened in Asia:

1. Problems in the banking system eroded international confidence in these economies.
2. Loss of confidence raised risk premiums and interest rates.
3. Rising interest rates, together with the loss of confidence, depressed the prices of stock and other assets.
4. Falling asset prices reduced the value of collateral being used for bank loans.
5. Reduced collateral increased default rates on bank loans.
6. Greater defaults exacerbated problems in the banking system. Now return to step 1 to complete and continue the circle.

Some economists have used this vicious-circle argument to suggest that the Asian crisis was a self-fulfilling prophecy: bad things happened merely because people expected bad things to happen. Most economists, however, thought the political corruption of the banking system was a real problem, which was then compounded by this vicious circle of reduced confidence.

As the Asian crisis developed, the IMF and the United States tried to restore confidence, much as they had with Mexico a few years earlier. In particular, the IMF made loans to the Asian countries to help them over the crisis; in exchange for these loans, it exacted promises that the governments would reform their banking systems and eliminate crony capitalism. The IMF's hope was that the short-term loans and longer-term reforms would restore confidence, lower the risk premium, and turn the vicious circle into a virtuous circle. This policy seems to have worked: the Asian economies recovered quickly from their crisis.

12-5 Should Exchange Rates Be Floating or Fixed?

Having analyzed how an economy works under floating and fixed exchange rates, let's consider which exchange-rate regime is better.

Pros and Cons of Different Exchange-Rate Systems

The primary argument for a floating exchange rate is that it allows monetary policy to be used for other purposes. Under fixed rates, monetary policy is committed to the single goal of maintaining the exchange rate at its announced level. Yet the exchange rate is only one of many macroeconomic variables that monetary policy can influence. A system of floating exchange rates leaves monetary policymakers free to pursue other goals, such as stabilizing employment or prices.

"Then it's agreed. Until the dollar firms up, we let the clamshell float."

Advocates of fixed exchange rates argue that exchange-rate uncertainty makes international trade more difficult. After the world abandoned the Bretton Woods system of fixed exchange rates in the early 1970s, both real and nominal exchange rates became (and have remained) much more volatile than anyone had expected. Some economists attribute this volatility to irrational and destabilizing speculation by international investors. Business executives often claim that this volatility is harmful because it increases the uncertainty that accompanies international business transactions. Despite this exchange-rate volatility, however, the amount of world trade has continued to rise under floating exchange rates.

Advocates of fixed exchange rates sometimes argue that a commitment to a fixed exchange rate is one way to discipline a nation's monetary authority and prevent excessive growth in the money supply. Yet there are many other policy rules to which the central bank could be committed. In Chapter 14, for instance, we discuss policy rules such as targets for nominal GDP or the inflation rate. Fixing the exchange rate has the advantage of being simpler to implement than these other policy rules, because the money supply adjusts automatically, but this policy may lead to greater volatility in income and employment.

In practice, the choice between floating and fixed rates is not as stark as it may seem at first. Under systems of fixed exchange rates, countries can change the value of their currency if maintaining the exchange rate conflicts too severely with other goals. Under systems of floating exchange rates, countries often use formal or informal targets for the exchange rate when deciding whether to expand or contract the money supply. We rarely observe exchange rates that are completely fixed or completely floating. Instead, under both systems, stability of the exchange rate is usually one among many of the central bank's objectives.

CASE STUDY

Monetary Union in the United States and Europe

If you have ever driven the 3,000 miles from New York City to San Francisco, you may recall that you never needed to change your money from one form of currency to another. In all fifty U.S. states, local residents are happy to accept the U.S. dollar for the items you buy. Such a *monetary union* is the most extreme form of a fixed exchange rate. The exchange rate between New York dollars and San Francisco dollars is so irrevocably fixed that you may not even know that there is a difference between the two. (What's the difference? Each dollar bill is issued by one of the dozen local Federal Reserve Banks. Although the bank of origin can be identified from the bill's markings, you don't care which type of dollar you hold because everyone else, including the Federal Reserve System, is ready to trade them one for one.)

If you made a similar 3,000-mile trip across Europe during the 1990s, however, your experience was very different. You didn't have to travel far before needing to exchange your French francs for German marks, Dutch guilders, Spanish pesetas, or Italian lira. The large number of currencies in Europe made traveling less convenient and more expensive. Every time you crossed a border, you had to wait in line at a bank to get the local money, and you had to pay the bank a fee for the service.

Today, however, the situation in Europe is more like that in the United States. Many European countries have given up having their own currencies and have formed a monetary union that uses a common currency called the *Euro*. As a result, the exchange rate between France and Germany is now as fixed as the exchange rate between New York and California.

The introduction of a common currency has its costs. The most important is that the nations of Europe are no longer able to conduct their own monetary policies. Instead, the European Central Bank, with the participation of all member countries, sets a single monetary policy for all of Europe. The central banks of the individual countries play a role similar to that of regional Federal Reserve Banks: they monitor local conditions but they have no control over the money supply or interest rates. Critics of the move toward a common currency argue that the cost of losing national monetary policy is large. When a recession hits one country but not others in Europe, that country does not have the tool of monetary policy to combat the downturn. This argument is one reason some European nations, such as the United Kingdom, have chosen not to give up their own currency in favor of the Euro.

Why, according to the Euro critics, is monetary union a bad idea for Europe if it works so well in the United States? These economists argue that the United States is different from Europe in two important ways. First, labor is more mobile among U.S. states than among European countries. This is in part because the United States has a common language and in part because most Americans are descended from immigrants, who have shown a willingness to move. Therefore, when a regional recession occurs, U.S. workers are more likely to move from high-unemployment states to low-unemployment states. Second, the United States has a strong central government that can use fiscal policy—such as the federal income tax—to redistribute resources among regions. Because Europe does not have these two advantages, it bears a larger cost when it restricts itself to a single monetary policy.

Advocates of a common currency believe that the loss of national monetary policy is more than offset by other gains. With a single currency in all of Europe, travelers and businesses no longer need to worry about exchange rates, and this encourages more international trade. In addition, a common currency may have the political advantage of making Europeans feel more connected to one another. The twentieth century was marked by two world wars, both of which were sparked by European discord. If a common currency makes the nations of Europe more harmonious, it benefits the entire world.

Speculative Attacks, Currency Boards, and Dollarization

Imagine that you are a central banker of a small country. You and your fellow policymakers decide to fix your currency—let's call it the peso—against the U.S. dollar. From now on, one peso will sell for one dollar.

As we discussed earlier, you now have to stand ready to buy and sell pesos for a dollar each. The money supply will adjust automatically to make the equilibrium exchange rate equal your target. There is, however, one potential problem with this plan: you might run out of dollars. If people come to the central bank to sell large quantities of pesos, the central bank's dollar reserves might dwindle to zero. In this case, the central bank has no choice but to abandon the fixed exchange rate and let the peso depreciate.

This fact raises the possibility of a *speculative attack*—a change in investors' perceptions that makes the fixed exchange rate untenable. Suppose that, for no good reason, a rumor spreads that the central bank is going to abandon the exchange-rate peg. People would respond by rushing to the central bank to convert pesos into dollars before the pesos lose value. This rush would drain the central bank's reserves and could force the central bank to abandon the peg. In this case, the rumor would prove self-fulfilling.

To avoid this possibility, some economists argue that a fixed exchange rate should be supported by a *currency board*, such as that used by Argentina in the 1990s. A currency board is an arrangement by which the central bank holds enough foreign currency to back each unit of the domestic currency. In our example, the central bank would hold one U.S. dollar (or one dollar invested in a U.S. government bond) for every peso. No matter how many pesos turned up at the central bank to be exchanged, the central bank would never run out of dollars.

Once a central bank has adopted a currency board, it might consider the natural next step: it can abandon the peso altogether and let its country use the U.S. dollar. Such a plan is called *dollarization*. It happens on its own in high-inflation economies, where foreign currencies offer a more reliable store of value than the domestic currency. But it can also occur as a matter of public policy, as in Panama. If a country really wants its currency to be irrevocably fixed to the dollar, the most reliable method is to make its currency the dollar. The only loss from dollarization is the seigniorage revenue that a government gives up by relinquishing its control over the printing press. The U.S. government then gets the revenue that is generated by growth in the money supply.[5]

The Impossible Trinity

The analysis of exchange-rate regimes leads to a simple conclusion: you can't have it all. To be more precise, it is impossible for a nation to have free capital flows, a fixed exchange rate, and independent monetary policy. This fact, often called the *impossible trinity*, is illustrated in Figure 12-12. A nation must choose one side of this triangle, giving up the institutional feature at the opposite corner.

The first option is to allow free flows of capital and to conduct an independent monetary policy, as the United States has done in recent years. In this case, it is impossible to have a fixed exchange rate. Instead, the exchange rate must float to equilibrate the market for foreign-currency exchange.

The second option is to allow free flows of capital and to fix the exchange rate, as Hong Kong has done in recent years. In this case, the nation loses the ability to run an independent monetary policy. The money supply must adjust to keep the

[5] Dollarization may also lead to a loss in national pride from seeing American portraits on the currency. If it wanted, the U.S. government could fix this problem by leaving blank the center space that now has George Washington's portrait. Each nation using the U.S. dollar could insert the face of its own local hero.

FIGURE 12-12

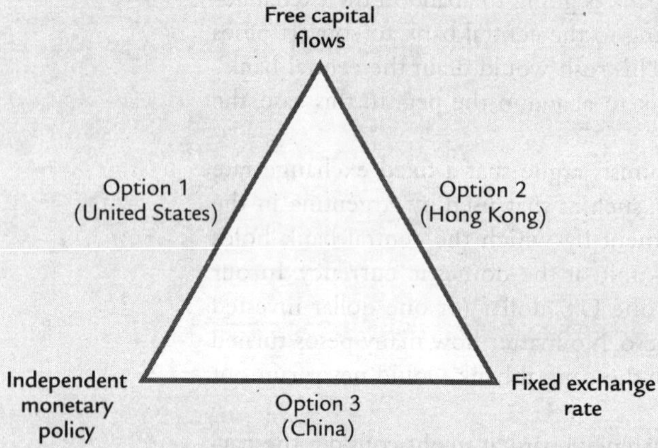

The Impossible Trinity It is impossible for a nation to have free capital flows, a fixed exchange rate, and independent monetary policy. A nation must choose one side of this triangle, giving up the opposite corner.

exchange rate at its predetermined level. In a sense, when a nation fixes its currency to that of another nation, it is adopting that other nation's monetary policy.

The third option is to restrict the international flow of capital in and out of the country, as China has done in recent years. In this case, the interest rate is no longer fixed by world interest rates but is determined by domestic forces, much as is the case in a completely closed economy. It is then possible to both fix the exchange rate and conduct an independent monetary policy.

History has shown that nations can, and do, choose different sides of the trinity. Every nation must ask itself the following question: Does it want to live with exchange-rate volatility (option 1), does it want to give up the use of monetary policy for purposes of domestic stabilization (option 2), or does it want to restrict its citizens from participating in world financial markets (option 3)? The impossible trinity says that no nation can avoid making one of these choices.

CASE STUDY

The Chinese Currency Controversy

From 1995 to 2005 the Chinese currency, the yuan, was pegged to the dollar at an exchange rate of 8.28 yuan per U.S. dollar. In other words, the Chinese central bank stood ready to buy and sell yuan at this price. This policy of fixing the exchange rate was combined with a policy of restricting international capital flows. Chinese citizens were not allowed to convert their savings into dollars or Euros and invest abroad.

Many observers believed that by the early 2000s, the yuan was significantly undervalued. They suggested that if the yuan were allowed to float, it would increase in value relative to the dollar. The evidence in favor of this hypothesis was that to maintain the fixed exchange rate, China was accumulating large dollar reserves. That is, the Chinese central bank had to supply yuan and demand dollars in foreign-exchange markets to keep the yuan at the pegged level. If this intervention in the currency market ceased, the yuan would rise in value compared to the dollar.

The pegged yuan became a contentious political issue in the United States. U.S. producers that competed against Chinese imports complained that the undervalued yuan made Chinese goods cheaper, putting the U.S. producers at a disadvantage. (Of course, U.S. consumers benefited from inexpensive imports, but in the politics of international trade, producers usually shout louder than consumers.) In response to these concerns, President Bush called on China to let its currency float. Charles Schumer, Senator from New York, proposed a more drastic step—a tariff of 27.5 percent on Chinese imports until China adjusted the value of its currency.

In July 2005 China announced that it would move in the direction of a floating exchange rate. Under the new policy, it would still intervene in foreign-exchange markets to prevent large and sudden movements in the exchange rate, but it would permit gradual changes. Moreover, it would judge the value of the yuan not just relative to the dollar but relative to a broad basket of currencies. Five months later, the exchange rate had moved to 8.08 yuan per dollar—a 2.4 percent appreciation of the yuan, far smaller than the 20 to 30 percent that Senator Schumer and other China critics were looking for.

Was the yuan really undervalued by such a large amount? To answer this question, we must first ask, compared to what? The critics of Chinese policy may well have been correct that the yuan would have appreciated substantially if the Chinese had stopped intervening in foreign-exchange markets while keeping their other policies the same. But a movement to a fully floating exchange rate could well have been coupled with a movement toward free capital mobility. If so, the currency implications could have been very different, as many Chinese citizens might have tried to move some of their savings abroad. While the central bank would no longer have been demanding dollars to fix the exchange rate, private investors would have been demanding dollars to add U.S. assets to their own portfolios. In this case, the change in policy could well have caused the yuan to depreciate rather than appreciate.

As this book was going to press, it was unclear whether China would continue on the path toward a floating exchange rate and freer capital mobility. The issue remains a topic of intense international negotiation.

12-6 From the Short Run to the Long Run: The Mundell-Fleming Model With a Changing Price Level

So far we have used the Mundell-Fleming model to study the small open economy in the short run when the price level is fixed. We now consider what happens when the price level changes. Doing so will show how the Mundell-Fleming model provides a theory of the aggregate demand curve in a small open economy. It will also show how this short-run model relates to the long-run model of the open economy we examined in Chapter 5.

Because we now want to consider changes in the price level, the nominal and real exchange rates in the economy will no longer be moving in tandem. Thus, we must distinguish between these two variables. The nominal exchange rate is *e* and the real exchange rate is ϵ, which equals eP/P^*, as you should recall from Chapter 5. We can write the Mundell-Fleming model as

$$Y = C(Y - T) + I(r^*) + G + NX(\epsilon) \qquad IS^*,$$
$$M/P = L(r^*, Y) \qquad LM^*.$$

These equations should be familiar by now. The first equation describes the *IS** curve, and the second equation describes the *LM** curve. Note that net exports depend on the real exchange rate.

Figure 12-13 shows what happens when the price level falls. Because a lower price level raises the level of real money balances, the *LM** curve shifts to the right, as in panel (a) of Figure 12-13. The real exchange rate depreciates, and the equilibrium level of income rises. The aggregate demand curve summarizes this negative relationship between the price level and the level of income, as shown in panel (b) of Figure 12-13.

FIGURE 12-13

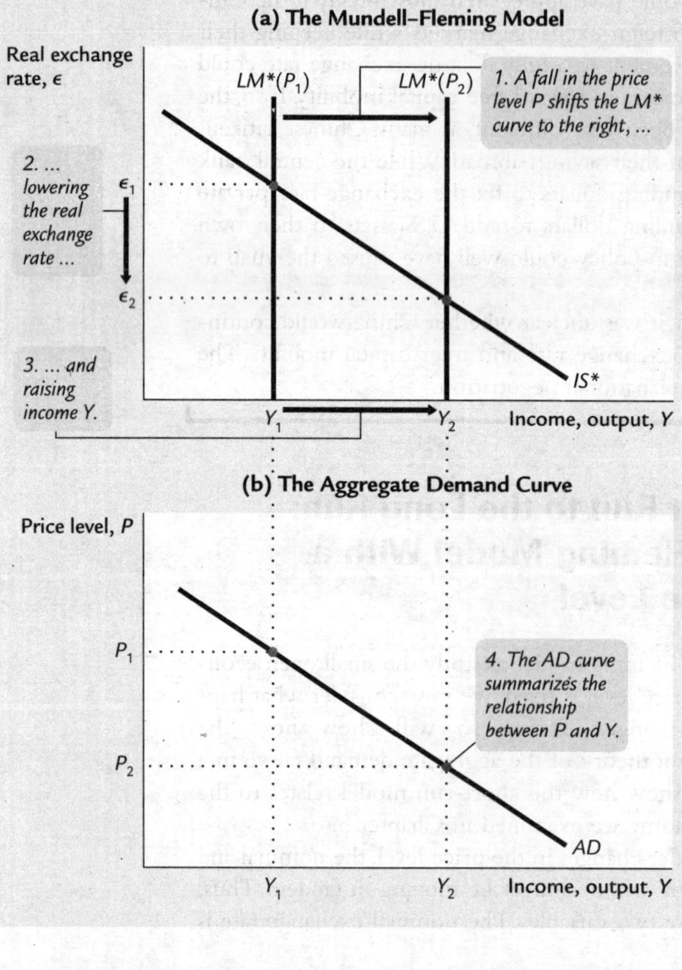

Mundell-Fleming as a Theory of Aggregate Demand Panel (a) shows that when the price level falls, the *LM** curve shifts to the right. The equilibrium level of income rises. Panel (b) shows that this negative relationship between *P* and *Y* is summarized by the aggregate demand curve.

Thus, just as the *IS-LM* model explains the aggregate demand curve in a closed economy, the Mundell-Fleming model explains the aggregate demand curve for a small open economy. In both cases, the aggregate demand curve shows the set of equilibria in the goods and money markets that arise as the price level varies. And in both cases, anything that changes equilibrium income, other than a change in the price level, shifts the aggregate demand curve. Policies and events that raise income for a given price level shift the aggregate demand curve to the right; policies and events that lower income for a given price level shift the aggregate demand curve to the left.

We can use this diagram to show how the short-run model in this chapter is related to the long-run model in Chapter 5. Figure 12-14 shows the short-run

FIGURE 12-14

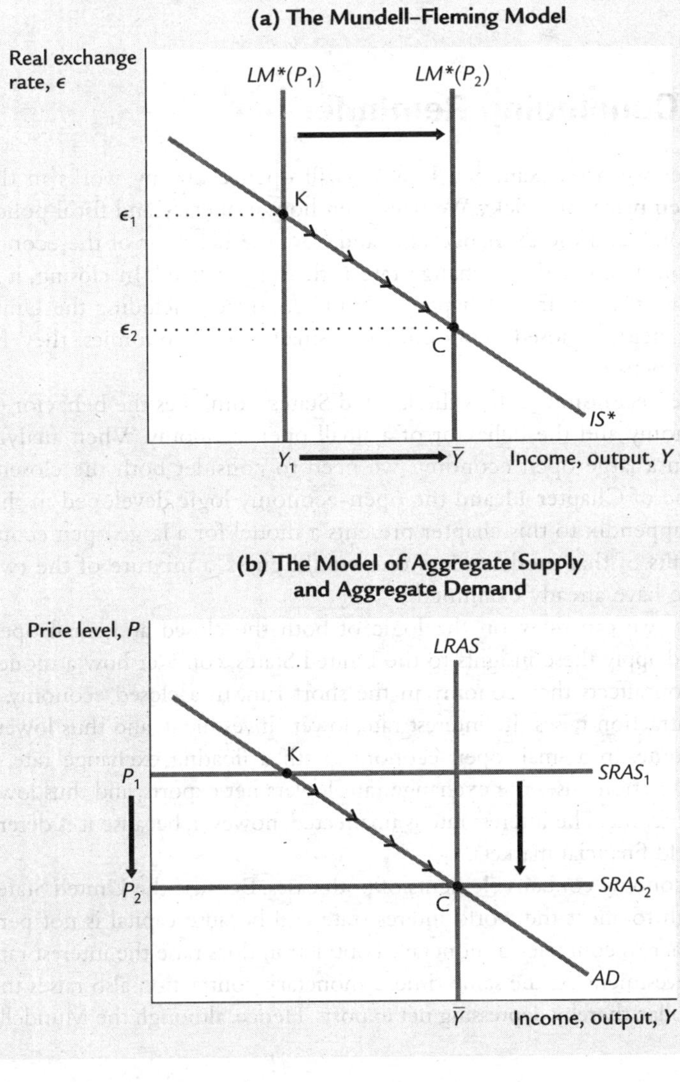

The Short-Run and Long-Run Equilibria in a Small Open Economy Point K in both panels shows the equilibrium under the Keynesian assumption that the price level is fixed at P_1. Point C in both panels shows the equilibrium under the classical assumption that the price level adjusts to maintain income at its natural level $\bar{Y}$.

and long-run equilibria. In both panels of the figure, point K describes the short-run equilibrium because it assumes a fixed price level. At this equilibrium, the demand for goods and services is too low to keep the economy producing at its natural level. Over time, low demand causes the price level to fall. The fall in the price level raises real money balances, shifting the LM^* curve to the right. The real exchange rate depreciates, so net exports rise. Eventually, the economy reaches point C, the long-run equilibrium. The speed of transition between the short-run and long-run equilibria depends on how quickly the price level adjusts to restore the economy to the natural level of output.

The levels of income at point K and point C are both of interest. Our central concern in this chapter has been how policy influences point K, the short-run equilibrium. In Chapter 5 we examined the determinants of point C, the long-run equilibrium. Whenever policymakers consider any change in policy, they need to consider both the short-run and long-run effects of their decision.

12-7 A Concluding Reminder

In this chapter we have examined how a small open economy works in the short run when prices are sticky. We have seen how monetary and fiscal policy influence income and the exchange rate, and how the behavior of the economy depends on whether the exchange rate is floating or fixed. In closing, it is worth repeating a lesson from Chapter 5. Many countries, including the United States, are neither closed economies nor small open economies: they lie somewhere in between.

A large open economy, such as the United States, combines the behavior of a closed economy and the behavior of a small open economy. When analyzing policies in a large open economy, we need to consider both the closed-economy logic of Chapter 11 and the open-economy logic developed in this chapter. The appendix to this chapter presents a model for a large open economy. The results of that model are, as one would guess, a mixture of the two polar cases we have already examined.

To see how we can draw on the logic of both the closed and small open economies and apply these insights to the United States, consider how a monetary contraction affects the economy in the short run. In a closed economy, a monetary contraction raises the interest rate, lowers investment, and thus lowers aggregate income. In a small open economy with a floating exchange rate, a monetary contraction raises the exchange rate, lowers net exports, and thus lowers aggregate income. The interest rate is unaffected, however, because it is determined by world financial markets.

The U.S. economy contains elements of both cases. Because the United States is large enough to affect the world interest rate and because capital is not perfectly mobile across countries, a monetary contraction does raise the interest rate and depress investment. At the same time, a monetary contraction also raises the value of the dollar, thereby depressing net exports. Hence, although the Mundell-

Fleming model does not precisely describe an economy like that of the United States, it does predict correctly what happens to international variables such as the exchange rate, and it shows how international interactions alter the effects of monetary and fiscal policies.

Summary

1. The Mundell-Fleming model is the *IS-LM* model for a small open economy. It takes the price level as given and then shows what causes fluctuations in income and the exchange rate.
2. The Mundell-Fleming model shows that fiscal policy does not influence aggregate income under floating exchange rates. A fiscal expansion causes the currency to appreciate, reducing net exports and offsetting the usual expansionary impact on aggregate income. Fiscal policy does influence aggregate income under fixed exchange rates.
3. The Mundell-Fleming model shows that monetary policy does not influence aggregate income under fixed exchange rates. Any attempt to expand the money supply is futile because the money supply must adjust to ensure that the exchange rate stays at its announced level. Monetary policy does influence aggregate income under floating exchange rates.
4. If investors are wary of holding assets in a country, the interest rate in that country may exceed the world interest rate by some risk premium. According to the Mundell-Fleming model, an increase in the risk premium causes the interest rate to rise and the currency of that country to depreciate.
5. There are advantages to both floating and fixed exchange rates. Floating exchange rates leave monetary policymakers free to pursue objectives other than exchange rate stability. Fixed exchange rates reduce some of the uncertainty in international business transactions. When deciding on an exchange-rate regime, policymakers are constrained by the fact that it is impossible for a nation to have free capital flows, a fixed exchange rate, and independent monetary policy.

KEY CONCEPTS

Mundell-Fleming model
Floating exchange rates
Fixed exchange rates
Devaluation
Revaluation

QUESTIONS FOR REVIEW

1. In the Mundell-Fleming model with floating exchange rates, explain what happens to aggregate income, the exchange rate, and the trade balance when taxes are raised. What would happen if exchange rates were fixed rather than floating?

2. In the Mundell-Fleming model with floating exchange rates, explain what happens to aggregate income, the exchange rate, and the trade balance when the money supply is reduced. What would happen if exchange rates were fixed rather than floating?

3. In the Mundell-Fleming model with floating exchange rates, explain what happens to aggregate income, the exchange rate, and the trade balance when a quota on imported cars is removed. What would happen if exchange rates were fixed rather than floating?

4. What are the advantages of floating exchange rates and fixed exchange rates?

5. Describe the impossible trinity.

PROBLEMS AND APPLICATIONS

1. Use the Mundell-Fleming model to predict what would happen to aggregate income, the exchange rate, and the trade balance under both floating and fixed exchange rates in response to each of the following shocks:

   a. A fall in consumer confidence about the future induces consumers to spend less and save more.

   b. The introduction of a stylish line of Toyotas makes some consumers prefer foreign cars over domestic cars.

   c. The introduction of automatic teller machines reduces the demand for money.

2. A small open economy with a floating exchange rate is in recession with balanced trade. If policymakers want to reach full employment while maintaining balanced trade, what combination of monetary and fiscal policy should they choose?

3. The Mundell-Fleming model takes the world interest rate r^* as an exogenous variable. Let's consider what happens when this variable changes.

   a. What might cause the world interest rate to rise?

   b. In the Mundell-Fleming model with a floating exchange rate, what happens to aggregate income, the exchange rate, and the trade balance when the world interest rate rises?

   c. In the Mundell-Fleming model with a fixed exchange rate, what happens to aggregate income, the exchange rate, and the trade balance when the world interest rate rises?

4. Business executives and policymakers are often concerned about the "competitiveness" of American industry (the ability of U.S. industries to sell their goods profitably in world markets).

   a. How would a change in the exchange rate affect competitiveness?

   b. Suppose you wanted to make domestic industries more competitive but did not want to alter aggregate income. According to the Mundell-Fleming model, what combination of monetary and fiscal policies should you pursue?

5. Suppose that higher income implies higher imports and thus lower net exports. That is, the net exports function is

$$NX = NX(e, Y).$$

Examine the effects in a small open economy of a fiscal expansion on income and the trade balance under

   a. A floating exchange rate.

   b. A fixed exchange rate.

How does your answer compare to the results in Table 12-1?

6. Suppose that money demand depends on disposable income, so that the equation for the money market becomes

$$M/P = L(r, Y - T).$$

Analyze the impact of a tax cut in a small open economy on the exchange rate and income under both floating and fixed exchange rates.

7. Suppose that the price level relevant for money demand includes the price of imported goods and that the price of imported goods depends on the exchange rate. That is, the money market is described by

$$M/P = L(r, Y),$$

where

$$P = \lambda P_d + (1 - \lambda)P_f/e.$$

The parameter λ is the share of domestic goods in the price index P. Assume that the price of domestic goods P_d and the price of foreign goods measured in foreign currency P_f are fixed.

a. Suppose we graph the LM^* curve for given values of P_d and P_f (instead of the usual P). Explain why in this model this LM^* curve is upward sloping rather than vertical.

b. What is the effect of expansionary fiscal policy under floating exchange rates in this model? Explain. Contrast with the standard Mundell-Fleming model.

c. Suppose that political instability increases the country risk premium and, thereby, the interest rate. What is the effect on the exchange rate, the price level, and aggregate income in this model? Contrast with the standard Mundell-Fleming model.

8. Use the Mundell-Fleming model to answer the following questions about the state of California (a small open economy).

a. If California suffers from a recession, should the state government use monetary or fiscal policy to stimulate employment? Explain. (*Note:* For this question, assume that the state government can print dollar bills.)

b. If California prohibited the import of wines from the state of Washington, what would happen to income, the exchange rate, and the trade balance? Consider both the short-run and the long-run impacts.

A Short-Run Model of the Large Open Economy

When analyzing policies in an economy such as the United States, we need to combine the closed-economy logic of the *IS-LM* model and the small-open-economy logic of the Mundell-Fleming model. This appendix presents a model for the intermediate case of a large open economy.

As we discussed in the appendix to Chapter 5, a large open economy differs from a small open economy because its interest rate is not fixed by world financial markets. In a large open economy, we must consider the relationship between the interest rate and the flow of capital abroad. The net capital outflow is the amount that domestic investors lend abroad minus the amount that foreign investors lend here. As the domestic interest rate falls, domestic investors find foreign lending more attractive, and foreign investors find lending here less attractive. Thus, the net capital outflow is negatively related to the interest rate. Here we add this relationship to our short-run model of national income.

The three equations of the model are

$$Y = C(Y - T) + I(r) + G + NX(e),$$

$$M/P = L(r, Y),$$

$$NX(e) = CF(r).$$

The first two equations are the same as those used in the Mundell-Fleming model of this chapter. The third equation, taken from the appendix to Chapter 5, states that the trade balance NX equals the net capital outflow CF, which in turn depends on the domestic interest rate.

To see what this model implies, substitute the third equation into the first, so the model becomes

$$Y = C(Y - T) + I(r) + G + CF(r) \qquad IS,$$

$$M/P = L(r, Y) \qquad LM.$$

These two equations are much like the two equations of the closed-economy *IS-LM* model. The only difference is that expenditure now depends on the interest rate for two reasons. As before, a higher interest rate reduces investment. But now, a higher interest rate also reduces the net capital outflow and thus lowers net exports.

To analyze this model, we can use the three graphs in Figure 12-15. Panel (a) shows the *IS-LM* diagram. As in the closed-economy model in Chapters 10 and 11, the interest rate r is on the vertical axis, and income Y is on the horizontal axis. The *IS* and *LM* curves together determine the equilibrium level of income and the equilibrium interest rate.

The new net-capital-outflow term in the *IS* equation, $CF(r)$, makes this *IS* curve flatter than it would be in a closed economy. The more responsive international capital flows are to the interest rate, the flatter the *IS* curve is. You might

FIGURE 12-15

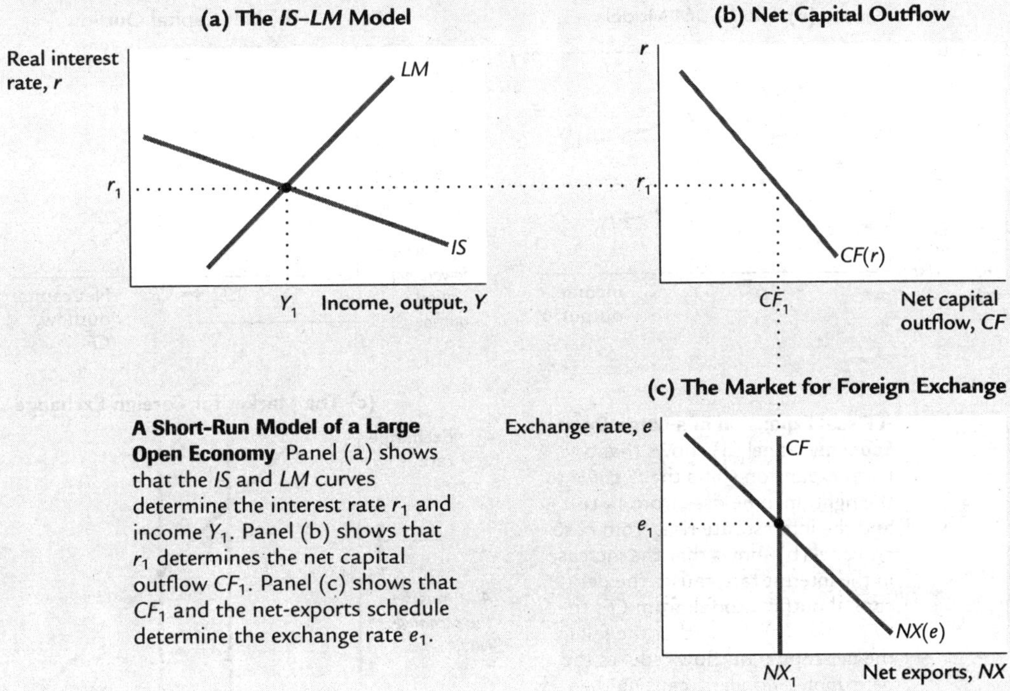

A Short-Run Model of a Large Open Economy Panel (a) shows that the *IS* and *LM* curves determine the interest rate r_1 and income Y_1. Panel (b) shows that r_1 determines the net capital outflow CF_1. Panel (c) shows that CF_1 and the net-exports schedule determine the exchange rate e_1.

recall from the Chapter 5 appendix that the small open economy represents the extreme case in which the net capital outflow is infinitely elastic at the world interest rate. In this extreme case, the *IS* curve is completely flat. Hence, a small open economy would be depicted in this figure with a horizontal *IS* curve.

Panels (b) and (c) show how the equilibrium from the *IS-LM* model determines the net capital outflow, the trade balance, and the exchange rate. In panel (b) we see that the interest rate determines the net capital outflow. This curve slopes downward because a higher interest rate discourages domestic investors from lending abroad and encourages foreign investors to lend here. In panel (c) we see that the exchange rate adjusts to ensure that net exports of goods and services equal the net capital outflow.

Now let's use this model to examine the impact of various policies. We assume that the economy has a floating exchange rate, because this assumption is correct for most large open economies such as the United States.

Fiscal Policy

Figure 12-16 examines the impact of a fiscal expansion. An increase in government purchases or a cut in taxes shifts the *IS* curve to the right. As panel (a) illustrates, this shift in the *IS* curve leads to an increase in the level of income and an

FIGURE 12-16

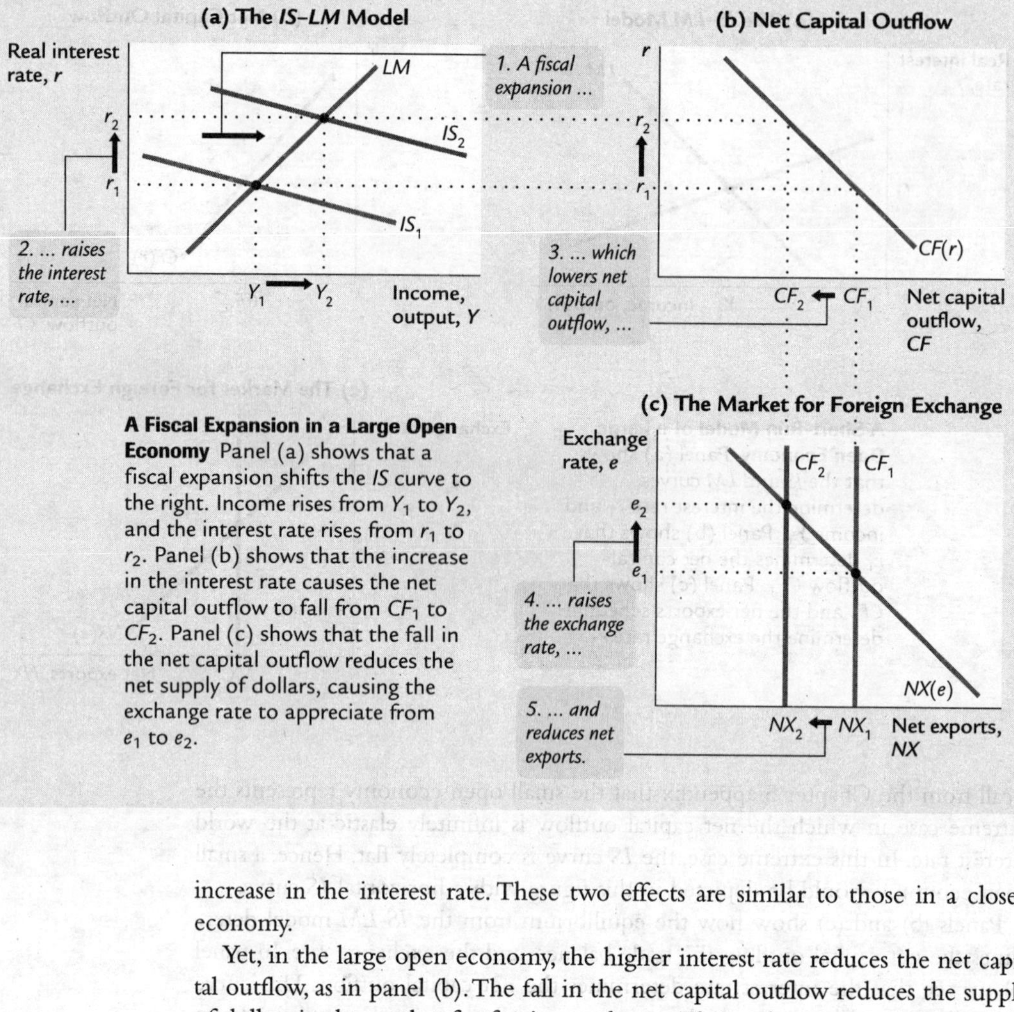

A Fiscal Expansion in a Large Open Economy Panel (a) shows that a fiscal expansion shifts the *IS* curve to the right. Income rises from Y_1 to Y_2, and the interest rate rises from r_1 to r_2. Panel (b) shows that the increase in the interest rate causes the net capital outflow to fall from CF_1 to CF_2. Panel (c) shows that the fall in the net capital outflow reduces the net supply of dollars, causing the exchange rate to appreciate from e_1 to e_2.

increase in the interest rate. These two effects are similar to those in a closed economy.

Yet, in the large open economy, the higher interest rate reduces the net capital outflow, as in panel (b). The fall in the net capital outflow reduces the supply of dollars in the market for foreign exchange. The exchange rate appreciates, as in panel (c). Because domestic goods become more expensive relative to foreign goods, net exports fall.

Figure 12-16 shows that a fiscal expansion does raise income in the large open economy, unlike in a small open economy under a floating exchange rate. The impact on income, however, is smaller than in a closed economy. In a closed economy, the expansionary impact of fiscal policy is partially offset by the crowding out of investment: as the interest rate rises, investment falls, reducing the fiscal-policy multipliers. In a large open economy, there is yet another offsetting factor: as the interest rate rises, the net capital outflow falls, the exchange rate appreciates, and net exports fall. Together these effects are not large enough to make fiscal policy powerless, as it is in a small open economy, but they do reduce fiscal policy's impact.

Monetary Policy

Figure 12-17 examines the effect of a monetary expansion. An increase in the money supply shifts the *LM* curve to the right, as in panel (a). The level of income rises, and the interest rate falls. Once again, these effects are similar to those in a closed economy.

Yet, as panel (b) shows, the lower interest rate leads to a higher net capital outflow. The increase in *CF* raises the supply of dollars in the market for foreign exchange. The exchange rate depreciates, as in panel (c). As domestic goods become cheaper relative to foreign goods, net exports rise.

We can now see that the monetary transmission mechanism works through two channels in a large open economy. As in a closed economy, a monetary expansion lowers the interest rate, which stimulates investment. As in a small open economy, a monetary expansion causes the currency to depreciate in the market for foreign exchange, which stimulates net exports. Both effects result in a higher level of aggregate income.

FIGURE 12-17

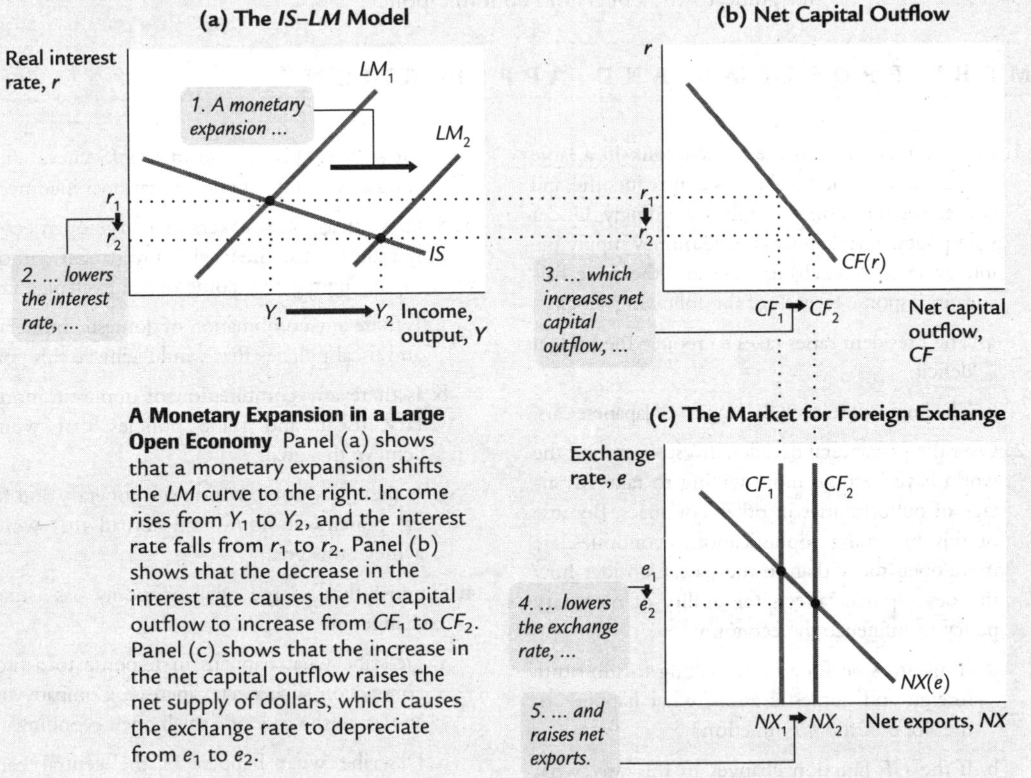

A Monetary Expansion in a Large Open Economy Panel (a) shows that a monetary expansion shifts the *LM* curve to the right. Income rises from Y_1 to Y_2, and the interest rate falls from r_1 to r_2. Panel (b) shows that the decrease in the interest rate causes the net capital outflow to increase from CF_1 to CF_2. Panel (c) shows that the increase in the net capital outflow raises the net supply of dollars, which causes the exchange rate to depreciate from e_1 to e_2.

A Rule of Thumb

This model of the large open economy describes well the U.S. economy today. Yet it is somewhat more complicated and cumbersome than the model of the closed economy we studied in Chapters 10 and 11 and the model of the small open economy we developed in this chapter. Fortunately, there is a useful rule of thumb to help you determine how policies influence a large open economy without remembering all the details of the model: *The large open economy is an average of the closed economy and the small open economy. To find how any policy will affect any variable, find the answer in the two extreme cases and take an average.*

For example, how does a monetary contraction affect the interest rate and investment in the short run? In a closed economy, the interest rate rises, and investment falls. In a small open economy, neither the interest rate nor investment changes. The effect in the large open economy is an average of these two cases: a monetary contraction raises the interest rate and reduces investment, but only somewhat. The fall in the net capital outflow mitigates the rise in the interest rate and the fall in investment that would occur in a closed economy. But unlike in a small open economy, the international flow of capital is not so strong as to negate fully these effects.

This rule of thumb makes the simple models all the more valuable. Although they do not describe perfectly the world in which we live, they do provide a useful guide to the effects of economic policy.

MORE PROBLEMS AND APPLICATIONS

1. Imagine that you run the central bank in a large open economy. Your goal is to stabilize income, and you adjust the money supply accordingly. Under your policy, what happens to the money supply, the interest rate, the exchange rate, and the trade balance in response to each of the following shocks?
   a. The president raises taxes to reduce the budget deficit.
   b. The president restricts the import of Japanese cars.
2. Over the past several decades, investors around the world have become more willing to take advantage of opportunities in other countries. Because of this increasing sophistication, economies are more open today than in the past. Consider how this development affects the ability of monetary policy to influence the economy.
   a. If investors become more willing to substitute foreign and domestic assets, what happens to the slope of the *CF* function?
   b. If the *CF* function changes in this way, what happens to the slope of the *IS* curve?
   c. How does this change in the *IS* curve affect the Fed's ability to control the interest rate?
   d. How does this change in the *IS* curve affect the Fed's ability to control national income?
3. Suppose that policymakers in a large open economy want to raise the level of investment without changing aggregate income or the exchange rate.
   a. Is there any combination of domestic monetary and fiscal policies that would achieve this goal?
   b. Is there any combination of domestic monetary, fiscal, and trade policies that would achieve this goal?
   c. Is there any combination of monetary and fiscal policies at home and abroad that would achieve this goal?
4. Suppose that a large open economy has a fixed exchange rate.
   a. Describe what happens in response to a fiscal contraction, such as a tax increase. Compare your answer to the case of a small open economy.
   b. Describe what happens if the central bank expands the money supply by buying bonds from the public. Compare your answer to the case of a small open economy.

CHAPTER

13

Aggregate Supply and the Short-run Tradeoff Between Inflation and Unemployment

Probably the single most important macroeconomic relationship is the Phillips curve.

— *George Akerlof*

There is always a temporary tradeoff between inflation and unemployment; there is no permanent tradeoff. The temporary tradeoff comes not from inflation per se, but from unanticipated inflation, which generally means, from a rising rate of inflation.

— *Milton Friedman*

Most economists analyze short-run fluctuations in aggregate income and the price level using the model of aggregate demand and aggregate supply. In the previous three chapters, we examined aggregate demand in some detail. The *IS-LM* model—together with its open-economy cousin the Mundell-Fleming model—shows how changes in monetary and fiscal policy and shocks to the money and goods markets shift the aggregate demand curve. In this chapter, we turn our attention to aggregate supply and develop theories that explain the position and slope of the aggregate supply curve.

When we introduced the aggregate supply curve in Chapter 9, we established that aggregate supply behaves differently in the short run than in the long run. In the long run, prices are flexible, and the aggregate supply curve is vertical. When the aggregate supply curve is vertical, shifts in the aggregate demand curve affect the price level, but the output of the economy remains at its natural level. By contrast, in the short run, prices are sticky, and the aggregate supply curve is not vertical. In this case, shifts in aggregate demand do cause fluctuations in output. In Chapter 9 we took a simplified view of price stickiness by drawing the short-run aggregate supply curve as a horizontal line, representing the extreme situation in which all prices are fixed. Our task now is to refine this understanding of short-run aggregate supply to better reflect the real world in which some prices are sticky and others are not.

Unfortunately, one fact makes our task more difficult: economists disagree about how best to explain aggregate supply. As a result, this chapter begins by presenting three models of the short-run aggregate supply curve. Among economists, each of these models has some prominent adherents (as well as some prominent critics), and you can decide for yourself which you find most plausible. Although these models differ in some significant details, they are related in an important way: they share a common theme about what makes the short-run and long-run aggregate supply curves differ and a common conclusion that the short-run aggregate supply curve is upward sloping.

After examining the models, we examine an implication of the short-run aggregate supply curve. We show that this curve implies a tradeoff between two measures of economic performance—inflation and unemployment. This tradeoff, called the *Phillips curve*, tell us that to reduce the rate of inflation policymakers must temporarily raise unemployment, and to reduce unemployment they must accept higher inflation. As the quotation from Milton Friedman at the beginning of the chapter suggests, the tradeoff between inflation and unemployment is only temporary. One goal of this chapter is to explain why policymakers face such a tradeoff in the short run and, just as important, why they do not face it in the long run.

13-1 Three Models of Aggregate Supply

When classes in physics study balls rolling down inclined planes, they often begin by assuming away the existence of friction. This assumption makes the problem simpler and is useful in many circumstances, but no good engineer would ever take this assumption as a literal description of how the world works. Similarly, this book began with classical macroeconomic theory, but it would be a mistake to assume that this model is always true. Our job now is to look more deeply into the "frictions" of macroeconomics.

We do this by examining three prominent models of aggregate supply. In all the models, some market imperfection (that is, some type of friction) causes the output of the economy to deviate from its natural level. As a result, the short-run aggregate supply curve is upward sloping, rather than vertical, and shifts in the aggregate demand curve cause output to fluctuate. These temporary deviations of output from its natural level represent the booms and busts of the business cycle.

Although each of the three models takes us down a different theoretical route, each route ends up in the same place. That final destination is a short-run aggregate supply equation of the form

$$Y = \bar{Y} + \alpha(P - P^e), \qquad \alpha > 0,$$

where Y is output, $\bar{Y}$ is the natural level of output, P is the price level, and P^e is the expected price level. This equation states that output deviates from its natural level when the price level deviates from the expected price level. The parameter α indicates how much output responds to unexpected changes in the price level; $1/\alpha$ is the slope of the aggregate supply curve.

Each of the three models tells a different story about what lies behind this short-run aggregate supply equation. In other words, each model highlights a particular reason why unexpected movements in the price level are associated with fluctuations in aggregate output.

The Sticky-Price Model

Our first explanation for the upward-sloping short-run aggregate supply curve is called the **sticky-price model**. This model emphasizes that firms do not instantly adjust the prices they charge in response to changes in demand. Sometimes prices are set by long-term contracts between firms and customers. Even without formal agreements, firms may hold prices steady in order not to annoy their regular customers with frequent price changes. Some prices are sticky because of the way markets are structured: once a firm has printed and distributed its catalog or price list, it is costly to alter prices.

To see how sticky prices can help explain an upward-sloping aggregate supply curve, we first consider the pricing decisions of individual firms and then add together the decisions of many firms to explain the behavior of the economy as a whole. Notice that this model encourages us to depart from the assumption of perfect competition, which we have used since Chapter 3. Perfectly competitive firms are price takers rather than price setters. If we want to consider how firms set prices, it is natural to assume that these firms have at least some monopoly control over the prices they charge.

Consider the pricing decision facing a typical firm. The firm's desired price p depends on two macroeconomic variables:

- The overall level of prices P. A higher price level implies that the firm's costs are higher. Hence, the higher the overall price level, the more the firm would like to charge for its product.
- The level of aggregate income Y. A higher level of income raises the demand for the firm's product. Because marginal cost increases at higher levels of production, the greater the demand, the higher the firm's desired price.

We write the firm's desired price as

$$p = P + a(Y - \bar{Y}).$$

This equation says that the desired price p depends on the overall level of prices P and on the level of aggregate output relative to the natural level $Y - \bar{Y}$. The parameter a (which is greater than zero) measures how much the firm's desired price responds to the level of aggregate output.[1]

Now assume that there are two types of firms. Some have flexible prices: they always set their prices according to this equation. Others have sticky prices: they

[1] *Mathematical note:* The firm cares most about its relative price, which is the ratio of its nominal price to the overall price level. If we interpret p and P as the logarithms of the firm's price and the price level, then this equation states that the desired relative price depends on the deviation of output from its natural level.

announce their prices in advance based on what they expect economic conditions to be. Firms with sticky prices set prices according to

$$p = P^e + a(Y^e - \overline{Y}^e),$$

where, as before, a superscript "e" represents the expected value of a variable. For simplicity, assume that these firms expect output to be at its natural level, so that the last term, $a(Y^e - \overline{Y}^e)$, is zero. Then these firms set the price

$$p = P^e.$$

That is, firms with sticky prices set their prices based on what they expect other firms to charge.

We can use the pricing rules of the two groups of firms to derive the aggregate supply equation. To do this, we find the overall price level in the economy, which is the weighted average of the prices set by the two groups. If s is the fraction of firms with sticky prices and $1 - s$ the fraction with flexible prices, then the overall price level is

$$P = sP^e + (1 - s)[P + a(Y - \overline{Y})].$$

The first term is the price of the sticky-price firms weighted by their fraction in the economy, and the second term is the price of the flexible-price firms weighted by their fraction. Now subtract $(1 - s)P$ from both sides of this equation to obtain

$$sP = sP^e + (1 - s)[a(Y - \overline{Y})].$$

Divide both sides by s to solve for the overall price level:

$$P = P^e + [(1 - s)a/s](Y - \overline{Y}).$$

The two terms in this equation are explained as follows:

- When firms expect a high price level, they expect high costs. Those firms that fix prices in advance set their prices high. These high prices cause the other firms to set high prices also. Hence, a high expected price level P^e leads to a high actual price level P.
- When output is high, the demand for goods is high. Those firms with flexible prices set their prices high, which leads to a high price level. The effect of output on the price level depends on the proportion of firms with flexible prices.

Hence, the overall price level depends on the expected price level and on the level of output.

Algebraic rearrangement puts this aggregate pricing equation into a more familiar form:

$$Y = \overline{Y} + \alpha(P - P^e),$$

where $\alpha = s/[(1 - s)a]$. The sticky-price model says that the deviation of output from the natural level is positively associated with the deviation of the price level from the expected price level.[2]

[2] For a more advanced development of the sticky-price model, see Julio Rotemberg, "Monopolistic Price Adjustment and Aggregate Output," *Review of Economic Studies* 49 (1982): 517–531.

The Sticky-Wage Model

To explain why the short-run aggregate supply curve is upward sloping, many economists stress the sluggish adjustment of nominal wages. In many industries, nominal wages are set by long-term contracts, so wages cannot adjust quickly when economic conditions change. Even in industries not covered by formal contracts, implicit agreements between workers and firms may limit wage changes. Wages may also depend on social norms and notions of fairness that evolve slowly. For these reasons, many economists believe that nominal wages are sticky in the short run.

The **sticky-wage model** shows what a sticky nominal wage implies for aggregate supply. To preview the model, consider what happens to the amount of output produced when the price level rises:

1. When the nominal wage is stuck, a rise in the price level lowers the real wage, making labor cheaper.
2. The lower real wage induces firms to hire more labor.
3. The additional labor hired produces more output.

This positive relationship between the price level and the amount of output means that the aggregate supply curve slopes upward during the time when the nominal wage cannot adjust to a change in the price level.

To develop this story of aggregate supply more formally, assume that workers and firms bargain over and agree on the nominal wage before they know what the price level will be when their agreement takes effect. The bargaining parties—the workers and the firms—have in mind a target real wage. The target may be the real wage that equilibrates labor supply and demand. More likely, the target real wage is higher than the equilibrium real wage: as discussed in Chapter 6, union power and efficiency-wage considerations tend to keep real wages above the level that brings labor supply and labor demand into balance.

The workers and firms set the nominal wage W based on the target real wage ω and on their expectation of the price level P^e. The nominal wage they set is

$$W \quad = \quad \omega \quad \times \quad P^e$$

$$\text{Nominal Wage} = \text{Target Real Wage} \times \text{Expected Price Level.}$$

After the nominal wage has been set and before labor has been hired, firms learn the actual price level P. The real wage turns out to be

$$W/P \quad = \quad \omega \quad \times \quad (P^e/P)$$

$$\text{Real Wage} = \text{Target Real Wage} \times \frac{\text{Expected Price Level}}{\text{Actual Price Level}}.$$

This equation shows that the real wage deviates from its target if the actual price level differs from the expected price level. When the actual price level is greater than expected, the real wage is less than its target; when the actual price level is less than expected, the real wage is greater than its target.

The final assumption of the sticky-wage model is that employment is determined by the quantity of labor that firms demand. In other words, the bargain between the workers and the firms does not determine the level of employment in advance; instead, the workers agree to provide as much labor as the firms wish to buy at the predetermined wage. We describe the firms' hiring decisions by the labor demand function

$$L = L^d(W/P),$$

which states that the lower the real wage, the more labor firms hire. The labor demand curve is shown in panel (a) of Figure 13-1. Output is determined by the production function

$$Y = F(L),$$

which states that the more labor is hired, the more output is produced. This is shown in panel (b) of Figure 13-1.

FIGURE 13-1

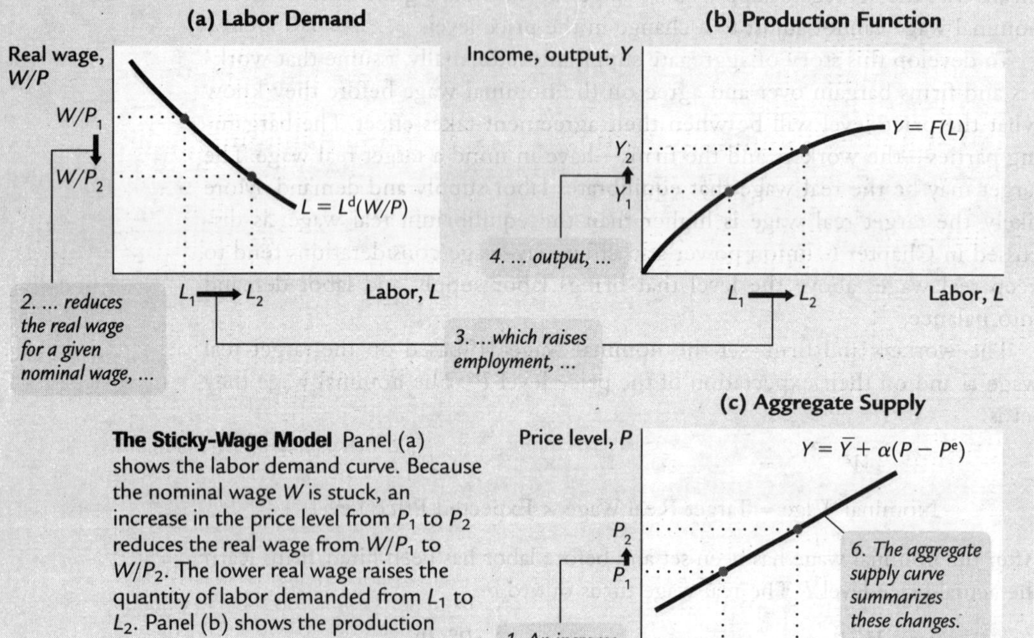

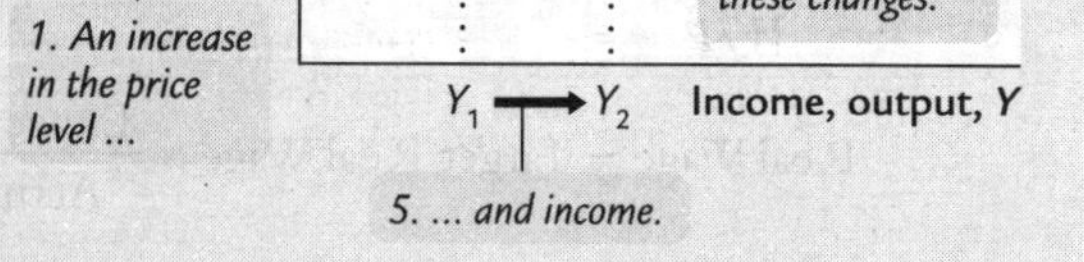

The Sticky-Wage Model Panel (a) shows the labor demand curve. Because the nominal wage W is stuck, an increase in the price level from P_1 to P_2 reduces the real wage from W/P_1 to W/P_2. The lower real wage raises the quantity of labor demanded from L_1 to L_2. Panel (b) shows the production function. An increase in the quantity of labor from L_1 to L_2 raises output from Y_1 to Y_2. Panel (c) shows the aggregate supply curve summarizing this relationship between the price level and output. An increase in the price level from P_1 to P_2 raises output from Y_1 to Y_2.

Panel (c) of Figure 13-1 shows the resulting aggregate supply curve. Because the nominal wage is sticky, an unexpected change in the price level moves the real wage away from the target real wage, and this change in the real wage influences the amounts of labor hired and output produced. The aggregate supply curve can be written as

$$Y = \bar{Y} + \alpha(P - P^e).$$

Output deviates from its natural level when the price level deviates from the expected price level.[3]

CASE STUDY

The Cyclical Behavior of the Real Wage

In any model with an unchanging labor demand curve, such as the model we just discussed, employment rises when the real wage falls. In the sticky-wage model, an unexpected rise in the price level lowers the real wage and thereby raises the quantity of labor hired and the amount of output produced. Thus, the real wage should be *countercyclical*: it should fluctuate in the opposite direction from employment and output. Keynes himself wrote in *The General Theory* that "an increase in employment can only occur to the accompaniment of a decline in the rate of real wages."

The earliest attacks on *The General Theory* came from economists challenging Keynes's prediction. Figure 13-2 is a scatterplot of the percentage change in real compensation per hour and the percentage change in real GDP using annual data for the U.S. economy from 1960 to 2004. If Keynes's prediction were correct, the dots in this figure would show a downward-sloping pattern, indicating a negative relationship. Yet the figure shows only a weak correlation between the real wage and output, and it is the opposite of what Keynes predicted. That is, if the real wage is cyclical at all, it is slightly *procyclical*: the real wage tends to rise when output rises. Abnormally high labor costs cannot explain the low employment and output observed in recessions.

How should we interpret this evidence? Most economists conclude that the sticky-wage model cannot fully explain aggregate supply. They advocate models in which the labor demand curve shifts over the business cycle. These shifts may arise because firms have sticky prices: when prices are stuck too high, firms sell less of their output and reduce their demand for labor. Alternatively, the labor demand curve may shift because shocks to technology alter labor

---

[3] For more on the sticky-wage model, see Jo Anna Gray, "Wage Indexation: A Macroeconomic Approach," *Journal of Monetary Economics* 2 (April 1976): 221–235; and Stanley Fischer, "Long-term Contracts, Rational Expectations, and the Optimal Money Supply Rule," *Journal of Political Economy* 85 (February 1977): 191–205.

FIGURE 13-2

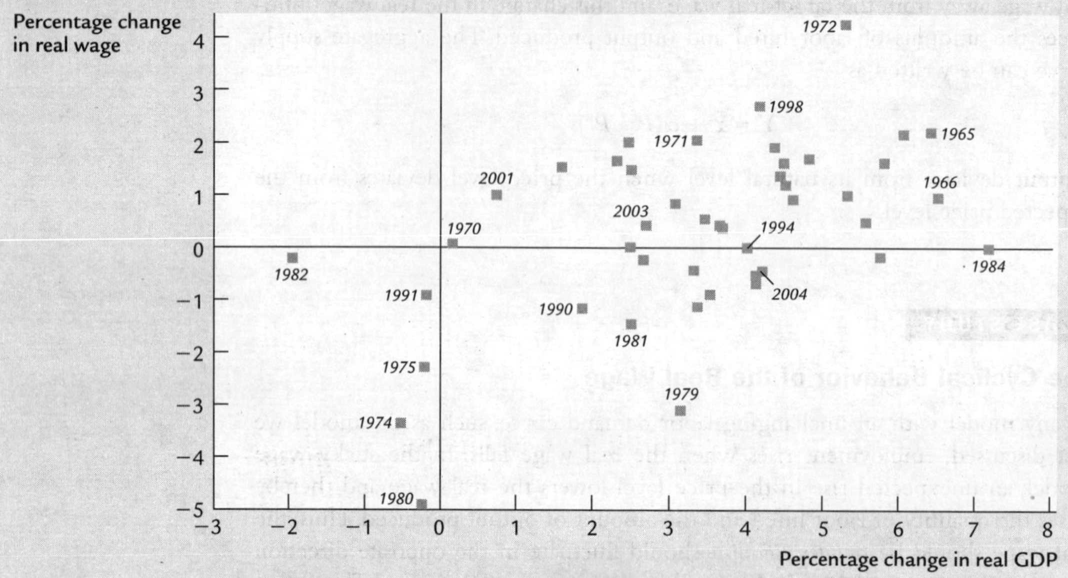

The Cyclical Behavior of the Real Wage This scatterplot shows the percentage change in real GDP and the percentage change in the real wage (measured here as real private hourly earnings). As output fluctuates, the real wage typically moves in the same direction. That is, the real wage is somewhat procyclical. This observation is inconsistent with the sticky-wage model.

Source: U.S. Department of Commerce and U.S. Department of Labor.

productivity. The theory we discuss in Chapter 19, called the theory of real business cycles, gives a prominent role to technology shocks as a source of economic fluctuations.[4]

The Imperfect-Information Model

The third explanation for the upward slope of the short-run aggregate supply curve is called the **imperfect-information model**. Unlike the previous two models, this model assumes that markets clear—that is, all wages and prices are free to adjust to balance supply and demand. In this model, the short-run and

[4] For some of the recent work on the cyclical behavior of the real wage, see Scott Sumner and Stephen Silver, "Real Wages, Employment, and the Phillips Curve," *Journal of Political Economy* 97 (June 1989): 706–720; and Gary Solon, Robert Barsky, and Jonathan A. Parker, "Measuring the Cyclicality of Real Wages: How Important Is Composition Bias?" *Quarterly Journal of Economics* 109 (February 1994): 1–25.

long-run aggregate supply curves differ because of temporary misperceptions about prices.

The imperfect-information model assumes that each supplier in the economy produces a single good and consumes many goods. Because the number of goods is so large, suppliers cannot observe all prices at all times. They monitor closely the prices of what they produce but less closely the prices of all the goods they consume. Because of imperfect information, they sometimes confuse changes in the overall level of prices with changes in relative prices. This confusion influences decisions about how much to supply, and it leads to a positive relationship between the price level and output in the short run.

Consider the decision facing a single supplier—a wheat farmer, for instance. Because the farmer earns income from selling wheat and uses this income to buy goods and services, the amount of wheat she chooses to produce depends on the price of wheat relative to the prices of other goods and services in the economy. If the relative price of wheat is high, the farmer is motivated to work hard and produce more wheat, because the reward is great. If the relative price of wheat is low, she prefers to enjoy more leisure and produce less wheat.

Unfortunately, when the farmer makes her production decision, she does not know the relative price of wheat. As a wheat producer, she monitors the wheat market closely and always knows the nominal price of wheat. But she does not know the prices of all the other goods in the economy. She must, therefore, estimate the relative price of wheat using the nominal price of wheat and her expectation of the overall price level.

Consider how the farmer responds if all prices in the economy, including the price of wheat, increase. One possibility is that she expected this change in prices. When she observes an increase in the price of wheat, her estimate of its relative price is unchanged. She does not work any harder.

The other possibility is that the farmer did not expect the price level to increase (or to increase by this much). When she observes the increase in the price of wheat, she is not sure whether other prices have risen (in which case wheat's relative price is unchanged) or whether only the price of wheat has risen (in which case its relative price is higher). The rational inference is that some of each has happened. In other words, the farmer infers from the increase in the nominal price of wheat that its relative price has risen somewhat. She works harder and produces more.

Our wheat farmer is not unique. When the price level rises unexpectedly, all suppliers in the economy observe increases in the prices of the goods they produce. They all infer, rationally but mistakenly, that the relative prices of the goods they produce have risen. They work harder and produce more.

To sum up, the imperfect-information model says that when actual prices exceed expected prices, suppliers raise their output. The model implies an aggregate supply curve with the familiar form:

$$Y = \bar{Y} + \alpha(P - P^e).$$

Output deviates from the natural level when the price level deviates from the expected price level.[5]

CASE STUDY

International Differences in the Aggregate Supply Curve

Although all countries experience economic fluctuations, these fluctuations are not exactly the same everywhere. International differences are intriguing puzzles in themselves, and they often provide a way to test alternative economic theories. Examining international differences has been especially fruitful in research on aggregate supply.

When economist Robert Lucas proposed the imperfect-information model, he derived a surprising interaction between aggregate demand and aggregate supply: according to his model, the slope of the aggregate supply curve should depend on the volatility of aggregate demand. In countries where aggregate demand fluctuates widely, the aggregate price level fluctuates widely as well. Because most movements in prices in these countries do not represent movements in relative prices, suppliers should have learned not to respond much to unexpected changes in the price level. Therefore, the aggregate supply curve should be relatively steep (that is, α will be small). Conversely, in countries where aggregate demand is relatively stable, suppliers should have learned that most price changes are relative price changes. Accordingly, in these countries, suppliers should be more responsive to unexpected price changes, making the aggregate supply curve relatively flat (that is, α will be large).

Lucas tested this prediction by examining international data on output and prices. He found that changes in aggregate demand have the biggest effect on output in those countries where aggregate demand and prices are most stable. Lucas concluded that the evidence supports the imperfect-information model.[6]

The sticky-price model also makes predictions about the slope of the short-run aggregate supply curve. In particular, it predicts that the average rate of inflation should influence the slope of the short-run aggregate supply curve. When the average rate of inflation is high, it is very costly for firms to keep prices fixed for long intervals. Thus, firms adjust prices more frequently. More frequent price

---

[5] Two economists who have emphasized the role of imperfect information for understanding the short-run effects of monetary policy are the Nobel Prize winners Milton Friedman and Robert Lucas. See Milton Friedman, "The Role of Monetary Policy," *American Economic Review* 58 (March 1968): 1–17; and Robert E. Lucas, Jr., "Understanding Business Cycles," *Stabilization of the Domestic and International Economy,* vol. 5 of Carnegie-Rochester Conference on Public Policy (Amsterdam: North-Holland, 1977), 7–29.

[6] Robert E. Lucas, Jr., "Some International Evidence on Output-Inflation Tradeoffs," *American Economic Review* 63 (June 1973): 326–334.

adjustment in turn allows the overall price level to respond more quickly to shocks to aggregate demand. Hence, a high rate of inflation should make the short-run aggregate supply curve steeper.

International data support this prediction of the sticky-price model. In countries with low average inflation, the short-run aggregate supply curve is relatively flat: fluctuations in aggregate demand have large effects on output and are slowly reflected in prices. High-inflation countries have steep short-run aggregate supply curves. In other words, high inflation appears to erode the frictions that cause prices to be sticky.[7]

Note that the sticky-price model can also explain Lucas's finding that countries with variable aggregate demand have steep aggregate supply curves. If the price level is highly variable, few firms will commit to prices in advance (s will be small). Hence, the aggregate supply curve will be steep (α will be small).

Summary and Implications

We have seen three models of aggregate supply and the market imperfection that each uses to explain why the short-run aggregate supply curve is upward sloping. One model assumes the prices of some goods are sticky; the second assumes nominal wages are sticky; the third assumes information about prices is imperfect. Keep in mind that these models are not incompatible with one another. We need not accept one model and reject the others. The world may contain all three of these market imperfections, and all may contribute to the behavior of short-run aggregate supply.

Although the three models of aggregate supply differ in their assumptions and emphases, their implications for aggregate output are similar. All can be summarized by the equation

$$Y = \bar{Y} + \alpha(P - P^e).$$

This equation states that deviations of output from the natural level are related to deviations of the price level from the expected price level. *If the price level is higher than the expected price level, output exceeds its natural level. If the price level is lower than the expected price level, output falls short of its natural level.* Figure 13-3 graphs this equation. Notice that the short-run aggregate supply curve is drawn for a given expectation P^e and that a change in P^e would shift the curve.

Now that we have a better understanding of aggregate supply, let's put aggregate supply and aggregate demand back together. Figure 13-4 uses our aggregate supply equation to show how the economy responds to an unexpected increase

[7] Laurence Ball, N. Gregory Mankiw, and David Romer, "The New Keynesian Economics and the Output-Inflation Tradeoff," *Brookings Papers on Economic Activity* 1(1988): 1–65.

FIGURE 13-3

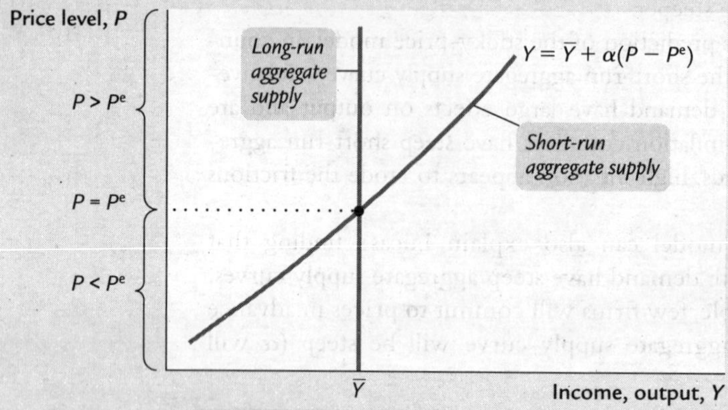

The Short-Run Aggregate Supply Curve Output deviates from its natural level $\bar{Y}$ if the price level P deviates from the expected price level P^e.

in aggregate demand attributable, say, to an unexpected monetary expansion. In the short run, the equilibrium moves from point A to point B. The increase in aggregate demand raises the actual price level from P_1 to P_2. Because people did not expect this increase in the price level, the expected price level remains at P_2^e, and output rises from Y_1 to Y_2, which is above the natural level $\bar{Y}$. Thus, the unexpected expansion in aggregate demand causes the economy to boom.

Yet the boom does not last forever. In the long run, the expected price level rises to catch up with reality, causing the short-run aggregate supply curve to shift upward. As the expected price level rises from P_2^e to P_3^e, the equilibrium of

FIGURE 13-4

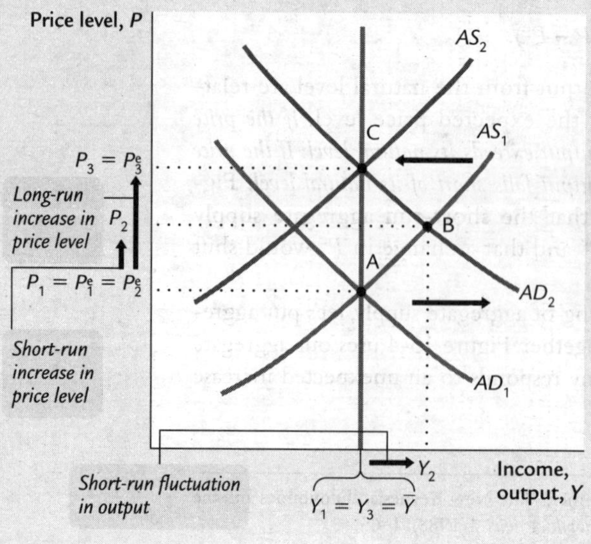

How Shifts in Aggregate Demand Lead to Short-Run Fluctuations Here the economy begins in a long-run equilibrium, point A. When aggregate demand increases unexpectedly, the price level rises from P_1 to P_2. Because the price level P_2 is above the expected price level P_2^e, output rises temporarily above the natural level, as the economy moves along the short-run aggregate supply curve from point A to point B. In the long run, the expected price level rises to P_3^e, causing the short-run aggregate supply curve to shift upward. The economy returns to a new long-run equilibrium, point C, where output is back at its natural level.

the economy moves from point B to point C. The actual price level rises from P_2 to P_3, and output falls from Y_2 to Y_3. In other words, the economy returns to the natural level of output in the long run, but at a much higher price level.

This analysis shows an important principle, which holds for each of the three models of aggregate supply: long-run monetary neutrality and short-run monetary *non*neutrality are perfectly compatible. Short-run nonneutrality is represented here by the movement from point A to point B, and long-run monetary neutrality is represented by the movement from point A to point C. We reconcile the short-run and long-run effects of money by emphasizing the adjustment of expectations about the price level.

13-2 Inflation, Unemployment, and the Phillips Curve

Two goals of economic policymakers are low inflation and low unemployment, but often these goals conflict. Suppose, for instance, that policymakers were to use monetary or fiscal policy to expand aggregate demand. This policy would move the economy along the short-run aggregate supply curve to a point of higher output and a higher price level. (Figure 13-4 shows this as the change from point A to point B.) Higher output means lower unemployment, because firms employ more workers when they produce more. A higher price level, given the previous year's price level, means higher inflation. Thus, when policymakers move the economy up along the short-run aggregate supply curve, they reduce the unemployment rate and raise the inflation rate. Conversely, when they contract aggregate demand and move the economy down the short-run aggregate supply curve, unemployment rises and inflation falls.

This tradeoff between inflation and unemployment, called the *Phillips curve*, is our topic in this section. As we have just seen (and will derive more formally in a moment), the Phillips curve is a reflection of the short-run aggregate supply curve: as policymakers move the economy along the short-run aggregate supply curve, unemployment and inflation move in opposite directions. The Phillips curve is a useful way to express aggregate supply because inflation and unemployment are such important measures of economic performance.

Deriving the Phillips Curve From the Aggregate Supply Curve

The **Phillips curve** in its modern form states that the inflation rate depends on three forces:

- Expected inflation
- The deviation of unemployment from the natural rate, called *cyclical unemployment*
- Supply shocks.

These three forces are expressed in the following equation:

$$\pi = \pi^e - \beta(u - u^n) + v$$

$$\text{Inflation} = \text{Expected Inflation} - (\beta \times \text{Cyclical Unemployment}) + \text{Supply Shock},$$

where β is a parameter measuring the response of inflation to cyclical unemployment. Notice that there is a minus sign before the cyclical unemployment term: other things equal, higher unemployment is associated with lower inflation.

Where does this equation for the Phillips curve come from? Although it may not seem familiar, we can derive it from our equation for aggregate supply. To see how, write the aggregate supply equation as

$$P = P^e + (1/\alpha)(Y - \bar{Y}).$$

With one addition, one subtraction, and one substitution, we can transform this equation into the Phillips curve relationship between inflation and unemployment.

Here are the three steps. First, add to the right-hand side of the equation a supply shock v to represent exogenous events (such as a change in world oil prices) that alter the price level and shift the short-run aggregate supply curve:

$$P = P^e + (1/\alpha)(Y - \bar{Y}) + v.$$

Next, to go from the price level to inflation rates, subtract last year's price level P_{-1} from both sides of the equation to obtain

$$(P - P_{-1}) = (P^e - P_{-1}) + (1/\alpha)(Y - \bar{Y}) + v.$$

The term on the left-hand side, $P - P_{-1}$, is the difference between the current price level and last year's price level, which is inflation π.[8] The term on the right-hand side, $P^e - P_{-1}$, is the difference between the expected price level and last year's price level, which is expected inflation π^e. Therefore, we can replace $P - P_{-1}$ with π and $P^e - P_{-1}$ with π^e:

$$\pi = \pi^e + (1/\alpha)(Y - \bar{Y}) + v.$$

Third, to go from output to unemployment, recall from Chapter 9 that Okun's law gives a relationship between these two variables. One version of Okun's law states that the deviation of output from its natural level is inversely related to the deviation of unemployment from its natural rate; that is, when output is higher than the natural level of output, unemployment is lower than the natural rate of unemployment. We can write this as

$$(1/\alpha)(Y - \bar{Y}) = -\beta(u - u^n).$$

---

[8] *Mathematical note:* This statement is not precise, because inflation is really the *percentage* change in the price level. To make the statement more precise, interpret P as the logarithm of the price level. By the properties of logarithms, the change in P is roughly the inflation rate. The reason is that $dP = d(\text{log price level}) = d(\text{price level})/\text{price level}$.

FYI The History of the Modern Phillips Curve

The Phillips curve is named after New Zealand-born economist A. W. Phillips. In 1958 Phillips observed a negative relationship between the unemployment rate and the rate of wage inflation in data for the United Kingdom.[9] The Phillips curve that economists use today differs in three ways from the relationship Phillips examined.

First, the modern Phillips curve substitutes price inflation for wage inflation. This difference is not crucial, because price inflation and wage inflation are closely related. In periods when wages are rising quickly, prices are rising quickly as well.

Second, the modern Phillips curve includes expected inflation. This addition is due to the work of Milton Friedman and Edmund Phelps. In developing early versions of the imperfect-information model in the 1960s, these two economists emphasized the importance of expectations for aggregate supply.

Third, the modern Phillips curve includes supply shocks. Credit for this addition goes to OPEC, the Organization of Petroleum Exporting Countries. In the 1970s OPEC caused large increases in the world price of oil, which made economists more aware of the importance of shocks to aggregate supply.

Using this Okun's law relationship, we can substitute $-\beta(u - u^{n})$ for $(1/\alpha)(Y - \bar{Y})$ in the previous equation to obtain:

$$\pi = \pi^{e} - \beta(u - u^{n}) + v.$$

Thus, we can derive the Phillips-curve equation from the aggregate supply equation.

All this algebra is meant to show one thing: the Phillips-curve equation and the short-run aggregate supply equation represent essentially the same macroeconomic ideas. In particular, both equations show a link between real and nominal variables that causes the classical dichotomy (the theoretical separation of real and nominal variables) to break down in the short run. According to the short-run aggregate supply equation, output is related to unexpected movements in the price level. According to the Phillips-curve equation, unemployment is related to unexpected movements in the inflation rate. The aggregate supply curve is more convenient when we are studying output and the price level, whereas the Phillips curve is more convenient when we are studying unemployment and inflation. But we should not lose sight of the fact that the Phillips curve and the aggregate supply curve are two sides of the same coin.

Adaptive Expectations and Inflation Inertia

To make the Phillips curve useful for analyzing the choices facing policymakers, we need to say what determines expected inflation. A simple and often plausible assumption is that people form their expectations of inflation based on recently

---

[9] A. W. Phillips, "The Relationship Between Unemployment and the Rate of Change of Money Wages in the United Kingdom, 1861-1957," *Economica* 25 (November 1958): 283–299.

observed inflation. This assumption is called **adaptive expectations**. For example, suppose that people expect prices to rise this year at the same rate as they did last year. Then expected inflation π^e equals last year's inflation π_{-1}:

$$\pi^e = \pi_{-1}.$$

In this case, we can write the Phillips curve as

$$\pi = \pi_{-1} - \beta(u - u^n) + v,$$

which states that inflation depends on past inflation, cyclical unemployment, and a supply shock. When the Phillips curve is written in this form, the natural rate of unemployment is sometimes called the *Non-Accelerating Inflation Rate of Unemployment*, or *NAIRU*.

The first term in this form of the Phillips curve, π_{-1}, implies that inflation has inertia. That is, like an object moving through space, inflation keeps going unless something acts to stop it. In particular, if unemployment is at the NAIRU and if there are no supply shocks, the continued rise in price level neither speeds up nor slows down. This inertia arises because past inflation influences expectations of future inflation and because these expectations influence the wages and prices that people set. Robert Solow captured the concept of inflation inertia well when, during the high inflation of the 1970s, he wrote, "Why is our money ever less valuable? Perhaps it is simply that we have inflation because we expect inflation, and we expect inflation because we've had it."

In the model of aggregate supply and aggregate demand, inflation inertia is interpreted as persistent upward shifts in both the aggregate supply curve and the aggregate demand curve. Consider first aggregate supply. If prices have been rising quickly, people will expect them to continue to rise quickly. Because the position of the short-run aggregate supply curve depends on the expected price level, the short-run aggregate supply curve will shift upward over time. It will continue to shift upward until some event, such as a recession or a supply shock, changes inflation and thereby changes expectations of inflation.

The aggregate demand curve must also shift upward to confirm the expectations of inflation. Most often, the continued rise in aggregate demand is due to persistent growth in the money supply. If the Fed suddenly halted money growth, aggregate demand would stabilize, and the upward shift in aggregate supply would cause a recession. The high unemployment in the recession would reduce inflation and expected inflation, causing inflation inertia to subside.

Two Causes of Rising and Falling Inflation

The second and third terms in the Phillips-curve equation show the two forces that can change the rate of inflation.

The second term, $\beta(u - u^n)$, shows that cyclical unemployment—the deviation of unemployment from its natural rate—exerts upward or downward pressure on inflation. Low unemployment pulls the inflation rate up. This is called **demand-pull inflation** because high aggregate demand is responsible for this type of inflation. High unemployment pulls the inflation rate down. The parameter β measures how responsive inflation is to cyclical unemployment.

The third term, v, shows that inflation also rises and falls because of supply shocks. An adverse supply shock, such as the rise in world oil prices in the 1970s, implies a positive value of v and causes inflation to rise. This is called **cost-push inflation** because adverse supply shocks are typically events that push up the costs of production. A beneficial supply shock, such as the oil glut that led to a fall in oil prices in the 1980s, makes v negative and causes inflation to fall.

CASE STUDY

Inflation and Unemployment in the United States

Because inflation and unemployment are such important measures of economic performance, macroeconomic developments are often viewed through the lens of the Phillips curve. Figure 13-5 displays the history of inflation and unemployment in the United States since 1960. This almost half century of data illustrates some of the causes of rising or falling inflation.

The 1960s showed how policymakers can, in the short run, lower unemployment at the cost of higher inflation. The tax cut of 1964, together with expansionary monetary policy, expanded aggregate demand and pushed the unemployment rate below 5 percent. This expansion of aggregate demand continued in the late 1960s largely as a by-product of government spending for the Vietnam War. Unemployment fell lower and inflation rose higher than policymakers intended.

FIGURE 13-5

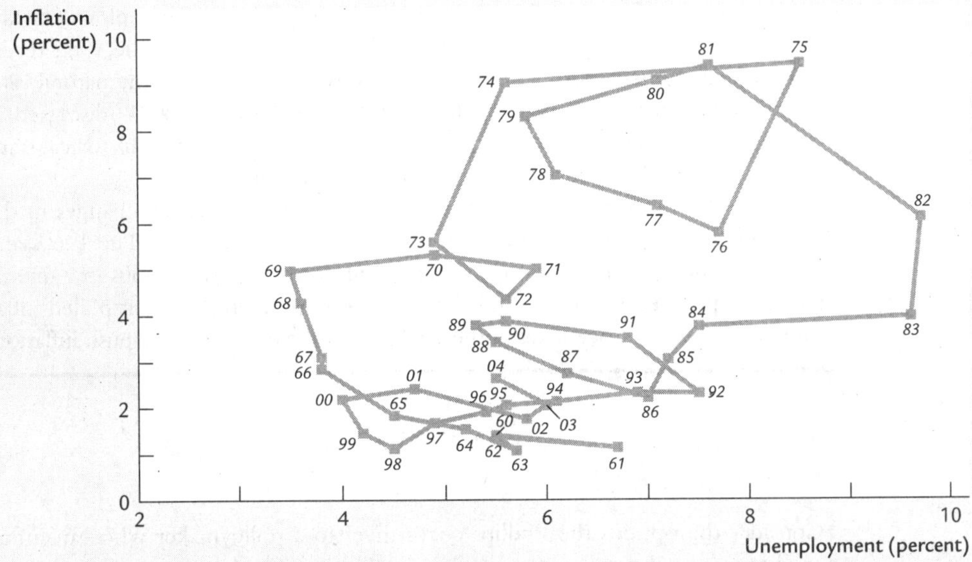

Inflation and Unemployment in the United States Since 1960 This figure uses annual data on the unemployment rate and the inflation rate (percentage change in the GDP deflator) to illustrate macroeconomic developments in almost a half century of U.S. history.

Source: U.S. Department of Commerce and U.S. Department of Labor.

The 1970s were a period of economic turmoil. The decade began with policymakers trying to lower the inflation inherited from the 1960s. President Nixon imposed temporary controls on wages and prices, and the Federal Reserve engineered a recession through contractionary monetary policy, but the inflation rate fell only slightly. The effects of wage and price controls ended when the controls were lifted, and the recession was too small to counteract the inflationary impact of the boom that had preceded it. By 1972 the unemployment rate was the same as a decade earlier, while inflation was 3 percentage points higher.

Beginning in 1973 policymakers had to cope with the large supply shocks caused by the Organization of Petroleum Exporting Countries (OPEC). OPEC first raised oil prices in the mid-1970s, pushing the inflation rate up to about 10 percent. This adverse supply shock, together with temporarily tight monetary policy, led to a recession in 1975. High unemployment during the recession reduced inflation somewhat, but further OPEC price hikes pushed inflation up again in the late 1970s.

The 1980s began with high inflation and high expectations of inflation. Under the leadership of Chairman Paul Volcker, the Federal Reserve doggedly pursued monetary policies aimed at reducing inflation. In 1982 and 1983 the unemployment rate reached its highest level in 40 years. High unemployment, aided by a fall in oil prices in 1986, pulled the inflation rate down from about 10 percent to about 3 percent. By 1987 the unemployment rate of about 6 percent was close to most estimates of the natural rate. Unemployment continued to fall through the 1980s, however, reaching a low of 5.2 percent in 1989 and beginning a new round of demand-pull inflation.

Compared to the preceding 30 years, the 1990s and early 2000s were relatively quiet. The 1990s began with a recession caused by several contractionary shocks to aggregate demand: tight monetary policy, the savings-and-loan crisis, and a fall in consumer confidence coinciding with the Gulf War. The unemployment rate rose to 7.3 percent in 1992, and inflation fell slightly. Unlike in the 1982 recession, unemployment in the 1990 recession was never far above the natural rate, so the effect on inflation was small. Similarly, a recession in 2001 (discussed in chapter 11) raised unemployment, but the downturn was mild by historical standards, and the impact on inflation was once again slight.

Thus, U.S. macroeconomic history exhibits the two causes of changes in the inflation rate that we encountered in the Phillips curve equation. The 1960s and the 1980s show the two sides of demand-pull inflation: in the 1960s low unemployment pulled inflation up, and in the 1980s high unemployment pulled inflation down. The oil price hikes of the 1970s show the effects of cost-push inflation.

The Short-Run Tradeoff Between Inflation and Unemployment

Consider the options the Phillips curve gives to a policymaker who can influence aggregate demand with monetary or fiscal policy. At any moment, expected inflation and supply shocks are beyond the policymaker's immediate control. Yet, by changing aggregate demand, the policymaker can alter output, unemployment, and inflation. The policymaker can expand aggregate demand to lower unemployment and raise inflation. Or the policymaker can depress aggregate demand to raise unemployment and lower inflation.

FIGURE 13-6

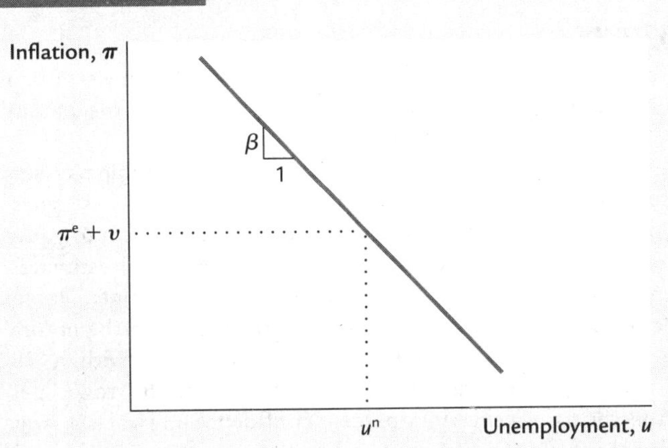

The Short-Run Tradeoff Between Inflation and Unemployment In the short run, inflation and unemployment are negatively related. At any point in time, a policymaker who controls aggregate demand can choose a combination of inflation and unemployment on this short-run Phillips curve.

Figure 13-6 plots the Phillips-curve equation and shows the short-run tradeoff between inflation and unemployment. When unemployment is at its natural rate ($u = u^n$), inflation depends on expected inflation and the supply shock ($\pi = \pi^e + v$). The parameter β determines the slope of the tradeoff between inflation and unemployment. In the short run, for a given level of expected inflation, policymakers can manipulate aggregate demand to choose any combination of inflation and unemployment on this curve, called the *short-run Phillips curve.*

Notice that the position of the short-run Phillips curve depends on the expected rate of inflation. If expected inflation rises, the curve shifts upward, and the policymaker's tradeoff becomes less favorable: inflation is higher for any level of unemployment. Figure 13-7 shows how the tradeoff depends on expected inflation.

FIGURE 13-7

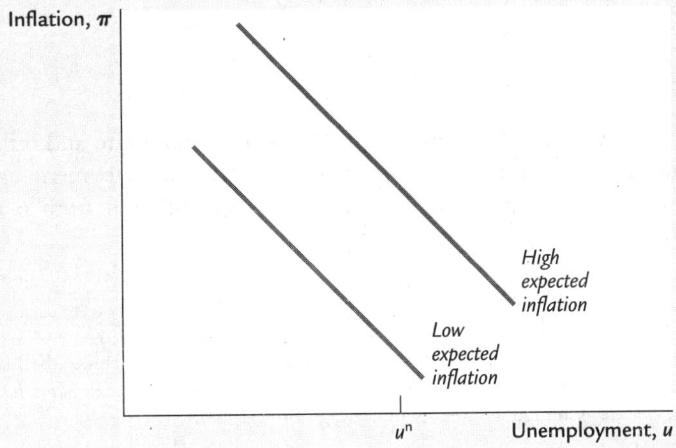

Shifts in the Short-Run Tradeoff The short-run tradeoff between inflation and unemployment depends on expected inflation. The curve is higher when expected inflation is higher.

FYI

How Precise Are Estimates of the Natural Rate of Unemployment?

If you ask an astronomer how far a particular star is from our sun, he'll give you a number, but it won't be accurate. Man's ability to measure astronomical distances is still limited. Another astronomer might well take better measurements and conclude that a star is really twice or half as far away as he previously thought.

Estimates of the natural rate of unemployment, or NAIRU, are also far from precise. One problem is supply shocks. Shocks to oil supplies, farm harvests, or technological progress can cause inflation to rise or fall in the short run. When we observe rising inflation, therefore, we can not be sure if it is evidence that the unemployment rate is below the natural rate or evidence that the economy is experiencing an adverse supply shock.

A second problem is that the natural rate changes over time. Demographic changes (such as the aging of the baby-boom generation), policy changes (such as minimum-wage laws), and institutional changes (such as the declining role of unions) all influence the economy's normal level of unemployment. Estimating the natural rate is like hitting a moving target.

Economists deal with these problems using statistical techniques that yield a best guess about the natural rate and allow them to gauge the uncertainty associated with their estimates. In one such study, Douglas Staiger, James Stock, and Mark Watson estimated the natural rate to be 6.2 percent in 1990, with a 95-percent confidence interval from 5.1 to 7.7 percent. A 95-percent confidence interval is a range such that the statistician is 95-percent confident that the true value falls in that range. The large confidence interval here of 2.6 percentage points shows that estimates of the natural rate are not at all precise.

This conclusion has profound implications. Policymakers may want to keep unemployment close to its natural rate, but their ability to do so is limited by the fact that they cannot be sure what that natural rate is.[10]

Because people adjust their expectations of inflation over time, the tradeoff between inflation and unemployment holds only in the short run. The policymaker cannot keep inflation above expected inflation (and thus unemployment below its natural rate) forever. Eventually, expectations adapt to whatever inflation rate the policymaker has chosen. In the long run, the classical dichotomy holds, unemployment returns to its natural rate, and there is no tradeoff between inflation and unemployment.

Disinflation and the Sacrifice Ratio

Imagine an economy in which unemployment is at its natural rate and inflation is running at 6 percent. What would happen to unemployment and output if the central bank pursued a policy to reduce inflation from 6 to 2 percent?

[10] Douglas Staiger, James H. Stock, and Mark W. Watson, "How Precise Are Estimates of the Natural Rate of Unemployment?" in Christina D. Romer and David H. Romer, eds., *Reducing Inflation: Motivation and Strategy* (Chicago: University of Chicago Press, 1997).

The Phillips curve shows that in the absence of a beneficial supply shock, lowering inflation requires a period of high unemployment and reduced output. But by how much and for how long would unemployment need to rise above the natural rate? Before deciding whether to reduce inflation, policymakers must know how much output would be lost during the transition to lower inflation. This cost can then be compared with the benefits of lower inflation.

Much research has used the available data to examine the Phillips curve quantitatively. The results of these studies are often summarized in a number called the **sacrifice ratio**, the percentage of a year's real GDP that must be forgone to reduce inflation by 1 percentage point. Although estimates of the sacrifice ratio vary substantially, a typical estimate is about 5: for every percentage point that inflation is to fall, 5 percent of one year's GDP must be sacrificed.[11]

We can also express the sacrifice ratio in terms of unemployment. Okun's law says that a change of 1 percentage point in the unemployment rate translates into a change of 2 percentage points in GDP. Therefore, reducing inflation by 1 percentage point requires about 2.5 percentage points of cyclical unemployment.

We can use the sacrifice ratio to estimate by how much and for how long unemployment must rise to reduce inflation. If reducing inflation by 1 percentage point requires a sacrifice of 5 percent of a year's GDP, reducing inflation by 4 percentage points requires a sacrifice of 20 percent of a year's GDP. Equivalently, this reduction in inflation requires a sacrifice of 10 percentage points of cyclical unemployment.

This disinflation could take various forms, each totaling the same sacrifice of 20 percent of a year's GDP. For example, a rapid disinflation would lower output by 10 percent for 2 years: this is sometimes called the *cold-turkey* solution to inflation. A moderate disinflation would lower output by 5 percent for 4 years. An even more gradual disinflation would depress output by 2 percent for a decade.

Rational Expectations and the Possibility of Painless Disinflation

Because the expectation of inflation influences the short-run tradeoff between inflation and unemployment, it is crucial to understand how people form expectations. So far, we have been assuming that expected inflation depends on recently observed inflation. Although this assumption of adaptive expectations is plausible, it is probably too simple to apply in all circumstances.

An alternative approach is to assume that people have **rational expectations**. That is, we might assume that people optimally use all the available information, including information about current government policies, to forecast the future. Because monetary and fiscal policies influence inflation, expected inflation should also depend on the monetary and fiscal policies in effect. According to

---

[11] Arthur M. Okun, "Efficient Disinflationary Policies," *American Economic Review* 68 (May 1978): 348–352; Robert J. Gordon and Stephen R. King, "The Output Cost of Disinflation in Traditional and Vector Autoregressive Models," *Brookings Papers on Economic Activity* 1(1982): 205–245.

the theory of rational expectations, a change in monetary or fiscal policy will change expectations, and an evaluation of any policy change must incorporate this effect on expectations. If people do form their expectations rationally, then inflation may have less inertia than it first appears.

Here is how Thomas Sargent, a prominent advocate of rational expectations, describes its implications for the Phillips curve:

> An alternative "rational expectations" view denies that there is any inherent momentum to the present process of inflation. This view maintains that firms and workers have now come to expect high rates of inflation in the future and that they strike inflationary bargains in light of these expectations. However, it is held that people expect high rates of inflation in the future precisely because the government's current and prospective monetary and fiscal policies warrant those expectations. . . . Thus inflation only seems to have a momentum of its own; it is actually the long-term government policy of persistently running large deficits and creating money at high rates which imparts the momentum to the inflation rate. An implication of this view is that inflation can be stopped much more quickly than advocates of the "momentum" view have indicated and that their estimates of the length of time and the costs of stopping inflation in terms of foregone output are erroneous. . . . [Stopping inflation] would require a change in the policy regime: there must be an abrupt change in the continuing government policy, or strategy, for setting deficits now and in the future that is sufficiently binding as to be widely believed. . . . How costly such a move would be in terms of foregone output and how long it would be in taking effect would depend partly on how resolute and evident the government's commitment was.[12]

Thus, advocates of rational expectations argue that the short-run Phillips curve does not accurately represent the options that policymakers have available. They believe that if policymakers are credibly committed to reducing inflation, rational people will understand the commitment and will quickly lower their expectations of inflation. Inflation can then come down without a rise in unemployment and fall in output. According to the theory of rational expectations, traditional estimates of the sacrifice ratio are not useful for evaluating the impact of alternative policies. Under a credible policy, the costs of reducing inflation may be much lower than estimates of the sacrifice ratio suggest.

In the most extreme case, one can imagine reducing the rate of inflation without causing any recession at all. A painless disinflation has two requirements. First, the plan to reduce inflation must be announced before the workers and firms who set wages and prices have formed their expectations. Second, the workers and firms must believe the announcement; otherwise, they will not reduce their expectations of inflation. If both requirements are met, the announcement will immediately shift the short-run tradeoff between inflation and unemployment downward, permitting a lower rate of inflation without higher unemployment.

Although the rational-expectations approach remains controversial, almost all economists agree that expectations of inflation influence the short-run tradeoff

---

[12] Thomas J. Sargent, "The Ends of Four Big Inflations," in Robert E. Hall, ed., *Inflation: Causes and Effects* (Chicago: University of Chicago Press, 1982).

between inflation and unemployment. The credibility of a policy to reduce inflation is therefore one determinant of how costly the policy will be. Unfortunately, it is often difficult to predict whether the public will view the announcement of a new policy as credible. The central role of expectations makes forecasting the results of alternative policies far more difficult.

CASE STUDY

The Sacrifice Ratio in Practice

The Phillips curve with adaptive expectations implies that reducing inflation requires a period of high unemployment and low output. By contrast, the rational-expectations approach suggests that reducing inflation can be much less costly. What happens during actual disinflations?

Consider the U.S. disinflation in the early 1980s. This decade began with some of the highest rates of inflation in U.S. history. Yet because of the tight monetary policies the Fed pursued under Chairman Paul Volcker, the rate of inflation fell substantially in the first few years of the decade. This episode provides a natural experiment with which to estimate how much output is lost during the process of disinflation.

The first question is, how much did inflation fall? As measured by the GDP deflator, inflation reached a peak of 9.7 percent in 1981. It is natural to end the episode in 1985 because oil prices plunged in 1986—a large, beneficial supply shock unrelated to Fed policy. In 1985, inflation was 3.0 percent, so we can estimate that the Fed engineered a reduction in inflation of 6.7 percentage points over four years.

The second question is, how much output was lost during this period? Table 13-1 shows the unemployment rate from 1982 to 1985. Assuming that the natural rate of unemployment was 6 percent, we can compute the amount of cyclical unemployment in each year. In total over this period, there were 9.5 percentage points of cyclical unemployment. Okun's law says that 1 percentage point of unemployment translates into 2 percentage points of GDP. Therefore, 19.0 percentage points of annual GDP were lost during the disinflation.

TABLE 13-1

Unemployment During the Volcker Disinflation

Year	Unemployment Rate u	Natural Rate u^n	Cyclical Unemployment $u - u^n$
1982	9.5%	6.0%	3.5%
1983	9.5	6.0	3.5
1984	7.4	6.0	1.4
1985	7.1	6.0	1.1
			Total 9.5%

Now we can compute the sacrifice ratio for this episode. We know that 19.0 percentage points of GDP were lost and that inflation fell by 6.7 percentage points. Hence, 19.0/6.7, or 2.8, percentage points of GDP were lost for each percentage-point reduction in inflation. The estimate of the sacrifice ratio from the Volcker disinflation is 2.8.

This estimate of the sacrifice ratio is smaller than the estimates made before Volcker was appointed Fed chairman. In other words, Volcker reduced inflation at a smaller cost than many economists had predicted. One explanation is that Volcker's tough stand was credible enough to influence expectations of inflation directly. Yet the change in expectations was not large enough to make the disinflation painless: in 1982 unemployment reached its highest level since the Great Depression.

Although the Volcker disinflation is only one historical episode, this kind of analysis can be applied to other disinflations. A recent study documented the results of 65 disinflations in 19 countries. In almost all cases, the reduction in inflation came at the cost of temporarily lower output. Yet the size of the output loss varied from episode to episode. Rapid disinflations usually had smaller sacrifice ratios than slower ones. That is, in contrast to what the Phillips curve with adaptive expectations suggests, a cold-turkey approach appears less costly than a gradual one. Moreover, countries with more flexible wage-setting institutions, such as shorter labor contracts, had smaller sacrifice ratios. These findings indicate that reducing inflation always has some cost, but that policies and institutions can affect its magnitude.[13]

Hysteresis and the Challenge to the Natural-Rate Hypothesis

Our discussion of the cost of disinflation—and indeed our entire discussion of economic fluctuations in the past four chapters—has been based on an assumption called the **natural-rate hypothesis**. This hypothesis is summarized in the following statement:

> *Fluctuations in aggregate demand affect output and employment only in the short run. In the long run, the economy returns to the levels of output, employment, and unemployment described by the classical model.*

The natural-rate hypothesis allows macroeconomists to study separately short-run and long-run developments in the economy. It is one expression of the classical dichotomy.

Recently, some economists have challenged the natural-rate hypothesis by suggesting that aggregate demand may affect output and employment even in the long run. They have pointed out a number of mechanisms through which recessions might leave permanent scars on the economy by altering the natural rate

[13] Laurence Ball, "What Determines the Sacrifice Ratio?" in N. Gregory Mankiw, ed., *Monetary Policy* (Chicago: University of Chicago Press, 1994).

of unemployment. **Hysteresis** is the term used to describe the long-lasting influence of history on the natural rate.

A recession can have permanent effects if it changes the people who become unemployed. For instance, workers might lose valuable job skills when unemployed, lowering their ability to find a job even after the recession ends. Alternatively, a long period of unemployment may change an individual's attitude toward work and reduce his desire to find employment. In either case, the recession permanently inhibits the process of job search and raises the amount of frictional unemployment.

Another way in which a recession can permanently affect the economy is by changing the process that determines wages. Those who become unemployed may lose their influence on the wage-setting process. Unemployed workers may lose their status as union members, for example. More generally, some of the *insiders* in the wage-setting process become *outsiders.* If the smaller group of insiders cares more about high real wages and less about high employment, then the recession may permanently push real wages further above the equilibrium level and raise the amount of structural unemployment.

Hysteresis remains a controversial theory. Some economists believe the theory helps explain persistently high unemployment in Europe, because the rise in European unemployment starting in the early 1980s coincided with disinflation but continued after inflation stabilized. Moreover, the increase in unemployment tended to be larger for those countries that experienced the greatest reductions in inflations, such as Ireland, Italy, and Spain. Yet there is still no consensus whether the hysteresis phenomenon is significant, or why it might be more pronounced in some countries than in others. (Other explanations of high European unemployment, discussed in Chapter 6, give little role to the disinflation.) If it is true, however, the theory is important, because hysteresis greatly increases the cost of recessions. Put another way, hysteresis raises the sacrifice ratio, because output is lost even after the period of disinflation is over.[14]

13-3 Conclusion

We began this chapter by discussing three models of aggregate supply, each of which focuses on a different reason why, in the short run, output rises above its natural level when the price level rises above the level that people had expected. All three models explain why the short-run aggregate supply curve is upward sloping, and all of them yield a short-run tradeoff between inflation and unemployment. A convenient way to express and analyze that tradeoff is with the

[14] Olivier J. Blanchard and Lawrence H. Summers, "Beyond the Natural Rate Hypothesis," *American Economic Review* 78 (May 1988): 182–187; Laurence Ball, "Disinflation and the NAIRU," in Christina D. Romer and David H. Romer, eds., *Reducing Inflation: Motivation and Strategy* (Chicago: University of Chicago Press, 1997), 167-185.

Phillips-curve equation, according to which inflation depends on expected inflation, cyclical unemployment, and supply shocks.

Keep in mind that not all economists endorse all the ideas discussed here. There is widespread disagreement, for instance, about the practical importance of rational expectations and the relevance of hysteresis. If you find it difficult to fit all the pieces together, you are not alone. The study of aggregate supply remains one of the most unsettled—and therefore one of the most exciting—research areas in macroeconomics.

Summary

1. The three theories of aggregate supply—the sticky-price, sticky-wage, and imperfect-information models—attribute deviations of output and employment from their natural levels to various market imperfections. According to all three theories, output rises above its natural level when the price level exceeds the expected price level, and output falls below its natural level when the price level is less than the expected price level.
2. Economists often express aggregate supply in a relationship called the Phillips curve. The Phillips curve says that inflation depends on expected inflation, the deviation of unemployment from its natural rate, and supply shocks. According to the Phillips curve, policymakers who control aggregate demand face a short-run tradeoff between inflation and unemployment.
3. If expected inflation depends on recently observed inflation, then inflation has inertia, which means that reducing inflation requires either a beneficial supply shock or a period of high unemployment and reduced output. If people have rational expectations, however, then a credible announcement of a change in policy might be able to influence expectations directly and, therefore, reduce inflation without causing a recession.
4. Most economists accept the natural-rate hypothesis, according to which fluctuations in aggregate demand have only short-run effects on output and unemployment. Yet some economists have suggested ways in which recessions can leave permanent scars on the economy by raising the natural rate of unemployment.

KEY CONCEPTS

Sticky-price model
Sticky-wage model
Imperfect-information model
Phillips curve
Adaptive expectations
Demand-pull inflation
Cost-push inflation
Sacrifice ratio
Rational expectations
Natural-rate hypothesis
Hysteresis

QUESTIONS FOR REVIEW

1. Explain the three theories of aggregate supply. On what market imperfection does each theory rely? What do the theories have in common?

2. How is the Phillips curve related to aggregate supply?

3. Why might inflation be inertial?

4. Explain the differences between demand-pull inflation and cost-push inflation.

5. Under what circumstances might it be possible to reduce inflation without causing a recession?

6. Explain two ways in which a recession might raise the natural rate of unemployment.

PROBLEMS AND APPLICATIONS

1. In the sticky-price model, describe the aggregate supply curve in the following special cases. How do these cases compare to the short-run aggregate supply curve we discussed in Chapter 9?

   a. No firms have flexible prices ($s = 1$).

   b. The desired price does not depend on aggregate output ($a = 0$).

2. Consider the following changes in the sticky-wage model.

   a. Suppose that labor contracts specify that the nominal wage be fully indexed for inflation. That is, the nominal wage is to be adjusted to fully compensate for changes in the consumer price index. How does full indexation alter the aggregate supply curve in this model?

   b. Suppose now that indexation is only partial. That is, for every increase in the CPI, the nominal wage rises, but by a smaller percentage. How does partial indexation alter the aggregate supply curve in this model?

3. Suppose that an economy has the Phillips curve

$$\pi = \pi_{-1} - 0.5(u - 0.06).$$

   a. What is the natural rate of unemployment?

   b. Graph the short-run and long-run relationships between inflation and unemployment.

   c. How much cyclical unemployment is necessary to reduce inflation by 5 percentage points? Using Okun's law, compute the sacrifice ratio.

   d. Inflation is running at 10 percent. The Fed wants to reduce it to 5 percent. Give two scenarios that will achieve that goal.

4. According to the rational-expectations approach, if everyone believes that policymakers are committed to reducing inflation, the cost of reducing inflation—the sacrifice ratio—will be lower than if the public is skeptical about the policymakers' intentions. Why might this be true? How might credibility be achieved?

5. Assume that people have rational expectations and that the economy is described by the sticky-wage or sticky-price model. Explain why each of the following propositions is true:

   a. Only unanticipated changes in the money supply affect real GDP. Changes in the money supply that were anticipated when wages and prices were set do not have any real effects.

   b. If the Fed chooses the money supply at the same time as people are setting wages and prices, so that everyone has the same information about the state of the economy, then monetary policy cannot be used systematically to stabilize output. Hence, a policy of keeping the money supply constant will have the same real effects as a policy of adjusting the money supply in response to the state of the economy. (This is called the *policy irrelevance proposition.*)

   c. If the Fed sets the money supply well after people have set wages and prices, so the Fed has collected more information about the state of the economy, then monetary policy can be used systematically to stabilize output.

6. Suppose that an economy has the Phillips curve

$$\pi = \pi_{-1} - 0.5(u - u^n),$$

and that the natural rate of unemployment is given by an average of the past two years' unemployment:

$$u^n = 0.5(u_{-1} + u_{-2}).$$

a. Why might the natural rate of unemployment depend on recent unemployment (as is assumed in the preceding equation)?

b. Suppose that the Fed follows a policy to reduce permanently the inflation rate by 1 percentage point. What effect will that policy have on the unemployment rate over time?

c. What is the sacrifice ratio in this economy? Explain.

d. What do these equations imply about the short-run and long-run tradeoffs between inflation and unemployment?

7. Some economists believe that taxes have an important effect on labor supply. They argue that higher taxes cause people to want to work less and that lower taxes cause them to want to work more. Consider how this effect alters the macroeconomic analysis of tax changes.

a. If this view is correct, how does a tax cut affect the natural level of output?

b. How does a tax cut affect the aggregate demand curve? The long-run aggregate supply curve? The short-run aggregate supply curve?

c. What is the short-run impact of a tax cut on output and the price level? How does your answer differ from the case without the labor-supply effect?

d. What is the long-run impact of a tax cut on output and the price level? How does your answer differ from the case without the labor-supply effect?

8. Economist Alan Blinder, whom Bill Clinton appointed to be Vice Chairman of the Federal Reserve, once wrote the following:

> The costs that attend the low and moderate inflation rates experienced in the United States and in other industrial countries appear to be quite modest—more like a bad cold than a cancer on society. . . . As rational individuals, we do not volunteer for a lobotomy to cure a head cold. Yet, as a collectivity, we routinely prescribe the economic equivalent of lobotomy (high unemployment) as a cure for the inflationary cold.[15]

What do you think Blinder meant by this? What are the policy implications of the viewpoint Blinder is advocating? Do you agree? Why or why not?

9. Go to the Web site of the Bureau of Labor Statistics (www.bls.gov). For each of the past five years, find the inflation rate as measured by the consumer price index (all items) and as measured by the CPI excluding food and energy. Compare these two measures of inflation. Why might they be different? What might the difference tell you about shifts in the aggregate supply curve and in the short-run Phillips curve?

[15] Alan Blinder, *Hard Heads, Soft Hearts: Tough-Minded Economics for a Just Society* (Reading, MA: Addison-Wesley, 1987), 51.

A Big, Comprehensive Model

In the previous chapters, we have seen many models of how the economy works. When learning these models, it can be hard to see how they are related. Now that we have finished developing the model of aggregate demand and aggregate supply, this is a good time to look back at what we have learned. This appendix sketches a large model that incorporates much of the theory we have already seen, including the classical theory presented in Part Two and the business cycle theory presented in Part Four. The notation and equations should be familiar from previous chapters.

The model has seven equations:

$Y = C(Y - T) + I(r) + G + NX(\epsilon)$	*IS*: Goods Market Equilibrium
$M/P = L(i, Y)$	*LM*: Money Market Equilibrium
$NX(\epsilon) = CF(r - r^*)$	Foreign Exchange Market Equilibrium
$i = r + \pi^e$	Relationship Between Real and Nominal Interest Rates
$\epsilon = eP/P^*$	Relationship Between Real and Nominal Exchange Rates
$Y = \bar{Y} + \alpha(P - P^e)$	Aggregate Supply
$\bar{Y} = F(\bar{K}, \bar{L})$	Natural Level of Output

These seven equations determine the equilibrium values of seven endogenous variables: output Y, the natural level of output $\bar{Y}$, the real interest rate r, the nominal interest rate i, the real exchange rate ϵ, the nominal exchange rate e, and the price level P.

There are many exogenous variables that influence these endogenous variables. They include the money supply M, government purchases G, taxes T, the capital stock K, the labor force L, the world price level P^*, and the world real interest rate r^*. In addition, there are two expectation variables: the expectation of future inflation π^e and the expectation of the current price level formed in the past P^e. As written, the model takes these expectations as exogenous, although additional equations could be added to make them endogenous.

Although mathematical techniques are available to analyze this seven-equation model, they are beyond the scope of this book. But this large model is still useful, because we can use it to see how the smaller models we have examined are related to one another. In particular, *many of the models we have been studying are special cases of this large model.* Let's consider six special cases.

Special Case 1: The Classical Closed Economy Suppose that $P^e = P$, $L(i, Y) = (1/V)Y$, and $CF(r - r^*) = 0$. In words, this means that expectations of the price level adjust so that expectations are correct, that money demand is proportional to income, and that there are no international capital flows. In this case, output is always at its natural level, the real interest rate adjusts to equilibrate the goods market, the price level moves parallel with the money supply, and the nominal interest rate adjusts one-for-one with expected inflation. This special case corresponds to the economy analyzed in Chapters 3 and 4.

Special Case 2: The Classical Small Open Economy Suppose that $P^e = P$, $L(i, Y) = (1/V)Y$, and $CF(r - r^*)$ is infinitely elastic. Now we are examining the special case when international capital flows respond greatly to any differences between the domestic and world interest rates. This means that $r = r^*$ and that the trade balance NX equals the difference between saving and investment at the world interest rate. This special case corresponds to the economy analyzed in Chapter 5.

Special Case 3: The Basic Model of Aggregate Demand and Aggregate Supply Suppose that α is infinite and $L(i, Y) = (1/V)Y$. In this case, the short-run aggregate supply curve is horizontal, and the aggregate demand curve is determined only by the quantity equation. This special case corresponds to the economy analyzed in Chapter 9.

Special Case 4: The *IS-LM* Model Suppose that α is infinite and $CF(r - r^*) = 0$. In this case, the short-run aggregate supply curve is horizontal, and there are no international capital flows. For any given level of expected inflation π^e, the level of income and interest rate must adjust to equilibrate the goods market and the money market. This special case corresponds to the economy analyzed in Chapters 10 and 11.

Special Case 5: The Mundell-Fleming Model With a Floating Exchange Rate Suppose that α is infinite and $CF(r - r^*)$ is infinitely elastic. In this case, the short-run aggregate supply curve is horizontal, and international capital flows are so great as to ensure that $r = r^*$. The exchange rate floats freely to reach its equilibrium level. This special case corresponds to the first economy analyzed in Chapter 12.

Special Case 6: The Mundell-Fleming Model With a Fixed Exchange Rate Suppose that α is infinite, $CF(r - r^*)$ is infinitely elastic, and e is fixed. In this case, the short-run aggregate supply curve is horizontal, huge international capital flows ensure that $r = r^*$, but the exchange rate is set by the central bank. The exchange rate is now an exogenous policy variable, but the money supply M is an endogenous variable that must adjust to ensure the exchange rate hits the fixed level. This special case corresponds to the second economy analyzed in Chapter 12.

You should now see the value in this big model. Even though the model is too large to be useful in developing an intuitive understanding of how the economy works, it shows that the different models we have been studying are closely related. Each model shows a different facet of the larger and more realistic model presented here. In each chapter, we made some simplifying assumptions to make the big model smaller and easier to understand. When thinking about the real world, it is important to keep the simplifying assumptions in mind and to draw on the insights learned in each of the chapters.

MORE PROBLEMS AND APPLICATIONS

1. Let's consider some more special cases of this large model. Starting with the large model, what extra assumptions would you need to yield each of the following models:
   a. The model of the classical large open economy in the appendix to Chapter 5.
   b. The Keynesian cross in the first half of Chapter 10.
   c. The *IS-LM* model for the large open economy in the appendix to Chapter 12.

PART V

Macroeconomic Policy Debates

CHAPTER 14

Stabilization Policy

The Federal Reserve's job is to take away the punch bowl just as the party gets going.

— William McChesney Martin

What we need is not a skilled monetary driver of the economic vehicle continuously turning the steering wheel to adjust to the unexpected irregularities of the route, but some means of keeping the monetary passenger who is in the back seat as ballast from occasionally leaning over and giving the steering wheel a jerk that threatens to send the car off the road.

— Milton Friedman

How should government policymakers respond to the business cycle? The two quotations above—the first from a former chairman of the Federal Reserve, the second from a prominent critic of the Fed—show the diversity of opinion over how this question is best answered.

Some economists, such as William McChesney Martin, view the economy as inherently unstable. They argue that the economy experiences frequent shocks to aggregate demand and aggregate supply. Unless policymakers use monetary and fiscal policy to stabilize the economy, these shocks will lead to unnecessary and inefficient fluctuations in output, unemployment, and inflation. According to the popular saying, macroeconomic policy should "lean against the wind," stimulating the economy when it is depressed and slowing the economy when it is overheated.

Other economists, such as Milton Friedman, view the economy as naturally stable. They blame bad economic policies for the large and inefficient fluctuations we have sometimes experienced. They argue that economic policy should not try to "fine tune" the economy. Instead, economic policymakers should admit their limited abilities and be satisfied if they do no harm.

This debate has persisted for decades with numerous protagonists advancing various arguments for their positions. The fundamental issue is how policymakers should use the theory of short-run economic fluctuations developed in the preceding chapters. In this chapter we ask two questions that arise in this debate. First, should monetary and fiscal policy take an active role in trying to stabilize the economy, or should policy remain passive? Second, should policymakers be free to use their discretion in responding to changing economic conditions, or should they be committed to following a fixed policy rule?

14-1 Should Policy Be Active or Passive?

Policymakers in the federal government view economic stabilization as one of their primary responsibilities. The analysis of macroeconomic policy is a regular duty of the Council of Economic Advisers, the Congressional Budget Office, the Federal Reserve, and other government agencies. As we have seen in the preceding chapters, monetary and fiscal policy can exert a powerful impact on aggregate demand and, thereby, on inflation and unemployment. When Congress or the president is considering a major change in fiscal policy, or when the Federal Reserve is considering a major change in monetary policy, foremost in the discussion are how the change will influence inflation and unemployment and whether aggregate demand needs to be stimulated or restrained.

Although the government has long conducted monetary and fiscal policy, the view that it should use these policy instruments to try to stabilize the economy is more recent. The Employment Act of 1946 was a landmark piece of legislation in which the government first held itself accountable for macroeconomic performance. The act states that "it is the continuing policy and responsibility of the Federal Government to . . . promote full employment and production." This law was written when the memory of the Great Depression was still fresh. The lawmakers who wrote it believed, as many economists do, that in the absence of an active government role in the economy, events like the Great Depression could occur regularly.

To many economists the case for active government policy is clear and simple. Recessions are periods of high unemployment, low incomes, and increased economic hardship. The model of aggregate demand and aggregate supply shows how shocks to the economy can cause recessions. It also shows how monetary and fiscal policy can prevent (or at least soften) recessions by responding to these shocks. These economists consider it wasteful not to use these policy instruments to stabilize the economy.

Other economists are critical of the government's attempts to stabilize the economy. These critics argue that the government should take a hands-off approach to macroeconomic policy. At first, this view might seem surprising. If our model shows how to prevent or reduce the severity of recessions, why do these critics want the government to refrain from using monetary and fiscal policy for economic stabilization? To find out, let's consider some of their arguments.

Lags in the Implementation and Effects of Policies

Economic stabilization would be easy if the effects of policy were immediate. Making policy would be like driving a car: policymakers would simply adjust their instruments to keep the economy on the desired path.

Making economic policy, however, is less like driving a car than it is like piloting a large ship. A car changes direction almost immediately after the steering wheel is turned. By contrast, a ship changes course long after the pilot adjusts the rudder, and once the ship starts to turn, it continues turning long after the rudder is set back to normal. A novice pilot is likely to oversteer and, after noticing the mistake, overreact by steering too much in the opposite direction. The ship's path could become unstable, as the novice responds to previous mistakes by making larger and larger corrections.

Like a ship's pilot, economic policymakers face the problem of long lags. Indeed, the problem for policymakers is even more difficult, because the lengths of the lags are hard to predict. These long and variable lags greatly complicate the conduct of monetary and fiscal policy.

Economists distinguish between two lags that are relevant for the conduct of stabilization policy: the inside lag and the outside lag. The **inside lag** is the time between a shock to the economy and the policy action responding to that shock. This lag arises because it takes time for policymakers first to recognize that a shock has occurred and then to put appropriate policies into effect. The **outside lag** is the time between a policy action and its influence on the economy. This lag arises because policies do not immediately influence spending, income, and employment.

A long inside lag is a central problem with using fiscal policy for economic stabilization. This is especially true in the United States, where changes in spending or taxes require the approval of the president and both houses of Congress. The slow and cumbersome legislative process often leads to delays, which make fiscal policy an imprecise tool for stabilizing the economy. This inside lag is shorter in countries with parliamentary systems, such as the United Kingdom, because there the party in power can often enact policy changes more rapidly.

Monetary policy has a much shorter inside lag than fiscal policy, because a central bank can decide on and implement a policy change in less than a day, but monetary policy has a substantial outside lag. Monetary policy works by changing the money supply and interest rates, which in turn influence investment and aggregate demand. Many firms make investment plans far in advance, however, so a change in monetary policy is thought not to affect economic activity until about six months after it is made.

The long and variable lags associated with monetary and fiscal policy certainly make stabilizing the economy more difficult. Advocates of passive policy argue that, because of these lags, successful stabilization policy is almost impossible. Indeed, attempts to stabilize the economy can be destabilizing. Suppose that the economy's condition changes between the beginning of a policy action and its impact on the economy. In this case, active policy may end up stimulating the economy when it is heating up or depressing the economy when it is cooling off. Advocates of active policy admit that such lags do require policymakers to be cautious. But, they argue, these lags do not necessarily mean that policy should be completely passive, especially in the face of a severe and protracted economic downturn.

Some policies, called **automatic stabilizers**, are designed to reduce the lags associated with stabilization policy. Automatic stabilizers are policies that stimulate or depress the economy when necessary without any deliberate policy change. For example, the system of income taxes automatically reduces taxes when the economy goes into a recession, without any change in the tax laws, because individuals and corporations pay less tax when their incomes fall. Similarly, the unemployment-insurance and welfare systems automatically raise transfer payments when the economy moves into a recession, because more people apply for benefits. One can view these automatic stabilizers as a type of fiscal policy without any inside lag.

The Difficult Job of Economic Forecasting

Because policy influences the economy only after a long lag, successful stabilization policy requires the ability to predict accurately future economic conditions. If we cannot predict whether the economy will be in a boom or a recession in six months or a year, we cannot evaluate whether monetary and fiscal policy should now be trying to expand or contract aggregate demand. Unfortunately, economic developments are often unpredictable, at least given our current understanding of the economy.

One way forecasters try to look ahead is with *leading indicators*. As we discussed in Chapter 9, a leading indicator is a data series that fluctuates in advance of the economy. A large fall in a leading indicator signals that a recession is more likely to occur in the coming months.

Another way forecasters look ahead is with macroeconometric models, which have been developed both by government agencies and by private firms for forecasting and policy analysis. As we discussed in Chapter 11, these large-scale computer models are made up of many equations, each representing a part of the economy. After making assumptions about the path of the exogenous variables, such as monetary policy, fiscal policy, and oil prices, these models yield predictions about unemployment, inflation, and other endogenous variables. Keep in mind, however, that the validity of these predictions is only as good as the model and the forecasters' assumptions about the exogenous variables.

"It's true, Caesar. Rome is declining, but I expect it to pick up in the next quarter."

CASE STUDY

Mistakes in Forecasting

"Light showers, bright intervals, and moderate winds." This was the forecast offered by the renowned British national weather service on October 14, 1987. The next day Britain was hit by its worst storm in more than two centuries.

Like weather forecasts, economic forecasts are a crucial input to private and public decisionmaking. Business executives rely on economic forecasts when deciding how much to produce and how much to invest in plant and equipment. Government policymakers also rely on forecasts when developing economic policies. Unfortunately, like weather forecasts, economic forecasts are far from precise.

The most severe economic downturn in U.S. history, the Great Depression of the 1930s, caught economic forecasters completely by surprise. Even after the stock market crash of 1929, they remained confident that the economy would not suffer a substantial setback. In late 1931, when the economy was clearly in bad shape, the eminent economist Irving Fisher predicted that it would recover quickly. Subsequent events showed that these forecasts were much too optimistic: the unemployment rate continued to rise until 1933, and it remained elevated for the rest of the decade.[1]

Figure 14-1 shows how economic forecasters did during the recession of 1982, the most severe economic downturn in the United States since the Great Depression. This figure shows the actual unemployment rate (in red) and six

FIGURE 14-1

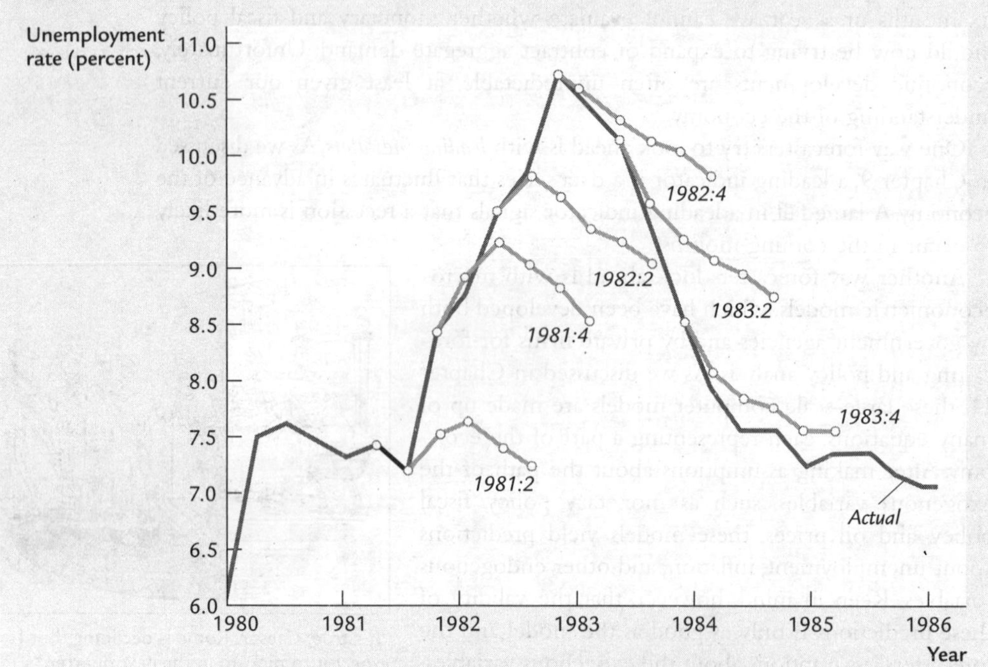

Forecasting the Recession of 1982 The red line shows the actual unemployment rate from the first quarter of 1980 to the first quarter of 1986. The green lines show the unemployment rate predicted at six points in time: the second quarter of 1981, the fourth quarter of 1981, the second quarter of 1982, and so on. For each forecast, the symbols mark the current unemployment rate and the forecast for the subsequent five quarters. Notice that the forecasters failed to predict both the rapid rise in the unemployment rate and the subsequent rapid decline.

Source: The unemployment rate is from the Department of Labor. The predicted unemployment rate is the median forecast of about 20 forecasters surveyed by the American Statistical Association and the National Bureau of Economic Research.

[1] Kathryn M. Dominguez, Ray C. Fair, and Matthew D. Shapiro, "Forecasting the Depression: Harvard versus Yale," *American Economic Review* 78 (September 1988): 595–612. This article shows how badly economic forecasters did during the Great Depression, and it argues that they could not have done any better with the modern forecasting techniques available today.

attempts to predict it for the following five quarters (in green). You can see that the forecasters did well predicting unemployment one quarter ahead. The more distant forecasts, however, were often inaccurate. For example, in the second quarter of 1981, forecasters were predicting little change in the unemployment rate over the next five quarters; yet only two quarters later unemployment began to rise sharply. The rise in unemployment to almost 11 percent in the fourth quarter of 1982 caught the forecasters by surprise. After the depth of the recession became apparent, the forecasters failed to predict how rapid the subsequent decline in unemployment would be.

These two episodes—the Great Depression and the recession of 1982—show that many of the most dramatic economic events are unpredictable. Although private and public decisionmakers have little choice but to rely on economic forecasts, they must always keep in mind that these forecasts come with a large margin of error.

Ignorance, Expectations, and the Lucas Critique

The prominent economist Robert Lucas once wrote, "As an advice-giving profession we are in way over our heads." Even many of those who advise policymakers would agree with this assessment. Economics is a young science, and there is still much that we do not know. Economists cannot be completely confident when they assess the effects of alternative policies. This ignorance suggests that economists should be cautious when offering policy advice.

In his writings on macroeconomic policymaking, Lucas has emphasized that economists need to pay more attention to the issue of how people form expectations of the future. Expectations play a crucial role in the economy because they influence all sorts of behavior. For instance, households decide how much to consume based on how much they expect to earn in the future, and firms decide how much to invest based on their expectations of future profitability. These expectations depend on many things, but one factor, according to Lucas, is especially important: the policies being pursued by the government. When policymakers estimate the effect of any policy change, therefore, they need to know how people's expectations will respond to the policy change. Lucas has argued that traditional methods of policy evaluation—such as those that rely on standard macroeconometric models—do not adequately take into account the impact of policy on expectations. This criticism of traditional policy evaluation is known as the **Lucas critique**.[2]

An important example of the Lucas critique arises in the analysis of disinflation. As you may recall from Chapter 13, the cost of reducing inflation is often measured by the sacrifice ratio, which is the number of percentage points of GDP that must be forgone to reduce inflation by 1 percentage point. Because

[2] Robert E. Lucas, Jr., "Econometric Policy Evaluation: A Critique," *Carnegie Rochester Conference on Public Policy* 1 (Amsterdam: North-Holland, 1976): 19–46. Lucas won the Nobel Prize for this and other work in 1995.

estimates of the sacrifice ratio are often large, they have led some economists to argue that policymakers should learn to live with inflation, rather than incur the large cost of reducing it.

According to advocates of the rational-expectations approach, however, these estimates of the sacrifice ratio are unreliable because they are subject to the Lucas critique. Traditional estimates of the sacrifice ratio are based on adaptive expectations, that is, on the assumption that expected inflation depends on past inflation. Adaptive expectations may be a reasonable premise in some circumstances, but if the policymakers make a credible change in policy, workers and firms setting wages and prices will rationally respond by adjusting their expectations of inflation appropriately. This change in inflation expectations will quickly alter the short-run tradeoff between inflation and unemployment. As a result, reducing inflation can potentially be much less costly than is suggested by traditional estimates of the sacrifice ratio.

The Lucas critique leaves us with two lessons. The narrow lesson is that economists evaluating alternative policies need to consider how policy affects expectations and, thereby, behavior. The broad lesson is that policy evaluation is hard, so economists engaged in this task should be sure to show the requisite humility.

The Historical Record

In judging whether government policy should play an active or passive role in the economy, we must give some weight to the historical record. If the economy has experienced many large shocks to aggregate supply and aggregate demand, and if policy has successfully insulated the economy from these shocks, then the case for active policy should be clear. Conversely, if the economy has experienced few large shocks, and if the fluctuations we have observed can be traced to inept economic policy, then the case for passive policy should be clear. In other words, our view of stabilization policy should be influenced by whether policy has historically been stabilizing or destabilizing. For this reason, the debate over macroeconomic policy frequently turns into a debate over macroeconomic history.

Yet history does not settle the debate over stabilization policy. Disagreements over history arise because it is not easy to identify the sources of economic fluctuations. The historical record often permits more than one interpretation.

The Great Depression is a case in point. Economists' views on macroeconomic policy are often related to their views on the cause of the Depression. Some economists believe that a large contractionary shock to private spending caused the Depression. They assert that policymakers should have responded by using the tools of monetary and fiscal policy to stimulate aggregate demand. Other economists believe that the large fall in the money supply caused the Depression. They assert that the Depression would have been avoided if the Fed had been pursuing a passive monetary policy of increasing the money supply at a steady rate. Hence, depending on one's beliefs about its cause, the Great Depression can be viewed either as an example of why active monetary and fiscal policy is necessary or as an example of why it is dangerous.

CASE STUDY

Is the Stabilization of the Economy a Figment of the Data?

Keynes wrote *The General Theory* in the 1930s, and in the wake of the Keynesian revolution, governments around the world began to view economic stabilization as a primary responsibility. Some economists believe that the development of Keynesian theory has had a profound influence on the behavior of the economy. Comparing data from before World War I and after World War II, they find that real GDP and unemployment have become much more stable. This, some Keynesians claim, is the best argument for active stabilization policy: it has worked.

In a series of provocative and influential papers, economist Christina Romer has challenged this assessment of the historical record. She argues that the measured reduction in volatility reflects not an improvement in economic policy and performance but rather an improvement in the economic data. The older data are much less accurate than the newer data. Romer claims that the higher volatility of unemployment and real GDP reported for the period before World War I is largely a figment of the data.

Romer uses various techniques to make her case. One is to construct more accurate data for the earlier period. This task is difficult because data sources are not readily available. A second way is to construct *less* accurate data for the recent period—that is, data that are comparable to the older data and thus suffer from the same imperfections. After constructing new "bad" data, Romer finds that the recent period appears almost as volatile as the early period, suggesting that the volatility of the early period may be largely an artifact of how the data were assembled.

Romer's work is part of the continuing debate over whether macroeconomic policy has improved the performance of the economy. Although her work remains controversial, most economists now believe that the economy in the immediate aftermath of the Keynesian revolution was only slightly more stable than it had been before.[3]

CASE STUDY

The Remarkable Stability of the Modern Economy

Although economists who take a long historical view debate how much the economy has stabilized over time, there is less controversy about the more recent experience. Everyone agrees that the 1990s and early 2000s stand out as a period of remarkable stability for the U.S. economy.

[3] Christina D. Romer, "Spurious Volatility in Historical Unemployment Data," *Journal of Political Economy* 94 (February 1986): 1–37; and Christina D. Romer, "Is the Stabilization of the Postwar Economy a Figment of the Data?" *American Economic Review* 76 (June 1986): 314–334.

Figure 14-2 shows the volatility of economic growth and inflation over the past several decades. Panel (a) shows the standard deviation of real GDP growth, and panel (b) shows the standard deviation of inflation. The standard deviation measures the volatility of a variable: the higher the standard deviation, the more volatile the variable is. One striking result from this figure is the low volatility in both variables during the 1990s and early 2000s.

FIGURE 14-2

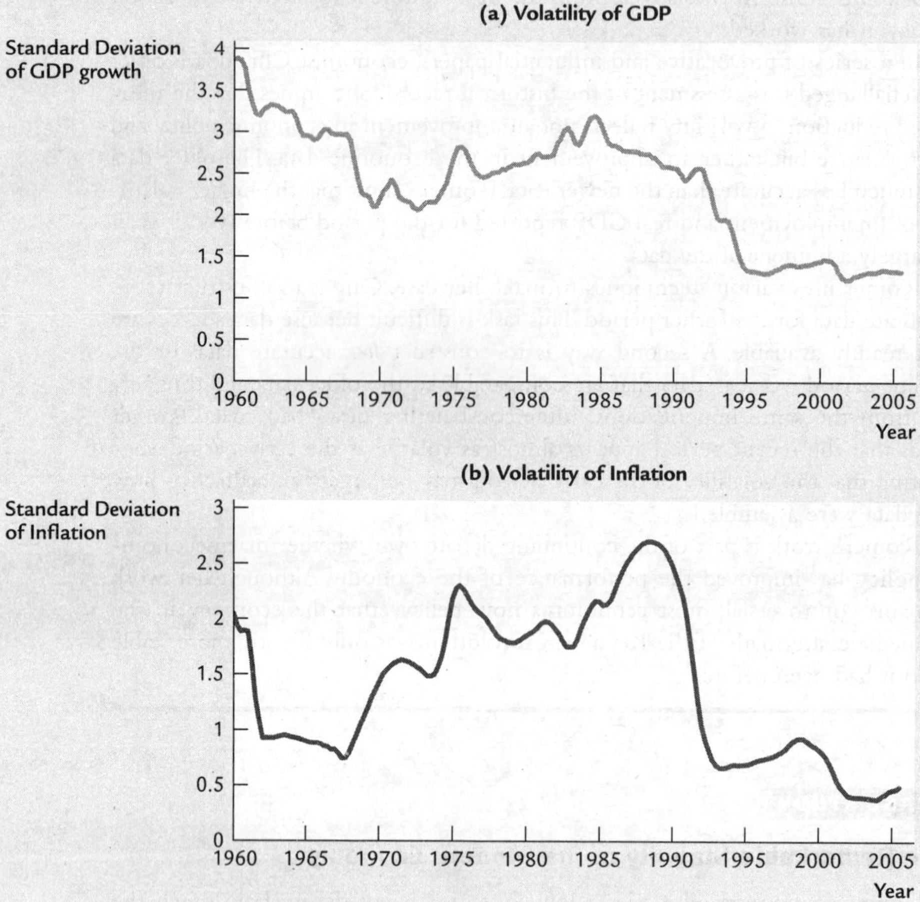

Macroeconomic Volatility. Panel (a) shows the standard deviation of economic growth. Panel (b) shows the standard deviation of inflation. By both measures, the 1990s and early 2000s were a period of remarkable macroeconomic stability.

Note: Economic growth is measured as the percentage change in real GDP from four quarters earlier. Inflation is measured as the percentage change in the GDP deflator from four quarters earlier. For each date, the standard deviation is computed using the preceding 40 quarters of data.
Source: U.S. Department of Commerce and author's calculations.

What accounts for the stability of the recent period? There are several hypotheses:

- *Structural change.* The U.S. economy today is more service-based and less manufacturing-based than it was in the past, and service industries are less volatile than manufacturing industries.
- *Good luck.* In recent years, the U.S. economy did not have to deal with, for example, adverse supply shocks as severe as the oil price shocks of the 1970s.
- *Good policy.* Many economists give credit to Alan Greenspan, who was chairman of the Federal Reserve from 1987 to 2006. His management of interest rates and the money supply kept the economy on track, avoiding both deep recessions and runaway inflation.

There may well be elements of truth to all three of these explanations. To the extent that good policy gets credit for the improved performance, part of that credit should perhaps go to advances in macroeconomic science.[4]

14-2 Should Policy Be Conducted by Rule or by Discretion?

A second topic debated among economists is whether economic policy should be conducted by rule or by discretion. Policy is conducted by rule if policymakers announce in advance how policy will respond to various situations and commit themselves to following through on this announcement. Policy is conducted by discretion if policymakers are free to size up events as they occur and choose whatever policy the policymakers consider appropriate at the time.

The debate over rules versus discretion is distinct from the debate over passive versus active policy. Policy can be conducted by rule and yet be either passive or active. For example, a passive policy rule might specify steady growth in the money supply of 3 percent per year. An active policy rule might specify that

$$\text{Money Growth} = 3\% + (\text{Unemployment Rate} - 6\%).$$

Under this rule, the money supply grows at 3 percent if the unemployment rate is 6 percent, but for every percentage point by which the unemployment rate exceeds 6 percent, money growth increases by an extra percentage point. This rule tries to stabilize the economy by raising money growth when the economy is in a recession.

We begin this section by discussing why policy might be improved by a commitment to a policy rule. We then examine several possible policy rules.

[4] For one study of this topic, see James H. Stock and Mark W. Watson, "Has the Business Cycle Changed and Why?" *NBER Macroeconomics Annual* (2002): 159–230.

Distrust of Policymakers and the Political Process

Some economists believe that economic policy is too important to be left to the discretion of policymakers. Although this view is more political than economic, evaluating it is central to how we judge the role of economic policy. If politicians are incompetent or opportunistic, then we may not want to give them the discretion to use the powerful tools of monetary and fiscal policy.

Incompetence in economic policy arises for several reasons. Some economists view the political process as erratic, perhaps because it reflects the shifting power of special interest groups. In addition, macroeconomics is complicated, and politicians often do not have sufficient knowledge of it to make informed judgments. This ignorance allows charlatans to propose incorrect but superficially appealing solutions to complex problems. The political process often cannot weed out the advice of charlatans from that of competent economists.

Opportunism in economic policy arises when the objectives of policymakers conflict with the well-being of the public. Some economists fear that politicians use macroeconomic policy to further their own electoral ends. If citizens vote on the basis of economic conditions prevailing at the time of the election, then politicians have an incentive to pursue policies that will make the economy look good during election years. A president might cause a recession soon after coming into office to lower inflation and then stimulate the economy as the next election approaches to lower unemployment; this would ensure that both inflation and unemployment are low on election day. Manipulation of the economy for electoral gain, called the **political business cycle**, has been the subject of extensive research by economists and political scientists.[5]

Distrust of the political process leads some economists to advocate placing economic policy outside the realm of politics. Some have proposed constitutional amendments, such as a balanced-budget amendment, that would tie the hands of legislators and insulate the economy from both incompetence and opportunism.

The Time Inconsistency of Discretionary Policy

If we assume that we can trust our policymakers, discretion at first glance appears superior to a fixed policy rule. Discretionary policy is, by its nature, flexible. As long as policymakers are intelligent and benevolent, there might appear to be little reason to deny them flexibility in responding to changing conditions.

---

[5] William Nordhaus, "The Political Business Cycle," *Review of Economic Studies* 42 (1975): 169–190; and Edward Tufte, *Political Control of the Economy* (Princeton, NJ: Princeton University Press, 1978).

Yet a case for rules over discretion arises from the problem of **time inconsistency** of policy. In some situations policymakers may want to announce in advance the policy they will follow to influence the expectations of private decisionmakers. But later, after the private decisionmakers have acted on the basis of their expectations, these policymakers may be tempted to renege on their announcement. Understanding that policymakers may be inconsistent over time, private decisionmakers are led to distrust policy announcements. In this situation, to make their announcements credible, policymakers may want to make a commitment to a fixed policy rule.

Time inconsistency is illustrated most simply in a political rather than an economic example—specifically, public policy about negotiating with terrorists over the release of hostages. The announced policy of many nations is that they will not negotiate over hostages. Such an announcement is intended to deter terrorists: if there is nothing to be gained from kidnapping hostages, rational terrorists won't kidnap any. In other words, the purpose of the announcement is to influence the expectations of terrorists and thereby their behavior.

But, in fact, unless the policymakers are credibly committed to the policy, the announcement has little effect. Terrorists know that once hostages are taken, policymakers face an overwhelming temptation to make some concession to obtain the hostages' release. The only way to deter rational terrorists is to take away the discretion of policymakers and commit them to a rule of never negotiating. If policymakers were truly unable to make concessions, the incentive for terrorists to take hostages would be largely eliminated.

The same problem arises less dramatically in the conduct of monetary policy. Consider the dilemma of a Federal Reserve that cares about both inflation and unemployment. According to the Phillips curve, the tradeoff between inflation and unemployment depends on expected inflation. The Fed would prefer everyone to expect low inflation so that it will face a favorable tradeoff. To reduce expected inflation, the Fed might announce that low inflation is the paramount goal of monetary policy.

But an announcement of a policy of low inflation is by itself not credible. Once households and firms have formed their expectations of inflation and set wages and prices accordingly, the Fed has an incentive to renege on its announcement and implement expansionary monetary policy to reduce unemployment. People understand the Fed's incentive to renege and therefore do not believe the announcement in the first place. Just as a president facing a hostage crisis is sorely tempted to negotiate their release, a Federal Reserve with discretion is sorely tempted to inflate in order to reduce unemployment. And just as terrorists discount announced policies of never negotiating, households and firms discount announced policies of low inflation.

The surprising outcome of this analysis is that policymakers can sometimes better achieve their goals by having their discretion taken away from them. In the case of rational terrorists, fewer hostages will be taken and killed if policymakers are committed to following the seemingly harsh rule of refusing to negotiate for hostages' freedom. In the case of monetary policy, there will be lower inflation without higher unemployment if the Fed is committed to a policy of zero inflation. (This conclusion about monetary policy is modeled more explicitly in the appendix to this chapter.)

The time inconsistency of policy arises in many other contexts. Here are some examples:

- To encourage investment, the government announces that it will not tax income from capital. But after factories have been built, the government is tempted to renege on its promise to raise more tax revenue from them.
- To encourage research, the government announces that it will give a temporary monopoly to companies that discover new drugs. But after a drug has been discovered, the government is tempted to revoke the patent or to regulate the price to make the drug more affordable.
- To encourage good behavior, a parent announces that he or she will punish a child whenever the child breaks a rule. But after the child has misbehaved, the parent is tempted to forgive the transgression, because punishment is unpleasant for the parent as well as for the child.
- To encourage you to work hard, your professor announces that this course will end with an exam. But after you have studied and learned all the material, the professor is tempted to cancel the exam so that he or she won't have to grade it.

In each case, rational agents understand the incentive for the policymaker to renege, and this expectation affects their behavior. And in each case, the solution is to take away the policymaker's discretion with a credible commitment to a fixed policy rule.

CASE STUDY

Alexander Hamilton Versus Time Inconsistency

Time inconsistency has long been a problem associated with discretionary policy. In fact, it was one of the first problems that confronted Alexander Hamilton when President George Washington appointed him the first U.S. Secretary of the Treasury in 1789.

Hamilton faced the question of how to deal with the debts that the new nation had accumulated as it fought for its independence from Britain. When the revolutionary government incurred the debts, it promised to honor them when the war was over. But after the war, many Americans advocated defaulting on the debt because repaying the creditors would require taxation, which is always costly and unpopular.

Hamilton opposed the time-inconsistent policy of repudiating the debt. He knew that the nation would likely need to borrow again sometime in the future.

In his *First Report on the Public Credit*, which he presented to Congress in 1790, he wrote

> If the maintenance of public credit, then, be truly so important, the next inquiry which suggests itself is: By what means is it to be effected? The ready answer to which question is, by good faith; by a punctual performance of contracts. States, like individuals, who observe their engagements are respected and trusted, while the reverse is the fate of those who pursue an opposite conduct.

Thus, Hamilton proposed that the nation make a commitment to the policy rule of honoring its debts.

The policy rule that Hamilton originally proposed has continued for more than two centuries. Today, unlike in Hamilton's time, when Congress debates spending priorities, no one seriously proposes defaulting on the public debt as a way to reduce taxes. In the case of public debt, everyone now agrees that the government should be committed to a fixed policy rule.

Rules for Monetary Policy

Even if we are convinced that policy rules are superior to discretion, the debate over macroeconomic policy is not over. If the Fed were to commit to a rule for monetary policy, what rule should it choose? Let's discuss briefly three policy rules that various economists advocate.

Some economists, called **monetarists**, advocate that the Fed keep the money supply growing at a steady rate. The quotation at the beginning of this chapter from Milton Friedman—the most famous monetarist—exemplifies this view of monetary policy. Monetarists believe that fluctuations in the money supply are responsible for most large fluctuations in the economy. They argue that slow and steady growth in the money supply would yield stable output, employment, and prices.

Although a monetarist policy rule might have prevented many of the economic fluctuations we have experienced historically, most economists believe that it is not the best possible policy rule. Steady growth in the money supply stabilizes aggregate demand only if the velocity of money is stable. But sometimes the economy experiences shocks, such as shifts in money demand, that cause velocity to be unstable. Most economists believe that a policy rule needs to allow the money supply to adjust to various shocks to the economy.

A second policy rule that economists widely advocate is nominal GDP targeting. Under this rule, the Fed announces a planned path for nominal GDP. If nominal GDP rises above the target, the Fed reduces money growth to dampen aggregate demand. If it falls below the target, the Fed raises money growth to stimulate aggregate demand. Because a nominal GDP target allows monetary policy to adjust to changes in the velocity of money, most economists believe it would lead to greater stability in output and prices than a monetarist policy rule.

A third policy rule that is often advocated is **inflation targeting**. Under this rule, the Fed would announce a target for the inflation rate (usually a low one) and then adjust the money supply when the actual inflation rate deviates from the target. Like nominal GDP targeting, inflation targeting insulates the economy from changes in the velocity of money. In addition, an inflation target has the political advantage that it is easy to explain to the public.

Notice that all these rules are expressed in terms of some nominal variable—the money supply, nominal GDP, or the price level. One can also imagine policy rules expressed in terms of real variables. For example, the Fed might try to target the unemployment rate at 5 percent. The problem with such a rule is that no one knows exactly what the natural rate of unemployment is. If the Fed chose a target for the unemployment rate below the natural rate, the result would be accelerating inflation. Conversely, if the Fed chose a target for the unemployment rate above the natural rate, the result would be accelerating deflation. For this reason, economists rarely advocate rules for monetary policy expressed solely in terms of real variables, even though real variables such as unemployment and real GDP are the best measures of economic performance.

CASE STUDY

Inflation Targeting: Rule or Constrained Discretion?

Since the late 1980s, many of the world's central banks—including those of Australia, Canada, Finland, Israel, New Zealand, Spain, Sweden, and the United Kingdom—have adopted some form of inflation targeting. Sometimes inflation targeting takes the form of a central bank announcing its policy intentions. Other times it takes the form of a national law that spells out the goals of monetary policy. For example, the Reserve Bank of New Zealand Act of 1989 told the central bank "to formulate and implement monetary policy directed to the economic objective of achieving and maintaining stability in the general level of prices." The act conspicuously omitted any mention of any other competing objective, such as stability in output, employment, interest rates, or exchange rates.

Should we interpret inflation targeting as a type of precommitment to a policy rule? Not completely. In all the countries that have adopted inflation targeting, central banks are left with a fair amount of discretion. Inflation targets are usually set as a range—an inflation rate of 1 to 3 percent, for instance—rather than a particular number. Thus, the central bank can choose where in the range it wants to be: it can stimulate the economy and be near the top of the range, or dampen the economy and be near the bottom. In addition, the central banks are sometimes allowed to adjust their targets for inflation, at least temporarily, if some exogenous event (such as an easily identified supply shock) pushes inflation outside of the range that was previously announced.

In light of this flexibility, what is the purpose of inflation targeting? Although inflation targeting leaves the central bank with some discretion, the policy does constrain how this discretion is used. When a central bank is told simply to "do the right thing," it is hard to hold the central bank accountable, because people can argue forever about what the right thing is in any specific circumstance. By contrast, when a central bank has announced a specific inflation target, or even a target range, the public can more easily judge whether the central bank is meeting its objectives. Thus, although inflation targeting does not tie the hands of the central bank, it does increase the transparency of monetary policy and, by doing so, makes central bankers more accountable for their actions.

The Federal Reserve has not adopted an explicit policy of inflation targeting (although some commentators have suggested that it is, implicitly, targeting inflation at about 2 percent). One prominent advocate of inflation targeting is Ben Bernanke, a former professor of economics whom President Bush appointed to succeed Alan Greenspan as chairman of the Federal Reserve. Bernanke took over the job in 2006. In the future, the Federal Reserve may move toward inflation targeting as the explicit framework for monetary policy.[6]

CASE STUDY

John Taylor's Rule for Monetary Policy

If you wanted to set interest rates to achieve stable prices while avoiding large fluctuations in output and employment, how would you do it? This is exactly the question that the governors of the Federal Reserve must ask themselves every day. The short-term policy instrument that the Fed now sets is the *federal funds rate*—the short-term interest rate at which banks make loans to one another. Whenever the Federal Open Market Committee meets, it chooses a target for the federal funds rate. The Fed's bond traders are then told to conduct open-market operations in order to hit the desired target.

The hard part of the Fed's job is choosing the target for the federal funds rate. Two general guidelines are clear. First, when inflation heats up, the federal funds rate should rise. An increase in the interest rate will mean a smaller money supply and, eventually, lower investment, lower output, higher unemployment, and reduced inflation. Second, when real economic activity slows—as reflected in real GDP or unemployment—the federal funds rate should fall. A decrease in the interest rate will mean a larger money supply and, eventually, higher investment, higher output, and lower unemployment.

The Fed needs to go beyond these general guidelines, however, and decide exactly how much to respond to changes in inflation and real economic activity.

[6] See Ben S. Bernanke and Frederic S. Mishkin, "Inflation Targeting: A New Framework for Monetary Policy?" *Journal of Economic Perspectives* 11 (Spring 1997): 97–116.

FIGURE 14-3

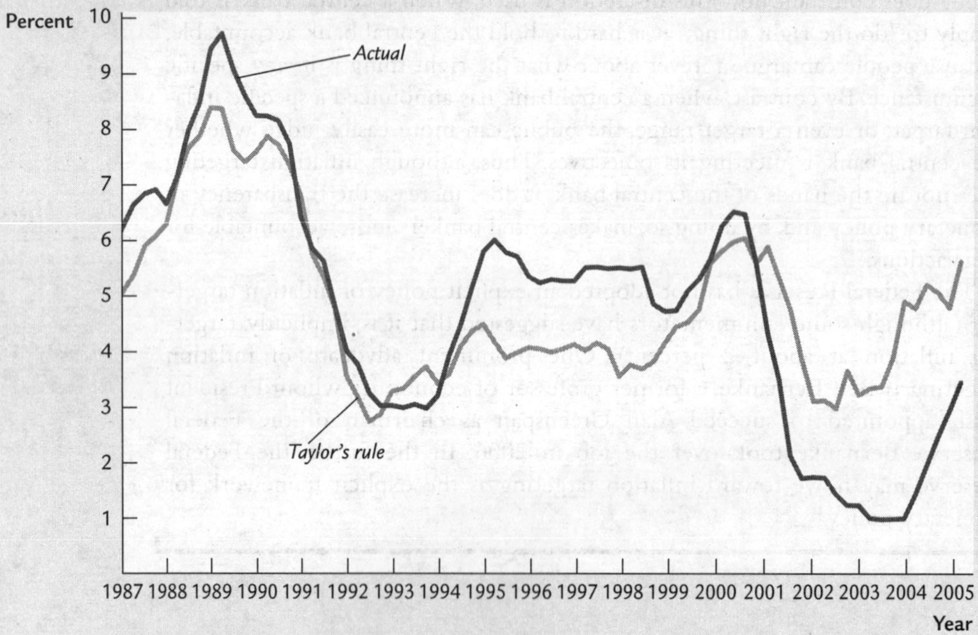

The Federal Funds Rate: Actual and Suggested This figure shows the federal funds rate—the short-term interest rate at which banks make loans to each other. It also shows the federal funds rate suggested by John Taylor's monetary rule. Notice that the two series move closely together.

Source: Federal Reserve Board, U.S. Department of Commerce, U.S. Department of Labor, and author's calculations. To implement the Taylor rule, the inflation rate is measured as the percentage change in the GDP deflator over the previous four quarters, and the GDP gap is measured as twice the deviation of the unemployment rate from its natural rate (as shown in Figure 6-1).

To help it make this decision, economist John Taylor has proposed a simple rule for the federal funds rate:

$$\text{Nominal Federal Funds Rate} = \text{Inflation} + 2.0 + 0.5\,(\text{Inflation} - 2.0) - 0.5\,(\text{GDP gap}).$$

The GDP gap is the percentage shortfall of real GDP from an estimate of its natural level.

The **Taylor rule** has the real federal funds rate—the nominal rate minus inflation—responding to inflation and the GDP gap. According to this rule, the real federal funds rate equals 2 percent when inflation is 2 percent and GDP is at its natural level. For each percentage point by which inflation rises above 2 percent, the real federal funds rate rises by 0.5 percent. For each percentage point by which real GDP falls below its natural level, the real federal funds rate falls by

0.5 percent. If GDP rises above its natural level, so that the GDP gap is negative, the real federal funds rate rises accordingly.

One way to view the Taylor rule is as a complement to (rather than a substitute for) inflation targeting. As the previous case study discussed, inflation targeting offers a plan for the central bank in the medium run, but it does not tightly constrain its month-to-month policy decisions. The Taylor rule may be a good short-run operating procedure for hitting a medium-run inflation target. According to the Taylor rule, monetary policy responds directly to inflation—as any inflation-targeting central bank must. But it also responds to the output gap, which can be viewed as a measure of inflationary pressures.

Taylor's rule for monetary policy is not only simple and reasonable but it also resembles actual Fed behavior in recent years. Figure 14-3 shows the actual federal funds rate and the target rate as determined by Taylor's proposed rule. Notice the two series tend to move together. John Taylor's monetary rule may be more than an academic suggestion. To some degree, it may be the rule that the Federal Reserve Governors have been subconsciously following.[7]

CASE STUDY

Central-Bank Independence

Suppose you were put in charge of writing the constitution and laws for a country. Would you give the president of the country authority over the policies of the central bank? Or would you allow the central bank to make decisions free from such political influence? In other words, assuming that monetary policy is made by discretion rather than by rule, who should exercise that discretion?

Countries vary greatly in how they choose to answer this question. In some countries, the central bank is a branch of the government; in others, the central bank is largely independent. In the United States, Fed governors are appointed by the president for 14-year terms, and they cannot be recalled if the president is unhappy with their decisions. This institutional structure gives the Fed a degree of independence similar to that of the U.S. Supreme Court.

Many researchers have investigated the effects of constitutional design on monetary policy. They have examined the laws of different countries to construct an index of central-bank independence. This index is based on various characteristics, such as the length of bankers' terms, the role of government officials on the bank board, and the frequency of contact between the government and the central bank. The researchers then examined

[7] John B. Taylor, "Discretion Versus Policy Rules in Practice," *Carnegie-Rochester Conference Series on Public Policy* 39 (1993): 195–214.

FIGURE 14-4

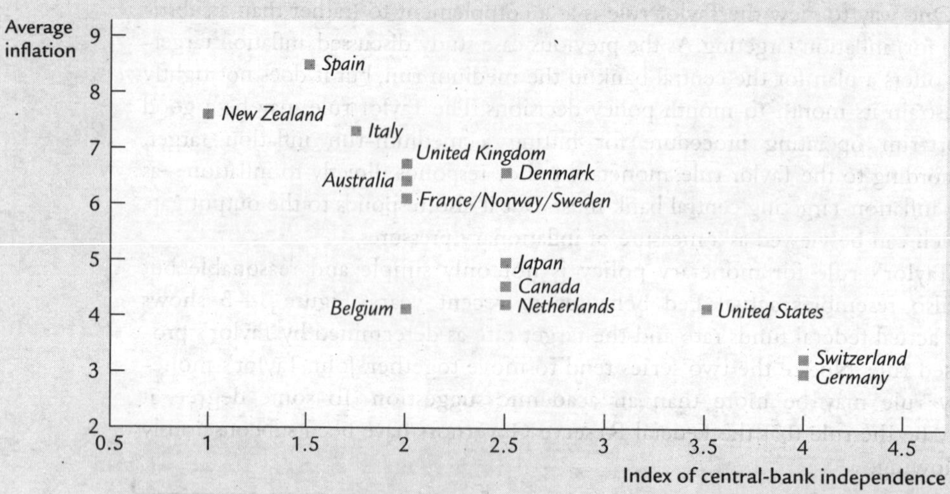

Inflation and Central-Bank Independence This scatterplot presents the international experience with central-bank independence. The evidence shows that more independent central banks tend to produce lower rates of inflation.

Source: Figure 1a, page 155, of Alberto Alesina and Lawrence H. Summers, "Central Bank Independence and Macroeconomic Performance: Some Comparative Evidence," *Journal of Money, Credit, and Banking* 25 (May 1993): 151–162. Average inflation is for the period 1955–1988.

the correlation between central-bank independence and macroeconomic performance.

The results of these studies are striking: more independent central banks are strongly associated with lower and more stable inflation. Figure 14-4 shows a scatterplot of central-bank independence and average inflation for the period 1955 to 1988. Countries that had an independent central bank, such as Germany, Switzerland, and the United States, tended to have low average inflation. Countries that had central banks with less independence, such as New Zealand and Spain, tended to have higher average inflation.

Researchers have also found there is no relationship between central-bank independence and real economic activity. In particular, central-bank independence is not correlated with average unemployment, the volatility of unemployment, the average growth of real GDP, or the volatility of real GDP. Central-bank independence appears to offer countries a free lunch: it has the benefit of lower inflation without any apparent cost. This finding has led some countries, such as New Zealand, to rewrite their laws to give their central banks greater independence.[8]

[8] For a more complete presentation of these findings and references to the large literature on central-bank independence, see Alberto Alesina and Lawrence H. Summers, "Central Bank Independence and Macroeconomic Performance: Some Comparative Evidence," *Journal of Money, Credit,*

14-3 Conclusion: Making Policy in an Uncertain World

In this chapter we have examined whether policy should take an active or passive role in responding to economic fluctuations and whether policy should be conducted by rule or by discretion. There are many arguments on both sides of these questions. Perhaps the only clear conclusion is that there is no simple and compelling case for any particular view of macroeconomic policy. In the end, you must weigh the various arguments, both economic and political, and decide for yourself what kind of role the government should play in trying to stabilize the economy.

For better or worse, economists play a key role in the formulation of economic policy. Because the economy is complex, this role is often difficult. Yet it is also inevitable. Economists cannot sit back and wait until our knowledge of the economy has been perfected before giving advice. In the meantime, someone must advise economic policymakers. That job, difficult as it sometimes is, falls to economists.

The role of economists in the policymaking process goes beyond giving advice to policymakers. Even economists cloistered in academia influence policy indirectly through their research and writing. In the conclusion of *The General Theory,* John Maynard Keynes wrote that

> the ideas of economists and political philosophers, both when they are right and when they are wrong, are more powerful than is commonly understood. Indeed, the world is ruled by little else. Practical men, who believe themselves to be quite exempt from intellectual influences, are usually the slaves of some defunct economist. Madmen in authority, who hear voices in the air, are distilling their frenzy from some academic scribbler of a few years back.

This is as true today as it was when Keynes wrote it in 1936—except now that academic scribbler is often Keynes himself.

and Banking 25 (May 1993): 151–162. For a study that questions the link between inflation and central-bank independence, see Marta Campillo and Jeffrey A. Miron, "Why Does Inflation Differ Across Countries?," in Christina D. Romer and David H. Romer, eds., *Reducing Inflation: Motivation and Strategy* (Chicago: University of Chicago Press, 1997), 335–362.

Summary

1. Advocates of active policy view the economy as subject to frequent shocks that will lead to unnecessary fluctuations in output and employment unless monetary or fiscal policy responds. Many believe that economic policy has been successful in stabilizing the economy.
2. Advocates of passive policy argue that because monetary and fiscal policies work with long and variable lags, attempts to stabilize the economy are likely to end up being destabilizing. In addition, they believe that our present understanding of the economy is too limited to be useful in formulating successful stabilization policy and that inept policy is a frequent source of economic fluctuations.
3. Advocates of discretionary policy argue that discretion gives more flexibility to policymakers in responding to various unforeseen situations.
4. Advocates of policy rules argue that the political process cannot be trusted. They believe that politicians make frequent mistakes in conducting economic policy and sometimes use economic policy for their own political ends. In addition, advocates of policy rules argue that a commitment to a fixed policy rule is necessary to solve the problem of time inconsistency.

KEY CONCEPTS

Inside and outside lags
Automatic stabilizers
Lucas critique
Political business cycle
Time inconsistency
Monetarists
Inflation targeting
Taylor rule

QUESTIONS FOR REVIEW

1. What are the inside lag and the outside lag? Which has the longer inside lag—monetary or fiscal policy? Which has the longer outside lag? Why?
2. Why would more accurate economic forecasting make it easier for policymakers to stabilize the economy? Describe two ways economists try to forecast developments in the economy.
3. Describe the Lucas critique.
4. How does a person's interpretation of macroeconomic history affect his view of macroeconomic policy?
5. What is meant by the "time inconsistency" of economic policy? Why might policymakers be tempted to renege on an announcement they made earlier? In this situation, what is the advantage of a policy rule?
6. List three policy rules that the Fed might follow. Which of these would you advocate? Why?

PROBLEMS AND APPLICATIONS

1. Suppose that the tradeoff between unemployment and inflation is determined by the Phillips curve:

$$u = u^n - \alpha(\pi - \pi^e),$$

where u denotes the unemployment rate, u^n the natural rate, π the rate of inflation, and π^e the expected rate of inflation. In addition, suppose that the Democratic party always follows a policy of high money growth and the Republican party always follows a policy of low money growth. What "political business cycle" pattern of inflation and unemployment would you predict under the following conditions?

   a. Every four years, one of the parties takes control based on a random flip of a coin. [*Hint*: What will expected inflation be prior to the election?]

   b. The two parties take turns.

2. When cities pass laws limiting the rent landlords can charge on apartments, the laws usually apply to existing buildings and exempt any buildings not yet built. Advocates of rent control argue that this exemption ensures that rent control does not discourage the construction of new housing. Evaluate this argument in light of the time-inconsistency problem.

3. Go to the Web site of the Federal Reserve (www.federalreserve.gov). Find and read a press release, congressional testimony, or report about recent monetary policy. What does it say? What is the Fed doing? Why? What do you think about the Fed's recent policy decisions?

Time Inconsistency and the Tradeoff Between Inflation and Unemployment

In this appendix, we examine more formally the time-inconsistency argument for rules rather than discretion. This analysis is relegated to an appendix because we need to use some calculus.[9]

Suppose that the Phillips curve describes the relationship between inflation and unemployment. Letting u denote the unemployment rate, u^n the natural rate of unemployment, π the rate of inflation, and π^e the expected rate of inflation, unemployment is determined by

$$u = u^n - \alpha(\pi - \pi^e).$$

Unemployment is low when inflation exceeds expected inflation and high when inflation falls below expected inflation. The parameter α determines how much unemployment responds to surprise inflation.

For simplicity, suppose also that the Fed chooses the rate of inflation. Of course, more realistically, the Fed controls inflation only imperfectly through its control of the money supply. But for purposes of illustration, it is useful to assume that the Fed can control inflation perfectly.

The Fed likes low unemployment and low inflation. Suppose that the cost of unemployment and inflation, as perceived by the Fed, can be represented as

$$L(u, \pi) = u + \gamma\pi^2,$$

where the parameter γ represents how much the Fed dislikes inflation relative to unemployment. $L(u, \pi)$ is called the *loss function*. The Fed's objective is to make the loss as small as possible.

Having specified how the economy works and the Fed's objective, let's compare monetary policy made under a fixed rule and under discretion.

We begin by considering policy under a fixed rule. A rule commits the Fed to a particular level of inflation. As long as private agents understand that the Fed is committed to this rule, the expected level of inflation will be the level the Fed is committed to produce. Because expected inflation equals actual inflation ($\pi^e = \pi$), unemployment will be at its natural rate ($u = u^n$).

What is the optimal rule? Because unemployment is at its natural rate regardless of the level of inflation legislated by the rule, there is no benefit to having

---

[9] The material in this appendix is derived from Finn E. Kydland and Edward C. Prescott, "Rules Rather Than Discretion: The Inconsistency of Optimal Plans," *Journal of Political Economy* 85 (June 1977): 473–492; and Robert J. Barro and David Gordon, "A Positive Theory of Monetary Policy in a Natural Rate Model," *Journal of Political Economy* 91 (August 1983): 589–610. Kydland and Prescott won the Nobel Prize for this and other work in 2004.

any inflation at all. Therefore, the optimal fixed rule requires that the Fed produce zero inflation.

Now let's consider discretionary monetary policy. Under discretion, the economy works as follows:

1. Private agents form their expectations of inflation π^e.
2. The Fed chooses the actual level of inflation π.
3. Based on expected and actual inflation, unemployment is determined.

Under this arrangement, the Fed minimizes its loss $L(u, \pi)$ subject to the constraint that the Phillips curve imposes. When making its decision about the rate of inflation, the Fed takes expected inflation as already determined.

To find what outcome we would obtain under discretionary policy, we must examine what level of inflation the Fed would choose. By substituting the Phillips curve into the Fed's loss function, we obtain

$$L(u, \pi) = u^n - \alpha(\pi - \pi^e) + \gamma\pi^2.$$

Notice that the Fed's loss is negatively related to unexpected inflation (the second term in the equation) and positively related to actual inflation (the third term). To find the level of inflation that minimizes this loss, differentiate with respect to π to obtain

$$dL/d\pi = -\alpha + 2\gamma\pi.$$

The loss is minimized when this derivative equals zero.[10] Solving for π, we get

$$\pi = \alpha/(2\gamma).$$

Whatever level of inflation private agents expected, this is the "optimal" level of inflation for the Fed to choose. Of course, rational private agents understand the objective of the Fed and the constraint that the Phillips curve imposes. They therefore expect that the Fed will choose this level of inflation. Expected inflation equals actual inflation [$\pi^e = \pi = \alpha/(2\gamma)$], and unemployment equals its natural rate ($u = u^n$).

Now compare the outcome under optimal discretion to the outcome under the optimal rule. In both cases, unemployment is at its natural rate. Yet discretionary policy produces more inflation than does policy under the rule. *Thus, optimal discretion is worse than the optimal rule.* This is true even though the Fed under discretion was attempting to minimize its loss, $L(u, \pi)$.

At first it may seem strange that the Fed can achieve a better outcome by being committed to a fixed rule. Why can't the Fed with discretion mimic the Fed committed to a zero-inflation rule? The answer is that the Fed is playing a game against private decisionmakers who have rational expectations. Unless it is committed to a fixed rule of zero inflation, the Fed cannot get private agents to expect zero inflation.

---

[10] The second derivative, $d^2L/d\pi^2 = 2\gamma$, is positive, ensuring that we are solving for a minimum of the loss function rather than a maximum!

Suppose, for example, that the Fed simply announces that it will follow a zero-inflation policy. Such an announcement by itself cannot be credible. After private agents have formed their expectations of inflation, the Fed has the incentive to renege on its announcement in order to decrease unemployment. (As we have just seen, once expectations are given, the Fed's optimal policy is to set inflation at $\pi = \alpha/(2\gamma)$, regardless of π^e.) Private agents understand the incentive to renege and therefore do not believe the announcement in the first place.

This theory of monetary policy has an important corollary. Under one circumstance, the Fed with discretion achieves the same outcome as the Fed committed to a fixed rule of zero inflation. If the Fed dislikes inflation much more than it dislikes unemployment (so that γ is very large), inflation under discretion is near zero, because the Fed has little incentive to inflate. This finding provides some guidance to those who have the job of appointing central bankers. An alternative to imposing a fixed rule is to appoint an individual with a fervent distaste for inflation. Perhaps this is why even liberal politicians (Jimmy Carter, Bill Clinton) who are more concerned about unemployment than inflation sometimes appoint conservative central bankers (Paul Volcker, Alan Greenspan) who are more concerned about inflation.

MORE PROBLEMS AND APPLICATIONS

1. In the 1970s in the United States, the inflation rate and the natural rate of unemployment both rose. Let's use this model of time inconsistency to examine this phenomenon. Assume that policy is discretionary.
   a. In the model as developed so far, what happens to the inflation rate when the natural rate of unemployment rises?
   b. Let's now change the model slightly by supposing that the Fed's loss function is quadratic in both inflation and unemployment. That is,
   $$L(u, \pi) = u^2 + \gamma\pi^2.$$
   Follow steps similar to those in the text to solve for the inflation rate under discretionary policy.
   c. Now what happens to the inflation rate when the natural rate of unemployment rises?
   d. In 1979, President Jimmy Carter appointed the conservative central banker Paul Volcker to head the Federal Reserve. According to this model, what should have happened to inflation and unemployment?

CHAPTER 15

Government Debt

Blessed are the young, for they shall inherit the national debt.

— *Herbert Hoover*

When a government spends more than it collects in taxes, it has a budget deficit, which it finances by borrowing from the private sector. The accumulation of past borrowing is the government debt.

Debate about the appropriate amount of government debt in the United States is as old as the country itself. Alexander Hamilton believed that "a national debt, if it is not excessive, will be to us a national blessing," while James Madison argued that "a public debt is a public curse." Indeed, the location of the nation's capital was chosen as part of a deal in which the federal government assumed the Revolutionary War debts of the states: because the Northern states had larger outstanding debts, the capital was located in the South.

This chapter considers various aspects of the debate over the economic effects of government debt. We begin by looking at the numbers. Section 15-1 examines the size of the U.S. government debt, comparing it to the debt of other countries and to the debt that the United States has had during its own past. It also takes a brief look at what the future may hold. Section 15-2 discusses why measuring changes in government indebtedness is not as straightforward as it might seem. Indeed, some economists argue that traditional measures are so misleading that they should be completely ignored.

We then look at how government debt affects the economy. Section 15-3 describes the traditional view of government debt, according to which government borrowing reduces national saving and crowds out capital accumulation. This view is held by most economists and has been implicit in the discussion of fiscal policy throughout this book. Section 15-4 discusses an alternative view, called *Ricardian equivalence,* which is held by a small but influential minority of economists. According to the Ricardian view, government debt does not influence national saving and capital accumulation. As we will see, the debate between the traditional and Ricardian views of government debt arises from disagreements over how consumers respond to the government's debt policy.

Section 15-5 then looks at other facets of the debate over government debt. It begins by discussing whether the government should always try to balance its budget and, if not, when a budget deficit or surplus is desirable. It also examines the effects of government debt on monetary policy, the political process, and a nation's role in the world economy.

15-1 The Size of the Government Debt

Let's begin by putting the government debt in perspective. In 2005, the debt of the U.S. federal government was $4.7 trillion. If we divide this number by 297 million, the number of people in the United States, we find that each person's share of the government debt was about $15,800. Obviously, this is not a trivial number—few people sneeze at $15,800. Yet if we compare this debt to the more than $1 million a typical person will earn over his or her working life, the government debt does not look like the catastrophe it is sometimes made out to be.

One way to judge the size of a government's debt is to compare it to the amount of debt other countries have accumulated. Table 15-1 shows the amount of government debt for 27 major countries expressed as a percentage of each country's GDP. On the top of the list are the heavily indebted countries of Japan and Italy, which have accumulated a debt that exceeds annual GDP. At the bottom are Luxembourg and Australia, which have accumulated relatively small debts. The United States is in the middle of the pack. By international standards, the U.S. government is neither especially profligate nor especially frugal.

Over the course of U.S. history, the indebtedness of the federal government has varied substantially. Figure 15-1 shows the ratio of the federal debt to GDP since 1791. The government debt, relative to the size of the economy, varies from close to zero in the 1830s to a maximum of 107 percent of GDP in 1945.

Historically, the primary cause of increases in the government debt is war. The debt-GDP ratio rises sharply during major wars and falls slowly during peacetime.

TABLE 15-1

How Indebted Are the World's Governments?

Country	Government Debt as a Percentage of GDP	Country	Government Debt as a Percentage of GDP
Japan	158.9	Poland	53.3
Italy	125.4	Finland	53.3
Greece	108.1	Norway	51.7
Belgium	98.5	Denmark	49.7
France	76.7	Spain	49.1
Portugal	76.5	United Kingdom	46.8
Germany	69.9	Czech Republic	42.8
Canada	69.3	Iceland	32.0
Austria	69.2	Ireland	29.9
United States	63.8	New Zealand	26.0
Netherlands	63.7	Korea	20.3
Hungary	62.5	Australia	15.3
Sweden	61.5	Luxembourg	8.6
Slovak Republic	56.8		

Source: OECD Economic Outlook. Data are based on estimates of gross government financial liabilities and nominal GDP for 2005.

FIGURE 15-1

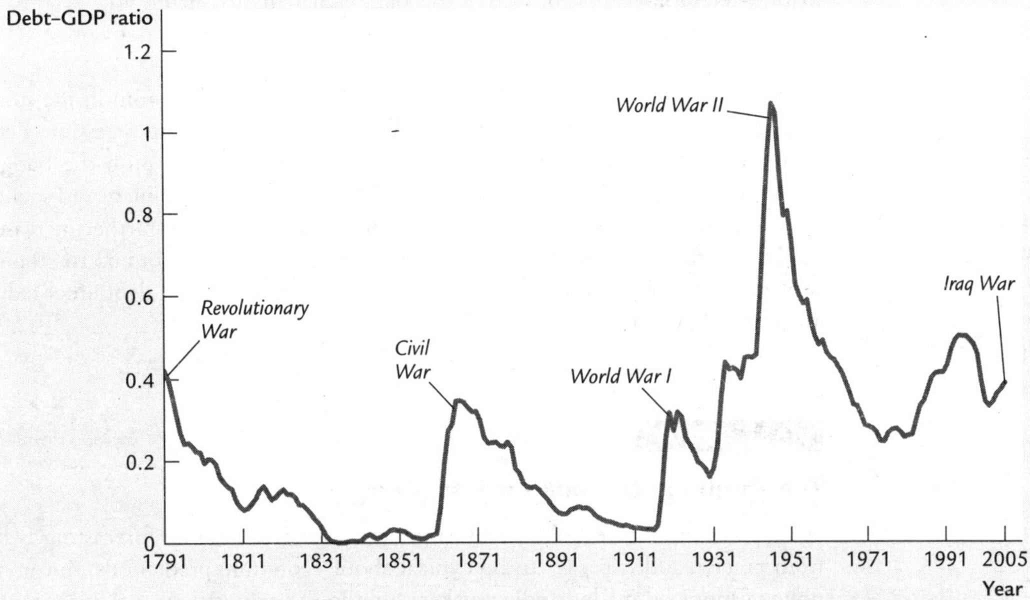

The Ratio of Government Debt to GDP Since 1790 The U.S. federal government debt held by the public, relative to the size of the U.S. economy, rises sharply during wars and declines slowly during peacetime. A major exception is the period from 1980 to 1995, when the ratio of debt to GDP rose without the occurrence of a major military conflict.

Source: U.S. Department of Treasury, U.S. Department of Commerce, and T.S. Berry, "Production and Population Since 1789," Bostwick Paper No. 6, Richmond, 1988.

Many economists think that this historical pattern is the appropriate way to run fiscal policy. As we will discuss more fully later in this chapter, deficit financing of wars appears optimal for reasons of both tax smoothing and generational equity.

One instance of a large increase in government debt in peacetime began in the early 1980s. When Ronald Reagan was elected President in 1980, he was committed to reducing taxes and increasing military spending. These policies, coupled with a deep recession attributable to tight monetary policy, began a long period of substantial budget deficits. The government debt expressed as a percentage of GDP roughly doubled from 26 percent in 1980 to 50 percent in 1995. The United States had never before experienced such a large increase in government debt during a period of peace and prosperity. Many economists have criticized this increase in government debt as imposing an unjustifiable burden on future generations.

The increase in government debt during the 1980s caused significant concern among many policymakers as well. The first President Bush raised taxes to reduce the deficit, breaking his "Read my lips: No new taxes" campaign pledge and, according to some political commentators, costing him reelection. In 1993, when

President Clinton took office, he raised taxes yet again. These tax increases, together with spending restraint and rapid economic growth due to the information-technology boom, caused the budget deficits to shrink and eventually turn into budget surpluses. The government debt fell from 50 percent of GDP in 1995 to 33 percent in 2001.

When George W. Bush took office in 2001, the high-tech boom in the stock market was reversing course, and the economy was heading into recession. Economic downturns automatically cause tax revenue to fall and push the budget toward deficit. In addition, tax cuts to combat the recession and increased spending on homeland security and for wars in Afghanistan and Iraq further increased the budget deficit. From 2001 to 2005, government debt rose from 33 to 39 percent of GDP. Once again, the long-term effects of government debt emerged as a major policy concern.

CASE STUDY

The Troubling Outlook for Fiscal Policy

What does the future hold for fiscal policymakers? Economic forecasting is far from precise, and it is easy to be cynical about economic predictions. But good policy cannot be made if policymakers only look backward. As a result, economists in the Congressional Budget Office (CBO) and other government agencies are always trying to look ahead to see what problems and opportunities are likely to develop. When these economists conduct long-term projections of U.S. fiscal policy, they paint a troubling picture.

One reason is demographic. Advances in medical technology have been increasing life expectancy, while improvements in birth-control techniques and changing social norms have reduced the number of children people have. Because of these developments, the elderly are becoming a larger share of the population. In 1950, the elderly population (aged 65 and older) equaled about 14 percent of the working-age population (aged 20 to 64). Now the elderly are about 21 percent of the working-age population, and that figure will rise to about 40 percent over the next fifty years. About one-third of the budget of the U.S. federal government is devoted to providing the elderly with pensions (mainly through the Social Security program) and health care. As more people become eligible for these "entitlements," as they are sometimes called, government spending will automatically rise over time.

A second, related reason for the troubling fiscal picture is the rising cost of health care. The government provides health care to the elderly through the Medicare system and to the poor through Medicaid. As the cost of health care increases, government spending on these programs increases as well. Policymakers have proposed various ways to stem the rise in health care costs, such as reducing the burden of lawsuits, encouraging more competition among health care providers, and promoting greater use of information technology, but most health economists believe such measures will have only limited impact. The main reason for rising health care costs is medical advances that provide new, better, but often expensive ways to extend and improve our lives.

The combination of the aging population and rising health care costs will have a major impact on the federal budget. Government spending on Social Security, Medicare, and Medicaid has already risen from less than 1 percent of GDP in 1950 to about 8 percent today. The upward trajectory is not about to stop. The Congressional Budget Office estimates that if no changes are made, spending on these programs will rise to about 20 percent of GDP over the next half century.

How the United States will handle these spending pressures is an open question. Simply increasing the budget deficit is not feasible. A budget deficit just pushes the cost of government spending onto a future generation of taxpayers. In the long run, the government needs to raise tax revenue to pay for the benefits it provides.

The big question is how the required fiscal adjustment will be split between tax increases and spending reductions. Some economists believe that to pay for these commitments, we will need to raise taxes substantially as a percentage of GDP. Given the projected increases in spending on Social Security, Medicare, and Medicaid, paying for these benefits would require increasing all taxes by approximately one-third. Other economists believe that such high tax rates would impose too great a cost on younger workers. They believe that policymakers should reduce the promises now being made to the elderly of the future and that, at the same time, people should be encouraged to take a greater role caring for themselves as they age. This might entail increasing the normal retirement age, while giving people more incentive to save during their working years to prepare for their own retirement and health costs. Resolving this debate will likely be one of the great policy challenges in the decades ahead.

15-2 Problems in Measurement

The government budget deficit equals government spending minus government revenue, which in turn equals the amount of new debt the government needs to issue to finance its operations. This definition may sound simple enough, but in fact debates over fiscal policy sometimes arise over how the budget deficit should be measured. Some economists believe that the deficit as currently measured is not a good indicator of the stance of fiscal policy. That is, they believe that the budget deficit does not accurately gauge either the impact of fiscal policy on today's economy or the burden being placed on future generations of taxpayers. In this section we discuss four problems with the usual measure of the budget deficit.

Measurement Problem 1: Inflation

The least controversial of the measurement issues is the correction for inflation. Almost all economists agree that the government's indebtedness should be measured in real terms, not in nominal terms. The measured deficit should equal the change in the government's real debt, not the change in its nominal debt.

The budget deficit as commonly measured, however, does not correct for inflation. To see how large an error this induces, consider the following example. Suppose that the real government debt is not changing; in other words, in real terms, the budget is balanced. In this case, the nominal debt must be rising at the rate of inflation. That is,

$$\Delta D/D = \pi,$$

where π is the inflation rate and D is the stock of government debt. This implies

$$\Delta D = \pi D.$$

The government would look at the change in the nominal debt ΔD and would report a budget deficit of πD. Hence, most economists believe that the reported budget deficit is overstated by the amount πD.

We can make the same argument in another way. The deficit is government expenditure minus government revenue. Part of expenditure is the interest paid on the government debt. Expenditure should include only the real interest paid on the debt rD, not the nominal interest paid iD. Because the difference between the nominal interest rate i and the real interest rate r is the inflation rate π, the budget deficit is overstated by πD.

This correction for inflation can be large, especially when inflation is high, and it can often change our evaluation of fiscal policy. For example, in 1979, the federal government reported a budget deficit of \$28 billion. Inflation was 8.6 percent, and the government debt held at the beginning of the year by the public (excluding the Federal Reserve) was \$495 billion. The deficit was therefore overstated by

$$\begin{aligned}\pi D &= 0.086 \times \$495 \text{ billion} \\ &= \$43 \text{ billion.}\end{aligned}$$

Corrected for inflation, the reported budget deficit of \$28 billion turns into a budget surplus of \$15 billion! In other words, even though nominal government debt was rising, real government debt was falling.

Measurement Problem 2: Capital Assets

Many economists believe that an accurate assessment of the government's budget deficit requires taking into account the government's assets as well as its liabilities. In particular, when measuring the government's overall indebtedness, we should subtract government assets from government debt. Therefore, the budget deficit should be measured as the change in debt minus the change in assets.

Certainly, individuals and firms treat assets and liabilities symmetrically. When a person borrows to buy a house, we do not say that he is running a budget deficit. Instead, we offset the increase in assets (the house) against the increase in debt (the mortgage) and record no change in net wealth. Perhaps we should treat the government's finances the same way.

A budget procedure that accounts for assets as well as liabilities is called **capital budgeting**, because it takes into account changes in capital. For example, suppose that the government sells one of its office buildings or some of its land and uses the proceeds to reduce the government debt. Under current budget procedures, the reported deficit would be lower. Under capital budgeting, the revenue received from the sale would not lower the deficit, because the reduction in debt would be offset by a reduction in assets. Similarly, under capital budgeting, government borrowing to finance the purchase of a capital good would not raise the deficit.

The major difficulty with capital budgeting is that it is hard to decide which government expenditures should count as capital expenditures. For example, should the interstate highway system be counted as an asset of the government? If so, what is its value? What about the stockpile of nuclear weapons? Should spending on education be treated as expenditure on human capital? These difficult questions must be answered if the government is to adopt a capital budget.

Economists and policymakers disagree about whether the federal government should use capital budgeting. (Many state governments already use it.) Opponents of capital budgeting argue that, although the system is superior in principle to the current system, it is too difficult to implement in practice. Proponents of capital budgeting argue that even an imperfect treatment of capital assets would be better than ignoring them altogether.

Measurement Problem 3: Uncounted Liabilities

Some economists argue that the measured budget deficit is misleading because it excludes some important government liabilities. For example, consider the pensions of government workers. These workers provide labor services to the government today, but part of their compensation is deferred to the future. In essence, these workers are providing a loan to the government. Their future pension benefits represent a government liability not very different from government debt. Yet this liability is not included as part of the government debt, and the accumulation of this liability is not included as part of the budget deficit. According to some estimates, this implicit liability is almost as large as the official government debt.

Similarly, consider the Social Security system. In some ways, the system is like a pension plan. People pay some of their income into the system when young and expect to receive benefits when old. Perhaps accumulated future Social Security benefits should be included in the government's liabilities. Estimates suggest that the government's future Social Security liabilities (less future Social Security taxes) are more than three times the government debt as officially measured.

One might argue that Social Security liabilities are different from government debt because the government can change the laws determining Social Security benefits. Yet, in principle, the government could always choose not to repay all of its debt: the government honors its debt only because it chooses to do so. Promises to pay the holders of government debt may not be fundamentally different from promises to pay the future recipients of Social Security.

A particularly difficult form of government liability to measure is the *contingent liability*—the liability that is due only if a specified event occurs. For example, the government guarantees many forms of private credit, such as student loans, mortgages for low- and moderate-income families, and deposits in banks and savings and loan institutions. If the borrower repays the loan, the government pays nothing; if the borrower defaults, the government makes the repayment. When the government provides this guarantee, it undertakes a liability contingent on the borrower's default. Yet this contingent liability is not reflected in the budget deficit, in part because it is not clear what dollar value to attach to it.

Measurement Problem 4: The Business Cycle

Many changes in the government's budget deficit occur automatically in response to a fluctuating economy. For example, when the economy goes into a recession, incomes fall, so people pay less in personal income taxes. Profits fall, so corporations pay less in corporate income taxes. More people become eligible for government assistance, such as welfare and unemployment insurance, so government spending rises. Even without any change in the laws governing taxation and spending, the budget deficit increases.

These automatic changes in the deficit are not errors in measurement, because the government truly borrows more when a recession depresses tax revenue and boosts government spending. But these changes do make it more difficult to use the deficit to monitor changes in fiscal policy. That is, the deficit can rise or fall either because the government has changed policy or because the economy has changed direction. For some purposes, it would be good to know which is occurring.

To solve this problem, the government calculates a **cyclically adjusted budget deficit** (sometimes called the *full-employment budget deficit*). The cyclically adjusted deficit is based on estimates of what government spending and tax revenue would be if the economy were operating at its natural level of output and employment. The cyclically adjusted deficit is a useful measure because it reflects policy changes but not the current stage of the business cycle.

Summing Up

Economists differ in the importance they place on these measurement problems. Some believe that the problems are so severe that the budget deficit as normally measured is almost meaningless. Most take these measurement problems seriously but still view the measured budget deficit as a useful indicator of fiscal policy.

The undisputed lesson is that to evaluate fully what fiscal policy is doing, economists and policymakers must look at more than just the measured budget deficit. And, in fact, they do. The budget documents prepared annually by the Office of Management and Budget contain much detailed information about the government's finances, including data on capital expenditures and credit programs.

No economic statistic is perfect. Whenever we see a number reported in the media, we need to know what it is measuring and what it is leaving out. This is especially true for data on government debt and budget deficits.

15-3 The Traditional View of Government Debt

Imagine that you are an economist working for the Congressional Budget Office (CBO). You receive a letter from the chair of the Senate Budget Committee:

> Dear CBO Economist:
>
> Congress is about to consider the president's request to cut all taxes by 20 percent. Before deciding whether to endorse the request, my committee would like your analysis. We see little hope of reducing government spending, so the tax cut would mean an increase in the budget deficit. How would the tax cut and budget deficit affect the economy and the economic well-being of the country?
>
> Sincerely,
> Committee Chair

Before responding to the senator, you open your favorite economics textbook—this one, of course—to see what the models predict for such a change in fiscal policy.

To analyze the long-run effects of this policy change, you turn to the models in Chapters 3 through 8. The model in Chapter 3 shows that a tax cut stimulates consumer spending and reduces national saving. The reduction in saving raises the interest rate, which crowds out investment. The Solow growth model introduced in Chapter 7 shows that lower investment eventually leads to a lower steady-state capital stock and a lower level of output. Because we concluded in Chapter 8 that the U.S. economy has less capital than in the Golden Rule steady state (the steady state with maximum consumption), the fall in steady-state capital means lower consumption and reduced economic well-being.

To analyze the short-run effects of the policy change, you turn to the *IS-LM* model in Chapters 10 and 11. This model shows that a tax cut stimulates consumer spending, which implies an expansionary shift in the *IS* curve. If there is no change in monetary policy, the shift in the *IS* curve leads to an expansionary shift in the aggregate demand curve. In the short run, when prices are sticky, the expansion in aggregate demand leads to higher output and lower unemployment. Over time, as prices adjust, the economy returns to the natural level of output, and the higher aggregate demand results in a higher price level.

To see how international trade affects your analysis, you turn to the open-economy models in Chapters 5 and 12. The model in Chapter 5 shows that when national saving falls, people start financing investment by borrowing from abroad, causing a trade deficit. Although the inflow of capital from abroad lessens the effect of the fiscal policy change on U.S. capital accumulation, the United

States becomes indebted to foreign countries. The fiscal policy change also causes the dollar to appreciate, which makes foreign goods cheaper in the United States and domestic goods more expensive abroad. The Mundell-Fleming model in Chapter 12 shows that the appreciation of the dollar and the resulting fall in

FYI Taxes and Incentives

Throughout this book we have summarized the tax system with a single variable *T*. In our models, the policy instrument is the level of taxation that the government chooses; we have ignored the issue of how the government raises this tax revenue. In practice, however, taxes are not lump-sum payments but are levied on some type of economic activity. The U.S. federal government raises some revenue by taxing personal income (43 percent of tax revenue), some by taxing payrolls (39 percent), some by taxing corporate profits (10 percent), and some from other sources (8 percent).

Courses in public finance spend much time studying the pros and cons of alternative types of taxes. One lesson emphasized in such courses is that taxes affect incentives. When people are taxed on their labor earnings, they have less incentive to work hard. When people are taxed on the income from owning capital, they have less incentive to save and invest in capital. As a result, when taxes change, incentives change, and this can have macroeconomic effects. If lower tax rates encourage increased work and investment, the aggregate supply of goods and services increases.

Some economists, called *supply-siders,* believe that the incentive effects of taxes are large. Some supply-siders go so far as to suggest that tax cuts can be self-financing: a cut in tax rates induces such a large increase in aggregate supply that tax revenue increases, despite the fall in tax rates. Although all economists agree that taxes affect incentives and that incentives affect aggregate supply to some degree, most believe that the incentive effects are not large enough to make tax cuts self-financing in most circumstances.

In recent years, there has been much debate about how to reform the tax system to reduce the disincentives that impede the economy from reaching its full potential. A proposal endorsed by many economists is to move from the current income tax system toward a consumption tax. Compared to an income tax, a consumption tax would provide more incentives for saving, investment, and capital accumulation. One way of taxing consumption would be to expand the availability of tax-advantaged saving accounts, such as individual retirement accounts and 401(k) plans, which exempt saving from taxation until that saving is later withdrawn and spent. Another way of taxing consumption would be to adopt a value-added tax, a tax on consumption paid by producers rather than consumers, now used by many European countries to raise government revenue.[1]

[1] To read more about how taxes affect the economy through incentives, the best place to start is an undergraduate textbook in public finance, such as Harvey Rosen, *Public Finance*, 7th ed. (New York: McGraw-Hill, 2004). In the more advanced literature that links *public finance* and macroeconomics, a classic reference is Christophe Chamley, "Optimal Taxation of Capital Income in a General Equilibrium Model with Infinite Lives," *Econometrica* 54 (May 1986): 607–622. Chamley establishes conditions under which the tax system should not distort the incentive to save (that is, conditions under which consumption taxation is superior to income taxation). The robustness of this conclusion is investigated in Andrew Atkeson, V.V. Chari, and Patrick J. Kehoe, "Taxing Capital Income: A Bad Idea," *Federal Reserve Bank of Minneapolis Quarterly Review* 23 (Summer 1999): 3–17.

net exports reduce the short-run expansionary impact of the fiscal change on output and employment.

With all these models in mind, you draft a response:

Dear Senator:

A tax cut financed by government borrowing would have many effects on the economy. The immediate impact of the tax cut would be to stimulate consumer spending. Higher consumer spending affects the economy in both the short run and the long run.

In the short run, higher consumer spending would raise the demand for goods and services and thus raise output and employment. Interest rates would also rise, however, as investors competed for a smaller flow of saving. Higher interest rates would discourage investment and would encourage capital to flow in from abroad. The dollar would rise in value against foreign currencies, and U.S. firms would become less competitive in world markets.

In the long run, the smaller national saving caused by the tax cut would mean a smaller capital stock and a greater foreign debt. Therefore, the output of the nation would be smaller, and a greater share of that output would be owed to foreigners.

The overall effect of the tax cut on economic well-being is hard to judge. Current generations would benefit from higher consumption and higher employment, although inflation would likely be higher as well. Future generations would bear much of the burden of today's budget deficits: they would be born into a nation with a smaller capital stock and a larger foreign debt.

Your faithful servant,
CBO Economist

The senator replies:

Dear CBO Economist:

Thank you for your letter. It made sense to me. But yesterday my committee heard testimony from a prominent economist who called herself a "Ricardian" and who reached quite a different conclusion. She said that a tax cut by itself would not stimulate consumer spending. She concluded that the budget deficit would therefore not have all the effects you listed. What's going on here?

Sincerely,
Committee Chair

After studying the next section, you write back to the senator, explaining in detail the debate over Ricardian equivalence.

15-4 The Ricardian View of Government Debt

The traditional view of government debt presumes that when the government cuts taxes and runs a budget deficit, consumers respond to their higher after-tax income by spending more. An alternative view, called **Ricardian equivalence**, questions this presumption. According to the Ricardian view, consumers are forward-looking and, therefore, base their spending decisions not only on their current income but also on their expected future income. As we explore more fully in Chapter 16, the forward-looking consumer is at the heart of many modern theories of consumption. The Ricardian view of government debt applies the logic of the forward-looking consumer to analyze the effects of fiscal policy.

The Basic Logic of Ricardian Equivalence

Consider the response of a forward-looking consumer to the tax cut that the Senate Budget Committee is considering. The consumer might reason as follows:

> The government is cutting taxes without any plans to reduce government spending. Does this policy alter my set of opportunities? Am I richer because of this tax cut? Should I consume more?
>
> Maybe not. The government is financing the tax cut by running a budget deficit. At some point in the future, the government will have to raise taxes to pay off the debt and accumulated interest. So the policy really represents a tax cut today coupled with a tax hike in the future. The tax cut merely gives me transitory income that eventually will be taken back. I am not any better off, so I will leave my consumption unchanged.

The forward-looking consumer understands that government borrowing today means higher taxes in the future. A tax cut financed by government debt does not reduce the tax burden; it merely reschedules it. It therefore should not encourage the consumer to spend more.

One can view this argument another way. Suppose that the government borrows $1,000 from the typical citizen to give that citizen a $1,000 tax cut. In essence, this policy is the same as giving the citizen a $1,000 government bond as a gift. One side of the bond says, "The government owes you, the bondholder, $1,000 plus interest." The other side says, "You, the taxpayer, owe the government $1,000 plus interest." Overall, the gift of a bond from the government to the typical citizen does not make the citizen richer or poorer, because the value of the bond is offset by the value of the future tax liability.

The general principle is that government debt is equivalent to future taxes, and if consumers are sufficiently forward-looking, future taxes are equivalent to current taxes. Hence, financing the government by debt is equivalent to financing it by taxes. This view is called *Ricardian equivalence* after the famous nineteenth-century economist David Ricardo, because he first noted the theoretical argument.

The implication of Ricardian equivalence is that a debt-financed tax cut leaves consumption unaffected. Households save the extra disposable income to pay the future tax liability that the tax cut implies. This increase in private saving exactly offsets the decrease in public saving. National saving—the sum of private and public saving—remains the same. The tax cut therefore has none of the effects that the traditional analysis predicts.

The logic of Ricardian equivalence does not mean that all changes in fiscal policy are irrelevant. Changes in fiscal policy do influence consumer spending if they influence present or future government purchases. For example, suppose that the government cuts taxes today because it plans to reduce government purchases in the future. If the consumer understands that this tax cut does not require an increase in future taxes, he feels richer and raises his consumption. But note that it is the reduction in government purchases, rather than the reduction in taxes, that stimulates consumption: the announcement of a future reduction in government purchases would raise consumption today even if current taxes were unchanged, because it would imply lower taxes at some time in the future.

Consumers and Future Taxes

The essence of the Ricardian view is that when people choose their consumption, they rationally look ahead to the future taxes implied by government debt. But how forward-looking are consumers? Defenders of the traditional view of government debt believe that the prospect of future taxes does not have as large an influence on current consumption as the Ricardian view assumes. Here are some of their arguments.[2]

Myopia Proponents of the Ricardian view of fiscal policy assume that people are rational when making decisions such as choosing how much of their income to consume and how much to save. When the government borrows to pay for current spending, rational consumers look ahead to the future taxes required to support this debt. Thus, the Ricardian view presumes that people have substantial knowledge and foresight.

One possible argument for the traditional view of tax cuts is that people are shortsighted, perhaps because they do not fully comprehend the implications of government budget deficits. It is possible that some people follow simple and not fully rational rules of thumb when choosing how much to save. Suppose, for example, that a person acts on the assumption that future taxes will be the same as current taxes. This person will fail to take account of future changes in taxes required by current government policies. A debt-financed tax cut will lead this person to believe that his lifetime income has increased, even if it hasn't. The tax cut will therefore lead to higher consumption and lower national saving.

Borrowing Constraints The Ricardian view of government debt assumes that consumers base their spending not on their current income but on their lifetime income, which includes both current and expected future income. According to the Ricardian view, a debt-financed tax cut increases current income, but it does not alter lifetime income or consumption. Advocates of the traditional view of government debt argue that current income is more important than lifetime income for those consumers who face binding borrowing constraints. A *borrowing constraint* is a limit on how much an individual can borrow from banks or other financial institutions.

A person who would like to consume more than his current income—perhaps because he expects higher income in the future—has to do so by borrowing. If

[2] For a survey of the debate over Ricardian equivalence, see Douglas Bernheim, "Ricardian Equivalence: An Evaluation of Theory and Evidence," *NBER Macroeconomics Annual* (1987): 263–303. See also the symposium on budget deficits in the Spring 1989 issue of the *Journal of Economic Perspectives.*

he cannot borrow to finance current consumption, or can borrow only a limited amount, his current income determines his spending, regardless of what his lifetime income might be. In this case, a debt-financed tax cut raises current income and thus consumption, even though future income is lower. In essence, when the government cuts current taxes and raises future taxes, it is giving taxpayers a loan. For a person who wanted to obtain a loan but was unable to, the tax cut expands his opportunities and stimulates consumption.

CASE STUDY

George Bush's Withholding Experiment

In early 1992, President George Bush pursued a novel policy to deal with the lingering recession in the United States. By executive order, he lowered the amount of income taxes that were being withheld from workers' paychecks. The order did not reduce the amount of taxes that workers owed; it merely delayed payment. The higher take-home pay that workers received during 1992 was to be offset by higher tax payments, or smaller tax refunds, when income taxes were due in April 1993.

What effect would you predict for this policy? According to the logic of Ricardian equivalence, consumers should realize that their lifetime resources were unchanged and, therefore, save the extra take-home pay to meet the upcoming tax liability. Yet George Bush claimed his policy would provide "money people can use to help pay for clothing, college, or to get a new car." That is, he believed that consumers would spend the extra income, thereby stimulating aggregate demand and helping the economy recover from the recession. Bush seemed to be assuming that consumers were shortsighted or faced binding borrowing constraints.

Gauging the actual effects of this policy is difficult with aggregate data, because many other things were happening at the same time. Yet some evidence comes from a survey two economists conducted shortly after the policy was announced. The survey asked people what they would do with the extra income. Fifty-seven percent of the respondents said they would save it, use it to repay debts, or adjust their withholding in order to reverse the effect of Bush's executive order. Forty-three percent said they would spend the extra income. Thus, for this policy change, a majority of the population was planning to act as Ricardian theory posits. Nonetheless, Bush was partly right: many people planned to spend the extra income, even though they understood that the following year's tax bill would be higher.[3]

Future Generations Besides myopia and borrowing constraints, a third argument for the traditional view of government debt is that consumers expect the implied future taxes to fall not on them but on future generations. Suppose, for

[3] Matthew D. Shapiro and Joel Slemrod, "Consumer Response to the Timing of Income: Evidence From a Change in Tax Withholding," *American Economic Review* 85 (March 1995): 274–283.

example, that the government cuts taxes today, issues 30-year bonds to finance the budget deficit, and then raises taxes in 30 years to repay the loan. In this case, the government debt represents a transfer of wealth from the next generation of taxpayers (which faces the tax hike) to the current generation of taxpayers (which gets the tax cut). This transfer raises the lifetime resources of the current generation, so it raises their consumption. In essence, a debt-financed tax cut stimulates consumption because it gives the current generation the opportunity to consume at the expense of the next generation.

"What's this I hear about you adults mortgaging my future?"

Economist Robert Barro has provided a clever rejoinder to this argument to support the Ricardian view. Barro argues that because future generations are the children and grandchildren of the current generation, we should not view them as independent economic actors. Instead, he argues, the appropriate assumption is that current generations care about future generations. This altruism between generations is evidenced by the gifts that many people give their children, often in the form of bequests at the time of their deaths. The existence of bequests suggests that many people are not eager to take advantage of the opportunity to consume at their children's expense.

According to Barro's analysis, the relevant decisionmaking unit is not the individual, whose life is finite, but the family, which continues forever. In other words, an individual decides how much to consume based not only on his own income but also on the income of future members of his family. A debt-financed tax cut may raise the income an individual receives in his lifetime, but it does not raise his family's overall resources. Instead of consuming the extra income from the tax cut, the individual saves it and leaves it as a bequest to his children, who will bear the future tax liability.

We can see now that the debate over government debt is really a debate over consumer behavior. The Ricardian view assumes that consumers have a long time horizon. Barro's analysis of the family implies that the consumer's time horizon, like the government's, is effectively infinite. Yet it is possible that consumers do not look ahead to the tax liabilities of future generations. Perhaps they expect their children to be richer than they are and therefore welcome the opportunity to consume at their children's expense. The fact that many people leave zero or minimal bequests to their children is consistent with this hypothesis. For these zero-bequest families, a debt-financed tax cut alters consumption by redistributing wealth among generations.[4]

[4] Robert J. Barro, "Are Government Bonds Net Wealth?" *Journal of Political Economy* 81 (1974): 1095–1117.

CASE STUDY

Why Do Parents Leave Bequests?

The debate over Ricardian equivalence is partly a debate over how different generations are linked to one another. Robert Barro's defense of the Ricardian view is based on the assumption that parents leave their children bequests because they care about them. But is altruism really the reason that parents leave bequests?

One group of economists has suggested that parents use bequests to control their children. Parents often want their children to do certain things for them, such as phoning home regularly and visiting on holidays. Perhaps parents use the implicit threat of disinheritance to induce their children to be more attentive.

To test this "strategic bequest motive," these economists examined data on how often children visit their parents. They found that the more wealthy the parent, the more often the children visit. Even more striking was another result: only wealth that can be left as a bequest induces more frequent visits. Wealth that cannot be bequeathed, such as pension wealth which reverts to the pension company in the event of an early death, does not encourage children to visit. These findings suggest that there may be more to the relationships among generations than mere altruism.[5]

Making a Choice

Having seen the traditional and Ricardian views of government debt, you should ask yourself two sets of questions.

First, with which view do you agree? If the government cuts taxes today, runs a budget deficit, and raises taxes in the future, how will the policy affect the economy? Will it stimulate consumption, as the traditional view holds? Or will consumers understand that their lifetime income is unchanged and, therefore, offset the budget deficit with higher private saving?

Second, why do you hold the view that you do? If you agree with the traditional view of government debt, what is the reason? Do consumers fail to understand that higher government borrowing today means higher taxes tomorrow? Or do they ignore future taxes, either because they are borrowing-constrained or because future taxes fall on future generations with which they do not feel an economic link? If you hold the Ricardian view, do you believe that consumers have the foresight to see that government borrowing today will result in future taxes levied on them or their descendants? Do you believe that consumers will save the extra income to offset that future tax liability?

We might hope that the evidence could help us decide between these two views of government debt. Yet when economists examine historical episodes of large budget deficits, the evidence is inconclusive. History can be interpreted in different ways.

[5] B. Douglas Bernheim, Andrei Shleifer, and Lawrence H. Summers, "The Strategic Bequest Motive," *Journal of Political Economy* 93 (1985): 1045–1076.

FYI Ricardo on Ricardian Equivalence

David Ricardo was a millionaire stockbroker and one of the great economists of all time. His most important contribution to the field was his 1817 book *Principles of Political Economy and Taxation,* in which he developed the theory of comparative advantage, which economists still use to explain the gains from international trade. Ricardo was also a member of the British Parliament, where he put his own theories to work and opposed the corn laws, which restricted international trade in grain.

Ricardo was interested in the alternative ways in which a government might pay for its expenditure. In an 1820 article called *Essay on the Funding System,* he considered an example of a war that cost 20 million pounds. He noted that if the interest rate were 5 percent, this expense could be financed with a one-time tax of 20 million pounds, a perpetual tax of 1 million pounds, or a tax of 1.2 million pounds for 45 years. He wrote

> In point of economy, there is no real difference in either of the modes; for twenty million in one payment, one million per annum for ever, or 1,200,000 pounds for 45 years, are precisely of the same value.

Ricardo was aware that the issue involved the linkages among generations:

> It would be difficult to convince a man possessed of 20,000 pounds, or any other sum, that a perpetual payment of 50 pounds per annum was equally burdensome with a single tax of 1000 pounds. He would have some vague notion that the 50 pounds per annum would be paid by posterity, and would not be paid by him; but if he leaves his fortune to his son, and leaves it charged with this perpetual tax, where is the difference whether he leaves him 20,000 pounds with the tax, or 19,000 pounds without it?

Although Ricardo viewed these alternative methods of government finance as equivalent, he did not think other people would view them as such:

> The people who pay taxes . . . do not manage their private affairs accordingly. We are apt to think that the war is burdensome only in proportion to what we are at the moment called to pay for it in taxes, without reflecting on the probable duration of such taxes.

Thus, Ricardo doubted that people were rational and farsighted enough to look ahead fully to their future tax liabilities.

As a policymaker, Ricardo took seriously the government debt. Before the British Parliament, he once declared,

> This would be the happiest country in the world, and its progress in prosperity would go beyond the powers of imagination to conceive, if we got rid of two great evils—the national debt and the corn laws.

It is one of the great ironies in the history of economic thought that Ricardo rejected the theory that now bears his name!

Consider, for example, the experience of the 1980s. The large budget deficits, caused partly by the Reagan tax cut of 1981, seem to offer a natural experiment to test the two views of government debt. At first glance, this episode appears decisively to support the traditional view. The large budget deficits coincided with low national saving, high real interest rates, and a large trade deficit. Indeed, advocates of the traditional view of government debt often claim that the experience of the 1980s confirms their position.

Yet those who hold the Ricardian view of government debt interpret these events differently. Perhaps saving was low in the 1980s because people were optimistic about future economic growth—an optimism that was also reflected in a booming stock market. Or perhaps saving was low because people expected that the tax cut would eventually lead not to higher taxes but, as Reagan promised, to lower government spending. Because it is hard to rule out any of these interpretations, both views of government debt survive.

15-5 Other Perspectives on Government Debt

The policy debates over government debt have many facets. So far we have considered the traditional and Ricardian views of government debt. According to the traditional view, a government budget deficit expands aggregate demand and stimulates output in the short run but crowds out capital and depresses economic growth in the long run. According to the Ricardian view, a government budget deficit has none of these effects, because consumers understand that a budget deficit represents merely the postponement of a tax burden. With these two theories as background, we now consider several other perspectives on government debt.

Balanced Budgets Versus Optimal Fiscal Policy

In the United States, many state constitutions require the state government to run a balanced budget. A recurring topic of political debate is whether the federal constitution should require a balanced budget for the federal government as well. Most economists oppose a strict rule requiring the government to balance its budget. There are three reasons why optimal fiscal policy may at times call for a budget deficit or surplus.

Stabilization A budget deficit or surplus can help stabilize the economy. In essence, a balanced-budget rule would revoke the automatic stabilizing powers of the system of taxes and transfers. When the economy goes into a recession, taxes automatically fall, and transfers automatically rise. Although these automatic responses help stabilize the economy, they push the budget into deficit. A strict balanced-budget rule would require that the government raise taxes or reduce spending in a recession, but these actions would further depress aggregate demand.

Tax Smoothing A budget deficit or surplus can be used to reduce the distortion of incentives caused by the tax system. As we discussed earlier, high tax rates impose a cost on society by discouraging economic activity. A tax on labor earnings, for instance, reduces the incentive that people have to work long hours. Because this disincentive becomes particularly large at very high tax rates, the total social cost of taxes is minimized by keeping tax rates relatively stable rather than making them high in some years and low in others. Economists call this policy *tax smoothing.* To keep tax rates smooth, a deficit is necessary in years of unusually low income (recessions) or unusually high expenditure (wars).

Intergenerational Redistribution A budget deficit can be used to shift a tax burden from current to future generations. For example, some economists argue that if the current generation fights a war to preserve freedom, future generations benefit as well and should bear some of the burden. To pass on some of the war's costs, the current generation can finance the war with a budget deficit. The government can later retire the debt by levying taxes on the next generation.

These considerations lead most economists to reject a strict balanced-budget rule. At the very least, a rule for fiscal policy needs to take account of the recurring episodes, such as recessions and wars, during which it is reasonable for the government to run a budget deficit.

Fiscal Effects on Monetary Policy

In 1985, Paul Volcker told Congress that "the actual and prospective size of the budget deficit . . . heightens skepticism about our ability to control the money supply and contain inflation." A decade later, Alan Greenspan claimed that "a substantial reduction in the long-term prospective deficit of the United States will significantly lower very long-term inflation expectations." Both of these Fed chairmen apparently saw a link between fiscal policy and monetary policy.

We first discussed such a possibility in Chapter 4. As we saw, one way for a government to finance a budget deficit is simply to print money—a policy that leads to higher inflation. Indeed, when countries experience hyperinflation, the typical reason is that fiscal policymakers are relying on the inflation tax to pay for some of their spending. The ends of hyperinflations almost always coincide with fiscal reforms that include large cuts in government spending and therefore a reduced need for seigniorage.

In addition to this link between the budget deficit and inflation, some economists have suggested that a high level of debt might also encourage the government to create inflation. Because most government debt is specified in nominal terms, the real value of the debt falls when the price level rises. This is the usual redistribution between creditors and debtors caused by unexpected inflation—here the debtor is the government and the creditor is the private sector. But this debtor, unlike others, has access to the monetary printing press. A high level of debt might encourage the government to print money, thereby raising the price level and reducing the real value of its debts.

Despite these concerns about a possible link between government debt and monetary policy, there is little evidence that this link is important in most developed countries. In the United States, for instance, inflation was high in the 1970s, even though government debt was low relative to GDP. Monetary policymakers got inflation under control in the early 1980s, just as fiscal policymakers started running large budget deficits and increasing the government debt. Thus, although monetary policy might be driven by fiscal policy in some situations, such as during the classic hyperinflations, this situation appears not to be the norm in most countries today. There are several reasons for this. First, most governments can finance deficits by selling debt and don't need to rely on seigniorage. Second, central banks often have enough independence to resist political pressure for more expansionary monetary policy. Third, and most important, policymakers in all parts of government know that inflation is a poor solution to fiscal problems.

Debt and the Political Process

Fiscal policy is made not by angels but by an imperfect political process. Some economists worry that the possibility of financing government spending by issuing debt makes that political process all the worse.

This idea has a long history. Nineteenth-century economist Knut Wicksell claimed that if the benefit of some type of government spending exceeded its cost, it should be possible to finance that spending in a way that would receive unanimous support from the voters. He concluded that government spending should be undertaken only when support was, in fact, nearly unanimous. In the case of debt finance, however, Wicksell was concerned that "the interests [of future taxpayers] are not represented at all or are represented inadequately in the tax-approving assembly."

Many economists have echoed this theme more recently. In their 1977 book *Democracy in Deficit,* James Buchanan and Richard Wagner argued for a balanced-budget rule for fiscal policy on the grounds that it "will have the effect of bringing the real costs of public outlays to the awareness of decision makers; it will tend to dispel the illusory 'something for nothing' aspects of fiscal choice." Similarly, Martin Feldstein (once an economic advisor to Ronald Reagan and a long-time critic of budget deficits) argues that "only the 'hard budget constraint' of having to balance the budget" can force politicians to judge whether spending's "benefits really justify its costs."

These arguments have led some economists to favor a constitutional amendment that would require Congress to pass a balanced budget. Often these proposals have escape clauses for times of national emergency, such as wars and depressions, when a budget deficit is a reasonable policy response. Some critics of these proposals argue that, even with the escape clauses, such a constitutional amendment would tie the hands of policymakers too severely. Others claim that Congress would easily evade the balanced-budget requirement with accounting tricks. As this discussion makes clear, the debate over the desirability of a balanced-budget amendment is as much political as economic.

International Dimensions

Government debt may affect a nation's role in the world economy. As we first saw in Chapter 5, when a government budget deficit reduces national saving, it often leads to a trade deficit, which in turn is financed by borrowing from abroad. For instance, many observers have blamed U.S. fiscal policy for the recent switch of the United States from a major creditor in the world economy to a major debtor. This link between the budget deficit and the trade deficit leads to two further effects of government debt.

First, high levels of government debt may increase the risk that an economy will experience capital flight—an abrupt decline in the demand for a country's assets in world financial markets. International investors are aware that a government can always deal with its debt simply by defaulting. This approach was used as far back as 1335, when England's King Edward III defaulted on his debt to Italian bankers. More recently, several Latin American countries defaulted on their debts in the 1980s, and Russia did the same in 1998. The higher the level of the government debt, the greater the temptation of default. Thus, as government debt increases, international investors may come to fear default and curtail their lending. If this loss of confidence occurs suddenly, the result could be the classic symptoms of capital flight: a collapse in the value of the currency and an increase in interest rates. As we discussed in Chapter 12, this is precisely what happened to Mexico in the early 1990s when default appeared likely.

Second, high levels of government debt financed by foreign borrowing may reduce a nation's political clout in world affairs. This fear was emphasized by economist Ben Friedman in his 1988 book *Day of Reckoning.* He wrote, "World power and influence have historically accrued to creditor countries. It is not coincidental that America emerged as a world power simultaneously with our transition from a debtor nation . . . to a creditor supplying investment capital to the rest of the world." Friedman suggests that if the United States continues to run large trade deficits, it will eventually lose some of its international influence. So far, the record has not been kind to this hypothesis: the United States has run trade deficits throughout the 1980s, 1990s, and early 2000s and remains a leading superpower. But perhaps other events—such as the collapse of the Soviet Union—offset the fall in political clout that the United States would have experienced because of its increased indebtedness.

CASE STUDY

The Benefits of Indexed Bonds

In 1997, the U.S. Treasury Department started to issue bonds that pay a return based on the consumer price index. These bonds pay a low interest rate of about 3.5 percent, so a $1,000 bond pays only $35 per year in interest. But that interest payment grows with the overall price level as measured by the CPI. In addition, when the $1,000 of principal is repaid, that amount is also adjusted for changes in the CPI. The 3.5 percent, therefore, is a real interest rate. No longer do professors of macroeconomics need to define the real interest rate as an abstract construct. They can open the *New York Times,* point to the credit report, and say, "Look here, this is a nominal interest rate, and this is a real interest rate." (Professors in the United Kingdom and several other countries have long enjoyed this luxury because indexed bonds have been trading in other countries for years.)

Of course, making macroeconomics easier to teach was not the reason that the Treasury chose to index some of the government debt. That was just a positive externality. Its goal was to introduce a new type of government bond that should benefit bondholder and taxpayer alike. These bonds are a win-win proposition because they insulate both sides of the transaction from inflation risk. Bondholders should care about the real interest rate they earn, and taxpayers should care about the real interest rate they pay. When government bonds are specified in nominal terms, both sides take on risk that is neither productive nor necessary. The new indexed bonds eliminate this inflation risk.

In addition, the new bonds have three other benefits:

First, the bonds may encourage the private sector to begin issuing its own indexed securities. Financial innovation is, to some extent, a public good. Once an innovation has been introduced into the market, the idea is nonexcludable (people cannot be prevented from using it) and nonrival (one person's use of the idea does not diminish other people's use of it). Just as a free market will not adequately supply the public goods of national defense and basic research, it will not adequately supply financial innovation. The Treasury's new bonds can be viewed as a remedy for that market failure.

Second, the bonds reduce the government's incentive to produce surprise inflation. After the large budget deficits of the past few decades, the U.S. government is now a substantial debtor, and its debts are specified almost entirely in dollar terms. What is unique about the federal government, in contrast to most debtors, is that it can print the money it needs. The greater the government's nominal debts, the more incentive the government has to inflate away its debt. The Treasury's switch toward indexed debt reduces this potentially problematic incentive.

Third, the bonds provide data that might be useful for monetary policy. Many macroeconomic theories point to expected inflation as a key variable to explain the relationship between inflation and unemployment. But what is expected inflation? One way to measure it is to survey private forecasters. Another way is to look at the difference between the yield on nominal bonds and the yield on real bonds.

In the past, economists have proposed a variety of rules that could be used to conduct monetary policy, as we discussed in the preceding chapter. The new indexed bonds expand the number of possible rules. Here is one idea: the Fed announces a target for the inflation rate. Then, every day, the Fed measures expected inflation as the spread between the yield on nominal debt and the yield on indexed debt. If expected inflation is above the target, the Fed contracts the money supply. If expected inflation is below the target, the Fed expands the money supply. In this way, the Fed can use the bond market's inflation forecast to ensure that the money supply is growing at the rate needed to keep inflation close to its target.

The Treasury's new indexed bonds, therefore, will likely produce many benefits: less inflation risk, more financial innovation, better government incentives, more informed monetary policy, and easier lives for students and teachers of macroeconomics.[6]

15-6 Conclusion

Fiscal policy and government debt are central in the U.S. political debate. This chapter discussed some of the economic issues that lie behind the policy decisions. As we have seen, economists are not in complete agreement about the measurement or effects of government indebtedness. Nor are economists in agreement about the best budget policy. Given the profound importance of this topic, there seems little doubt that the debates will continue in the years to come.

[6] To read more about indexed bonds, see John Y. Campbell and Robert J. Shiller, "A Scorecard for Indexed Government Debt," *NBER Macroeconomics Annual* (1996): 155–197; and David W. Wilcox, "Policy Watch: The Introduction of Indexed Government Debt in the United States," *The Journal of Economic Perspectives* 12 (Winter 1998): 219–227.

Summary

1. The current debt of the U.S. federal government is of moderate size compared to the debt of other countries or compared to the debt that the United States has had throughout its own history. The 1980s and early 1990s were unusual in that the ratio of debt to GDP increased during a period of peace and prosperity. From 1995 to 2001, the ratio of debt to GDP declined significantly, but after 2001 it started to rise again.

2. Standard measures of the budget deficit are imperfect measures of fiscal policy because they do not correct for the effects of inflation, do not offset changes in government liabilities with changes in government assets, omit some liabilities altogether, and do not correct for the effects of the business cycle.

3. According to the traditional view of government debt, a debt-financed tax cut stimulates consumer spending and lowers national saving. This increase in consumer spending leads to greater aggregate demand and higher income in the short run, but it leads to a lower capital stock and lower income in the long run.

4. According to the Ricardian view of government debt, a debt-financed tax cut does not stimulate consumer spending because it does not raise consumers' overall resources—it merely reschedules taxes from the present to the future. The debate between the traditional and Ricardian views of government debt is ultimately a debate over how consumers behave. Are consumers rational or shortsighted? Do they face binding borrowing constraints? Are they economically linked to future generations through altruistic bequests? Economists' views of government debt hinge on their answers to these questions.

5. Most economists oppose a strict rule requiring a balanced budget. A budget deficit can sometimes be justified on the basis of short-run stabilization, tax smoothing, or intergenerational redistribution of the tax burden.

6. Government debt can potentially have other effects. Large government debt or budget deficits may encourage excessive monetary expansion and, therefore, lead to greater inflation. The possibility of running budget deficits may encourage politicians to unduly burden future generations when setting government spending and taxes. A high level of government debt may risk capital flight and diminish a nation's influence around the world. Economists differ in which of these effects they consider most important.

KEY CONCEPTS

Capital budgeting

Cyclically adjusted budget deficit

Ricardian equivalence

QUESTIONS FOR REVIEW

1. What was unusual about U.S. fiscal policy from 1980 to 1995?

2. Why do many economists project increasing budget deficits and government debt over the next several decades?

3. Describe four problems affecting measurement of the government budget deficit.

4. According to the traditional view of government debt, how does a debt-financed tax cut affect public saving, private saving, and national saving?

5. According to the Ricardian view of government debt, how does a debt-financed tax cut affect public saving, private saving, and national saving?

6. Do you believe the traditional or the Ricardian view of government debt? Why?

7. Give three reasons why a budget deficit might be a good policy choice.

8. Why might the level of government debt affect the government's incentives regarding money creation?

PROBLEMS AND APPLICATIONS

1. On April 1, 1996, Taco Bell, the fast-food chain, ran a full-page ad in the *New York Times* with this news: "In an effort to help the national debt, Taco Bell is pleased to announce that we have agreed to purchase the Liberty Bell, one of our country's most historic treasures. It will now be called the *Taco Liberty Bell* and will still be accessible to the American public for viewing. We hope our move will prompt other corporations to take similar action to do their part to reduce the country's debt." Would such actions by U.S. corporations actually reduce the national debt as it is now measured? How would your answer change if the U.S. government adopted capital budgeting? Do you think these actions represent a true reduction in the government's indebtedness? Do you think Taco Bell was serious about this plan? (*Hint:* Note the date.)

2. Draft a letter to the senator described in Section 15-3, explaining and evaluating the Ricardian view of government debt.

3. The Social Security system levies a tax on workers and pays benefits to the elderly. Suppose that Congress increases both the tax and the benefits. For simplicity, assume that the Congress announces that the increases will last for one year only.

   a. How do you suppose this change would affect the economy? (*Hint:* Think about the marginal propensities to consume of the young and the old.)

   b. Does your answer depend on whether generations are altruistically linked?

4. Some economists have proposed the rule that the cyclically adjusted budget deficit always be balanced. Compare this proposal to a strict balanced-budget rule. Which is preferable? What problems do you see with the rule requiring a balanced cyclically adjusted budget?

5. Using the library or the Internet, find some recent projections for the future path of the U.S. government debt as a percentage of GDP. What assumptions are made about government spending, taxes, and economic growth? Do you think these assumptions are reasonable? If the U.S. experiences a productivity slowdown, how will reality differ from this projection? (*Hint:* A good place to look is www.cbo.gov.)

PART VI

More on the Microeconomics Behind Macroeconomics

CHAPTER 16

Consumption

Consumption is the sole end and purpose of all production.

— Adam Smith

How do households decide how much of their income to consume today and how much to save for the future? This is a microeconomic question because it addresses the behavior of individual decision-makers. Yet its answer has important macroeconomic consequences. As we have seen in previous chapters, households' consumption decisions affect the way the economy as a whole behaves both in the long run and in the short run.

The consumption decision is crucial for long-run analysis because of its role in economic growth. The Solow growth model of Chapters 7 and 8 shows that the saving rate is a key determinant of the steady-state capital stock and thus of the level of economic well-being. The saving rate measures how much of its income the present generation is not consuming but is instead putting aside for its own future and for future generations.

The consumption decision is crucial for short-run analysis because of its role in determining aggregate demand. Consumption is two-thirds of GDP, so fluctuations in consumption are a key element of booms and recessions. The *IS-LM* model of Chapters 10 and 11 shows that changes in consumers' spending plans can be a source of shocks to the economy, and that the marginal propensity to consume is a determinant of the fiscal-policy multipliers.

In previous chapters we explained consumption with a function that relates consumption to disposable income: $C = C(Y - T)$. This approximation allowed us to develop simple models for long-run and short-run analysis, but it is too simple to provide a complete explanation of consumer behavior. In this chapter we examine the consumption function in greater detail and develop a more thorough explanation of what determines aggregate consumption.

Since macroeconomics began as a field of study, many economists have written about the theory of consumer behavior and suggested alternative ways of interpreting the data on consumption and income. This chapter presents the views of six prominent economists to show the diverse approaches to explaining consumption.

16-1 John Maynard Keynes and the Consumption Function

We begin our study of consumption with John Maynard Keynes's *General Theory,* which was published in 1936. Keynes made the consumption function central to his theory of economic fluctuations, and it has played a key role in macroeconomic analysis ever since. Let's consider what Keynes thought about the consumption function, and then see what puzzles arose when his ideas were confronted with the data.

Keynes's Conjectures

Today, economists who study consumption rely on sophisticated techniques of data analysis. With the help of computers, they analyze aggregate data on the behavior of the overall economy from the national income accounts and detailed data on the behavior of individual households from surveys. Because Keynes wrote in the 1930s, however, he had neither the advantage of these data nor the computers necessary to analyze such large data sets. Instead of relying on statistical analysis, Keynes made conjectures about the consumption function based on introspection and casual observation.

First and most important, Keynes conjectured that the **marginal propensity to consume**—the amount consumed out of an additional dollar of income—is between zero and one. He wrote that the "fundamental psychological law, upon which we are entitled to depend with great confidence, . . . is that men are disposed, as a rule and on the average, to increase their consumption as their income increases, but not by as much as the increase in their income." That is, when a person earns an extra dollar, he typically spends some of it and saves some of it. As we saw in Chapter 10 when we developed the Keynesian cross, the marginal propensity to consume was crucial to Keynes's policy recommendations for how to reduce widespread unemployment. The power of fiscal policy to influence the economy—as expressed by the fiscal-policy multipliers—arises from the feedback between income and consumption.

Second, Keynes posited that the ratio of consumption to income, called the **average propensity to consume**, falls as income rises. He believed that saving was a luxury, so he expected the rich to save a higher proportion of their income than the poor. Although not essential for Keynes's own analysis, the postulate that the average propensity to consume falls as income rises became a central part of early Keynesian economics.

Third, Keynes thought that income is the primary determinant of consumption and that the interest rate does not have an important role. This conjecture stood in stark contrast to the beliefs of the classical economists who preceded him. The classical economists held that a higher interest rate encourages saving and discourages consumption. Keynes admitted that the interest rate could influence consumption as a matter of theory. Yet he wrote that "the main conclusion suggested by experience,

FIGURE 16-1

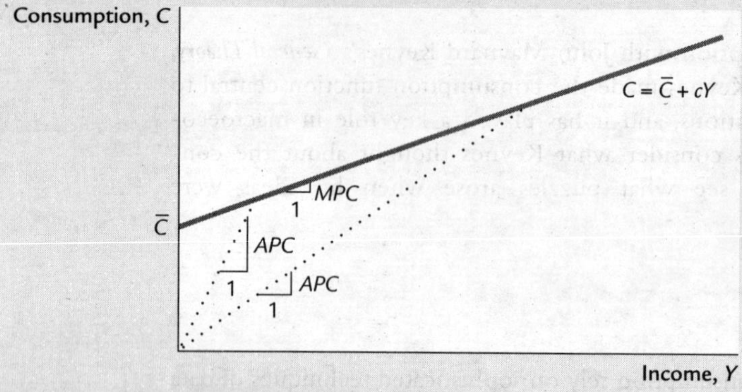

The Keynesian Consumption Function This figure graphs a consumption function with the three properties that Keynes conjectured. First, the marginal propensity to consume c is between zero and one. Second, the average propensity to consume falls as income rises. Third, consumption is determined by current income.

Note: The marginal propensity to consume, *MPC*, is the slope of the consumption function. The average propensity to consume, $APC = C/Y$, equals the slope of a line drawn from the origin to a point on the consumption function.

I think, is that the short-period influence of the rate of interest on individual spending out of a given income is secondary and relatively unimportant."

On the basis of these three conjectures, the Keynesian consumption function is often written as

$$C = \overline{C} + cY, \qquad \overline{C} > 0, \quad 0 < c < 1,$$

where C is consumption, Y is disposable income, $\overline{C}$ is a constant, and c is the marginal propensity to consume. This consumption function, shown in Figure 16-1, is graphed as a straight line. $\overline{C}$ determines the intercept on the vertical axis, and c determines the slope.

Notice that this consumption function exhibits the three properties that Keynes posited. It satisfies Keynes's first property because the marginal propensity to consume c is between zero and one, so that higher income leads to higher consumption and also to higher saving. This consumption function satisfies Keynes's second property because the average propensity to consume APC is

$$APC = C/Y = \overline{C}/Y + c.$$

As Y rises, $\overline{C}/Y$ falls, and so the average propensity to consume C/Y falls. And finally, this consumption function satisfies Keynes's third property because the interest rate is not included in this equation as a determinant of consumption.

The Early Empirical Successes

Soon after Keynes proposed the consumption function, economists began collecting and examining data to test his conjectures. The earliest studies indicated that the Keynesian consumption function is a good approximation of how consumers behave.

In some of these studies, researchers surveyed households and collected data on consumption and income. They found that households with higher income consumed more, which confirms that the marginal propensity to consume is greater than zero. They also found that households with higher income saved more, which confirms that the marginal propensity to consume is less than one. In addition, these researchers found that higher-income households saved a larger fraction of their income, which confirms that the average propensity to consume falls as income rises. Thus, these data verified Keynes's conjectures about the marginal and average propensities to consume.

In other studies, researchers examined aggregate data on consumption and income for the period between the two world wars. These data also supported the Keynesian consumption function. In years when income was unusually low, such as during the depths of the Great Depression, both consumption and saving were low, indicating that the marginal propensity to consume is between zero and one. In addition, during those years of low income, the ratio of consumption to income was high, confirming Keynes's second conjecture. Finally, because the correlation between income and consumption was so strong, no other variable appeared to be important for explaining consumption. Thus, the data also confirmed Keynes's third conjecture that income is the primary determinant of how much people choose to consume.

Secular Stagnation, Simon Kuznets, and the Consumption Puzzle

Although the Keynesian consumption function met with early successes, two anomalies soon arose. Both concern Keynes's conjecture that the average propensity to consume falls as income rises.

The first anomaly became apparent after some economists made a dire—and, it turned out, erroneous—prediction during World War II. On the basis of the Keynesian consumption function, these economists reasoned that as incomes in the economy grew over time, households would consume a smaller and smaller fraction of their incomes. They feared that there might not be enough profitable investment projects to absorb all this saving. If so, the low consumption would lead to an inadequate demand for goods and services, resulting in a depression once the wartime demand from the government ceased. In other words, on the basis of the Keynesian consumption function, these economists predicted that the economy would experience what they called *secular stagnation*—a long depression of indefinite duration—unless the government used fiscal policy to expand aggregate demand.

Fortunately for the economy, but unfortunately for the Keynesian consumption function, the end of World War II did not throw the country into another depression. Although incomes were much higher after the war than before, these higher incomes did not lead to large increases in the rate of saving. Keynes's conjecture that the average propensity to consume would fall as income rose appeared not to hold.

The second anomaly arose when economist Simon Kuznets constructed new aggregate data on consumption and income dating back to 1869. Kuznets assembled these data in the 1940s and would later receive the Nobel Prize for this work. He discovered that the ratio of consumption to income was remarkably stable from decade to decade, despite large increases in income over the period he studied. Again, Keynes's conjecture that the average propensity to consume would fall as income rose appeared not to hold.

The failure of the secular-stagnation hypothesis and the findings of Kuznets both indicated that the average propensity to consume is fairly constant over long periods of time. This fact presented a puzzle that motivated much of the subsequent research on consumption. Economists wanted to know why some studies confirmed Keynes's conjectures and others refuted them. That is, why did Keynes's conjectures hold up well in the studies of household data and in the studies of short time-series, but fail when long time-series were examined?

Figure 16-2 illustrates the puzzle. The evidence suggested that there were two consumption functions. For the household data or for the short time-series, the Keynesian consumption function appeared to work well. Yet for the long time-series, the consumption function appeared to have a constant average propensity to consume. In Figure 16-2, these two relationships between consumption and income are called the short-run and long-run consumption functions. Economists needed to explain how these two consumption functions could be consistent with each other.

In the 1950s, Franco Modigliani and Milton Friedman each proposed explanations of these seemingly contradictory findings. Both economists later won Nobel Prizes, in part because of their work on consumption. But before we see

FIGURE 16-2

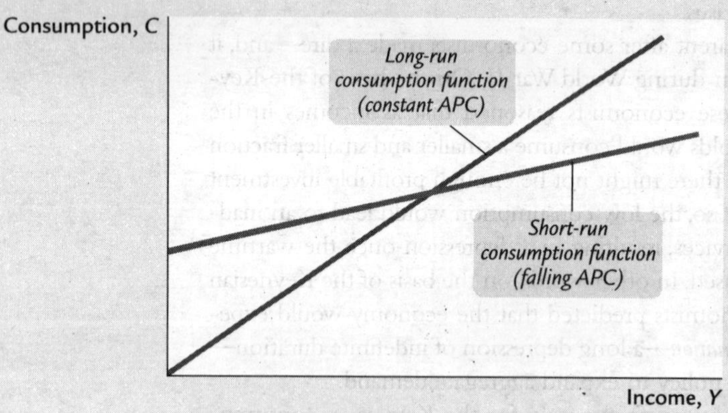

The Consumption Puzzle Studies of household data and short time-series found a relationship between consumption and income similar to the one Keynes conjectured. In the figure, this relationship is called the short-run consumption function. But studies of long time-series found that the average propensity to consume did not vary systematically with income. This relationship is called the long-run consumption function. Notice that the short-run consumption function has a falling average propensity to consume, whereas the long-run consumption function has a constant average propensity to consume.

how Modigliani and Friedman tried to solve the consumption puzzle, we must discuss Irving Fisher's contribution to consumption theory. Both Modigliani's life-cycle hypothesis and Friedman's permanent-income hypothesis rely on the theory of consumer behavior proposed much earlier by Irving Fisher.

16-2 Irving Fisher and Intertemporal Choice

The consumption function introduced by Keynes relates current consumption to current income. This relationship, however, is incomplete at best. When people decide how much to consume and how much to save, they consider both the present and the future. The more consumption they enjoy today, the less they will be able to enjoy tomorrow. In making this tradeoff, households must look ahead to the income they expect to receive in the future and to the consumption of goods and services they hope to be able to afford.

The economist Irving Fisher developed the model with which economists analyze how rational, forward-looking consumers make intertemporal choices—that is, choices involving different periods of time. Fisher's model illuminates the constraints consumers face, the preferences they have, and how these constraints and preferences together determine their choices about consumption and saving.

The Intertemporal Budget Constraint

Most people would prefer to increase the quantity or quality of the goods and services they consume—to wear nicer clothes, eat at better restaurants, or see more movies. The reason people consume less than they desire is that their consumption is constrained by their income. In other words, consumers face a limit on how much they can spend, called a *budget constraint.* When they are deciding how much to consume today versus how much to save for the future, they face an **intertemporal budget constraint**, which measures the total resources available for consumption today and in the future. Our first step in developing Fisher's model is to examine this constraint in some detail.

To keep things simple, we examine the decision facing a consumer who lives for two periods. Period one represents the consumer's youth, and period two represents the consumer's old age. The consumer earns income Y_1 and consumes C_1 in period one, and earns income Y_2 and consumes C_2 in period two. (All variables are real—that is, adjusted for inflation.) Because the consumer has the opportunity to borrow and save, consumption in any single period can be either greater or less than income in that period.

Consider how the consumer's income in the two periods constrains consumption in the two periods. In the first period, saving equals income minus consumption. That is,

$$S = Y_1 - C_1,$$

where S is saving. In the second period, consumption equals the accumulated saving, including the interest earned on that saving, plus second-period income. That is,

$$C_2 = (1 + r)S + Y_2,$$

where r is the real interest rate. For example, if the real interest rate is 5 percent, then for every \$1 of saving in period one, the consumer enjoys an extra \$1.05 of consumption in period two. Because there is no third period, the consumer does not save in the second period.

Note that the variable S can represent either saving or borrowing and that these equations hold in both cases. If first-period consumption is less than first-period income, the consumer is saving, and S is greater than zero. If first-period consumption exceeds first-period income, the consumer is borrowing, and S is less than zero. For simplicity, we assume that the interest rate for borrowing is the same as the interest rate for saving.

To derive the consumer's budget constraint, combine the two preceding equations. Substitute the first equation for S into the second equation to obtain

$$C_2 = (1 + r)(Y_1 - C_1) + Y_2.$$

To make the equation easier to interpret, we must rearrange terms. To place all the consumption terms together, bring $(1 + r)C_1$ from the right-hand side to the left-hand side of the equation to obtain

$$(1 + r)C_1 + C_2 = (1 + r)Y_1 + Y_2.$$

Now divide both sides by $1 + r$ to obtain

$$C_1 + \frac{C_2}{1 + r} = Y_1 + \frac{Y_2}{1 + r}.$$

This equation relates consumption in the two periods to income in the two periods. It is the standard way of expressing the consumer's intertemporal budget constraint.

The consumer's budget constraint is easily interpreted. If the interest rate is zero, the budget constraint shows that total consumption in the two periods equals total income in the two periods. In the usual case in which the interest rate is greater than zero, future consumption and future income are discounted by a factor $1 + r$. This **discounting** arises from the interest earned on savings. In essence, because the consumer earns interest on current income that is saved, future income is worth less than current income. Similarly, because future consumption is paid for out of savings that have earned interest, future consumption costs less than current consumption. The factor $1/(1 + r)$ is the price of second-period consumption measured in terms of first-period consumption: it is the amount of first-period consumption that the consumer must forgo to obtain 1 unit of second-period consumption.

Figure 16-3 graphs the consumer's budget constraint. Three points are marked on this figure. At point A, the consumer consumes exactly his income in each period ($C_1 = Y_1$ and $C_2 = Y_2$), so there is neither saving nor borrowing between the two periods. At point B, the consumer consumes nothing in the first period ($C_1 = 0$) and

FIGURE 16-3

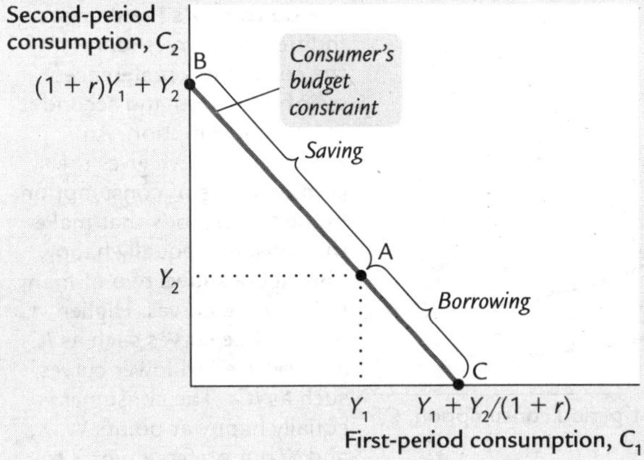

The Consumer's Budget Constraint This figure shows the combinations of first-period and second-period consumption the consumer can choose. If he chooses points between A and B, he consumes less than his income in the first period and saves the rest for the second period. If he chooses points between A and C, he consumes more than his income in the first period and borrows to make up the difference.

saves all income, so second-period consumption C_2 is $(1 + r)Y_1 + Y_2$. At point C, the consumer plans to consume nothing in the second period ($C_2 = 0$) and borrows as much as possible against second-period income, so first-period consumption C_1 is $Y_1 + Y_2/(1 + r)$. Of course, these are only three of the many combinations of first- and second-period consumption that the consumer can afford: all the points on the line from B to C are available to the consumer.

FYI Present Value, or Why a $1,000,000 Prize Is Worth Only $623,000

The use of discounting in the consumer's budget constraint illustrates an important fact of economic life: a dollar in the future is less valuable than a dollar today. This is true because a dollar today can be deposited in an interest-bearing bank account and produce more than one dollar in the future. If the interest rate is 5 percent, for instance, then a dollar today can be turned into $1.05 dollars next year, $1.1025 in two years, $1.1576 in three years, . . ., or $2.65 in 20 years.

Economists use a concept called *present value* to compare dollar amounts from different times. The present value of any amount in the future is the amount that would be needed today, given available interest rates, to produce that future amount. Thus, if you are going to be paid X dollars in T years and the interest rate is r, then the present value of that payment is

$$\text{Present Value} = X/(1+r)^T.$$

In light of this definition, we can see a new interpretation of the consumer's budget constraint in our two-period consumption problem. The intertemporal budget constraint states that the present value of consumption must equal the present value of income.

The concept of present value has many applications. Suppose, for instance, that you won a million-dollar lottery. Such prizes are usually paid out over time—say, $50,000 a year for 20 years. What is the present value of such a delayed prize? By applying the above formula to each of the 20 payments and adding up the result, we learn that the million-dollar prize, discounted at an interest rate of 5 percent, has a present value of only $623,000. (If the prize were paid out as a dollar a year for a million years, the present value would be a mere $20!) Sometimes a million dollars isn't all it's cracked up to be.

FIGURE 16-4

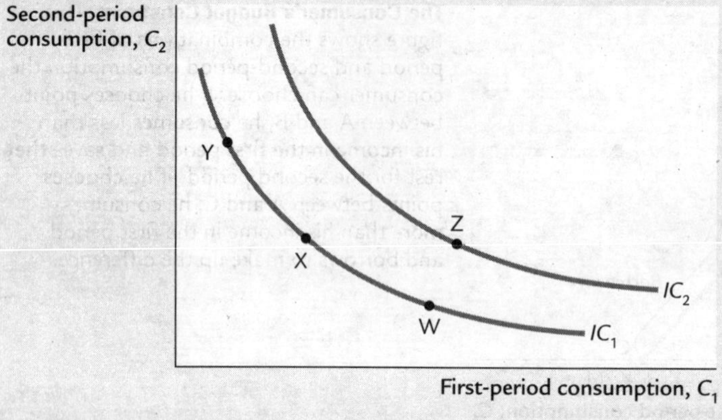

The Consumer's Preferences Indifference curves represent the consumer's preferences over first-period and second-period consumption. An indifference curve gives the combinations of consumption in the two periods that make the consumer equally happy. This figure shows two of many indifference curves. Higher indifference curves such as IC_2 are preferred to lower curves such as IC_1. The consumer is equally happy at points W, X, and Y, but prefers point Z to points W, X, or Y.

Consumer Preferences

The consumer's preferences regarding consumption in the two periods can be represented by **indifference curves**. An indifference curve shows the combinations of first-period and second-period consumption that make the consumer equally happy.

Figure 16-4 shows two of the consumer's many indifference curves. The consumer is indifferent among combinations W, X, and Y, because they are all on the same curve. Not surprisingly, if the consumer's first-period consumption is reduced, say from point W to point X, second-period consumption must increase to keep him equally happy. If first-period consumption is reduced again, from point X to point Y, the amount of extra second-period consumption he requires for compensation is greater.

The slope at any point on the indifference curve shows how much second-period consumption the consumer requires in order to be compensated for a 1-unit reduction in first-period consumption. This slope is the **marginal rate of substitution** between first-period consumption and second-period consumption. It tells us the rate at which the consumer is willing to substitute second-period consumption for first-period consumption.

Notice that the indifference curves in Figure 16-4 are not straight lines and, as a result, the marginal rate of substitution depends on the levels of consumption in the two periods. When first-period consumption is high and second-period consumption is low, as at point W, the marginal rate of substitution is low: the consumer requires only a little extra second-period consumption to give up 1 unit of first-period consumption. When first-period consumption is low and second-period consumption is high, as at point Y, the marginal rate of substitution is high: the consumer requires much additional second-period consumption to give up 1 unit of first-period consumption.

The consumer is equally happy at all points on a given indifference curve, but he prefers some indifference curves to others. Because he prefers more consumption to less, he prefers higher indifference curves to lower ones. In Figure 16-4, the consumer prefers any of the points on curve IC_2 to any of the points on curve IC_1.

The set of indifference curves gives a complete ranking of the consumer's preferences. It tells us that the consumer prefers point Z to point W, but that may be obvious because point Z has more consumption in both periods. Yet compare point Z and point Y: point Z has more consumption in period one and less in period two. Which is preferred, Z or Y? Because Z is on a higher indifference curve than Y, we know that the consumer prefers point Z to point Y. Hence, we can use the set of indifference curves to rank any combinations of first-period and second-period consumption.

Optimization

Having discussed the consumer's budget constraint and preferences, we can consider the decision about how much to consume in each period of time. The consumer would like to end up with the best possible combination of consumption in the two periods—that is, on the highest possible indifference curve. But the budget constraint requires that the consumer also end up on or below the budget line, because the budget line measures the total resources available to him.

Figure 16-5 shows that many indifference curves cross the budget line. The highest indifference curve that the consumer can obtain without violating the budget constraint is the indifference curve that just barely touches the budget line, which is curve IC_3 in the figure. The point at which the curve and line touch—point O for "optimum"—is the best combination of consumption in the two periods that the consumer can afford.

FIGURE 16-5

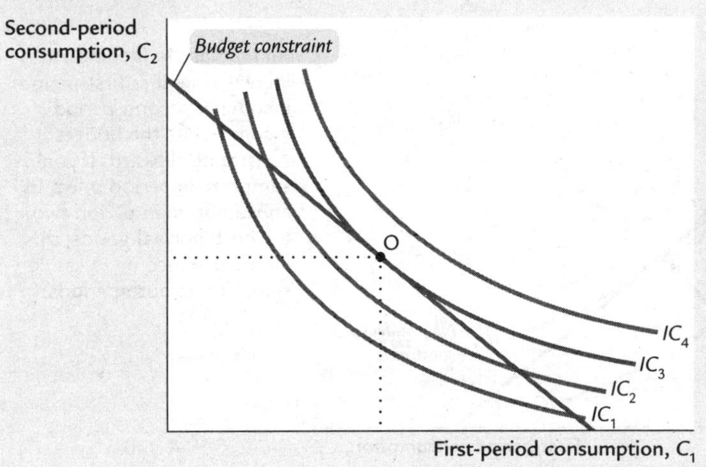

The Consumer's Optimum The consumer achieves his highest level of satisfaction by choosing the point on the budget constraint that is on the highest indifference curve. At the optimum, the indifference curve is tangent to the budget constraint.

Notice that, at the optimum, the slope of the indifference curve equals the slope of the budget line. The indifference curve is *tangent* to the budget line. The slope of the indifference curve is the marginal rate of substitution *MRS*, and the slope of the budget line is 1 plus the real interest rate. We conclude that at point O,

$$MRS = 1 + r.$$

The consumer chooses consumption in the two periods so that the marginal rate of substitution equals 1 plus the real interest rate.

How Changes in Income Affect Consumption

Now that we have seen how the consumer makes the consumption decision, let's examine how consumption responds to an increase in income. An increase in either Y_1 or Y_2 shifts the budget constraint outward, as in Figure 16-6. The higher budget constraint allows the consumer to choose a better combination of first- and second-period consumption—that is, the consumer can now reach a higher indifference curve.

In Figure 16-6, the consumer responds to the shift in his budget constraint by choosing more consumption in both periods. Although it is not implied by the logic of the model alone, this situation is the most usual. If a consumer wants more of a good when his or her income rises, economists call it a **normal good**. The indifference curves in Figure 16-6 are drawn under the assumption that consumption in period one and consumption in period two are both normal goods.

The key conclusion from Figure 16-6 is that regardless of whether the increase in income occurs in the first period or the second period, the consumer spreads it over consumption in both periods. This behavior is sometimes called

FIGURE 16-6

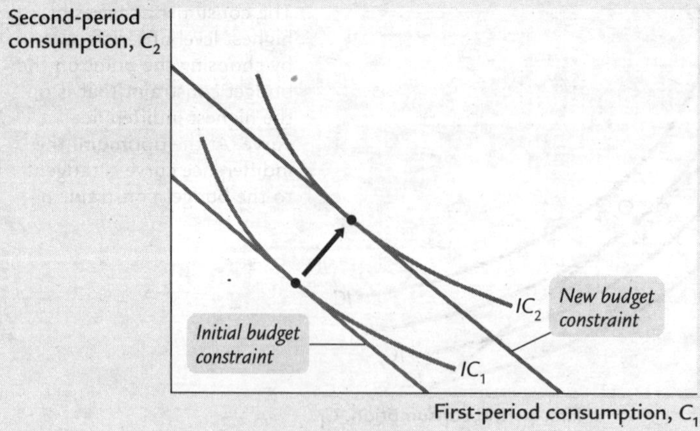

An Increase in Income An increase in either first-period income or second-period income shifts the budget constraint outward. If consumption in period one and consumption in period two are both normal goods, this increase in income raises consumption in both periods.

consumption smoothing. Because the consumer can borrow and lend between periods, the timing of the income is irrelevant to how much is consumed today (except that future income is discounted by the interest rate). The lesson of this analysis is that consumption depends on the present value of current and future income, which can be written as

$$\text{Present Value of Income} = Y_1 + \frac{Y_2}{1 + r}.$$

Notice that this conclusion is quite different from that reached by Keynes. *Keynes posited that a person's current consumption depends largely on his current income. Fisher's model says, instead, that consumption is based on the income the consumer expects over his entire lifetime.*

How Changes in the Real Interest Rate Affect Consumption

Let's now use Fisher's model to consider how a change in the real interest rate alters the consumer's choices. There are two cases to consider: the case in which the consumer is initially saving and the case in which he is initially borrowing. Here we discuss the saving case; Problem 1 at the end of the chapter asks you to analyze the borrowing case.

Figure 16-7 shows that an increase in the real interest rate rotates the consumer's budget line around the point (Y_1, Y_2) and, thereby, alters the amount of

FIGURE 16-7

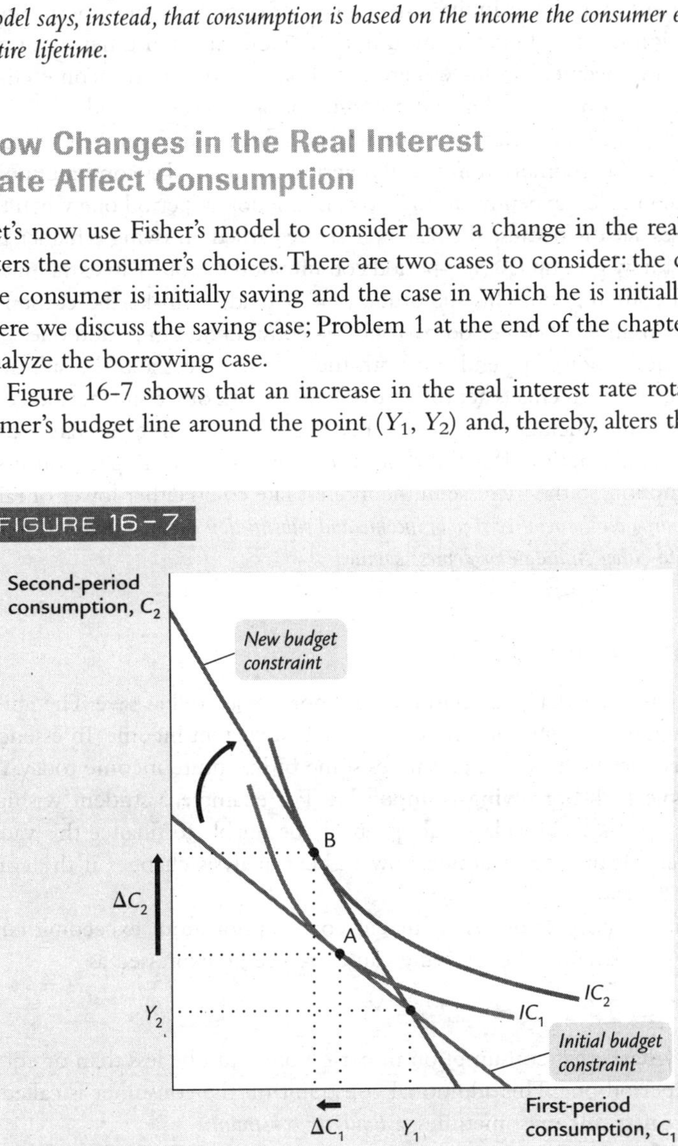

An Increase in the Interest Rate An increase in the interest rate rotates the budget constraint around the point (Y_1, Y_2). In this figure, the higher interest rate reduces first-period consumption by ΔC_1 and raises second-period consumption by ΔC_2.

consumption he chooses in both periods. Here, the consumer moves from point A to point B. You can see that for the indifference curves drawn in this figure first-period consumption falls and second-period consumption rises.

Economists decompose the impact of an increase in the real interest rate on consumption into two effects: an **income effect** and a **substitution effect**. Textbooks in microeconomics discuss these effects in detail. We summarize them briefly here.

The *income effect* is the change in consumption that results from the movement to a higher indifference curve. Because the consumer is a saver rather than a borrower (as indicated by the fact that first-period consumption is less than first-period income), the increase in the interest rate makes him better off (as reflected by the movement to a higher indifference curve). If consumption in period one and consumption in period two are both normal goods, the consumer will want to spread this improvement in his welfare over both periods. This income effect tends to make the consumer want more consumption in both periods.

The *substitution effect* is the change in consumption that results from the change in the relative price of consumption in the two periods. In particular, consumption in period two becomes less expensive relative to consumption in period one when the interest rate rises. That is, because the real interest rate earned on saving is higher, the consumer must now give up less first-period consumption to obtain an extra unit of second-period consumption. This substitution effect tends to make the consumer choose more consumption in period two and less consumption in period one.

The consumer's choice depends on both the income effect and the substitution effect. Because both effects act to increase the amount of second-period consumption, we can conclude that an increase in the real interest rate raises second-period consumption. But the two effects have opposite impacts on first-period consumption, so the increase in the interest rate could either lower or raise it. *Hence, depending on the relative size of income and substitution effects, an increase in the interest rate could either stimulate or depress saving.*

Constraints on Borrowing

Fisher's model assumes that the consumer can borrow as well as save. The ability to borrow allows current consumption to exceed current income. In essence, when the consumer borrows, he consumes some of his future income today. Yet for many people such borrowing is impossible. For example, a student wishing to enjoy spring break in Florida would probably be unable to finance this vacation with a bank loan. Let's examine how Fisher's analysis changes if the consumer cannot borrow.

The inability to borrow prevents current consumption from exceeding current income. A constraint on borrowing can therefore be expressed as

$$C_1 \leq Y_1.$$

This inequality states that consumption in period one must be less than or equal to income in period one. This additional constraint on the consumer is called a **borrowing constraint** or, sometimes, a *liquidity constraint.*

FIGURE 16-8

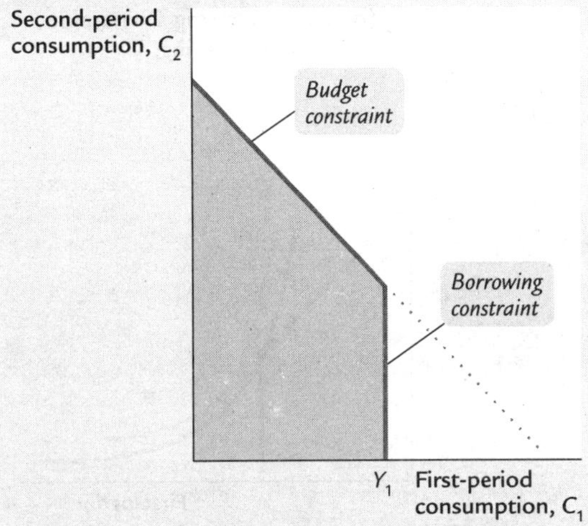

A Borrowing Constraint If the consumer cannot borrow, he faces the additional constraint that first-period consumption cannot exceed first-period income. The shaded area represents the combinations of first-period and second-period consumption the consumer can choose.

Figure 16-8 shows how this borrowing constraint restricts the consumer's set of choices. The consumer's choice must satisfy both the intertemporal budget constraint and the borrowing constraint. The shaded area represents the combinations of first-period consumption and second-period consumption that satisfy both constraints.

Figure 16-9 shows how this borrowing constraint affects the consumption decision. There are two possibilities. In panel (a), the consumer wishes to consume less in period one than he earns. The borrowing constraint is not binding and, therefore, does not affect consumption. In panel (b), the consumer would like to choose point D, where he consumes more in period one than he earns, but the borrowing constraint prevents this outcome. The best the consumer can do is to consume his first-period income, represented by point E.

The analysis of borrowing constraints leads us to conclude that there are two consumption functions. For some consumers, the borrowing constraint is not binding, and consumption in both periods depends on the present value of lifetime income, $Y_1 + [Y_2/(1 + r)]$. For other consumers, the borrowing constraint binds, and the consumption function is $C_1 = Y_1$ and $C_2 = Y_2$. *Hence, for those consumers who would like to borrow but cannot, consumption depends only on current income.*

"What I'd like, basically, is a temporary line of credit just to tide me over the rest of my life."

FIGURE 16-9

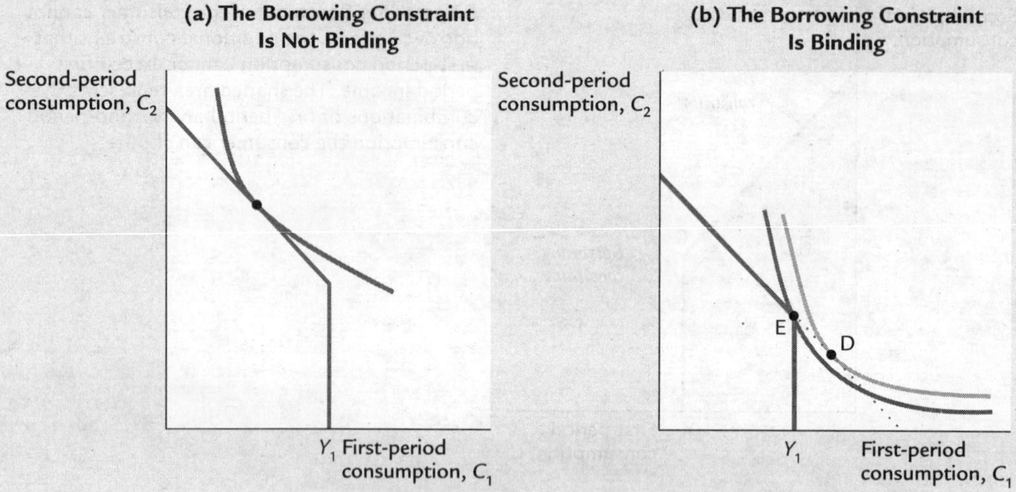

The Consumer's Optimum With a Borrowing Constraint When the consumer faces a borrowing constraint, there are two possible situations. In panel (a), the consumer chooses first-period consumption to be less than first-period income, so the borrowing constraint is not binding and does not affect consumption in either period. In panel (b), the borrowing constraint is binding. The consumer would like to borrow and choose point D. But because borrowing is not allowed, the best available choice is point E. When the borrowing constraint is binding, first-period consumption equals first-period income.

CASE STUDY

The High Japanese Saving Rate

Japan has historically had one of the world's highest saving rates—far higher than the United States. This fact is important for understanding both the long-run and short-run performance of its economy. On the one hand, many economists believe that the high Japanese saving rate is a key to the rapid growth Japan experienced in the decades after World War II. The Solow growth model developed in Chapters 7 and 8 shows that the saving rate is a primary determinant of a country's steady-state level of income. On the other hand, some economists have argued that the high Japanese saving rate contributed to Japan's slump during the 1990s. High saving means low consumer spending, which according to the *IS–LM* model of Chapters 10 and 11 translates into low aggregate demand and reduced income.

Why have the Japanese consumed a much smaller fraction of their income than Americans? One reason is that it is harder for households to borrow in Japan. As Fisher's model shows, a household facing a binding borrowing constraint consumes less than it would without the borrowing constraint. Hence, societies in which borrowing constraints are common will tend to have higher rates of saving.

One reason that households often wish to borrow is to buy a home. In the United States, a person can usually buy a home with a down payment of 10 percent. A homebuyer in Japan cannot borrow nearly this much: down payments of 40 percent are common. Moreover, housing prices are very high in Japan, primarily because land prices are high. A Japanese family must save a great deal if it is ever to afford its own home.

Although constraints on borrowing are part of the explanation of high Japanese saving, there are many other differences between Japan and the United States that contribute to the difference in the saving rates. The Japanese tax system encourages saving by taxing capital income very lightly. In addition, cultural differences may lead to differences in consumer preferences regarding present and future consumption. One prominent Japanese economist writes, "The Japanese are simply *different*. They are more risk averse and more patient. If this is true, the long-run implication is that Japan will absorb all the wealth in the world. I refuse to comment on this explanation."[1]

Over time, the high rates of saving in Japan have diminished to some degree and are now closer to those in the United States. But even in the early 2000s, most measures suggested that Japanese households save more than American households. This is one reason the Japanese economy was experiencing capital outflows and trade surpluses, while the U.S. economy was experiencing capital inflows and trade deficits. It would be a mistake to worry that "Japan will absorb all the wealth in the world," but it is true that U.S. investment and growth are in part financed by Japanese saving.

16-3 Franco Modigliani and the Life-Cycle Hypothesis

In a series of papers written in the 1950s, Franco Modigliani and his collaborators Albert Ando and Richard Brumberg used Fisher's model of consumer behavior to study the consumption function. One of their goals was to solve the consumption puzzle—that is, to explain the apparently conflicting pieces of evidence that came to light when Keynes's consumption function was brought to the data. According to Fisher's model, consumption depends on a person's lifetime income. Modigliani emphasized that income varies systematically over people's lives and that saving allows consumers to move income from those times in life when income is high to those times when it is low. This interpretation of consumer behavior formed the basis for his **life-cycle hypothesis**.[2]

[1] Fumio Hayashi, "Why Is Japan's Saving Rate So Apparently High?" *NBER Macroeconomics Annual* (1986): 147–210.

[2] For references to the large body of work on the life-cycle hypothesis, a good place to start is the lecture Modigliani gave when he won the Nobel Prize. Franco Modigliani, "Life Cycle, Individual Thrift, and the Wealth of Nations," *American Economic Review* 76 (June 1986): 297–313. For an example of more recent research in this tradition, see Pierre-Olivier Gourinchas and Jonathan A. Parker, "Consumption Over the Life Cycle," *Econometrica* 70 (January 2002): 47–89.

The Hypothesis

One important reason that income varies over a person's life is retirement. Most people plan to stop working at about age 65, and they expect their incomes to fall when they retire. Yet they do not want a large drop in their standard of living, as measured by their consumption. To maintain their level of consumption after retirement, people must save during their working years. Let's see what this motive for saving implies for the consumption function.

Consider a consumer who expects to live another T years, has wealth of W, and expects to earn income Y until she retires R years from now. What level of consumption will the consumer choose if she wishes to maintain a smooth level of consumption over her life?

The consumer's lifetime resources are composed of initial wealth W and lifetime earnings of $R \times Y$. (For simplicity, we are assuming an interest rate of zero; if the interest rate were greater than zero, we would need to take account of interest earned on savings as well.) The consumer can divide up her lifetime resources among her T remaining years of life. We assume that she wishes to achieve the smoothest possible path of consumption over her lifetime. Therefore, she divides this total of $W + RY$ equally among the T years and each year consumes

$$C = (W + RY)/T.$$

We can write this person's consumption function as

$$C = (1/T)W + (R/T)Y.$$

For example, if the consumer expects to live for 50 more years and work for 30 of them, then $T = 50$ and $R = 30$, so her consumption function is

$$C = 0.02W + 0.6Y.$$

This equation says that consumption depends on both income and wealth. An extra $1 of income per year raises consumption by $0.60 per year, and an extra $1 of wealth raises consumption by $0.02 per year.

If every individual in the economy plans consumption like this, then the aggregate consumption function is much the same as the individual one. In particular, aggregate consumption depends on both wealth and income. That is, the economy's consumption function is

$$C = \alpha W + \beta Y,$$

where the parameter α is the marginal propensity to consume out of wealth, and the parameter β is the marginal propensity to consume out of income.

Implications

Figure 16-10 graphs the relationship between consumption and income predicted by the life-cycle model. For any given level of wealth W, the model yields a conventional consumption function similar to the one shown in Figure 16-1.

FIGURE 16-10

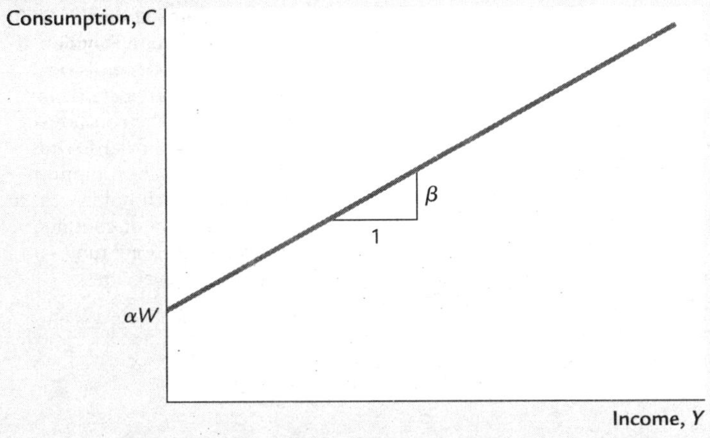

The Life-Cycle Consumption Function The life-cycle model says that consumption depends on wealth as well as income. As a result, the intercept of the consumption function αW depends on wealth.

Notice, however, that the intercept of the consumption function, which shows what would happen to consumption if income ever fell to zero, is not a fixed value, as it is in Figure 16-1. Instead, the intercept here is αW and, thus, depends on the level of wealth.

This life-cycle model of consumer behavior can solve the consumption puzzle. According to the life-cycle consumption function, the average propensity to consume is

$$C/Y = \alpha(W/Y) + \beta.$$

Because wealth does not vary proportionately with income from person to person or from year to year, we should find that high income corresponds to a low average propensity to consume when looking at data across individuals or over short periods of time. But, over long periods of time, wealth and income grow together, resulting in a constant ratio W/Y and thus a constant average propensity to consume.

To make the same point somewhat differently, consider how the consumption function changes over time. As Figure 16-10 shows, for any given level of wealth, the life-cycle consumption function looks like the one Keynes suggested. But this function holds only in the short run when wealth is constant. In the long run, as wealth increases, the consumption function shifts upward, as in Figure 16-11. This upward shift prevents the average propensity to consume from falling as income increases. In this way, Modigliani resolved the consumption puzzle posed by Simon Kuznets's data.

The life-cycle model makes many other predictions as well. Most important, it predicts that saving varies over a person's lifetime. If a person begins adulthood with no wealth, she will accumulate wealth during her working years and then

FIGURE 16-11

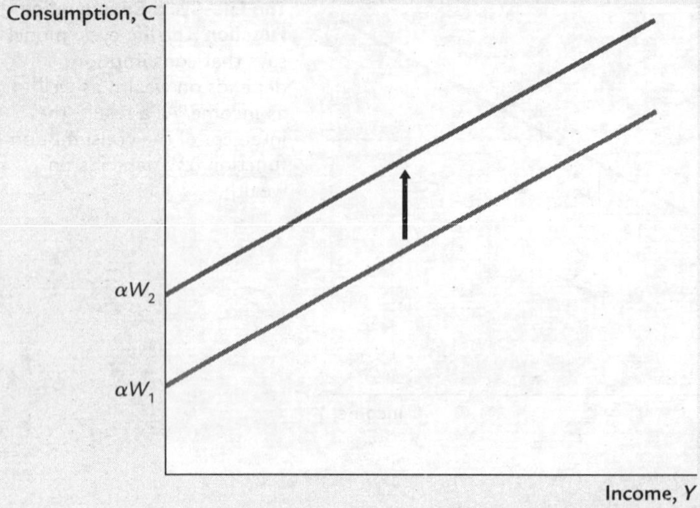

How Changes in Wealth Shift the Consumption Function If consumption depends on wealth, then an increase in wealth shifts the consumption function upward. Thus, the short-run consumption function (which holds wealth constant) will not continue to hold in the long run (as wealth rises over time).

run down her wealth during her retirement years. Figure 16-12 illustrates the consumer's income, consumption, and wealth over her adult life. According to the life-cycle hypothesis, because people want to smooth consumption over their lives, the young who are working save, while the old who are retired dissave.

FIGURE 16-12

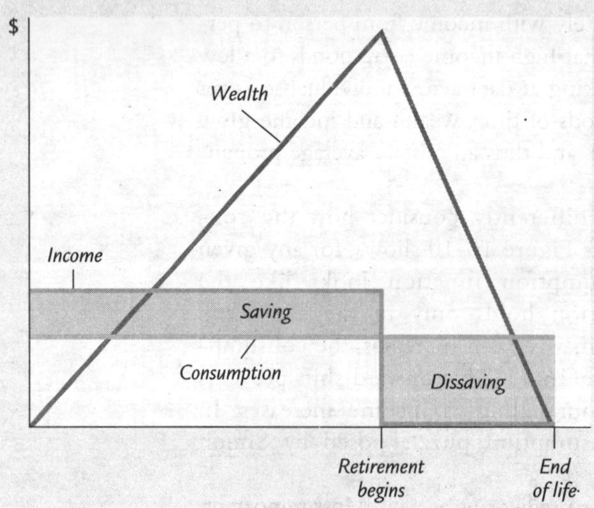

Consumption, Income, and Wealth Over the Life Cycle If the consumer smooths consumption over her life (as indicated by the horizontal consumption line), she will save and accumulate wealth during her working years and then dissave and run down her wealth during retirement.

CASE STUDY

The Consumption and Saving of the Elderly

Many economists have studied the consumption and saving of the elderly. Their findings present a problem for the life-cycle model. It appears that the elderly do not dissave as much as the model predicts. In other words, the elderly do not run down their wealth as quickly as one would expect if they were trying to smooth their consumption over their remaining years of life.

There are two chief explanations for why the elderly do not dissave to the extent that the model predicts. Each suggests a direction for further research on consumption.

The first explanation is that the elderly are concerned about unpredictable expenses. Additional saving that arises from uncertainty is called **precautionary saving**. One reason for precautionary saving by the elderly is the possibility of living longer than expected and thus having to provide for a longer than average span of retirement. Another reason is the possibility of illness and large medical bills. The elderly may respond to this uncertainty by saving more in order to be better prepared for these contingencies.

The precautionary-saving explanation is not completely persuasive, because the elderly can largely insure against these risks. To protect against uncertainty regarding life span, they can buy *annuities* from insurance companies. For a fixed fee, annuities offer a stream of income that lasts as long as the recipient lives. Uncertainty about medical expenses should be largely eliminated by Medicare, the government's health insurance plan for the elderly, and by private insurance plans.

The second explanation for the failure of the elderly to dissave is that they may want to leave bequests to their children. Economists have proposed various theories of the parent-child relationship and the bequest motive. In Chapter 15 we discussed some of these theories and their implications for consumption and fiscal policy.

Overall, research on the elderly suggests that the simplest life-cycle model cannot fully explain consumer behavior. There is no doubt that providing for retirement is an important motive for saving, but other motives, such as precautionary saving and bequests, appear important as well.[3]

[3] To read more about the consumption and saving of the elderly, see Albert Ando and Arthur Kennickell, "How Much (or Little) Life Cycle Saving Is There in Micro Data?" in Rudiger Dornbusch, Stanley Fischer, and John Bossons, eds., *Macroeconomics and Finance: Essays in Honor of Franco Modigliani* (Cambridge, MA: MIT Press, 1986); and Michael Hurd, "Research on the Elderly: Economic Status, Retirement, and Consumption and Saving," *Journal of Economic Literature* 28 (June 1990): 565–589.

16-4 Milton Friedman and the Permanent-Income Hypothesis

In a book published in 1957, Milton Friedman proposed the **permanent-income hypothesis** to explain consumer behavior. Friedman's permanent-income hypothesis complements Modigliani's life-cycle hypothesis: both use Irving Fisher's theory of the consumer to argue that consumption should not depend on current income alone. But unlike the life-cycle hypothesis, which emphasizes that income follows a regular pattern over a person's lifetime, the permanent-income hypothesis emphasizes that people experience random and temporary changes in their incomes from year to year.[4]

The Hypothesis

Friedman suggested that we view current income Y as the sum of two components, **permanent income** Y^P and **transitory income** Y^T. That is,

$$Y = Y^P + Y^T.$$

Permanent income is the part of income that people expect to persist into the future. Transitory income is the part of income that people do not expect to persist. Put differently, permanent income is average income, and transitory income is the random deviation from that average.

To see how we might separate income into these two parts, consider these examples:

- Maria, who has a law degree, earned more this year than John, who is a high-school dropout. Maria's higher income resulted from higher permanent income, because her education will continue to provide her a higher salary.
- Sue, a Florida orange grower, earned less than usual this year because a freeze destroyed her crop. Bill, a California orange grower, earned more than usual because the freeze in Florida drove up the price of oranges. Bill's higher income resulted from higher transitory income, because he is no more likely than Sue to have good weather next year.

These examples show that different forms of income have different degrees of persistence. A good education provides a permanently higher income, whereas good weather provides only transitorily higher income. Although one can imagine intermediate cases, it is useful to keep things simple by supposing that there are only two kinds of income: permanent and transitory.

Friedman reasoned that consumption should depend primarily on permanent income, because consumers use saving and borrowing to smooth consumption

[4] Milton Friedman, *A Theory of the Consumption Function* (Princeton, NJ: Princeton University Press, 1957).

in response to transitory changes in income. For example, if a person received a permanent raise of \$10,000 per year, his consumption would rise by about as much. Yet if a person won \$10,000 in a lottery, he would not consume it all in one year. Instead, he would spread the extra consumption over the rest of his life. Assuming an interest rate of zero and a remaining life span of 50 years, consumption would rise by only \$200 per year in response to the \$10,000 prize. Thus, consumers spend their permanent income, but they save rather than spend most of their transitory income.

Friedman concluded that we should view the consumption function as approximately

$$C = \alpha Y^{P},$$

where α is a constant that measures the fraction of permanent income consumed. The permanent-income hypothesis, as expressed by this equation, states that consumption is proportional to permanent income.

Implications

The permanent-income hypothesis solves the consumption puzzle by suggesting that the standard Keynesian consumption function uses the wrong variable. According to the permanent-income hypothesis, consumption depends on permanent income Y^{P}; yet many studies of the consumption function try to relate consumption to current income Y. Friedman argued that this *errors-in-variables problem* explains the seemingly contradictory findings.

Let's see what Friedman's hypothesis implies for the average propensity to consume. Divide both sides of his consumption function by Y to obtain

$$APC = C/Y = \alpha Y^{P}/Y.$$

According to the permanent-income hypothesis, the average propensity to consume depends on the ratio of permanent income to current income. When current income temporarily rises above permanent income, the average propensity to consume temporarily falls; when current income temporarily falls below permanent income, the average propensity to consume temporarily rises.

Now consider the studies of household data. Friedman reasoned that these data reflect a combination of permanent and transitory income. Households with high permanent income have proportionately higher consumption. If all variation in current income came from the permanent component, the average propensity to consume would be the same in all households. But some of the variation in income comes from the transitory component, and households with high transitory income do not have higher consumption. Therefore, researchers find that high-income households have, on average, lower average propensities to consume.

Similarly, consider the studies of time-series data. Friedman reasoned that year-to-year fluctuations in income are dominated by transitory income. Therefore, years of high income should be years of low average propensities to consume. But over long periods of time—say, from decade to decade—the variation in income comes from the permanent component. Hence, in long time-series, one should observe a constant average propensity to consume, as in fact Kuznets found.

CASE STUDY

The 1964 Tax Cut and the 1968 Tax Surcharge

The permanent-income hypothesis can help us to interpret how the economy responds to changes in fiscal policy. According to the *IS-LM* model of Chapters 10 and 11, tax cuts stimulate consumption and raise aggregate demand, and tax increases depress consumption and reduce aggregate demand. The permanent-income hypothesis, however, predicts that consumption responds only to changes in permanent income. Therefore, transitory changes in taxes will have only a negligible effect on consumption and aggregate demand. If a change in taxes is to have a large effect on aggregate demand, it must be permanent.

Two changes in fiscal policy—the tax cut of 1964 and the tax surcharge of 1968—illustrate this principle. The tax cut of 1964 was popular. It was announced to be a major and permanent reduction in tax rates. As we discussed in Chapter 10, this policy change had the intended effect of stimulating the economy.

The tax surcharge of 1968 arose in a very different political climate. It became law because the economic advisors of President Lyndon Johnson believed that the increase in government spending from the Vietnam War had excessively stimulated aggregate demand. To offset this effect, they recommended a tax increase. But Johnson, aware that the war was already unpopular, feared the political repercussions of higher taxes. He finally agreed to a temporary tax surcharge—in essence, a one-year increase in taxes. The tax surcharge did not have the desired effect of reducing aggregate demand. Unemployment continued to fall, and inflation continued to rise. This is precisely what the permanent-income hypothesis would lead us to predict: the tax increase only affected transitory income, so consumption behavior and aggregate demand were not greatly affected.

The lesson to be learned from these episodes is that a full analysis of tax policy must go beyond the simple Keynesian consumption function; it must take into account the distinction between permanent and transitory income. If consumers expect a tax change to be temporary, it will have a smaller impact on consumption and aggregate demand.

16-5 Robert Hall and the Random-Walk Hypothesis

The permanent-income hypothesis is based on Fisher's model of intertemporal choice. It builds on the idea that forward-looking consumers base their consumption decisions not only on their current income but also on the income they expect to receive in the future. Thus, the permanent-income hypothesis highlights that consumption depends on people's expectations.

Recent research on consumption has combined this view of the consumer with the assumption of rational expectations. The rational-expectations assumption states that people use all available information to make optimal forecasts about the future. As we saw in Chapter 13, this assumption can have profound implications for the costs of stopping inflation. It can also have profound implications for the study of consumer behavior.

The Hypothesis

The economist Robert Hall was the first to derive the implications of rational expectations for consumption. He showed that if the permanent-income hypothesis is correct, and if consumers have rational expectations, then changes in consumption over time should be unpredictable. When changes in a variable are unpredictable, the variable is said to follow a **random walk**. According to Hall, the combination of the permanent-income hypothesis and rational expectations implies that consumption follows a random walk.

Hall reasoned as follows. According to the permanent-income hypothesis, consumers face fluctuating income and try their best to smooth their consumption over time. At any moment, consumers choose consumption based on their current expectations of their lifetime incomes. Over time, they change their consumption because they receive news that causes them to revise their expectations. For example, a person getting an unexpected promotion increases consumption, whereas a person getting an unexpected demotion decreases consumption. In other words, changes in consumption reflect "surprises" about lifetime income. If consumers are optimally using all available information, then they should be surprised only by events that were entirely unpredictable. Therefore, changes in their consumption should be unpredictable as well.[5]

Implications

The rational-expectations approach to consumption has implications not only for forecasting but also for the analysis of economic policies. *If consumers obey the permanent-income hypothesis and have rational expectations, then only unexpected policy changes influence consumption. These policy changes take effect when they change expectations.* For example, suppose that today Congress passes a tax increase to be effective next year. In this case, consumers receive the news about their lifetime incomes when Congress passes the law (or even earlier if the law's passage was predictable). The arrival of this news causes consumers to revise their expectations and reduce their consumption. The following year, when the tax hike goes into effect, consumption is unchanged because no news has arrived.

Hence, if consumers have rational expectations, policymakers influence the economy not only through their actions but also through the public's

[5] Robert E. Hall, "Stochastic Implications of the Life Cycle-Permanent Income Hypothesis: Theory and Evidence," *Journal of Political Economy* 86 (April 1978): 971–987.

expectation of their actions. Expectations, however, cannot be observed directly. Therefore, it is often hard to know how and when changes in fiscal policy alter aggregate demand.

CASE STUDY

Do Predictable Changes in Income Lead to Predictable Changes in Consumption?

Of the many facts about consumer behavior, one is impossible to dispute: income and consumption fluctuate together over the business cycle. When the economy goes into a recession, both income and consumption fall, and when the economy booms, both income and consumption rise rapidly.

By itself, this fact doesn't say much about the rational-expectations version of the permanent-income hypothesis. Most short-run fluctuations are unpredictable. Thus, when the economy goes into a recession, the typical consumer is receiving bad news about his lifetime income, so consumption naturally falls. And when the economy booms, the typical consumer is receiving good news, so consumption rises. This behavior does not necessarily violate the random-walk theory that changes in consumption are impossible to forecast.

Yet suppose we could identify some *predictable* changes in income. According to the random-walk theory, these changes in income should not cause consumers to revise their spending plans. If consumers expected income to rise or fall, they should have adjusted their consumption already in response to that information. Thus, predictable changes in income should not lead to predictable changes in consumption.

Data on consumption and income, however, appear not to satisfy this implication of the random-walk theory. When income is expected to fall by $1, consumption will on average fall at the same time by about $0.50. In other words, predictable changes in income lead to predictable changes in consumption that are roughly half as large.

Why is this so? One possible explanation of this behavior is that some consumers may fail to have rational expectations. Instead, they may base their expectations of future income excessively on current income. Thus, when income rises or falls (even predictably), they act as if they received news about their lifetime resources and change their consumption accordingly. Another possible explanation is that some consumers are borrowing-constrained and, therefore, base their consumption on current income alone. Regardless of which explanation is correct, Keynes's original consumption function starts to look more attractive. That is, current income has a larger role in determining consumer spending than the random-walk hypothesis suggests.[6]

---

[6] John Y. Campbell and N. Gregory Mankiw, "Consumption, Income, and Interest Rates: Reinterpreting the Time-Series Evidence," *NBER Macroeconomics Annual* (1989): 185–216; Jonathan Parker, "The Response of Household Consumption to Predictable Changes in Social Security Taxes," *American Economic Review* 89 (September 1999): 959–973; Nicholas S. Souleles, "The Response of Household Consumption to Income Tax Refunds," *American Economic Review* 89 (September 1999): 947–958.

16-6 David Laibson and the Pull of Instant Gratification

Keynes called the consumption function a "fundamental psychological law." Yet, as we have seen, psychology has played little role in the subsequent study of consumption. Most economists assume that consumers are rational maximizers of utility who are always evaluating their opportunities and plans in order to obtain the highest lifetime satisfaction. This model of human behavior was the basis for all the work on consumption theory from Irving Fisher to Robert Hall.

More recently, economists have started to return to psychology. They have suggested that consumption decisions are not made by the ultrarational *homo economicus* but by real human beings whose behavior can be far from rational. This new subfield infusing psychology into economics is called *behavioral economics.* The most prominent behavioral economist studying consumption is Harvard professor David Laibson.

Laibson notes that many consumers judge themselves to be imperfect decisionmakers. In one survey of the American public, 76 percent said they were not saving enough for retirement. In another survey of the baby-boom generation, respondents were asked the percentage of income that they save and the percentage that they thought they should save. The saving shortfall averaged 11 percentage points.

According to Laibson, the insufficiency of saving is related to another phenomenon: the pull of instant gratification. Consider the following two questions:

Question 1: Would you prefer (A) a candy today or (B) two candies tomorrow?

Question 2: Would you prefer (A) a candy in 100 days or (B) two candies in 101 days?

Many people confronted with such choices will answer A to the first question and B to the second. In a sense, they are more patient in the long run than they are in the short run.

This raises the possibility that consumers' preferences may be *time-inconsistent*: they may alter their decisions simply because time passes. A person confronting question 2 may choose B and wait the extra day for the extra candy. But after 100 days pass, he finds himself in a new short run, confronting question 1. The pull of instant gratification may induce him to change his mind.

We see this kind of behavior in many situations in life. A person on a diet may have a second helping at dinner, while promising himself that he will eat less tomorrow. A person may smoke one more cigarette, while promising himself that this is the last one. And a consumer may splurge at the shopping center, while promising himself that tomorrow he will cut back his spending and start saving more for retirement. But when tomorrow arrives, the promises are in the past, and a new self takes control of the decisionmaking, with its own desire for instant gratification.

These observations raise as many questions as they answer. Will the renewed focus on psychology among economists offer a better understanding of consumer behavior? Will it offer new and better prescriptions regarding, for instance, tax policy toward saving? It is too early to give a full evaluation, but without a doubt, these questions are on the forefront of the research agenda.[7]

CASE STUDY

How to Get People to Save More

Many economists believe that it would be desirable for Americans to increase the fraction of their income that they save. There are several reasons for this conclusion. From a microeconomic perspective, greater saving would mean that people would be better prepared for retirement; this goal is especially important because Social Security, the public program that provides retirement income, is projected to run into financial difficulties in the years ahead as the population ages. From a macroeconomic perspective, greater saving would increase the supply of loanable funds available to finance investment; the Solow growth model shows that increased capital accumulation leads to higher income. From an open-economy perspective, greater saving would mean that less domestic investment would be financed by capital flows from abroad; a smaller capital inflow pushes the trade balance from deficit toward surplus. Finally, the fact that many Americans say that they are not saving enough may be sufficient reason to think that increased saving should be a national goal.

The difficult issue is how to get Americans to save more. The burgeoning field of behavioral economics offers some answers.

One approach is to make saving the path of least resistance. For example, consider 401(k) plans, the tax-advantaged retirement savings accounts available to many workers through their employers. In most firms, participation in the plan is an option that workers can choose by filling out a simple form. In some firms, however, workers are automatically enrolled in the plan but can opt out by filling out a simple form. Studies have shown that workers are far more likely to participate in the second case than in the first. If workers were rational maximizers, as is so often assumed in economic theory, they would choose the optimal amount of retirement saving, regardless of whether they had to choose to enroll or were enrolled automatically. In fact, workers' behavior appears to exhibit substantial inertia. Policymakers who want to increase saving can take advantage of this inertia by making automatic enrollment in these savings plans more common.

A second approach to increase saving is to give people the opportunity to control their desires for instant gratification. One intriguing possibility is the "Save More Tomorrow" program proposed by economist Richard Thaler. The essence of this program is that people commit in advance to putting a portion of

[7] For more on this topic, see David Laibson, "Golden Eggs and Hyperbolic Discounting," *Quarterly Journal of Economics* 62 (May 1997): 443–477; George-Marios Angeletos, David Laibson, Andrea Repetto, Jeremy Tobacman, and Stephen Weinberg, "The Hyperbolic Buffer Stock Model: Calibration, Simulation, and Empirical Evidence," *Journal of Economic Perspectives* 15 (Summer 2001): 47–68.

their future salary increases into a retirement savings account. When a worker signs up, he or she makes no sacrifice of lower consumption today but, instead, commits to reducing consumption growth in the future. When this plan was implemented in several firms, it had a large impact. A high proportion (78 percent) of those offered the plan joined. In addition, of those enrolled, the vast majority (80 percent) stayed with the program through at least the fourth annual pay raise. The average saving rates for those in the program increased from 3.5 percent to 13.6 percent over the course of 40 months.

How successful would more widespread applications of these ideas be in increasing the U.S. national saving rate? It is impossible to say for sure. But given the importance of saving to both personal and national economic prosperity, many economists believe these proposals are worth a try.[8]

16-7 Conclusion

In the work of six prominent economists, we have seen a progression of views on consumer behavior. Keynes proposed that consumption depends largely on current income. Since then, economists have argued that consumers understand that they face an intertemporal decision. Consumers look ahead to their future resources and needs, implying a more complex consumption function than the one that Keynes proposed. Keynes suggested a consumption function of the form

$$\text{Consumption} = f(\text{Current Income}).$$

Recent work suggests instead that

$$\text{Consumption} = f(\text{Current Income, Wealth, Expected Future Income, Interest Rates}).$$

In other words, current income is only one determinant of aggregate consumption.

Economists continue to debate the importance of these determinants of consumption. There remains disagreement about, for example, the influence of interest rates on consumer spending, the prevalence of borrowing constraints, and the importance of psychological effects. Economists sometimes disagree about economic policy because they assume different consumption functions. For instance, as we saw in the previous chapter, the debate over the effects of government debt is in part a debate over the determinants of consumer spending. The key role of consumption in policy evaluation is sure to maintain economists' interest in studying consumer behavior for many years to come.

[8] James J. Choi, David I. Laibson, Brigitte Madrian, and Andrew Metrick, "Defined Contribution Pensions: Plan Rules, Participant Decisions, and the Path of Least Resistance," in James Poterba, ed., *Tax Policy and the Economy* (Cambridge, MA: MIT Press, 2002), 16:67–113; Richard H. Thaler and Shlomo Benartzi, "Save More Tomorrow: Using Behavioral Economics to Increase Employee Saving," *Journal of Political Economy* 112 (2004): S164–S187.

Summary

1. Keynes conjectured that the marginal propensity to consume is between zero and one, that the average propensity to consume falls as income rises, and that current income is the primary determinant of consumption. Studies of household data and short time-series confirmed Keynes's conjectures. Yet studies of long time-series found no tendency for the average propensity to consume to fall as income rises over time.

2. Recent work on consumption builds on Irving Fisher's model of the consumer. In this model, the consumer faces an intertemporal budget constraint and chooses consumption for the present and the future to achieve the highest level of lifetime satisfaction. As long as the consumer can save and borrow, consumption depends on the consumer's lifetime resources.

3. Modigliani's life-cycle hypothesis emphasizes that income varies somewhat predictably over a person's life and that consumers use saving and borrowing to smooth their consumption over their lifetimes. According to this hypothesis, consumption depends on both income and wealth.

4. Friedman's permanent-income hypothesis emphasizes that individuals experience both permanent and transitory fluctuations in their income. Because consumers can save and borrow, and because they want to smooth their consumption, consumption does not respond much to transitory income. Consumption depends primarily on permanent income.

5. Hall's random-walk hypothesis combines the permanent-income hypothesis with the assumption that consumers have rational expectations about future income. It implies that changes in consumption are unpredictable, because consumers change their consumption only when they receive news about their lifetime resources.

6. Laibson has suggested that psychological effects are important for understanding consumer behavior. In particular, because people have a strong desire for instant gratification, they may exhibit time-inconsistent behavior and may end up saving less than they would like.

KEY CONCEPTS

Marginal propensity to consume
Average propensity to consume
Intertemporal budget constraint
Discounting
Indifference curves
Marginal rate of substitution
Normal good
Income effect
Substitution effect
Borrowing constraint
Life-cycle hypothesis
Precautionary saving
Permanent-income hypothesis
Permanent income
Transitory income
Random walk

QUESTIONS FOR REVIEW

1. What were Keynes's three conjectures about the consumption function?
2. Describe the evidence that was consistent with Keynes's conjectures and the evidence that was inconsistent with them.
3. How do the life-cycle and permanent-income hypotheses resolve the seemingly contradictory pieces of evidence regarding consumption behavior?
4. Use Fisher's model of consumption to analyze an increase in second-period income. Compare the case in which the consumer faces a binding borrowing constraint and the case in which he does not.
5. Explain why changes in consumption are unpredictable if consumers obey the permanent-income hypothesis and have rational expectations.
6. Give an example in which someone might exhibit time-inconsistent preferences.

PROBLEMS AND APPLICATIONS

1. The chapter uses the Fisher model to discuss a change in the interest rate for a consumer who saves some of his first-period income. Suppose, instead, that the consumer is a borrower. How does that alter the analysis? Discuss the income and substitution effects on consumption in both periods.
2. Jack and Jill both obey the two-period Fisher model of consumption. Jack earns \$100 in the first period and \$100 in the second period. Jill earns nothing in the first period and \$210 in the second period. Both of them can borrow or lend at the interest rate *r*.
   a. You observe both Jack and Jill consuming \$100 in the first period and \$100 in the second period. What is the interest rate *r*?
   b. Suppose the interest rate increases. What will happen to Jack's consumption in the first period? Is Jack better off or worse off than before the interest rate rise?
   c. What will happen to Jill's consumption in the first period when the interest rate increases? Is Jill better off or worse off than before the interest rate increase?
3. The chapter analyzes Fisher's model for the case in which the consumer can save or borrow at an interest rate of *r* and for the case in which the consumer can save at this rate but cannot borrow at all. Consider now the intermediate case in which the consumer can save at rate r_s and borrow at rate r_b, where $r_s < r_b$.
   a. What is the consumer's budget constraint in the case in which he consumes less than his income in period one?
   b. What is the consumer's budget constraint in the case in which he consumes more than his income in period one?
   c. Graph the two budget constraints and shade the area that represents the combination of first-period and second-period consumption the consumer can choose.
   d. Now add to your graph the consumer's indifference curves. Show three possible outcomes: one in which the consumer saves, one in which he borrows, and one in which he neither saves nor borrows.
   e. What determines first-period consumption in each of the three cases?
4. Explain whether borrowing constraints increase or decrease the potency of fiscal policy to influence aggregate demand in each of the following two cases:
   a. A temporary tax cut.
   b. An announced future tax cut.
5. In the discussion of the life-cycle hypothesis in the text, income is assumed to be constant during the period before retirement. For most people, however, income grows over their lifetimes. How does this growth in income influence the lifetime pattern of consumption and wealth accumulation shown in Figure 16-12 under the following conditions?

a. Consumers can borrow, so their wealth can be negative.

b. Consumers face borrowing constraints that prevent their wealth from falling below zero.

Do you consider case (a) or case (b) to be more realistic? Why?

6. Demographers predict that the fraction of the population that is elderly will increase over the next 20 years. What does the life-cycle model predict for the influence of this demographic change on the national saving rate?

7. One study found that the elderly who do not have children dissave at about the same rate as the elderly who do have children. What might this finding imply about the reason the elderly do not dissave as much as the life-cycle model predicts?

8. Consider two savings accounts that pay the same interest rate. One account lets you take your money out on demand. The second requires that you give 30-day advance notification before withdrawals. Which account would you prefer? Why? Can you imagine a person who might make the opposite choice? What do these choices say about the theory of the consumption function?

CHAPTER 17

Investment

The social object of skilled investment should be to defeat the dark forces of time and ignorance which envelope our future.

— *John Maynard Keynes*

While spending on consumption goods provides utility to households today, spending on investment goods is aimed at providing a higher standard of living at a later date. Investment is the component of GDP that links the present and the future.

Investment spending plays a key role not only in long-run growth but also in the short-run business cycle because it is the most volatile component of GDP. When expenditure on goods and services falls during a recession, much of the decline is usually due to a drop in investment. In the severe U.S. recession of 1982, for example, real GDP fell \$105 billion from its peak in the third quarter of 1981 to its trough in the fourth quarter of 1982. Investment spending over the same period fell \$152 billion, accounting for more than the entire fall in spending.

Economists study investment to better understand fluctuations in the economy's output of goods and services. The models of GDP we saw in previous chapters, such as the *IS–LM* model in Chapters 10 and 11, were based on a simple investment function relating investment to the real interest rate: $I = I(r)$. That function states that an increase in the real interest rate reduces investment. In this chapter we look more closely at the theory behind this investment function.

There are three types of investment spending. **Business fixed investment** includes the equipment and structures that businesses buy to use in production. **Residential investment** includes the new housing that people buy to live in and that landlords buy to rent out. **Inventory investment** includes those goods that businesses put aside in storage, including materials and supplies, work in process, and finished goods. Figure 17-1 plots total investment and its three components in the United States between 1970 and 2005. You can see that all types of investment fall substantially during recessions, which are shown as shaded areas in the figure.

In this chapter we build models of each type of investment to explain these fluctuations. The models will shed light on the following questions:

- Why is investment negatively related to the interest rate?

FIGURE 17-1

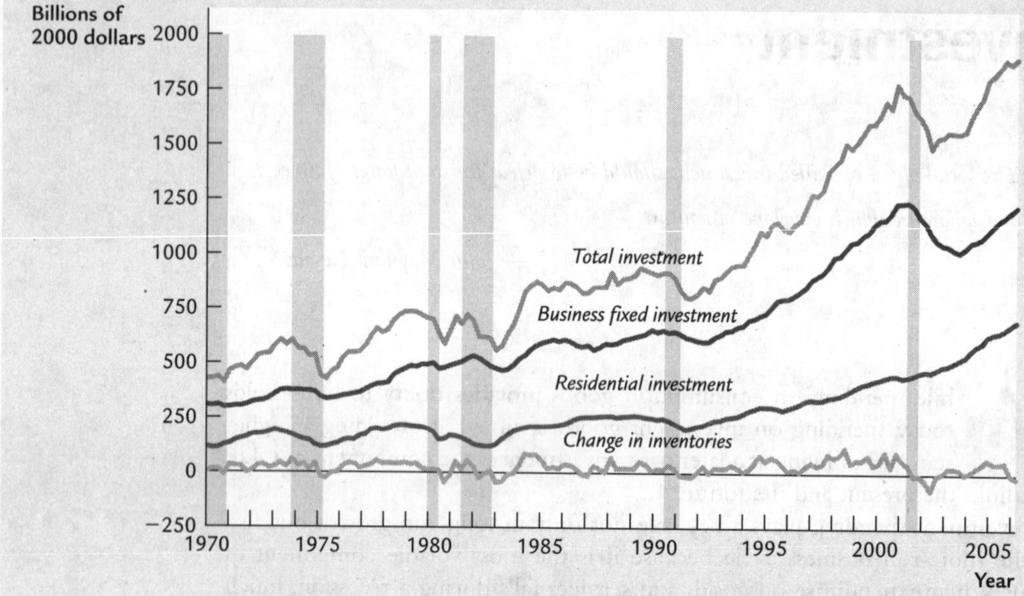

The Three Components of Investment This figure shows total investment, business fixed investment, residential investment, and inventory investment in the United States from 1970 to 2005. Notice that all types of investment fall substantially during recessions, which are indicated here by the shaded areas.

Source: U.S. Department of Commerce.

- What causes the investment function to shift?
- Why does investment rise during booms and fall during recessions?

At the end of the chapter, we return to these questions and summarize the answers that the models offer.

17-1 Business Fixed Investment

The largest piece of investment spending, accounting for about three-quarters of the total, is business fixed investment. The term "business" means that these investment goods are bought by firms for use in future production. The term "fixed" means that this spending is for capital that will stay put for a while, as opposed to inventory investment, which will be used or sold within a short time. Business fixed investment includes everything from fax machines to factories, computers to company cars.

The standard model of business fixed investment is called the **neoclassical model of investment**. The neoclassical model examines the benefits and costs to firms of owning capital goods. The model shows how the level of investment—the addition to the stock of capital—is related to the marginal product of capital, the interest rate, and the tax rules affecting firms.

To develop the model, imagine that there are two kinds of firms in the economy. *Production firms* produce goods and services using capital that they rent. *Rental firms* make all the investments in the economy; they buy capital and rent it out to the production firms. Most firms in the real world perform both functions: they produce goods and services, and they invest in capital for future production. We can simplify our analysis and clarify our thinking, however, if we separate these two activities by imagining that they take place in different firms.

The Rental Price of Capital

Let's first consider the typical production firm. As we discussed in Chapter 3, this firm decides how much capital to rent by comparing the cost and benefit of each unit of capital. The firm rents capital at a rental rate R and sells its output at a price P; the real cost of a unit of capital to the production firm is R/P. The real benefit of a unit of capital is the marginal product of capital MPK—the extra output produced with one more unit of capital. The marginal product of capital declines as the amount of capital rises: the more capital the firm has, the less an additional unit of capital will add to its output. Chapter 3 concluded that, to maximize profit, the firm rents capital until the marginal product of capital falls to equal the real rental price.

Figure 17-2 shows the equilibrium in the rental market for capital. For the reasons just discussed, the marginal product of capital determines the demand curve. The demand curve slopes downward because the marginal product of capital is low when the level of capital is high. At any point in time, the amount of

FIGURE 17-2

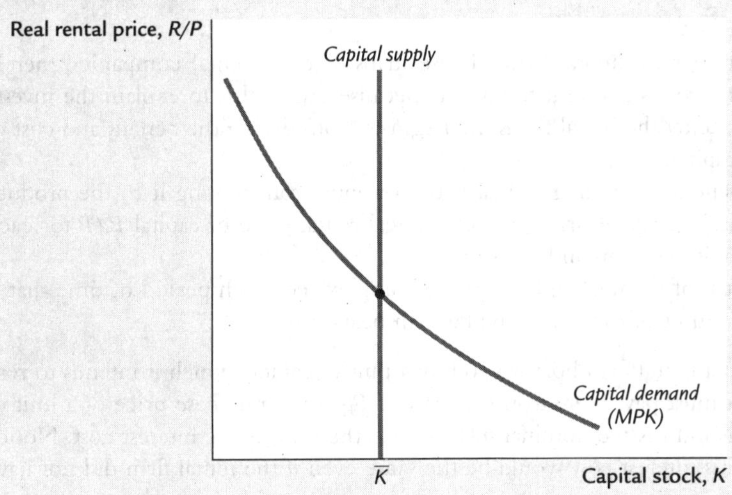

The Rental Price of Capital The real rental price of capital adjusts to equilibrate the demand for capital (determined by the marginal product of capital) and the fixed supply.

capital in the economy is fixed, so the supply curve is vertical. The real rental price of capital adjusts to equilibrate supply and demand.

To see what variables influence the equilibrium rental price, let's consider a particular production function. As we saw in Chapter 3, many economists consider the Cobb-Douglas production function a good approximation of how the actual economy turns capital and labor into goods and services. The Cobb-Douglas production function is

$$Y = AK^{\alpha}L^{1-\alpha},$$

where Y is output, K capital, L labor, A a parameter measuring the level of technology, and α a parameter between zero and one that measures capital's share of output. The marginal product of capital for the Cobb-Douglas production function is

$$MPK = \alpha A(L/K)^{1-\alpha}.$$

Because the real rental price R/P equals the marginal product of capital in equilibrium, we can write

$$R/P = \alpha A(L/K)^{1-\alpha}.$$

This expression identifies the variables that determine the real rental price. It shows the following:

- The lower the stock of capital, the higher the real rental price of capital.
- The greater the amount of labor employed, the higher the real rental price of capital.
- The better the technology, the higher the real rental price of capital.

Events that reduce the capital stock (an earthquake), or raise employment (an expansion in aggregate demand), or improve the technology (a scientific discovery) raise the equilibrium real rental price of capital.

The Cost of Capital

Next consider the rental firms. These firms, like car-rental companies, merely buy capital goods and rent them out. Because our goal is to explain the investments made by the rental firms, we begin by considering the benefit and cost of owning capital.

The benefit of owning capital is the revenue from renting it to the production firms. The rental firm receives the real rental price of capital R/P for each unit of capital it owns and rents out.

The cost of owning capital is more complex. For each period of time that it rents out a unit of capital, the rental firm bears three costs:

1. When a rental firm borrows to buy a unit of capital, which it intends to rent out, it must pay interest on the loan. If P_K is the purchase price of a unit of capital and i is the nominal interest rate, then iP_K is the interest cost. Notice that this interest cost would be the same even if the rental firm did not have

to borrow: if the rental firm buys a unit of capital using cash on hand, it loses out on the interest it could have earned by depositing this cash in the bank. In either case, the interest cost equals iP_K.

2. While the rental firm is renting out the capital, the price of capital can change. If the price of capital falls, the firm loses, because the firm's asset has fallen in value. If the price of capital rises, the firm gains, because the firm's asset has risen in value. The cost of this loss or gain is $-\Delta P_K$. (The minus sign is here because we are measuring costs, not benefits.)

3. While the capital is rented out, it suffers wear and tear, called **depreciation**. If δ is the rate of depreciation—the fraction of capital's value lost per period because of wear and tear—then the dollar cost of depreciation is δP_K.

The total cost of renting out a unit of capital for one period is therefore

$$\begin{aligned}\text{Cost of Capital} &= iP_K - \Delta P_K + \delta P_K \\ &= P_K(i - \Delta P_K/P_K + \delta).\end{aligned}$$

The cost of capital depends on the price of capital, the interest rate, the rate at which capital prices are changing, and the depreciation rate.

For example, consider the cost of capital to a car-rental company. The company buys cars for \$10,000 each and rents them out to other businesses. The company faces an interest rate i of 10 percent per year, so the interest cost iP_K is \$1,000 per year for each car the company owns. Car prices are rising at 6 percent per year, so, excluding wear and tear, the firm gets a capital gain ΔP_K of \$600 per year. Cars depreciate at 20 percent per year, so the loss due to wear and tear δP_K is \$2,000 per year. Therefore, the company's cost of capital is

$$\begin{aligned}\text{Cost of Capital} &= \$1{,}000 - \$600 + \$2{,}000 \\ &= \$2{,}400.\end{aligned}$$

The cost to the car-rental company of keeping a car in its capital stock is \$2,400 per year.

To make the expression for the cost of capital simpler and easier to interpret, we assume that the price of capital goods rises with the prices of other goods. In this case, $\Delta P_K/P_K$ equals the overall rate of inflation π. Because $i - \pi$ equals the real interest rate r, we can write the cost of capital as

$$\text{Cost of Capital} = P_K(r + \delta).$$

This equation states that the cost of capital depends on the price of capital, the real interest rate, and the depreciation rate.

Finally, we want to express the cost of capital relative to other goods in the economy. The **real cost of capital**—the cost of buying and renting out a unit of capital measured in units of the economy's output—is

$$\text{Real Cost of Capital} = (P_K/P)(r + \delta).$$

This equation states that the real cost of capital depends on the relative price of a capital good P_K/P, the real interest rate r, and the depreciation rate δ.

The Determinants of Investment

Now consider a rental firm's decision about whether to increase or decrease its capital stock. For each unit of capital, the firm earns real revenue R/P and bears the real cost $(P_K/P)(r + \delta)$. The real profit per unit of capital is

$$\text{Profit Rate} = \text{Revenue} - \text{Cost}$$
$$= R/P - (P_K/P)(r + \delta).$$

Because the real rental price in equilibrium equals the marginal product of capital, we can write the profit rate as

$$\text{Profit Rate} = MPK - (P_K/P)(r + \delta).$$

The rental firm makes a profit if the marginal product of capital is greater than the cost of capital. It incurs a loss if the marginal product is less than the cost of capital.

We can now see the economic incentives that lie behind the rental firm's investment decision. The firm's decision regarding its capital stock—that is, whether to add to it or to let it depreciate—depends on whether owning and renting out capital is profitable. The change in the capital stock, called **net investment**, depends on the difference between the marginal product of capital and the cost of capital. *If the marginal product of capital exceeds the cost of capital, firms find it profitable to add to their capital stock. If the marginal product of capital falls short of the cost of capital, they let their capital stock shrink.*

We can also now see that the separation of economic activity between production and rental firms, although useful for clarifying our thinking, is not necessary for our conclusion regarding how firms choose how much to invest. For a firm that both uses and owns capital, the benefit of an extra unit of capital is the marginal product of capital, and the cost is the cost of capital. Like a firm that owns and rents out capital, this firm adds to its capital stock if the marginal product exceeds the cost of capital. Thus, we can write

$$\Delta K = I_n\,[MPK - (P_K/P)(r + \delta)],$$

where $I_n(\,)$ is the function showing how much net investment responds to the incentive to invest.

We can now derive the investment function. Total spending on business fixed investment is the sum of net investment and the replacement of depreciated capital. The investment function is

$$I = I_n\,[MPK - (P_K/P)(r + \delta)] + \delta K.$$

Business fixed investment depends on the marginal product of capital, the cost of capital, and the amount of depreciation.

This model shows why investment depends on the interest rate. A decrease in the real interest rate lowers the cost of capital. It therefore raises the amount of profit from owning capital and increases the incentive to accumulate more capital. Similarly, an increase in the real interest rate raises the cost of capital and leads firms to reduce their investment. For this reason, the investment schedule relating investment to the interest rate slopes downward, as in panel (a) of Figure 17-3.

FIGURE 17-3

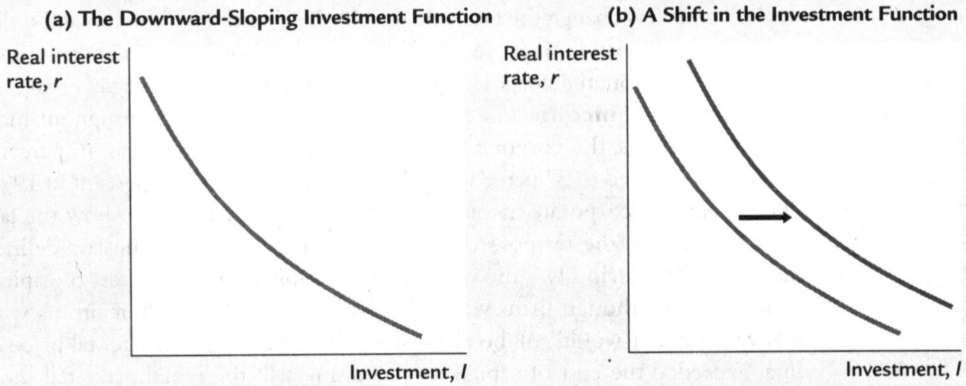

The Investment Function Panel (a) shows that business fixed investment increases when the interest rate falls. This is because a lower interest rate reduces the cost of capital and therefore makes owning capital more profitable. Panel (b) shows an outward shift in the investment function, which might be due to an increase in the marginal product of capital.

The model also shows what causes the investment schedule to shift. Any event that raises the marginal product of capital increases the profitability of investment and causes the investment schedule to shift outward, as in panel (b) of Figure 17-3. For example, a technological innovation that increases the production function parameter A raises the marginal product of capital and, for any given interest rate, increases the amount of capital goods that rental firms wish to buy.

Finally, consider what happens as this adjustment of the capital stock continues over time. If the marginal product begins above the cost of capital, the capital stock will rise and the marginal product will fall. If the marginal product of capital begins below the cost of capital, the capital stock will fall and the marginal product will rise. Eventually, as the capital stock adjusts, the marginal product of capital approaches the cost of capital. When the capital stock reaches a steady-state level, we can write

$$MPK = (P_K/P)(r + \delta).$$

Thus, in the long run, the marginal product of capital equals the real cost of capital. The speed of adjustment toward the steady state depends on how quickly firms adjust their capital stock, which in turn depends on how costly it is to build, deliver, and install new capital.[1]

[1] Economists often measure capital goods in units such that the price of 1 unit of capital equals the price of 1 unit of other goods and services ($P_K = P$). This was the approach taken implicitly in Chapters 7 and 8, for example. In this case, the steady-state condition says that the marginal product of capital net of depreciation, $MPK - \delta$, equals the real interest rate r.

Taxes and Investment

Tax laws influence firms' incentives to accumulate capital in many ways. Sometimes policymakers change the tax code to shift the investment function and influence aggregate demand. Here we consider two of the most important provisions of corporate taxation: the corporate income tax and the investment tax credit.

The **corporate income tax** is a tax on corporate profits. Throughout most of the past 40 years, the corporate tax rate in the United States was 46 percent. The rate was lowered to 34 percent in 1986 and then raised to 35 percent in 1993.

The effect of a corporate income tax on investment depends on how the law defines "profit" for the purpose of taxation. Suppose, first, that the law defined profit as we did previously—the rental price of capital minus the cost of capital. In this case, even though firms would be sharing a fraction of their profits with the government, it would still be rational for them to invest if the rental price of capital exceeded the cost of capital, and to disinvest if the rental price fell short of the cost of capital. A tax on profit, measured in this way, would not alter investment incentives.

Yet, because of the tax law's definition of profit, the corporate income tax does affect investment decisions. There are many differences between the law's definition of profit and ours. For example, one difference is the treatment of depreciation. Our definition of profit deducts the *current* value of depreciation as a cost. That is, it bases depreciation on how much it would cost today to replace worn-out capital. By contrast, under the corporate tax laws, firms deduct depreciation using *historical* cost. That is, the depreciation deduction is based on the price of the capital when it was originally purchased. In periods of inflation, replacement cost is greater than historical cost, so the corporate tax tends to understate the cost of depreciation and overstate profit. As a result, the tax law sees a profit and levies a tax even when economic profit is zero, which makes owning capital less attractive. For this and other reasons, many economists believe that the corporate income tax discourages investment.

Policymakers often change the rules governing the corporate income tax in an attempt to encourage investment, or at least mitigate the disincentive the tax provides. One example is the **investment tax credit**, a tax provision that reduces a firm's taxes by a certain amount for each dollar spent on capital goods. Because a firm recoups part of its expenditure on new capital in lower taxes, the credit reduces the effective purchase price of a unit of capital P_K. Thus, the investment tax credit reduces the cost of capital and raises investment.

In 1985 the investment tax credit was 10 percent. Yet the Tax Reform Act of 1986, which reduced the corporate income tax rate, also eliminated the investment tax credit. When Bill Clinton ran for president in 1992, he campaigned on a platform of reinstituting the investment tax credit, but he did not succeed in getting this proposal through Congress. Many economists agreed with Clinton that the investment tax credit is an effective way to stimulate investment, and the idea of reinstating the investment tax credit still arises from time to time.

The tax rules regarding depreciation are another example of how policymakers can influence the incentives for investment. When George W. Bush became president, the economy was sliding into recession, attributable in large measure to a significant decline in business investment. The tax cuts Bush signed into law during his first term included provisions for temporary "bonus depreciation." This meant that for purposes of calculating their corporate tax liability, firms could deduct the cost of depreciation earlier in the life of an investment project. This bonus, however, was available only for investments made before the end of 2004. The goal of the policy was to encourage investment at a time when the economy particularly needed a boost to aggregate demand. According to a recent study by economists Christopher House and Matthew Shapiro, the goal was achieved to some degree. They write, "While their aggregate effects were probably modest, the 2002 and 2003 bonus depreciation policies had noticeable effects on the economy. For the U.S. economy as a whole, these policies may have increased GDP by $10 to $20 billion and may have been responsible for the creation of 100,000 to 200,000 jobs."[2]

The Stock Market and Tobin's *q*

Many economists see a link between fluctuations in investment and fluctuations in the stock market. The term **stock** refers to the shares in the ownership of corporations, and the **stock market** is the market in which these shares are traded. Stock prices tend to be high when firms have many opportunities for profitable investment, because these profit opportunities mean higher future income for the shareholders. Thus, stock prices reflect the incentives to invest.

The Nobel-Prize-winning economist James Tobin proposed that firms base their investment decisions on the following ratio, which is now called **Tobin's *q***:

$$q = \frac{\text{Market Value of Installed Capital}}{\text{Replacement Cost of Installed Capital}}.$$

The numerator of Tobin's q is the value of the economy's capital as determined by the stock market. The denominator is the price of that capital if it were purchased today.

Tobin reasoned that net investment should depend on whether q is greater or less than 1. If q is greater than 1, then the stock market values installed capital at more than its replacement cost. In this case, managers can raise the market value of their firms' stock by buying more capital. Conversely, if q is less than 1, the stock market values capital at less than its replacement cost. In this case, managers will not replace capital as it wears out.

Although at first the q theory of investment may appear quite different from the neoclassical model developed previously, in fact the two theories are closely related. To see the relationship, note that Tobin's q depends on current and future expected profits from installed capital. If the marginal product of capital exceeds

[2] A classic study of how taxes influence investment is Robert E. Hall and Dale W. Jorgenson, "Tax Policy and Investment Behavior," *American Economic Review* 57 (June 1967): 391–414. For the study of the recent corporate tax changes, see Christopher L. House and Matthew D. Shapiro, "Temporary Investment Tax Incentives: Theory With Evidence From Bonus Depreciation," University of Michigan, 2005.

the cost of capital, then firms are earning profit on their installed capital. These profits make the firms more desirable to own, which raises the market value of these firms' stock, implying a high value of q. Similarly, if the marginal product of capital falls short of the cost of capital, then firms are incurring losses on their installed capital, implying a low market value and a low value of q.

The advantage of Tobin's q as a measure of the incentive to invest is that it reflects the expected future profitability of capital as well as the current profitability. For example, suppose that Congress legislates a reduction in the corporate income tax beginning next year. This expected fall in the corporate tax means greater profits for the owners of capital. These higher expected profits raise the value of stock today, raise Tobin's q, and therefore encourage investment today. Thus, Tobin's q theory of investment emphasizes that investment decisions depend not only on current economic policies but also on policies expected to prevail in the future.[3]

CASE STUDY

The Stock Market as an Economic Indicator

"The stock market has predicted nine out of the last five recessions." So goes Paul Samuelson's famous quip about the stock market's reliability as an economic indicator. The stock market is in fact quite volatile, and it can give false signals about the future of the economy. Yet one should not ignore the link between the stock market and the economy. Figure 17-4 shows that changes in the stock market often reflect changes in real GDP. Whenever the stock market experiences a substantial decline, there is reason to fear that a recession may be around the corner.

Why do stock prices and economic activity tend to fluctuate together? One reason is given by Tobin's q theory, together with the model of aggregate demand and aggregate supply. Suppose, for instance, that you observe a fall in stock prices. Because the replacement cost of capital is fairly stable, a fall in the stock market is usually associated with a fall in Tobin's q. A fall in q reflects investors' pessimism about the current or future profitability of capital. This means that the investment function has shifted inward: investment is lower at any given interest rate. As a result, the aggregate demand for goods and services contracts, leading to lower output and employment.

There are two additional reasons why stock prices are associated with economic activity. First, because stock is part of household wealth, a fall in stock prices makes people poorer and thus depresses consumer spending, which also reduces aggregate demand. Second, a fall in stock prices might reflect bad news about technological progress and long-run economic growth. If so, this means that the natural level of output—and thus aggregate supply—will be growing more slowly in the future than was previously expected.

These links between the stock market and the economy are not lost on policymakers, such as those at the Federal Reserve. Indeed, because the stock mar-

[3] To read more about the relationship between the neoclassical model of investment and q theory, see Fumio Hayashi, "Tobin's Marginal q and Average q: A Neoclassical Approach," *Econometrica* 50 (January 1982): 213–224; and Lawrence H. Summers, "Taxation and Corporate Investment: A q-Theory Approach," *Brookings Papers on Economic Activity* 1 (1981): 67–140.

FIGURE 17-4

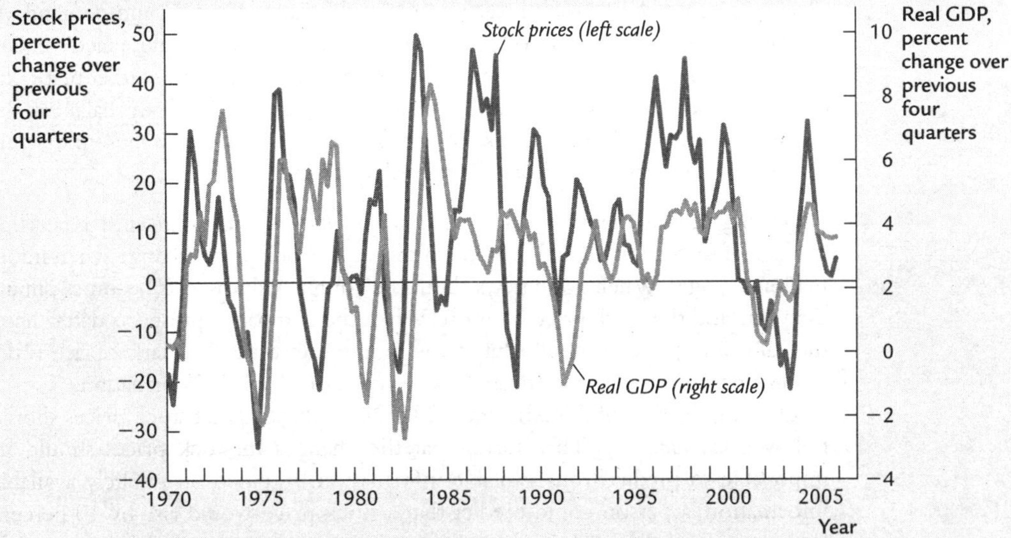

The Stock Market and the Economy This figure shows the association between the stock market and real economic activity. Using quarterly data from 1970 to 2005, it presents the percentage change from one year earlier in the Dow Jones Industrial Average (an index of stock prices of major industrial companies) and in real GDP. The figure shows that the stock market and GDP tend to move together but that the association is far from precise.

Source: U.S. Department of Commerce and Global Financial Data.

ket often anticipates changes in real GDP, and because data on the stock market are available more quickly than data on GDP, the stock market is a closely watched economic indicator.

Alternative Views of the Stock Market: The Efficient Markets Hypothesis Versus Keynes's Beauty Contest

One continuing source of debate among economists is whether stock market fluctuations are rational.

Some economists subscribe to the **efficient markets hypothesis**, according to which the market price of a company's stock is the fully rational valuation of the company's value, given current information about the company's business prospects. This hypothesis rests on two foundations:

1. Each company listed on a major stock exchange is followed closely by many professional portfolio managers, such as the individuals who run mutual funds. Every day, these managers monitor news stories to try to determine

the company's value. Their job is to buy a stock when its price falls below its value, and to sell it when its price rises above its value.

2. The price of each stock is set by the equilibrium of supply and demand. At the market price, the number of shares being offered for sale exactly equals the number of shares that people want to buy. That is, at the market price, the number of people who think the stock is overvalued exactly balances the number of people who think it's undervalued. As judged by the typical person in the market, the stock must be fairly valued.

According to this theory, the stock market is *informationally efficient*: It reflects all available information about the value of the asset. Stock prices change when information changes. When good news about the company's prospects becomes public, the value and the stock price both rise. When the company's prospects deteriorate, the value and price both fall. But at any moment in time, the market price is the rational best guess of the company's value based on available information.

One implication of the efficient markets hypothesis is that stock prices should follow a *random walk*. This means that the changes in stock prices should be impossible to predict from available information. If, based on publicly available information, a person could predict that a stock price would rise by 10 percent tomorrow, then the stock market must be failing to incorporate that information today. According to this theory, the only thing that can move stock prices is news that changes the market's perception of the company's value. But news must be unpredictable—otherwise, it wouldn't really be news. For the same reason, changes in stock prices should be unpredictable as well.

What is the evidence for the efficient markets hypothesis? Its proponents point out that it is hard to beat the market by buying allegedly undervalued stocks and selling allegedly overvalued stocks. Statistical tests show that stock prices are random walks, or at least approximately so. Moreover, index funds, which buy all companies in a stock market index, outperform most actively managed mutual funds run by professional money managers.

Although the efficient markets hypothesis has many proponents, some economists are less convinced that the stock market is so rational. These economists point out that many movements in stock prices are hard to attribute to news. They suggest that when buying and selling, stock investors are less focused on companies' fundamental values and more focused on what they expect other investors will later pay.

John Maynard Keynes proposed a famous analogy to explain stock market speculation. In his day, some newspapers held "beauty contests" in which the paper printed the picture of 100 women and readers were invited to submit a list of the five most beautiful. A prize went to the reader whose choices most closely matched those of the consensus of the other entrants. A naïve entrant would have simply picked the five most beautiful women in his eyes. But a slightly more sophisticated strategy would have been to guess the five women whom other people considered the most beautiful. Other people, however, were likely thinking along the same lines. So an even more sophisticated strategy would have been to try to guess whom other people thought other people thought were the most beautiful women. And so on. In the end of the process, judging true beauty would be less important to winning the contest than guessing other people's opinions of other people's opinions.

Similarly, Keynes reasoned that because stock market investors will eventually sell their shares to others, they were more concerned about other people's valuation of a company than the company's true worth. The best stock investors, in his view, were those who were good at outguessing mass psychology. He believed that movements in stock prices often reflect irrational waves of optimism and pessimism, which he called the "animal spirits" of investors.

The two views of the stock market persist to this day. Some economists see the stock market through the lens of the efficient markets hypothesis. They believe fluctuations in stock prices are a rational reflection of changes in underlying economic fundamentals. Other economists, however, take Keynes's beauty contest as a metaphor for stock speculation. In their view, the stock market often fluctuates for no good reason, and because the stock market influences the aggregate demand for goods and services, these fluctuations are a source of short-run economic fluctuations.[4]

Financing Constraints

When a firm wants to invest in new capital, say by building a new factory, it often raises the necessary funds in financial markets. This financing may take several forms: obtaining loans from banks, selling bonds to the public, or selling shares in future profits on the stock market. The neoclassical model assumes that if a firm is willing to pay the cost of capital, the financial markets will make the funds available.

Yet sometimes firms face **financing constraints**—limits on the amount they can raise in financial markets. Financing constraints can prevent firms from undertaking profitable investments. When a firm is unable to raise funds in financial markets, the amount it can spend on new capital goods is limited to the amount it is currently earning. Financing constraints influence the investment behavior of firms just as borrowing constraints influence the consumption behavior of households. Borrowing constraints cause households to determine their consumption on the basis of current rather than permanent income; financing constraints cause firms to determine their investment on the basis of their current cash flow rather than expected profitability.

To see the impact of financing constraints, consider the effect of a short recession on investment spending. A recession reduces employment, the rental price of capital, and profits. If firms expect the recession to be short-lived, however, they will want to continue investing, knowing that their investments will be profitable in the future. That is, a short recession will have only a small effect on Tobin's q. For firms that can raise funds in financial markets, the recession should have only a small effect on investment.

[4] A classic reference on the efficient markets hypothesis is Eugene Fama, "Efficient Capital Markets: A Review of Theory and Empirical Work," *Journal of Finance* 25 (1970): 383–417. For the alternative view, see Robert J. Shiller, "From Efficient Markets Theory to Behavioral Finance," *Journal of Economic Perspectives* 17 (Winter 2003): 83–104.

Quite the opposite is true for firms that face financing constraints. The fall in current profits restricts the amount that these firms can spend on new capital goods and may prevent them from making profitable investments. Thus, financing constraints make investment more sensitive to current economic conditions.[5]

CASE STUDY

Banking Crises and Credit Crunches

Throughout history, problems in the banking system have often coincided with downturns in economic activity. This was true, for instance, during the Great Depression of the 1930s (which we discussed in Chapter 11). Soon after the Depression's onset, many banks found themselves insolvent, as the value of their assets fell below the value of their liabilities. These banks were forced to suspend operations. Many economists believe the widespread bank failures during this period help explain the Depression's depth and persistence.

Similar patterns, although less severe, can be observed more recently. In the United States, the 1990 recession came on the heels of the savings and loan crisis. Problems in the banking system were also part of the recent slump in Japan (as we saw in Chapter 11) and the recent financial crisis in Indonesia and other Asian economies (Chapter 12).

Why are banking crises so often at the center of economic crises? Banks have an important role in allocating financial resources: they serve as *intermediaries* between those people who have income they want to save and those people who have profitable investment projects but need to borrow to invest. When banks become insolvent or nearly so, they are less able to serve this function. Financing constraints become more common, and some investors are forced to forgo potentially profitable investment projects. Such an increase in financing constraints is sometimes called a *credit crunch*.

We can use the *IS-LM* model to interpret the short-run effects of a credit crunch. When some would-be investors are denied credit, the demand for investment goods falls at every interest rate. The result is a contractionary shift in the *IS* curve. This reduces aggregate demand, production, and employment.

The long-run effects of a credit crunch are best understood from the perspective of growth theory, with its emphasis on capital accumulation as a source of growth. When a credit crunch prevents some firms from investing, the financial markets fail to allocate national saving to its best use. Less productive investment projects may take the place of more productive projects, reducing the economy's potential for producing goods and services.

Because of these effects, policymakers at the Fed and other parts of government are always trying to monitor the health of the nation's banking

---

[5] For empirical work supporting the importance of these financing constraints, see Steven M. Fazzari, R. Glenn Hubbard, and Bruce C. Petersen, "Financing Constraints and Corporate Investment," *Brookings Papers on Economic Activity* 1 (1988): 141–195.

system. Their goal is to avert banking crises and credit crunches and, when they do occur, to respond quickly to minimize the resulting disruption to the economy.[6]

17-2 Residential Investment

In this section we consider the determinants of residential investment. We begin by presenting a simple model of the housing market. Residential investment includes the purchase of new housing both by people who plan to live in it themselves and by landlords who plan to rent it to others. To keep things simple, however, it is useful to imagine that all housing is owner-occupied.

The Stock Equilibrium and the Flow Supply

There are two parts to the model. First, the market for the existing stock of houses determines the equilibrium housing price. Second, the housing price determines the flow of residential investment.

Panel (a) of Figure 17-5 shows how the relative price of housing P_H/P is determined by the supply and demand for the existing stock of houses. At any point in time, the supply of houses is fixed. We represent this stock with a vertical supply curve. The demand curve for houses slopes downward, because high prices

FIGURE 17-5

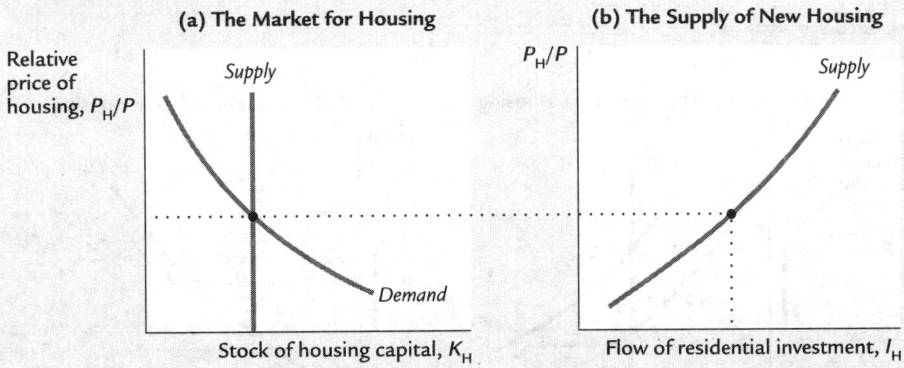

The Determination of Residential Investment The relative price of housing adjusts to equilibrate supply and demand for the existing stock of housing capital. The relative price then determines residential investment, the flow of new housing that construction firms build.

[6] For an analysis of the U.S. experience in 1990, see Ben S. Bernanke and Cara Lown, "The Credit Crunch," *Brookings Papers on Economic Activity* 2 (1991): 205–228.

cause people to live in smaller houses, to share residences, or sometimes even to become homeless. The price of housing adjusts to equilibrate supply and demand.

Panel (b) of Figure 17-5 shows how the relative price of housing determines the supply of new houses. Construction firms buy materials and hire labor to build houses, and then sell the houses at the market price. Their costs depend on the overall price level P (which reflects the cost of wood, bricks, plaster, etc.), and their revenue depends on the price of houses P_H. The higher the relative price of housing, the greater the incentive to build houses, and the more houses are built. The flow of new houses—residential investment—therefore depends on the equilibrium price set in the market for existing houses.

This model of residential investment is similar to the q theory of business fixed investment. According to the q theory, business fixed investment depends on the market price of installed capital relative to its replacement cost; this relative price, in turn, depends on the expected profits from owning installed capital. According to this model of the housing market, residential investment depends on the relative price of housing. The relative price of housing, in turn, depends on the demand for housing, which depends on the imputed rent that individuals expect to receive from their housing. Hence, the relative price of housing plays much the same role for residential investment as Tobin's q does for business fixed investment.

Changes in Housing Demand

When the demand for housing shifts, the equilibrium price of housing changes, and this change in turn affects residential investment. The demand curve for housing can shift for various reasons. An economic boom raises national income and therefore the demand for housing. A large increase in the population, perhaps because of immigration, also raises the demand for housing. Panel (a) of Figure 17-6 shows that

FIGURE 17-6

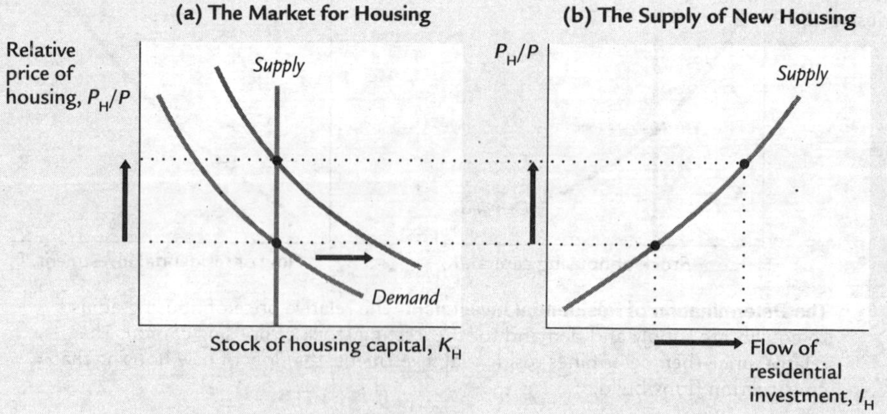

An Increase in Housing Demand An increase in housing demand, perhaps attributable to a fall in the interest rate, raises housing prices and residential investment.

FYI What Price House Can You Afford?

When someone takes out a mortgage to buy a house, the bank often places a ceiling on the size of the loan. That ceiling depends on the person's income and the market interest rate. A typical bank requirement is that the monthly mortgage payment—including both interest and repayment of principal—not exceed 28 percent of the borrower's monthly income.

Table 17-1 shows how the interest rate affects the loan ceiling. The home buyer in the example has an income of $30,000 and is applying for a 30-year mortgage. The bank is assumed to use the standard 28 percent limit on the size of the loan.

As you can see, if the home buyer is up against the borrowing limit, as many are, small changes in the interest rate can have a large influence on the amount he or she can spend on a house. An increase in the interest rate from 8 to 10 percent reduces the maximum loan from $95,398 to $79,766—a fall of 16 percent. An increase in the interest rate therefore reduces housing demand, which in turn depresses housing prices and residential investment.

It is noteworthy—and a bit puzzling—that banks make this calculation using the nominal rather than the real interest rate. The real interest rate measures the true cost of borrowing to buy a house, because the price of the house will normally rise at the overall rate of inflation. Yet bank rules use nominal interest rates when computing mortgage eligibility. Because of these bank rules, residential investment depends on nominal as well as real interest rates.

TABLE 17-1

How High Interest Rates Reduce Mortgage Eligibility and Housing Demand

Assumptions: **30-year mortgage, $30,000 annual income, 28-percent limit on mortgage payment**

Interest Rate	Maximum Possible Loan
5%	$130,397
6	116,754
7	105,215
8	95,398
9	86,997
10	79,766
11	73,504
12	68,053

an expansionary shift in demand raises the equilibrium price. Panel (b) shows that the increase in the housing price increases residential investment.

One important determinant of housing demand is the real interest rate. Many people take out loans—mortgages—to buy their homes; the interest rate is the cost of the loan. Even the few people who do not have to borrow to purchase a home will respond to the interest rate, because the interest rate is the opportunity cost of holding their wealth in housing rather than putting it in a bank. A reduction in the interest rate therefore raises housing demand, housing prices, and residential investment.

The Tax Treatment of Housing

Just as the tax laws affect the accumulation of business fixed investment, they also affect the accumulation of residential investment. In this case, however, their effects are nearly the opposite. Rather than discouraging investment, as the corporate income tax does for businesses, the personal income tax encourages households to invest in housing.

One can view a homeowner as a landlord with himself as a tenant. But he is a landlord with a special tax treatment. The U.S. income tax does not require him to pay tax on the imputed rent (the rent he "pays" himself), yet it allows him to deduct mortgage interest. In essence, when computing his taxable income, he can subtract part of the cost of owning a home, but he does not have to add any of the benefit.

The size of this subsidy to homeownership depends on the rate of inflation. The reason is that the tax law allows homeowners to deduct their *nominal* interest payments when computing taxable income. Because the nominal interest rate on mortgages rises when inflation rises, the value of this subsidy is higher at higher rates of inflation. When inflation and nominal interest rates rose substantially in the 1970s, the tax benefits of homeownership rose as well. When inflation and nominal interest rates fell in the 1980s and early 1990s, the tax benefits became smaller.

Many economists have criticized the tax treatment of homeownership. They believe that, because of this subsidy, the United States invests too much in housing compared to other forms of capital. They advocate reducing the subsidy, perhaps by eliminating the deductibility of mortgage interest and using the extra tax revenue to lower tax rates. The political reaction to this idea is mixed: although voters like lower tax rates, homeowners are not eager to give up the mortgage interest subsidy that they have enjoyed for many years.

17-3 Inventory Investment

Inventory investment—the goods that businesses put aside in storage—is at the same time negligible and of great significance. It is one of the smallest components of spending, averaging about 1 percent of GDP. Yet its remarkable volatility makes it central to the study of economic fluctuations. In recessions, firms stop replenishing their inventory as goods are sold, and inventory investment becomes negative. In a typical recession, more than half the fall in spending comes from a decline in inventory investment.

Reasons for Holding Inventories

Inventories serve many purposes. Before presenting a model to explain fluctuations in inventory investment, let's discuss some of the motives firms have for holding inventories.

One use of inventories is to smooth the level of production over time. Consider a firm that experiences temporary booms and busts in sales. Rather than adjusting production to match the fluctuations in sales, the firm may find it cheaper to produce goods at a steady rate. When sales are low, the firm produces more than it sells and puts the extra goods into inventory. When sales are high, the firm produces less than it sells and takes goods out of inventory. This motive for holding inventories is called **production smoothing**.

A second reason for holding inventories is that they may allow a firm to operate more efficiently. Retail stores, for example, can sell merchandise more effectively if they have goods on hand to show to customers. Manufacturing firms keep inventories of spare parts to reduce the time that the assembly line is shut down when a machine breaks. In some ways, we can view **inventories as a factor of production**: the larger the stock of inventories a firm holds, the more output it can produce.

A third reason for holding inventories is to avoid running out of goods when sales are unexpectedly high. Firms often have to make production decisions before knowing the level of customer demand. For example, a publisher must decide how many copies of a new book to print before knowing whether the book will be popular. If demand exceeds production and there are no inventories, the good will be out of stock for a period, and the firm will lose sales and profit. Inventories can prevent this from happening. This motive for holding inventories is called **stock-out avoidance**.

A fourth explanation of inventories is dictated by the production process. Many goods require a number of steps in production and, therefore, take time to produce. When a product is only partly completed, its components are counted as part of a firm's inventory. These inventories are called **work in process**.

The Accelerator Model of Inventories

Because there are many motives for holding inventories, there are many models of inventory investment. One simple model that explains the data well, without endorsing a particular motive, is the **accelerator model**. This model was developed about half a century ago, and it is sometimes applied to all types of investment. Here we apply it to the type for which it works best—inventory investment.

The accelerator model of inventories assumes that firms hold a stock of inventories that is proportional to the firms' level of output. There are various reasons for this assumption. When output is high, manufacturing firms need more materials and supplies on hand, and they have more goods in the process of being completed. When the economy is booming, retail firms want to have more merchandise on the shelves to show customers. Thus, if N is the economy's stock of inventories and Y is output, then

$$N = \beta Y,$$

where β is a parameter reflecting how much inventory firms wish to hold as a proportion of output.

Inventory investment I is the change in the stock of inventories ΔN. Therefore,

$$I = \Delta N = \beta \Delta Y.$$

The accelerator model predicts that inventory investment is proportional to the change in output. When output rises, firms want to hold a larger stock of inventory, so inventory investment is high. When output falls, firms want to hold a smaller stock of inventory, so they allow their inventory to run down, and inventory investment is negative.

We can now see how the model earned its name. Because the variable Y is the rate at which firms are producing goods, ΔY is the "acceleration" of production. The model says that inventory investment depends on whether the economy is speeding up or slowing down.

To see how well the accelerator model fits the data, look at Figure 17-7. This figure is a scatterplot of annual data from the national income accounts for the United States. On the horizontal axis is the change in real GDP. On the vertical axis is real inventory investment.

The positive association between the change in GDP and inventory investment supports the prediction of the accelerator model. The line drawn through these points shows the following relationship:

$$I = 0.16\ \Delta Y.$$

For every \$1 that GDP rises, there is 16 cents of inventory investment.

FIGURE 17-7

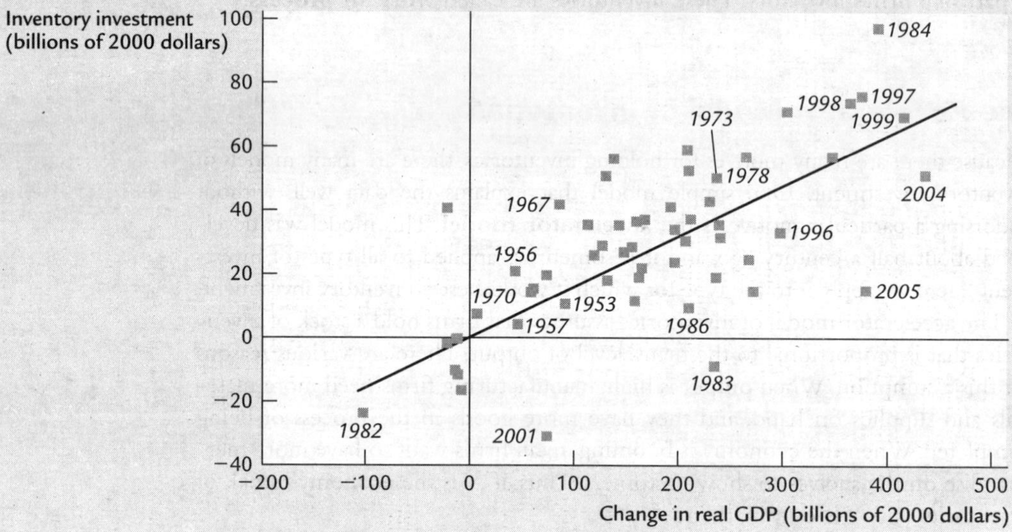

The Evidence for the Accelerator Model This scatterplot shows that inventory investment is high in years when real GDP rises and low in years when real GDP falls, just as the accelerator model of inventory investment predicts.

Source: U.S. Department of Commerce.

Inventories and the Real Interest Rate

Like other components of investment, inventory investment depends on the real interest rate. When a firm holds a good in inventory and sells it tomorrow rather than selling it today, it gives up the interest it could have earned between today and tomorrow. Thus, the real interest rate measures the opportunity cost of holding inventories.

When the real interest rate rises, holding inventories becomes more costly, so rational firms try to reduce their stock. Therefore, an increase in the real interest rate depresses inventory investment. For example, in the 1980s many firms adopted "just-in-time" production plans, which were designed to reduce the amount of inventory by producing goods just before sale. The high real interest rates that prevailed during most of this decade are one possible explanation for this change in business strategy.

17-4 Conclusion

The purpose of this chapter has been to examine the determinants of investment in detail. Looking back on the various models of investment, we can see three themes.

First, all types of investment spending are inversely related to the real interest rate. A higher interest rate raises the cost of capital for firms that invest in plant and equipment, raises the cost of borrowing for home buyers, and raises the cost of holding inventories. Thus, the models of investment developed here justify the investment function we have used throughout this book.

Second, there are various causes of shifts in the investment function. An improvement in the available technology raises the marginal product of capital and raises business fixed investment. An increase in the population raises the demand for housing and raises residential investment. Most important, various economic policies, such as changes in the investment tax credit and the corporate income tax, alter the incentives to invest and thus shift the investment function.

Third, it is natural to expect investment to be volatile over the business cycle, because investment spending depends on the output of the economy as well as on the interest rate. In the neoclassical model of business fixed investment, higher employment raises the marginal product of capital and the incentive to invest. Higher output also raises firms' profits and, thereby, relaxes the financing constraints that some firms face. In addition, higher income raises the demand for houses, in turn raising housing prices and residential investment. Higher output raises the stock of inventories firms wish to hold, stimulating inventory investment. Our models predict that an economic boom should stimulate investment and a recession should depress it. This is exactly what we observe.

Summary

1. The marginal product of capital determines the real rental price of capital. The real interest rate, the depreciation rate, and the relative price of capital goods determine the cost of capital. According to the neoclassical model, firms invest if the rental price is greater than the cost of capital, and they disinvest if the rental price is less than the cost of capital.
2. Various parts of the federal tax code influence the incentive to invest. The corporate income tax discourages investment, and the investment tax credit—which has now been repealed in the United States—encourages it.
3. An alternative way of expressing the neoclassical model is to state that investment depends on Tobin's q, the ratio of the market value of installed capital to its replacement cost. This ratio reflects the current and expected future profitability of capital. The higher is q, the greater is the market value of installed capital relative to its replacement cost, and the greater is the incentive to invest.
4. Economists debate whether fluctuations in the stock market are a rational reflection of companies' true value or are driven by irrational waves of optimism and pessimism.
5. In contrast to the assumption of the neoclassical model, firms cannot always raise funds to finance investment. Financing constraints make investment sensitive to firms' current cash flow.
6. Residential investment depends on the relative price of housing. Housing prices in turn depend on the demand for housing and the current fixed supply. An increase in housing demand, perhaps attributable to a fall in the interest rate, raises housing prices and residential investment.
7. Firms have various motives for holding inventories of goods: smoothing production, using them as a factor of production, avoiding stock-outs, and storing work in process. One model of inventory investment that works well without endorsing a particular motive is the accelerator model. According to this model, the stock of inventories depends on the level of GDP, and inventory investment depends on the change in GDP.

KEY CONCEPTS

Business fixed investment
Residential investment
Inventory investment
Neoclassical model of investment
Depreciation
Real cost of capital
Net investment
Corporate income tax
Investment tax credit
Stock
Stock market
Tobin's q
Efficient markets hypothesis
Financing constraints
Production smoothing
Inventories as a factor of production
Stock-out avoidance
Work in process
Accelerator model

QUESTIONS FOR REVIEW

1. In the neoclassical model of business fixed investment, under what conditions will firms find it profitable to add to their capital stock?
2. What is Tobin's q, and what does it have to do with investment?
3. Explain why an increase in the interest rate reduces the amount of residential investment.
4. List four reasons firms might hold inventories.

PROBLEMS AND APPLICATIONS

1. Use the neoclassical model of investment to explain the impact of each of the following on the rental price of capital, the cost of capital, and investment:
   a. Anti-inflationary monetary policy raises the real interest rate.
   b. An earthquake destroys part of the capital stock.
   c. Immigration of foreign workers increases the size of the labor force.
2. Suppose that the government levies a tax on oil companies equal to a proportion of the value of the company's oil reserves. (The government assures the firms that the tax is for one time only.) According to the neoclassical model, what effect will the tax have on business fixed investment by these firms? What if these firms face financing constraints?
3. The *IS-LM* model developed in Chapters 10 and 11 assumes that investment depends only on the interest rate. Yet our theories of investment suggest that investment might also depend on national income: higher income might induce firms to invest more.
   a. Explain why investment might depend on national income.
   b. Suppose that investment is determined by
   $$I = \bar{I} + aY,$$
   where a is a constant between zero and one, which measures the influence of national income on investment. With investment set this way, what are the fiscal-policy multipliers in the Keynesian cross model? Explain.
   c. Suppose that investment depends on both income and the interest rate. That is, the investment function is
   $$I = \bar{I} + aY - br,$$
   where a is a constant between zero and one, which measures the influence of national income on investment, and b is a constant greater than zero, which measures the influence of the interest rate on investment. Use the *IS-LM* model to consider the short-run impact of an increase in government purchases on national income Y, the interest rate r, consumption C, and investment I. How might this investment function alter the conclusions implied by the basic *IS-LM* model?
4. When the stock market crashes, as it did in October 1929 and October 1987, how should the Federal Reserve respond? Why?
5. It is an election year, and the economy is in a recession. The opposition candidate campaigns on a platform of passing an investment tax credit, which would be effective next year after she takes office. What impact does this campaign promise have on economic conditions during the current year?
6. The United States experienced a large increase in the number of births in the 1950s. People in this baby-boom generation reached adulthood and started forming their own households in the 1970s.
   a. Use the model of residential investment to predict the impact of this event on housing prices and residential investment.
   b. For the years 1970 and 1980, compute the real price of housing, measured as the residential investment deflator divided by the GDP deflator. What do you find? Is this finding consistent with the model? (*Hint*: A good source of data is the *Economic Report of the President*, which is published annually.)
7. The U.S. tax laws encourage investment in housing and discourage investment in business capital. What are the long-run effects of this policy? (*Hint*: Think about the labor market.)

CHAPTER

18 Money Supply and Money Demand

There have been three great inventions since the beginning of time: fire, the wheel, and central banking.

— Will Rogers

The supply and demand for money are crucial to many issues in macroeconomics. In Chapter 4, we discussed how economists use the term "money," how the central bank controls the quantity of money, and how monetary policy affects prices and interest rates in the long run when prices are flexible. In Chapters 10 and 11, we saw that the money market is a key element of the *IS-LM* model, which describes the economy in the short run when prices are sticky.

This chapter examines money supply and money demand more closely. In Section 18-1 we see that the banking system plays a key role in determining the money supply, and we discuss various policy instruments that the central bank can use to alter the money supply. In Section 18-2 we consider the motives behind money demand, and we analyze the individual household's decision about how much money to hold. We also discuss how recent changes in the financial system have blurred the distinction between money and other assets and how this development complicates the conduct of monetary policy.

18-1 Money Supply

Chapter 4 introduced the concept of "money supply" in a highly simplified manner. In that chapter we defined the quantity of money as the number of dollars held by the public, and we assumed that the Federal Reserve controls the supply of money by increasing or decreasing the number of dollars in circulation through open-market operations. Although this explanation is a good first approximation, it is incomplete, because it omits the role of the banking system in determining the money supply. We now present a more complete explanation.

In this section we see that the money supply is determined not only by Fed policy but also by the behavior of households (which hold money) and banks (in which money is held). We begin by recalling that the money supply includes both currency in the hands of the public and deposits at banks that households can use on demand for transactions, such as checking accounts. That is, letting M denote the money supply, C currency, and D demand deposits, we can write

$$\text{Money Supply} = \text{Currency} + \text{Demand Deposits}$$
$$M = C + D.$$

To understand the money supply, we must understand the interaction between currency and demand deposits and how Fed policy influences these two components of the money supply.

100-Percent-Reserve Banking

We begin by imagining a world without banks. In such a world, all money takes the form of currency, and the quantity of money is simply the amount of currency that the public holds. For this discussion, suppose that there is $1,000 of currency in the economy.

Now introduce banks. At first, suppose that banks accept deposits but do not make loans. The only purpose of the banks is to provide a safe place for depositors to keep their money.

The deposits that banks have received but have not lent out are called **reserves**. Some reserves are held in the vaults of local banks throughout the country, but most are held at a central bank, such as the Federal Reserve. In our hypothetical economy, all deposits are held as reserves: banks simply accept deposits, place the money in reserve, and leave the money there until the depositor makes a withdrawal or writes a check against the balance. This system is called **100-percent-reserve banking**.

Suppose that households deposit the economy's entire $1,000 in Firstbank. Firstbank's **balance sheet**—its accounting statement of assets and liabilities—looks like this:

FIRSTBANK'S BALANCE SHEET

Assets		Liabilities	
Reserves	$1,000	Deposits	$1,000

The bank's assets are the $1,000 it holds as reserves; the bank's liabilities are the $1,000 it owes to depositors. Unlike banks in our economy, this bank is not making loans, so it will not earn profit from its assets. The bank presumably charges depositors a small fee to cover its costs.

What is the money supply in this economy? Before the creation of Firstbank, the money supply was the $1,000 of currency. After the creation of Firstbank, the money supply is the $1,000 of demand deposits. A dollar deposited in a bank reduces currency by one dollar and raises deposits by one dollar, so the money supply remains the same. *If banks hold 100 percent of deposits in reserve, the banking system does not affect the supply of money.*

Fractional-Reserve Banking

Now imagine that banks start to use some of their deposits to make loans—for example, to families who are buying houses or to firms that are investing in new plants and equipment. The advantage to banks is that they can charge interest on the loans. The banks must keep some reserves on hand so that reserves are available whenever depositors want to make withdrawals. But as long as the amount of new deposits approximately equals the amount of withdrawals, a bank need not keep all its deposits in reserve. Thus, bankers have an incentive to make loans. When they do so, we have **fractional-reserve banking**, a system under which banks keep only a fraction of their deposits in reserve.

Here is Firstbank's balance sheet after it makes a loan:

FIRSTBANK'S BALANCE SHEET

Assets		Liabilities	
Reserves	$200	Deposits	$1,000
Loans	$800		

This balance sheet assumes that the *reserve-deposit ratio*—the fraction of deposits kept in reserve—is 20 percent. Firstbank keeps $200 of the $1,000 in deposits in reserve and lends out the remaining $800.

Notice that Firstbank increases the supply of money by $800 when it makes this loan. Before the loan is made, the money supply is $1,000, equaling the deposits in Firstbank. After the loan is made, the money supply is $1,800: the depositor still has a demand deposit of $1,000, but now the borrower holds $800 in currency. *Thus, in a system of fractional-reserve banking, banks create money.*

The creation of money does not stop with Firstbank. If the borrower deposits the $800 in another bank (or if the borrower uses the $800 to pay someone who then deposits it), the process of money creation continues. Here is the balance sheet of Secondbank:

SECONDBANK'S BALANCE SHEET

Assets		Liabilities	
Reserves	$160	Deposits	$800
Loans	$640		

Secondbank receives the $800 in deposits, keeps 20 percent, or $160, in reserve, and then loans out $640. Thus, Secondbank creates $640 of money. If this $640 is eventually deposited in Thirdbank, this bank keeps 20 percent, or $128, in reserve and loans out $512, resulting in this balance sheet:

THIRDBANK'S BALANCE SHEET

Assets		Liabilities	
Reserves	$128	Deposits	$640
Loans	$512		

The process goes on and on. With each deposit and loan, more money is created.

Although this process of money creation can continue forever, it does not create an infinite amount of money. Letting *rr* denote the reserve-deposit ratio, the amount of money that the original \$1,000 creates is

$$
\begin{aligned}
\text{Original Deposit} &= \$1{,}000 \\
\text{Firstbank Lending} &= (1 - rr) \times \$1{,}000 \\
\text{Secondbank Lending} &= (1 - rr)^2 \times \$1{,}000 \\
\text{Thirdbank Lending} &= (1 - rr)^3 \times \$1{,}000 \\
&\ \ \vdots \\
\hline
\text{Total Money Supply} &= [1 + (1 - rr) + (1 - rr)^2 \\
&\quad + (1 - rr)^3 + \cdots] \times \$1{,}000 \\
&= (1/rr) \times \$1{,}000.
\end{aligned}
$$

Each \$1 of reserves generates $\$(1/rr)$ of money. In our example, $rr = 0.2$, so the original \$1,000 generates \$5,000 of money.[1]

The banking system's ability to create money is the primary difference between banks and other financial institutions. As we first discussed in Chapter 3, financial markets have the important function of transferring the economy's resources from those households that wish to save some of their income for the future to those households and firms that wish to borrow to buy investment goods to be used in future production. The process of transferring funds from savers to borrowers is called **financial intermediation**. Many institutions in the economy act as financial intermediaries: the most prominent examples are the stock market, the bond market, and the banking system. Yet, of these financial institutions, only banks have the legal authority to create assets (such as checking accounts) that are part of the money supply. Therefore, banks are the only financial institutions that directly influence the money supply.

Note that although the system of fractional-reserve banking creates money, it does not create wealth. When a bank loans out some of its reserves, it gives borrowers the ability to make transactions and therefore increases the supply of money. The borrowers are also undertaking a debt obligation to the bank, however, so the loan does not make them wealthier. In other words, the creation of money by the banking system increases the economy's liquidity, not its wealth.

---

[1] *Mathematical note:* The last step in the derivation of the total money supply uses the algebraic result for the sum of an infinite geometric series (which we used previously in computing the multiplier in Chapter 10). According to this result, if x is a number between −1 and 1, then

$$1 + x + x^2 + x^3 + \cdots = 1/(1 - x).$$

In this application, $x = (1 - rr)$.

A Model of the Money Supply

Now that we have seen how banks create money, let's examine in more detail what determines the money supply. Here we present a model of the money supply under fractional-reserve banking. The model has three exogenous variables:

- The **monetary base** B is the total number of dollars held by the public as currency C and by the banks as reserves R. It is directly controlled by the Federal Reserve.
- The **reserve-deposit ratio** rr is the fraction of deposits that banks hold in reserve. It is determined by the business policies of banks and the laws regulating banks.
- The **currency-deposit ratio** cr is the amount of currency C people hold as a fraction of their holdings of demand deposits D. It reflects the preferences of households about the form of money they wish to hold.

Our model shows how the money supply depends on the monetary base, the reserve-deposit ratio, and the currency-deposit ratio. It allows us to examine how Fed policy and the choices of banks and households influence the money supply.

We begin with the definitions of the money supply and the monetary base:

$$M = C + D,$$
$$B = C + R.$$

The first equation states that the money supply is the sum of currency and demand deposits. The second equation states that the monetary base is the sum of currency and bank reserves. To solve for the money supply as a function of the three exogenous variables (B, rr, and cr), we begin by dividing the first equation by the second to obtain

$$\frac{M}{B} = \frac{C + D}{C + R}.$$

Then divide both the top and bottom of the expression on the right by D.

$$\frac{M}{B} = \frac{C/D + 1}{C/D + R/D}.$$

Note that C/D is the currency-deposit ratio cr, and that R/D is the reserve-deposit ratio rr. Making these substitutions, and bringing the B from the left to the right side of the equation, we obtain

$$M = \frac{cr + 1}{cr + rr} \times B.$$

This equation shows how the money supply depends on the three exogenous variables.

We can now see that the money supply is proportional to the monetary base. The factor of proportionality, $(cr + 1)/(cr + rr)$, is denoted m and is called the **money multiplier**. We can write

$$M = m \times B.$$

Each dollar of the monetary base produces m dollars of money. Because the monetary base has a multiplied effect on the money supply, the monetary base is sometimes called **high-powered money**.

Here's a numerical example that approximately describes the U.S. economy today. Suppose that the monetary base B is \$800 billion, the reserve-deposit ratio rr is 0.1, and the currency-deposit ratio cr is 0.8. In this case, the money multiplier is

$$m = \frac{0.8 + 1}{0.8 + 0.1} = 2.0,$$

and the money supply is

$$M = 2.0 \times \$800 \text{ billion} = \$1,600 \text{ billion}.$$

Each dollar of the monetary base generates two dollars of money, so the total money supply is \$1,600 billion.

We can now see how changes in the three exogenous variables—B, rr, and cr—cause the money supply to change.

1. The money supply is proportional to the monetary base. Thus, an increase in the monetary base increases the money supply by the same percentage.
2. The lower the reserve-deposit ratio, the more loans banks make, and the more money banks create from every dollar of reserves. Thus, a decrease in the reserve-deposit ratio raises the money multiplier and the money supply.
3. The lower the currency-deposit ratio, the fewer dollars of the monetary base the public holds as currency, the more base dollars banks hold as reserves, and the more money banks can create. Thus, a decrease in the currency-deposit ratio raises the money multiplier and the money supply.

With this model in mind, we can discuss the ways in which the Fed influences the money supply.

The Three Instruments of Monetary Policy

In previous chapters we made the simplifying assumption that the Federal Reserve controls the money supply directly. In fact, the Fed controls the money supply indirectly by altering either the monetary base or the reserve-deposit ratio. To do this, the Fed has at its disposal three instruments of monetary policy: open-market operations, reserve requirements, and the discount rate.

Open-market operations are the purchases and sales of government bonds by the Fed. When the Fed buys bonds from the public, the dollars it pays for the bonds increase the monetary base and thereby increase the money supply. When the Fed sells bonds to the public, the dollars it receives reduce the monetary base and thus decrease the money supply. Open-market operations are the policy instrument that the Fed uses most often. In fact, the Fed conducts open-market operations in New York bond markets almost every weekday.

Reserve requirements are Fed regulations that impose on banks a minimum reserve-deposit ratio. An increase in reserve requirements raises the reserve-deposit ratio and thus lowers the money multiplier and the money supply. Changes in reserve requirements are the least frequently used of the Fed's three policy instruments.

The **discount rate** is the interest rate that the Fed charges when it makes loans to banks. Banks borrow from the Fed when they find themselves with too few reserves to meet reserve requirements. The lower the discount rate, the cheaper are borrowed reserves, and the more banks borrow at the Fed's discount window. Hence, a reduction in the discount rate raises the monetary base and the money supply.

Although these three instruments—open-market operations, reserve requirements, and the discount rate—give the Fed substantial power to influence the money supply, the Fed cannot control the money supply perfectly. Bank discretion in conducting business can cause the money supply to change in ways the Fed did not anticipate. For example, banks may choose to hold **excess reserves**—that is, reserves above the reserve requirement. The higher the amount of excess reserves, the higher the reserve-deposit ratio, and the lower the money supply. As another example, the Fed cannot precisely control the amount banks borrow from the discount window. The less banks borrow, the smaller the monetary base, and the smaller the money supply. Hence, the money supply sometimes moves in ways the Fed does not intend.

CASE STUDY

Bank Failures and the Money Supply in the 1930s

Between August 1929 and March 1933, the money supply fell 28 percent. As we discussed in Chapter 11, some economists believe that this large decline in the money supply was the primary cause of the Great Depression. But we did not discuss why the money supply fell so dramatically.

The three variables that determine the money supply—the monetary base, the reserve-deposit ratio, and the currency-deposit ratio—are shown in Table 18-1 for 1929 and 1933. You can see that the fall in the money supply cannot be attributed to a fall in the monetary base: in fact, the monetary base rose 18 percent over this period. Instead, the money supply fell because the money multiplier fell 38 percent. The money multiplier fell because the currency-deposit and reserve-deposit ratios both rose substantially.

Most economists attribute the fall in the money multiplier to the large number of bank failures in the early 1930s. From 1930 to 1933, more than 9,000 banks suspended operations, often defaulting on their depositors. The bank failures caused the money supply to fall by altering the behavior of both depositors and bankers.

Bank failures raised the currency-deposit ratio by reducing public confidence in the banking system. People feared that bank failures would continue, and they began to view currency as a more desirable form of money than demand deposits. When they withdrew their deposits, they drained the banks of reserves. The process of money creation reversed itself, as banks responded to lower reserves by reducing their outstanding balance of loans.

TABLE 18-1

The Money Supply and Its Determinants: 1929 and 1933

	August 1929	March 1933
Money Supply	**26.5**	**19.0**
Currency	3.9	5.5
Demand deposits	22.6	13.5
Monetary Base	**7.1**	**8.4**
Currency	3.9	5.5
Reserves	3.2	2.9
Money Multiplier	**3.7**	**2.3**
Reserve-deposit ratio	0.14	0.21
Currency-deposit ratio	0.17	0.41

Source: Adapted from Milton Friedman and Anna Schwartz, *A Monetary History of the United States, 1867–1960* (Princeton, N.J.: Princeton University Press, 1963), Appendix A.

In addition, the bank failures raised the reserve-deposit ratio by making bankers more cautious. Having just observed many bank runs, bankers became apprehensive about operating with a small amount of reserves. They therefore increased their holdings of reserves to well above the legal minimum. Just as households responded to the banking crisis by holding more currency relative to deposits, bankers responded by holding more reserves relative to loans. Together these changes caused a large fall in the money multiplier.

Although it is easy to explain why the money supply fell, it is more difficult to decide whether to blame the Federal Reserve. One might argue that the monetary base did not fall, so the Fed should not be blamed. Critics of Fed policy during this period make two counterarguments. First, they claim that the Fed should have taken a more vigorous role in preventing bank failures by acting as a *lender of last resort* when banks needed cash during bank runs. This would have helped maintain confidence in the banking system and prevented the large fall in the money multiplier. Second, they point out that the Fed could have responded to the fall in the money multiplier by increasing the monetary base even more than it did. Either of these actions would likely have prevented such a large fall in the money supply, which in turn might have reduced the severity of the Great Depression.

Since the 1930s, many policies have been put into place that make such a large and sudden fall in the money multiplier less likely today. Most important, the system of federal deposit insurance protects depositors when a bank fails. This policy maintains public confidence in the banking system and thus prevents large swings in the currency-deposit ratio. Deposit insurance has a cost: in the late 1980s and early 1990s, the federal government incurred the large expense of bailing out many insolvent savings and loan institutions. Yet deposit insurance helps stabilize the banking system and the money supply.

18-2 Money Demand

We now turn to the other side of the money market and examine what determines money demand. In previous chapters, we used simple money demand functions. We started with the quantity theory, which assumes that the demand for real balances is proportional to income. That is, the quantity theory assumes

$$(M/P)^d = kY,$$

where k is a constant measuring how much money people want to hold for every dollar of income. We then considered a more general and realistic money demand function that assumes the demand for real money balances depends on both the interest rate and income:

$$(M/P)^d = L(i, Y).$$

We used this money demand function when we discussed the link between money and prices in Chapter 4 and when we developed the *IS-LM* model in Chapters 10 and 11.

There is, of course, much more to say about what determines how much money people choose to hold. Just as studies of the consumption function rely on microeconomic models of the consumption decision, studies of the money demand function rely on microeconomic models of the money demand decision. In this section we first discuss in broad terms the different ways to model money demand. We then develop one prominent model.

Recall that money serves three functions: it is a unit of account, a store of value, and a medium of exchange. The first function—money as a unit of account—does not by itself generate any demand for money, because one can quote prices in dollars without holding any. By contrast, money can serve its other two functions only if people hold it. Theories of money demand emphasize the role of money either as a store of value or as a medium of exchange.

Portfolio Theories of Money Demand

Theories of money demand that emphasize the role of money as a store of value are called **portfolio theories**. According to these theories, people hold money as part of their portfolio of assets. The key insight is that money offers a different combination of risk and return than other assets. In particular, money offers a safe (nominal) return, whereas the prices of stocks and bonds may rise or fall. Thus, some economists have suggested that households choose to hold money as part of their optimal portfolio.[2]

Portfolio theories predict that the demand for money should depend on the risk and return offered by money and by the various assets households can hold instead of money. In addition, money demand should depend on total wealth,

---

[2] James Tobin, "Liquidity Preference as Behavior Toward Risk," *Review of Economic Studies* 25 (February 1958): 65–86.

because wealth measures the size of the portfolio to be allocated among money and the alternative assets. For example, we might write the money demand function as

$$(M/P)^d = L(r_s, r_b, \pi^e, W),$$

where r_s is the expected real return on stock, r_b is the expected real return on bonds, π^e is the expected inflation rate, and W is real wealth. An increase in r_s or r_b reduces money demand, because other assets become more attractive. An increase in π^e also reduces money demand, because money becomes less attractive. (Recall that $-\pi^e$ is the expected real return to holding money.) An increase in W raises money demand, because greater wealth means a larger portfolio.

From the standpoint of portfolio theories, we can view our money demand function, $L(i, Y)$, as a useful simplification. First, it uses real income Y as a proxy for real wealth W. Second, the only return variable it includes is the nominal interest rate, which is the sum of the real return on bonds and expected inflation (that is, $i = r_b + \pi^e$). According to portfolio theories, however, the money demand function should include the expected returns on other assets as well.

Are portfolio theories useful for studying money demand? The answer depends on which measure of money we are considering. The narrowest measures of money, such as *M*1, include only currency and deposits in checking accounts. These forms of money earn zero or very low rates of interest. There are other assets—such as savings accounts, Treasury bills, certificates of deposit, and money market mutual funds—that earn higher rates of interest and have the same risk characteristics as currency and checking accounts. Economists say that money (*M*1) is a **dominated asset**: as a store of value, it exists alongside other assets that are always better. Thus, it is not optimal for people to hold money as part of their portfolio, and portfolio theories cannot explain the demand for these dominated forms of money.

Portfolio theories are more plausible as theories of money demand if we adopt a broad measure of money. The broad measures include many of those assets that dominate currency and checking accounts. *M*2, for example, includes savings accounts and money market mutual funds. When we examine why people hold assets in the form of *M*2, rather than bonds or stock, the portfolio considerations of risk and return may be paramount. Hence, although the portfolio approach to money demand may not be plausible when applied to *M*1, it may be a good theory to explain the demand for *M*2 or *M*3.

CASE STUDY

Currency and the Underground Economy

How much currency are you holding right now in your wallet? How many $100 bills?

In the United States today, the amount of currency per person is about $2,000. About half of that is in $100 bills. Most people find this fact surprising, because they hold much smaller amounts and in smaller denominations.

Some of this currency is used by people in the underground economy—that is, by those engaged in illegal activity such as the drug trade and by those trying to hide income to evade taxes. People whose wealth was earned illegally may have fewer options for investing their portfolio, because by holding wealth in banks, bonds, or stock, they assume a greater risk of detection. For criminals, currency may not be a dominated asset: it may be the best store of value available.

Some economists point to the large amount of currency in the underground economy as one reason that some inflation may be desirable. Recall that inflation is a tax on the holders of money, because inflation erodes the real value of money. A drug dealer holding $20,000 in cash pays an inflation tax of $2,000 per year when the inflation rate is 10 percent. The inflation tax is one of the few taxes those in the underground economy cannot evade.[3]

Transactions Theories of Money Demand

Theories of money demand that emphasize the role of money as a medium of exchange are called **transactions theories**. These theories acknowledge that money is a dominated asset and stress that people hold money, unlike other assets, to make purchases. These theories best explain why people hold narrow measures of money, such as currency and checking accounts, as opposed to holding assets that dominate them, such as savings accounts or Treasury bills.

Transactions theories of money demand take many forms, depending on how one models the process of obtaining money and making transactions. All these theories assume that money has the cost of earning a low rate of return and the benefit of making transactions more convenient. People decide how much money to hold by trading off these costs and benefits.

To see how transactions theories explain the money demand function, let's develop one prominent model of this type. The **Baumol-Tobin model** was developed in the 1950s by economists William Baumol and James Tobin, and it remains a leading theory of money demand.[4]

The Baumol-Tobin Model of Cash Management

The Baumol-Tobin model analyzes the costs and benefits of holding money. The benefit of holding money is convenience: people hold money to avoid making a trip to the bank every time they wish to buy something. The cost of this convenience is the forgone interest they would have received had they left the money deposited in a savings account that paid interest.

[3] To read more about the large quantity of currency, see Case M. Sprenkle, "The Case of the Missing Currency," *Journal of Economic Perspectives* 7 (Fall 1993): 175–184.

[4] William Baumol, "The Transactions Demand for Cash: An Inventory Theoretic Approach," *Quarterly Journal of Economics* 66 (November 1952): 545–556; and James Tobin, "The Interest Elasticity of the Transactions Demand for Cash," *Review of Economics and Statistics* (August 1956): 241–247.

To see how people trade off these benefits and costs, consider a person who plans to spend Y dollars gradually over the course of a year. (For simplicity, assume that the price level is constant, so real spending is constant over the year.) How much money should he hold in the process of spending this amount? That is, what is the optimal size of average cash balances?

Consider the possibilities. He could withdraw the Y dollars at the beginning of the year and gradually spend the money. Panel (a) of Figure 18-1 shows his money holdings over the course of the year under this plan. His money holdings begin the year at Y and end the year at zero, averaging $Y/2$ over the year.

A second possible plan is to make two trips to the bank. In this case, he withdraws $Y/2$ dollars at the beginning of the year, gradually spends this amount over the first half of the year, and then makes another trip to withdraw $Y/2$ for the second half of the year. Panel (b) of Figure 18-1 shows that money holdings over the year vary between $Y/2$ and zero, averaging $Y/4$. This plan has the advantage that less money is held on average, so the individual forgoes less interest, but it has the disadvantage of requiring two trips to the bank rather than one.

More generally, suppose the individual makes N trips to the bank over the course of the year. On each trip, he withdraws Y/N dollars; he then spends the money gradually over the following $1/N$th of the year. Panel (c) of Figure 18-1 shows that money holdings vary between Y/N and zero, averaging $Y/(2N)$.

The question is, what is the optimal choice of N? The greater N is, the less money the individual holds on average and the less interest he forgoes. But as N increases, so does the inconvenience of making frequent trips to the bank.

FIGURE 18-1

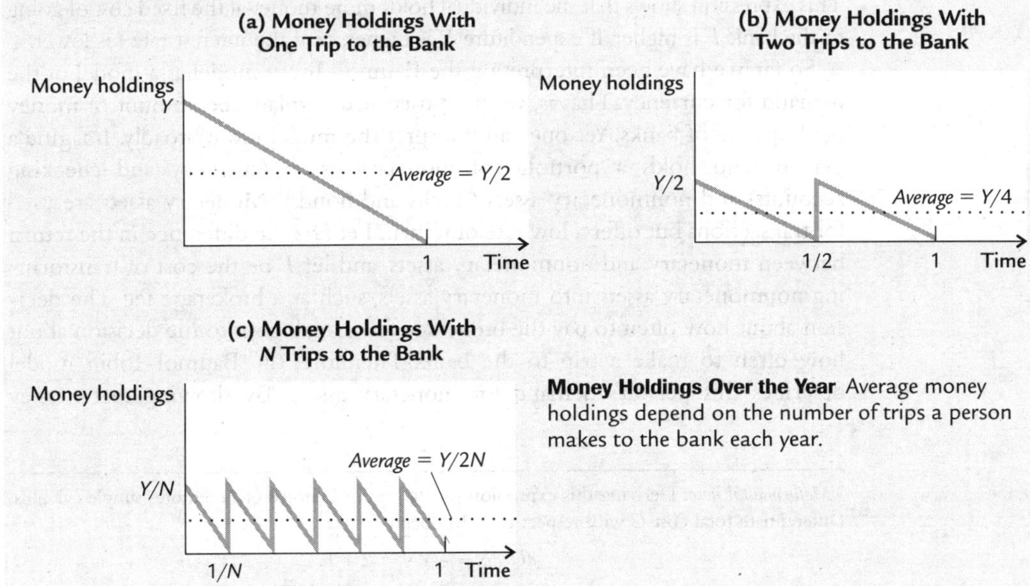

Money Holdings Over the Year Average money holdings depend on the number of trips a person makes to the bank each year.

Suppose that the cost of going to the bank is some fixed amount F. We can view F as representing the value of the time spent traveling to and from the bank and waiting in line to make the withdrawal. For example, if a trip to the bank takes 15 minutes and a person's wage is \$12 per hour, then F is \$3. Also, let i denote the interest rate; because money does not bear interest, i measures the opportunity cost of holding money.

Now we can analyze the optimal choice of N, which determines money demand. For any N, the average amount of money held is $Y/(2N)$, so the forgone interest is $iY/(2N)$. Because F is the cost per trip to the bank, the total cost of making trips to the bank is FN. The total cost the individual bears is the sum of the forgone interest and the cost of trips to the bank:

$$\begin{aligned}\text{Total Cost} &= \text{Forgone Interest} + \text{Cost of Trips}\\ &= \quad iY/(2N) \quad + \quad FN.\end{aligned}$$

The larger the number of trips N, the smaller the forgone interest, and the larger the cost of going to the bank.

Figure 18-2 shows how total cost depends on N. There is one value of N that minimizes total cost. The optimal value of N, denoted N^*, is[5]

$$N^* = \sqrt{\frac{iY}{2F}}.$$

Average money holding is

$$\begin{aligned}\text{Average Money Holding} &= Y/(2N^*)\\ &= \sqrt{\frac{YF}{2i}}.\end{aligned}$$

This expression shows that the individual holds more money if the fixed cost of going to the bank F is higher, if expenditure Y is higher, or if the interest rate i is lower.

So far, we have been interpreting the Baumol–Tobin model as a model of the demand for currency. That is, we have used it to explain the amount of money held outside of banks. Yet one can interpret the model more broadly. Imagine a person who holds a portfolio of monetary assets (currency and checking accounts) and nonmonetary assets (stocks and bonds). Monetary assets are used for transactions but offer a low rate of return. Let i be the difference in the return between monetary and nonmonetary assets, and let F be the cost of transforming nonmonetary assets into monetary assets, such as a brokerage fee. The decision about how often to pay the brokerage fee is analogous to the decision about how often to make a trip to the bank. Therefore, the Baumol–Tobin model describes this person's demand for monetary assets. By showing that money

---

[5] *Mathematical note:* Deriving this expression for the optimal choice of N requires simple calculus. Differentiate total cost C with respect to N to obtain

$$dC/dN = -iYN^{-2}/2 + F.$$

At the optimum, $dC/dN = 0$, which yields the formula for N^*.

FIGURE 18-2

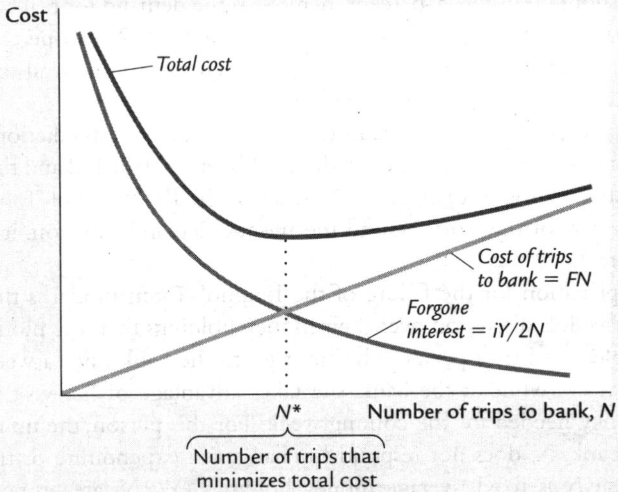

The Cost of Money Holding Forgone interest, the cost of trips to the bank, and total cost depend on the number of trips *N*. One value of *N*, denoted *N**, minimizes total cost.

demand depends positively on expenditure *Y* and negatively on the interest rate *i*, the model provides a microeconomic justification for the money demand function, *L*(*i*, *Y*), that we have used throughout this book.

One implication of the Baumol-Tobin model is that any change in the fixed cost of going to the bank *F* alters the money demand function—that is, it changes the quantity of money demanded for any given interest rate and income. It is easy to imagine events that might influence this fixed cost. The spread of automatic teller machines, for instance, reduces *F* by reducing the time it takes to withdraw money. Similarly, the introduction of Internet banking reduces *F* by making it easier to transfer funds among accounts. On the other hand, an increase in real wages increases *F* by increasing the value of time. And an increase in banking fees increases *F* directly. Thus, although the Baumol-Tobin model gives us a very specific money demand function, it does not give us reason to believe that this function will necessarily be stable over time.

CASE STUDY

Empirical Studies of Money Demand

Many economists have studied the data on money, income, and interest rates to learn more about the money demand function. One purpose of these studies is to estimate how money demand responds to changes in income and the interest rate. The sensitivity of money demand to these two variables determines the slope of the *LM* curve; it thus influences how monetary and fiscal policy affect the economy.

Another purpose of the empirical studies is to test the theories of money demand. The Baumol-Tobin model, for example, makes precise predictions for how income and interest rates influence money demand. The model's square-root formula implies that the income elasticity of money demand is 1/2: a 10-percent increase in income should lead to a 5-percent increase in the demand for real balances. It also says that the interest elasticity of money demand is 1/2: a 10-percent increase in the interest rate (say, from 10 percent to 11 percent) should lead to a 5-percent decrease in the demand for real balances.

Most empirical studies of money demand do not confirm these predictions. They find that the income elasticity of money demand is larger than 1/2 and that the interest elasticity is smaller than 1/2. Thus, although the Baumol-Tobin model may capture part of the story behind the money demand function, it is not completely correct.

One possible explanation for the failure of the Baumol-Tobin model is that some people may have less discretion over their money holdings than the model assumes. For example, consider a person who must go to the bank once a week to deposit her paycheck; while at the bank, she takes advantage of her visit to withdraw the currency needed for the coming week. For this person, the number of trips to the bank, N, does not respond to changes in expenditure or the interest rate. Because N is fixed, average money holdings ($Y/2N$) are proportional to expenditure and insensitive to the interest rate.

Now imagine that the world is populated with two sorts of people. Some obey the Baumol-Tobin model, so they have income and interest elasticities of 1/2. The others have a fixed N, so they have an income elasticity of 1 and an interest elasticity of zero. In this case, the overall demand for money looks like a weighted average of the demands of the two groups. The income elasticity will be between 1/2 and 1, and the interest elasticity will be between 1/2 and zero, as the empirical studies find.[6]

Financial Innovation, Near Money, and the Demise of the Monetary Aggregates

Traditional macroeconomic analysis groups assets into two categories: those used as a medium of exchange as well as a store of value (currency, checking accounts) and those used only as a store of value (stocks, bonds, savings accounts). The first category of assets is called "money." In this chapter we have discussed its supply and demand.

Although the distinction between monetary and nonmonetary assets remains a useful theoretical tool, in recent years it has become more difficult to use in practice. In part because of deregulation of banks and other financial institutions, and in part because of improved computer technology, the past two decades have seen rapid financial innovation. Monetary assets such as checking accounts once paid no interest; today they earn market interest rates and are comparable to non-

[6] To learn more about the empirical studies of money demand, see Stephen M. Goldfeld and Daniel E. Sichel, "The Demand for Money," *Handbook of Monetary Economics*, vol. 1 (Amsterdam: North-Holland, 1990), 299–356; and David Laidler, *The Demand for Money: Theories and Evidence*, 3d ed. (New York: Harper & Row, 1985).

monetary assets as stores of value. Nonmonetary assets such as stocks and bonds were once inconvenient to buy and sell; today mutual funds allow depositors to hold stocks and bonds and to make withdrawals simply by writing checks from their accounts. These nonmonetary assets that have acquired some of the liquidity of money are called **near money**.

The existence of near money complicates monetary policy by making the demand for money unstable. Because money and near money are close substitutes, households can easily switch their assets from one form to the other. Such changes can occur for minor reasons and do not necessarily reflect changes in spending. Thus, the velocity of money becomes unstable, and the quantity of money gives faulty signals about aggregate demand.

One response to this problem is to use a broad definition of money that includes near money. Yet, because there is a continuum of assets in the world with varying characteristics, it is not clear how to choose a subset to label "money." Moreover, if we adopt a broad definition of money, the Fed's ability to control this quantity may be limited, because many forms of near money have no reserve requirement.

The instability in money demand caused by near money has been an important practical problem for the Federal Reserve. In February 1993, Fed Chairman Alan Greenspan announced that the Fed would pay less attention to the monetary aggregates than it had in the past. The aggregates, he said, "do not appear to be giving reliable indications of economic developments and price pressures." It's easy to see why he reached this conclusion when he did. Over the preceding 12 months, $M1$ had grown at an extremely high 12-percent rate, while $M2$ had grown at an extremely low 0.5-percent rate. Depending on how much weight was given to each of these two measures, monetary policy was either very loose, very tight, or somewhere in between.

Since then, the Fed has conducted policy by setting a target for the *federal funds rate*, the short-term interest rate at which banks make loans to one another. It adjusts the target interest rate in response to changing economic conditions. (Recall from Chapter 14 our discussion of the Taylor rule, according to which the target interest rate increases when inflation increases and when output rises above its natural level.) Under such a policy, the money supply becomes endogenous: it is allowed to adjust to whatever level is necessary to keep the interest rate on target. If the subsequent performance of the economy is any guide, this policy of ignoring data on the monetary aggregates has proven a remarkably effective operating procedure. In the period after this announcement, the United States enjoyed better-than-average macroeconomic stability.

18-3 Conclusion

Money is at the heart of much macroeconomic analysis. Models of money supply and money demand can help shed light on the long-run determinants of the price level and the short-run causes of economic fluctuations. The rise of near money in recent years has shown that there is still much to be learned. Building reliable microeconomic models of money and near money remains a central challenge for macroeconomists.

Summary

1. The system of fractional-reserve banking creates money, because each dollar of reserves generates many dollars of demand deposits.
2. The supply of money depends on the monetary base, the reserve-deposit ratio, and the currency-deposit ratio. An increase in the monetary base leads to a proportionate increase in the money supply. A decrease in the reserve-deposit ratio or in the currency-deposit ratio increases the money multiplier and thus the money supply.
3. The Federal Reserve changes the money supply using three policy instruments. It can increase the monetary base by making an open-market purchase of bonds or by lowering the discount rate. It can reduce the reserve-deposit ratio by relaxing reserve requirements.
4. Portfolio theories of money demand stress the role of money as a store of value. They predict that the demand for money depends on the risk and return on money and alternative assets.
5. Transactions theories of money demand, such as the Baumol-Tobin model, stress the role of money as a medium of exchange. They predict that the demand for money depends positively on expenditure and negatively on the interest rate.
6. Financial innovation has led to the creation of assets with many of the attributes of money. These near monies make the demand for money less stable, which complicates the conduct of monetary policy.

KEY CONCEPTS

Reserves
100-percent-reserve banking
Balance sheet
Fractional-reserve banking
Financial intermediation
Monetary base
Reserve-deposit ratio
Currency-deposit ratio
Money multiplier
High-powered money
Open-market operations
Reserve requirements
Discount rate
Excess reserves
Portfolio theories
Dominated asset
Transactions theories
Baumol-Tobin model
Near money

QUESTIONS FOR REVIEW

1. Explain how banks create money.
2. What are the three ways in which the Federal Reserve can influence the money supply?
3. Why might a banking crisis lead to a fall in the money supply?
4. Explain the difference between portfolio and transactions theories of money demand.
5. According to the Baumol-Tobin model, what determines how often people go to the bank? What does this decision have to do with money demand?
6. In what way does the existence of near money complicate the conduct of monetary policy? How has the Federal Reserve responded to this complication?

PROBLEMS AND APPLICATIONS

1. The money supply fell during the years 1929 to 1933 because both the currency-deposit ratio and the reserve-deposit ratio increased. Use the model of the money supply and the data in Table 18-1 to answer the following hypothetical questions about this episode.

   a. What would have happened to the money supply if the currency-deposit ratio had risen but the reserve-deposit ratio had remained the same?

   b. What would have happened to the money supply if the reserve-deposit ratio had risen but the currency-deposit ratio had remained the same?

   c. Which of the two changes was more responsible for the fall in the money supply?

2. To increase tax revenue, the U.S. government in 1932 imposed a two-cent tax on checks written on deposits in bank accounts. (In today's dollars, this tax was about 25 cents per check.)

   a. How do you think the check tax affected the currency-deposit ratio? Explain.

   b. Use the model of the money supply under fractional-reserve banking to discuss how this tax affected the money supply.

   c. Now use the *IS-LM* model to discuss the impact of this tax on the economy. Was the check tax a good policy to implement in the middle of the Great Depression?

3. Suppose that an epidemic of street crime sweeps the country, making it more likely that your wallet will be stolen. Using the Baumol-Tobin model, explain (in words, not equations) how this crime wave will affect the optimal frequency of trips to the bank and the demand for money.

4. Let's see what the Baumol-Tobin model says about how often you should go to the bank to withdraw cash.

   a. How much do you buy per year with currency (as opposed to checks or credit cards)? This is your value of Y.

   b. How long does it take you to go to the bank? What is your hourly wage? Use these two figures to compute your value of F.

   c. What interest rate do you earn on the money you leave in your bank account? This is your value of i. (Be sure to write i in decimal form—that is, 6 percent should be expressed 0.06.)

   d. According to the Baumol-Tobin model, how many times should you go to the bank each year, and how much should you withdraw each time?

   e. In practice, how often do you go to the bank, and how much do you withdraw?

   f. Compare the predictions of the Baumol-Tobin model to your behavior. Does the model describe how you actually behave? If not, why not? How would you change the model to make it a better description of your behavior?

5. In Chapter 4, we defined the velocity of money as the ratio of nominal expenditure to the quantity of money. Let's now use the Baumol-Tobin model to examine what determines velocity.

   a. Recalling that average money holdings equal $Y/(2N)$, write velocity as a function of the number of trips to the bank N. Explain your result.

   b. Use the formula for the optimal number of trips to express velocity as a function of expenditure Y, the interest rate i, and the cost of a trip to the bank F.

   c. What happens to velocity when the interest rate rises? Explain.

   d. What happens to velocity when the price level rises? Explain.

   e. As the economy grows, what should happen to the velocity of money? (*Hint:* Think about how economic growth will influence Y and F.)

   f. Suppose now that the number of trips to the bank is fixed rather than discretionary. What does this assumption imply about velocity?

CHAPTER 19

Advances in Business Cycle Theory

Every great advance in science has issued from a new audacity of imagination.

— John Dewey

Your theory is crazy, but it's not crazy enough to be true.

— Niels Bohr

What is the best way to explain short-run fluctuations in output and employment? How should monetary and fiscal policy respond to these fluctuations? Most economists believe that these questions are best answered using the model of aggregate demand and aggregate supply, which this book has developed and applied thoroughly. Yet as we approach the end of the book, let's take a step closer to the frontier of modern economic research and examine the continuing debate over the theory of short-run economic fluctuations. This chapter discusses two recent strands of research—**real business cycle theory** and **new Keynesian economics.**

We begin by examining the theory of real business cycles—a viewpoint held by a small but significant minority of economists. According to this theory, short-run economic fluctuations should be explained while maintaining the assumptions of the classical model, which we have used to study the long run. Most important, real business cycle theory assumes that prices are fully flexible, even in the short run. Almost all microeconomic analysis is based on the premise that prices adjust to clear markets. Advocates of real business cycle theory argue that macroeconomic analysis should be based on the same assumption.

Because real business cycle theory assumes complete price flexibility, it is consistent with the classical dichotomy: in this theory, nominal variables, such as the money supply and the price level, do not influence real variables, such as output and employment. To explain fluctuations in real variables, real business cycle theory emphasizes real changes in the economy, such as changes in production technologies. The "real" in real business cycle theory refers to the theory's exclusion of nominal variables in explaining short-run economic fluctuations.

By contrast, new Keynesian economics is based on the premise that market-clearing models such as real business cycle theory cannot explain short-run economic fluctuations. In *The General Theory*, Keynes urged economists to abandon the classical presumption that wages and prices adjust quickly to equilibrate markets. He emphasized that aggregate demand is a primary determinant of national income in the short run. New Keynesian economists accept these basic conclusions, and so they advocate models with sticky wages and prices.

In their research, new Keynesian economists try to develop more fully the Keynesian approach to economic fluctuations. Many new Keynesians accept the *IS-LM* model as the theory of aggregate demand and, in their research, try to refine the theory of aggregate supply. This work tries to explain how wages and prices behave in the short run by identifying more precisely the market imperfections that make wages and prices sticky and that cause output to deviate from its natural level. We discuss this research in the second half of the chapter.

In presenting the work of these two schools of thought, this chapter takes an approach that is more descriptive than analytic. Studying recent theoretical developments in detail would require more mathematics than is appropriate for this book. Yet, even without the formal models, we can discuss the direction of this research and get a sense of how different economists are applying microeconomic thinking to better understand macroeconomic fluctuations.[1]

19-1 The Theory of Real Business Cycles

When we studied economic growth in Chapters 7 and 8, we described a relatively smooth process. Output grew as population, capital, and the available technology evolved over time. In the Solow growth model, the economy approaches a steady state in which most variables grow together at a rate determined by the constant rate of technological progress.

But is the process of economic growth necessarily as steady as the Solow model assumes? Perhaps technological progress and economic growth occur unevenly. Perhaps there are shocks to the economy that induce short-run fluctuations in the natural levels of output and employment. To see how this might be so, we consider a famous allegory that economists have borrowed from author Daniel Defoe.

The Economics of Robinson Crusoe

Robinson Crusoe is a sailor stranded on a desert island. Because Crusoe lives alone, his life is simple. Yet he has to make many economic decisions. Considering Crusoe's decisions—and how they change in response to changing circumstances—sheds light on the decisions that people face in larger, more complex economies.

[1] For a more formal treatment of the issues discussed here, see the superb graduate-level textbook by David Romer, *Advanced Macroeconomics*, 3rd ed. (New York: McGraw-Hill, 2006).

To keep things simple, imagine that Crusoe engages in only a few activities. Crusoe spends some of his time enjoying leisure, perhaps swimming at his island's beaches. He spends the rest of his time working, either catching fish or collecting vines to make into fishing nets. Both forms of work produce a valuable good: fish are Crusoe's consumption, and nets are Crusoe's investment. If we were to compute GDP for Crusoe's island, we would add together the number of fish caught and the number of nets made (weighted by some "price" to reflect Crusoe's relative valuation of these two goods).

Crusoe allocates his time among swimming, fishing, and making nets based on his preferences and the opportunities available to him. It is reasonable to assume that Crusoe optimizes. That is, he chooses the quantities of leisure, consumption, and investment that are best for him given the constraints that nature imposes.

Over time, Crusoe's decisions change as shocks impinge on his life. For example, suppose that one day a big school of fish passes by the island. GDP rises in the Crusoe economy for two reasons. First, Crusoe's productivity rises: with a large school in the water, Crusoe catches more fish per hour of fishing. Second, Crusoe's employment rises. That is, he decides to reduce temporarily his enjoyment of leisure to work harder and take advantage of this unusual opportunity to catch fish. The Crusoe economy is booming.

Similarly, suppose that a storm arrives one day. Because the storm makes outdoor activity difficult, productivity falls: each hour spent fishing or making nets yields a smaller output. In response, Crusoe decides to spend less time working and to wait out the storm in his hut. Consumption of fish and investment in nets both fall, so GDP falls as well. The Crusoe economy is in recession.

Suppose that one day Crusoe is attacked by natives. While he is defending himself, Crusoe has less time to enjoy leisure. Thus, the increased demand for defense spurs employment in the Crusoe economy, especially in the "defense industry." To some extent, Crusoe spends less time fishing for consumption. To a larger extent, he spends less time making nets, because this task is easy to put off for a while. Thus, defense spending crowds out investment. Because Crusoe spends more time at work, GDP (which now includes the value of national defense) rises. The Crusoe economy is experiencing a wartime boom.

What is notable about this story of booms and recessions is its simplicity. *In this story, fluctuations in output, employment, consumption, investment, and productivity are all the natural and desirable response of an individual to the inevitable changes in his environment.* In the Crusoe economy, fluctuations have nothing to do with monetary policy, sticky prices, or any type of market failure.

According to the theory of real business cycles, fluctuations in our economy are much the same as fluctuations in Robinson Crusoe's. Shocks to our ability to produce goods and services (like the changing weather on Crusoe's island) alter the natural levels of employment and output. These shocks are not necessarily desirable, but they are inevitable. Once the shocks occur, it is desirable for GDP, employment, and other real macroeconomic variables to fluctuate in response.

The parable of Robinson Crusoe, like any model in economics, is not intended to be a literal description of how the economy works. Instead, it tries to get at the essence of the complex phenomenon that we call the business cycle. Does the parable achieve this goal? Are the booms and recessions in modern industrial economies really like the fluctuations on Robinson Crusoe's island? Economists disagree about the answer to this question and, therefore, disagree about the validity of real business cycle theory. At the heart of the debate are four basic issues:

- The interpretation of the labor market: Do fluctuations in employment reflect voluntary changes in the quantity of labor supplied?
- The importance of technology shocks: Does the economy's production function experience large, exogenous shifts in the short run?
- The neutrality of money: Do changes in the money supply have only nominal effects?
- The flexibility of wages and prices: Do wages and prices adjust quickly and completely to balance supply and demand?

Regardless of whether you view the parable of Robinson Crusoe as a plausible allegory for the business cycle, considering these four issues is instructive, because each of them raises fundamental questions about how the economy works.

The Interpretation of the Labor Market

Real business cycle theory emphasizes the idea that the quantity of labor supplied at any given time depends on the incentives that workers face. Just as Robinson Crusoe changes his work effort voluntarily in response to changing circumstances, workers are willing to work more hours when they are well rewarded and are willing to work fewer hours when they are poorly rewarded. Sometimes, if the reward for working is sufficiently small, workers choose to forgo working altogether—at least temporarily. This willingness to reallocate hours of work over time is called the **intertemporal substitution of labor**.

To see how intertemporal substitution affects labor supply, consider the following example. A college student finishing her sophomore year has two summer vacations left before graduation. She wishes to work for one of these summers (so she can buy a car after she graduates) and to relax at the beach during the other summer. How should she choose which summer to work?

Let W_1 be her real wage in the first summer and W_2 the real wage she expects in the second summer. To choose which summer to work, the student compares these two wages. Yet, because she can earn interest on money earned earlier, a dollar earned in the first summer is more valuable than a dollar earned in the second summer. Let r be the real interest rate. If the student works in the first summer and saves her earnings, she will have $(1 + r)W_1$ a year later. If she works in the second summer, she will have W_2. The intertemporal relative wage—that is, the earnings from working the first summer relative to the earnings from working the second summer—is

$$\text{Intertemporal Relative Wage} = \frac{(1 + r)W_1}{W_2}.$$

Working the first summer is more attractive if the interest rate is high or if the wage is high relative to the wage expected to prevail in the future.

According to real business cycle theory, all workers perform this cost-benefit analysis when deciding whether to work or to enjoy leisure. If the wage is temporarily high or if the interest rate is high, it is a good time to work. If the wage is temporarily low or if the interest rate is low, it is a good time to enjoy leisure.

Real business cycle theory uses the intertemporal substitution of labor to explain why employment and output fluctuate. Shocks to the economy that cause the interest rate to rise or the wage to be temporarily high cause people to want to work more; the increase in work effort raises employment and production. Shocks that cause the interest rate to fall or the wage to be temporarily low decrease employment and production.

Critics of real business cycle theory believe that fluctuations in employment do not reflect changes in the amount people want to work. They believe that *desired* employment is not very sensitive to the real wage and the real interest rate. They point out that the unemployment rate fluctuates substantially over the business cycle. The high unemployment in recessions suggests that the labor market does not clear: if people were voluntarily choosing not to work in recessions, they would not call themselves unemployed. These critics conclude that wages do not adjust to equilibrate labor supply and labor demand, as real business cycle models assume.

In reply, advocates of real business cycle theory argue that unemployment statistics are difficult to interpret. The mere fact that the unemployment rate is high does not mean that intertemporal substitution of labor is unimportant. Individuals who voluntarily choose not to work may call themselves unemployed so they can collect unemployment-insurance benefits. Or they may call themselves unemployed because they would be willing to work if they were offered the wage they receive in most years.

CASE STUDY

Looking for Intertemporal Substitution

Because intertemporal substitution of labor is central to real business cycle theory, much research has been aimed at examining whether it is an important determinant of labor supply. This research looks at data on wages and hours to see whether people alter the amount they work in response to small changes in the real wag If leisure were highly intertemporally substitutable, then individuals expecting increases in the real wage should work little today and much in the future. Those expecting decreases in their real wage should work hard today and enjoy leisure in the future.

Most studies of labor supply find that expected changes in the real wage lead to only small changes in hours worked. Individuals appear not to respond to expected real-wage changes by substantially reallocating leisure over time. This evidence suggests that intertemporal substitution is not as important a determinant of labor supply as real business cycle theorists claim.

This evidence does not convince everyone, however. One reason is that the data are often far from perfect. For example, to study labor supply, we need data on wages; yet when a person is not working, we do not observe the wage that person could have earned by taking a job. Thus, although most studies of labor supply find little evidence for intertemporal substitution, they do not end the debate over real business cycle theory.[2]

The Importance of Technology Shocks

The Crusoe economy fluctuates because of changes in the weather, which induce Crusoe to alter his work effort. In real business cycle theory, the analogous variable is technology, which determines an economy's ability to turn inputs (capital and labor) into output (goods and services). The theory assumes that our economy experiences fluctuations in technology and that these fluctuations in technology cause fluctuations in output and employment. When the available production technology improves, the economy produces more output, and real wages rise. Because of intertemporal substitution of labor, the improved technology also leads to greater employment. Real business cycle theorists often explain recessions as periods of "technological regress." According to these models, output and employment fall during recessions because the available production technology deteriorates, lowering output and reducing the incentive to work.

Critics of real business cycle theory are skeptical that the economy experiences large shocks to technology. It is a more common presumption that technological progress occurs gradually. Critics argue that technological regress is especially implausible: the accumulation of technological knowledge may slow down, but it is hard to imagine that it would go in reverse.

Advocates respond by taking a broad view of shocks to technology. They argue that there are many events that, although not literally technological, affect the economy much as technology shocks do. For example, bad weather, the passage of strict environmental regulations, or increases in world oil prices have effects similar to adverse changes in technology: they all reduce our ability to turn capital and labor into goods and services. Whether such events are sufficiently common to explain the frequency and magnitude of business cycles is an open question.

---

[2] The classic article emphasizing the role of intertemporal substitution in the labor market is Robert E. Lucas, Jr. and Leonard A. Rapping, "Real Wages, Employment, and Inflation," *Journal of Political Economy* 77 (September/October 1969): 721–754. For some of the empirical work that casts doubt on this hypothesis, see Joseph G. Altonji, "Intertemporal Substitution in Labor Supply: Evidence From Micro Data," *Journal of Political Economy* 94 (June 1986, Part 2): S176–S215; and Laurence Ball, "Intertemporal Substitution and Constraints on Labor Supply: Evidence From Panel Data," *Economic Inquiry* 28 (October 1990): 706–724. For a recent study reporting evidence in favor of the hypothesis, see Casey B. Mulligan, "Substitution Over Time: Another Look at Life Cycle Labor Supply," *NBER Macroeconomics Annual* 13 (1998).

CASE STUDY

The Solow Residual and the Business Cycle

To demonstrate the role of technology shocks in generating business cycles, economist Edward Prescott looked at data on the economy's inputs (capital and labor) and its output (GDP). For every year, he computed the **Solow residual**—the percentage change in output minus the percentage change in inputs, where the different inputs are weighted by their factor shares. The Solow residual measures the portion of output growth that cannot be explained by growth in capital or labor. Prescott interprets it as a measure of the rate of technological progress.[3]

Figure 19-1 shows the Solow residual and the growth in output for the period 1960 to 2002. Notice that the Solow residual fluctuates substantially. It tells us, for example, that technology worsened in 1982 and improved in 1984. In addition, the Solow residual moves closely with output: in years when output falls, technology worsens. According to Prescott, these large fluctuations in the Solow residual show that technology shocks are an important source of economic fluctuations.

Prescott's interpretation of this figure is controversial, however. Many economists believe that the Solow residual does not accurately represent changes in technology over short periods of time. The standard explanation of the cyclical behavior of the Solow residual is that it results from two measurement problems.

First, during recessions, firms may continue to employ workers they do not need, so that they will have these workers on hand when the economy recovers. This phenomenon, called **labor hoarding**, means that labor input is overestimated in recessions, because the hoarded workers are probably not working as hard as usual. As a result, the Solow residual is more cyclical than the available production technology. In a recession, productivity as measured by the Solow residual falls even if technology has not changed simply because hoarded workers are sitting around waiting for the recession to end.

Second, when demand is low, firms may produce things that are not easily measured. In recessions, workers may clean the factory, organize the inventory, get some training, and do other useful tasks that standard measures of output fail to include. If so, then output is underestimated in recessions, which would also make the measured Solow residual cyclical for reasons other than technology.

Thus, economists can interpret the cyclical behavior of the Solow residual in different ways. Real business cycle theorists point to the low productivity in recessions as evidence for adverse technology shocks. Other economists believe that measured productivity is low in recessions because workers are not working as hard as usual and because more of their output is not measured. Unfortunately,

---

[3] The appendix to Chapter 8 shows that the Solow residual is

$$\frac{\Delta A}{A} = \frac{\Delta Y}{Y} - \alpha\frac{\Delta K}{K} - (1 - \alpha)\frac{\Delta L}{L},$$

where A is total factor productivity, Y output, K capital, L labor, and α capital's share of income.

FIGURE 19-1

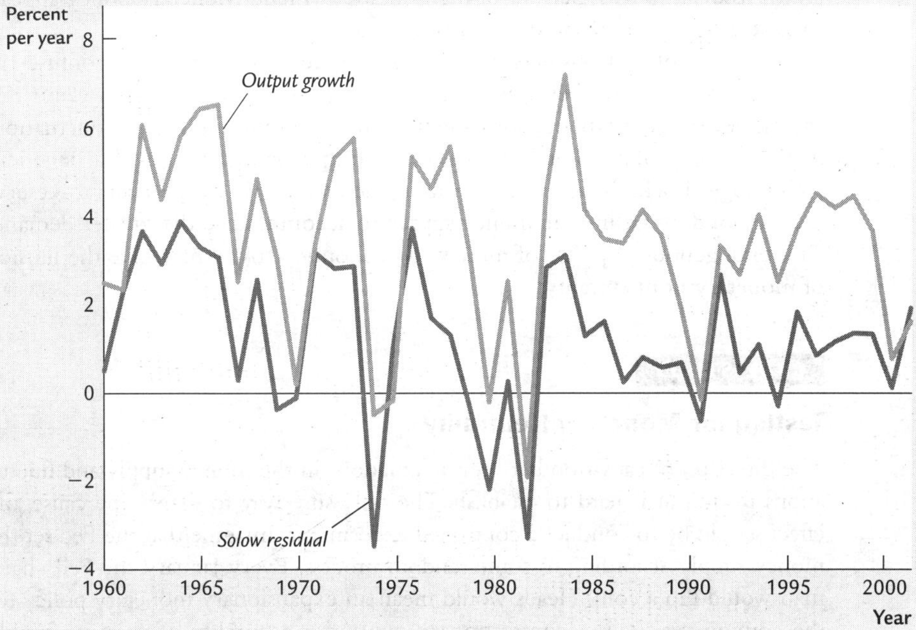

Growth in Output and the Solow Residual The Solow residual, which some economists interpret as a measure of technology shocks, fluctuates with the economy's output of goods and services.

Source: U.S. Department of Commerce, U.S. Department of Labor, and author's calculations.

there is no clear evidence on the importance of labor hoarding and the cyclical mismeasurement of output. Therefore, different interpretations of Figure 19-1 persist. This disagreement is one part of the debate between advocates and critics of real business cycle theory.[4]

The Neutrality of Money

Just as money has no role in the Crusoe economy, real business cycle theory assumes that money in our economy is neutral, even in the short run. That is, monetary policy is assumed not to affect real variables such as output and employment. Not only does the neutrality of money give real business cycle theory its name, but neutrality is also the theory's most radical assumption.

[4] For the two sides of this debate, see Edward C. Prescott, "Theory Ahead of Business Cycle Measurement," and Lawrence H. Summers, "Some Skeptical Observations on Real Business Cycle Theory." Both are in *Quarterly Review*, Federal Reserve Bank of Minneapolis (Fall 1986).

Critics argue that the evidence does not support short-run monetary neutrality. They point out that reductions in money growth and inflation are almost always associated with periods of high unemployment. Monetary policy appears to have a strong influence on the real economy.

Advocates of real business cycle theory argue that their critics confuse the direction of causation between money and output. These advocates claim that the money supply is endogenous: fluctuations in output might cause fluctuations in the money supply. For example, when output rises because of a beneficial technology shock, the quantity of money demanded rises. The Federal Reserve may respond by raising the money supply to accommodate the greater demand. This endogenous response of money to economic activity may give the illusion of monetary nonneutrality.[5]

CASE STUDY

Testing for Monetary Neutrality

The direction of causation between fluctuations in the money supply and fluctuations in output is hard to establish. The only sure way to determine cause and effect would be to conduct a controlled experiment. Imagine that the Fed set the money supply according to some random process. Every January, the Fed chairman would flip a coin. Heads would mean an expansionary monetary policy for the coming year; tails a contractionary one. After a number of years we would know with confidence the effects of monetary policy. If output and employment usually rose after the coin came up heads and usually fell after it came up tails, then we would conclude that monetary policy has real effects. Yet if the flip of the Fed's coin were unrelated to subsequent economic performance, then we would conclude that real business cycle theorists are right about the neutrality of money.

Unfortunately for scientific progress, but fortunately for the economy, economists are not allowed to conduct such experiments. Instead, we must glean what we can from the data that history gives us.

One classic study in the history of monetary policy is the 1963 book by Milton Friedman and Anna Schwartz, *A Monetary History of the United States, 1867–1960.* This book describes the historical events that shaped decisions over monetary policy and the economic events that resulted from those decisions. Friedman and Schwartz claim, for instance, that the death in 1928 of Benjamin Strong, the president of the New York Federal Reserve Bank, was one cause of the Great Depression of the 1930s: Strong's death left a power vacuum at the Fed, which prevented the Fed from responding vigorously as economic conditions deteriorated. In other words, Strong's death, like the Fed's coin coming up tails, was a random event leading to more contractionary monetary policy.[6]

A more recent study by Christina Romer and David Romer follows in the footsteps of Friedman and Schwartz. The Romers carefully read through the

---

[5] Robert G. King and Charles I. Plosser, "Money, Credit, and Prices in a Real Business Cycle," *American Economic Review* 74 (June 1984): 363–380.

[6] Milton Friedman and Anna J. Schwartz, *A Monetary History of the United States, 1867–1960* (Princeton, NJ: Princeton University Press, 1960).

minutes of the meetings of the Federal Reserve's Open Market Committee, which sets monetary policy. From these minutes, they identified dates when the Fed appears to have shifted its policy toward reducing the rate of inflation. The Romers argue that these dates are, in essence, the equivalent of the Fed's coin coming up tails. They then show that the economy experienced a decline in output and employment after each of these dates. Thus, the Romers' evidence appears to establish the short-run nonneutrality of money.[7]

Interpretations of history, however, are always open to dispute. No one can be sure what would have happened during the 1930s had Benjamin Strong lived. Similarly, not everyone is convinced that the Romers' dates are as exogenous as a coin's flip: perhaps the Fed was actually responding to events that would have caused declining output and employment even without Fed action. Thus, although most economists are convinced that monetary policy has an important role in the business cycle, this judgment is based on the accumulation of evidence from many studies. There is no "smoking gun" that convinces absolutely everyone.

The Flexibility of Wages and Prices

Real business cycle theory assumes that wages and prices adjust quickly to clear markets, just as Crusoe always achieves his optimal level of GDP without any impediment from a market imperfection. Advocates of this theory believe that the market imperfection of sticky wages and prices is not important for understanding economic fluctuations. They also believe that the assumption of flexible prices is superior methodologically to the assumption of sticky prices, because it ties macroeconomic theory more closely to microeconomic theory.

Critics point out that many wages and prices are not flexible. They believe that this inflexibility explains both the existence of unemployment and the nonneutrality of money. To explain why prices are sticky, they rely on the various new Keynesian theories that we discuss in the next section.[8]

19-2 New Keynesian Economics

Most economists are skeptical of the theory of real business cycles and believe that short-run fluctuations in output and employment represent deviations from the natural levels of these variables. They think these deviations occur because wages and prices are slow to adjust to changing economic conditions. As we

[7] Christina Romer and David Romer, "Does Monetary Policy Matter? A New Test in the Spirit of Friedman and Schwartz," *NBER Macroeconomics Annual* (1989): 121–170.

[8] To read more about real business cycle theory, see N. Gregory Mankiw, "Real Business Cycles: A New Keynesian Perspective," *Journal of Economic Perspectives* 3 (Summer 1989): 79–90; Bennett T. McCallum, "Real Business Cycle Models," in R. Barro, ed., *Modern Business Cycle Theory* (Cambridge, MA: Harvard University Press, 1989), 16–50; and Charles I. Plosser, "Understanding Real Business Cycles," *Journal of Economic Perspectives* 3 (Summer 1989): 51–77.

discussed in Chapters 9 and 13, this stickiness makes the short-run aggregate supply curve upward sloping rather than vertical. As a result, fluctuations in aggregate demand cause short-run fluctuations in output and employment.

But why exactly are prices sticky? New Keynesian research has attempted to answer this question by examining the microeconomics behind short-run price adjustment. By doing so, it tries to put the traditional theories of short-run fluctuations on a firmer theoretical foundation.

Small Menu Costs and Aggregate-Demand Externalities

One reason prices do not adjust immediately in the short run is that there are costs to price adjustment. To change its prices, a firm may need to send out new catalogs to customers, distribute new price lists to its sales staff, or, in the case of a restaurant, print new menus. These costs of price adjustment, called **menu costs**, lead firms to adjust prices intermittently rather than continuously.

Economists disagree about whether menu costs explain the short-run stickiness of prices. Skeptics point out that menu costs are usually very small. How can small menu costs help to explain recessions, which are very costly for society? Proponents reply that small does not mean inconsequential: even though menu costs are small for the individual firm, they can have large effects on the economy as a whole.

According to proponents of the menu-cost hypothesis, to understand why prices adjust slowly, we must acknowledge that there are externalities to price adjustment: a price reduction by one firm benefits other firms in the economy. When a firm lowers the price it charges, it slightly lowers the average price level and thereby raises real money balances. The increase in real money balances expands aggregate income (by shifting the *LM* curve outward). The economic expansion in turn raises the demand for the products of all firms. This macroeconomic impact of one firm's price adjustment on the demand for all other firms' products is called an **aggregate-demand externality**.

In the presence of this aggregate-demand externality, small menu costs can make prices sticky, and this stickiness can have a large cost to society. Suppose that a firm originally sets its price too high and later must decide whether to cut its price. The firm makes this decision by comparing the benefit of a price cut—higher sales and profit—to the cost of price adjustment. Yet because of the aggregate-demand externality, the benefit to society of the price cut would exceed the benefit to the firm. The firm ignores this externality when making its decision, so it may decide not to pay the menu cost and cut its price even though the price cut is socially desirable. *Hence, sticky prices may be optimal for those setting prices, even though they are undesirable for the economy as a whole.*[9]

[9] For more on this topic, see N. Gregory Mankiw, "Small Menu Costs and Large Business Cycles: A Macroeconomic Model of Monopoly," *Quarterly Journal of Economics* 100 (May 1985): 529–537; George A. Akerlof and Janet L. Yellen, "A Near Rational Model of the Business Cycle, With Wage and Price Inertia," *Quarterly Journal of Economics* 100 (Supplement 1985): 823–838; and Olivier Jean Blanchard and Nobuhiro Kiyotaki, "Monopolistic Competition and the Effects of Aggregate Demand," *American Economic Review* 77 (September 1987): 647–666.

CASE STUDY

How Large Are Menu Costs?

When microeconomists discuss a firm's costs, they usually emphasize the labor, capital, and raw materials that are needed to produce the firm's output. The cost of changing prices is rarely mentioned. For many purposes, this omission is a reasonable simplification. Yet the cost of changing prices is not zero, as was established by a study of price changes in five large supermarket chains.

In this study, a group of economists examined a unique store-level data set to determine how large menu costs really are. They found that price adjustment "is a complex process, requiring dozens of steps and a nontrivial amount of resources." These resources include the labor cost of changing shelf prices, the costs of printing and delivering new price tags, and the cost of supervising the process. The data included detailed measurements of these costs; when necessary, a stopwatch was used to measure the labor input.

The study reported that for a typical store in a supermarket chain, menu costs add up to \$105,887 a year. This amount equals 0.70 percent of a store's revenue, or 35 percent of net profits. If that total is divided by the number of price changes that a store institutes in a given year on all of its products, the result is that each price change costs \$0.52.

A notable finding from this research is that the cost of changing prices depends on the legal environment. One supermarket chain examined in the study was operating in a state with an "item-pricing law," which required that a separate price tag be placed on each individual item sold (in addition to the price tag on the shelf). The law raised the estimated cost of a price change from \$0.52 to \$1.33. As one would expect, the higher cost of changing prices reduced the frequency of price adjustment: the supermarket chain operating under the item-pricing law changed 6.3 percent of product prices per week, compared to 15.6 percent for other chains.

These findings apply to only a single industry, so one should be cautious about extrapolating the results to the entire economy. Nonetheless, the authors of the study conclude that "the magnitude of the menu costs we find is large enough to be capable of having macroeconomic significance."[10]

Recessions as Coordination Failure

Some new Keynesian economists suggest that recessions result from a failure of coordination among economic decisionmakers. In recessions, output is low, workers are unemployed, and factories sit idle. It is possible to imagine allocations of resources in which everyone is better off: the high output and employment of the 1920s, for example, were clearly preferable to the low output and employment of the 1930s. If society fails to reach an outcome that is feasible and

[10] Daniel Levy, Mark Bergen, Shantanu Dutta, and Robert Venable, "The Magnitude of Menu Costs: Direct Evidence From Large Supermarket Chains," *Quarterly Journal of Economics* 112 (August 1997): 791–825. All dollar figures in this case study are expressed in 1991 dollars, because that is the year when the data were collected. If expressed in 2005 dollars, they would be about 40 percent larger.

that everyone prefers, then the members of society have failed to coordinate their behavior in some way.

Coordination problems can arise in the setting of wages and prices because those who set them must anticipate the actions of other wage and price setters. Union leaders negotiating wages are concerned about the concessions other unions will win. Firms setting prices are mindful of the prices other firms will charge.

To see how a recession could arise as a failure of coordination, consider the following parable. The economy is made up of two firms. After a fall in the money supply, each firm must decide whether to cut its price, based on its goal of maximizing profit. Each firm's profit, however, depends not only on its pricing decision but also on the decision made by the other firm.

The choices facing each firm are listed in Figure 19-2, which shows how the profits of the two firms depend on their actions. If neither firm cuts its price, real money balances are low, a recession ensues, and each firm makes a profit of only \$15. If both firms cut their prices, real money balances are high, a recession is avoided, and each firm makes a profit of \$30. Although both firms prefer to avoid a recession, neither can do so by its own actions. If one firm cuts its price and the other does not, a recession follows. The firm making the price cut makes only \$5, while the other firm makes \$15.

The essence of this parable is that each firm's decision influences the set of outcomes available to the other firm. When one firm cuts its price, it improves the position of the other firm, because the other firm can then act to avoid the recession. This positive impact of one firm's price cut on the other firm's profit opportunities might arise from an aggregate-demand externality.

What outcome should we expect in this economy? On the one hand, if each firm expects the other to cut its price, both will cut prices, resulting in the preferred outcome in which each makes \$30. On the other hand, if each firm expects the other to maintain its price, both will maintain their prices, resulting in the inferior outcome in which each makes \$15. Either of these outcomes is possible: economists say that there are *multiple equilibria.*

FIGURE 19-2

		Firm 2: Cut Price	Firm 2: Keep High Price
Firm 1	Cut Price	**Firm 1** makes \$30 **Firm 2** makes \$30	**Firm 1** makes \$5 **Firm 2** makes \$15
	Keep High Price	**Firm 1** makes \$15 **Firm 2** makes \$5	**Firm 1** makes \$15 **Firm 2** makes \$15

Price Setting and Coordination Failure This figure shows a hypothetical "game" between two firms, each of which is deciding whether to cut prices after a fall in the money supply. Each firm must choose a strategy without knowing the strategy the other firm will choose. What outcome would you expect?

The inferior outcome, in which each firm makes $15, is an example of a **coordination failure**. If the two firms could coordinate, they would both cut their price and reach the preferred outcome. In the real world, unlike in our parable, coordination is often difficult because the number of firms setting prices is large. *The moral of the story is that prices can be sticky simply because people expect them to be sticky, even though stickiness is in no one's interest.*[11]

The Staggering of Wages and Prices

Not everyone in the economy sets new wages and prices at the same time. Instead, the adjustment of wages and prices throughout the economy is staggered. Staggering slows the process of coordination and price adjustment. In particular, *staggering makes the overall level of wages and prices adjust gradually, even when individual wages and prices change frequently*.

Consider the following example. Suppose first that price setting is synchronized: every firm adjusts its price on the first day of every month. If the money supply and aggregate demand rise on May 10, output will be higher from May 10 to June 1 because prices are fixed during this interval. But on June 1 all firms will raise their prices in response to the higher demand, ending the boom.

Now suppose that price setting is staggered: half the firms set prices on the first of each month and half on the fifteenth. If the money supply rises on May 10, then half the firms can raise their prices on May 15. But these firms will probably not raise their prices very much. Because half the firms will not be changing their prices on the fifteenth, a price increase by any firm will raise that firm's *relative* price, causing it to lose customers. (By contrast, if all firms are synchronized, all firms can raise prices together, leaving relative prices unaffected.) If the May 15 price setters make little adjustment in their prices, then the other firms will make little adjustment when their turn comes on June 1, because they also want to avoid relative price changes. And so on. The price level rises slowly as the result of small price increases on the first and the fifteenth of each month. Hence, staggering makes the overall price level adjust sluggishly, because no firm wishes to be the first to post a substantial price increase.

Staggering also affects wage determination. Consider, for example, how a fall in the money supply works its way through the economy. A smaller money supply reduces aggregate demand, which in turn requires a proportionate fall in nominal wages to maintain full employment. Each worker might be willing to take a lower nominal wage if all other wages were to fall proportionately. But each worker is reluctant to be the first to take a pay cut, knowing that this means, at least temporarily, a fall in his or her relative wage. Because the setting of wages is staggered, the reluctance of each worker to reduce his or her wage first makes

---

[11] For more on coordination failure, see Russell Cooper and Andrew John, "Coordinating Coordination Failures in Keynesian Models," *Quarterly Journal of Economics* 103 (1988): 441–463; and Laurence Ball and David Romer, "Sticky Prices as Coordination Failure," *American Economic Review* 81 (June 1991): 539–552.

the overall level of wages slow to respond to changes in aggregate demand. In other words, the staggered setting of individual wages makes the overall level of wages sticky.[12]

CASE STUDY

If You Want to Know Why Firms Have Sticky Prices, Ask Them

How sticky are prices, and why are they sticky? As we have seen, these questions are at the heart of new Keynesian theories of short-run economic fluctuations (as well as of the traditional model of aggregate demand and aggregate supply). In an intriguing study, economist Alan Blinder attacked these questions directly by surveying firms about their price adjustment decisions.

Blinder began by asking firm managers how often they change prices. The answers, summarized in Table 19-1, yielded two conclusions. First, sticky prices are quite common. The typical firm in the economy adjusts its prices once or twice a year. Second, there are large differences among firms in the frequency of price adjustment. About 10 percent of firms change prices more often than once a week, and about the same number change prices less often than once a year.

TABLE 19-1

The Frequency of Price Adjustment

This table is based on answers to the question: How often do the prices of your most important products change in a typical year?

Frequency	Percentage of Firms
Less than once	10.2
Once	39.3
1.01 to 2	15.6
2.01 to 4	12.9
4.01 to 12	7.5
12.01 to 52	4.3
52.01 to 365	8.6
More than 365	1.6

Source: Table 4.1, Alan S. Blinder, "On Sticky Prices: Academic Theories Meet the Real World," in N. G. Mankiw, ed., *Monetary Policy* (Chicago: University of Chicago Press, 1994), 117–154.

[12] For more on the effects of staggering, see John Taylor, "Staggered Price Setting in a Macro Model," *American Economic Review* 69 (May 1979): 108–113; and Olivier J. Blanchard, "Price Asynchronization and Price Level Inertia," in R. Dornbusch and Mario Henrique Simonsen, eds., *Inflation, Debt, and Indexation* (Cambridge, MA: MIT Press, 1983), 3–24.

Blinder then asked the firm managers why they don't change prices more often. In particular, he explained to the managers 12 economic theories of sticky prices and asked them to judge how well each of these theories describe their firms. Table 19-2 summarizes the theories and ranks them by the percentage of managers who accepted the theory. Notice that each of the theories was endorsed by some of the managers, and each was rejected by a large number as well. One interpretation is that different theories apply to different firms, depending on industry characteristics, and that price stickiness is a macroeconomic phenomenon without a single microeconomic explanation.

TABLE 19-2

Theories of Price Stickiness

Theory and Brief Description	Percentage of Managers Who Accepted Theory
Coordination failure: Firms hold back on price changes, waiting for others to go first	60.6
Cost-based pricing with lags: Price rises are delayed until costs rise	55.5
Delivery lags, service, etc.: Firms prefer to vary other product attributes, such as delivery lags, service, or product quality	54.8
Implicit contracts: Firms tacitly agree to stabilize prices, perhaps out of "fairness" to customers	50.4
Nominal contracts: Prices are fixed by explicit contracts	35.7
Costs of price adjustment: Firms incur costs by changing prices	30.0
Procyclical elasticity: Demand curves become less elastic as they shift in	29.7
Pricing points: Certain prices (e.g., $9.99) have special psychological significance	24.0
Inventories: Firms vary inventory stocks instead of prices	20.9
Constant marginal cost: Marginal cost is flat and markups are constant	19.7
Hierarchical delays: Bureaucratic delays slow down decisions	13.6
Judging quality by price: Firms fear customers will mistake price cuts for reductions in quality	10.0

Source: Tables 4.3 and 4.4, Alan S. Blinder, "On Sticky Prices: Academic Theories Meet the Real World," in N. G. Mankiw, ed., *Monetary Policy* (Chicago: University of Chicago Press, 1994), 117–154.

Among the dozen theories, coordination failure tops the list. According to Blinder, this is an important finding, because it suggests that the theory of coordination failure explains price stickiness, which in turn explains why the economy experiences short-run fluctuations around its natural rate. He writes, "The most obvious policy implication of the model is that more coordinated wage and price setting—somehow achieved—could improve welfare. But if this proves difficult or impossible, the door is opened to activist monetary policy to cure recessions."[13]

19-3 Conclusion

Recent developments in the theory of short-run economic fluctuations remind us that we do not understand economic fluctuations as well as we would like. Fundamental questions about the economy remain open to dispute. Is the stickiness of wages and prices a key to understanding economic fluctuations? Does monetary policy have real effects?

The way economists answer these questions affects how they view the role of economic policy. Economists who believe that wages and prices are sticky, such as those pursuing new Keynesian theories, often believe that monetary and fiscal policy should be used to try to stabilize the economy. Price stickiness is a type of market imperfection, and it leaves open the possibility that government policies can raise economic well-being for society as a whole.

By contrast, real business cycle theory suggests that the government's influence on the economy is limited and that even if the government could stabilize the economy, it should not try to do so. According to this theory, the ups and downs of the business cycle are the natural and efficient response of the economy to changing technological possibilities. The standard real business cycle model does not include any type of market imperfection. In this model, the "invisible hand" of the marketplace guides the economy to an optimal allocation of resources.

To evaluate alternative views of the economy, research economists bring to bear a wide variety of evidence, as we have seen in this chapter's five case studies. They have used micro data to study intertemporal substitution, macro data to examine the cyclical behavior of technology, the minutes of Fed meetings to test monetary neutrality, business studies to measure the magnitude of menu costs, and surveys to judge theories of price stickiness. Economists differ in which pieces of evidence they find most convincing, and so the theory of economic fluctuations remains a source of debate.

Although this chapter has divided recent research into two distinct camps, not all economists fall entirely into one camp or the other. Over time, more economists

[13] To read more about this study, see Alan S. Blinder, "On Sticky Prices: Academic Theories Meet the Real World," in N. G. Mankiw, ed., *Monetary Policy* (Chicago: University of Chicago Press, 1994), 117–154; or Alan S. Blinder, Elie R.D. Canetti, David E. Lebow, and Jeremy E. Rudd, *Asking About Prices: A New Approach to Understanding Price Stickiness,* (New York: Russell Sage Foundation, 1998).

have been trying to incorporate the strengths of both approaches into their research. Real business cycle theory emphasizes intertemporal optimization and forward-looking behavior, whereas new Keynesian theory stresses the importance of sticky prices and other market imperfections. Increasingly, theories at the research frontier meld many of these elements to advance our understanding of economic fluctuations. It is this kind of work that makes macroeconomics an exciting field of study.[14]

Summary

1. The theory of real business cycles is an explanation of short-run economic fluctuations built on the assumptions of the classical model, including the classical dichotomy and the flexibility of wages and prices. According to this theory, economic fluctuations are the natural and efficient response of the economy to changing economic circumstances, especially changes in technology.
2. Advocates and critics of real business cycle theory disagree about whether employment fluctuations represent intertemporal substitution of labor, whether technology shocks cause most economic fluctuations, whether monetary policy affects real variables, and whether the short-run stickiness of wages and prices is important for understanding economic fluctuations.
3. New Keynesian research on short-run economic fluctuations builds on the traditional model of aggregate demand and aggregate supply and tries to provide a better explanation of why wages and prices are sticky in the short run. One new Keynesian theory suggests that even small costs of price adjustment can have large macroeconomic effects because of aggregate-demand externalities. Another theory suggests that recessions occur as a type of coordination failure. A third theory suggests that staggering in price adjustment makes the overall price level sluggish in response to changing economic conditions.

KEY CONCEPTS

Real business cycle theory
New Keynesian economics
Intertemporal substitution of labor
Solow residual
Labor hoarding
Menu costs
Aggregate-demand externality
Coordination failure

[14] For some research that brings together the different approaches, see Marvin Goodfriend and Robert King, "The New Neoclassical Synthesis and the Role of Monetary Policy," *NBER Macroeconomics Annual* (1997): 231–283; Julio Rotemberg and Michael Woodford, "An Optimization-Based Econometric Framework for the Evaluation of Monetary Policy," *NBER Macroeconomics Annual* (1997): 297–346; Richard Clarida, Jordi Gali, and Mark Gertler, "The Science of Monetary Policy: A New Keynesian Perspective," *Journal of Economic Literature* 37 (December 1999): 1661–1707. These papers examine models in which both forward-looking optimizing behavior and sticky prices play central roles in explaining the business cycle and the short-run effects of monetary policy.

QUESTIONS FOR REVIEW

1. How does real business cycle theory explain fluctuations in employment?
2. What are the four central disagreements in the debate over real business cycle theory?
3. How does the staggering of price adjustments by individual firms affect the adjustment of the overall price level to a monetary contraction?
4. According to surveys, how often does the typical firm change its prices? How do firm managers explain the stickiness of their prices?

PROBLEMS AND APPLICATIONS

1. According to real business cycle theory, permanent and transitory shocks to technology should have very different effects on the economy. Use the parable of Robinson Crusoe to compare the effects of a transitory shock (good weather expected to last only a few days) and a permanent shock (a beneficial change in weather patterns). Which shock would have a greater effect on Crusoe's work effort? On GDP? Is it possible that one of these shocks might reduce work effort?
2. Suppose that prices are fully flexible and that the output of the economy fluctuates because of shocks to technology, as real business cycle theory claims.
   a. If the Federal Reserve holds the money supply constant, what will happen to the price level as output fluctuates?
   b. If the Federal Reserve adjusts the money supply to stabilize the price level, what will happen to the money supply as output fluctuates?
   c. Many economists have observed that fluctuations in the money supply are positively correlated with fluctuations in output. Is this evidence against real business cycle theory?
3. Coordination failure is an idea with many applications. Here is one: Andy and Ben are running a business together. If both work hard, the business is a success, and they each earn \$100 in profit. If one of them fails to work hard, the business is less successful, and they each earn \$70. If neither works hard, the business is even less successful, and they each earn \$60 in profit. Working hard takes \$20 worth of effort.
   a. Set up this "game" as in Figure 19-2.
   b. What outcome would Andy and Ben prefer?
   c. What outcome would occur if each expected his partner to work hard?
   d. What outcome would occur if each expected his partner to be lazy?
   e. Is this a good description of the relationship among partners? Why or why not?
4. (This problem uses basic microeconomics.) The chapter discusses the price-adjustment decisions of firms with menu costs. This problem asks you to consider that issue more analytically in the simple case of a single firm.
   a. Draw a diagram describing a monopoly firm, including a downward-sloping demand curve and a cost curve. (For simplicity, assume that marginal cost is constant, so the cost curve is a horizontal line.) Show the profit-maximizing price and quantity. Show the areas that represent profit and consumer surplus at this optimum.
   b. Now suppose the firm has previously announced a price slightly above the optimum. Show this price and the quantity sold. Show the area representing the lost profit from the excessive price. Show the area representing the lost consumer surplus.
   c. The firm decides whether to cut its price by comparing the extra profit from a lower price to the menu cost. In making this decision, what externality is the firm ignoring? In what sense is the firm's price-adjustment decision inefficient from the standpoint of society as a whole?

What We Know, What We Don't

If all economists were laid end to end, they would not reach a conclusion.

— *George Bernard Shaw*

The theory of economics does not furnish a body of settled conclusions immediately applicable to policy. It is a method rather than a doctrine, an apparatus of the mind, which helps its possessor to draw correct conclusions.

— *John Maynard Keynes*

The first chapter of this book states that the purpose of macroeconomics is to understand economic events and to improve economic policy. Now that we have developed and used many of the most important models in the macroeconomist's toolbox, we can assess whether macroeconomists have achieved these goals.

Any fair assessment of macroeconomics today must admit that the science is incomplete. There are some principles that almost all macroeconomists accept and on which we can rely when trying to analyze events or formulate policies. Yet there are also many questions about the economy that remain open to debate. In this last chapter we briefly review the central lessons of macroeconomics, and we discuss the most pressing unresolved questions.

The Four Most Important Lessons of Macroeconomics

We begin with four lessons that have recurred throughout this book and that most economists today would endorse. Each lesson tells us how policy can influence a key economic variable—output, inflation, or unemployment—either in the long run or in the short run.

Lesson 1: In the long run, a country's capacity to produce goods and services determines the standard of living of its citizens.

Of all the measures of economic performance introduced in Chapter 2 and used throughout this book, the one that best measures economic well-being is GDP. Real GDP measures the economy's total output of goods and services and, therefore, a country's ability to satisfy the needs and desires of its citizens. Nations with higher GDP per person have more of almost everything—bigger homes, more cars, higher literacy, better health care, longer life expectancy, and more Internet connections. Perhaps the most important question in macroeconomics is what determines the level and the growth of GDP.

The models in Chapters 3, 7, and 8 identify the long-run determinants of GDP. In the long run, GDP depends on the factors of production—capital and labor—and on the technology for turning capital and labor into output. GDP grows when the factors of production increase or when the economy becomes better at turning these inputs into an output of goods and services.

This lesson has an obvious but important corollary: public policy can raise GDP in the long run only by improving the productive capability of the economy. There are many ways in which policymakers can attempt to do this. Policies that raise national saving—either through higher public saving or higher private saving—eventually lead to a larger capital stock. Policies that raise the efficiency of labor—such as those that improve education or increase technological progress—lead to a more productive use of capital and labor. Policies that improve a nation's institutions—such as crackdowns on official corruption—lead to both greater capital accumulation and a more efficient use of the economy's resources. All these policies increase the economy's output of goods and services and, thereby, improve the standard of living. It is less clear, however, which of these policies is the best way to raise an economy's productive capability.

Lesson 2: In the short run, aggregate demand influences the amount of goods and services that a country produces.

Although the economy's ability to *supply* goods and services is the sole determinant of GDP in the long run, in the short run GDP depends also on the aggregate *demand* for goods and services. Aggregate demand is of key importance because prices are sticky in the short run. The *IS-LM* model developed in Chapters 10 and 11 shows what causes changes in aggregate demand and, therefore, short-run fluctuations in GDP.

Because aggregate demand influences output in the short run, all the variables that affect aggregate demand can influence economic fluctuations. Monetary policy, fiscal policy, and shocks to the money and goods markets are often responsible for year-to-year changes in output and employment. Because changes in aggregate demand are crucial to short-run fluctuations, policymakers monitor the economy closely. Before making any change in monetary or fiscal policy, they want to know whether the economy is booming or heading into a recession.

Lesson 3: In the long run, the rate of money growth determines the rate of inflation, but it does not affect the rate of unemployment.

In addition to GDP, inflation and unemployment are among the most closely watched measures of economic performance. Chapter 2 discussed how these two variables are measured, and subsequent chapters developed models to explain how they are determined.

The long-run analysis of Chapter 4 stresses that growth in the money supply is the ultimate determinant of inflation. That is, in the long run, a currency loses real value over time if and only if the central bank prints more and more of it. This lesson can explain the decade-to-decade variation in the inflation rate that we have observed in the United States, as well as the far more dramatic hyperinflations that various countries have experienced from time to time.

We have also seen many of the long-run effects of high money growth and high inflation. In Chapter 4 we saw that, according to the Fisher effect, high inflation raises the nominal interest rate (so that the real interest rate remains unaffected). In Chapter 5 we saw that high inflation leads to a depreciation of the currency in the market for foreign exchange.

"And please let Ben Bernanke accept the things he cannot change, give him the courage to change the things he can and the wisdom to know the difference."

The long-run determinants of unemployment are very different. According to the classical dichotomy—the irrelevance of nominal variables in the determination of real variables—growth in the money supply does not affect unemployment in the long run. As we saw in Chapter 6, the natural rate of unemployment is determined by the rates of job separation and job finding, which in turn are determined by the process of job search and by the rigidity of the real wage.

Thus, we concluded that persistent inflation and persistent unemployment are unrelated problems. To combat inflation in the long run, policymakers must reduce the growth in the money supply. To combat unemployment, they must alter the structure of labor markets. In the long run, there is no tradeoff between inflation and unemployment.

Lesson 4: In the short run, policymakers who control monetary and fiscal policy face a tradeoff between inflation and unemployment.

Although inflation and unemployment are not related in the long run, in the short run there is a tradeoff between these two variables, which is illustrated by the short-run Phillips curve. As we discussed in Chapter 13, policymakers can use monetary and fiscal policies to expand aggregate demand, which lowers unemployment and raises inflation. Or they can use these policies to contract aggregate demand, which raises unemployment and lowers inflation.

Policymakers face a fixed tradeoff between inflation and unemployment only in the short run. Over time, the short-run Phillips curve shifts for two reasons. First, supply shocks, such as changes in the price of oil, change the short-run tradeoff; an adverse supply shock offers policymakers the difficult choice of higher inflation or higher unemployment. Second, when people change their expectations of inflation, the short-run tradeoff between inflation and unemployment changes. The adjustment of expectations ensures that the tradeoff exists only in the short run. That is, only in the short run does unemployment deviate from its natural rate, and only in the short run does monetary policy have real effects. In the long run, the classical model of Chapters 3 through 8 describes the world.

The Four Most Important Unresolved Questions of Macroeconomics

So far, we have been discussing some of the broad lessons about which most economists would agree. We now turn to four questions about which there is continuing debate. Some of the disagreements concern the validity of alternative economic theories; others concern how economic theory should be applied to economic policy.

Question 1: How should policymakers try to promote growth in the economy's natural level of output?

The economy's natural level of output depends on the amount of capital, the amount of labor, and the level of technology. Any policy designed to raise output in the long run must aim to increase the amount of capital, improve the use of labor, or enhance the available technology. There is, however, no simple and cost-free way to achieve these goals.

The Solow growth model of Chapters 7 and 8 shows that increasing the amount of capital requires raising the economy's rate of saving and investment. Therefore, many economists advocate policies to increase national saving. Yet the Solow model also shows that raising the capital stock requires a period of reduced consumption for current generations. Some argue that policymakers should not encourage current generations to make this sacrifice, because technological progress will ensure that future generations are better off than current generations. (One waggish economist asked, "What has posterity ever done for me?") Even those who advocate increased saving and investment disagree about how to encourage additional saving and whether the investment should be in privately owned plants and equipment or in public infrastructure, such as roads and schools.

To improve the economy's use of its labor force, most policymakers would like to lower the natural rate of unemployment. As we discussed in Chapter 6, the large differences in unemployment that we observe across countries, and the large changes in unemployment we observe over time within countries, suggest that the natural rate is not an immutable constant but depends on a nation's policies and institutions. Yet reducing unemployment is a task fraught with perils. The natural rate of unemployment could likely be reduced by decreasing unemployment-insurance benefits (and thus increasing the search effort of the unemployed) or by decreasing the minimum wage (and thus bringing wages closer to equilibrium levels). Yet these policies would also hurt some of those members of society most in need and, therefore, do not command a consensus among economists.

In many countries, the natural level of output is depressed by a lack of institutions that people in developed nations take for granted. U.S. citizens today do not worry about revolutions, coups, or civil wars. For the most part, they trust the police and the court system to respect the laws, maintain order, protect property rights, and enforce private contracts. In nations without such institutions, however, people face the wrong incentives: if creating something of economic value is a less reliable path to riches than is stealing from a neighbor, an economy is unlikely to prosper. All economists agree that setting up the right institutions is a prerequisite for increasing growth in the world's poor nations, but changing a nation's institutions requires overcoming some difficult political hurdles.

Increasing the rate of technological progress is, according to some economists, the most important objective for public policy. The Solow growth model shows that persistent growth in living standards requires continuing technological progress. Despite much work on the new theories of endogenous growth, which highlight the societal decisions that determine technological progress, economists cannot offer a reliable recipe to ensure rapid advances in technology. The good news is that around 1995, productivity growth in the United States accelerated, ending the productivity slowdown that began in the mid-1970s. Yet it remains unclear how long this propitious development will last and whether it will spread to the rest of the world.

Question 2: Should policymakers try to stabilize the economy?

The model of aggregate supply and aggregate demand developed in Chapters 9 through 13 shows how various shocks to the economy cause economic fluctuations and how monetary and fiscal policy can influence these fluctuations. Some economists believe that policymakers should use this analysis in an attempt to stabilize the economy. They believe that monetary and fiscal policy should try to offset shocks in order to keep output and employment close to their natural levels.

Yet, as we discussed in Chapter 14, others are skeptical about our ability to stabilize the economy. These economists cite the long and variable lags inherent in economic policymaking, the poor record of economic forecasting, and our still-limited understanding of the economy. They conclude that the best policy is a passive one. In addition, many economists believe that policymakers are all too often opportunistic or follow time-inconsistent policies. They conclude that policymakers should not have discretion over monetary and fiscal policy but should be committed to following a fixed policy rule. Or, at the very least, their discretion should be somewhat constrained, as is the case when central banks adopt a policy of inflation targeting.

A related question is whether the benefits of economic stabilization—assuming stabilization could be achieved—would be large or small. Without any change in the natural rate of unemployment, stabilization policy can only reduce the magnitude of fluctuations around the natural rate. Thus, successful stabilization policy would eliminate booms as well as recessions. Some economists have suggested that the average gain from stabilization would be small.

Finally, not all economists endorse the model of economic fluctuations developed in Chapters 9 through 13, which assumes sticky prices and monetary nonneutrality. According to real business cycle theory, which we discussed in Chapter 19, economic fluctuations are the optimal response of the economy to changing technology. This theory suggests that policymakers should not stabilize the economy, even if this were possible.

Question 3: How costly is inflation, and how costly is reducing inflation?

Whenever prices are rising, policymakers confront the question of whether to pursue policies to reduce the rate of inflation. To make this decision, they must compare the cost of allowing inflation to continue at its current rate to the cost of reducing inflation. Yet economists cannot offer accurate estimates of either of these two costs.

The cost of inflation is a topic on which economists and laymen often disagree. When inflation reached 10 percent per year in the late 1970s, opinion polls showed that the public viewed inflation as a major economic problem. Yet, as we discussed in Chapter 4, when economists try to identify the social costs of inflation, they can point only to shoeleather costs, menu costs, the costs of a nonindexed tax system, and so on. These costs become large when countries experience hyperinflation, but they seem relatively minor at the moderate rates of inflation experienced in most major economies. Some economists believe that the public confuses inflation with other economic problems that coincide with inflation. For example, growth in productivity and real wages slowed in the 1970s; some laymen might have viewed inflation as the cause of the slowdown in real wages. Yet it is also possible that economists are mistaken: perhaps inflation is in fact very costly, and we have yet to figure out why.

The cost of reducing inflation is a topic on which economists often disagree among themselves. As we discussed in Chapter 13, the standard view—as described by the short-run Phillips curve—is that reducing inflation requires a period of low output and high unemployment. According to this view, the cost of reducing inflation is measured by the sacrifice ratio, which is the number of percentage points of a year's GDP that must be forgone to reduce inflation by 1 percentage point.

Some economists think that the cost of reducing inflation can be much smaller than standard estimates of the sacrifice ratio indicate. According to the rational-expectations approach discussed in Chapter 13, if a disinflationary policy is announced in advance and is credible, people will adjust their expectations quickly, so the disinflation need not cause a recession. According to the real business cycle models discussed in Chapter 19, prices are flexible and money is neutral, so disinflationary monetary policy will not affect the economy's output of goods and services.

Other economists believe that the cost of reducing inflation is much larger than standard estimates of the sacrifice ratio indicate. The theories of hysteresis discussed in Chapter 13 suggest that a recession caused by disinflationary policy could raise the natural rate of unemployment. If so, the cost of reducing inflation is not merely a temporary recession but a persistently higher level of unemployment.

Because the costs of inflation and disinflation remain open to debate, economists sometimes offer conflicting advice to policymakers. Perhaps with further research, we can reach a consensus on the benefits of low inflation and the best way to achieve it.

Question 4: How big a problem are government budget deficits?

Government debt is a perennial topic of debate among policymakers. In the United States, large budget deficits caused the ratio of government debt to GDP to double from 1980 to 1995—an event unprecedented in peacetime. The federal government's budget was under control by the late 1990s and even turned into a surplus, but the situation reversed in the early 2000s, as recession, war, and changes in tax policy caused deficits to reemerge. Even more troublesome, however, is the long-term fiscal picture. Many economists believe that budget deficits will get even larger when the large baby-boom generation reaches retirement age and starts drawing on the Social Security and Medicare benefits that the government provides to the elderly.

Most models in this book, and most economists, take the traditional view of government debt. According to this view, when the government runs a budget deficit and issues debt, it reduces national saving, which in turn leads to lower investment and a trade deficit. In the long run, it leads to a smaller steady-state capital stock and a larger foreign debt. Those who hold the traditional view conclude that government debt places a burden on future generations.

Yet, as we discussed in Chapter 15, some economists are skeptical of this assessment. Advocates of the Ricardian view of government debt stress that a budget deficit merely represents a substitution of future taxes for current taxes. As long as consumers are forward-looking, as the theories of consumption presented in Chapter 16 assume, they will save today to meet their or their children's future tax liability. These economists believe that government debt has only a minor effect on the economy.

Still other economists believe that standard measures of fiscal policy are too flawed to be of much use. Although the government's choices regarding taxes and spending have great influence on the welfare of different generations, many of these choices are not reflected in the size of the government debt. The level of Social Security benefits and taxes, for instance, determines the welfare of the elder beneficiaries versus the working-age taxpayers, but measures of the budget deficit do not reflect this policy choice. According to some economists, we should stop focusing on the government's current budget deficit and concentrate instead on the longer-term generational impacts of fiscal policy.

Conclusion

Economists and policymakers must deal with ambiguity. The current state of macroeconomics offers many insights, but it also leaves many questions open. The challenge for economists is to find answers to these questions and to expand our knowledge. The challenge for policymakers is to use the knowledge we now have to improve economic performance. Both challenges are formidable, but neither is insuperable.

glossary

Accelerator model: The model according to which investment depends on the change in output.

Accommodating policy: A policy that yields to the effect of a shock and thereby prevents the shock from being disruptive; for example, a policy that raises aggregate demand in response to an adverse supply shock, sustaining the effect of the shock on prices and keeping output at its natural level.

Accounting profit: The amount of revenue remaining for the owners of a firm after all the factors of production except capital have been compensated. (Cf. economic profit, profit.)

Acyclical: Moving in no consistent direction over the business cycle. (Cf. countercyclical, procyclical.)

Adaptive expectations: An approach that assumes that people form their expectation of a variable based on recently observed values of the variable. (Cf. rational expectations.)

Adverse selection: An unfavorable sorting of individuals by their own choices; for example, in efficiency-wage theory, when a wage cut induces good workers to quit and bad workers to remain with the firm.

Aggregate: Total for the whole economy.

Aggregate demand curve: The negative relationship between the price level and the aggregate quantity of output demanded that arises from the interaction between the goods market and the money market.

Aggregate-demand externality: The macroeconomic impact of one firm's price adjustment on the demand for all other firms' products.

Aggregate supply curve: The relationship between the price level and the aggregate quantity of output firms produce.

Animal spirits: Exogenous and perhaps self-fulfilling waves of optimism and pessimism about the state of the economy that, according to some economists, influence the level of investment.

Appreciation: A rise in the value of a currency relative to other currencies in the market for foreign exchange. (Cf. depreciation.)

Arbitrage: The act of buying an item in one market and selling it at a higher price in another market in order to profit from the price differential in the two markets.

Automatic stabilizer: A policy that reduces the amplitude of economic fluctuations without regular and deliberate changes in economic policy; for example, an income tax system that automatically reduces taxes when income falls.

Average propensity to consume (*APC*): The ratio of consumption to income (C/Y).

Balance sheet: An accounting statement that shows assets and liabilities.

Balanced budget: A budget in which receipts equal expenditures.

Balanced trade: A situation in which the value of imports equals the value of exports, so net exports equal zero.

Baumol–Tobin model: A model of money demand positing that people choose optimal money holdings by comparing the opportunity cost of the forgone interest from holding money and the benefit of making less frequent trips to the bank.

Bond: A document representing an interest-bearing debt of the issuer, usually a corporation or the government.

Borrowing constraint: A restriction on the amount a person can borrow from financial institutions, limiting that person's ability to spend his or her future income today; also called a liquidity constraint.

Budget constraint: The limit that income places on expenditure. (Cf. intertemporal budget constraint.)

Budget deficit: A shortfall of receipts from expenditure.

Budget surplus: An excess of receipts over expenditure.

Business cycle: Economy-wide fluctuations in output, incomes, and employment.

Business fixed investment: Equipment and structures that businesses buy for use in future production.

Capital: 1. The stock of equipment and structures used in production. 2. The funds to finance the accumulation of equipment and structures.

Capital budgeting: An accounting procedure that measures both assets and liabilities.

Central bank: The institution responsible for the conduct of monetary policy, such as the Federal Reserve in the United States.

Classical dichotomy: The theoretical separation of real and nominal variables in the classical model, which implies that nominal variables do not influence real variables. (Cf. neutrality of money.)

Classical model: A model of the economy derived from the ideas of the classical, or pre-Keynesian, economists; a model based on the assumptions that wages and prices adjust to clear markets and that monetary policy does not influence real variables. (Cf. Keynesian model.)

Closed economy: An economy that does not engage in international trade. (Cf. open economy.)

Cobb–Douglas production function: A production function of the form $F(K, L) = AK^{\alpha}L^{1-\alpha}$, where K is capital, L is labor, and A and α are parameters.

Commodity money: Money that is intrinsically useful and would be valued even if it did not serve as money. (Cf. fiat money, money.)

Competition: A situation in which there are many individuals or firms, so that the actions of any one of them do not influence market prices.

Constant returns to scale: A property of a production function whereby a proportionate increase in all factors of production leads to an increase in output of the same proportion.

Consumer price index (CPI): A measure of the overall level of prices that shows the cost of a fixed basket of consumer goods relative to the cost of the same basket in a base year.

Consumption: Goods and services purchased by consumers.

Consumption function: A relationship showing the determinants of consumption; for example, a relationship between consumption and disposable income, $C = C(Y - T)$.

Contractionary policy: Policy that reduces aggregate demand, real income, and employment. (Cf. expansionary policy.)

Coordination failure: A situation in which decision makers reach an outcome that is inferior for all of them because of their inability to jointly choose strategies that would result in a preferred outcome.

Corporate income tax: The tax levied on the accounting profit of corporations.

Cost of capital: The amount forgone by holding a unit of capital for one period, including interest, depreciation, and the gain or loss from the change in the price of capital.

Cost-push inflation: Inflation resulting from shocks to aggregate supply. (Cf. demand-pull inflation.)

Countercyclical: Moving in the opposite direction from output, incomes, and employment over the business cycle; rising during recessions and falling during recoveries. (Cf. acyclical, procyclical.)

CPI: *See* consumer price index.

Crowding out: The reduction in investment that results when expansionary fiscal policy raises the interest rate.

Currency: The sum of outstanding paper money and coins.

Cyclical unemployment: The unemployment associated with short-run economic fluctuations; the deviation of the unemployment rate from the natural rate.

Cyclically adjusted budget deficit: The budget deficit adjusted for the influence of the business cycle on government spending and tax revenue; the budget deficit that would occur if the economy's production and employment were at their natural levels. Also called full-employment budget deficit.

Debt-deflation: A theory according to which an unexpected fall in the price level redistributes real wealth from debtors to creditors and, therefore, reduces total spending in the economy.

Deflation: A decrease in the overall level of prices. (Cf. disinflation, inflation.)

Deflator: *See* GDP deflator.

Demand deposits: Assets that are held in banks and can be used on demand to make transactions, such as checking accounts.

Demand-pull inflation: Inflation resulting from shocks to aggregate demand. (Cf. cost-push inflation.)

Demand shocks: Exogenous events that shift the aggregate demand curve.

Depreciation: 1. The reduction in the capital stock that occurs over time because of aging and use. 2. A fall in the value of a currency relative to other currencies in the market for foreign exchange. (Cf. appreciation.)

Depression: A very severe recession.

Devaluation: An action by the central bank to decrease the value of a currency under a system of fixed exchange rates. (Cf. revaluation.)

Diminishing marginal product: A characteristic of a production function whereby the marginal product of a factor falls as the amount of the factor increases while all other factors are held constant.

Discount rate: The interest rate that the Fed charges when it makes loans to banks.

Discounting: The reduction in value of future expenditure and receipts, compared to current expenditure and receipts, resulting from the presence of a positive interest rate.

Discouraged workers: Individuals who have left the labor force because they believe that there is little hope of finding a job.

Disinflation: A reduction in the rate at which prices are rising. (Cf. deflation, inflation.)

Disposable income: Income remaining after the payment of taxes.

Dominated asset: An asset that offers an inferior return compared to another asset in all possible realizations of future uncertainty.

Double coincidence of wants: A situation in which two individuals each have precisely the good that the other wants.

Economic profit: The amount of revenue remaining for the owners of a firm after all the factors of production have been compensated. (Cf. accounting profit, profit.)

Efficiency of labor: A variable in the Solow growth model that measures the health, education, skills, and knowledge of the labor force.

Efficiency units of labor: A measure of the labor force that incorporates both the number of workers and the efficiency of each worker.

Efficiency-wage theories: Theories of real-wage rigidity and unemployment according to which firms raise labor productivity and profits by keeping real wages above the equilibrium level.

Efficient markets hypothesis: The theory that asset prices reflect all publicly available information about the value of an asset.

Elasticity: The percentage change in a variable caused by a 1-percent change in another variable.

Endogenous growth theory: Models of economic growth that try to explain the rate of technological change.

Endogenous variable: A variable that is explained by a particular model; a variable whose value is determined by the model's solution. (Cf. exogenous variable.)

Equilibrium: A state of balance between opposing forces, such as the balance of supply and demand in a market.

Euler's theorem: The mathematical result economists use to show that economic profit must be zero if the production function has constant returns to scale and if factors are paid their marginal products.

***Ex ante* real interest rate:** The real interest rate anticipated when a loan is made; the nominal interest rate minus expected inflation. (Cf. *ex post* real interest rate.)

***Ex post* real interest rate:** The real interest rate actually realized; the nominal interest rate minus actual inflation. (Cf. *ex ante* real interest rate.)

Excess reserves: Reserves held by banks above the amount mandated by reserve requirements.

Exchange rate: The rate at which a country makes exchanges in world markets. (Cf. nominal exchange rate, real exchange rate.)

Exogenous variable: A variable that a particular model takes as given; a variable whose value is independent of the model's solution. (Cf. endogenous variable.)

Expansionary policy: Policy that raises aggregate demand, real income, and employment. (Cf. contractionary policy.)

Exports: Goods and services sold to other countries.

Factor of production: An input used to produce goods and services; for example, capital or labor.

Factor price: The amount paid for one unit of a factor of production.

Factor share: The proportion of total income being paid to a factor of production.

Federal Reserve (the Fed): The central bank of the United States.

Fiat money: Money that is not intrinsically useful and is valued only because it is used as money. (Cf. commodity money, money.)

Financial intermediation: The process by which resources are allocated from those individuals who wish to save some of their income for future consumption to those individuals and firms who wish to borrow to buy investment goods for future production.

Financing constraint: A limit on the quantity of funds a firm can raise—such as through borrowing—in order to buy capital.

Fiscal policy: The government's choice regarding levels of spending and taxation.

Fisher effect: The one-for-one influence of expected inflation on the nominal interest rate.

Fisher equation: The equation stating that the nominal interest rate is the sum of the real interest rate and expected inflation ($i = r + \pi^e$).

Fixed exchange rate: An exchange rate that is set by the central bank's willingness to buy and sell the domestic currency for foreign currencies at a predetermined price. (Cf. floating exchange rate.)

Flexible prices: Prices that adjust quickly to equilibrate supply and demand. (Cf. sticky prices.)

Floating exchange rate: An exchange rate that the central bank allows to change in response to changing economic conditions and economic policies. (Cf. fixed exchange rate.)

Flow: A variable measured as a quantity per unit of time. (Cf. stock.)

Fractional-reserve banking: A system in which banks keep only some of their deposits on reserve. (Cf. 100-percent-reserve banking.)

Frictional unemployment: The unemployment that results because it takes time for workers to search for the jobs that best suit their skills and tastes. (Cf. structural unemployment.)

Full-employment budget deficit: *See* cyclically adjusted budget deficit.

GDP: *See* gross domestic product.

GDP deflator: The ratio of nominal GDP to real GDP; a measure of the overall level of prices that shows the cost of the currently produced basket of goods relative to the cost of that basket in a base year.

General equilibrium: The simultaneous equilibrium of all the markets in the economy.

GNP: *See* gross national product.

Gold standard: A monetary system in which gold serves as money or in which all money is convertible into gold at a fixed rate.

Golden rule: The saving rate in the Solow growth model that leads to the steady state in which consumption per worker (or consumption per efficiency unit of labor) is maximized.

Government purchases: Goods and services bought by the government. (Cf. transfer payments.)

Government-purchases multiplier: The change in aggregate income resulting from a one-dollar change in government purchases.

Gross domestic product (GDP): The total income earned domestically, including the income earned by foreign-owned factors of production; the total expenditure on domestically produced goods and services.

Gross national product (GNP): The total income of all residents of a nation, including the income from factors of production used abroad; the total expenditure on the nation's output of goods and services.

High-powered money: The sum of currency and bank reserves; also called the monetary base.

Hyperinflation: Extremely high inflation.

Hysteresis: The long-lasting influence of history, such as on the natural rate of unemployment.

Imperfect-information model: The model of aggregate supply emphasizing that individuals do not always know the overall price level because they cannot observe the prices of all goods and services in the economy.

Import quota: A legal limit on the amount of a good that can be imported.

Imports: Goods and services bought from other countries.

Imputed value: An estimate of the value of a good or service that is not sold in the marketplace and therefore does not have a market price.

Income effect: The change in consumption of a good resulting from a movement to a higher or lower indifference curve, holding the relative price constant. (Cf. substitution effect.)

Index of leading indicators: *See* leading indicators.

Indifference curves: A graphical representation of preferences that shows different combinations of goods producing the same level of satisfaction.

Inflation: An increase in the overall level of prices. (Cf. deflation, disinflation.)

Inflation targeting: A monetary policy under which the central bank announces a specific target, or target range, for the inflation rate.

Inflation tax: The revenue raised by the government through the creation of money; also called seigniorage.

Inside lag: The time between a shock hitting the economy and the policy action taken to respond to the shock. (Cf. outside lag.)

Insiders: Workers who are already employed and therefore have an influence on wage bargaining. (Cf. outsiders.)

Interest rate: The market price at which resources are transferred between the present and the future; the return to saving and the cost of borrowing.

Intermediation: *See* financial intermediation.

Intertemporal budget constraint: The budget constraint applying to expenditure and income in more than one period of time. (Cf. budget constraint.)

Intertemporal substitution of labor: The willingness of people to trade off working in one period for working in future periods.

Inventory investment: The change in the quantity of goods that firms hold in storage, including materials and supplies, work in process, and finished goods.

Investment: Goods purchased by individuals and firms to add to their stock of capital.

Investment tax credit: A provision of the corporate income tax that reduces a firm's tax when it buys new capital goods.

***IS* curve:** The negative relationship between the interest rate and the level of income that arises in the market for goods and services. (Cf. *IS–LM* model, *LM* curve.)

***IS–LM* model:** A model of aggregate demand that shows what determines aggregate income for a given price level by analyzing the interaction between the goods market and the money market. (Cf. *IS* curve, *LM* curve.)

Keynesian cross: A simple model of income determination, based on the ideas in Keynes's *General Theory,* which shows how changes in spending can have a multiplied effect on aggregate income.

Keynesian model: A model derived from the ideas of Keynes's *General Theory*; a model based on the assumptions that wages and prices do not adjust to clear markets and that aggregate demand determines the economy's output and employment. (Cf. classical model.)

Labor-augmenting technological progress: Advances in productive capability that raise the efficiency of labor.

Labor force: Those in the population who have a job or are looking for a job.

Labor-force participation rate: The percentage of the adult population in the labor force.

Labor hoarding: The phenomenon of firms employing workers whom they do not need when the demand for their products is low, so that they will still have these workers when demand recovers.

Large open economy: An open economy that can influence its domestic interest rate; an economy that, by virtue of its size, can have a substantial impact on world markets and, in particular, on the world interest rate. (Cf. small open economy.)

Laspeyres price index: A measure of the level of prices based on a fixed basket of goods. (Cf. Paasche price index.)

Leading indicators: Economic variables that fluctuate in advance of the economy's output and thus signal the direction of economic fluctuations.

Life-cycle hypothesis: The theory of consumption that emphasizes the role of saving and borrowing as transferring resources from those times in life when income is high to those times in life when income is low, such as from working years to retirement.

Liquid: Readily convertible into the medium of exchange; easily used to make transactions.

Liquidity constraint: A restriction on the amount a person can borrow from a financial institution, which limits the person's ability to spend his future income today; also called a borrowing constraint.

Liquidity-preference theory: A simple model of the interest rate, based on the ideas in Keynes's *General Theory*, which says that the interest rate adjusts to equilibrate the supply and demand for real money balances.

***LM* curve:** The positive relationship between the interest rate and the level of income (while holding the price level fixed) that arises in the market for real money balances. (Cf. *IS–LM* model, *IS* curve.)

Loanable funds: The flow of resources available to finance capital accumulation.

Lucas critique: The argument that traditional policy analysis does not adequately take into account the impact of policy changes on people's expectations.

***M*1, *M*2, *M*3:** Various measures of the stock of money, where larger numbers signify a broader definition of money.

Macroeconometric model: A model that uses data and statistical techniques to describe the economy quantitatively, rather than just qualitatively.

Macroeconomics: The study of the economy as a whole. (Cf. microeconomics.)

Marginal product of capital (*MPK*): The amount of extra output produced when the capital input is increased by one unit.

Marginal product of labor (*MPL*): The amount of extra output produced when the labor input is increased by one unit.

Marginal propensity to consume (*MPC*): The increase in consumption resulting from a one-dollar increase in disposable income.

Marginal rate of substitution (*MRS*): The rate at which a consumer is willing to give up some of one good in exchange for more of another; the slope of the indifference curve.

Market-clearing model: A model that assumes that prices freely adjust to equilibrate supply and demand.

Medium of exchange: The item widely accepted in transactions for goods and services; one of the functions of money. (Cf. store of value, unit of account.)

Menu cost: The cost of changing a price.

Microeconomics: The study of individual markets and decisionmakers. (Cf. macroeconomics.)

Model: A simplified representation of reality, often using diagrams or equations, that shows how variables interact.

Monetarism: The doctrine according to which changes in the money supply are the primary cause of economic fluctuations, implying that a stable money supply would lead to a stable economy.

Monetary base: The sum of currency and bank reserves; also called high-powered money.

Monetary neutrality: *See* neutrality of money.

Monetary policy: The central bank's choice regarding the supply of money.

Monetary transmission mechanism: The process by which changes in the money supply influence the amount that households and firms wish to spend on goods and services.

Monetary union: A group of economies that have decided to share a common currency and thus a common monetary policy.

Money: The stock of assets used for transactions. (Cf. commodity money, fiat money.)

Money demand function: A function showing the determinants of the demand for real money balances; for example, $(M/P)^d = L(i, Y)$.

Money multiplier: The increase in the money supply resulting from a one-dollar increase in the monetary base.

Moral hazard: The possibility of dishonest behavior in situations in which behavior is imperfectly monitored; for example, in efficiency-wage theory, the possibility that low-wage workers may shirk their responsibilities and risk getting caught and fired.

Multiplier: *See* government-purchases multiplier, money multiplier, or tax multiplier.

Mundell–Fleming model: The *IS–LM* model for a small open economy.

Mundell–Tobin effect: The fall in the real interest rate that results when an increase in expected inflation raises the nominal interest rate, lowers real money balances and real wealth, and thereby reduces consumption and raises saving.

NAIRU: Non-accelerating inflation rate of unemployment.

National income accounting: The accounting system that measures GDP and many other related statistics.

National income accounts identity: The equation showing that GDP is the sum of consumption, investment, government purchases, and net exports.

National saving: A nation's income minus consumption and government purchases; the sum of private and public saving.

Natural rate of unemployment: The steady-state rate of unemployment; the rate of unemployment toward which the economy gravitates in the long run.

Natural-rate hypothesis: The premise that fluctuations in aggregate demand influence output, employment, and unemployment only in the short run, and that in the long run these variables return to the levels implied by the classical model.

Near money: Assets that are almost as useful as money for engaging in transactions and, therefore, are close substitutes for money.

Neoclassical model of investment: The theory according to which investment depends on the deviation of the marginal product of capital from the cost of capital.

Net capital outflow: The net flow of funds being invested abroad; domestic saving minus domestic investment; also called net foreign investment.

Net exports: Exports minus imports.

Net foreign investment: *See* net capital outflow.

Net investment: The amount of investment after the replacement of depreciated capital; the change in the capital stock.

Neutrality of money: The property that a change in the money supply does not influence real variables. (Cf. classical dichotomy.)

New Keynesian economics: The school of thought according to which economic fluctuations can be explained only by admitting a role for some microeconomic imperfection, such as sticky wages or prices.

Nominal: Measured in current dollars; not adjusted for inflation. (Cf. real.)

Nominal exchange rate: The rate at which one country's currency trades for another country's currency. (Cf. exchange rate, real exchange rate.)

Nominal interest rate: The return to saving and the cost of borrowing without adjustment for inflation. (Cf. real interest rate.)

Normal good: A good that a consumer demands in greater quantity when his or her income rises.

Okun's law: The negative relationship between unemployment and real GDP, according to which a decrease in unemployment of 1 percentage point is associated with additional growth in real GDP of approximately 2 percent.

100-percent-reserve banking: A system in which banks keep all deposits on reserve. (Cf. fractional-reserve banking.)

Open economy: An economy in which people can freely engage in international trade in goods and capital. (Cf. closed economy.)

Open-market operations: The purchase or sale of government bonds by the central bank for the purpose of increasing or decreasing the money supply.

Outside lag: The time between a policy action and its influence on the economy. (Cf. inside lag.)

Outsiders: Workers who are not employed and therefore have no influence on wage bargaining. (Cf. insiders.)

Paasche price index: A measure of the level of prices based on a changing basket of goods. (Cf. Laspeyres price index.)

Permanent income: Income that people expect to persist into the future; normal income. (Cf. transitory income.)

Permanent-income hypothesis: The theory of consumption according to which people choose consumption based on their permanent income, and use saving and borrowing to smooth consumption in response to transitory variations in income.

Phillips curve: A negative relationship between inflation and unemployment; in its modern form, a relationship among inflation, cyclical unemployment, expected inflation, and supply shocks, derived from the short-run aggregate supply curve.

Pigou effect: The increase in consumer spending that results when a fall in the price level raises real money balances and, thereby, consumers' wealth.

Political business cycle: The fluctuations in output and employment resulting from the manipulation of the economy for electoral gain.

Portfolio theories of money demand: Theories that explain how much money people choose to hold and that stress the role of money as a store of value. (Cf. transactions theories of money demand.)

Precautionary saving: The extra saving that results from uncertainty regarding, for example, longevity or future income.

Present value: The amount today that is equivalent to an amount to be received in the future, taking into account the interest that could be earned over the interval of time.

Private saving: Disposable income minus consumption.

Procyclical: Moving in the same direction as output, incomes, and employment over the business cycle; falling during recessions and rising during recoveries. (Cf. acyclical, countercyclical.)

Production function: The mathematical relationship showing how the quantities of the factors of production determine the quantity of goods and services produced; for example, $Y = F(K, L)$.

Production smoothing: The motive for holding inventories according to which a firm can reduce its costs by keeping the amount of output it produces steady and allowing its stock of inventories to respond to fluctuating sales.

Profit: The income of firm owners; firm revenue minus firm costs. (Cf. accounting profit, economic profit.)

Public saving: Government receipts minus government spending; the budget surplus.

Purchasing-power parity: The doctrine according to which goods must sell for the same price in every country, implying that the nominal exchange rate reflects differences in price levels.

***q* theory of investment:** The theory according to which expenditure on capital goods depends on the ratio of the market value of installed capital to its replacement cost.

Quantity equation: The identity stating that the product of the money supply and the velocity of money equals nominal expenditure ($MV = PY$); coupled with the assumption of stable velocity, an explanation of nominal expenditure called the quantity theory of money.

Quantity theory of money: The doctrine emphasizing that changes in the quantity of money lead to changes in nominal expenditure.

Quota: *See* import quota.

Random walk: The path followed by a variable whose changes over time are unpredictable.

Rational expectations: An approach that assumes that people optimally use all available information—including information about current and prospective policies—to forecast the future. (Cf. adaptive expectations.)

Real: Measured in constant dollars; adjusted for inflation. (Cf. nominal.)

Real business cycle theory: The theory according to which economic fluctuations can be explained by real changes in the economy (such as changes in technology) and without any role for nominal variables (such as the money supply).

Real exchange rate: The rate at which one country's goods trade for another country's goods. (Cf. exchange rate, nominal exchange rate.)

Real interest rate: The return to saving and the cost of borrowing after adjustment for inflation. (Cf. nominal interest rate.)

Real money balances: The quantity of money expressed in terms of the quantity of goods and services it can buy; the quantity of money divided by the price level (M/P).

Recession: A sustained period of falling real income.

Rental price of capital: The amount paid to rent one unit of capital.

Reserve requirements: Regulations imposed on banks by the central bank that specify a minimum reserve–deposit ratio.

Reserves: The money that banks have received from depositors but have not used to make loans.

Residential investment: New housing bought by people to live in and by landlords to rent out.

Revaluation: An action undertaken by the central bank to raise the value of a currency under a system of fixed exchange rates. (Cf. devaluation.)

Ricardian equivalence: The theory according to which forward-looking consumers fully anticipate the future taxes implied by government debt, so that government borrowing today coupled with a tax increase in the future to repay the debt has the same effect on the economy as a tax increase today.

Sacrifice ratio: The number of percentage points of a year's real GDP that must be forgone to reduce inflation by 1 percentage point.

Saving: *See* national saving, private saving, and public saving.

Seasonal adjustment: The removal of the regular fluctuations in an economic variable that occur as a function of the time of year.

Sectoral shift: A change in the composition of demand among industries or regions.

Seigniorage: The revenue raised by the government through the creation of money; also called the inflation tax.

Shock: An exogenous change in an economic relationship, such as the aggregate demand or aggregate supply curve.

Shoeleather cost: The cost of inflation from reducing real money balances, such as the inconvenience of needing to make more frequent trips to the bank.

Small open economy: An open economy that takes its interest rate as given by world financial markets; an economy that, by virtue of its size, has a negligible impact on world markets and, in particular, on the world interest rate. (Cf. large open economy.)

Solow growth model: A model showing how saving, population growth, and technological progress determine the level of and growth in the standard of living.

Solow residual: The growth in total factor productivity, measured as the percentage change in output minus the percentage change in inputs, where the inputs are weighted by their factor shares. (Cf. total factor productivity.)

Stabilization policy: Public policy aimed at reducing the severity of short-run economic fluctuations.

Stagflation: A situation of falling output and rising prices; combination of stagnation and inflation.

Steady state: A condition in which key variables are not changing.

Sticky prices: Prices that adjust sluggishly and, therefore, do not always equilibrate supply and demand. (Cf. flexible prices.)

Sticky-price model: The model of aggregate supply emphasizing the slow adjustment of the prices of goods and services.

Sticky-wage model: The model of aggregate supply emphasizing the slow adjustment of nominal wages.

Stock: 1. A variable measured as a quantity at a point in time. (Cf. flow.) 2. Shares of ownership in a corporation.

Stock market: A market in which shares of ownership in corporations are bought and sold.

Stock-out avoidance: The motive for holding inventories according to which firms keep extra goods on hand to prevent running out if sales are unexpectedly high.

Store of value: A way of transferring purchasing power from the present to the future; one of the functions of money. (Cf. medium of exchange, unit of account.)

Structural unemployment: The unemployment resulting from wage rigidity and job rationing. (Cf. frictional unemployment.)

Substitution effect: The change in consumption of a good resulting from a movement along an indifference curve because of a change in the relative price. (Cf. income effect.)

Supply shocks: Exogenous events that shift the aggregate supply curve.

Tariff: A tax on imported goods.

Tax multiplier: The change in aggregate income resulting from a one-dollar change in taxes.

Taylor rule: A rule for monetary policy according to which the central bank sets the interest rate as a positive function of inflation and a negative function of the shortfall of output from its natural level.

Time inconsistency: The tendency of policymakers to announce policies in advance in order to influence the expectations of private decisionmakers, and then to follow different policies after those expectations have been formed and acted upon.

Tobin's *q*: The ratio of the market value of installed capital to its replacement cost.

Total factor productivity: A measure of the level of technology; the amount of output per unit of input, where different inputs are combined on the basis of their factor shares. (Cf. Solow residual.)

Trade balance: The receipts from exports minus the payments for imports.

Transactions theories of money demand: Theories that explain how much money people choose to hold and that stress the role of money as a medium of exchange. (Cf. portfolio theories of money demand.)

Transfer payments: Payments from the government to individuals that are not in exchange for goods and services, such as Social Security payments. (Cf. government purchases.)

Transitory income: Income that people do not expect to persist into the future; current income minus normal income. (Cf. permanent income.)

Underground economy: Economic transactions that are hidden in order to evade taxes or conceal illegal activity.

Unemployment insurance: A government program under which unemployed workers can collect benefits for a certain period of time after losing their jobs.

Unemployment rate: The percentage of those in the labor force who do not have jobs.

Unit of account: The measure in which prices and other accounting records are recorded; one of the functions of money. (Cf. medium of exchange, store of value.)

Value added: The value of a firm's output minus the value of the intermediate goods the firm purchased.

Velocity of money: The ratio of nominal expenditure to the money supply; the rate at which money changes hands.

Wage: The amount paid for one unit of labor.

Wage rigidity: The failure of wages to adjust to equilibrate labor supply and labor demand.

Work in process: Goods in inventory that are in the process of being completed.

Worker-misperception model: The model of aggregate supply emphasizing that workers sometimes perceive incorrectly the overall level of prices.

World interest rate: The interest rate prevailing in world financial markets.

index

Note: *Page numbers followed by* f *indicate figures; page numbers followed by* n *indicate footnotes; page numbers followed by* t *indicate tables.*

Abel, Andrew B., 226n
Accelerator model of inventories, 505
Account, money as unit of, 77–78
Accounting profit, 54
Accounting scandals, 311–312
Acemoglu, Daron, 230
Actual expenditure, 280
AD. See Aggregate demand *(AD)*
Adaptive expectations, inflation inertia and, 387–388
Adverse selection, 170
Aggregate demand *(AD)*, 261–264
  algebra of, 331–332
  as determinant of GDP, 548
  downward slope of curve, 264
  IS-LM model and. *See IS-LM* model
  quantity equation as, 263, 263f
  shifts in curve, 264, 265f
  shocks to, 271f, 271–272
Aggregate-demand externalities, 538–539
Aggregate supply *(AS)*, 261–262, 265–270, 374–385
  imperfect-information model of, 380–383
  international differences in, 382–383
  long-run, 265–267, 266f, 268–270
  Phillips curve derivation from, 385–387
  shocks to, 272–275, 273f
  short-run, 267f, 267–270, 268f
  sticky-price model of, 375–376
  sticky-wage model of, 377–379, 378f
Aggregate supply-aggregate demand model, 261–262, 402. *See also* Aggregate demand *(AD)*; Aggregate supply *(AS)*
Aghion, Philippe, 240
Aging population, 343, 435
Akerlof, George A., 13, 103n, 538n
Alesina, Alberto, 181, 425n
Altonji, Joseph G., 533n
American Revolution, 90–91, 431
Ando, Albert, 471, 475n
Angeletos, George-Marios, 482n
Angell, Norman, 80n
Animal spirits, 310
Annuities, 475
Appreciation of currency, 132
Arbitrageurs, 141–142
  international gold standard and, 347
Argentina
  Big Mac price and exchange rate in, 144t
  inflation and money growth in, 89f
  investment rate and income per person in, 197f
AS. See Aggregate supply *(AS)*
Asia. *See also specific countries*
  financial crisis of 1997-1998 in, 355–356
Asian Tigers. *See also* Hong Kong; Singapore; South Korea; Taiwan
  economic growth of, 248–249
Assets
  capital, measurement of government debt and, 436–437
  depreciation of, 28, 132, 491, 494
  dominated, 519
Assumptions, simplifying, 10–12
Aten, Bettina, 197n
Atkeson, Andrew, 440n
Australia
  Big Mac price and exchange rate in, 144t
  central bank of, 424f
  inflation and exchange rate in, 141f
  inflation targeting in, 420
  legal system in, 229
  population growth and income per person in, 210f
  unions in, 169t
Austria
  government debt of, 432t
  unions in, 169t
Automatic stabilizers, 408–409
Average capital productivity, 57
Average labor productivity, 57
Average propensity to consume, 457

Baby-boom generation, 174
Balanced budgets, 62
  optimal fiscal policy versus, 448
Balanced growth, 220–221
Balanced trade, 119
Balances, real money, 85
Balance sheets of banks, 511
Ball, Laurence, 175n, 383n, 396n, 397n, 533n, 541n
Bangladesh, standard of living in, 187t
Banking system. *See also* Central banks; Federal Reserve (Fed)
  balance sheet of banks and, 511
  bank failures during Great Depression and, 319, 500, 516–517, 517t
  money creation by banks and, 512
  problems in, credit crunches and, 500–501
Barro, Robert J., 68n, 69n, 222n, 428n, 445, 446
Barsky, Robert B., 30n, 95n, 380n
Base-year prices, 23
Baum, L. Frank, 102
Baumol, William, 520
Baumol-Tobin model of cash management, 520–524, 521f, 523f
Behavioral economics, 481
Belarus, inflation and money growth in, 89f
Belgium
  central bank of, 424f
  economic growth of, 224
  government debt of, 432t
  population growth and income per person in, 210f
  unions in, 169t
Benartzi, Shlomo, 483n
Benjamin, Daniel K., 69n
Bequests, reasons parents leave, 446
Bergen, Mark, 539n
Bernanke, Ben S., 319n, 421, 501n
Bernheim, B. Douglas, 443n, 446n
Big, comprehensive economic model, 401–402
Big Mac prices, exchange rates and, 143–145, 144t
Bilateral trade balances, irrelevance of, 120
Birthrate, change in, 174
Black Death, factor prices and, 54–55
Blanchard, Olivier Jean, 181, 397n, 538n, 542n
Blinder, Alan S., 98n, 261n, 542, 543n, 544n
BLS (Bureau of Labor Statistics), 31, 34, 35, 168n, 176
  Current Population Survey of, 35–39, 36f, 167
Bolivia, inflation in, 104–105
Bonds
  indexed, 451–452
  junk, 63
  municipal, 63
Borrowing constraints, 443–444
  intertemporal choice and, 468–471, 469f, 470f
Boskin, Michael, 34
Brazil
  Big Mac price and exchange rate in, 144t
  inflation and nominal interest rates in, 93f
  investment rate and income per person in, 197f
  population growth and income per person in, 210f
  standard of living in, 187t
Break-even investment, 207f, 207–208
Breit, William, 13n
Bretton Woods system, 344–345, 356
Brown, Charles, 167n
Brown, E. Cary, 320n
Brumberg, Richard, 471

Brunner, Karl, 318n
Bryan, William Jennings, 102
Bubonic plague, factor prices and, 54–55
Buchanan, James, 450
Budget constraint, intertemporal, 461–463, 463f
Budget deficits, 45, 62, 226, 553–554
  cyclically adjusted (full-employment), 438
Budget surpluses, 45, 62, 226
Bulgaria, inflation and nominal interest rates in, 93f
Bulow, Jeremy I., 171n
Bureau of Economic Analysis, 17, 24
Bureau of Labor Statistics (BLS), 31, 34, 35, 168n, 176
  Current Population Survey of, 35–39, 36f, 167
Burundi
  investment rate and income per person in, 197, 197f
  population growth and income per person in, 210f
Bush, George H.W., 3, 129, 433, 444
Bush, George W., 3, 129, 287, 361, 434, 494–495
Business Cycle Dating Committee, 253–254
Business cycles. *See also* Depressions; Economic fluctuations; Great Depression; New Keynesian economics; Real business cycle theory; Recessions
  measurement of government debt and, 438
  political, 416
Business fixed investment, 487, 488f, 488–501
  cost of capital and, 490–491
  determinants of, 492–493, 493f
  efficient markets hypothesis versus Keynes's beauty contests and, 497–499
  financing constraints and, 499–501
  rental price of capital and, 489f, 489–490
  stock market and Tobin's *q* and, 495–497
  taxes and, 494–495

Cagan, Phillip, 112n
Cagan model, 97, 112–114
Cameroon, investment rate and income per person in, 197f
Campbell, John Y., 452n, 480n
Campillo, Marta, 425n
Canada
  Big Mac price and exchange rate in, 144t
  central bank of, 424f
  economic growth of, 231t
  government debt of, 432t
  imports and exports as percentage of GDP in, 115, 116f
  inflation and exchange rate in, 141f
  inflation targeting in, 420
  unions in, 169t
Canetti, Elie R. D., 544n
Capital
  cost of, 490–491
  demand for, 53
  failure to flow to poor countries, 130–131
  fixed, consumption of, 28
  Golden Rule level of. *See* Golden Rule level of capital
  human, 130, 227
  increases in, economic growth and, 244–246
  international flow of. *See* International flows of capital and goods
  marginal product of, 53
  net outflow of, 118–120
  real rental price of, 53
  rental price of, 489f, 489–490
Capital accumulation, 187–198
  growth in capital stock and steady state and, 190f–192f, 190–192
  numerical example of approach to steady state and, 192–195, 194t
  saving effects on growth and, 195–198, 196f
  supply and demand for goods and, 187–190
  in United States, 439–440
Capital assets
  depreciation of, 28, 132, 491, 494
  measurement of government debt and, 436–437
Capital budgeting, 436–437
Capitalism, Socialism, and Democracy (Schumpeter), 239
Capital mobility
  Mundell-Fleming model and, 336
  world interest rate and, 121–122
Capital outflow, net, 118–120
  in large open economies, 149–151, 150f, 156–157, 157f
Capital productivity, average, 57
Capital stock, growth in, steady state and, 190f–192f, 190–192
Card, David, 167n
Carter, Jimmy, 3
CBO (Congressional Budget Office), 407, 434
Cecchetti, Stephen G., 261n
Central banks, 81
  German, 108
  independence of, 422–425, 424f
  U.S.. *See* Federal Reserve (Fed)
Chain-weighted measures of real GDP, 24
Chamley, Christopher, 440n
Chari, V.V., 440n
Chile
  Big Mac price and exchange rate in, 144t
  investment rate and income per person in, 197f
China
  Big Mac price and exchange rate in, 144t
  capital flow restriction by, 360–361
  failure to enforce intellectual property rights, 231
  investment rate and income per person in, 197f
  population growth and income per person in, 209–210, 210f
  standard of living in, 187t
  trade surplus of, 130
  U.S. trade balance with, 120
Choi, James J., 483n
Cigarettes as money, 79, 79n
Cipolla, Carlo M., 55n
Circular flow diagram, 17–19, 18f, 44–46, 45f, 63
Civil War, 222, 270
Clarida, Richard, 545n
Clark, Kim B., 172n
Classical dichotomy, 109
Clinton, Bill, 3, 129, 228, 434, 494
Closed economies, 59, 401–402
C money measure, 82, 82t
Cobb, Charles, 55
Cobb-Douglas production function, 55–59, 57f, 130, 490
COLAs (cost-of-living allowances), 33
Cold-turkey solution to inflation, 393
Collective bargaining, wage rigidity and, 168–170, 169t
Colosio, Luis Donaldo, 354
Commodity money, 78
Comparative advantage, 223–224
Compensation of employees in national income, 29
Competitive firms
  decisions facing, 49–50
  demand for factors of, 50–53, 51f, 52f
  profit and, 50
Comprehensive economic model, 401–402
Computer revolution, 233–234
Conditional convergence, 222
Conference board, 258
Congressional Budget Office (CBO), 407, 434
Consols, 69
Constant returns to scale, 47
Consumer preferences
  intertemporal choice and, 464f, 464–465
  time-inconsistent, 481
Consumer price index (CPI), 16, 30–34
  GDP deflator versus, 31–34, 33f
  overstatement of inflation by, 33–34
  price of basket of goods and, 31
Consumption, 26, 59–60, 60f, 456–484
  business cycles and, 254, 255f
  of elderly, 475
  of fixed capital, 28

  instant gratification and, 481–483
  intertemporal choice and. *See* Intertemporal choice
  Keynes and, 457–461, 458f
  life-cycle hypothesis of, 471–475
  MPC and, 60, 60f
  permanent-income hypothesis of, 476–478
  random-walk hypothesis of, 478–480
  of small open economy, 123
  steady-state, 199, 200f
Consumption function, 60
  demand for goods and, 188–190
Consumption puzzle, 460, 460f
Consumption smoothing, 467
Continental Congress, 90, 91
Contingent liabilities, measurement of, 437–438
Contractionary monetary policy, 270
Convergence, 221–222
  conditional, 222
Cooper, Russell, 541n
Coordination failure, recessions as, 539–541, 540f
Corporate income tax, 494
Corporate profits in national income, 29
Costa Rica, population growth and income per person in, 210f
Cost-of-living allowances (COLAs), 33
Cost-push inflation, 389
Costs
  of capital, 490–491
  of holding money, 95
  of inflation, 552–553
  of living, CPI as measure of, 30–34
  social, of inflation. *See* Social costs of inflation
Côte d'Ivoire, population growth and income per person in, 210f
Council of Economic Advisers, 287, 407
Country risk, interest-rate differentials and, 351, 352
CPI. *See* Consumer price index (CPI)
Credit cards, 83
Credit crunches, banking crises and, 500–501
Credit risk, interest rates and, 63
Crowding out, 67
Crusoe, Robinson, 529–531
Currency, 82. *See also* Money
  appreciation of, 132
  depreciation of, 132
  devaluation of, 348–349
  exchange rates and. *See* Exchange rates; Fixed exchange rates; Floating exchange rates; Nominal exchange rates; Real exchange rates
  greenbacks, 270
  revaluation of, 348, 349
  strengthening of, 132
  underground economy and, 519–520
Currency boards, 359
Currency-deposit ratio, 514
Current Population Survey, 35–39, 36f, 167
Cyclically adjusted budget deficit, 438
Czech Republic, Big Mac price and exchange rate in, 144t

Data Resources Incorporated (DRI) model, 309t, 309–310
David, Paul A., 234n
Day of Reckoning (Friedman), 451
Debit cards, 83
Debt crises
  Asian, of 1997-1998, 355–356
  Latin American defaults and, 450
  Mexican, of 1994-1995, 353–355
Debt-deflation theory, 321–322
Deficits. *See* Budget deficits; Trade deficits
Deflation, 4–5
  destabilizing effects of, 321–323, 322f
  stabilizing effects of, 321
Delta, 52
Demand
  aggregate. *See* Aggregate demand *(AD)*
  for capital, 53
  consumption function and, 188–190
  determinants of, 59–63
  at equilibrium. *See* Equilibrium
  for factors, of firm, 50–53
  fiscal policy and, 67f, 67–69, 68f
  for goods and services, 59–63, 64–65, 188–190
  for housing, changes in, 502f, 502–503
  for investment. *See* Investment demand
  for labor, 51–53, 52f
  for loanable funds. *See* Investment
  for money. *See* Money demand
Demand deposits, 82
Demand-pull inflation, 388, 390
Demand shocks, 270, 271f, 271–272
Democracy in Deficit (Buchanan and Wagner), 450
Denmark
  Big Mac price and exchange rate in, 144t
  central bank of, 424f
  devaluation in, 349
  inflation and exchange rate in, 141f
Deposits, demand, 82
Depreciation, 28, 132, 491
  taxes and, 494
Depreciation rate, 191
Depressions, 4, 5. *See also* Great Depression
  Japanese, of 1990s, 324–325
Devaluation, 348–349
Dickens, William T., 103n
Diminishing marginal product, 50–51
Discounting, 462
Discount rate, 516
Discouraged workers, 35, 176, 176t
Discretionary policy, time inconsistency of, 416–419, 429
Discretion for conduct of stabilization policy, 415–425
Disinflation
  rational expectations and, 393–395
  sacrifice ratio and, 392–393, 395t, 395–396
  under Volcker, 395t, 395–396
Disposable income, 60
Disposable personal income, 30
Di Tella, Rafael, 180n
Dollarization, 359
Dominated assets, 519
Dominguez, Kathryn M., 410n
Dornbusch, Rudiger, 106n
Double coincidence of wants, 78
Douglas, Paul, 55
DRI (Data Resources Incorporated) model, 309t, 309–310
Dulberger, Ellen, 34
Dutta, Shantanu, 539n

Earned income tax credit, 167
East Asian Tigers. *See also* Hong Kong; Singapore; South Korea; Taiwan
  economic growth of, 248–249
Eckstein, Otto, 309n
Economic fluctuations, 252–276. *See also* Business cycles; Depressions; Great Depression; New Keynesian economics; Real business cycle theory; Recessions
  aggregate demand and, 262–264
  aggregate supply and, 265–270
  GDP and its components and, 253–254, 254f, 255f
  IS-LM model explanations of, 304–313
  leading economic indicators and, 258–259
  stabilization policy and, 270–275
  time horizons and, 259–262
  unemployment and Okun's law and, 255–257, 256f, 257f
Economic forecasting, 409–411, 410f
Economic growth
  balanced, 220–221
  in East Asian Tigers, 248–249
  endogenous growth theory and, 235–240
  free trade and, 223–224
  of Germany, 194–195, 196
  of Japan, 194–195, 196
  as process of creative destruction, 239–240
  saving and, 195–198, 196f
  Solow growth model and. *See* Solow growth model
  sources of, 244–249
  in United States, 248, 248t
  worldwide slowdown in, during 1972-1995, 231t, 231–233

Economic indicators
  leading, 258–259, 409
  stock market as, 496–497, 497f
Economic models, 6–11. *See also specific models*
  big, comprehensive, 401–402
  endogenous and exogenous variables and, 7f–9f, 7–10
  microeconomic thinking and, 12
  number of, 11
  simplifying assumptions, 10–12
  simplifying assumptions and, 10–12
Economic policies. *See also* Fiscal policy; Monetary policy; Public policy; Stabilization policy; Trade policy
  evaluating, 127–131
  industrial, 228
  to promote growth, 224–234
  trade balance and, 124–127
Economic profit, 53–54
Economic statistics. *See also specific statistics, e.g.,* Unemployment rate
  seasonally adjusted, 30
Economies
  closed, 59
  open. *See* Large open economies; Mundell-Fleming model; Open economies; Small open economies
  underground. *See* Underground economy
Economists. *See also specific economists*
  on inflation, 98–99
  Nobel Prize–winning, 13
Ecuador, inflation and money growth in, 89f
Edward III, King of England, 450
Efficiency of labor, technological progress and, 217–218
Efficiency-wage theories, 170–171
Efficient markets hypothesis, 497–498
Egypt, Big Mac price and exchange rate in, 144t
Eichengreen, Barry, 347n, 349n
Elderly population
  consumption and saving of, 475
  growth of, 343, 435
Employment Act of 1946, 407
Endogenous growth theory, 235–240
  basic model of, 235–236
  microeconomics of research and development and, 237–240
  two-sector model of, 236–237
Endogenous variables, 7f–9f, 7–10
Enron, 311–312
Equilibrium, 63–71
  changes in, 9f, 9–10
  in financial markets, 65–66, 66f
  fiscal policy and, 67–69
  investment demand and, 69–71, 70f, 71f
  Keynesian cross and, 282f, 282–283
  long-run, steady state as, 191
  in market for goods and services, 64–65
  short-run. *See* Short-run equilibrium
Errors-in-variables problem, 477
Essay on the Funding System (Ricardo), 447
An Essay on the Principle of Population as It Affects the Future Improvement of Society (Malthus), 211
Ethiopia
  investment rate and income per person in, 197, 197f
  population growth and income per person in, 210f
Euler's theorem, 54
Euro, 358
Euro Area
  Big Mac price and exchange rate in, 144t
  inflation and money growth in, 89f
Euro-Barometer Survey Series, 179
Europe. *See also specific countries*
  Black Death in, factor prices and, 54–55
  monetary union in, 357–358
  rise of leisure in, 180f, 180–181
  unemployment in, 176–160, 397
  unemployment insurance in, 177
European Central Bank, 358
Ex ante real interest rate, 94
Excess reserves, 516
Exchange, money as medium of, 78
Exchange rates, 131–145
  Big Mac prices and, 143–145, 144t
  expected changes in, interest-rate differentials and, 351–352
  fixed. *See* Fixed exchange rates
  floating. *See* Floating exchange rates
  impossible trinity and, 359–361, 360f
  newspaper reporting of, 132
  nominal. *See* Nominal exchange rates
  purchasing-power parity and, 141–145, 142f
  real. *See* Real exchange rates
  real versus nominal, 346
  trade policies and, 138f, 138–139
Exogenous variables, 7f–9f, 7–10
Expansionary fiscal policy, domestic, in large open economy, 153–155, 154f
Expansionary monetary policy, 312
Expectations
  adaptive, inflation inertia and, 387–388
  for exchange rate changes, interest-rate differentials and, 351–352
  Lucas critique and, 411–412
  rational, disinflation and, 393–395
Expected inflation
  costs of, 99–100
  Phillips curve and, 387
Expenditures
  actual, 280
  circular flow and, 17–19, 18f
  components of, 25–28. *See also* Consumption; Government purchases; Investment; Net exports
  planned, Keynesian cross and, 280–281, 281f
Experience rating of unemployment insurance, 164
Exports
  net. *See* Net exports
  as percentage of GDP, 115, 116f
Ex post real interest rate, 94
Externalities
  aggregate-demand, 538–539
  technological, 228

Factor accumulation, production efficiency versus, 222–224
Factor prices, 48–49, 49f
  Black Death and, 54–55
Factors of production, 46, 48–59. *See also* Capital; Capital accumulation; Labor
  Cobb-Douglas production function and, 55–59, 57f
  decisions facing competitive firm and, 49–50
  firm's demand for, 50–53
  increases in, economic growth and, 244–246
  inventories as, 505
  national income distribution among markets for, 53–55
  prices of, 48–49, 49f
Fair, Ray C., 410n
Fair Labor Standards Act of 1938, 166
Fama, Eugene, 499n
Fazzari, Steven M., 500n
Federal Deposit Insurance, 323
Federal funds rate, 312, 421, 525
Federal Open Market Committee (FOMC), 81, 312
Federal Reserve (Fed), 81, 407. *See also* Monetary policy
  Great Depression and, 321
  interest rates and, 312–313
  as lender of last resort, 517
  money supply and. *See* Money supply
  monitoring of CPI by, 33
  power vacuum at, Great Depression and, 536
  supply shocks and, 272, 274
Federal Reserve Board, 81
Federal Reserve Notes, 81
Fed watchers, 93
Feldstein, Martin, 450
Fiat money, 78, 79–80
Financial innovation, 524
Financial intermediation, 513
Financial markets, equilibrium in, 65–66, 66f
Financing constraints, 499–501
Finland
  devaluation in, 349

inflation targeting in, 420
unions in, 169t
Firms. *See* Business fixed investment; Capital; Competitive firms; Corporate *entries;* Factor prices; Factors of production; Inventories; Inventory investment; Labor; Production *entries*
First Report on the Public Credit, 419
Fiscal policy
abroad, real exchange rate and, 136, 137f
abroad, trade balance and, 125–126, 126f
domestic, in large open economy, 153–155, 154f
domestic, real exchange rate and, 136, 136f
domestic, trade balance and, 124–125, 125f
effectiveness of, 332–333
fixed exchange rates and, 347f, 347–348
floating exchange rates and, 340–342, 341f
future of, 434–435
government purchases and, 283–286, 284f, 286f
Great Depression and, 319–320
interaction with monetary policy, 307, 308f, 309–310, 449
IS curve and, 289, 290f, 304f, 304–306, 305f
lags associated with, 408
optimal, balanced budgets versus, 448
and saving, 67f, 67–69, 68f
short-run equilibrium and, 304f, 304–306, 305f
short-run model of large open economy and, 369–370, 370f
summary of effects in Mundell-Fleming model, 350, 351t
Fischer, Stanley, 90n, 106n, 379n
Fisher, Irving, 91, 94, 461
Fisher effect, 91–93, 94, 97, 295
Fisher equation, 91–92
Fisher index, 32n
Fixed capital, consumption of, 28
Fixed exchange rates, 344–350, 346f
fiscal policy and, 347f, 347–348
gold standard and, 346–347
impossible trinity and, 359–361, 360f
monetary policy and, 348f, 348–349
Mundell-Fleming model with, 402
pros and cons of, 356–358
speculative attacks, currency boards, and dollarization and, 358–359
trade policy and, 349–350, 350f
Fleming, J. Marcus, 334n
Flexible prices, 12
Flinders Island, 212
Floating exchange rates, 340–343
fiscal policy and, 340–342, 341f
impossible trinity and, 359–361, 360f
monetary policy and, 342f, 342–343
Mundell-Fleming model with, 402
pros and cons of, 356–358
speculative attacks, currency boards, and dollarization and, 358–359
trade policy and, 343, 344f
Flows, 19, 19f
FOMC (Federal Open Market Committee), 81, 312
Ford, Henry, 171
Ford Motor Company, 171
Foreign exchange. *See also* Exchange rates; Fixed exchange rates; Floating exchange rates; Nominal exchange rates; Real exchange rates
market for, in large open economy, 152f, 152–153
Foreign investment, net, 118–120
Fractional-reserve banking, 512–513
France
central bank of, 424f
economic growth of, 231t
exchange rate in, 349
government debt of, 432t
imports and exports as percentage of GDP in, 116f
leisure in, 180f, 181
unemployment rate in, 176–178, 177f
unions in, 169t
Frankel, Jeffrey, 224
Free Silver movement, 101–102
Free trade, economic growth and, 223–224
Frictional unemployment, 162–165
public policy and, 163–165
unemployment insurance and, 164–165
Friedman, Ben, 451
Friedman, Milton, 13, 87–88, 318n, 320, 382n, 387, 406, 419, 460, 461, 476, 477, 536
Full-employment budget deficit, 438
Functions to express relationships among variables, 10

Gali, Jordi, 545n
Galor, Oded, 211n
GDP. *See* Gross domestic product (GDP)
GDP deflator, 23–24
CPI versus, 31–34, 33f
GDP targeting, 419
General equilibrium model, 71
The General Theory of Employment, Interest, and Money (Keynes), 278, 280, 292, 379, 413, 425, 457, 528–529
Germany
central bank of, 424f
economic growth of, 194–195, 196, 231t
exchange rate in, 349
government debt of, 432t
imports and exports as percentage of GDP in, 115, 116f
inflation and nominal interest rates in, 93f
inflation in, 76, 104, 106, 107f, 108
leisure in, 180f, 181
standard of living in, 187t
unemployment rate in, 176–178, 177f
unions in, 169t
Gertler, Mark, 545n
Ghana, investment rate and income per person in, 197f
Glaeser, Edward, 181
GNP (gross national product), 28
Golden Rule level of capital, 198–206, 220
comparing steady states and, 198–201, 200f, 201f
numerical example of finding steady state and, 202t, 202–203
transition to steady state and, 203–206, 204f, 205f
Goldfeld, Stephen M., 524n
Gold standard, 78
Free Silver movement in, 101–102
international, 346–347
return to, following Civil War, 270
Goodfriend, Marvin, 545n
Goods and services
demand for, 59–63, 187–190
equilibrium in market for, 64–65
intermediate, 21
international flow of. *See* International flows of capital and goods
normal goods and, 466
supply of, 47–48, 64–65, 187–190
used, 20
Goods market in Mundell-Fleming model, 336–338, 337f
Gordon, David, 428n
Gordon, Robert J., 34, 240n, 393n
Gourinchas, Pierre-Olivier, 471n
Government bonds, 451–452
Government debt, 431–453. *See also* Budget deficits
balanced budgets versus optimal fiscal policy and, 448
fiscal effects on monetary policy and, 449
international issues related to, 450–452
measuring, problems in, 435–439
political process and, 449–450
Ricardian view of, 441–447
size of, 431, 432t, 432–435, 433f
traditional view of, 439–441
in United States, 431, 432t, 432–435, 433f
Government purchases, 26–27, 62–63
increase in, 67, 67f
IS curve shifts and changes in short-run equilibrium due to, 304f, 304–305
Government-purchases multiplier, 283–285, 284f
Gray, Jo Anna, 379n

Great Depression, 5, 233, 252, 278, 317–325, 318t–319t, 459
 bank failures during, 500, 516–517, 517t
 devaluation and recovery from, 349
 failure of forecasters to predict, 409–410
 money hypothesis of, 320–323, 322f
 possibility of recurrence, 323–325
 power vacuum at Fed and, 536
 spending hypothesis of, 318–320
 stabilization policy and, 412
Greece
 government debt of, 432t
 investment rate and income per person in, 197f
 seigniorage in, 90
Greenback Party, 270
Greenbacks, 270
Greenspan, Alan, 421, 449, 525
Griliches, Zvi, 34, 238n
Gross domestic product (GDP), 16, 17–30, 44–73, 45f
 arithmetic tricks for working with percentage changes and, 25
 components of expenditure and, 25–28
 computation of, 18–22
 definition of, 19–20
 determinants of, 46–48, 548. *See also* Factors of production; Production function
 GDP deflator and, 23–24
 imports and exports as percentage of, 115, 116f
 income, expenditure, and circular flow and, 17–19, 18f
 nominal, 22–23
 Okun's law and, 258
 other measures of income compared with, 28–30
 real. *See* Real GDP
 sources and uses of, 44–46, 45f
 stocks and flows and, 19, 19f
Gross national product (GNP), 28
Growth accounting, 244–249
 increases in factors of production and, 244–246
 sources of growth in United States and, 248t, 248–249
 technological progress and, 246–247
Growth effect, 196
Guatemala, investment rate and income per person in, 197f
Guinea-Bissau
 investment rate and income per person in, 197f
 population growth and income per person in, 210f
Gulf War, 390

Haiti, inflation and money growth in, 89f
Hall, Robert E., 160n, 222n, 479, 495n
Hamilton, Alexander, 91, 418–419, 431
Hamilton, John D., 275n
Hansen, Gary D., 211n
Hayashi, Fumio, 471n, 496n
Health care costs, 343, 435
Heston, Alan, 197n
Hicks, John R., 280n
High-powered money, 515
Hirsch, Barry T., 13n
Honduras, population growth and income per person in, 210f
Hong Kong
 economic growth of, 248–249
 exchange rate in, 359
 investment rate and income per person in, 197f
 population growth and income per person in, 210f
House, Christopher L., 495
Housing
 in GDP, 21
 investment in. *See* Residential investment
Howitt, Peter, 240
Hubbard, R. Glenn, 500n
Human capital, 130, 227
Hume, David, 83
Hungary
 Big Mac price and exchange rate in, 144t
 government debt of, 432t
Hurd, Michael, 475n
Hyperinflation, 76, 77, 103–108
 Bolivian, 104–105
 causes of, 105–106
 costs of, 103–105
 German, 76, 104, 106, 107f, 108
Hysteresis, 397

Iceland, inflation and exchange rate in, 141f
Ideas, depletion of, productivity slowdown and, 233
Identities, 26
 quantity equation as, 84
IMF (International Monetary Fund), 354, 356
Imperfect-information model, 380–383
Implicit price deflator for GDP. *See* GDP deflator
Imports as percentage of GDP, 115, 116f
Impossible trinity, 359–361, 360f
Imputations in GDP, 21–22
Imputed value, 21–22
Income, 28–30
 circular flow and, 17–19, 18f
 consumption and, 466f, 466–467, 480
 disposable, 60
 LM curve, 295–296, 296f
 measures of, 28. *See also* Gross domestic product (GDP)
 national, 29. *See also* Gross domestic product (GDP)
 permanent, 476–478
 personal, 29–30
 proprietors', in national income, 29
 rental, in national income, 29
 transitory, 476
Income effect, 468
Income velocity of money, 85
Indexation, 101
Indexed bonds, 451–452
Index of leading economic indicators, 258–259
India
 investment rate and income per person in, 197f
 legal system in, 229
 population growth and income per person in, 210f
 standard of living in, 187t
Indifference curves, 464f, 464–465
Indonesia
 Big Mac price and exchange rate in, 144t
 financial crisis of 1997-1998 in, 355–356
 inflation and money growth in, 89f
 population growth and income per person in, 210f
 standard of living in, 187t
Industrial policy, 228
Inflation. *See also* Deflation; Disinflation; Hyperinflation
 benefit of, 102–103
 cold-turkey solution to, 393
 cost-push, 389
 costs of, 552–553
 definition of, 76
 demand-pull, 388, 390
 economists and public on, 98–99
 expected, costs of, 99–100
 Fisher effect and, 91–93
 in Germany, 76
 inertia of, adaptive expectations and, 387–388
 interest rates and, 91–95
 measurement of government debt and, 435–436
 menu costs of, 99, 104
 Mexican, 140
 nominal exchange rates and, 140–141, 141f
 nominal interest rates and, 92f, 92–93, 93f
 overstatement by CPI, 33–34
 quantity theory of money and, 86–89
 rate of money growth and, 549
 shoeleather cost of, 99, 103
 social costs of. *See* Social costs of inflation
 tradeoff with unemployment. *See* Phillips curve
 unexpected, costs of, 100–102
 in United States, 76, 88, 88f, 89f, 389f, 389–390

Inflation rate, 3
in United States, 4–5, 5f
Inflation targeting, 420–421
Inflation tax, 77, 90
Information, imperfect, 380–383
Information technology, new economy and, 233–234
Infrastructure, 227
Inside lag, 408
Insiders, 169–170, 397
Instant gratification, 481–483
Institutions, production efficiency and, 229–230
Instrumental variables, 224
Insurance
Medicaid, 343, 435
Medicare, 343, 435, 553
social, in Europe, 177
social, in United States, 34, 101, 343, 435, 437, 553
unemployment. *See* Unemployment insurance
Interest, net, in national income, 29
Interest-rate differentials, 351–356
Asian financial crisis and, 355–356
country risk and exchange-rate expectations and, 351–352
Mexican financial crisis and, 353–355
in Mundell-Fleming model, 352–353, 353f
Interest rates, 61, 62f
differences among, 63
federal funds, 312, 421, 525
as Fed policy instrument, 312–313
Fisher effect and, 91–93
inflation and, 91–95
IS curve and, 288f, 288–289
monetary policy and, 295
money and prices linked to, 96f
nominal. *See* Nominal interest rates
real. *See* Real interest rates
wars and, 68f, 68–69
world, capital mobility and, 121–122
Intergenerational redistribution, balanced budgets and, 448
Intermediaries, 500
Intermediate goods in GDP, 21
International flows of capital and goods, 116–121
example of, 120–121
net exports and, 116–118
trade balance and, 118–120, 119t
International Monetary Fund (IMF), 354, 356
International trade, 439–440
Intertemporal budget constraint, 461–463, 463f
Intertemporal choice, 461–471
borrowing constraint and, 468–471, 469f, 470f
budget constraint and, 461–463, 463f
consumer preferences and, 464f, 464–465
income and, 466f, 466–467
optimization and, 465f, 465–466
real interest rate and, 467f, 467–468
Intertemporal substitution of labor, 531–533
Inventories
as factor of production, 505
in GDP, 20–21
Inventory investment, 487, 488f, 504–507
accelerator model of inventories and, 505–506, 506f
real interest rate and, 507
reasons for holding inventories and, 504–505
Investment, 26, 61, 62f, 487–508
allocating, 227–228
break-even, 207f, 207–208
business cycles and, 254, 255f
business fixed. *See* Business fixed investment
crowding out of, 67
foreign, net, 118–120
growth in capital stock and, 190f–192f, 190–192
in housing, Great Depression and, 319
international differences in, 196–198, 197f
inventory, 487, 488f, 504–507
IS curve and, 288f, 288–289
neoclassical model of, 488–489
net, 492
residential. *See* Residential investment
shifts in demand for, trade balance and, 126f, 126–127
in small open economies. *See* Small open economies
Investment demand, 69–71, 70f, 71f
shifts in, in large open economy, 155, 155f
shifts in, real exchange rate and, 137f, 137–138
Investment tax credit, 494
Ireland, inflation in, 397
IS curve, 279–280. *See also IS-LM* model
algebra of, 329–330
fiscal policy and, 289, 290f
interest rate and investment and, 288f, 288–289
Keynesian cross and, 280–287, 281f–284f, 286f
loanable-funds interpretation of, 290–292
*IS** curve, 337f, 337–339, 340f
IS-LM model, 264, 278–301, 303–327, 402, 439, 470. *See also IS* curve; *LM* curve
aggregate demand and, 279, 279f, 313–314, 314f, 315f, 331–333
as aggregate demand theory, 313–317
algebra of, 329–331
credit crunches and, 500
fluctuations explained by, 304–313
Great Depression and, 317–325, 318t–319t
in short and long run, 315–317, 316f
short-run model of large open economy and, 368f, 368–372
Israel
inflation and nominal interest rates in, 93f
inflation targeting in, 420
investment rate and income per person in, 197f
population growth and income per person in, 210f
Italy
central bank of, 424f
economic growth of, 231t
exchange rate in, 349
government debt of, 432, 432t
imports and exports as percentage of GDP in, 116f
inflation in, 397
legal system in, 229
leisure in, 180f
population growth and income per person in, 210f
seigniorage in, 90
unemployment rate in, 176–178, 177f

Jamaica, population growth and income per person in, 210f
Japan
Big Mac price and exchange rate in, 144t
central bank of, 424f
depression during 1990s in, 324–325
economic growth of, 194–195, 196, 224, 231t
government debt of, 432, 432t
imports and exports as percentage of GDP in, 116f
inflation and exchange rate in, 141f
investment rate and income per person in, 197, 197f
saving rate in, 470–471
standard of living in, 187t
unions in, 169t
John, Andrew, 541n
Johnson, Lyndon, 478
Johnson, Simon, 230
Jones, Charles I., 222n, 235n
Jordan, population growth and income per person in, 210f
Jorgenson, Dale W., 34, 495n
Junk bonds, 63

Katz, Lawrence F., 165n, 167n, 171n
Kehoe, Patrick J., 440n
Kennedy, John F., 287
Kennickel, Arthur, 475n

Keynes, John Maynard, 76, 278, 280, 292, 379, 413, 425, 460, 467, 483, 528–529
beauty contests of, 498–499
consumption function and, 457–461, 458f
Keynesian cross, 280–287, 281f–284f, 286f
King, Robert G., 229n, 536, 545n
King, Stephen R., 393n
Kiyotaki, Nobuhiro, 538n
Klenow, Peter J., 222n
Knowledge spillovers, 228
Kochin, Levis A., 69n
Kremer, Michael, 211–212
Krueger, Alan B., 167n, 175n
Krugman, Paul R., 178n, 325n
Kuttner, Kenneth, 325n
Kuznets, Simon, 459–460, 473
Kydland, Finn E., 428n

Labor. *See also* Unemployment; Unemployment rate; Unions
efficiency of, technological progress and, 217–218
increases in, economic growth and, 245–246
intertemporal substitution of, 531–533
marginal product of, 50–53, 51f, 52f
Labor-augmenting technological progress, 218
Labor demand, 51–53, 52f
Labor force, 35. *See also* Unemployment; Unemployment rate; Unions
transitions into and out of, 175–176, 176t
U.S., changing composition of, 174
Labor-force participation rate, 35–37, 37f
Labor hoarding, 534
Labor markets, benefit of inflation in, 102–103
Labor productivity
average, 57
as key determinant of real wages, 58t, 58–59
Lags in implementation and effects of policies, 407–409
Laibson, David I., 481, 482n, 483n
Laidler, David, 524n
La Porta, Rafael, 229n
Large, comprehensive economic model, 401–402
Large open economies, 149–157
model of, 151–153
net capital outflow and, 149–151, 150f
policies in, 153f, 153–157
short-run model of, 368f, 368–372
trade deficits of, 145
United States as, 145–146, 364–365
Laspeyres index, 32

Latin America. *See also specific countries*
debt defaults in, 450
legal system in, 229
Law of one price, 141–142
Leading indicators, 258–259, 409
Learning by doing, 228
Lebow, David E., 544n
Legal systems, 229
Leisure in Europe, 180f, 180–181
Lender of last resort, 517
Level effect, 196
Levine, Ross, 229n
Levy, Daniel, 539n
Liabilities
contingent, measurement of, 437–438
uncounted, measurement of government debt and, 437–438
Life-cycle hypothesis, 471–475, 473f, 474f
Lilien, David M., 175n
Liquidity, 78
Liquidity constraint, 468
Liquidity preference, theory of, 292–295, 293f, 294f
Liquidity traps, 325
Living standard. *See* Gross domestic product (GDP); Standard of living
LM curve, 279, 280, 292–298. *See also IS-LM* model
algebra of, 330–331
income and money demand and, 295–296, 296f
liquidity preference and, 292–295, 293f, 294f
monetary policy and, 297, 297f
quantity-equation interpretation of, 298
*LM** curve, 338, 339f
Loanable funds, 66
demand for. *See* Investment
IS curve and, 290–292, 291f
market for, in large open economy, 151–152, 152f
Long run
Mundell-Fleming model and, 361–364, 362f, 363f
short run versus, 260–261
Long-run aggregate supply curve (*LRAS*), 265–267, 266f, 268–270
Lopez-de-Silanes, Florencio, 229n
Loss function, 428
Lown, Cara, 501n
LRAS (long-run aggregate supply curve), 265–267, 266f, 268–270
Lucas, Robert E., Jr., 13, 131n, 235n, 382, 382n, 411, 533n
Lucas critique, 411–412
Luddites, 239–240
Luxembourg
investment rate and income per person in, 197f
population growth and income per person in, 210f

MacCulloch, Robert J., 180n
Macroeconomic models, policy analysis with, 309t, 309–310
Macroeconomics
definition of, 2
most important lessons of, 547–550
questions studied by, 2–5
unresolved questions of, 550–554
Maddison, Angus, 231n
Madison, James, 431
Madrian, Brigitte, 483n
Malaysia, Big Mac price and exchange rate in, 144t
Malthus, Thomas Robert, 211
Mankiw, N. Gregory, 222n, 226n, 227n, 383n, 480n, 537n, 538n
Mann, Catherine L., 129n
Marginally attached workers, 176t
Marginal product, diminishing, 50–51
Marginal product of capital (*MPK*), 53
Marginal product of labor (*MPL*), 50–51, 51f
labor demand and, 51–53, 52f
Marginal propensity to consume (*MPC*), 60, 60f, 457
Marginal rate of substitution, 464
Market clearing assumption, 11–12
Martin, William McChesney, 406
Marx, Karl, 48
Mauro, Paulo, 229n
McCallum, Bennett T., 537n
McKinley, William, 102
Measurement problems, productivity slowdown and, 232
Medicaid, 343, 435
Medicare, 343, 435, 553
Medium of exchange, money as, 78
Men, labor-force participation rate of, 36, 37f
Menu costs
aggregate-demand externalities and, 538–539
of inflation, 99, 104
Metrick, Andrew, 483n
Mexico
Big Mac price and exchange rate in, 144t
financial crisis of 1994-1995 in, 353–355
inflation and exchange rate in, 140, 141f
investment rate and income per person in, 197f, 198
standard of living in, 187t
Meyer, Bruce D., 165n
Microeconomics, 12
Minimum-wage laws, 166–168
Mint Act of 1792, 91
Miron, Jeffrey A., 30n, 425n
Mishkin, Frederic S., 421n
*M*1 money measure, 82, 82t
*M*2 money measure, 82, 82t
*M*3 money measure, 82, 82t

Model of aggregate supply and aggregate demand, 261–262, 402. *See also* Aggregate demand *(AD)*; Aggregate supply *(AS)*
Models, 7. *See also* Economic models; *specific models*
Modigliani, Franco, 13, 460, 461, 471, 473
Moffitt, Robert, 175n
Monetarists, 419
Monetary aggregates, demise of, 525
Monetary base, 514
  Great Depression and, 516, 517t
A Monetary History of the United States, 1867–1960 (Friedman and Schwartz), 536
Monetary neutrality, 109
Monetary policy, 81, 371, 371f
  contractionary, 270
  effectiveness of, 332–333
  expansionary, 312
  fixed exchange rates and, 348f, 348–349
  floating exchange rates and, 342f, 342–343
  instruments of, 515–517
  interaction with fiscal policy, 307, 308f, 309–310, 449
  interest rates and, 295
  IS curve shifts and changes in short-run equilibrium due to, 306f, 306–307
  lags associated with, 408
  LM curve and, 297, 297f
  to reduce inflation, 390
  rules for, 419–425
  summary of effects in Mundell-Fleming model, 350, 351t
Monetary transmission mechanism, 307
Monetary union, 357–358
Money, 77–83
  commodity, 78
  cost of holding, 95
  creation by banks, 512
  definition of, 77
  demand for. *See* Money demand
  fiat, 78, 79–80
  functions of, 77–78
  future, current prices and, 96f, 96–97, 112–114
  gold standard and, 78
  high-powered, 515
  income velocity of, 85
  neutrality of, 535–537
  in POW camp, 79
  prices and interest rates linked to, 96f
  quantity theory of. *See* Quantity theory of money
  seigniorage and, 89–91
  supply of. *See* Money supply
  transactions velocity of, 84
  on Yap Island, 80
Money demand, 518–525
  empirical studies of, 523–524
  financial innovation, near money, and demise of monetary aggregates and, 524–525
  LM curve, 295–296, 296f
  nominal interest rate and, 95–97
  portfolio theories of, 518–520
  transactions theories of, 520–524, 521f, 523f
Money demand function, 85–86
Money hypothesis of Great Depression, 320–323, 322f
Money market in Mundell-Fleming model, 338–339, 339f, 340f
Money multiplier, 514–515
  Great Depression and, 516, 517t
Money supply, 510–517
  control of, 81
  fractional-reserve banking and, 512–513
  Great Depression and, 320–323, 322f, 516, 517t
  inflation and, 87–89, 88f, 89f, 105
  instruments of monetary policy and, 515–517
  measurement of, 81–83, 82t
  model of, 514–515
  100-percent-reserve banking and, 511
  rate of growth of, inflation and unemployment and, 549
  in United States, 88, 88f, 89f
Moore's law, 233–234
Moral hazard, 170–171
Mortgages, borrowing limit on, 503, 503t
MPC (marginal propensity to consume), 60, 60f, 457
MPK (marginal product of capital), 53
MPL (marginal product of labor), 50–51, 51f
  labor demand and, 51–53, 52f
Mulligan, Casey B., 533n
Multipliers
  government-purchases, 283–285, 284f
  money, 514–515, 516, 517t
  tax, 285–286, 286f
Mundell, Robert A., 334, 335
Mundell-Fleming model, 334–365, 340f
  with changing price level, 361–364, 362f, 363f
  fixed exchange rates and, 344–350, 356–361, 402
  floating exchange rates and, 340–343, 356–361, 402
  goods market and *IS** curve and, 336–338, 337f
  interest-rate differentials and, 351–356
  money market and *LM** curve and, 338, 339f
  short-run model of large open economy and, 368f, 368–372
Municipal bonds, 63
Mussa, Michael, 108n
NAFTA (North American Free Trade Agreement), 354
NAIRU (Non-Accelerating Inflation Rate of Unemployment), 388
  precision of estimates of, 392
National Bureau of Economic Research (NBER), 253–254
National income, 29. *See also* Gross domestic product (GDP)
  distribution of, 53–55
National income accounting, 17
  GDP and. *See* Gross domestic product (GDP)
National income accounts identity, 26, 118
National saving, 65–66, 66f. *See also* Saving
  government influence on, 226–227
Natural level of output, promoting growth of, 550–551
Natural-rate hypothesis, 396–397
Natural rate of unemployment, 159–162, 392
  job loss and job finding and, 160–162, 161f
  precision of estimates of, 392
NBER (National Bureau of Economic Research), 253–254
Near money, 525
Neoclassical model of investment, 488–489
Neoclassical theory of distribution, 48
Net capital outflow, 118–120
Net exports, 27, 116–118. *See also* Trade balances
Net foreign investment, 118–120
Netherlands
  central bank of, 424f
  exchange rate in, 349
  government debt of, 432t
  unions in, 169t
Net interest in national income, 29
Net investment, 492
Net national product (NNP), 28
Neumark, David, 167n
Neutrality of money, 535–537
Nevins, Alan, 171
New Keynesian economics, 528–529, 537–544
  recessions as coordination failure and, 539–541, 540f
  small menu costs and aggregate-demand externalities and, 538–539
  staggering of wages and prices and, 541–544
Newton, Isaac, 238
New Zealand, 425
  Big Mac price and exchange rate in, 144t
  central bank of, 424f
  economic growth of, 224
  inflation and exchange rate in, 141f
  inflation targeting in, 420
  unions in, 169t

Nickell, Stephen, 179n
Niger, population growth and income per person in, 210f
Nigeria
investment rate and income per person in, 197f
standard of living in, 187t
Nixon, Richard M., 3, 390
NNP (net national product), 28
Nominal exchange rates, 131, 346
determinants of, 139–141
inflation and, 140–141, 141f
Nominal GDP, real GDP versus, 22–23
Nominal interest rates, 61, 91
demand for money and, 95–97
inflation and, 92f, 92–93, 93f
in nineteenth century, 94–95
Nominal variables, 108–109
Non-Accelerating Inflation Rate of Unemployment (NAIRU), 388
precision of estimates of, 392
Nordhaus, William, 416n
Normal goods, 466
North American Free Trade Agreement (NAFTA), 354
Norway
central bank of, 424f
devaluation in, 349
inflation and exchange rate in, 141f
investment rate and income per person in, 197f
unions in, 169t

Okun, Arthur M., 256, 393n
Okun's law, 256–257, 257f, 386–387, 393, 395
100 percent experience rated unemployment insurance, 164
100-percent-reserve banking, 511
OPEC. *See* Organization of Petroleum Exporting Countries (OPEC)
Open economies, 59, 115–146. *See also* Exchange rates; International flows of capital and goods; Large open economies; Mundell-Fleming model; Small open economies
Open-market operations, 81, 312, 515
Optimization, intertemporal choice and, 465f, 465–466
Organization of Petroleum Exporting Countries (OPEC), 387
productivity slowdown and, 232
shocks caused by, 274–275, 390
unemployment and, 174
Oswald, Andrew J., 180n
Output. *See also* Gross domestic product (GDP); National income
natural level of, promoting growth of, 550–551
of small open economy, 123
Outside lag, 408
Outsiders, 169–170, 397

Paasche index, 32
Pakistan
inflation and exchange rate in, 141f
inflation and nominal interest rates in, 93f
investment rate and income per person in, 197f
standard of living in, 187t
Panama, investment rate and income per person in, 197f
Parker, Jonathan A., 380n, 471n, 480n
Partially experience rated unemployment insurance, 164
Percentage changes, arithmetic tricks for working with, 25
Permanent income, 476–478
Permanent-income hypothesis, 476–478
Perry, George L., 38n, 103n
Personal income, 29–30
disposable, 30
Petersen, Bruce C., 500n
Phelps, Edmund, 199n, 387
Philippines, standard of living in, 187t
Phillips, A.W., 387
Phillips curve, 374, 385–398, 549–550
adaptive expectations and inflation inertia and, 387–388
causes of rising and falling inflation and, 388–390, 389f
challenge to natural-rate hypothesis and, 396–397
derivation from aggregate supply curve, 385–387
disinflation and sacrifice ratio and, 392–393, 395t, 395–396
modern, history of, 387
precision of estimates of natural rate of unemployment and, 392
rational expectations and, 393–395
short-run tradeoff and, 390–392, 391f
time inconsistency and, 428–430
Pigou, Arthur, 321
Pigou effect, 321
Plague, factor prices and, 54–55
Planned expenditure, Keynesian cross and, 280–281, 281f
Plosser, Charles I., 536, 537n
Poland, Big Mac price and exchange rate in, 144t
Policy analysis with macroeconomic models, 309t, 309–310
Policymakers, distrust of, 416
Political business cycle, 416
Political process
distrust of, 416
government debt and, 449–450
Population growth, 206–212
effects of, 208f, 208–210
international comparison of, 209–210, 210f
Kremerian model of, 211–212
Malthusian model of, 211
Solow model of, 206–210
steady state with, 206–208, 207f
in United States, 206
Portfolio theories of money demand, 518–520
Portugal
government debt of, 432t
unions in, 169t
Posen, Adam S., 325n
POW (prisoner of war) camps, money in, 79
Precautionary saving, 475
Prescott, Edward C., 13, 181, 211n, 428n, 535n
Present value, 463
Price levels. *See also* Deflation; Disinflation; Hyperinflation; Inflation
changing, Mundell-Fleming model with, 361–364, 362f, 363f
Prices. *See also* Consumer price index (CPI); Deflation; Disinflation; Hyperinflation; Inflation
adjustment of, staggering of, 541–544
base-year, 23
of basket of goods, 31
of Big Macs, exchange rates and, 143–145, 144t
current, future money and, 96f, 96–97, 112–114
of factors of production, 48–49, 49f, 54–55
falling, money hypothesis of Great Depression and, 321–323, 322f
flexibility of, business cycles and, 537
flexible, 12
inflation of, 387. *See also* Inflation
money and interest rates linked to, 96f
quantity theory of money and, 86–89
sticky, 12, 260–261, 375–376, 382–383, 538–539, 542t, 542–543, 543t
of stock, random walk and, 498
Price shocks, 272
Principles of Economics (Samuelson), 13
Principles of Political Economy and Taxation (Ricardo), 447
Prisoner of war (POW) camps, money in, 79
Private saving, 65
government influence on, 226–227
Production efficiency, factor accumulation versus, 222–224
Production function, 47
Cobb-Douglas, 55–59, 57f, 130, 490
MPL and, 51, 51f
supply of goods and, 188, 189f
Production smoothing, 505
Productivity

capital, average, 57
growth of, unemployment and, 174–175
labor. *See* Labor productivity
total factor, 232, 247
Profits, 50
accounting, 54
corporate, in national income, 29
economic, 53–54
Proprietors' income in national income, 29
Public finance, 440n
Public policy, frictional unemployment and, 163–165
Public saving, 45, 65
Purchasing-power parity, 141–145, 142f

Quantity equation, 83–84
as aggregate demand, 263, 263f
money demand function and, 85–86
Quantity theory of money, 83–89
constant velocity assumption and, 86
LM curve and, 298
money, prices, and inflation and, 86–89
money demand function and, 85–86
quantity equation and, 83–84, 85–86
transactions and, 83–85

Radford, R. A., 79n
Raff, Daniel M. G., 171n
Random-walk hypothesis, 478–480
Rapping, Leonard A., 533n
Rational expectations, disinflation and, 393–395
Reagan, Ronald, 3, 129, 433, 447, 450
Real business cycle theory, 528, 529–537
economics of Robinson Crusoe and, 529–531
intertemporal substitution of labor and, 531–533
neutrality of money and, 535–537
technology shocks and, 533–535
wage and price flexibility and, 537
Real exchange rates, 133–139, 346
determinants of, 135, 135f
policies influencing, 136f, 136–138, 137f
purchasing-power parity and, 141–145, 142f
trade balance and, 134, 134f
trade policies and, 138f, 138–139
Real GDP, 3
chain-weighted measures of, 24
economic fluctuations and. *See* Economic fluctuations
nominal GDP versus, 22–23
per person in United States, 4, 4f
of United States, 186, 187t
Real interest rates, 61, 62f
consumption and, 467f, 467–468
ex ante, 94
ex post, 94
Real money balances, 85
Real rental price of capital, 53
Real variables, 108–109
Real wages, 52–53
cyclical behavior of, 379–380, 380f
labor productivity as key determinant of, 58t, 58–59
Recessions, 4, 5, 252
as coordination failure, 539–541, 540f
of 1873-1879, 270
of 1982, 410–411
of 1990, 500
of 2001, 311–312
OPEC, 274–275
Reichsbank, 108
Rental income in national income, 29
Rental price of capital, 489f, 489–490
Rentenbank, 108
Repetto, Andrea, 482n
Research and development, microeconomics of, 237–240
Reserve Bank of New Zealand Act of 1989, 420
Reserve-deposit ratio, 514
Reserve requirements, 515–516
Reserves, 511
excess, 516
Residential investment, 487, 488f, 501–504
changes in housing demand and, 502f, 502–503
mortgage ceilings and, 503, 503t
stock equilibrium and flow supply and, 501f, 501–502
taxes and, 504
Returns to scale, constant, 47
Revaluation, 348, 349
Revenue Act of 1932, 320
Revolutionary War, 90–91, 431
Ricardian equivalence, 431, 441–447
basic logic of, 442–443
consumers and future taxes and, 443–446
Ricardo, David, 223–224, 442, 447
Risk aversion, 101
Robinson, James A., 230
Rodriguez-Clare, Andres, 222n
Rogoff, Kenneth, 334n
Romania, inflation and nominal interest rates in, 93f
Romer, Christina D., 413, 536–537
Romer, David, 222n, 224, 227n, 383n, 529n, 536–537, 541n
Romer, Paul M., 228n, 235n
Rosen, Harvey, 440n
Rotemberg, Julio, 376n, 545n
Rudd, Jeremy E., 544n
Rule for conduct of stabilization policy, 415–425, 429
Russia
Big Mac price and exchange rate in, 144t
debt default by, 450
standard of living in, 187t
trade surplus of, 130

Sacerdote, Bruce, 181
Sachs, Jeffrey D., 223–224, 224n, 349n
Sacrifice ratio, 393, 395t, 395–396
Sala-i-Martin, Xavier, 222n
Samuelson, Paul A., 13
Sargent, Thomas J., 106n, 107n, 394
Saving, 65–66, 66f
of elderly, 475
evaluating rate of, 225–226
fiscal policy and, 67f, 67–69, 68f
growth and, 195–198, 196f
increasing, 482–483
international differences in, 196–198, 197f
national, 65–66, 66f
precautionary, 475
private, 65
public, 45, 65
in small open economies. *See* Small open economies
Saving rate
changing, 226–227
Golden Rule level of capital and, 201, 201f
Japanese, 470–471
Scale, constant returns to, 47
Schumer, Charles, 361
Schumpeter, Joseph, 239, 240
Schwartz, Anna J., 87–88, 318n, 320, 536
Seasonal adjustment, 30
Sectoral shifts, 163
Secular stagnation, 459, 460
Seigniorage, 89–91, 270
Senate Budget Committee, 442
Senate Finance Committee, 34
Services. *See also* Goods and services
demand for, determinants of, 59–63
supply of, 47–48
Shapiro, Matthew D., 34n, 410n, 444n, 495
Shiller, Robert J., 98, 99n, 452n, 499n
Shimer, Robert, 175n
Shleifer, Andrei, 229n, 446n
Shocks, 270
demand, 270, 271f, 271–272
in *IS-LM* model, 310–312
price, 272
supply, 270, 272–275, 273f, 387
technology, business cycles and, 533–535
Shoeleather cost of inflation, 99, 103
Short run
long run versus, 260–261
Phillips curve in, 390–392, 391f

Short-run aggregate supply curve
(*SRAS*), 267f, 267–270, 268f
Short-run equilibrium, 299f, 299–300, 300f
shifting by fiscal policy, 304f, 304–306, 305f
shifting by monetary policy, 306f, 306–307
Sichel, Daniel E., 524n
Silver
Free Silver movement and, 101–102
Silver, Stephen, 380n
Simplifying assumptions, 10–12
Singapore
Big Mac price and exchange rate in, 144t
economic growth of, 248–249
inflation and exchange rate in, 141f
inflation and money growth in, 89f
legal system in, 229
trade surplus of, 130
Slemrod, Joel, 444n
Slovak Republic, government debt of, 432t
Small open economies, 121–131, 402
assumption of, 122–123
capital mobility and world interest rate and, 121–122
countries qualifying as, 122
evaluating economic policy and, 127–131
investment of, 123
model of, 123–124, 124f
policies influencing trade balance and, 124–127
Smith, Adam, 223–224, 224, 229
Social costs of inflation, 97–103
benefit of inflation and, 102–103
of expected inflation, 99–100
layman's view and classical response to, 97–99
of unexpected inflation, 100–102
Social insurance in Europe, 177
Social Security, 34, 343, 435, 437, 553
indexation of, 101
Solon, Gary, 380n
Solow, Robert M., 13, 120, 175n, 187n, 234, 247
Solow growth model, 186–213, 216–235, 249, 456, 470
balanced growth and, 220–221
capital accumulation and. *See* Capital accumulation
convergence and, 221–222
factor accumulation versus production efficiency and, 222–224
Golden Rule level of capital and, 187–198
policies to promote growth and, 224–234
population growth and, 206–212
technological progress in, 217–220
Solow residual, 247
business cycles and, 534–535, 535f
Souleles, Nicholas S., 480n
South Africa
Big Mac price and exchange rate in, 144t
inflation and exchange rate in, 141f
investment rate and income per person in, 197f
population growth and income per person in, 210f
South Korea
Big Mac price and exchange rate in, 144t
economic growth of, 224, 248–249
financial crisis of 1997-1998 in, 355–356
inflation and exchange rate in, 141f
investment rate and income per person in, 197f
trade deficits of, 127
trade surplus of, 130
Soviet Union, cigarettes as money in, 79n
Spain
central bank of, 424f
inflation in, 397
inflation targeting in, 420
investment rate and income per person in, 197f
legal system in, 229
unions in, 169t
Speculative attacks, 359
Spending hypothesis of Great Depression, 318–320
Spiegelman, Robert G., 165n
Sprenkle, Case M., 520n
SRAS (short-run aggregate supply curve), 267f, 267–270, 268f
Stabilization, 551–552
balanced budgets and, 448
Stabilization policy, 270–275, 406–426
active versus passive, 407–415
economic forecasting and, 409–411
historical record of, 412–415
lags in implementation and effects of policies and, 407–409
Lucas critique and, 411–412
rule versus discretion for conducting, 415–425
shocks to aggregate demand and, 271f, 271–272
shocks to aggregate supply and, 272–275, 273f
Stagflation, 272, 274–275
Stagnation, secular, 459, 460
Staiger, Douglas, 392
Standard of living. *See also* Gross domestic product (GDP)
international differences in, 186, 187t
population growth and, 209–210, 210f
Statistics. *See also specific statistics, e.g.,* Unemployment rate
seasonally adjusted, 30
Steady state
Golden Rule level of capital and, 198–206
growth in capital stock and, 190f–192f, 190–192
with population growth, 206–208, 207f
with technological progress, 218–219, 219f
Steady-state level of capital, 190f–192f, 190–192
approaching, numerical example of, 192–195, 194t
Sticky-price model, 375–376, 382–383
Sticky prices, 12, 260–261, 538, 542t, 542–543, 543t
Sticky-wage model, 377–379, 378f
Stock, 495
Stock, James H., 392, 415n
Stock market, 495
as economic indicator, 496–497, 497f
efficient markets hypothesis versus Keynes's beauty contests and, 497–499
informational efficiency of, 498
Tobin's *q* and, 495–497
Stock-out avoidance, 505
Stock prices
Great Depression and, 319
random walk and, 498
shocks causing fall in, 311–312
Stocks, 19, 19f
Store of value, money as, 77
Strong, Benjamin, 536
Structural unemployment, 165–171, 166f
efficiency wages and, 170–171
minimum-wage laws and, 166–168
unions and collective bargaining and, 168–170, 169t
Substitution
intertemporal, of labor, 531–533
marginal rate of, 464
Substitution effect, 468
Summers, Lawrence H., 171n, 172n, 226n, 397n, 425n, 446n, 496n, 535n
Summers, Robert, 197n
Sumner, Scott, 380n
Supply
aggregate. *See* Aggregate supply *(AS)*
at equilibrium. *See* Equilibrium
of goods, production function and, 188, 189f
of goods and services, 47–48, 64–65
of housing, 501f, 501–502
of money. *See* Money supply
Supply-and-demand diagram, 8f, 8–10, 9f
Supply shocks, 270, 272–275, 273f
Phillips curve and, 387
Supply-siders, 287, 440

Surpluses
  budget, 45, 62, 226
  trade, 119, 130
Sweden
  Big Mac price and exchange rate in, 144t
  central bank of, 424f
  devaluation in, 349
  government debt of, 432t
  inflation and exchange rate in, 141f
  inflation targeting in, 420
  unions in, 169t, 169–170
Switzerland
  Big Mac price and exchange rate in, 144t
  central bank of, 424f
  inflation and exchange rate in, 141, 141f
  inflation and money growth in, 89f
  inflation and nominal interest rates in, 93f
  investment rate and income per person in, 197f
  unions in, 169t

Taiwan
  Big Mac price and exchange rate in, 144t
  economic growth of, 248–249
Tanzania
  investment rate and income per person in, 197f
  population growth and income per person in, 210f
Tax cuts
  budget deficit and, 447
  demand and, 69
  to stimulate economy, 287, 478
Taxes
  demand for investment and, 70
  Great Depression and, 320
  housing and, 504
  incentives and, 440
  inflation, 77, 90
  interest rates and, 63
  investment and, 494–495
  IS curve shifts and changes in short-run equilibrium due to changes in, 305f, 305–306
  labor supply and, 181
  lowering or withholding for, 444
  surcharge and, 478
  trade deficits and, 129
Tax multiplier, 285–286, 286f
Tax Reform Act of 1986, 494
Tax smoothing, balanced budgets and, 448
Tax surcharges, 478
Taylor, John B., 422, 542n
Taylor rule, 421–422
Technological externalities, 228
Technological progress, 217–220
  demand for investment and, 70
  economic growth and, 246–247
  effects of, 219t, 219–220
  efficiency of labor and, 217–218
  encouraging, 230–234
  labor-augmenting, 218
  steady state with, 218–219, 219f
Technology shocks, business cycles and, 533–535
Teenagers, minimum wage and, 166–167
Temin, Peter, 318n
Term, interest rates and, 63
Terms of trade. *See* Real exchange rates
Terrorist attacks of 9/11/2001, 311
Thailand
  Big Mac price and exchange rate in, 144t
  financial crisis of 1997-1998 in, 355–356
  investment rate and income per person in, 197f
Thaler, Richard H., 482, 483n
Theory. *See* Economic models; *specific models*
Theory of liquidity preference, 292–295, 293f, 294f
Time horizons, macroeconomic, 259–262
Time inconsistency
  of discretionary policy, 416–419
  Phillips curve and, 428–430
Time-inconsistent consumer preferences, 481
Tobacman, Jeremy, 482n
Tobin, James, 13, 495, 518n, 520
Tobin's *q*, 495–497
Total factor productivity, 232, 247
Trade. *See also* Net exports
  balanced, 119
  free, economic growth and, 223–224
  imports and exports as percentage of GDP and, 115, 116f
  terms of. *See* Real exchange rates
Trade balances
  bilateral, irrelevance of, 120
  determination of, 124
  international capital flows and, 118–120, 119t
  policies influencing, 124–127
  real exchange rate and, 134, 134f
Trade deficits, 119
  of South Korea, 127
  of United States, 127, 128f, 129, 145
Trade policy
  fixed exchange rates and, 349–350, 350f
  floating exchange rates and, 343, 344f
  in large open economy, 155–156, 156f
  real exchange rate and, 138f, 138–139
  summary of effects in Mundell-Fleming model, 350, 351t
Trade surpluses, 119, 130
Transactions theories of money demand, 520–524, 521f, 523f
Transactions velocity of money, 84
Transitory income, 476
Tufte, Edward, 416n
Turkey
  inflation and money growth in, 89, 89f
  inflation and nominal interest rates in, 93f
Twin deficits, 129

Underground economy, 22
  currency and, 519–520
  labor supply and, 181
  Soviet, 79n
Unemployment, 159–183
  business cycles and, 255–257, 256f, 257f
  duration of, 172–173
  European, 176–180, 177f
  frictional, 162–165
  rate of money growth and, 549
  structural, 165–171, 166f
  teenage, minimum wage and, 166–167
  tradeoff with inflation. *See* Phillips curve
  transitions into and out of labor force and, 175–176, 176t
  trends in, 174–175
  in United States, 172–176, 256f, 278, 389f, 389–390
Unemployment insurance, 163–165
  in Europe, 177
  rate of job finding and, 164–165
  in United States, 177
Unemployment rate, 3, 16–17, 34–39
  definition of, 35
  establishment survey of, 38–39
  household survey of, 35–37, 36f, 38
  natural, 159–162, 161f, 392
  Non-Accelerating Inflation Rate of Unemployment, 388, 392
  steady-state, 161–162
  in United States, 5, 6f
  variation across demographic groups, 173t, 173–174
Unexpected inflation, costs of, 100–102
Unions
  labor supply and, 181
  unemployment and, 178–179
  wage rigidity and, 168–170, 169t
United Kingdom
  Big Mac price and exchange rate in, 144t
  central bank of, 424f
  currency of, 358
  devaluation in, 349
  economic growth of, 231t
  imports and exports as percentage of GDP in, 116f
  indexed bonds in, 451
  inflation and exchange rate in, 141f
  inflation targeting in, 420
  unemployment rate in, 176–178, 177f
  unions in, 169t
  wars and interest rates in, 68f, 68–69

United States
Asian financial crisis and, 356
Big Mac price and exchange rate in, 144t
budget deficits of, 553–554
capital accumulation in, 439–440
capital flow in, 359
central bank of, 424f
Civil War in, 222, 270
economic growth of, 231t, 248, 248t
Free Silver movement in, 101–102
government debt in, 431, 432t, 432–435, 433f
historical performance of economy in, 3–5, 4f–6f
imports and exports as percentage of GDP in, 116f
indexation in, 101
inflation and exchange rate in, 141
inflation and nominal interest rates in, 93f
inflation in, 4–5, 5f, 76, 88, 88f, 89f, 389f, 389–390
investment rate and income per person in, 197, 197f
as large open economy, 145–146
large open economy of, 364–365
legal system in, 229
leisure in, 180f
minimum wage in, 167
money supply in, 88, 88f, 89f
population growth and income per person in, 210f
population growth in, 206
real GDP of, 186, 187t
real GDP per person in, 4, 4f
recessions in, 410–411
seigniorage in, 90–91
as small open economy, 122
taxes and incentives and, 440
trade balance with China, 120
trade deficits of, 127, 128f, 129
unemployment in, 5, 6f, 172–176, 256f, 278, 389f, 389–390
unemployment insurance in, 164, 165, 177
unions in, 168, 169, 169t
U.S. Department of Commerce, 17, 22
U.S. Department of Labor, 31
Unit of account, money as, 77–78
Used goods in GDP, 20

Value
imputed, 21–22
money as store of, 77
present, 463
Value added, GDP and, 21
Variables
in economic models, 7f–9f, 7–10
functions to express relationships among, 10
nominal, 108–109
real, 108–109
Velocity of money
constant, assumption in quantity theory of money, 86
stability of, 419
Venable, Robert, 539n
Vietnam
economic growth of, 224
standard of living in, 187t
Vietnam War, 478
Vishny, Robert, 229n
Volcker, Paul, 295, 390, 395, 396, 449

Wage rigidity, 165
structural unemployment and, 165–171, 166f
Wages
adjustment of, staggering of, 541–544
efficiency, 170–171
flexibility of, business cycles and, 537
inflation of, 387
real. *See* Real wages
sticky, 377–379, 378f
Wagner, Richard, 450
Wal-Mart, 239–240
Warner, Andrew, 223–224, 224n
Wars
Civil War, 222, 270
Gulf War, 390
interest rates and, 68f, 68–69
Revolutionary, 431
Vietnam, 478
World War II, 233
Wascher, William, 167n
Washington, George, 418
Watson, Mark W., 392, 415n
The Wealth of Nations (Smith), 223–224
Weil, David N., 211n, 222n, 227n, 235n
Weinberg, Stephen, 482n
West Germany, economic growth of, 231t
Wicksell, Knut, 449
Wilcox, David W., 34n, 452n
The Wizard of Oz (Baum), 102
Women, labor-force participation rate of, 36–37, 37f
Woodbury, Stephen A., 165n
Woodford, Michael, 545n
Worker quality, productivity slowdown and, 232–233
Work in process, 505
WorldCom, 311–312
World interest rate, capital mobility and, 121–122
World War II, 233

Yap Island, money on, 80
Yellen, Janet L., 171n, 538n
Young, Alwyn, 249n

Zambia, investment rate and income per person in, 197f, 198
Zeckhauser, Richard J., 226n
Zimbabwe
inflation and nominal interest rates in, 93f
population growth and income per person in, 210f

U.S. Federal Government Budget Deficit (Adjusted for Inflation)

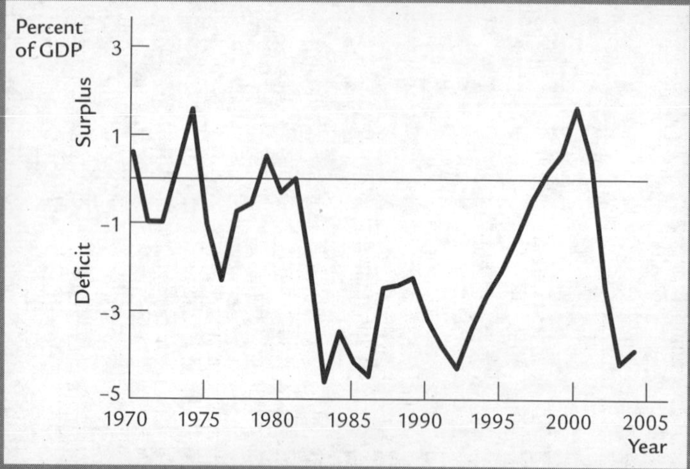

Source: U.S. Congressional Budget Office, U.S. Department of Commerce, and author's calculations.

Money Growth (*M*2)

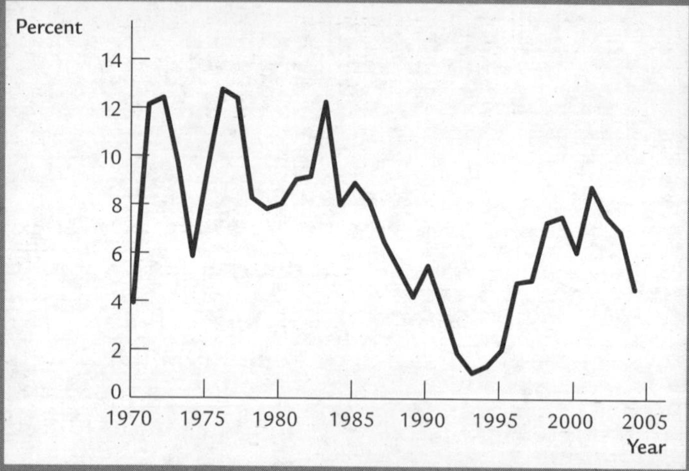

Source: U.S. Federal Reserve

U.S. Net Exports of Goods and Services

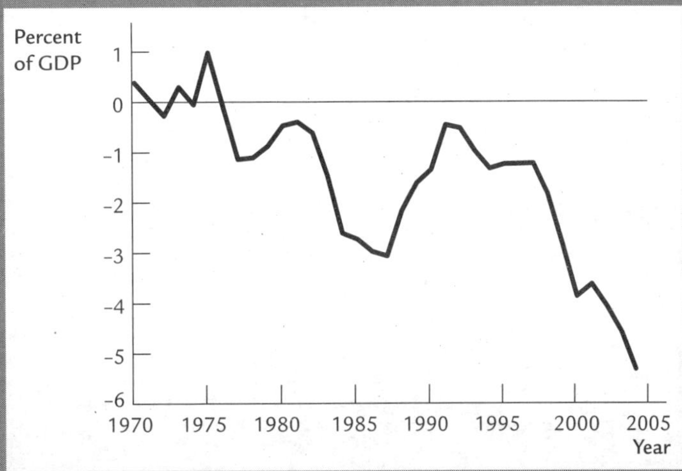

Source: U.S. Department of Commerce

U.S. Trade-weighted Real Exchange Rate

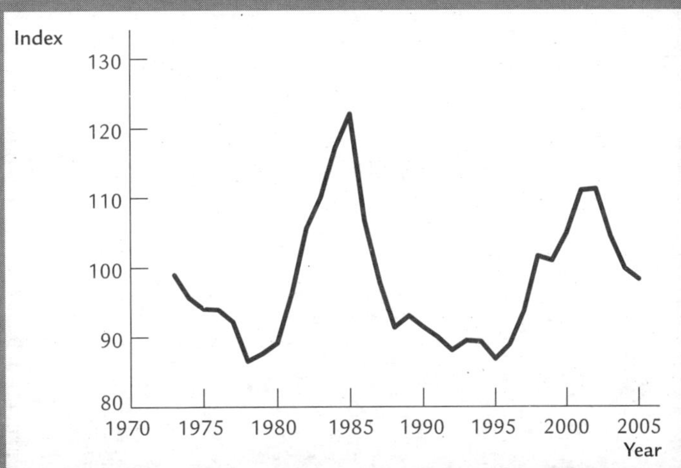

Source: U.S. Federal Reserve